# To Survive
# SOBIBOR

## DOV FREIBERG

gefen publishing house
JERUSALEM ◆ NEW YORK

First Published in Hebrew, July 1988

Project coordinator: Atara Ciechanover
Translated from the Hebrew by Barbara Doron
Layout: Marzel A.S. — Jerusalem
Cover design: Studio Paz
Cover painting: "The Binding of Isaac" by Menashe Kadishman

ISBN: 978-965–229-388-6
Edition   1  3  5  7  9  8  6  4  2

Gefen Publishing House Ltd.
6 Hatzvi St.
Jerusalem 94386, Israel
972–2–538–0247
orders@gefenpublishing.com

Gefen Books
600 Broadway
Lynbrook, NY 11563, USA
1–516–593–1234
orders@gefenpublishing.com

**www.israelbooks.com**

Printed in Israel                    *Send for our free catalogue*

# CONTENTS

The publication of this book in English
was made possible by the generous
contribution of Mr. Sidney Frank
and the Sidney E Frank Foundation

*My heartfelt thanks to*
*Sarah, my wife,*
*who has accompanied me along the way.*

**The author would like to thank**

Atara Ciechanover

Barbara Doron

Yaacov Sharett

Menashke Kadishman

This book is dedicated to my family who were killed
during the Holocaust without my knowing how or where,

To the hundreds of thousands of Jews
who were murdered in the death camp Sobibor,

To my friends who fell
during the revolt in the camp and afterward.

# Author's Note

A personal compulsion of many years has impelled me to write what I experienced during an era of tragedy for the Jewish people and to express the last will and testament of those who were put to death and whose cries during their last moments still echo in my ears. They are the forefathers of this book.

I have attempted to tell my own story, as I remember it, the story of an individual who remained alive among the millions who were destroyed — each of them individuals, unique, each with his or her own song of life. Nevertheless, I believe that this story of one will contribute to the study of the history of a complete nation.

The story has been written forty years after the events occurred, but their memory has not been blunted. I have tried to recreate the details and to be as faithful as I could in everything I have described. As I was writing, the scenes of those days became sharper in my memory and appeared to me as if they had occurred only yesterday.

I intentionally began with the years of my childhood and our family life before the Holocaust, and I concluded with events which took place in Poland and Germany after the war, culminating in my immigration on the *Exodus*. I believe that it is important to describe Jewish life in Poland before its destruction as well as the survivors' struggle for sanity, searching for a new life and for a sanctuary from the images of the past, as these too are part of the story of our nation during a fateful period in its history.

Dov Freiberg
1988

# Lodz

## Summer 1939—Winter 1939

The years leading up to 1939 were the best of years for our family.

My father, Moshe Freiberg, was born in the town of Turobin, in the district of Lublin, Poland. He had been drafted into the Polish army during World War I and saw action at the front. He was subsequently stationed at the fortress in Warsaw, the Citadel. He met my mother, Rivka Hurvitz, while in Warsaw. After he was released from the army, they married, and he began work in a sweater factory. He never again lived in the city of his birth.

He worked hard and earned little, but saved what he could, bit by bit, until he finally had enough money to purchase a second-hand knitting machine and become a subcontractor. The machine was placed in the center of the small room that served as living quarters for the young couple. My father worked from early morning until late into the night, my mother at his side. She wound wool at the primitive coiling machine and then sewed for hours on end at an old sewing machine my father had added to the room, hoping to realize his stubborn ambition of being an independent businessman, producing sweaters and selling them to shops. When life in the room, which served as both living quarters and workshop, became intolerable, my father rented small, cave-like quarters at no. 4 Mila Street, where he set up his new workshop. Over time, machines were added and my father was able to hire workers. Although he soon had enough orders to employ subcontractors of his own, he and my mother continued to work from dawn to dusk.

The business flourished, and our family moved to a larger apartment. Everything was going well, until the great economic collapse of 1929 destroyed my father's business, as it did many others. My father lost everything he had built by dint of years of hard work. It was only owing to his good reputation that he was able to gradually begin again, slowly and on a smaller scale. In 1935 we moved to Lodz, in the center of the country, where my father opened a factory in partnership with a capital investor. The business prospered, but the partnership ran into difficulties and the two separated. Business matters were settled by arbitration, with the result that my father had to buy out the share of his erstwhile partner. Father sank into debt. The success of the business helped him repay the money he owed, but he and my mother were forced to work even harder. The time finally came when Father could begin pleading with my mother to stop working, maintaining that we had enough money and that it was time for her to rest, but he did not really insist, as he had grown to depend on her help.

By 1939, we were a well-established family, enjoying the fruits of hard years of labor. The future looked secure and promising.

There were four children in our family. The eldest was my sister Dvora, who was called Dorka by her friends. In 1939, she was sixteen years old and a student at the commercial school in Warsaw. She had always been rebellious, ever fighting for what she regarded as justice. She was an outstanding student, but when my mother would return from parent-teacher meetings glowing with happiness at the teachers' praise of Dvora, my father would sigh and say: "Who knows what will become of your jewel of a daughter? She is moving farther and farther away from Judaism, and instead of helping in the house, she is always absorbed in those books of hers…" But when my mother was hospitalized for a week, Dvora completely took over the responsibilities of the household. My father, who had never even poured a cup of tea for himself, was helpless without my mother at home. Dvora took absolute charge.

During that week, a week of fear and terrible thoughts about what might happen to our mother, about whose illness we knew nothing, I noticed that relations between my father and my sister had changed. Those were days of mutual understanding between them, a "cease-fire," which had not existed previously and which would not exist in the future. That single week in their lives taught them to get to know and appreciate one another, although they both continued to hold their own opinions — my father with his religious piety and conservative capitalistic social views, and my sister with her left wing and anti-religious opinions. Perhaps my father did not know that Dvora was an active member of the Socialist *Hashomer Hatzair* (Young Guard) youth movement, or perhaps he did know, but understood that there would be no sense in fighting against it.

My brother Mottel, fourteen years old, was a talented yeshiva student. He was tall and broad-shouldered. Although he was only two years older than me, the difference between us seemed much greater. He was serious, scholarly, introspective and tended toward solitude. He had "golden hands," constructing objects that impressed everyone around him. My hands were completely useless and I was envious. Relations between Mottel and my father were not good. They quarreled frequently, and it sometimes seemed to me that my father did not love him. Father was afraid that Mottel would remain at yeshiva and tried to make him work, sitting him in front of a knitting machine. My mother would remonstrate with Father, saying, "He's still a child and you are asking him to work like one of your laborers!" Dvora and Mottel were constantly arguing and the quarrels usually ended in anger. At those times, I played the part of go-between.

I was the third child in the family. In 1939, I was twelve years old, short, thin and sickly. The youngest child was Yankele, seven, a handsome boy, but very spoiled. Everyone loved him but suffered from his demands, as well. He would latch on to one of us and not leave until he had gotten what he wanted.

In the summer of 1939, father rented a cottage at a summer inn that had just been built on the outskirts of the village of Czesarka-Timinka. To get to the village, which had a population of only a few hundred, we had to travel from Lodz to Glowno by bus and then continue for another eight kilometers by carriage. The inn and its cottages were on a hill overlooking forests and fields. Here and there, farmers' houses could be seen along with other cottages for rent. Our cottage stood alone, at the edge of a forest, not far from a farmer's home. The summer colonies and inns around Lodz were crowded with thousands of vacationers, and the cottages were usually so close together that there was the constant noise of people coming and going. We had privacy, as the cottages in our colony were far away from one another and surrounded by groves of trees.

The first week of our vacation Mother stayed with us, helping us get used to the new environment and teaching us how to behave, as this was the first time that we children had been sent to a summer colony where we would spend the holiday weekdays without her, under the supervision of the staff there. The first days were difficult for me. Before dinner, we had to shower and dress nicely. We were required to be exactly on time, and when we entered the dining hall all eyes turned toward us. But I quickly adjusted and soon fell in love with the place. In the morning, I would wake up to the sound of the birds singing and the rays of the sun filtering into my room through the shutters. I would go outside and gaze upon the peaceful rural view, enjoying the beauty I had not seen in Lodz, an industrial city. I was captivated by the freedom and by the privacy I had never had. I could do whatever I wanted. I would hike around the fields, in the forest, and often I would visit the nearby farmhouse, watching the farmer at work.

I made friends with the farmer's family, especially with one of the sons, who was my age. I would tell him about life in Lodz and Warsaw, about houses which had many stories, about the trams and the railroad traveling at top speed, about the cars and the policemen directing traffic, about the movie theaters and the parades of the Polish army on Independence Day. He gobbled up every word and kept asking me to tell him more and more. But I envied him and his independence — he was already capable of taking on the responsibility of farm work. He took care of the horse and cows that obeyed him as though he were an adult, and he ruled the hens and chicks as if he knew their language. My brother Mottel would get angry at me and would tell me not to play with non-Jews and warn me never to eat any of their food, not even a piece of dry bread, because it was not kosher. In the farmer's house, I was often invited to eat with the family or to taste something that the farmer's wife had baked. But I always refused, and one day the farmer explained to everyone that "Jews were not allowed to eat with Poles."

I also spent time with the children of other vacationers. After breakfast, we would run outside to play or have competitions. I was good at sports, but, as I was sickly, I obeyed my mother's request that I rest every day after lunch. I would lie down in a hammock hanging between two trees in a grove close to the house. I enjoyed watching the tops of the trees, and the branches at play with the sunbeams, listening to the breeze that would come in light gusts, quietly at first and then stronger and stronger, passing over my head. Everything was hushed; no voices penetrated the silence. It was as if I were in another world. Thoughts would run through my mind in my imaginary world, and sweet daydreams would alternate with more painful ones until I fell into such deep sleep that when I awoke, it was difficult to free myself from the web of dreams.

I loved the freedom, but on Fridays I anxiously awaited my parents' visit. In the morning, the first carriages and cars would arrive, bringing guests, and even though I knew that my parents would not be among the early ones, every noise of a carriage made me jump. In the afternoon, when the stream of guests increased, the village became crowded. I would sit on a hill overlooking the road with my brother Yankele, waiting impatiently for our parents. As the hours passed, my anxiety grew. For some reason, I was always afraid that something would happen to my father. I had bad dreams about this; in one dream, my father lay dead in his bed in the guest room, where there were three pits, with candles burning everywhere, the whole family standing quietly around the bed. Although I tried to forget the dream, it would not leave me, and of course, I could not tell Father about it. But as usual, our parents would arrive from the city with the last of the guests, and I would breathe a sigh of relief and jump up onto his carriage.

On Fridays we all hurriedly changed into our Shabbat clothing. After she had inspected our appearance from head to toe, my mother would tie a scarf around her head, bless the Shabbat candles, and bless us with "*Gut Shabbos.*" As she removed the scarf, she would gaze upon all of us with happiness.

My father, my brothers and I would go to synagogue, a small wooden building which stood in a grove next to the inn, its large windows open, with benches standing in the yard. This synagogue was very different from the one we had gone to in Lodz, which was in a rented apartment, dark and suffocating, smelling of candles and old books. After prayers, we went to the dining hall — an extended porch enclosed by large windows that reached to the ceiling. There were long tables, with lighted candles on each one. Vacationing families filled the room, everyone dressed in their Shabbat finery. As we seated ourselves at the table, we gazed upon our parents with pride. How handsome they were, I thought to myself. It was perhaps then, for the first time, that I became aware that my mother was a beautiful woman. I wanted to tell her how beautiful I thought she was. My father, as well, would send her pleased glances from time to time. Father poured wine for us and recited the Kiddush blessing, and then the waiters served dinner. Father would joke and mother would make sure that everything went smoothly. The dining hall would reverberate with Shabbat songs. I was too shy to sing, but after my father persuaded me, I would join in with my thin, clear voice — I had loved to sing since I was very young. When we returned home, we sat on our porch, eating sweets, drinking tea, and chatting, laughing and enjoying each other's company until exhaustion would overwhelm us. I would become sleepy, my eyes closing in spite of my efforts to remain awake with the family, not wanting to miss these wonderful moments. Half asleep, I would suddenly become conscious that my father was carrying me off to bed, and my mother was undressing me and covering me with a blanket.

One day my sister was making tea at the kerosene stove. She was adding some kerosene to the base when I saw her suddenly become engulfed in flames. She threw the kerosene tank aside and fire spread around the room. I leaped on my sister, tamping out the flames about her with my body and my hands, but I didn't notice the flames in the room. A woman who happened to be passing by the house began screaming, "Help! Help! Fire!" Other people heard her and joined the shouting while others hurried in with buckets of water, flooding the house and putting out the blaze in a few minutes. Many people gathered around the house and listened to the accounts of the witnesses. The woman who had shouted "Help!" described what had happened in great detail and related how I, a child, had saved my sister. In front of everyone she asked me, "Why didn't you shout for help? If I hadn't passed by, the whole house would have burned down!"

My sister and I sat there, paralyzed with shock. We still hadn't fully comprehended what had happened. And then someone said, "The girl is injured. She needs a doctor, quickly." My sister's face and hands had been burned. Some of her hair and her eyebrows had been singed, and her blouse looked like a torn rag. Someone called a carriage, and my sister, accompanied by one of the neighboring women and my older brother, was taken to the doctor. The crowd dispersed. People patted me on my head and muttered a few words. My little brother, Yankele, sat at my side, staring at me wide-eyed. After about two hours, my sister returned home, her hands and face bandaged and white salve spread here and there over her body. She was in good humor. She hugged and kissed me and when she looked at herself in the mirror, she burst out laughing. We all began to laugh with her, but her laughter soon turned to tears. "Why, I look…just like a scarecrow!" she said.

My brother Mottel was concerned, but calm. He told us that the doctor had said that the burns were not serious; after a week or two, she wouldn't even remember that she had been burned. At mealtime, my sister refused to come to the dining hall "with this face," and said that she wasn't at all hungry. I didn't want to go to the dining hall, either. I knew that people would ask me questions and say what they thought and I would blush and everyone would laugh. Just then, the owner of the inn came to visit, asking how we were. He told us that he had let our parents know about the accident, and they would be arriving that night. "And dinner is in a few minutes," he added, "don't be late."

We looked at each other silently. Finally my sister acquiesced, and we went to dinner. As we sat down, all eyes were focused upon us. People got up, came to our table, congratulated us and complimented me on what I had done. As usual, I blushed. Our frightened parents arrived later that night, calming down only after they had made sure that we were all right. That Shabbat, I went up to read from the Torah with my father and recited the *gomel*, the blessing one says upon deliverance from danger.

I don't remember exactly when I started reading newspapers, but the events in the Land of Israel in 1936 were what impelled me to begin. I had heard non-Jewish youngsters shouting derisively "Jews, go to Palestine!" many times, but we prayed daily for a return to Zion that could only occur when the Messiah came. Before I became interested in what would become the State of Israel, I only knew about the Western Wall, the Tomb of Rachel, the Tomb of the Patriarchs, and caravans of camels in the desert. The sources of my knowledge were the Torah and postcards that we received as New Year's greetings, which I collected. Suddenly, I discovered that alongside the land of our distant past, the land of Abraham, Isaac, Jacob and Moses, there was a land of our Forefathers that existed in the present, where Jews were actually living. I used to visit my Uncle Feivel, who read Zionist newspapers, and I would read about Eretz Israel and look at the pictures: pioneers working in the fields, in the kibbutzim, and villages of the Galilee and the Jezreel Valley; Tel Aviv, Petah Tikvah, signs in Hebrew, Jewish policemen directing traffic, parades in the streets of Tel Aviv... It was a bit strange to see grown men in shorts, but it seemed to me that everyone was happy and proud. I dreamed of being among them. I didn't understand exactly what was going on, however. Arab gangs, the British army, the Balfour Declaration, the "White Paper" — they were all vague ideas in my mind.

What exactly was going on in the British Mandate? I understood only that Jews were coming to the land to build a state for themselves. Every morning on my way to school, I would run to the news vendor and read the headlines about battles between Jews and Arabs, how many Jews had been killed and how many Arabs. According to my calculations, the Jews were winning, because the number of Arabs killed always seemed to be more than the number of Jews. But I had no one with whom to share my thoughts. The arguments that went on at home made me understand that my father rejected Zionism. One day I asked why we were living among non-Jews, and why we didn't leave for Israel. My father looked at me, surprised that a child would ask such a question. Then he smiled and said, "You are young. You don't understand many things." After a moment, he added, "When the Messiah comes, we will all live in the Land of Israel." My father's answer didn't satisfy me, but I knew that he, too, was not satisfied, because he continued to look at me. I didn't speak to him about the subject again, but I continued to try to follow what was going on and to dream about a future Israel.

I was conscious of quite a lot about what was going on in the world during those days of my childhood: the civil war in Spain and General Franco's victory; the Italian invasion of Ethiopia ordered by Mussolini; the rise of Hitler in Germany and the fact that everyone said that he was insane and would probably not lead such a cultured nation for very long; the increasing persecution of Jews in Germany; the annexation of Austria to the Third Reich; the struggle for control of the Sudeten region and the ultimate betrayal of Czechoslovakia by Chamberlain for an artificial peace lasting a few months; the Molotov-Ribbentrop Pact, the non-aggression treaty between Germany and Bolshevik Russia; and finally — the demand by Germany to cede parts of Poland, which led to the understanding that a world war was inevitable.

On the last few Shabbats of our vacation, the calm of the vacationers was disrupted. Sitting in deck chairs, they argued about the situation, but most thought that war would not break out, as Hitler, "the great leader," had been allowed to get everything he wanted; now, when it was clear to him that he would not receive anything else, he wouldn't take the risk of fighting against all of Europe, and perhaps even against the United States. But in spite of this consensus, fear crept into everyone's hearts. The propaganda war between Germany and Poland intensified from day to day. Here and there, border skirmishes broke out. General Rydz-Śmigły, commander-in-chief of the Polish Armed Forces, declared in a speech to the nation, "We will not give up even a button to anyone, and if the Germans declare war, we will fight them to victory."

The farmers told us that they had found confirming signs that war would break out: on the fruit trees, signs of larvae had appeared. A few families began to return home. My father, who had planned to spend the Jewish holidays in the country, was in no hurry to leave. He was optimistic that everything would turn out well, so Mottel, Dvora, Yankele and I were among the last to return to the city. Only two days before the war broke out, after a general mobilization had been declared and people were panicking, Father hurried around, trying to rent any kind of vehicle to get us home, finally locating a coach. We were frightened, feeling that we had been left alone and abandoned. What if the war that everyone was talking about broke out? We would be left in this forgotten place, and our father wouldn't be able to reach us and to take us home. I was also afraid that if we stayed in the country, I might miss the great experience called war. So it wasn't hard for me to leave the place I had loved, a place in which it seemed that I had spent the best summer of my life.

The trip home was difficult and slow. Traffic was heavy; there were wagons and army vehicles clogging the road. Our coach advanced sluggishly. Father was tense and restless, angry that he hadn't been able to find a faster way to get home. We, too, were tense. It was a hot, muggy day. The fields of chaff after the harvest were yellow. As we approached Lodz, we saw more and more army vehicles. At the edge of the road, units of armed soldiers were marching, dripping with perspiration. These were not the burnished soldiers that I remembered from the military parades. My father, who had served in World War I, explained to us about the qualities of the different types of arms and ammunition. The army vehicles were draped with branches, and when I asked my father why, he answered that this was camouflage against enemy aircraft. The idea seemed interesting to me, but I couldn't understand how the planes would not see trees traveling down the road. Everyone burst out laughing, and Father explained that when the enemy attacked, the vehicles parked on the shoulders of the road.

There was a strange atmosphere in the streets of the city. Groups of people stood and read notices which fluttered from the walls of the houses. Others stood around talking. The news vendors were shouting, "Special edition! Special edition!" People grabbed the newspapers from their hands and read them with worried faces.

It was good to get home after the tension of the past few days. We all felt cheerful, as though our home were a fortress which would defend us from all evil. Our neighbors were glad to have us back. After a careful examination it was declared that we had gained weight and that I was looking very well. My mother was happy.

That evening, we went to visit our grandparents, my father's parents. When we went into the house, we saw Grandfather sitting at the table, head lowered and eyes full of deep sorrow. Grandmother was sitting opposite him, crying. Our young uncle, Feivel, dressed in a soldier's uniform, was pacing the floor and speaking. I had met my Uncle Feivel only a few years previously, when my grandparents were still living in the town of Turobin and we had visited them for the summer. That summer, my uncle and I became good friends. He took me for walks in the surrounding villages, bought me sweets and told me stories. One day, he took me to the forest.

He was dressed in a uniform and was wearing a cap with the *Magen David* (Star of David) imprinted on it. On the way, he told me about the Betar youth Zionist movement and about its great leader, Ze'ev Jabotinsky, who was organizing thousands of young men who would, in time, go to the holy land and conquer it for the Jewish people. In the forest, there were dozens of young men, all dressed in uniforms. My uncle seated me to the side. The young men stood in rows and performed military training exercises. Afterward, they sat in a circle, and my uncle motioned for me to join them and sit next to him. Everyone sang songs in Yiddish and Hebrew, ate their fill of sandwiches, and sang again. I was deeply impressed.

My grandfather did not get along with my uncle. They would argue constantly and Grandfather would shout, "Criminal! Jew-hater!" Now, my uncle was wearing the uniform of the Polish army. He had been called up the previous day with the general mobilization, and was given two hours to say goodbye to his family. His unit would move up to the border the following day. Feivel was happy to see us and tried to break the tension by asking us about our vacation in the country and when we had returned. "Tell them that it is not the end of the world," he said, turning to my father. "You have already fought in a war…"

We said goodbye to Feivel. My grandmother was sobbing. My grandfather was crying, as well. Feivel looked sad, tried unsuccessfully to smile, and left the house quickly. That night, I couldn't stop thinking about him. I had always thought that my grandparents hated him; even my father had seemed not to like him and had acted indifferently toward him. Only my mother had been nice to him. And this evening, everything had been so different; everyone had seemed to care for him. I felt relieved that I wasn't the only one who loved him. In my imagination, I saw him riding a horse, fighting, and killing Germans. Then I imagined him with a head wound, wrapped in bloodstained bandages, and then wounded in his arm, which was in a sling, while he continued to fight with the other arm. I imagined him being killed, and although I tried to repress this thought, it returned from time to time. But I also saw him as a hero, returning home decorated with medals on his chest and the two of us walking, arm in arm, down busy Piotrkowska Street with everyone watching us.

The next morning, from the window, I saw my father and some neighbors digging pits in the yard. I went downstairs. My father was panting and sweating, but he seemed to be in good spirits. "I heard," said my father, "that there are long lines of people outside the banks wanting to withdraw money. The banks are only giving a limited amount to each person. I'll go take some money out of the bank." "How much money do you have in the bank, young man?" someone asked. "Thirty-six zlotys," I answered. Everyone laughed. I ran into the house, took out my bankbook and hurried to the bank. The line of people waiting was long. After two hours, I entered the bank and took out all of my money. My brother Mottel, who had a few hundred zlotys in the bank, got there a little later and could not withdraw anything. During the day, my father brought packs of sweaters from the factory and the children's bedroom was turned into a storeroom. My mother told us that food was disappearing from the shops.

When I woke up the next morning, my parents' faces were more somber than ever. "Berale, get up and get dressed," my father said. "We are at war!" Mother was pale. I glanced out of the window. It seemed to be a normal day, sunny with blue skies, as if nothing had changed. But the radio announcer said that the Germans had crossed the border and were attacking. Our brave army was battling to repel the invader. The nation was called upon to remain steadfast against the enemy.

Suddenly, explosions sounded as we heard the thunder of airplane engines. My father ordered us to go down to the cellar, which was usually used by the residents of the building to store vegetables and milk products. The rank smell of rotting vegetables and sour cheese filled the air. The residents of the building began crowding into the cellar, family after family. I stood close to my father, but he wasn't a person who could stand calmly by until someone came to announce that the attack had ended. After a few minutes, he told my mother that he was going outside to see what was happening and that he would be right back. My mother insisted that he stay in the cellar, but he didn't pay her any attention and went out. A few minutes later he returned, saying that there was no one in the street, and that from time to time, an army vehicle would pass by. After a while, although my mother begged him not to, he went outside again. I ran after him, unnoticed. I saw my father looking up at the sky, and when he saw me, he pointed up at a plane, which seemed the size of a bird. Abruptly, as if he had just come to his senses, he took me by the hand and returned me to the cellar. Neither of us told anyone about my adventure.

Meanwhile, people were getting used to the crowded cellar and there was an atmosphere of intimacy; the excitement, anxiety and feeling of shared fate had turned all of us into a kind of extended family. When the all-clear signal was sounded, we went outside into the fresh air. After the cold cellar, the warm sun was pleasant, and after being forced into a small space, we all enjoyed standing outside. None of us hurried back to our apartments.

The war had broken out only a few short hours ago, and the fighting was hundreds of kilometers from Lodz, but our lives had changed completely. Men did not go to work, and children did not go to school, even though it was September first and schools had opened. Families stayed together as they did on holidays. The residents of the building, who had not had any contact with each other for years, if they even knew one another, behaved as though they were all related. As we sought refuge in the cellar several times during the day, the environment became more comfortable. Each family found a place for itself, people conversed and the time passed more quickly.

Between sirens, we pasted paper over the windowpanes of our apartment so that no light could be seen from outside. My sister took command of this job to ensure that our work was aesthetic. My big brother handled the religious aspect — he made certain that no crosses were created by the papers we pasted on the windows. Aside from small differences of opinion about how the work should be done, we worked quietly and steadily. In a few hours, all the panes were covered with squares of paper and then with two diagonal strips from corner to corner for reinforcement. Mother was busy cooking and baking cookies, which could be stored for a long time. Whenever she entered the room, she was pleased to see her children working quietly and seriously, and the day passed quickly.

Night had fallen. This evening was different from any other I had known. I looked out the window. Outside, there was complete darkness; the opposite building looked like a blank wall. Here and there, a light went on in one of the apartments and immediately someone would call from the yard, "Turn off the light!" The light would go out in a second. In spite of my fear of the dark, I left the house, wanting to see the city in darkness. I quickly ran down the stairs, left the yard, and ran into the street. My heart beat quickly and I was panting with fear. I stood at the gate, where some of the neighbors were standing, happy not to be alone. My confidence returned. At first, the street seemed to have disappeared, along with its houses, the sidewalk and the road. Only our building existed, and around it, empty space. Cars passed me, their headlights colored in blue, looking like boats sailing down a river. When my eyes became accustomed to the dark, I could discern the houses next to ours as black blobs, reaching up to the sky. The people around me stood quietly, exchanging an infrequent word or two in whispers.

Suddenly there was a loud noise and we searched for the source. A black form was coming toward us — two units of armed soldiers marching down the street. The thought suddenly occurred to me: Maybe my uncle, Feivel, was among them? My heart beating rapidly, I approached the road and searched the faces of the soldiers. They all looked the same. I wanted to shout "Uncle Feivel!" but I was embarrassed. All of a sudden I felt uncomfortable and anxious, as though I were alone in the woods, and quickly ran home. When I walked in, Mottel greeted me with, "Where have you been?" Dvora joined him with, "Don't you know that there is a war going on? What were you looking for outside in the dark?" My brother and sister, who had never agreed about anything, who were always arguing, their opinions always conflicting, were unexpectedly in accord. And my mother and father, who had just entered the room, had nothing to add, but only looked at me with faces that seemed to repeat the words of anger I had just heard. Finally, my father gave me a serious look and said, "Berale, you will not leave the house again without my permission. Do you understand?" I nodded my head.

An uncomfortable atmosphere filled the house. No one knew exactly what to do. All of us were deep in thought, but we did not share our thoughts with one another, so we were silent, and the strange silence was unpleasant. Only young Yankele ran around, asking us to play with him. This time, nobody had the patience for him and he began to cry. At dinner, Father tried to joke in order to dispel our tension, and perhaps his own, as well, but he was unsuccessful.

War had broken out. No one knew how long it would last, what tomorrow would bring, what would happen to us, what we had to do. We were left to a fate that we could not predict. One thing was clear, however: that morning, the beginning of the war, was the end of an era. Our lives had changed and our behavior was different. Summer had ended, for our hopes, our expectations and our dreams. For us children, who had until then been living in paradise, the change was especially striking.

In the middle of the night we were awakened and ordered to go down to the cellar. The sirens outside sounded like a terrible wailing. I was trembling with cold in the cellar, although Mother had dressed us snugly. We stood close to one another to keep warm. Yankele remained fast asleep, completely unaware that he was being taken downstairs or that he was being carried back upstairs to the apartment when we were allowed to return.

The next morning, the radio announcer reported that there had been heavy fighting at the front: our forces had destroyed fifty of the enemy's tanks and had repelled the Germans. The public was warned to be careful of spies and of gossipmongers spreading stories that might depress the people. When I went downstairs with Father, the courtyard's gatekeeper greeted us with a happy face. "Have you heard the news, Mr. Freiberg? We have destroyed fifty tanks! We'll show those awful Swabians (slang for 'German') what it means to start a war with us." And more quietly, she told Father that our neighbor, who was a *Volksdeutsche*, a Pole of German descent, had not come home last night, and his wife and children didn't leave their house. "He's probably a spy. If they catch him, they should kill him on the spot!"

The gatekeeper's family and the *Volksdeutsche*, the only Christian families in the apartment building, were friendly with each other, so I was surprised to hear her say this. Near the gate, neighbors were standing and arguing in loud voices. The news of the destruction of the German tanks, and of the entry of England into the war, had raised spirits after a day of uncertainty. But along with the good news, there were also strange rumors. It was said that many spies were wandering around the city signaling to enemy planes with mirrors; a few of them had already been caught. There was also a rumor that German parachutists had been seen in various places, and we began suspecting every passerby. Throughout the day, the rumors proliferated and the news was bad. It was said that during the bombardment, a four-story building had been destroyed. It had collapsed like a box of matches; people in the vicinity had been thrown to a height of twenty meters from the shock wave. It was said that soldiers returning from the front had reported that the Germans were attacking relentlessly and the Polish defense lines had completely collapsed. The Polish army had been defeated and was fleeing in chaos; they could not even establish a new line of defense. Thousands had been killed and the army had been shattered. Soldiers, who were now without commanders, were stealing clothes from civilians, taking off their uniforms and throwing their guns away.

The good news broadcast on the radio, the exhortations not to believe rumors, coupled with the general human tendency to believe good news rather than bad, influenced people not to accept the dire rumors. However, although we tried to repress them, we could not ignore them, and they completely obliterated the happiness that we had felt in the morning.

When I got home, I ran into Yadzia, the family maid, who lived on the ground floor. Yadzia was a village girl of eighteen, of medium height, not fat, but nicely built, with an innocent face, as smooth as silk, and long blond hair usually arranged into a braid at work. Her eyes were blue, and she was almost always smiling. Her chest was well-rounded, and her clothes, which were always a bit too small for her, must have been remainders of a period when she had been thinner and emphasized the curves of her body.

I was not indifferent to her. I would frequently run into her at the stairs as I left for school in the morning, as though she had been waiting for me behind the door so that I would say "Good morning" to her. She would answer, "Good morning, sweet child," or "dear one" or some other affectionate greeting, and keep me there for a moment with a few questions, sometimes even patting me. Although I liked her, I tried to avoid her. Whenever I crossed the yard, I would look at the kitchen window to see if she was there. I admired her as you would a beautiful picture; I did not want to talk to her, and I certainly did not want her to touch me — her touch was pleasant, but it made me feel shame, as though I had sinned. Now she was standing opposite me, an old suitcase in her hand, a kerchief covering her hair, eyes red with tears. I felt sorry for her as she explained that she had decided to return to her village and to her family because the war had broken out and no one knew what would happen, but leaving her employers was difficult; she had gotten accustomed to living with us and loved us. She said through her tears, "Who knows if we will ever see each other again?" She unexpectedly bent down and hugged me hard, kissed my head and my cheek and then gave me a long, wet kiss on my mouth. I did not resist. I let her do whatever she wanted to. My head resting on her breast, her arms around me, her warm kiss, all awakened a pleasurable feeling in me that I had never felt before. It was difficult enough for me even to manage to say "Good-bye," although

I wanted to say other things that were in my heart. As she stood up, I felt as if I had been hypnotized. She answered, "Goodbye, my sweet child," and each of us continued walking in opposite directions. For a long time, I could not free myself from the experience of those moments of parting from Yadzia. At night, I would try to reconstruct every detail of my encounter with her.

I noticed that my father was becoming more and more somber and introverted, pacing the room with a gloomy face, as he had done during times of business crises — when a strike had broken out at the factory, or when he had quarreled with his partner. But at those times, he had also spoken, shouted, cursed, and this time he was quiet, whispering from time to time with my mother, and again wrapped in silence. Mother tried to be encouraging. We heard her say, "Thank God, you are with us and not in the army." But as the days passed, Father's mood worsened. One day, when he came home, he looked hopeless, as though he had been wrestling with a fateful decision. In the evening, my mother also looked very worried, and her face showed signs that she had been crying. I was seized with an irrational fear, but I didn't dare to ask them anything.

Most of that night, we remained in the cellar. From time to time, we heard muffled explosions, but we had become accustomed to them. When we finally returned to our apartment, trembling with cold and exhaustion, we sat down around the table. My mother served tea and cookies, and my father, who looked calmer and even smiled, spoke to us while we were drinking. "I want you all to listen. The situation at the front is not good. From what I have heard, the Germans are advancing rapidly and are not far from Lodz. I have decided that I will not fall into the hands of the Germans. I don't want to suffer their persecutions, the things they have done to the Jews of Austria and Czechoslovakia. If the Germans approach Lodz, I will take Mottel, who is old enough, and we will flee to Warsaw. There is no danger to women and children. While I'm in Warsaw, I will make arrangements to bring all of you there. If the Germans approach Warsaw, we will go to Bialystok (in the northeast), where I have good friends, and if they advance to Bialystok, we will try to cross the Russian border." He repeated again with emphasis, "I will not fall into German hands."

When my father realized that we were in shock, he added, "Don't be so upset. The war will not be over in a few days; the Germans won't succeed in conquering Poland so quickly. They are not yet at the gates of Lodz, and I am not leaving yet. Now let's all go to sleep." None of us asked any questions; none of us said a word.

Lying in bed, I tried to absorb what I had heard. Different scenarios jumbled through my mind, but nothing was clear. I prayed to God that we would stay together. When I woke in the morning, the conversation of the night before seemed like a dream. But when I saw that my brother was not in his bed, my heart began to pound. I ran to the next room and when I didn't see anyone, I ran to the kitchen. Everyone except my father was sitting around the table and eating breakfast. "Where is Father?" I asked. "He went to attend to some things," my mother answered with a smile, and when my sister smiled, as well, my fears disappeared. No, Father had not left us.

During the day, we witnessed quite a bit of army movement. Powerful explosions resounded in the area. We sat in the cellar for long hours. My father told us that he had visited our grandparents: Grandmother had been constantly crying, and Grandfather was praying for Uncle Feivel. That evening, the city was quiet and we fell into a peaceful sleep.

Suddenly, we were awakened by a sharp knocking at our door. It was one of the neighbors, who said agitatedly, "Why are you sleeping? Don't you know what's going on? The whole city is awake. A radio announcement has ordered all men to leave the city eastward. Everyone is leaving. The streets are filled with people and soldiers."

We immediately got up and dressed, and my father told Mottel to put on warm clothes. He hurriedly packed a suitcase and a parcel. Everyone was calm; we stood and watched as though it was all clear to us, and whatever was done, was done as a matter of course. Father asked us not to see them out, and kissed us all as he left. When he was saying goodbye to Mother on the doorstep, he suddenly burst into tears — and quickly left the house with my brother. Everything had happened so fast, there was no time to react. I had never seen my mother and my father kissing. My father never kissed us, the children, either. The last time he had kissed me was very long ago, when I was sick…and now he was kissing us all, even my big sister. And then, the last picture: my father and my mother hugging each other tightly, kissing, and my father sobbing like a little child. I was deeply shocked.

Those of us remaining at home sat close together and cried. My mother, who was holding little Yankele on her lap, told us to go to sleep. Lying in bed, I imagined my father and brother running in the darkness down roads crowded with people, holding each other's hands, and the Germans running after them. I was envious of my brother, chosen by father to accompany him on his flight. Why was I so small? If I had been taller, he would certainly have taken me, as well. I imagined the two of them returning to us, my brother relating the adventures they had had away from home, and becoming an object of everyone's admiration.

The next morning I stayed close to my mother, feeling that I should be near her. My sister did not leave the house, either. Mother seemed calmer, dressed nicely, her hair combed back. Only her eyes were red and tired. Her composure made me feel more relaxed and lessened the tension. But I still could not reconcile myself to my father's and brother's leaving home, just when I needed them so. We would stop and listen to every footstep from the yard or from the staircase. Every knock on the door made us jump. Where could they be? How did they get away — on foot or in some vehicle? I knew that there were no answers to my questions, but I felt the need to voice them.

"You are asking foolish questions. Who knows the answers?" replied my sister, her anger mixed with laughter, and Mother said, "Listen, children. Your father has often been in difficult situations. He knows how to take care of himself. It's a good thing that there are two of them — they can always help each other. And the moment he can, he will contact us. You don't have to worry." Mother asked Dvora to visit Grandmother and Grandfather, to tell them that Father and Mottel had fled during the night, and also to find out how they were getting along. Mother asked her not to stop anywhere and to come home quickly. My sister, who probably, like me, thought that Father and Mottel might return home at any moment, didn't want to leave the house and found a variety of excuses to postpone the errand. "I'll go," I said. "I'll be home in a few minutes." Mother considered this for a moment, packed some food, gave it to me and told me to be careful.

It was strange to see Yednastego-Listopada Street, one of the main streets of Lodz, completely empty. There were no trams, no cars, no policemen and no soldiers. I ran across the street. At Plac Wolności (Liberty Square), I saw a white flag flying over the city hall. I turned into Piotrkowska Street, the main street of the city and it, too, was quiet and empty. I entered my grandparents' apartment panting, and saw their surprise that I had come alone. Grandfather asked if I hadn't been afraid to come. I said that my mother had sent me and that Father and Mottel had left the city that night for Warsaw. "We know," said my grandfather. "They were here last night to say goodbye. But it was nice of you to come and tell us." "Have you heard anything from Uncle Feivel?" I asked. "No, child," answered Grandfather, and Grandmother began to cry. I was sorry that I had asked.

I ran home blindly. But then, near the house, I heard the roar of engines, and four motorcycles with sidecars swiftly appeared, driven by German soldiers. In each sidecar sat three armed German soldiers wearing grey raincoats and boots, helmets covering their heads. I watched them until they disappeared, then ran into the house shouting, "I've just seen Germans!" I described the soldiers. My mother and sister were quiet. My mother's face became pale. Seeing the Germans so impressed me that I forgot to tell them about my visit to our grandparents.

"None of you is to leave the house," my mother ordered. I knew why. I remembered the stories I had heard about the Great War — when units of Cossacks had marched through Jewish towns and had carried out pogroms, and then, after the Polish army had liberated the towns, rioting among the Jews.

In the afternoon hours, the noise of German vehicles and tanks in the streets increased. The threatening sounds made the window-panes shake. I was curious and wanted to see the German army moving though the streets, but I didn't dare ask my mother for permission. In the excitement, I had forgotten that it was Friday, but my mother hadn't. In the evening, she made us bathe and get dressed up in our Shabbat clothes, and, as on every Shabbat, she covered the table with a white tablecloth, put a bottle of wine on the table, challah bread covered with a cloth napkin, and four silver candlesticks with candles. She covered her head with a scarf, lit the candles and recited the blessing, crying silently. When she finished, she wiped away her tears and said, "*Gut Shabbos*. May we hear good news." We answered her with "Amen."

When we saw stars in the sky, I took the *siddur* (prayer book) and began to pray. I had never really paid attention to the meanings of the words of the prayers. I had prayed out of routine, skipping words and paragraphs, without noticing what I was reading. This time, I didn't miss a word, and even though I didn't understand everything, every time I came to the word *Elokim* (God), I pronounced it with emphasis. In the deep quiet that enveloped our home, I sensed that my mother and sister were praying with me. Even little Yankele was quiet and hardly disturbed us. After the evening prayer, we felt confused. The table was set as usual, but could we welcome in Shabbat without Father? How? Even sitting down to eat the Shabbat meal seemed impossible without him. Mother finally came to a decision and instructed us to sit down at the table. Everyone sat in his usual place; the chair at the head of the table and the one to the left of it remained empty. My mother turned to me and said, "Berale, make the Kiddush, recite the blessing over the wine…you are the head of the family now, until we are together again…"

I was full of a mixture of pride and fear. I stood up and recited the Kiddush. My voice shook, and I sang louder to hide the trembling, although I imagined that those listening understood my feelings and even saw my hand shaking. I recited the blessing over the challah, and I passed the knife over the bread, slicing it and handing everyone a slice. I dipped my slice in salt, doing everything the way I had seen it done throughout my childhood. I was afraid to raise my eyes, feeling that my mother and sister were staring at me. I was not hungry, but I ate everything my mother served, not wanting to behave like a spoiled child. I knew that I should sing Shabbat songs, but I was not capable of singing at that point, and no one asked me to. I recited the blessing thanking God for the food at the end of the meal. My mother came to me and kissed me, and I felt that my childhood had come to an end.

On Saturday morning, a German soldier appeared in our yard and shouted, "All Jews are to come downstairs to the yard!" We gathered in the yard, men, women and children, all of us fearful. One of our neighbors, a man of about fifty, said, "Don't be afraid. I've known the Germans since the Great War. I know how to get along with them." Then he walked over to the soldier and said a few words in German. The German looked at him with surprise — and suddenly slapped his face and shouted, "Jewish pig!" The man seemed to be in shock. Then the soldier turned to us and said, "I don't need women and children. I need men to work!" and he took the men with him. I was glad that my father and brother had run away. If they had stayed at home, they, too, would have been taken.

In front of the house, there was a truck filled with Jewish men who already had been selected to work. There were a large number of German soldiers in the street, which was full of people, especially Poles and Germans, in a variety of uniforms, all of them spotless and well-made. The soldiers were wearing shiny boots, which seemed to fit perfectly; each soldier was armed with a pistol and each was wearing a leather belt pulled diagonally over his chest, and a starched cap, adorned with stripes of silver or gold. Their boastful faces were threatening. Among those coming and going were Poles wearing streamers adorned with swastikas. These *Volksdeutsche* sprang up suddenly like mushrooms after the rain. There were also Jews hurrying to and fro.

That Saturday we spent the entire day in our apartment. We were thinking of Father and Mottel on the road. What had happened to them? Had they been lucky and made it to Warsaw? The news on the Polish radio stations did not clarify how far into Poland the Germans had advanced, but the residents of Warsaw had been ordered to set up barricades and to fight the Germans until the last drop of Polish blood had been shed.

Another radio announcement stated that Warsaw had been bombarded by the enemy and that there were dead and wounded. The residents of the city were asked to donate blood. It was also announced that long streams of refugees were reaching Warsaw, and residents were requested to welcome them and share whatever they had with them.

On Sunday morning, when I left the house, I saw people with loaves of white bread in their hands walking down the street. I walked in the direction from which they had come until I reached a bakery on a side street where people were standing in line, waiting to buy bread. A German soldier was keeping order. The fragrance of warm bread filled my nose. I ran home and asked for money to buy bread, then returned to the bakery and took my place in line. After a few minutes, a Polish girl who had been standing behind me approached me and said aggressively, "Jew, get out of here, you won't get any bread!" I ignored her and didn't move, nor did I answer her. The people standing around me ignored the incident, as though they were deaf and blind, and after a moment the girl came back and said, "I'm telling you that you won't get any bread! I'll tell the German soldier!"

I looked around me but I didn't see any Jewish faces. I began to feel anxious and as I got closer to the entrance to the bakery, I became more and more frightened, but I continued standing in line. There was something inside me that would not let me give in to the girl. As I reached the entrance and the German soldier standing next to it, the girl turned to the soldier and said, "*Jude! Jude!* (Jew! Jew!)" and pointed at me. The German shouted at me, "*Jude*, get out of here!" I ran away humiliated and in tears. After a while, the gatekeeper of the house came to our apartment and offered us a loaf of white bread at double the price. My mother bought it.

By the morning after the mass flight from the city, many had already begun returning home. These were people who had been pulled along in the panicky crowd without giving a thought to the significance of what they were doing, or those who had not been able to stand the long trek eastward. After several days, a large number had returned, even though they had managed to travel quite a ways eastward — and then they, too, were taken for work details by the Germans. News about those who had returned spread through the neighborhood and my mother ran here and there, trying to find someone who might have some information about my father and brother. She was not the only one; the homes of those who had returned were filled with people like her, looking for a sign of life from relatives who had fled. The returnees spoke animatedly about the difficulties they had encountered — how crowds of refugees had engulfed the road from Lodz to Warsaw, and along with them, the fleeing units of the Polish army; how German planes had flown over their heads without meeting any Polish resistance, dropping bombs on the fleeing crowd and strafing them with machine gun fire; how people had searched for their relatives among the dead in the chaos of the crowd, and how they could hear the cries of the wounded who were left untreated; how the crowds had set upon every well and had almost killed each other in the struggle to get a drop of water to drink; how, at the beginning, the farmers had welcomed those who were fleeing and given them food and drink and how, as time passed, this, too, had changed, and no one would allow them near their houses;

how Polish soldiers had thrown their weapons to the side of the road and searched for civilian clothes, even undressing the dead and taking their clothing; how special units of the German army had overtaken them and examined those whom they had caught, taking Polish soldiers and others prisoner after they had shot some of them on the spot.

My mother asked every person who had returned whether they had met my father and brother — showing them their photographs, describing them. She even found some who thought they had seen the two and related anecdotes about them, some reassuring and others frightening, but after persistent questioning my mother would conclude that the stories were figments of the imagination. One of those who had returned was sure that he had seen my father and brother alive and well, on their way back to Lodz, and was surprised that they had not yet arrived home. When my mother came home with that story, the house filled with happiness. We expected that any minute the door would open and my father and brother would walk in. For many days, I stood at the front of the house from morning till night, wanting to be the first to greet them, in vain...

My mother did not despair. Every day she spoke with those who had just returned, even those she had already spoken to, asking them more questions. Every evening she would return home exhausted, telling their stories or disappearing into her own thoughts. Almost the whole of Poland had been overrun by the Germans and the Russians by now; only besieged Warsaw continued to fight. Radio Warsaw broadcast regards from refugees every day, and we sat by the radio and listened to the thousands of names. But we did not hear our own. We were almost overwhelmed by despair and depression; no one smiled; everyone spoke in whispers and spent long hours in our own little corners of the apartment. My sister read for days on end. I wasn't able to do anything. But thoughts kept going around in my head. I didn't lose hope that my father and brother would return safely. I was afraid to think that something might have happened to them — I could not forget the orphan children whom I knew and pitied, and I could never understand how they were able to laugh and play. These children were often insolent, and the adults would say, "It's no wonder they behave like that, growing up without a father…"

I tried to fight off the gloomy thoughts, but they kept returning. Over and over I remembered my dream about the three open graves in our home. Once when I was asking myself what the number meant, I suddenly remembered Uncle Feivel. I was angry with myself; how could I think that my father, my brother and Uncle Feivel might be dead? I couldn't forgive myself. I prayed and asked God to forgive me for my evil thoughts. My mother, who understood my mental state, tried to raise my spirits by chatting with me about daily concerns. One day I heard her saying to the neighbors, "That boy worries me. I'm afraid that something might happen to him. He is always alone, sitting and thinking. I don't know what to do." I didn't understand what there was to worry about, but I didn't know how to make her stop worrying, either.

The days passed. Most of those who had fled had returned to their homes, and the others had managed to send word about where they were. Our neighbor on the ground floor received radio regards from her husband. He said that he was in Warsaw and that he was well. We waited, day after day, for some message, some sign from Father and Mottel, but we received nothing.

The fact that we were so anxious for some word influenced our dreams. Early in the morning, we would climb into Mother's bed and ask about each other's dreams. We all dreamed about Father and Mottel, and the dreams would provide us with some kind of hope. We interpreted all of the dreams positively. We never dared talk about bad dreams and so darken the mood of the others. One night, I dreamed that I was walking down Kamienna Street and I saw Father from afar, coming toward me in tattered clothing, two big packages in his hands. I looked at his face and saw an expression of pain and sorrow; it seemed as though his body would collapse under the heavy weight. He looked at me and began crying. I ran toward him to fall into his arms and hug him, but instead of coming nearer, he was going farther and farther away from me. I ran after him as fast as I could, but he continued to go farther away and finally disappeared into Kilińskiego Street. I started to shout, "Father!" but I couldn't get a word out. My throat hurt from the effort to shout until I finally managed a strange sound, and woke up, drenched in perspiration, my heart pounding.

I went over every detail of the dream over and over. I grieved. I had seen my father, but why did he look so terrible? Why had he been dressed so sloppily? Why had he cried? And why had he slipped away from me and disappeared? I had never seen him like that. I decided that I wouldn't tell anyone about this dream, and because I was afraid that my face would give me away, I closed my eyes and pretended I was asleep. I heard my mother tell my sister not to wake me up, and she left the house. I got up, but I couldn't stop thinking about the dream. Suddenly, without wanting to, I found myself telling the dream to my sister in all its detail. My sister's eyes filled with tears. The two of us decided not to tell Mother.

A few days later, I dreamed that we were at the Great Synagogue in Lodz. I had only been there once, on Rosh Hashanah, the Jewish New Year, thanks to Uncle Feivel. The Jewish soldiers of his unit had been allowed to pray there. I lived near the army camp, and I arrived there an hour before we were supposed to meet; I was standing at the gate when I saw my uncle and his comrades, about fifty of them, marching in threes, dressed in their well-brushed holiday uniforms, led by their sergeant. I accompanied them through the streets of Lodz to the synagogue, where their sergeant called them to order as the curious Jewish onlookers watched. When they were dismissed, I ran to my uncle, and the two of us entered the synagogue, hand in hand. The main hall was spacious, with a high ceiling and crystal chandeliers. The bright light, the lectern for reading the Torah, the "Eastern" wall and at its center, the Holy Ark covered by a thick velvet curtain sewn with gold thread, the cantor and the large choir, and the great number of people praying: all of these deeply impressed me.

Now, in my dream, I saw the hall of the Great Synagogue and it was more beautiful than I can describe. The bright light blinded my eyes. The hall was full of well-dressed, nice-looking people. I was there with the whole family, including my brother Mottel, and we stood in a row, next to one another. Suddenly, an old man with a long white beard called to my father by name, Moshe ben Arieh Leibish, to come up to read a portion from the Torah. My father went up to the platform, dressed in holiday clothing, looking wonderful, his face shining, his sparkling eyes expressing satisfaction and pride, and everyone was looking at him with admiration. I felt that the event was festive and important, that my father was the hero, and my heart was overflowing with pride.

When I awoke, I hurried to my mother and I told her about my dream, the words tumbling out of my mouth with happiness, awaiting signs of happiness and satisfaction in her eyes. But her face only became more serious, and at the end of my story, she burst into tears and hugged and kissed me. I was confused and frustrated. What terrible event had been in the dream that could have caused her to cry? I thought more about the dream and came to the conclusion that my father had died. His soul had gone up to Heaven. In my previous dream, Father hadn't been admitted to Paradise because of his sins. His terrible appearance, his crying and the heavy parcels he was carrying bore witness to his suffering. Without a doubt, his soul was wandering and knew no rest. I had heard stories of lost souls who had not been permitted to enter Paradise. At night, their wailing could be heard. But the second dream meant that Father had been purified and had been accepted into Heaven with great honor. And that was why my mother had burst into tears.

It was only after some time that I discovered the real reason for Mother's tears. Among the people who had returned to Lodz, she had found someone who, by all indications, had been with my father and brother; when he was talking to her about them, however, he had suddenly and inexplicably fallen silent, and the rest of the conversation had somehow been illogical. When my mother met him a second time and questioned him again, she felt that he was hiding something from her, and she understood that he had not become confused the first time they had met, but rather, wanted to avoid telling her some painful news. After my mother left him the first time, the man told the truth to his wife, and she had convinced him not to say anything in case it turned out to be a case of mistaken identity. On my mother's second visit, he gave in to her pleas and told her everything he knew: he had met my father and brother in a barn, where they had spent the night. They had continued walking together. When they reached the town of Prushkov, about twenty kilometers from Warsaw, a German unit searching for Polish soldiers caught up with them. They were stopping people and taking anyone who looked like a soldier with them. My father and brother had been taken. This man had later met some people who had told him that my father had been shot to death with another group of men, and my brother and other prisoners had been taken away by truck.

What he said sounded plausible, but the fact that he, himself, had not been a witness to the shooting gave my mother a glimmer of hope that my father had not been killed. So she didn't tell us what she had heard, trying to save us from unnecessary grief. After a time, we received a letter from my brother, writing from Germany. Although he was not yet fifteen, he had been sent to a prison camp with Polish soldiers. He wrote that he was healthy, and, as the youngest in the camp, everyone was taking care of him. Even when he had been sick and in the hospital, he had been well treated, and he hoped that he would be sent home soon. He said that he had been separated from Father when he was taken captive, and had not seen him nor heard anything of him since. He asked that we write him if we knew anything.

The atmosphere at home was a mixture of joy and sadness. After weeks of knowing nothing — a letter had come from my brother, written in his own hand, proving that he was alive and well. But what had happened to Father?

The news spread quickly. Neighbors gathered in our apartment, each of them reading the letter and adding comments and interpretations. Finally my mother said, "I will write to Mottel today and tell him that we have heard from Father and that he is in Warsaw. Who knows how much the boy has suffered, and what he is suffering right now..."

The bitter truth was that Mottel's letter had confirmed what my mother had heard, and left no room for hope that my father might still be alive. At that time, Warsaw had surrendered to the German army, and another stream of returning people had reached Lodz. We received regards from our relatives in Warsaw, and it was clear that Father had not reached them. Mother began gently hinting to us that our father was no longer alive, and then, after a time, she told us the whole story.

So what I feared had proven to be true. I had been orphaned. I no longer had a father. I knew that, in wars, people got killed, but it never occurred to me that anything like that might happen to my father. And why did it have to happen to us? Everyone we knew was alive. No one had been killed; no one had even been injured. Why did the Germans have to kill him, for no good reason? He was not a soldier and he had not fought against them. And what should I do? How should I behave now? Everyone told me that I "must be strong." But I didn't know how to be strong or what being strong meant. I couldn't stop thinking about my father and my throat kept choking up. Since my father and brother had left the house, I had not really thought about Mottel, nor had I thought about my uncle Feivel, whom I dearly loved. Only after the letter came from the prison camp did I begin to think about Mottel's life in the camp, about his expectations of coming home.

I refused to reconcile myself to the fact that my father was not alive. I didn't give up hope that he would return. I had heard stories about people who said that they had seen someone being killed, the families had sat *shiva* (the seven-day mourning period) for them — and the "dead" person had suddenly appeared, completely healthy. I was waiting for this miracle. I spent a lot of time sitting by the window, looking out into the street, waiting to see my father suddenly walking toward the building. Every day I waited for the postman, hoping for a letter from my father, which perhaps had been written from a different prison camp.

And my mother? She decided that she must find the remains of my father and bring them home for a Jewish burial. My father could not just be "missing," with his burial place unknown, without sitting *shiva* and without saying Kaddish for his soul. She saw this as her duty, of the utmost importance, that she must fulfill at any price — that was the only thing she could do for our father. Her friends tried in vain to convince her that the roads were dangerous, that she should not leave her home and children at a time like this, that her chances of finding my father were nonexistent.

As the railroads were being used for the most part by the German army, and any civilian trying to go by train needed a permit, and, as buses were not running at all, she looked for and found Jewish coachmen who were carrying people from Lodz to Warsaw and back. She set out after promising us to get back as quickly as she could.

It had only been a month earlier that my father and brother had left the house. Now my mother was going. I was frightened and worried — how could my mother set forth on the roads, a Jewish woman traveling alone among Poles and Germans? How would she find my father among the thousands of the dead? Were dead people scattered along the sides of the roads, as they said, or were they buried; and then, if he had been buried, how could she find Father? And if she found him, how could she bring him home? I wanted to see my father one more time. But up until then, I had never seen a dead person, and I was afraid to think about how my father's dead face would look. A coach with two black horses would certainly arrive, covered by black cloth, and my father would be put into a coffin, and I would walk beside my mother and my sister... And little Yankele, who didn't understand anything, would he be going with us? Would there be many people at the funeral? The funeral coach would probably travel through the streets of Lodz, as I had seen a few times — and how I used to pity the children who were walking behind the coffin! I never imagined that anything like that could happen to me. And at the cemetery, they would put my father into a pit, and maybe I would have to say Kaddish at the open grave. I hadn't reached my thirteenth birthday yet, the age at which I would be considered a man according to Jewish law, but my older brother was not there. I was the only one who could say Kaddish. These thoughts ran through my mind, and I was again choked up with tears. How could I say Kaddish at a grave?

I did not reveal my thoughts to anyone; I did not even tell my sister. I avoided my friends: they seemed so unfamiliar that I didn't want to see them. When I met one of them, I felt uncomfortable. They did not belong to my world. I prayed that my brother Mottel would come home quickly from the prison camp, so that I wouldn't be alone. He had always been at my side when I needed help. It was a good feeling knowing that you had an older brother, even though I didn't like it when he was angry with me or when he told me what to do or how to behave. When that had happened, I automatically resisted him, even though I often knew that he was right. Now I missed him. I needed him; I needed his closeness. I wanted to see how he would act in the new circumstances in which we found ourselves. I wanted him to show me how to go on living after what had happened to us. I needed him to relieve me of this heavy responsibility. It seemed to me that when he arrived, I would be able to tell him everything that was in my heart. That would bring me relief.

But most of my thoughts concerned my mother, who had gone to search for my dead father. A thousand images went through my mind, anything that could be imagined. I was very afraid. I was so worried about Mother that I thought less and less about Father. I counted the hours that had passed since she had left the house, and how much time remained until Friday — Mother had promised to be home for Shabbat. Time just didn't seem to move.

In order to make the time pass, I visited my grandparents every day; but whenever I walked into their house, I immediately wanted to leave. I could not look into their faces; I didn't know what to say to them, and they spoke only a few words to me. I knew that they had heard nothing from Feivel. I could feel their pain. My grandfather sat at the table, an open book in front of him, looking so sad. When I caught his glance, I felt a trembling pass through me. Grandmother sat in the corner of the room, hunched up as if she were frozen. Each of them was sealed in sorrow, and it seemed that there was no communication between them...as though they were strangers to one another. I didn't even know whether they wanted me to visit; I just seemed to be disturbing them. I felt as if the connection between us had been broken. I left with various excuses and went home using the main streets.

On Plac Wolności, the statue of Tadeusz Kosciuszko (the Polish war hero of the American Revolution) was gone — the Germans had blown it up one night, and there was no sign of it the next morning. The square stood empty and denuded without the statue. One of the large shops had been turned into German army head-quarters. On the street, there was a heavy machine gun, loaded with a chain of bullets, with two German soldiers sitting beside it. Armed German soldiers were stationed in front of public buildings. Flags with swastikas were waving in every direction. Some of the shops were closed; some of them had changed owners from Jews to Poles. Signs in German had been posted and those in Yiddish removed. The street was crowded with Poles, German soldiers and Germans in civilian clothes speaking German in loud voices. German army vehicles crowded the roads in every direction. The trolleys passed by filled with riders and ringing their bells. Life had gone back to normal, but not for the Jews. Jews were not seen walking or standing in the street — not in the doorways of the buildings nor in the entrances to the shops. Now they only crossed the streets quickly and disappeared.

When my mother left the house, she walked to one of the squares where the coachmen and their coaches stood. She traveled first to Glowno, where she stayed until evening, and then continued on her way all night in a coach filled with people. On the way, they passed through German army checkpoints, and toward morning, they reached Prushkov. When my mother told some Jews there why she had come, they advised her to speak to the town rabbi. The rabbi and his wife received her warmly, gave her a room and said that she could stay there as long as she wanted to. The rabbi heard her story and asked for details. He said that he would do anything he could to help her in her holy task. The rabbi invited Jews who were in contact with the surrounding villages to come, and asked them if they had heard about a group of Jews who had been shot by the Germans. He asked them to question the farmers in the area, and he spoke to the people who came to pray in the synagogue, telling them that it would be a mitzvah to help find my father's body.

My mother rented another coach and went out to the villages in the area. She went from house to house, asking, but usually met with lack of interest and short answers such as, "We don't know anything," or "We didn't hear anything," while some answered her with open hostility or even chased her away with threats. But there were also villagers who received her pleasantly and with understanding and helped her in her search. She visited churches and spoke with priests, left sums of money with them and asked them to request information from those who came to pray on Sundays. She promised a handsome reward to anyone who would bring her information about what she was seeking. In the evenings, she would return to the rabbi's house, where the rabbi and his wife would prepare a hot meal for her and offer encouragement. My mother continued searching day after day, from morning till night — with no success, but with the belief that she would ultimately succeed.

On Thursday morning, Mother came home. We were so happy to see her that for a moment, we forgot all of our troubles. Mother was home with us. After the initial moments had passed, we could see from Mother's face what she had been through over the past few days, including the exhaustion of the all-night journey by coach in the stormy weather of the Polish autumn. Her coat was drenched and creased, her shoes covered with mud. When she took off her kerchief, her hair was oddly plastered to her head. Her face, which had been red when she entered the house, was now wan, and her forehead was creased with wrinkles that we had never noticed before. Her eyes seemed smaller and it looked as though she had difficulty keeping them open. We sat with her silently. We didn't dare ask the painful question. But she saw the inquiry in our faces and said, "I haven't succeeded in finding Father. On Sunday, I'll continue my search. Now I must lie down to sleep awhile."

Mother slept deeply for many hours. In the meanwhile, my sister prepared lunch and we hungrily waited. When Mother awoke, she was angry that she had slept so long. After she had washed up and gotten dressed, she looked nice again, and she even smiled. During lunch she told us that she had many errands that must be done. She needed money and she didn't know how she could get it quickly. She wanted to meet again with the man who had told her about Father's death — perhaps she could find out more accurately where the shooting had taken place. She intended to leave again on Sunday morning, and she had to buy provisions and cook for the following week. She spoke firmly and confidently; she had no doubt that she would be able to withstand whatever she had to. She ate quickly and went out to do her errands. In the evening, she told us about her difficult week in Prushkov, about the rabbi's wonderful family, about her visits in the villages and her conversations with the people she had met. She described her searches for mass graves in the fields, about the moments of hope, fear and despair she had experienced. There was a pleasant atmosphere at home that Shabbat. It was good to wake up in the morning and to find our mother at home, to sit at the table in her company, to hear her speak to the people who came to visit us. I took in every word, wondering at her courage.

Since she had come home from her journey, Mother had greatly changed. She seemed more sure of herself, full of energy, confident in her ability to achieve what she had set out to do. In the past, she had taken care of the home and had helped Father with the business, but Father had been the one to make decisions and determine what was to be done in the business and in the family. Mother had never done anything without his agreement; she had never even bought anything, except household provisions, without him — despite the fact that he was always busy, father even used to go with all of us to buy clothes. When Father made an important deal, he would explain its importance to Mother until he had convinced her. More than once when Father had argued with people, Mother had disagreed with his strict and inflexible attitudes and had tried to bridge the gap and compromise, and this had greatly upset him. He would pace the floor, speaking, shouting, even begging my mother to agree with him, and when she maintained her own opinion, he would become downcast and silent for hours. My mother had enjoyed the fact that my father assumed all responsibility. But now that he was absent, everything had changed completely.

When my mother decided to seek my father's remains, she didn't take anything into consideration and she had no idea of what was ahead of her. She saw only the goal she had set for herself, ignoring the fact that she was alone without anyone to watch over her, who would decide or plan for her. She could plan, decide and do things that she never would have thought that she had the strength to do. This discovery was evident in her behavior.

Her intuition told her that she was close to finding Father; she had already planned to hire workers who would open the mass grave where he had been buried and bring him to a Jewish grave. She hesitated, though, about where it would be fitting to bury him. It was logical to lay his remains to rest in Prushkov, but in that case, she would have to come back to take my sister and me to the funeral. She couldn't leave little Yankele with our grandparents, who weren't able to care for him in their present state, so she arranged that he would stay with a neighbor when the time came. I heard her talking to the neighbor and I was filled with uneasiness. This time I wasn't afraid that something would happen to my mother; I was frightened of a meeting with death. I was afraid that I would not be able to stand face-to-face with the reality of my dead father. I secretly prayed that my mother would not find his remains.

As it turned out, Mother was not successful. On her second journey, rain fell constantly in the area, and the dusty paths turned to mud. The fields were covered with water; the tracks had been erased. All of my mother's efforts to search for Father ended in futility. Depressed and in despair, she took the advice of the priests, who told her to wait for the end of winter. In the spring, when the farmers began to plow their fields, they would discover the graves; they would remove the bodies and bring them to the cemetery. She would be able to identify my father's body then.

My mother returned to all of the villages in the vicinity of Prushkov, met with priests and the heads of the villages, left descriptions of my father, and left money with them, along with our address and the address of the rabbi in Prushkov. She came home disappointed, but satisfied that she had done everything she could, and still hopeful that her efforts eventually would be rewarded.

These were the last days of autumn, days of rain and wind. Everything was grey and depressing. The days were short and the nights were long. We sat at home and waited, without knowing what we were waiting for. In the evenings, the neighbor from the floor below us would visit, and my mother would speak to her of the past. I heard stories I had never heard before. Excited, glowing, her eyes bright, choking back the tears and unable to speak from time to time, Mother spoke of how father had appeared at her home for the first time, a young soldier, tall and thin, introducing himself as a far-removed relative, and saying that he was serving at the Citadel in Warsaw, and that his parents had given him their address so that he could have some contact with a "Jewish home" near there.

My mother went on to say that my father had been shy and diffident, unlike those sharp-tongued Warsaw youths that she knew. "But on the first evening, the young soldier captured my heart, and that night, I couldn't sleep a wink," she said. She waited impatiently for his second visit, afraid that he might not come. As he began to visit their home more frequently, he became less shy, and my mother would listen avidly to the stories of his adventures in the army and tales of the war, stories that were seasoned with humor. The first time my father invited my mother to go for a walk, she agreed without hesitation, although it was not customary for a young girl to go out walking with a soldier — and it might have cost her her good reputation. The two walked along the streets without talking very much, and during the walk, my father invited her out to a bakeshop to have some cake with him.

My mother was extremely happy. Whenever she heard my father's steps outside, she knew that he was coming to visit and she would already be at the window when he arrived. The other girls in the building looked out as well, and were envious. Just in case one of the girls might consider stealing my father's heart from her, she cut off all of her relationships with her friends.

My mother related that my father would leave the camp without permission to spend time with her, and she was always afraid that he would be caught and punished with imprisonment, but on the other hand, she was proud that he would take that chance just to be with her. One day, after he hadn't visited her for quite a while, she couldn't stand it any longer and went out looking for him. A Jewish girl walking near the gates of the Citadel alone was a rare sight. Soldiers gathered around her; some tried to court her, a few tried to help her find my father. "I wouldn't have gone there for any amount of money in the world," said my mother. "I don't know what gave me the strength to go there." In the end, a soldier came out and told her that my father was training with his unit in the fields, about three kilometers from the fortress. The soldier told her that it was an area forbidden to civilians, but my mother didn't listen to him.

"Not deliberately, without intending to, I found myself walking in the direction that the soldier had pointed out until I heard the shout, 'Halt!' A soldier ordered me to go back down the path I had come and to approach him. His rifle was aimed at me. When I neared him, he began shouting, 'What are you doing in a closed army area? Don't you know that you were walking through a minefield? You could have been killed!' When the soldier calmed down, he began to question me about what I was doing in an army area. I didn't know what to answer. I couldn't tell him that I was looking for my Moshe," said my mother, and she smiled contemplatively. "I told the soldier that I had just gone for a walk. The soldier looked into my eyes and said, 'You're lying. All right, you'll have to wait here until I bring a soldier to relieve me, and then, you'll have to come with me to headquarters. There are officers there who'll know how to get the truth out of you. Perhaps you are a spy?' I was very frightened. I thought I would be arrested and put in prison. They might send me to a military court and I could be sentenced to hanging for spying," continued my mother. She burst out laughing, but I swallowed my tears of emotion.

The German occupational regime, which was getting better-organized every day, issued a great number of decrees against Jews. Jews were fired from government and municipal jobs. Jews were forbidden to work in the free professions — there were no more Jewish teachers, lawyers or newspaper reporters. There were no more Jewish doctors in hospitals. There was no end to the anti-Jewish proclamations, which sometimes contradicted each other. One day an edict was issued ordering shops and businesses to open; the next day came another edict saying that shops wishing to open had to receive a license — and when Jews came to request a license, not only were they refused, they were not even allowed to enter the licensing office. The Germans began to loot and steal. Again and again, German trucks would stop near a shop, a business or storage facility belonging to Jews and soldiers would clear out the merchandise, often arresting the owners. The Germans found assistants quickly enough among Polish and Jewish informers. They seemed to be in every corner, and when they were seen traveling in German cars, everyone would be struck by fear and anxiety.

Actually, no one had any idea of what was going on — there was a total lack of information. The rumor mill churned out contradictory information with great speed. In every Jewish home, there were stormy arguments about what to do. Rumor followed rumor: the Germans had made an agreement with the Russians — they would soon evacuate Lodz and the Russians would come in their place (when I saw a convoy of German vehicles headed west, I told everyone that the Germans were already leaving the city); the Germans had decided to annex all of western Poland, including Lodz, to the Third Reich, and in other parts of Poland, they would set up a Polish government under German auspices; the Jews who had fled to Russia were receiving a warm welcome — people were returning for their families, and families were quietly leaving the city, leaving all of their possessions behind. Those who were returning from Russia, however, said that the situation there was worse than in Poland — many of those who crossed the border from Poland to the Soviet Union were being arrested and sent to Siberia, and those who hadn't been arrested were wandering around the streets, homeless and without a crust of bread to eat; thousands who had crossed the border from Poland to the Soviet Union had been chased back across the border by the Russians and the Germans had opened fire on them.

Two families had left our apartment building, and a German family now occupied the apartment on the floor above us. When my mother left the house in the morning, she met the German woman in the hall, who introduced herself, and they exchanged a few friendly words. My mother spoke a mixture of German and Yiddish with her and they were able to understand each other. When I went out into the hall, I was shocked to see the two of them speaking. The German woman was about forty years old, thin, tall and nice-looking. She was wearing a long, flowered housecoat. I didn't know how to react and wanted to go back inside, but the woman called to me in German and asked my name. In confusion I told her my name in a weak voice, and she laughed and patted me. Afterward, she told my mother that her husband had received a position in Lodz, and she hoped that there would be good, neighborly relations between us. She asked if my mother could lend her some household utensils to clean the apartment with until she could buy what she needed, and she came into our house, looked around, took what she asked for and thanked my mother. When she left, my mother sat down deep in thought.

The German woman visited us every morning after her husband had gone to work. She always apologized, finding some reason to knock at our door — asking for or returning some object and chatting about something while standing in the doorway. Sometimes, out of politeness, my mother would invite her in, but she always refused, saying that she had no time and that she had a lot of work in the apartment. More than once, she offered my mother help buying things that were hard for us to obtain; my mother thanked her but refused. One day, she told my mother that because of the war, unpleasant people had appeared who were taking advantage of the situation and making trouble for Jews; if we had any problems, we should not hesitate to speak to her. Her husband was an important man and he could do a lot for us.

One morning, Mother told us that Father had appeared to her in a dream and told her that she must open the factory, and that she had decided follow his request. This was difficult and dangerous for people with experience, let alone a woman whose only familiarity with the business had been helping her husband with production. My mother's first goal was to use the raw material we still had to manufacture the finished goods for sale; we could use the earnings if we decided to leave Lodz. She proceeded to work with great energy, spending her days looking for workers, negotiating with dealers, and of course, tackling difficulties at every step. In the evenings, she would come home exhausted, talking of the business all the time, making calculations, writing lists, and when people came to our home, she would show them the merchandise, explain and bargain about the price. The atmosphere at home changed. The house seemed to come to life — but this was only during the day. When late evening came, depression returned and enveloped us in its darkness.

Ultimately, Mother found two workers and a woman to do the sewing, and the three of them began to work in production. But the next problem was how to transfer the merchandise from place to place. This was forbidden without a license, and German guards patrolled the streets, stopping people who carried parcels. I told my mother that if I wrapped myself in bolts of cloth and then wore a wide coat, no one would notice. My suggestion was accepted and the smuggling went well. One day, I walked, wrapped in cloth, right past a German building. I knew that a sentry was standing at the gate of the building, so as I approached it I crossed to the other side of the street. But when I was just opposite the sentry, I glanced at him — and he called me over to him. I was very frightened. I was sure that the German had understood what I was doing; for a moment, I considered running away, but I was already too close to him. I stood before him, trembling, and he took a bill out of his pocket and ordered me to buy a pack of cigarettes for him. When I brought him the cigarettes and the change, he thanked me.

The direct meeting with the German soldier bolstered my confidence. I continued walking to the house of the woman who was going to do the sewing, in a good mood, but when I got home my mother immediately asked me, "Berale, what happened?" I must have been too excited. I told my mother what had happened and she said, "I'm not going to let you do that again." I protested; I asserted that I wasn't afraid anymore, but her intuition told her how strong the shock must have been and she wouldn't change her mind.

The next day, early in the morning, there was loud knocking at the door. Immediately, a group of four Germans came in — straight to the guest room. One, dressed in a brown uniform, aimed a pistol in his hand directly at us. Two were belted soldiers and two were wearing civilian clothing. One of them shouted "Heil Hitler!" We stood there, frightened. The German in the brown uniform shouted, "Why don't you answer?" We all replied "Heil Hitler!" They searched every room in the apartment and took out all of the packed boxes of merchandise that my father had brought home just before the war had begun. One of them opened the kitchen cabinet and took out the silver utensils that were arranged on the shelf — Kiddush cups, four candlesticks and a few other dishes, most of them gifts from previous years. We stood huddled together, frozen. The German in the brown uniform guarded us, keeping his gun pointed in our direction. My mother, to my surprise, began speaking to the German. She asked him to leave us a few sweaters. I was afraid that the German would shoot her, but he looked at us, thought for a moment, and with a smile called the soldier with the package. He took out four sweaters and threw them at us, looking at us as though he expected us to thank him for his kindheartedness. My mother murmured, "Thank you very much." When they finished taking out all of the merchandise, they left in great haste, awakening in us the suspicion that they had not been sent by the authorities but were just thieves acting on some information. After they left, my mother burst into tears.

As we were sitting in a state of shock, the German neighbor came into the apartment. When my mother told her what had just happened, she began to shout, "In the name of God, why didn't you call me? I wouldn't have let them do that to you." She questioned my mother and asked who the Germans were, whether they had presented a warrant from the government, whether they had given a receipt. She decided that they must have been thieves and advised us to speak to the Gestapo. She would speak to her husband, she said; the thieves might be found and our merchandise returned to us. When Mother told her friends about the advice we had received — to speak to the Gestapo — she heard hair-raising stories about people who had complained to the Gestapo and who had been beaten instead of being helped, or even disappeared, never to be seen again. From then on, our German neighbor stopped visiting us and tried not to run into us.

Mother finally came to the conclusion that she couldn't overcome the difficulties of running the business. She sold the raw material at a low price and changed the money into gold; and again, we sat at home, doing nothing. "When Mottel comes home from the prison camp," she said, "maybe times will have changed for the better, and we can start again." But in the meantime, we lacked any productive activity, and there would have been no better remedy than activity to get over the disaster of our failure. On the other hand, the short period of business activity had left a more relaxed and pleasant atmosphere in our home. We hadn't forgotten Father, but there had been other things to occupy our thoughts, and it had been good to see Mother busy and feeling useful.

My love for Mother deepened greatly during those days. My heart bled for her. I felt that there was no one in the world unhappier than she was; now, condemned to do nothing, she again became despondent. Mourning and depression returned and ruled our home. The spirit of our father haunted us and never left.

One day my mother came home and told us that our Uncle Feivel had been killed. Two soldiers who had served with him had come home from a prison camp and said that on the second day of the war, when their divisions had reached the front, the Germans attacked them even before they had managed to get organized. Some of the soldiers had been killed and the others taken prisoner. Since the beginning of the war there had been no word from Feivel. We knew, of course, that the Polish army had been defeated and was completely broken and splintered, but we still had hopes that Feivel had been taken prisoner, or perhaps had fled eastward, into Russia. Now all our hopes were shattered. My uncle, whom I had loved, was also dead. We would never see him again.

We all went to our grandparents' home, to stay with them through the seven days of *shiva*. Living with them was very difficult, at first. For days, we were all together in one room, deep in sorrow. I felt as though Uncle Feivel's spirit was hovering in the air. I used to love visiting my grandparents, and I especially loved to watch Piotrkowska Street, the main street of Lodz, through their window. On holidays, I would watch the army parades and marches. On other days, there were demonstrations and funerals of important people, and whatever was happening on the busy street interested me. Now, during the *shiva*, I didn't dare go near the window, even though I knew that watching the street would make me feel less depressed and would help me bear the somber atmosphere. After all, I had come to my grandparents' home to mourn, and I would not desecrate the mourning period. My grandfather prayed and recited Psalms all day. My grandmother sat without moving. Restless, I did not know what to do. My grandfather gave me a book of Psalms and ordered me to read. I sat, the book open in front of me, but I couldn't read one word. In the mornings and in the evenings, people would come to pray, and my grandfather would say Kaddish. Would I, too, have to say Kaddish for a full year, three times a day, for my father?

My resolve crumpled quickly; I went to the window that first morning. The street was especially busy. I saw many Germans in different uniforms, and a few Jews who walked quickly and disappeared into the yards of their buildings. Ladders extended from fire engines and the firemen had climbed up and were hanging huge flags on the fronts of the buildings and on the electricity poles, as they did on Polish national holidays. But this time, seeing the red flags with swastikas in the center turned the exciting spectacle into a source of frustration. I walked away from the window and decided not to look out again.

That day we discovered that the Germans had annexed Lodz to the Third Reich and had given the city a new name; from now on, the city would be called Litzmannstadt. Piotrkowski Street also had a new name: Hitlerstrasse. There were also rumors that Hitler himself would come to Lodz and observe a parade of the German army from the city square. The rumors and hopes that the Germans would leave Lodz had proven false.

In Uncle Feivel's room, I found a sealed treasure trove of books, booklets and old magazines. Most of them had been issued by Zionist organizations. I looked through them and they took me away to another world, a beautiful one, full of hopes and dreams. Engrossed in reading, I didn't notice the time passing. When my mother came in to see what I was doing, I awoke at once from my daydreams and blushed as though I had been caught in some sinful activity. I was sure that my mother would be angry with me for reading heretical literature, but she smiled and said, "Keep on reading, Berale." As she left the room I heard her say, "Berale is sitting and reading." My grandfather replied, "It's not good that he's reading that garbage," but my mother thought differently. "Nothing will happen to him," she said. "It is better for him to read than to be deep in thought all day. I'm afraid that the child will lose his mind from too much thinking, Heaven forbid."

There, in my uncle's little room, I discovered literature. During the six remaining days of *shiva*, I read from morning till night, and the days went by quickly. When we finally came home, our apartment seemed large and roomy, and we all felt relieved. Yankele, who had been quiet and reserved at Grandmother's house, began running around as though he had been released from a cage. As for me, the minute I entered the house thoughts of my father returned and weighed down upon me.

One day, a woman whom I had never seen before, about thirty years old, came to see my mother, and I noticed how my mother paled and then blushed when she saw her. I also noticed that Mother hesitated a bit before she invited the guest to come in. I wondered what gave the woman such an unusual appearance — her clothing, her hair style, or perhaps her sad face — and it was difficult for me to tell whether or not she was Jewish. For a moment, the woman and my mother sat silently opposite each other, and then the woman asked, "Do you know who I am?" "Yes, I know," my mother answered, and again there was silence. After a bit the woman said that she had heard about the disaster that had struck us. My mother introduced us to her, but because of the woman's embarrassment, asked us to leave the room. My curiosity was aroused. Who was this woman? I stood behind the door, trying to eavesdrop. The woman explained to my mother, "I came to you because I felt that I had to speak to someone from the family. My heart told me that you would not slam the door in my face, that you would listen to me."

Now I knew who the woman was. Long ago I had heard of a relative of my father who had converted to Christianity, married a Pole and was a high official in the municipality of Lodz. The sorrow and shame of this deed had been so great that no one from our family dared to mention the name of the convert. Everyone tried to forget her, as though she had never existed, and her parents had even sat *shiva* for her, cut off all contact with her, and isolated themselves from other people in shame and depression. The only person I knew from this part of my father's family was the woman's brother, who had often visited us. As he was extremely anti-religious, he had argued with my father many times, at first, in a reserved way, and then with more and more excitement and shouting, to my great anxiety. My mother tried to placate the two, usually unsuccessfully, but I had the feeling that she enjoyed the arguments themselves. My father's opponent claimed that the appearance of the ultra-Orthodox, the beards and the *payess* (sidelocks), their dress and behavior, which was different from that of everyone around them, would arouse anti-Semitism and bring destruction upon all of the Jews. My father would answer, "Look at what happened in Germany! There, the Jews were so integrated that they themselves had forgotten that they were Jews. Did that help them?"

The two would insult each other at every meeting, and more than once, I had the feeling that they really hated each other, but again and again they would be happy when they met. I never heard the man mention his sister; it seemed that there was some kind of unwritten agreement in the family never to touch this painful subject. As having a convert in the family seemed to me both horrible and mysterious, I never asked my mother or father about it; I felt that the subject was forbidden. About a year before the war broke out, the woman's mother died — it was said that she had died of sorrow — and when my parents came back from the funeral, I heard them arguing. "Where did she get the audacity to come to the funeral?" said my father, "She's the one who killed her!" But my mother defended her, "Do you think that it was easy for her to come, to sense the hatred that everyone feels toward her? Didn't you see how she was standing aside, alone and crying? Moshe, I'll tell you the truth. I wanted to go over and comfort her." My father reacted with a short laugh. "Yes," he said, "I can believe that you would do that. Even if the devil himself seemed sad, you would go over and comfort him."

Now this very woman, the convert, never to be mentioned, was sitting in our home and telling Mother the story of her life. She spoke fluently. She said that her marriage had not been a success; her husband had been a good man and she had loved him, but his family had been anti-Semitic and only saw her as a Jew, in spite of the fact that she had converted. They had purposely tormented her and had treated her as an unwanted stranger, causing tension between her and her husband. In the end, the family had been victorious. "They won," she said. "We were divorced. Two weeks ago, I was fired from my job in the municipality because I am Jewish. For non-Jews, I remained a Jew. For the Jews, I was a non-Jew. I have no place in this world."

Again there was silence. But after a moment, my mother invited the woman to have lunch with us. The woman refused and left us with a forced smile. At the door, my mother told her that our home would always be open to her and she could return and visit. The woman answered with a nod of her head. Mother was worried; she blamed herself for not finding the words to encourage the depressed woman. "I am afraid," she said, "that she might do something stupid and commit suicide." We never saw the woman again. In my imagination, I saw her jumping from the roof of a building.

The edict the Germans publicized stating that Jews must wear a yellow patch shocked us. The Jews of Poland had always known persecution, edicts, and pogroms, but we had learned to deal with them, as we had dealt with natural disasters and unforeseeable and unpreventable calamities. When governments had initiated and encouraged pogroms against Jews, they had never made their intentions public; it was enough for them that the Polish people did the dirty work. Hitler, on the other hand, came out openly against the Jewish nation and set up a special system to deal with Jews. From the day the Germans took control of our city, we began experiencing humiliation. The edicts made our lives difficult in every aspect and eliminated the basis of our livelihoods. With each new edict, we imagined that things could not get any worse. But after a short period of time, something more terrible would come — and this pattern was repeated again and again. It is difficult to describe the extent of the affront, the terrible feeling of being marked, separated from all others, identified publicly as inferior, lacking rights which every non-Jew enjoyed.

The order was as follows: every Jew, from young children to the elderly, with no exception, must wear a yellow patch in the form of a *Magen David* (Star of David) on his front and back, at all hours of the day, from the moment he left his home. This seemed very strange to me. I couldn't understand the meaning behind the patch. A *Magen David*, the symbol that decorated synagogues, the Torah scroll, our flag — a symbol of pride and hope — had been turned into a sign of humiliation by the Germans! My mother sewed yellow patches on all of our coats, trying to do it as accurately as possible for aesthetic reasons, and we sat around her, watching silently. My sister cried. She said that she wouldn't leave the house looking like an exhibit or a display.

The first time I left the house with a yellow patch sewn on both sides of my coat, I stopped at the gate and looked around. Among the people passing by, those wearing a yellow patch stuck out, but this wasn't the *Magen David* that decorated things that were dear to us; the patch was ugly and prominent. The Germans and the Poles looked at those who were wearing the patch as though they were strange beings, smiled, and sometimes even burst out laughing or cursed us. The marked ones, their faces serious and pale, walked quickly, keeping close to the walls of the buildings so as not to be too obvious. I walked out into the street. I felt that everyone was staring at me. Suddenly I was a stranger, even to those who knew me. I tried to avoid the eyes of people I knew.

The area where we lived was mixed, Jews and Poles living together; the closer I came to a more Jewish neighborhood, the more coats I saw with yellow patches — and I felt better. It quickly became clear that even with this edict, which was so shocking we couldn't imagine how we would be able to tolerate it, we would be able to get on with our lives. We got used to it. Lodz, a city where half the residents were Jewish, was divided into two camps — the camp of those who wore the yellow patch and the camp of those who were exempt. And such was the force of habit that it quickly began to seem that it had always been that way.

The Germans, who did not know how to distinguish between Jews and Poles, were sometimes helped by Poles to catch Jews for forced labor. The first victims were Jews with beards and *payess*, who wore traditional Jewish clothing. Many Jews, especially young people, shaved their beards and *payess*, changed their long coats to short ones, and donned "Jewish" visor hats, brimmed hats or regular visor hats so that they would not be easy prey for the Germans or objects of their cruelty. Again and again, I was surprised to come across Jews I knew who had changed their appearance and looked like non-Jews — as though the "image of God" had been removed from them. Then, however, the edict to wear the patch revealed the identities of Jews for all to see — a change of dress or appearance could no longer help, even for one who had been non-religious or had completely identified him or herself as a Pole for many years. Those who had distanced themselves from Judaism to the extent that they had even forgotten that they were Jews, who had forgotten the language and customs of their forefathers, could now be seen walking down the street wearing a yellow patch, belonging neither to the Jews nor to the non-Jews.

From the time that the Germans changed the name of Piotrkowski Street to Hitlerstrasse, Jews were forbidden to enter the street. Each day, the Germans would confiscate Jewish apartments and the Jews would be forced out, allowed to take with them only what they could carry. There was a widespread rumor that soon the Jews would be ordered to leave the street entirely. My grandparents, who lived on that street, could not leave their home. We had to provide them with everything they needed, and I would usually be the one to do this. To get to their street, I would have to walk about one hundred meters through areas off-limits to Jews.

When I got to the corner of the street, I would look in all directions, and after I had made sure that there were no Germans, I would run quickly; in a few minutes I was at the yard of my grandparents' building. The first few times I did this, I was so frightened that I sat in the doorway for a few minutes before I knocked at their door. As time passed, my fear almost disappeared; I felt almost as though I were going out to buy a pack of cigarettes, like my father used to ask me to do. In the evenings, when the stairway was dark, I would run up quickly and if I bumped into someone, or a startled cat, I would lose my breath from fright. I was always panting when I got home. Now that everyone could identify me by the yellow patch on my coat, my fear was even greater, especially since there were gangs of local German children — the *Volksdeutsche* — whose members, wearing fine-looking clothes adorned with a ribbon with a swastika on their sleeves, lay in wait for Jewish children at the corner of Hitlerstrasse. When one of us got caught, we were beaten mercilessly.

As I approached the street, I would hide in the doorways, peeking out to make sure that there were no gangs in the vicinity. If I saw them, I would wait a long time after they had gone, because I had been caught a few times as I ran the short distance to my grandparents' building by a gang that had suddenly appeared and run after me. Luckily, I was faster than they were. I had the feeling that they had given up trying to catch me until one day, as I was leaving my grandparents' building, one of them jumped out in front of me, caught me by my sleeve, and began shouting, "*Jude! Jude!*" He was shorter than me, but heavier. He shouted to his older friends, but no one came. I was confused and didn't know what to do, and it seemed to me that he was about to burst into tears. "Leave me alone," I said, but he kept holding on to me and muttering, "*Jude! Jude!*" I pushed him away to free myself and he fell down on the sidewalk. After I had run for a while, I turned to look behind me. A group of German boys was running after me in the distance. I didn't know whether they had seen me, or whether they were just looking for me. I hadn't intended to push the boy down

— I just wanted to free myself. But the fact remained: I had pushed down a German boy.

I kept running until I couldn't go any farther. My feet were tripping over themselves and my whole body was shaking. What would happen to me if they kept running and followed me to our house? I could bring disaster down upon my whole family! I entered the gate of one of the buildings not far from ours where some friends of my parents lived. I climbed the stairs but I didn't dare knock on their door, so I kept climbing until I had reached the attic. The door was locked. I sat on the floor, in a corner, and waited. Now and then I heard footsteps and became scared, but nothing happened. In the end, after more than an hour, I went downstairs and ran home. I didn't tell anyone what had happened to me; I didn't want to upset my mother. But deep inside, I was still afraid, even in the house. Every time I heard footsteps in the yard, I would run to the window to make sure it wasn't the group of German boys. If my brother Mottel had been at home, I would have told him about it. I missed him very much. The thought of the German gang looking for me weighed on my mind constantly. I sought a way to get to my grandparents' building by bypassing the dangerous part of the street. The next time my mother sent me to my grandparents' house, I made my way through side streets until I reached an exit to Hitlerstrasse that was directly opposite their house. Then, all I had to do was cross the forbidden street, which was less dangerous. From then on, this was the route my whole family took.

After a period of heavy wind and rain, snow fell one night and blanketed the city in white. The wind died down. Large flakes of snow continued to fall from a grey sky. Every year, my mother used to wake us in the morning after the first snowfall so we could see the white covering in which the world was enveloped. I would jump out of bed and stand by the window, hypnotized by the magical sight, each year experiencing the lovely sight as if I were seeing it for the first time. With the snow, silence covered the earth and life seemed to be a silent movie, or as if people walked on tiptoe, with hushed steps. The wagons and the coaches traveled slowly and quietly, and the only sound was the whinnying of the horses from time to time. The sleighs quickly appeared and slid along the white carpet, filling the air with the constant sound of the bells tied to the horses' necks, warning pedestrians of their approach. Instead of coming right home after school, I used to love to walk the streets, absorbing the special atmosphere of the first snowfall until the cold would pierce through me, forcing me home to the heater. My mother would look at me and say, "That boy is as frozen as ice." These were days of happiness and fun for children. We would make snowmen in the yards, have snowball fights with each other, go sliding on sleds, on pieces of flat board, or on the sides of our shoes, always knowing that a warm house would be waiting for us. But snow didn't always fall quietly; there were also snowstorms, which would hurl heavy wet snowflakes into our faces like whip lashes. The sidewalks would become slippery with ice, and walking was difficult and dangerous. Many people slipped and fell even if they were walking carefully, next to the walls of the buildings, trying to protect themselves against the gusts of wind. Everyone hurried home to the warmth and security of their own sheltering homes.

On the long winter evenings, so frosty and cold outside, the family would stay together in our house, which was so warm you could have walked around with no clothes on, as we used to say. Every guest was received with shouts of happiness and we would all dine on the treats that father would bring home; more than anything, I loved the hot sandwiches made with a variety of smoked meat and salami, and the delicious halva that father would buy for us. The usual routine of dinner rules was ignored; we didn't have to eat at a table covered by a tablecloth, and everyone would just take what they wanted and wash it down with hot tea.

That year, 1939, the snow fell just as it did in other years. Everything was covered in white as in every other year, and again, I stood by the window, watching the beautiful spectacle that nature was creating within the space of one evening. But my heart was filled with pain. Why couldn't this winter be like all of the others? Why had the snow ceased to be a sign of happiness and enjoyment? I wanted to believe that everything that had happened in the past few months had only been a terrifying dream, that everything would go back to normal, to the way it was before. I imagined that when I awakened from this dream, I wouldn't tell anyone about it, and I continued to watch the snowflakes falling…but I did not awaken. The nightmare continued, heralding unlimited horror.

A letter arrived from my brother Mottel. He wrote that he had been released from the prison camp, but while on his way home, he had gotten sick and was hospitalized in Krakow. For now he was staying with a Jewish family who had taken him under their wing, and soon he would be home. The house resounded with shouts of joy, our troubles momentarily forgotten. Mottel was coming home from the prison camp! But in our hearts, there was anger, pain. I was even afraid of the moment when Mottel would enter the house, alone, without Father. Mother was confused, first hurrying around the house and then, suddenly, stopping and thinking, talking to herself, not knowing exactly what to do. Should she go to Krakow and bring Mottel home? Perhaps he wasn't able to travel by himself. Perhaps he wasn't really well enough. But what if she left the house when he might knock at the door at any moment? Who knows how long it had taken for the letter to reach us?

The problem was solved on that very afternoon, when we received a telegram saying that Mottel would be arriving on the following day. Mother recovered and went into action. She rushed out and bought the best food she could find, and the kitchen went into operation as though it were a holiday evening, delicious smells filling the house. Mother didn't stop talking about the great suffering Mottel had experienced. "When he gets home," she said, "let him enjoy life for a bit, at least. We have to spoil him. Who knows what state his health is in… Why, he's only a child…" She worked hard, preparing the foods that he liked, and kept talking to herself in a loud voice. The kitchen was warm and pleasant. We all sat there and Mother turned to us and said, "I don't know what to do. Judging by the letters he sent us, Mottel doesn't know what happened to Father. Now he is coming home from hell. How can we tell him that Father is not alive? We must let him recover from what he has experienced. In the meantime, we'll tell him that we have received regards from Father and that he is in Russia. After that, we'll see..." Mother looked into my eyes, looking for approval for her idea. My sister and I remained quiet. We didn't have anything to say.

That night, I tried to imagine the meeting with Mottel. Only four months had passed since my father and Mottel had left home, but how far away it all seemed — so much had happened since then. Would the same Mottel who had left be coming back home? Would he be the same big brother with whom I had spent the summer in the village, the same brother who had sat with me in the forest, carving poplar branches for me more beautifully than anyone else could? I didn't know how I should act. My mother said that we should try to make Mottel happy; but how?

Early in the morning, I went out into the street and stood at the entrance to the house. It was winter, but the day wasn't very bitter; the cold snap had broken. The snow was grey, and beginning to melt, turning the streets and sidewalks into puddles of mud. Large drops of water and melting icicles fell from the windowsills onto the street, or onto people's heads. My eyes focused on every person who approached, on every trolley that stopped to let people off. The frost was over, but the damp cold penetrated my body through my wet shoes, spreading through me and pinching my heart. I hopped from foot to foot, but it didn't help. Every so often, I ran into the house to warm up, and then I returned to the street. Suddenly, I saw my brother as the trolley approached the station. I saw his head among the others, scanning the crowd. Our eyes met. He stood at the steps of the trolley car and stepped off before it had stopped. He had forgotten for a moment where he was standing when he saw me, and he hurried toward me. For a moment, he seemed to be walking on air — then he fell from the platform onto the muddy street. I ran to help him get up. People stopped for a moment and looked at us. Someone shouted at my brother loudly for getting off the trolley so carelessly. My brother got up, took his suitcase, and the two of us disappeared into the yard of the building.

At home, after a moment of excitement, kissing and crying, there was silence and embarrassment. We didn't know how to begin a conversation or what to talk about. Mother set the table, piling Mottel's plate with the delicious dishes she had prepared. My eyes measured him; it seemed to me that he had grown taller and thinner. His head had been shaved, and his appearance was strange; for some reason, he seemed to be a stranger among us. His eyes investigated every corner of the room, as if he didn't recognize the house. Would he return to himself and become my brother and my friend, as he had been in the past? Would I be able to tell him everything buried in my heart? Mother asked about his health and why he had been hospitalized. Mottel answered that while he had been in the prison camp, he had developed an infection and a high fever. He was taken to a hospital in a small village in Germany. He described the lovely small hospital in detail, the order and cleanliness, the quiet around him, the good treatment of the doctors and the nurses. He spoke of them by name, and the sound of the German names was strange coming from his lips.

Mottel told his story, stopping from time to time to concentrate on eating. He ate hungrily, and Mother, who had worried that perhaps she had prepared too much food, advised him to stop from time to time and not eat too much at once. Mottel acknowledged that she was right, but took another roll, spread butter on it and said with a smile, "It's so good…" While he was in the German hospital, he continued, there was an order to return him to the camp, as the prisoners were going to be released and sent back to Poland. The doctor who was taking care of Mottel objected, saying that his leg was not in good condition and he should remain in the hospital until it was completely healed. The director of the camp insisted. Mottel was returned to the camp in spite of the fact that he was still ill, and then he was put on a train to Poland. On the way, his condition worsened, and when he reached Krakow, he was taken to a Jewish hospital. He had been in danger of losing his left leg, but fortunately, the doctor there managed to save it. Mottel said that in Krakow, a woman he didn't know had come to visit him every day, taking care of his needs, and when he was released from the hospital she had taken him home, refusing to let him continue on his trip until he was well enough.

We sat and listened to Mottel's fascinating stories, and deep inside, I was envious that he had been in so many places and had experienced so much, in contrast to what I had done during this period. Suddenly, after about an hour of speaking, Mottel asked, "Has there been any news from Father?" A tense quiet fell over the room and I imagined that I could even hear the beating of my own heart. "Yes," said Mother, "we received regards from someone who had seen him on the Russian side of Poland, and since then, we haven't heard from him. They say that many refugees have been sent by the Russians to Siberia, and it is very difficult to get information from there…" I couldn't look into my brother's eyes. My sister lowered her gaze and tears filled her eyes. Mottel nodded, his eyes focused on the plate in front of him, but didn't say anything. I expected that he would ask more questions about Father, that he would talk about what had happened on their way to Warsaw and explain the reasons for their separation. Mottel was quiet, as though he were thinking about something else, and after a moment of silence asked how we were getting along. Only yesterday, I had been worried about what would happen when we began to talk about Father. I was sure that we wouldn't be able to hold up under the tension and father's death would be revealed immediately. But how easy it all was! Mottel had asked, my mother had lied — and he had accepted the lie without another thought, no questions asked, as if we had been speaking of something unimportant. All of a sudden it occurred to me that perhaps something was mentally wrong with my brother; I had heard that people who had undergone difficult experiences changed and behaved strangely. I was seized by fear.

"Mottel is tired from the trip. He has to rest," said Mother, and suggested that he go to sleep. Mottel got up, put his hand on my shoulder, gave me a warm look, and went to his room. He went to sleep while we continued to sit in the kitchen. "Thank God, Mottel didn't ask too many questions," said Mother. "He didn't ask about Father at all. He just ignored him," responded my sister in an angry tone. "Listen, children," Mother said to the two of us, "Mottel has come home after months of suffering and we haven't heard anything about them. You saw how thin he was? And how he wolfed down the food? It seems that he has been hungry for a long time. We must let him get used to living at home. We won't be able to keep this a secret for long. And maybe he doesn't want to ask us too many questions and make things too difficult for us."

Thanks to Mottel we were able to enjoy a holiday dinner, something we hadn't had for a long time. The atmosphere at home became freer. When we asked about Germany and about life in the prison camp, Mottel answered offhandedly, sometimes with jokes that made us all laugh. Only after some time, when our neighbor from the ground floor had come to visit us and we were all drinking tea together, did Mottel began to tell his story without our asking.

I had already heard quite a few stories about the mass flight to Warsaw and the terrible things that had occurred, but not in such detail and so vividly as Mottel told his story now. As I listened to him, I pictured the mobs of people moving along the road to Warsaw, the Polish army retreating in disorder, the shrieks of German planes over their heads, people fleeing and searching for cover, trapped by the assault from above and falling like flies. Mottel's pride in Father was evident as he told of how Father's army experience led him to know to pull Mottel to the side of the road and lie there with him the moment they heard the sound of planes approaching. Very few people followed suit when Father shouted at them to do as he did. Father told Mottel that when there was an explosion, they shouldn't be too close to one another; if one of them was hit, at least the other would survive. Father also confided to him one day that he thought he might have been wrong to leave the house — he shouldn't have left Mother and the rest of us alone.

As Mottel's story came closer to the fateful day when the Germans trapped them, the tension rose among us. Mottel stopped the flow of the story and sat quietly, lost in thought. For a moment it seemed as if he wouldn't begin speaking again, but suddenly he continued. That night, he said, the ground had trembled with the thunder of explosions, and barrages of fire could be heard from a variety of weapons. Father knew how to distinguish between the different types of explosions. "Those are artillery, that's mortar fire, those are heavy machine guns," he explained. He understood that the front was very close, but also that Warsaw was not far away; if they could just make one great effort they would be there. "The Germans won't get into Warsaw so quickly..."

And again Mottel was quiet; after a long pause, he looked at us and said, on the verge of tears, "It's my fault! Father wanted to continue running all night. If we had done what he wanted, we would have reached Warsaw. But both of my legs were injured. At each step, I felt as if I would faint from the pain. Father's feet were wounded, as well, but he wanted to continue. I didn't let him. I just couldn't go on. So we lay down to rest, and fell asleep. At dawn, we woke to shouts of 'Germans! Germans!' There was chaos. The Germans emerged from every direction. A long convoy of German vehicles was moving along the road. There was firing all around us. People were running and trampling each other in a frightened stampede. In the end, we stopped and sat down at the side of the road, not knowing how to continue. Then the Germans came, passed through the groups of people and pulled out those wearing uniforms or just any young people who were on the scene. For some reason, I don't know why, a German standing about fifty meters from us shouted, '*Du! Du!*' When father asked, 'Me?' the German answered, 'Yes, I want you!' Father stood up and I got up with him, but he said to me, 'You stay here; don't get up. He didn't ask for you.' I sat back down, but the German soldier shouted, 'You come, too!' They led us with some other people to a place where prisoners had been assembled and were being guarded by German soldiers. The German who chose us ordered Father to come with him. I was left with the other prisoners. I never saw Father again after that."

Everything he told us fit the information that we had already heard and verified what we had been told about father's death. Everyone in the room — except for my brother — knew what my father's fate had been. Embarrassed, we pretended that father was still alive. Our terrible secret created a barrier between Mottel and us. To ease the tension, Mother said, "Let's hope to hear good news in the future," and I wondered at the simplicity with which she told the lie and was surprised that my brother accepted her words with no hesitation. Mother asked Mottel to continue telling what had happened to him. He agreed, but now he spoke unwillingly and in a disordered way, and many times we had to encourage him to continue. He described the prison camp that the Germans had set up, and the suffering, the hunger, and the punishments. The Germans killed many of them. He said that he himself had had a relatively easy time of it; as the youngest, he had been considered a child, and everyone had helped him. Even the German soldiers had treated him better. As he continued speaking, his story became more general and lost focus. His face became frozen blank. His thoughts seemed to wander to faraway places that we couldn't imagine.

Life in our home, the routine, the meals, the behavior of each member of the family, had completely changed. Now there was a man in the house. There was someone who could be depended on. All of the heaviness of responsibility was lifted from my shoulders; after my brother returned, it seemed that I could go back to being a boy. My brother and mother spoke for hours about our financial situation. Mother had found someone to share this responsibility with. There was only one thing that didn't return — the friendly relationship that had existed between my brother and me.

Mottel had changed; all at once, he had become a grown man. He sometimes even seemed a stranger to me. The dream that I had had of pouring out everything in my heart to my big brother when he returned, of finding consolation in the strong bond between us, disappeared. The gap that had developed between us was unbridge-able. From then on, I tried not to find myself alone with Mottel, avoiding conversation with him. Everything I had wanted to tell him suddenly seemed less important compared to what he had been through. The secret of father's death also divided us, and I found it difficult to bear. Many times, we had to hold our tongues. One morning my sister said, "If father were alive…" and there was a moment of tension and shock, but she immediately corrected her-self, saying, "If only father were living with us here now…" There were other incidents like this one, but they were all successfully covered. As time passed, however, it became more and more dif-ficult to live with the lie, with the pretense. I couldn't understand how my brother hadn't perceived that we were lying to him, and on the other hand, why, when we spoke of Father, he himself would avoid the conversation and change the subject.

One evening, for no specific reason, Dvora broke down and told him the truth. At supper she suddenly shouted, "Let's stop playing this game. Father is dead! This whole story about 'regards' we received from Russia is a lie. The Germans shot him to death after you were separated, Mottel…," and she stopped and began to cry. We all cried with her. Mottel, who up till now had behaved more stoically than anyone else in the family, became as emotional as we all were. He sobbed and sobbed, the tears washing down his face. Afterward, he lifted his head, looked at us and said, "I knew that all the time. I also lied when I said that the German had taken Father and I hadn't heard anything else. That wasn't the truth! After Father was taken, I was terribly upset. I looked for him constantly, and kept hoping that he would return. I asked everyone I saw if they knew anything about him. In the meantime, the Germans were gathering more and more prisoners. The camp was getting bigger. The Germans walked around the camp among the prison-ers, taking some of them away with them. Shots could be heard everywhere. There was an atmosphere of terrible fear in the camp. Next to me in the barracks were two Jewish soldiers, who imme-diately began taking care of me and keeping my spirits up. When

I saw that Father wasn't returning, I was afraid that I wouldn't see him again. I couldn't bear to remain alone, without Father, among thousands of Polish soldiers who had become a shapeless flock, guarded by German soldiers. I didn't want to eat or to drink. I didn't care about what would happen to me. I just sat and cried. The Jewish soldiers kept whispering among themselves, and my intuition told me that they were hiding something from me. When night fell, they stayed close to me so that I could feel their bodies alongside mine. Their faces became serious. One of them turned to me and said, 'You are already a young man. I have to give you some bad news, and you must be strong. Your father was shot to death by the German who took him. That German killed a few other men, as well. We were witnesses. We're sorry, but we had to tell you so that you would know what happened to your father.'"

I looked at my brother. His face had become serious and from time to time became distorted while he spoke. It was clear that he was reliving everything that had taken place. It was hard for me to see his suffering. He told us that from our letters, he had concluded that we didn't know what had happened to Father, and that we were living on unreliable rumors that he was in Russia. "Until a few days before I got home, I was sure that when I arrived, I would tell you the truth. It seemed impossible and unfair to hide what had happened. But after I left the hospital in Krakow, I told the whole story to the family who had taken me in, and they advised me not to tell you about father's death immediately, so that I wouldn't turn my first day back with you into a day of mourning. How could I know that you already knew everything?"

When my sister blurted out the secret, I thought she had done something terrible. Now I knew that she had done the right thing and that it could not have been avoided. Each day had been more and more difficult — reunited, but living a lie. I felt that now, freed from all secrets, it would be easier for us to live together. Indeed, we now became stronger and more cohesive.

From the time that our city had been annexed to the Third Reich, it had been undergoing a process of "Germanization"

— posters in German multiplied from day to day, while street signs in Polish began to disappear. With all of the rumors that the Germans would be leaving and the Russians entering proven false, life became routine. The factories went back into production, the shops opened (although many of them had changed their Jewish owners for Polish ones, and at the entrances to the shops there were signs reading "Entrance to Jews and dogs forbidden"). The Poles reconciled themselves to the German occupation and tried to live under the new government as best they could. Some were even able to do better financially than ever by taking advantage of the terrible circumstances of the Jews. They bought merchandise from Jews at minimal prices, bought their shops and factories for almost nothing, or became partners without investing anything in order to put their names on the signs above the businesses, thereby making excellent profits. The cafés were filled with German soldiers who passed the time with Polish girls.

And the Jews? The Jews looked for ways to cope with the decrees that the Germans imposed on them, certain that the situation, although difficult, was only temporary, and they would just have to make do until it passed. Some Jews hoped to see the Germans defeated soon so that things would go back to normal. There were those who hoped that, when the battles and conquests had ended, the Germans would relax and allow the Jews to live peacefully. But in the meantime, the war wasn't ending and the Germans weren't relaxing — they confiscated Jewish property and imposed new limitations on Jews daily. It was said that the situation was better in the area of Poland under the German Protectorate, in central Poland, and many Jews moved there, some continuing on to the Russian border and succeeding in crossing it.

Night and day, my mother, my brother and my sister discussed our situation. What should we do? Mother asked friends for advice, but had difficulty deciding. In Lodz, we had no way to earn a living — we were surviving on the cash we had on hand; all of my mother's family were living in Warsaw. Also, our neighborhood was filling up with Germans and *Volksdeutsche*, and we felt more and more out of place. One Saturday, two German officers appeared at our home, looked over the apartment and said, "You have a very nice apartment!" We got the impression that it wouldn't be our apartment for long. On the other hand, we had possessions in Lodz — a well-equipped factory with machines worth large sums of money; equipment and tools, which could be operated easily and could be a source of livelihood for the family; a lovely apartment that lacked nothing... We knew that if we left the city, we couldn't take anything with us, neither from the factory nor from the apartment. We would be penniless refugees. On the other hand, if we went to Warsaw, at least we would have a home, as we could live with our grandparents.

The Germans helped us decide what to do. One morning, they imposed an order demanding that all Jews leave their homes and move to an area that would be reserved for Jews alone — a ghetto. The ghetto was located in an area crowded with poor Jews. It was difficult to imagine how the three hundred thousand Jews of Lodz could be concentrated into such a small area. Even though there had been rumors that the Germans were planning to consolidate the Jews into one area, in the face of the explicit order itself the Jews were stricken with stupefaction, many of them finding it difficult to believe that this was actually going to happen. After all, this meant leaving the home where you had been born and had lived all of your life, leaving all of your possessions behind, possessions that had been collected by generations of family members for hundreds of years. It meant leaving sources of livelihood, positions and customers, shops, storehouses, workshops and factories; it meant leaving synagogues, schools, libraries and community institutions; it meant losing contact with the rest of the city population; and more than anything else, it meant abandoning a steady routine for an unknown, incomprehensible world. This was simply inconceivable.

Thus, on the day that the Germans ordered the ghetto to be established, my mother decided that we must move from Lodz to Warsaw. The time of doubt and hesitation was over. Discussions were at an end. The choice was not between staying in one place and moving to another place, but between moving to Warsaw or to the ghetto. Without knowing why, I was anxious to leave Lodz for Warsaw. I knew that here in Lodz, I was unhappy, that I felt stifled. I hoped, without knowing why, that in Warsaw, things would change for the better. Perhaps I was attracted to the city where I had been born, where I had lived for the first few years of my life. In any case, from the moment that it was decided that we were moving to Warsaw, I was impatient to leave the city. My brother took me and someone my mother had hired to the factory to disassemble the machinery. The worker and my brother took apart machine after machine. Conversation kept to a minimum, they cleaned, oiled and wrapped each part, packing everything away in sacks. Thus, our workshop emptied before my very eyes and turned into just another large empty space, whose floor was covered with piles of pieces of machinery, instruments, tools and rags. The two worked without a break, and happily for me, from time to time they asked for my help. When the work was finished we took all of the machine parts down to the basement, where the worker closed off the entrance with bricks and plastered it over. I came home feeling that I had participated in a secret and important operation, and I was grateful to my brother for allowing me to be a partner in it. Mother was satisfied. "We have done all we can," she said. "Who knows? Maybe some day we will come back and take the machines out of the basement."

Once again, life at home changed completely. From doing nothing and not knowing what to expect, we went into a frenzy of activity, arranging our affairs as quickly as possible so we could leave the city. Mother tried to sell furniture and other objects we couldn't carry with us, but it was almost impossible to find a buyer, and those who were interested offered ridiculously low prices. The Poles knew that the Jews couldn't take all of their property into the ghetto, and that they could easily buy the most beautiful objects for almost no money and sometimes, for no money at all. The house quickly lost its importance to us. We became indifferent to what was going on around us; even when one of the *Volksdeutsche* families moved into one of the apartments in our building, we didn't care. In the streets, wagons reappeared, loaded with possessions, on their way to the ghetto. I watched them uninterestedly. We were going to leave the city and I was only waiting for that to happen.

Knowing that we would leave our furniture, our household utensils and other possessions to who knows who aroused feelings of contempt and hatred for our things and released a destructive instinct. Even though, at first, none of us broke anything on purpose, more and more dishes got broken, and when anything broke, we would all start laughing. Because of the pain we felt, seeing our home being destroyed before our very eyes, we began to get a kind of strange pleasure in destroying our own possessions, if only so that the next occupants of the apartment would not get any enjoyment from them. At the time, it was already very difficult to obtain coal for heating and the house was never warm enough. My brother looked at a chair, declared that it was "unstable, and not worth fixing" and began to take it apart to be burned for heat. The chair was in good condition and could have been used for decades, or even for hundreds of years, as all of grandfather's furniture could; indeed, it refused to give in to my brother's attempts to take it apart, and he struggled with it for a long time until it was in pieces. The dry wood burned quickly in the heater, though, and, from that moment on, we all went through the house, looking for furniture to burn. The heater incinerated every flammable object we put inside it. In spite of our seeming indifference, our hearts constricted again and again to see objects we had loved, which we had used for so many years, going up in flames. The house quickly lost its beauty and warmth and became strange and repulsive. This made us want to leave even more.

Mother spent her days trying to clarify what was the best way to get to Warsaw and transfer whatever we would need to live there. Since my brother had returned from the prison camp, everyone had gone back to treating me as a child. My mother arranged everything with my brother now, and each morning, when I awak-

ened, the two of them were already absorbed in discussion. I felt
superfluous. It is true that I felt that a load had been lifted from my
shoulders, but, at the same time, the freedom from responsibility
made me feel insulted and jealous of my brother.

One evening, when my mother came home, she told us that
there was a rumor that the border between the Third Reich and
the Protectorate would soon be closed and no one would be able
to leave the city. She decided that we would leave the next day; she
had already rented a wagon for tomorrow afternoon. The house
was quiet and tense. We were paralyzed — for a long moment, we
sat without saying a word. Then my mother said, "We have a long
evening ahead of us. We'll have enough time to pack. We won't be
able to take very much, so we must choose carefully what we are
taking and what we are leaving."

I never imagined that we had so many possessions. On the
floor of each room there were piles of bedclothes, clothing, shoes,
china, boxes, packages and bundles. I especially loved the Passover
dishes — dishes that were so different from the usual ones. They
were decorated with pictures of flowers in bright colors, and every
year, I had enjoyed watching my mother while she unpacked them,
wiped the dust with a towel, and put them in place of the dishes
we used the rest of the year. We would have to leave these behind.
My mother, concentrating, chose whatever she thought necessary
and had no difficulty deciding whether to take some object or to
leave it. So the work did not take long — after a few hours of effort,
everything was in order. Our suitcases and parcels were all packed.
My mother returned to the cupboards what we were leaving behind
so that the house looked as though we had just moved in. Finally,
we sat down to eat our last meal in our home. It seemed as if it
were the night before Passover, when we ate all of the *chametz*, the
leavened food forbidden to eat during Passover. After the meal,
my brother took two big glass carafes from the cupboard in the
bedroom. They were filled with cherry wine, waiting to be drunk
on Passover eve. Now my mother put a large bowl on the table
and my brother poured all the wine from one of the carafes into

the bowl. A wonderful smell of cherries filled the room, sharp and sweet. We all tasted the wine. It was delicious, but too sweet and thick. The cherries themselves were delicious — sour, but saturated in sweet juice, and we began eating them. Mother didn't allow us to eat too many for fear that we would get drunk or that we would get stomachaches. After a time, we couldn't even look at the cherries and it was their fate to be thrown away. The house was warm, as we had filled the heater with anything that could be burned. The wine left its mark on all of us. My head was whirling, and I quickly fell asleep as though in some strange dream.

The next morning, we waited for a long time for the wagon to come into our yard. We quickly brought down all of our parcels and loaded them onto it. From behind the curtains, our new neighbors were watching, Germans and Poles. There was only one other Jewish family still left in the building. The gatekeeper came over to us and my mother told her that we were leaving for the Jewish area of Lodz, and left her the keys to our apartment. I prayed that we would leave as quickly as possible. Every minute seemed like an hour to me. I felt that we were in an impossible situation. I was ashamed, as though we had committed some crime and were now being punished for it. But what crime had we committed? I was unable to look at the faces of people I knew, and until we left the neighborhood, I hid in the bottom of the wagon.

Four years before, following the economic depression that had struck many countries and had affected our family, as well, the Freiberg family, my family, had come to Lodz with knowledge and experience, both of my parents instilled with a strong ambition to succeed, the two of them ready to work hard. After a time, they had succeeded in building a solid business that was a source of faith in a secure future. Now we were leaving Lodz without the head of the family, almost without possessions, and what future was awaiting us? But none of us had time to consider our disaster. We had other worries: Would we reach Warsaw without difficulty? Would the few possessions we had remain with us, or would the Germans steal them on the way?

The wagon traveled through the streets and entered the Jewish area. The street was crowded. Almost everything was marked with a yellow *Magen David*. There were people offering objects for sale without holding anything that could be seen or pointing to samples that they were guarding in the rims of their coats. It was as noisy as a beehive. The wagon entered one of the yards, and the driver and my brother took a few bundles of holy books and disappeared with them into one of the rooms on the stairs. It would have been impossible to leave the books in the apartment, as the Poles would have destroyed them. We continued to drive through the sidewalk-less, narrow streets, among the old, deteriorating houses, past the many Jews standing in the streets, wearing worn clothing, their shoes falling apart. Abruptly, the streets crowded with Jews ended. Our wagon drove though an area of small houses surrounded by wooden fences and vegetable gardens. The spaces between the houses grew wider. The road was almost empty, and no one was wearing a yellow patch. We had reached the road from Lodz to Warsaw.

This was the third time this year that we had traveled the road to Warsaw. The first time had been on the way to our vacation village at the beginning of the summer. The fields had been green, the wild flowers had bloomed at the sides of the road, and we had been a happy family going off for a pleasant holiday. The second time, we had returned to the city just before the war had broken out, and the fields had been yellow with chaff. We had been apprehensive about what lay ahead. Now, the third time, the fields were muddy grey, and the fruit trees were leafless, as if dead. Only the forests were still a greenish dark brown. The cloudy sky above us also left a grey pall over everything.

We traveled at the side of the road. The German army vehicles continually passed us, spraying us with mud and leaving behind the odor of burning gasoline. I wanted to see everything, and when I fell asleep, I was terribly sorry afterward that I had missed things. I was sitting between my brother, Mottel, and my mother, who was holding my little brother Yankele on her lap, and he looked at me with his big eyes and smiled. I watched the quiet, peaceful country-side, and my mind filled with strange thoughts and questions with no answers. My throat choked up with unbidden tears.

Toward evening, we reached the outskirts of the city of Glowno, the city from which we used to walk on foot or take a coach to our vacation village. The wagon entered the backyard of an old house standing near the road that for many years had been used as an inn. Now, in addition, it was a smuggling point for people and merchandise. The owner of the inn, who had agreements with his German contacts and with guards at the border crossing point nearby, separating the Reich and the "General-Gouvernement" (the German Protectorate), had an arrangement that the wagons would arrive when "his" Germans were standing guard. Inside the inn there were strong smells, different odors of food, grain, animal skins and perfumes. Even though it was still light outside, the house was dark and there were a few oil lamps burning.

When my eyes adjusted to the darkness, I saw a large room, people sitting around a long table, and at the other end of the room, an oven and stove, with food cooking. The owner's wife came toward us, hugged my mother and received us happily — she knew my mother from former holidays, and now she served us tea and cookies. After that, each of us received a bowl of hot soup and a big slice of bread. We ate until the last morsel was finished. We didn't know exactly when we would be able to continue on our journey; we had been told that we would have to wait for about an hour, when the shift changed. The calm atmosphere and the jokes the waiting people told relaxed us. We waited patiently, and in the meanwhile, observed what was going on. Every so often someone would come in and report on what was happening at the border crossing point. Finally the word came; we could move on!

We went out into the cold, dark night. We reached the border in a few minutes, and a German soldier signaled with his light for us to stop. We waited, fearfully, behind another wagon while the Germans checked it. Now and then a German flashed his light over us, the light passing from person to person. When it was our turn to be checked, the wagon driver displayed documents to the German and added a few words. We were quickly allowed to continue on our way. We were relieved. We could speak again. We could laugh. Now, we organized ourselves for the long night trip. It was cold. The sky was cloudy and it was completely dark; there was no evidence of the existence of the villages in the area except for a few flashing lights and the barking of dogs.

I was exhausted. When I woke up a few hours later, it was already light. I looked around. We were in the heart of Warsaw, on Bonifraterska Street, close to our grandfather's home! Again, I regretted that I had slept and missed the entrance to the city, and felt as if I had fallen from the sky into the big city. I recognized the street at once, although there had been changes. In place of a few of the houses, there were piles of rubble: houses had turned into mere shells, their outer walls still standing like perforated boxes. The houses that remained whole had not changed — here were the same gates, the same shops that I remembered, here was the hospital for the mentally ill which had been left unharmed by the bombing.

We turned into Muranowska Street and again, everything was familiar to me, as though I had come home from a long journey. House no. 5, where I had studied at *cheder* (religious school) when I was four years old, remained only a skeleton in a pile of rubble. What had become of the old *melamed* (religious teacher) and his wife, I wondered. Were they still alive? And here was the gate to my grandfather's house! The gatekeeper, who had known my mother since childhood, received us with a warm welcome, exchanged a few words with her and opened the heavy iron gate. The wagon entered the yard of the building where I had been born and grown up, house no. 1 on Pshebyeg Street.

# Warsaw

## Spring 1940—Autumn 1941

O n Pshebyeg Street, a small street leading into Muranowska and Bonifraterska Streets, there were only four buildings, two on each side. It was a quiet street; you couldn't hear trolleys or cars, and very few people walked through it. The ones who did were usually taking a shortcut, crossing it as a kind of side gate into the city. Pshebyeg Street opened into a Jewish neighborhood, which included Muranowska, Mila, Nalewska, Bonifraterska and Franciszkanska Streets among others, busy streets with trolleys and other vehicles, which led to an open area of gardens and football fields, to the Citadel fortress, to the Vistula River and its bridges, and then on to the suburb of Praga on the other side of the river, and to the road leading to the new suburb of Zoliborz. House no. 1 on Pshebyeg Street was built as two identical square buildings, five stories each. The facade was attractive, painted light brown and decorated with openwork around the windows and between the floors. At the front of the building there was a shop, the grocery belonging to Reb Nahman, and next to it was a coal storeroom. On the other side of the gate was a copper workshop. On each floor, there were four large apartments, with windows looking out onto the street side and into the inner courtyard. Many of the residents were well-to-do. However, they did not visit the courtyard, nor did their children play there. The windows facing the yard in their apartments were always shuttered and locked from within, covered by heavy curtains. Only rarely could you see those residents looking into the courtyard; these richer tenants had no contact with the other inhabitants of the building.

In the middle of the inner courtyard stood a large waste disposal unit, with a big door at the side and a small covered opening on top for putting it in. A ladder was next to the unit for people to climb up to throw their garbage into the bin. Although rubbish was constantly being thrown in, from morning till night, the bin was never full. At midnight, while everyone slept, the trash collectors would empty it. Alongside the bin there was an apparatus for cleaning carpets and blankets, which was used by the children as a soccer net. In three of the corners of the inner courtyard, there were stairways leading to the upper floors of the building and the long halls, which led to the apartments. The stairs in the fourth corner led down to the cellar, where two strong Polish women operated the laundry room. It was hard work wringing the laundry out through the large rollers and then turning the wheels on both sides to iron the laundry. I used to watch as the two women worked skillfully, but their red and perspiring faces indicated how great a physical effort their work required. During their breaks, they would sit in the courtyard near the doorway to the cellar, speaking and laughing in loud voices.

The inhabitants of the building were extremely varied. There were the owners of businesses who occupied the larger apartments, and the simpler people, office workers, blue-collar workers and salespeople in the market, along with others about whom it was unclear how they earned their living. They lived in the smaller apartments, which in some cases served as workshops, as well. You could figure out what was being produced in the workshops by looking at the parcels that people carried in and out. But the residents were not interested in what was going on in their neighbors' homes; people lived their own private lives in their apartments. Only when something out of the ordinary occurred, when there were shouts of happiness, singing and music coming from the windows of one of the apartments and when guests dressed in holiday clothing came and went, would everyone ask what was being celebrated. The same would occur in cases of death — then they would ask if the mourners needed help, and if so, groups of virtuous women, my grandmother among them, would organize funds among the other tenants to collect money for those in need.

The courtyard of the second building was very different from the first. The asphalt surface was cracked, filled with potholes, and trash and discarded objects littered the ground. The paint and plaster on the surrounding walls were peeling. There was a mixture of odors: the pleasant smells of freshly baked goods or boiled sugar and wafers, and odors which were nauseating, like rotting meat and unprocessed animal skins. All of the cellars and the ground floor apartments of this part of the complex were workshops, most of which sold foodstuffs; one of the shops was Kaufman's Bakeshop, a large bakery famous for its dark bread, considered to be the best in Warsaw. Hundreds of people, perhaps thousands, lived in the little rooms on the five floors of the building surrounding the second courtyard. I did not know any of them, and I entered their yard very infrequently. There was almost no contact between the two yards, which were different worlds, but the tenants of the second courtyard passed though ours on their way to the street.

Although it was already light when we arrived, our courtyard was still enveloped in shadow. Mornings always came later here, and evenings came earlier. This, too, was as it always had been — nothing had changed since we had left. I looked around. People were looking at us from the windows; some of them certainly knew us. The stairway was dark, as usual. A small electric bulb in a corner lit the way. We reached the long hallway of the second floor in our side of the building, also completely dark. The first door on the right opened — and we were home!

From the moment we arrived in Warsaw, I was filled with a kind of special pleasure, which grew from moment to moment. When we arrived home, I didn't know what I wanted to do first. I ran from room to room, looking through every window into the courtyard; everything was so familiar, as if I had just left yesterday. I felt a great desire to go outside, to go walking through the streets of the neighborhood I had known from my first memories. It seemed to me that no one knew me, but that I knew everyone, and that feeling left me free of all embarrassment. But I didn't have much time alone to enjoy myself. Our whole family came to see us, group after group, each meeting accompanied by crying, sighing and discussion of our tragedy. The discomfiture increased and was unbearable. Again I was plunged into a world of suffering and unceasing despair. There were times, around then, that I had almost forgotten that I had lost a parent; I was in good spirits and little things gave me pleasure, but when I remembered my father, I would feel ashamed and angry with myself for my inappropriate behavior.

When my uncle Hershel came to visit, he assailed us with his kisses and began to cry. There was something ridiculous about his appearance — he looked like a weepy, overgrown child. Abruptly he stopped crying and cursed the Germans for a few minutes, his face flushed with anger. He then promised us formally, with his right hand on his chest, that he would take care of us and that he would make sure that we lacked for nothing. He sat with us for a few more minutes, looking again and again at his watch, apologized that he had to run, and left.

Aunt Sarah, my mother's sister, came with her husband and their daughter — and the weeping started anew. When I was a child, my aunt had played with me and told me stories. We had an understanding and trusting relationship, and I loved her very much. I had been anticipating an emotional meeting with her now, but it didn't happen. My aunt didn't show any special interest in me; I had the feeling that all of her attention was devoted to her daughter. Apparently, she had forgotten me.

We were all happy about the move from Lodz to Warsaw. My mother was happy about the fact that the journey had gone well: we had arrived successfully, with some of our possessions intact. It was good to be among relatives after the period of isolation in Lodz, after the tragedy of Father's death. For me, Warsaw was a paradise compared to Lodz, perhaps because our neighborhood was completely Jewish. It seemed that life in Warsaw was continuing just as it had before the war. I often walked through the streets of the city, and it looked as if nothing had changed. I met very few Germans, and I quickly got used to the skeletons of buildings and the piles of brick that stood in place of the structures destroyed in the bombings — and I had the feeling that everyone else had gotten used to them as well.

We soon realized, however, that the situation in Warsaw was no better than that in Lodz; here, too, the Germans were issuing orders and stealing property. Thousands of families had lost their livelihoods, and the number of needy was continually growing. The Jewish community had opened soup kitchens and was distributing food, and more and more 'respectable' people could be seen standing in line to receive a small quantity of diluted soup. Of course, for those with money, anything could be purchased in Warsaw. Although we thought that we had enough to sustain ourselves for a long time, we would obviously have to find some form of income. My uncle Hershel visited us often, usually at meal times. At first, he refused to eat with us, and joined us at the table only after my mother had insisted, but after a short while he would come and immediately sit down to eat as though it were a matter of course. My sister, Dvora, would be angry and say that he wasn't behaving decently, that he was just taking advantage of us. Sometimes he came with his young daughter, Fella, a beautiful little girl whom I loved, and for whom I was willing to do anything.

In spite of the war, and our unusual situation, we prepared for two occasions — the Passover holidays and my bar mitzvah. Whether we wanted to celebrate Passover or not, we still had to prepare special foods for the holiday. These were very difficult to get and their prices were naturally going up from day to day. My mother went out every morning to hunt for supplies and was happy to find any potatoes or eggs that she could. But she would come home and say that we must behave modestly and not be ostentatious, as so many people were unable to afford the items necessary for the holiday. Some tenants in the building organized a fund to help the needy and asked my mother to join them. She politely refused, but contributed generously to the fund.

As for my bar mitzvah, none of us had any desire or intention to celebrate, but we couldn't just ignore the occasion. For me, it was an unavoidable nuisance. A year ago, my father had spoken of my bar mitzvah as a very opulent event, and even then it had been a source of anxiety for me; it felt like he expected too much of me and that I might disappoint him if I couldn't meet his expectations. I was shy, and I dreaded an occasion where I would be the center of attention. Now, I knew that my bar mitzvah would be very modest, but even that seemed too difficult for me. However, there were things that must be done: I would have to buy a *tallis* (prayer shawl) and *tefillin* (phylacteries), and learn how to put them on. I would have to go to synagogue and read from the Torah, and I would have to learn to sing the *Haftorah* (the reading from the Prophets) with the appropriate melody. Mother understood how I felt when I said I didn't want to go to a rabbi to learn the *Haftorah*, and so it was agreed that my grandfather would prepare me for my Torah reading. It was a pleasure to study with him. He didn't pressure me and he enjoyed my every achievement. Indeed, I learned what I did only to please him.

One day, a special messenger came from the rabbi of Prushkov with some news: my father's body had been found in an unmarked grave, along with the corpses of two other Jews and three Poles. My mother's efforts had paid off: farmers who had been plowing their fields before seeding had uncovered the bodies. The messenger said that although the bodies were somewhat decomposed, the identification was certain. In my father's coat pocket they had found his wallet with some still-legible documents that included my father's name. The messenger said that we should go to Prushkov right away, that we could stay in the rabbi's home, and the next day we would give my father and the other two Jews a Jewish burial. The bodies were now in the town's Jewish cemetery, and they should be buried immediately. The messenger was an expert in how to get to Prushkov. He advised us to go by *kolieka*, a small railroad with narrow tracks that linked the neighboring towns and the city. It would be leaving in a few hours from the railroad station, which was not far from our home.

This sudden news left us all in shock. For a few minutes, we sat speechlessly listening to the messenger, my mother's face as white as a ghost, my grandfather's face so tormented that I couldn't look him in the eyes. But there was no time to get used to the news. Mother prepared lunch and we ate quickly, without speaking, without lifting our eyes from the table. Mother ordered us to shower, to put on clean shirts and holiday clothing, and in a short time we were ready for the journey. Yankele, who sensed that we were going to leave the house and that he would have to stay, cried inconsolably. Grandfather also wanted to go along and to be with us at this difficult time, but Mother explained to him that it was impossible. Grandmother sat silently in her corner, watching us. It was difficult to know what was going through her mind. I prayed that time would pass quickly; waiting to leave and doing nothing was unbearable. But time seemed to stand irritatingly still. I also prayed that no one would come to tell us how Father's body was found and that no one would start talking about his funeral again. I didn't want anyone else to go with us to Prushkov. I hoped that we would go by ourselves, and Mother confirmed that in this situation, it would be better if no one accompanied us to the funeral.

We finally left, and Mottel went out to bring a horse-drawn *droshka*. As we traveled to the station, it seemed that everyone was looking at us with pity, that everyone knew we were going to bury my father, and there was something strange and unnatural about this: Father had been killed a few months ago, but we were just going to bury him now. I hoped that I wouldn't see anyone and that no one would see me.

It had been a long time since I had ridden in a *droshka*. We usually traveled by trolley; we only went by *droshka* on special, festive occasions, and I had loved these journeys and was always sorry to reach our destination. And here we were traveling in a *droshka*, my brother at my side, and my mother and sister sitting opposite me. I looked outside, as I usually did, but this time, I didn't see anything. I tried to imagine the burial, my father's body, but I wasn't able to picture it fully — only flashes of images passed through my head from time to time.

Unlike the Central Railroad Station of Warsaw, which was always crowded, day and night, this station was small and quiet, with very few travelers. Only a few people were there when we arrived, and a German guard was on patrol. We sat in one of the corners, trying to be inconspicuous. The *kolieka* was already standing in the station and after Dvora bought tickets, we entered the train. We sat together, quietly, having nothing to say to each other. I felt Mother looking at me as her hand stroked me lightly. I wanted to look back at her, but I was afraid.

The trip to Prushkov took less than half an hour. Time was passing quickly now. I could look out of the window of the *kolieka* at the changing scene that was like a moving picture show. I observed everything closely. Until we left the outskirts of the city, the signs of war were everywhere — destroyed houses, gutted buildings, German army units. But when we left the built-up areas, we emerged into a country scene, and it seemed as though nothing had changed — the plowed fields, the lakes, the scattered villages, the farmers working their fields who turned their heads for a moment to look at the passing train — and everything seemed so peaceful I wanted to keep traveling and never stop. The whistle of the locomotive and the train slowing down as it entered the village brought me back to reality. We had just gotten off the train when a wagon driver approached us and said in Yiddish that the rabbi had sent him to pick us up. The sun was setting; its last strong rays emphasized the whiteness of the houses of Prushkov. The carriage stopped near a pleasant two-story house, painted white, which stood on the main street. All of the local government buildings were also on this street, and close by, I saw a German flag waving above one of the houses and a German soldier standing at its gate.

The rabbi and his wife welcomed us and quickly ushered us into their home. The expressions on their faces exuded friendliness and familiarity. My mother acted like one of the family and embraced the rabbi's wife, and the rabbi said to Mother, intending for us to hear him, "You are a woman of valor. You have done a wonderful thing. May God bless you." The rabbi's wife said that we would soon have supper, and in the meantime made us a cup of tea. The table had been set. The house itself was lovely and sparkling clean. The rabbi's wife showed us into a large room whose windows looked out on the main street. While we were drinking the tea, the rabbi and Mother exchanged a few inconsequential words, and when Mother asked to discuss the reason we had come, the rabbi said that we would talk after supper.

My brother and I went to another room with the rabbi, where some people were already waiting. We prayed *Mincha* (the late afternoon prayer) and *Ma'ariv* (the evening prayer). The people left and we sat down to the meal. The atmosphere at the table was somber. We were silent and had difficulty eating. Self-conscious, we children didn't know how to behave. The rabbi's wife tried to persuade us to eat, and Mother joined in her exhortations. We ate so as not to disappoint Mother and the rabbi's wife, but without tasting the food. We finished the meal quickly. Mother and the rabbi began to speak together in low voices, and after a few moments my mother asked me to go up to our room and go to sleep — she didn't want me to hear what the rabbi was going to tell her. I was anxious to know every detail about my father, so I said that I wasn't tired: I wanted to stay, and to go to sleep with everyone else. To my surprise, Mother agreed, saying, "If you want to, you can stay." She signaled the rabbi that he could begin his story. We had already heard the important details from the messenger, but we were anxious to know everything.

The rabbi took out a small parcel and put it down in front of him. He told us that since the snow had melted, when the farmers had begun plowing the fields, several mass graves had been uncovered. As they had previously agreed to do, the farmers reported what they found to the priest, who then informed the rabbi. Groups had gone out to try to identify the bodies, some of which had decomposed to such an extent that identification was impossible. "Near one of the villages," said the rabbi, "six bodies were found that couldn't be identified. When I was told of it, I decided to go to the site immediately with two other Jewish men. I was afraid that if the bodies weren't identified, they would be buried in the local cemetery, and what if, Heaven forbid, they were Jewish bodies? When we arrived at the village we saw the bodies were placed side by side. They were all decomposed. We searched for signs of identification in the remains of the clothing, and here is what we found."

The rabbi opened the parcel that he had placed on the table. A terrible odor filled the room. He carefully unrolled the wrapping and we saw Father's leather wallet and a few documents, some of them rotting. At the center of the wallet was the hole made by the bullet that had pierced father's heart. Inside the wallet was his fountain pen, which had been bent by the bullet, and among the documents was his passport. There was no doubt as to the identity of the body. The rabbi stopped and looked at us; we sat dumbfounded. And then the rabbi said, "Children, thanks to your mother, your father will have a Jewish burial tomorrow, and you will know the place where he is buried."

I was proud of my mother. Because of her efforts and persistence, Father had been found and would have a Jewish burial. This seemed very important to me. I had heard that as long as the deceased is not buried according to Jewish law, his soul is tortured and knows no rest. The soul of my father would be tortured no longer. The great distress was lifted from my heart, but suddenly I was terrified. Tomorrow I would have to go to a cemetery and participate in the burial of my father, and I had never been in a cemetery; I had never seen a dead person. How would the face of a dead person look? How were the dead buried? Could you see their faces? And what would I have to do at the cemetery?

Remembering rumors and stories I had heard here and there, I imagined frightening things. The rabbi had said that my father's body had been in "a state of decomposition." What did that mean?

How would my father look to me tomorrow? The terrible smell of his wallet was still in my nostrils and gave me no rest. It was not possible that the smell had come from my father... Deep in thought and filled with questions that had no answers, I fell asleep and dreamed that I was walking down a street in Lodz, down Piotrkowska. German children in brown shirts with swastika-festooned ribbons on their sleeves were running after me, and I was fleeing from them with all of my might. Suddenly, the street ended and I was running through the fields, and instead of children, dogs were running after me and getting closer. Abruptly a chasm opened ahead of me and I was falling, falling, trying to hold on to something and not succeeding. I wanted to shout but I couldn't hear my own voice. I woke up, drenched in perspiration, my heart beating quickly.

I was afraid to fall asleep again. I opened my eyes and looked around me. My brother was sleeping next to me. On the other side of the room slept my mother and sister. Quiet. How good it was that I had awoken from that horrible dream. And perhaps I hadn't woken from the dream — the dream was continuing and I wasn't really in this room in this village, and we hadn't really come here to bury my father — I was sleeping in our home in Lodz and tomorrow morning my father would wake me up because it was time to go to school. What a terrible dream this was, I thought to myself, this whole story that the rabbi had told about my father, in such great detail. Wasn't it the same dream I had had a year ago about my father's death? I surrendered to the sweet illusion and wanted it to continue, but I heard steps outside in the street, and they were getting closer. They were steps that could not be mistaken, the steps of the nailed boots of German soldiers. I tensed up. Fear overcame me as the steps came closer and closer, but the soldiers continued walking and the steps got farther away. After a few minutes I heard the steps getting louder again.

I got out of bed and went to the widow. Two German soldiers, their rifles bayoneted, were marching back and forth down the quiet, empty street. I don't know how long I stood by the window, looking out at the dark street and the German soldiers who passed from time to time. Then I heard a noise behind me. My mother had gotten out of bed and walked over to me. "Can't you sleep, Berale?" she said. The two of us listened to the sound of the soldiers' steps. "Those are German soldiers, marching back and forth all night," I told my mother to calm her. "You have been standing here a long time," she said. "Go to bed and try to sleep. Tomorrow will be a difficult day for us. We'll have to get up early." I went back to bed, but I didn't fall asleep until the light of dawn lit the room. The next day was a lovely fresh spring day, the kind of day that warms the heart. A day like that certainly did not suit the event awaiting us; perhaps it only emphasized the cruelty in life. It was as though nature was maliciously laughing at us.

We went to the cemetery with the rabbi and his wife. The Jews of the town whom we met on the way nodded their heads and sighed, and some of them came with us. When we neared the cemetery, Mother gently took my hand. I did not object. We walked down the path among the graves and the headstones. I didn't feel anything special; I looked around me indifferently. All at once I became aware of the same odor I had smelled the night before, growing stronger as we continued on our way to the end of the row of graves, where some Jewish men were waiting for us. Finally, we stopped. When the breeze blew, the odor became less intense, but when it stopped, the smell was unbearable. In front of us were three parallel pits, and in front of each of them was a body covered with a black cloth. Now there was no room for doubt: the terrible odor was coming from the bodies.

One of the men began to recite the Psalms. We stood and looked at the three bodies in front of us. There, as I stood before the body of my father, my first encounter with death, my senses suddenly were blunted and it was as if I were made of stone. I could hear the prayers and clearly see everything that was happening around me, but I was impervious. I was able to look at anything, nothing could shock me, nothing could make me collapse. It seemed to me that I had made my peace with death, that I had stopped being afraid of it. In fact, I felt that I belonged to death.

Two men approached and picked up the remains of my father, and, at that moment, the body lost its form and became a heap. It was evident that the parts of the body and the skeleton had come apart. Another two men quickly supported the center of the body and it was lowered into the grave. Afterward, the other two bodies were lowered into their graves, more prayers were said, and the graves were covered. My mother and sister cried quietly. When the graves were sealed, my brother and I stood before Father's grave, and two other Jewish men stood before the other graves, and we all said Kaddish, the prayer for the dead. The rabbi approached us, took out a penknife from his pocket and cut the lapel of my coat, signifying my state of mourning. It felt as though he were cutting my flesh.

The boy who came back from the cemetery was not the same boy who had entered it. All of the fear and the feeling of mystery I had felt about cemeteries and the dead had disappeared. Everything seemed so natural. Another three graves were added to the hundreds and thousands that had accumulated from generation to generation. I was happy that I hadn't broken down, that I hadn't fainted, that I hadn't burst into tears. But the image of the three bodies carved a permanent place in my consciousness that would never leave, and the odor claimed a place in my nostrils that would never disappear.

Mother was very worried about me. She spoke to the rabbi and said that my behavior at the cemetery had concerned her. "Berale is a weak child, and very sensitive," she said, "and, at the cemetery, he stood, frozen, and didn't react. He didn't even shed a tear. He just kept looking at his father's body. I wish he had cried — that would have given him some relief. Now all of his suffering will remain inside him…" The rabbi calmed my mother and said that in these situations, different people react in different ways, and she had nothing to fear. "Children get over their grief quickly," he said, "and Berale will also recover now that his father has been buried. Time will heal his wounds." At the rabbi's home, I gave her another reason to worry: the rabbi's wife had prepared a meal for us and wouldn't let us leave until we had eaten, but I couldn't eat anything, in spite of my mother's requests. I felt that if I ate anything, I would throw up.

On our way home, again traveling on the narrow railroad, fresh air entered our car and mixed with the terrible odor of the decomposing bodies that wouldn't leave me. Again, as we rode through fields, forests and lakes, I watched the views that aroused mixed feelings in me, and again made me feel as though I never wanted the railroad train to reach its destination.

We returned to Warsaw, and, as Jewish law demands, we sat *shiva*, the mourning period. Twice a day neighbors came to pray with us, and my brother and I said Kaddish. Members of the family, some of whom I didn't know, visited us and praised my mother, who had not given up until she had given my father a Jewish burial. Uncle Hershel visited us every day. One day, he came with his wife and both of his daughters, Mira, the eldest, and Fella, my friend. All of them were dressed up and the girls' facial expressions and behavior indicated that they had been instructed how to behave by my aunt. My aunt and the two girls approached us, shook hands and kissed each one of us on the cheek. Fella, too, kissed me and even hugged me, and I felt a quiver go through my body. While they were with us, I didn't speak to Fella, and that upset me. I thought that if I had the chance, I would confide in her, but, for some reason, I couldn't speak to her, even when we were together.

During the first days of the *shiva*, the neighbors would come to pray the services and when they had finished, they would hurry out. After we had gotten to know them better, however, they would sit with us in the evenings, after the prayers were over, and they would tell us the news they had heard during the day. We had few sources of information — they were mostly the Polish newspaper that the Germans published and the German radio station that could be heard from a loudspeaker installed on Muranowski Square. But some people secretly listened to Radio London and the other free stations, not to mention the flood of rumors that circulated endlessly. The local and neighborhood news was repeated over and over, day after day. There were daily robberies, humiliations and physical beatings. People were taken from their homes in the middle of the night and no one knew what had happened to them. Hunger and poverty were spreading and penniless refugees, expelled from their own houses and towns, came to Warsaw every day. Everyone would listen to the reports, sigh, lift their hands to the heavens and ask, "What more can happen? When will all this end?"

The official German news was depressing. In the spring, the Germans attacked Europe in a wide front and captured Holland and Belgium, Norway and Denmark. We sadly listened to news of German victories and how they were conquering country after country with incredible speed. But there were always people who could put a positive light on the news, pointing out that if the Germans had only conquered Poland, the world would have stood by without lifting a finger, but now that they were trying to conquer all of Europe, the world wouldn't let them. The United States was about to declare war on Germany, and the German defeat was closer than we thought.

Everyone considered England a "superpower." Every word that we heard from Radio London was sacred. Uncle Hershel told us that someone had heard on a newscast from London radio that now the English would remove their white gloves and teach the Germans a lesson. Everyone smiled with satisfaction at this, while I tried to understand the difference between fighting with white gloves and fighting without them. These conversations about the situation would usually end on a happy note, with an optimistic hope for a better future. We would only have to hold out until then.

The days were warm and spring-like. Most of the residents of the building opened the windows and doors to their terraces, which had been bolted throughout the winter. Heads looked out of the windows from time to time and people wanted to enjoy the clear spring air. In our apartment, everything remained closed, perhaps to preserve the sense of isolation from the outside world.

When I could no longer stand the heavy atmosphere, I would open the terrace and go out onto it, sitting in a corner so as not to be conspicuous. Before we left Warsaw for Lodz, because I was a sickly child, I had had to spend long periods of time at home, and I used to enjoy standing at the window or on the terrace, looking out at what was going on in the inner courtyard, never bored. The courtyard had not physically changed at all since then. Everything was in its place, exactly as it had been before we left Warsaw. Even most of the residents were the same; only the children had grown and looked a bit strange to me. But the atmosphere had changed completely. Everything had become quieter, slower. The well-known assortment of noises in the courtyard lacked happy sounds. Even the children didn't play with the same enthusiasm and were more restrained. Childhood memories started to pop up in my imagination. Here, in this courtyard, I had experienced the good and the bad, the beautiful and the ugly. I had learned more here than anywhere else. My parents had not let me play in the yard with the street children, concerned that I would pick up "bad things" from them, but they didn't forbid my watching everything that was happening from the terrace.

On the left side of the building, on the ground floor, had lived a family with many daughters. During the day, their apartment would turn into a sewing workshop and I would watch the girls sitting at their sewing machines and listen to the hum of the machines mixed with their singing. In the evenings, their apartment became a normal residence again, and this routine continued year after year. One morning, I awoke to the sounds of terrible shouting from their apartment. It soon became clear that the mother of the girls had died. When the funeral began, the courtyard was filled with people. The girls were sobbing, and everyone in the building watched what was happening from their windows and cried with them. The funeral coach, led by black horses and covered with a black cloth that reached to the ground, began its procession and left the yard. Now when I watched, I could see that no one was working, and there was no longer the hum of sewing machines in their apartment.

Above that apartment lived the Prinzental family, an elderly and wealthy couple who owned a well-known cutlery factory. They had a young live-in maid. I saw the tenants infrequently, but I watched the maid, who was cleaning every room and cooking in the kitchen from morning till night. Sometimes, on Shabbat and holidays, their children would come to dine with them, and friends would come after the Kiddush blessing. I could hear sounds of singing and the tumult of the guests. The apartment looked as though it hadn't changed, but the maid, who hadn't particularly attracted my attention when I was a child, caught my imagination now. One evening while I was watching the Prinzental apartment the girl turned off the lights in the kitchen, but I could still see her clearly by the light that was shining on her from the next room. She started to undress, and I couldn't take my eyes off her. I watched as she took off her dress and walked around the kitchen in her underwear. I kept watching until she took off her bra and I could dimly see her breasts. She suddenly saw me and quickly closed the door of the lighted room, and her magical figure became only a black blur. A strange feeling, one I had never felt before, passed through my body. I kept on standing by the window, even though I knew that I wouldn't see her again. The girl had opened the door to a period of mysterious pleasure and suffering that began taking its place in my life.

Also above the Prinzental apartment, on the third floor, there lived a family whose children I remembered well. They were always playing in the courtyard and their mother was continually calling them to come home, but they never listened. One Sunday, I was surprised to see a German SS officer come into the courtyard, whistle and shout, "Max!" A window opened from that same apartment on the third floor, and a young man looked out — he was one of the children who used to play in the yard. He answered in German, "I'll be right down!" A few minutes later, the young man appeared in the yard and left with the German, the two of them laughing.

Afterward, I found out that he was one of the most dangerous informers in the neighborhood and that everyone was afraid of him. In Lodz, I had heard stories of Jewish informers who worked for the Germans, but now, when I actually saw a young Jewish man collaborating with a German — it was said that he helped the Germans plan their robberies — I was in a state of shock. I couldn't understand how his family could let him cooperate with the Germans. Every time I saw him after that, I used to pray that he would be killed. I heard that he had told one of the tenants, "You have nothing to be afraid of. I won't bring any Germans here." But the residents of the building were not reassured. They said that when he had no one else to report on, he would bring the Germans to our building, as well.

When I had lived here as a child, I would categorize the regular visitors to the courtyard into a few groups: the first was a group of singers, musicians, jugglers and a variety of entertainment groups; the second were the various beggars; the third were the peddlers selling everything imaginable; and the fourth were the tradesmen, who would come with their tools and turn the courtyard into a workshop. More than the others, I used to enjoy watching the singers and the entertainment groups, and the tradesmen. Among the singers was an elderly Jewish man, both of whose legs had been amputated, and he would get from place to place in a homemade wagon, turning the wheels with his arms. The singer played an accordion and sang a fixed repertoire from which he never deviated in a strong metallic voice. One of his songs was about the *Titanic* disaster, and another was about Baruch Shulman, the young man who had been executed for assassinating the Jew-hater, Patlora. These were the words:

> Baruch Shulman of Passa Street
> Held a bomb in his hand.
> Do not cry my brother, my sister, do not cry,
> Because the best of all people —
> Will fall, and that is the way of the world…

Although they had heard his songs dozens of times, the women of the building were always moved when they heard them and always joined in his singing. My mother, as well, would sometimes sing along. Coins wrapped in paper would be thrown from the windows during the songs, and the children in the yard would collect them and give them to the singer. I really loved this disabled singer with his sad songs, and I pitied him, as well. The moment he appeared, I would run to my mother and ask her for some coins to throw out the window.

There were the street singers who were admired, and who would receive many coins, and then there were those who sang and played, looked up at the windows, but received only a few coins. Sometimes, a troupe of singers and musicians would come into the courtyard and stand in the center, playing popular songs and segments of operas. The yard would be turned into a stage and the building surrounding it would become a theater with many balconies, the terraces filled with people, heads looking out of the windows. Downstairs in the yard, a large circle of passersby would gather, including people who had left their work for a few moments and women who had stopped their housework — everyone taking the time to enjoy themselves, everyone expecting an entertaining experience. At the end of every song, there would be applause, accompanied by a shower of coins.

The jugglers and the circus people who entered the yard would bring a wave of children with them. The entertainers would do wonderful things — eat razor blades, breathe fire, walk on the palms of their hands, and other exciting tricks, but they would only earn a small number of coins, which made me feel sorry for them. Beggars would come on fixed days and hours, each one with a cry and a story. Some would ask for money, others would ask for food or old clothes. One tall, thin beggar, a sack hanging on her back, would sing, "Old bread! Old challah! Old rolls! Throw them down!"

The food peddlers would come early in the morning and display their wares — fruits and vegetables, freshly baked goods just out of the oven, sandwiches. Village women would bring homemade dairy products: they would take the heavy packs off their backs and sell sour cream from earthenware jugs, butter and cheese wrapped in coarse village cloth or in cabbage leaves, and eggs in baskets lined in straw. The notions peddlers would open their suitcases, which were full of interesting items. You could buy anything from a shoelace to a dress. Others would sell low quality goods at a bargain, or merchandise left over from the previous season. They would exhibit sweaters, shirts and other items, shouting that this was a "once in a lifetime opportunity," and the women would go down to look through the piles of clothing.

The repairmen and tradesmen would come carrying their tools and take broken or bent pots and utensils and, like magic, turn them into new ones. They worked calmly, patiently, sometimes completing their work in minutes; sometimes they would work for hours or for a full day, for example, when they changed the upholstery on sofas and chairs.

My curious eyes would take in everything, and of course I found great enjoyment watching the children's games, especially in the late afternoon and evening. I often felt that I would do anything to be able to join in their play.

The rabbi from Prushkov was right when he said that the moment a person is buried, the process of forgetting begins. From the day we buried my father, I began thinking about him less, although the sight of the three bodies lying in the cemetery next to the burial pits returned to my thoughts often, and the terrible odor never left me. Now, however, other things occupied me and gave me no rest as well, among them the changes that were occurring in my body, and the attraction I was feeling for women. I had known nothing of the mysterious path between a young man and a young woman, except for the things I had gleaned from the stories of children, which sounded coarse and made me feel embarrassed.

I knew that my thoughts were sinful, but it was as if a devil had entered me and wouldn't leave — I tried to deal with this demon, but I couldn't avoid my thoughts about women. I was attracted to them like a magnet: I wanted to solve the secret of women, although I had no clear idea of what it was exactly that I was looking for. I felt that if only I could be close to the body of a woman, it would free me from this great tension I felt. At the same time, I was afraid that my secret would become known, and then I would be lost; I couldn't go on living. Luckily, no one paid any attention to me. Even my mother left me alone, as she was busy looking for ways we could earn a living, and who knows, perhaps she was intentionally letting me do anything I wanted. As free as a bird, I would walk the streets of Warsaw, carried along by the swarm of humanity filling the Warsaw streets on the warm spring days, watching the women in their summer dresses and longing for contact with them...

My thoughts became focused on a young girl who lived on the third floor, opposite us, on the right side of the courtyard. At first, I only saw her face at the window as part of the general picture of the yard, and I didn't pay any particular attention to her. But without knowing how or why, for no special reason, one day I began to watch for her figure at the window. When I woke up in the morning, I would go out to the terrace and watch her window. When I saw her, I would silently thank her, as if she had appeared especially for me, and when I didn't see her, I would be upset, and sometimes I would wait for her for more than an hour. I couldn't see her face clearly from my terrace, but I had no doubt that she was the most beautiful girl I had ever seen. From time to time, I would see her crossing the courtyard with tiny, quick steps, and then, observing her more closely, I gathered that she was about thirteen or fourteen years old, slender, with legs as thin as a stork's. Her face was long, she had a high forehead, and her hair was parted in the center with a very long braid hanging down her back. Sometimes I would see her at their window, her face looking out from under a long mane of hair. I could never decide which way I loved her more — with her hair in a braid or unbound.

Every day, I desired her more and more, the girl on the third floor whose name I did not know and with whom I had never exchanged a word. Sometimes when I looked at her from our terrace, it seemed to me that she was looking back and smiling at me, and I would be content. I would walk for hours around the building, hoping to see her more closely. Once, we even passed each other, and then, I felt as if an electric current had passed through my body, and I was ecstatic. At night, I would see her close to me, looking at me with smiling eyes, and I would be stroking her head and holding her body close to mine. Were all of these new thoughts a result of my life of idleness? In any case, they gave my life purpose, and caused me to develop wonderful fantasies, better than anything I had imagined before, after a period in which I could find no reason to go on living, when it seemed that I couldn't go on without my father.

Mother began to talk about solving the problem of continuing my studies. We had heard that because of the situation in Warsaw, teachers were schooling groups of children in their homes, and my uncle promised to find me a teacher. Mother said that it would be difficult for me to catch up with my studies, but for some reason, a teacher was never found. The only private lessons I received were my studies with my grandfather, teaching me to read from the Torah at my bar mitzvah. Unlike my grandfather in Lodz, who, although I loved him, made me feel awed and even a bit afraid, my Warsaw grandfather was relaxed and calm, and I could distract his attention easily; I could begin and end the lesson with him whenever I wanted. But he was so forgiving, I couldn't exaggerate and take advantage of his kindheartedness, and I would study just to make him happy. I was grateful for his kind treatment.

Something else occupying my thoughts was our situation in general. I was anxious to know what was going on in the outside world. I searched for sources of information, trying to interpret signs of a German downfall in the near future. I found that people were so hungry for information that any news item would be snapped up, even if it came from a child like me. One day during morning prayers, when I was talking about something I had heard, everyone in the group listened to me with such seriousness that I blushed in embarrassment. My daily routine became influenced by my search for news. At ten in the morning I would have to be in Muranowski Square, near the loudspeaker that broadcast the official news, but I would always be there earlier, listening to the German marching music. The German news broadcast always included news from the front — a series of victories which seemed to have no end — the capture of cities, sectors, countries; the ships which had been sunk; the aircraft which had been brought down. This news would undermine any hope I had of a quick German defeat. After the news, the loudspeaker would broadcast announcements and orders, and occasionally I would be the first to bring these to the attention of the family.

From Muranowski Square, I would go visit my Aunt Sarah, who lived on Bonifraterska Street, where I would read the Polish newspapers. I had trouble reading the newspapers published by the Germans. I didn't really know the language and the long words seemed to be riddles to me, but my tremendous desire to know what the Germans were writing pushed me to make an effort to learn, and I quickly reached the stage where I could understand the headlines of the news reports from the front, and even read short articles. I would bury myself in the pile of newspapers, never finding anything to make me happy except for the articles memorializing German war victims, which would cover entire pages. I spent a lot of time on these. I found that most of them were written about officers and about those who had been awarded the Iron Cross.

From Aunt Sarah's house, I would continue to Nalewska Street. I enjoyed walking down this street because of the shops and the well-to-do crowds. I would stroll down the street for a while with no particular objective, and then I would go into my uncle's shop, where I sometimes heard rumors that had been passed on by people who secretly listened to foreign radio stations, the BBC in particular. I would also hear rumors whose sources no one knew, but which sprouted like mushrooms after the rain and spread with the speed of lightening. Some of these rumors would arouse false hopes, such as the one that kept circulating that claimed that the

Germans were about to leave the city, with the Russians taking their place.

I would return home with the news I had heard and report it to the family. At first, everyone would laugh and say, "Berale and his news…" But as time went by, they began listening seriously to every word, and when I returned from the "news hunt" they would ask, "Nu, what's going on?" I enjoyed being a source of information.

Passover is the loveliest of Jewish holidays, and the preparations are lengthy and thorough. As the holiday takes place in the spring, it provided a nice transition between the difficult Central European winter and the pleasant summer. Each year, the windows and doors of the terraces would be opened as the holiday approached, even if the weather was still cold and everyone in the house was shivering. The time had come to air out the house after the winter months, to fix everything needing repair, to give the house a thorough cleaning, and to repaint. Whenever I came home during this period, I would be greeted by the scent of fresh air mixed with the odors of paint and cleaning materials. A few weeks before the holiday, the courtyard of no. 1 Pshebyeg Street would be a flurry of activity. From morning till evening, the sound of carpets being beaten echoed in the air. Painters and their ladders came in and out. Every apartment was being cleaned, and the rubbish bin was too small to contain all of the refuse thrown into it from all sides. Every day the bin would be filled to overflowing and piles of rubbish would appear next to it, and at night, the trash collectors would carry it all away, and the next day the same scene would be repeated. In the end, the courtyard would be completely clean, and the apartments ten times as clean.

As the holiday grew nearer, everyone would receive new clothes. When we went to synagogue on the holiday, wearing our new clothes, I would be filled with pride. During Passover week, we did not use our usual dishes, but rather special Passover dishes, which were lovely and colorful. The food was also special, different from the food we ate the rest of the year. It was the most impressive of holidays. It was tangible in everything you did, felt and smelled. It was also a family holiday. We didn't invite anyone outside the family to our Seder meal, nor did we accept any invitations. The eight days of Passover were eight days of family happiness, with enjoyment of every festive detail. Such are the memories of childhood.

This year it was different. Now the holiday had become a needless annoyance, an occasion ill suited to our living conditions, something we had to endure because we had no choice. Every family prepared for the holiday as best they could, but the courtyard was not sparkling this year. We barely felt a holiday atmosphere. Everything was done modestly and quietly, so as not to depress those who could not celebrate, and also in fear of the unknown tomorrow.

Our apartment was prepared for the holiday and everything was ready for the Seder, but we felt nothing. Everything was done cheerlessly, as though we wanted to just get the holiday over with. When the Seder evening came, the courtyard was completely silent. No one could be seen, not even a child. We didn't go to synagogue. Abbreviated prayers were said in private houses, and everyone went home quickly. Candles were lit in every apartment, but in past years, the courtyard had been flooded with the lights shining from the windows. Now the yard was dark. No one lit all of the lights in his home, as had been customary. Fear was everywhere, the fear of being noticed. In fact, everyone was endeavoring to mark the holiday with restraint.

The Seder nights, which I had experienced every year as the ultimate uplifting experience, festive and beautiful, couldn't be like that again without my father. We sat down at the table indifferently, and sadness filled our hearts. Grandfather led the Seder and read the *Haggadah*, the retelling of the story of Passover, with a pained face, in a broken voice. I prayed that he would not break down, as it seemed to me that he was on the verge of tears. I knew that if he cried, I wouldn't be able to hold back my tears. But his voice became stronger as he read and we gained strength together with him. Yankele asked the Four Questions: "Why is this night different from all other nights?" We all silently asked ourselves, Why is this

Seder different from all other Seders we have known? Grandfather continued, "We were slaves to Pharaoh in Egypt, and God Almighty brought us out…" And what about us? Wasn't our situation worse than that of our forefathers in Egypt? What awaited us?

We continued reading the *Haggadah*: "In every generation they have tried to destroy us, and the Holy One, blessed be He, saved us…" The words penetrated our hearts. We had to believe that they were true. As God had saved us in the past, He would save us now, as well.

We read through the entire *Haggadah*, and nothing was lacking at the meal, yet the Seder went by quickly. None of us noticed how everything was done at a faster pace, with an inner compulsion to finish as quickly as possible. Afterward, we remained sitting around the table, drinking tea. Suddenly we heard the familiar sound of nailed boots, the boots of German soldiers. We sat frozen in our chairs. We heard the Germans climbing the stairs. Then we heard a loud knocking at the door to one of the apartments, and after a few seconds, we heard the sound of the Germans, this time leaving the courtyard. A Jew had been arrested on Seder night.

The circumstances of the Jews were so terrible it seemed that things couldn't get any worse. Jews had known persecution in Poland before, but at least they could lift their voices in a shout for help. After a pogrom, Jews throughout the world would offer aid to the victims. Now the Jews had been abandoned completely. Any German could humiliate a Jew, could behave with terrible cruelty, could beat Jews mercilessly, and could even kill — and the victim was not permitted to shout in protest, to complain.

Even more difficult was the financial situation, which worsened from day to day. Most of the sources of livelihood had been forbidden to Jews; money was running out, and more and more people were selling their valuables, their possessions, even their clothes. The *Wolavka*, the used goods market, was full of people and getting bigger every day. People of all classes, people who had never set foot there, one and all were selling their possessions — valuable sets of dishes, sets of silver, clothing, bedclothes, and even more modest objects — everything was being offered for sale. The Poles bought; Jewish merchants also bought cheaply from people who wanted to sell as quickly as possible, and then they sold the merchandise to the Poles at a profit. When a Pole came to the market expecting to sell something expensive at its worth, people would laugh at him. After standing in the market for an hour, which seemed like a year, the seller would set his price lower and lower; if he had come to sell something, that meant that he needed money, and quickly.

Many Jews who lived in mixed neighborhoods left their apartments — some expelled by Germans, some out of fear — and everyone moved into the Jewish quarter. The ghetto seemed to spring up naturally, without an edict, and the crowdedness, which increased as refugees came from the sector of Poland that had been annexed to the Reich, was unbearable. The streets were crammed full with people and seemed ready to explode. I couldn't understand how all of these people found places to sleep. As the sanitary conditions deteriorated, disease broke out, and typhus and dysentery claimed many victims. The Sanitation Department of the Jewish community did everything it could to get rid of the filth and rubbish and to prevent infectious diseases. Groups of sanitation workers sprayed for pests, took ill people to the hospitals, and tried to prevent further deterioration. But they couldn't keep up their efforts for long.

When we arrived from Lodz, my mother had with her quite a large sum of money, and it had seemed to us that we would be able to make do with it for a long time. But because we had no income, and expenses were greater than we had expected, our resources began to dwindle. My worried mother looked for ways to earn money. At first she tried selling sweaters, using Father's old Warsaw connections. She told us that everyone welcomed her warmly, but no one offered assistance. The financial situation of experienced Warsaw merchants was terrible; my mother had no chance of success and finally gave up.

My brother Mottel's hunt for work led him to a job as a laborer in a workshop making sweaters, which was located in a stuffy room in our building. Mottel had heard the sound of knitting machines, and when he discovered where the sounds were coming from he thought maybe he could find work there. The owner of the workshop was doubtful about Mottel's abilities, and told Mottel that it wasn't enough to be the son of the owner of a sweater factory to be able to operate a knitting machine. But Mottel proved he could do the work. Mottel, who had complained, "I'm sick of doing nothing — I can't go on studying; I can't concentrate," seemed content after he began working, but my mother and sister were upset. "Can't we manage without Mottel having to be someone's laborer?" mumbled my sister. Physical labor humiliated our family; it was a clear sign of a decrease in status for us. Everyone regarded my brother as an unfortunate, an object of pity. But I envied him — here he was again the focus of activity and interest, doing something for all of us, while I was unable to do anything.

From the time he started his job, Mottel enjoyed special treatment at home. Mother gave him extra food to make him stronger, and I would follow him around when he came home to have lunch. When he returned from work, I would ply him with questions like "How was it?" After some time, we got used to the new situation and Mottel stopped being the center of attention, but he began to change — he hardly spoke, he became introverted and seemed depressed. Only later did we find out the reason for his behavior. The two young men who worked with him at the workshop were uncouth, and when they found out that he wasn't crude like them, they tormented him. They cursed unceasingly, even in the presence of the girl who coiled the wool, but it didn't bother her — she even laughed — while my brother suffered. He worked there with them throughout the summer.

The rumor mill didn't stop churning out news for even a moment. Rumors came in waves, carrying everyone on their crests until they reached their peaks, then disappearing to make room for new rumors. No one knew where they were coming from or how new ones appeared. While we were still in Lodz we had heard that the Germans were leaving to make way for the Russians

— then the Germans annexed Lodz to the Third Reich and ordered the Jews into the ghetto. In Warsaw, as well, there were constant rumors that the Russians were coming, and these rumors intensified with the new rumor that the Germans and the Russians had reached an agreement. Hardly any of the Jews sympathized with the "Bolsheviks": they didn't want to live under a dictatorship, and certainly not a dictatorship of the proletariat; they were fearful of the Communist war against religion. Under normal circumstances, a Communist government would have been considered a national disaster for the Jews, but with the situation created by the war, the coming of the Russians in place of the Germans seemed to represent hope for rescue. So there was fertile ground for believing the rumor and there even seemed to be evidence of its truthfulness: it was enough for an apartment to be vacated by Germans for it to be taken as a sign that the Germans had begun leaving the city.

But there were also other rumors, like those spreading the news that a ghetto would soon be set up in Warsaw. This news, too, was cyclic, appearing and disappearing, but here and there, signs materialized indicating that this rumor would soon prove to be true. Every day, the Germans issued new limitations on where Jews could live.

On some streets, it was now forbidden to rent apartments to Jews; on others, Jews had been evicted from their apartments. More and more Jews were concentrated in the traditionally Jewish section of the city, and there were rumors that the area would be completely closed off, with no one allowed in or out.

The news from the front destroyed any optimism we might have had. Who could have imagined that France, which was considered a world power, defended by the unconquerable Maginot Line, the fortifications of which were equipped with the best weaponry, would collapse in a few days, despite the aid of the British? We began to fear that the German army was unstoppable, that the Germans actually would conquer the whole world. It would take a long time to reawaken our hopes of a German defeat.

The Jewish community authority issued an order in the name

of the German occupation authority: All men were required to work for the German occupation authority a number of days each month. Some who appeared for work, especially the younger ones, were taken by the Germans and sent to work camps. No one knew what happened to them; no one knew where they had gone. There were many stories about what went on in these camps. There were those who said that conditions were good and that the detainees would return after a month or two. There were also horror stories — the coerced labor force was being used to dry out swamps and worked from dawn to dusk; the work was terribly difficult and those who could not work were shot on the spot.

An atmosphere of terrible fear set in. The rich paid a "ransom" to be released from work or hired workers to take their places. When it became known that people were being sent to camps, fewer and fewer appeared for work — and the Germans responded by grabbing people from the city streets, taking every young man they could find, whether he had already worked or paid for a release or not. A crowded street would often clear out in a few seconds, and the Germans, tense and confused, would find no one to ensnare.

Before the war, Warsaw would empty out during the summer months, as many would leave for vacations in summer villages. My mother used to say, "Leaving for the country during the summer is a health matter." Now, no one even dared consider leaving for the country. Everyone was packed into the sweltering buildings, or tried to escape the heat by fleeing into the crowded streets and the tiny parks and squares in the Jewish neighborhood, as people were afraid to go out to other parks or to the open areas in the direction of the Vistula River.

Despite everything that was happening, the Jews quickly adjusted to the changing situation. Every day, new restaurants, delicatessens and cafés would open, and these would be filled with people. Young people found ways to spend their time, as well. All of the youth movements were functioning — secretly, of course — and there would be social gatherings, dances, singing and plays.

My sister, Dvora, belonged to *Hashomer Hatzair* and she would go to "movement activities" every day.

Our home once again filled with fear: now we feared that Mottel would be sent to a work camp. He was a tall, strong boy who looked older than his age. Mother was afraid that the Germans would just take him, not bothering to ask how old he was. He was at home most of the time, but, even so, Mother was worried. She would say, "Who knows what will happen today. I don't want to lose my son a second time." She was even more worried about Mottel because he had been getting thinner and paler, and he would have outbursts of anger that made us afraid to speak to him. Mottel didn't talk very much and it was difficult to know what he was going through. Except for my mother, whom he respected, I was the only one he was kind to. I often got angry with him, though, as it seemed to me that he was arrogant and added tension to our home. I couldn't stand the quarrels between Mottel and Dvora — I saw him as the head of the family, even though he was younger than Dvora, and I expected him to keep the peace at home.

Mother sent letters to Father's sisters in Turobin, asking about the situation there. The answers she received indicated that conditions there were much better than in Warsaw. They wrote that if the situation was very difficult in Warsaw, we could leave and come live with them. Mother suggested that Mottel go to Turobin, but he firmly refused to leave the house, saying that his place was with the family and he had to take care of us. I thought he was right. Indeed, he had already tried running away, at the beginning of the war.

I had a new partner watching the courtyard from the terrace — my brother, Yankele. He had changed from a spoiled, shouting, and at times unbearable child, to a quiet, attentive boy. He learned to enjoy the terrace, where he would sit next to me, asking questions and telling me stories. I had begun to pay more attention to him and I would even take him for walks without my mother asking me to. Could a child of seven understand that this was not the right time for being spoiled? Did he sense what was going on around us and suit his behavior to the situation?

The courtyard was like a nest of ants, full of people coming in and going out, stopping for a moment, exchanging a few words, and continuing on. There were many new faces, as quite a number of people had found shelter in our large building. There were new faces among the peddlers and the beggars, as well. Street singers, musicians and new bands also appeared. I had loved the old performers and their old songs, although they were seen less frequently now. Nothing much had changed in the windows surrounding us. The same faces looked out. Only the maid in the Prinzental apartment had disappeared, and knowing that I had done something forbidden by watching her undress and seeing her naked, I was happy that I wouldn't be tempted again, but I missed her, and often looked for her figure in the window. I also looked for the girl I was in love with and with whom I would sail on a sea of wonderful fantasies.

The first winds of autumn began to blow and they were stronger than usual. Our street faced an open area that continued on to the Vistula. When I was a child, my grandfather would take me to the synagogue on Bonifraterska Street, and when we got to the corner of the street, he would say, "Hold on to me so that the wind doesn't blow you away!" I would be alarmed and hold on tightly to his hand. The autumn winds were a sign of the coming winter, and we weren't prepared for it. In normal times we would ready the house for winter, filling the cellar with coal and wood for the fire, buying new winter clothes. This time, we prepared nothing, neither clothing nor coal. We only prayed for an easy winter. Rosh Hashanah and Yom Kippur, the High Holy Days, were approaching, holidays that terrified me; this was the time when the fates of men were sealed, "who shall live and who shall die, who by fire and who by water... It will be written on Rosh Hashanah and sealed on Yom Kippur..." Who knew if it wouldn't be decided that I, Berale, would die? I had sinned this year. Would God forgive me or not? And what about the people I knew who had sinned, eating non-kosher food, working on Shabbat and not going to synagogue, not even on Shabbat and holidays? Would anything happen to them?

One day Mother happily told us that we would begin attending school. I wasn't happy about it. I didn't feel that I could sit in a classroom and study. But, in the end, the school turned out to be just a rumor; no school opened. At the same time, rumors became more prevalent that a ghetto would be established. These rumors were not new and everyone hoped that they, too, would prove to be false. But the decrees came, one after another: a Jew who passed a German walking opposite him had to step off the sidewalk into the street. It was a strange sight to see a German soldier, sometimes just a youth, almost a boy, walk down a street crowded with Jews — and everyone, young and old, stepped off the sidewalk until he had passed by. After a short time, this became an automatic reaction, and from afar, you could see a river of people flowing into the street as a German soldier passed.

Next, Jews were forbidden to travel freely on the trolley cars; Jews were allotted a special car, and this was usually the last one. Not every trolley had a car for Jews, who sometimes had to wait for more than an hour. Nearly empty trolleys would pass them by, and when a trolley would finally pull up with one car for Jews, the first two cars would be half-empty and the last would always be overcrowded and there wouldn't be enough room for everybody.

Since the German occupation, prayer in synagogues had been forbidden, and Jews prayed in private homes. On Rosh Hashanah and Yom Kippur the situation became more serious as everyone, almost without exception, prayed on those days. Every other apartment was turned into a house of prayer, and on the eve of the holiday you could see people carrying Torah scrolls from the synagogues to private houses. Praying in groups in private homes was also forbidden, but we had to pray, even if it meant that we were in danger. We prayed with our grandparents at no. 31 Bonifraterska Street, in the apartment above my grandfather's synagogue. About a hundred people crowded into one room, and the women were crowded into an adjacent room, my mother among them. The people prayed in weeping voices, asking God to save their souls; could it be that God would not hear our voices? At the end of the service, we felt relief. We had opened our hearts to God, who was the only one who could save us. We wished each other Happy New Year, and when we got home, we celebrated the holiday according to tradition and dipped challah in honey, the sign of a sweet year to come.

We prayed the Yom Kippur service in the same place, but the room was even more suffocating as the number of people crowding into it had grown. The room was lit with candles and the windows had been bolted so that the sounds of our prayers could not be heard outside. The suffocation forced me out onto the stairway from time to time to get a breath of air. It was difficult for me to fast; I was constantly hungry. But I had no choice — if everyone else could hold out, I had to, as well.

During the afternoon prayers, someone came in and said that the radio had announced that a ghetto would be set up in Warsaw. The news came as a complete surprise and spread like wildfire. Everyone stopped praying and asked the man who had brought the news for more information, wondering whether it was true. The man said that he had heard the news himself on the loudspeaker in the street and the announcement had given details about the streets to be included in the ghetto. The faces of the people, which were already pale, became even paler. At first, everyone began talking at once, but after a few moments everyone was quiet, as if petrified, until someone reminded us that we had to continue praying. We returned, weeping bitterly, to our prayers.

Each time it had seemed to us that the situation was so bad that it couldn't get any worse. But again and again, we were proved wrong. The situation could always get worse, darker, with no sign of light. The rumors had circulated for months about a ghetto being set up in Warsaw, and we were very aware that the Germans were able to create one, as the ghetto in Lodz had been in existence for almost a year. The Germans could do even worse — in Krakow one fine day they had ordered all the Jews to leave the city forever. The Jews of Krakow had found themselves suddenly penniless, with no roofs over their heads, without livelihoods, refugees in the surrounding towns. The Jews of Warsaw, in spite of everything, had hoped that "that" would not happen to them. And when "that" happened, everyone was in shock.

The day after Yom Kippur, notices were pasted on walls and bulletin boards ordering all of the Jews living outside the area defined as Jewish to leave their homes and businesses and to move to the "Jewish area" within a month. All Christians living in the Jewish area were ordered to leave their homes and businesses and move to the "Aryan area." The order defined the streets of the ghetto and its borders. All that day, people studied the ghetto plan. Some of them thanked God that their apartments were within ghetto limits; some of them cried because their homes were outside of it. We were lucky. Our street was on the border of the ghetto, just inside it.

Questions arose. Within the ghetto there were many Christian institutions, including a church and a hospital for the chronically ill that was on our street. What would become of them? The Germans, out of the kindness of their hearts, said that the church had intentionally been included within the boundaries of the ghetto for those many Jews who had converted to Christianity, but that the order to live in the ghetto applied to them, as well; it seemed that the efforts of these Jews to leave Judaism (or that their fathers had converted in previous generations) had been in vain. With the help of the Poles, the Germans searched for and found converts, both those who had been born to Jewish parents and those who had only a Jewish grandparent: they were all considered Jews and had been forced to wear the Star of David, and now they had to move into the ghetto.

It was difficult to understand how there would be room for the tens of thousands, perhaps even hundreds of thousands, more Jews in the area designated as the ghetto, which was already overflowing. The price of apartments in the ghetto rose astronomically. Jews who lived in the area quickly took advantage of the distress of their fellows. During the first days after publication of the order, wagons filled with furniture and other property could be seen entering the Jewish area. These wagons had usually been rented by the richer people, who were trying to keep their possessions for as long as they could, as no one knew what the future would bring. As time passed, the number of loaded wagons increased. This was a good time for wagon drivers and porters, who, thanks to the great demand, could request high fees for their work. Many of the unemployed put together primitive, handmade wagons and earned some money carrying goods to the ghetto. Before the war, when there had been outbursts of anti-Semitism, and groups of Endeks (members of the anti-Semitic National Democratic Party) had rioted and shattered display windows of Jewish shops, Jews would joke and say that the Endeks were doing a favor for the poor Jewish glaziers; now there was an opportunity to make some money by becoming wagon drivers and porters, whose jobs had disappeared with the disappearance of commerce.

The poorer Jews, who were unable to rent apartments, waited to move in until the last possible day. A swarm of people flowed into the ghetto, with or without wagons. Whole families were moving, carrying baggage, pieces of furniture, kitchen utensils and other objects on everyone's shoulders. Unbelievable poverty was exposed for all to see. People who had nowhere to live organized themselves in the streets, in the courtyards and in the stairways — any place they could find. The community workers opened up the schools and other public institutions. No one knew whether the ghetto would be open or closed, and even though it was known that the Lodz Ghetto was completely closed and cut off from the outside world, in Warsaw we hoped that the ghetto would remain open and that we would not be isolated.

My brother was let go because there was no work for him. Our constant fear was that he would be sent to a work camp, and my mother again suggested that he leave the city before it was too late. The house became the center of constant argument, as my brother refused to leave. In the meantime, our financial situation was becoming more and more precarious, and this was reflected in the lower quality of our food. "Ironically," said my mother, "the war has brought one good thing — an increase in your appetite."

Before the war I was never hungry and I ate little; when I wanted to please my mother and I would eat more than usual, I would immediately throw up. Now my appetite had grown and I was able to eat greater and greater quantities of food. But our menu had changed. Butter, sour cream, eggs and meat appeared less and less often on our table, until they remained just a memory of times gone by. The demand for all foods had been growing.

The house committee, which had been set up by respected residents of the building, collected money and clothes for the needy. Committee members had visited our home several times. My mother always contributed generously, and friendly relations had developed between her and the members of the committee, some of whom she had known for a long time. Now Mother was afraid of another visit, saying that she couldn't deprive her own children to help other people. But she also didn't want it to be known that our financial situation had deteriorated to such an extent. Then, one evening, the house committee came for another visit. She poured them cups of tea as she always did, and they told her of their welfare activities. Mother gave them a small sum of money, and apologized that she couldn't contribute more. The committee members were surprised; they were used to receiving larger amounts from her. One woman remarked, "If you're having problems, perhaps you shouldn't contribute at all." Mother insisted on giving her small contribution, but when the visitors left, she burst into tears.

One morning when I went out into the street, I saw that at the corner, where our street met Bonifraterska Street, a wall was being built. Everyone passing by stopped to watch how the street was being blocked to keep us from going out into the wide area leading to the large parks, the fortress and the Vistula. Now, not only could we not walk in that direction, we couldn't even see the undeveloped area, which had remained a wide green expanse. It quickly became clear that this was not the only wall — dozens of walls were being built to completely seal off all of the streets of the ghetto. At the corner of Muranowska and Bonifraterska Streets, a barricade had been set up with a guardhouse. The manner in which the ghetto was sealed off indicated that it had been planned down to the smallest detail, and it was quickly carried out. Within a few days we found ourselves imprisoned in a jail with eight and a half million inmates.

For months I had repeatedly heard the word "ghetto," and I knew from my experience in Lodz that it was an area where all of the Jews were confined. I had also heard about the ghettos where Jews had lived during the Middle Ages. But I couldn't imagine how life could carry on inside a ghetto. My curiosity impelled me to spend my days wandering the streets of the city, among the crowds, paying attention to what was going on in the neighborhood. The boundaries of the ghetto, as if made of rubber, expanded every day to receive thousands of additional people and their possessions. More and more came and were swallowed up into the courtyards, and somehow, amazingly, there was room for all of them. But there was nothing really to wonder at; they simply crowded into any empty space and lived in inhuman conditions.

As I wandered, I was witness to the creation of the "kingdom" of the ghetto, along with all of its institutions. One day the Jewish police appeared, dressed in round black hats with a Star of David on the front. They looked very similar to the Polish police. They did not have uniforms, but they seemed to be wearing the same coats, most of them wore boots, and all of them carried batons tucked into their belts. There was also a special unit of "economic police" whose members wore green hats. These were called, for some reason, "the Thirteen," and were supposed to combat the dealers on the black market, but in actuality, everyone was afraid of them. In place of the trolley cars, which were now forbidden to Jews, horse-drawn carriages appeared in the streets with large Stars of David displayed above them. An entire system of Jewish government was established as the ghetto was being created. All civilian administration within the ghetto was transferred to the Jewish community. At the entrances to official buildings, signs appeared in Yiddish, and stores and shops also had Yiddish signs.

On my daily walks, I reached every corner of the wall or the barbed wire barricades which sealed off the ghetto, guarded by a German soldier, a Polish policeman and a Jewish policeman. When I visited my aunt on Bonifraterska Street, I discovered that one side of the street belonged to the ghetto and was blocked off with barbed wire, while across the road, the other side was not included. I had known this Jewish street since I was a child, and until a few days before, I had walked on a sidewalk that was now part of a different world, the world outside the ghetto, where no Jew could be seen. Every Jew who crossed to the other side of the street put his life in danger.

It seemed that there was nothing people couldn't get used to. Now we were all living in the ghetto, cut off from the world, in the situation we had talked about with trepidation for months; yet despite the extreme changes we had been witness to, life went on in its new course. The streets were full of people, all Jewish — "Aryans" were not allowed to enter the ghetto. Only the trolley cars crossing the ghetto contained non-Jews, but they traveled quickly, without stopping, and a Polish policeman stood guard ensuring that no one would get off or on the trolley while it was passing through.

The economic situation, which had been very bad even before the ghetto had been created, was now many times worse. The closure of the ghetto sealed off the last possible source of livelihood, commerce; how would people survive? Now we were dependent upon the Germans and what they would allow us to bring into the ghetto. But through all this, people got used to the new situation, trying to build their lives within the limits allowed them, making the best of what was happening and saying that we had to make do, that we would still see the defeat of the Germans. There were even those who saw this in a positive light — inside the ghetto we would be left to live our lives in peace.

As the ghetto was sealed, most necessities disappeared from the shops. Meat, milk products, eggs and fruit completely vanished. Ghetto residents were given food coupons to live on, with which individuals could receive a small amount of food, containing very few calories. Gradually, everything one might wish to buy could be found in the black market or at the back doors of the shops, but at very high prices which only a few could afford. A smuggling network sprang up and there was nothing that was not smuggled into the ghetto. People spoke of underground passages and passageways through walls common to both sides of the ghetto. They said that in one house, there was a pipe through which milk flowed constantly. Meat and fruit were smuggled into the ghetto; no one knew exactly how. And there were smugglers who operated publicly. I would stand for hours, watching the smuggling on the trolley cars that crossed the ghetto. At certain places, especially at sharp turns, after the car with the policeman had rounded the corner and he was unable to see what was going on behind him, smugglers would quickly throw out heavy sacks filled with flour, grain, beans or vegetables. The sacks would fall in the middle of the street, almost as if by accident, but the minute the trolley car had passed, people would come out of one of the building entrances, load the sacks and disappear the way they had come. These operations took no more than a few seconds and went on all through the day. The smugglers did not always succeed in throwing out their merchandise, as sometimes the policeman would hamper the operation or a German soldier might be standing near the smuggler on the trolley, and he would have to return with his sack and try his luck again. Sometimes the smuggler would have to jump off the trolley with the sack to avoid getting caught.

Smuggling of another type took place at the gates of the ghetto. Workers who were employed outside the ghetto and returned home in the evenings would buy food on the Aryan side, usually bread and vegetables, to feed their families, sometimes using their last coins. They would pad their bodies with food, and standing at the gate to be checked, pray that they would be lucky and not be discovered. Sometimes a group would pass through without being checked, and then you could see the happiness on the faces of the workers who knew that their families would have a bit more to eat. But more often than not, people were checked one by one, and were forced to open their long underclothing, unbutton their shirts, and roll up their sleeves. Potatoes, carrots and onions would drop out or sometimes, a loaf of bread, and less frequently, a packet of butter. There were workers who might only have a few potatoes or a piece of bread, but they, too, would have to leave these behind, and sometimes they would be beaten, as well. Then I would see them entering the ghetto, faces pale, and sometimes washed in tears.

The heavy rains and the strong winds sent the crowds from the streets into their homes. Along with the cold, there was a new form of suffering that we had not yet known, but which we had heard about in stories about the World War — hunger. Our family was still eating three meals a day, but the food, which lacked fats, did not satisfy us. Hunger did not leave me from the moment I opened my eyes in the morning until I fell asleep at night. And it was the same for every one of us. We waited impatiently for meals, tensely watching the food being divided. My mother, who felt that she was being inspected and manipulated, lost her self-confidence and sometimes erred in her division, which would lead to outbursts and arguments between Dvora and Mottel, who blamed each other. The arguments between the two of them were not about the division of food, but, without a doubt, the gnawing hunger that made each of us feel that someone else was receiving more food encouraged short tempers.

We noticed that our mother had almost stopped eating anything except for a bit of soup. When we mentioned it, she said that she was eating as much as she needed, and we didn't have to worry about her, but we decided that we wouldn't start eating until she had given herself a portion equal to the ones we received. She quarreled about this with us at every meal, but in the end, she had no choice and had to eat as much as we did.

A group of people began to gather in our home every night, most of them neighbors who sat for long hours, drinking tea sweetened with saccharine, talking about their experiences, arguing, and sometimes playing bingo. Now and then someone would bring candy, sometimes cookies. Why in our apartment? Perhaps it was because even though we were seven people living in two rooms, our apartment was quite large, and perhaps it was because my mother was the best hostess. Most of these evenings passed pleasantly. At the end of a hard day in the ghetto, people needed a break, a relief, a chance to talk about their troubles or forget the difficult realities, to recall the pleasant past which now seemed so far away, or to nurture illusions about a hopeful future. Discussions usually began with the news. Everyone would relate what they had heard or seen during the day, and when there was bad news, a stifling silence would settle over the room for a few minutes. Sometimes arguments would break out about what the future held for us, until someone would end the discussion by talking about the recent past, which now seemed so distant — stories about vacation homes, trips, parties and other pleasant pastimes. A wave of longing would pass over us, each of us wanting to add to the conversation that focused on happier times.

Among those who visited us in the evenings was a couple who were unusual — he was the son of one of the long-time residents of the building, an ultra-Orthodox family, and who, when he was younger, had "left the fold for bad company." He had joined a Zionist organization and gone to Israel, where he remained for three years. He hadn't been able to adjust there and had returned to Poland and gotten married. Now he was filled with regret that he had returned. He would tell us simple romantic stories about the country, about the hard work and the burning sun, about suffering from malaria, but also about the exciting experiences — about building Jewish settlements, the socialistic kibbutzim and moshavim, about Tel Aviv, Haifa and Jerusalem, about the bustling life in the "land of the Forefathers" while we were sitting here imprisoned in a ghetto, condemned to starvation, and there was nothing we could do. I swallowed up every word about Israel, as though I were hypnotized. I was captivated by the idea that there were Jews who were not living under German persecution, living in their own land.

Almost every evening would end with a discussion of food. People enjoyed telling about dishes that they had eaten on Shabbat and holidays, describing in great detail the tastes and aromas until you could actually smell them and feel them on the tip of your tongue. Faces would become sensual, eyes would be dreamy, but the ever-present hunger would eventually send everyone back home.

In spite of the autumn weather, the rains that fell in showers and the damp cold that chilled your bones, the streets were crowded all hours of the day. Every so often they would instantly empty out, when a car containing German soldiers appeared. When they came, they only added to our suffering. But when the car disappeared, the roads would quickly fill up again. Every day, people forced out of their previous professions opened new restaurants, cafés and bake shops, and in the streets, there would be more and more musical groups, cabaret singers, opera singers, acrobats and jugglers, all of whom had lost their jobs and were trying to earn some money in the streets, alongside the beggars. One day, I saw a crowd in Muranowski Square, and I heard music playing. I walked over. The music wasn't like that of the usual street musicians. These were older people, dressed formally, standing in a half-circle and playing violins with serious faces. The crowd was paying more attention to the serious group than to the music. Finally I heard someone standing near me say, "Do you know who these players are? They are the best musicians in Poland. They are members of the Warsaw Philharmonic Orchestra, and some of them are famous soloists." The man excitedly added, "How terrible for them and for us, that we have gotten to this." A few people put coins into the plate that had been placed on the ground, and I stood there for a long time listening to them play, listening to music which I was hearing for the first time.

The street was dangerous, for at any moment, a German could appear and attack you, beat you mercilessly, arrest you and send you to a work camp, or even shoot you to death for no reason at all, on a passing whim; but even so, something prodded people to leave their houses and go out into the street. After all, how could you sit at home with your wife and children and not do anything at all? It was better to try your luck in the street, where, perhaps, you could find something to do to earn some money, meet a friend who would help you find a job, or perhaps, while walking, some idea of what to do to earn a living would occur to you. Many hung around the doors of the Jewish community institutions, hoping that there would be something for them to do. Long lines formed near the soup kitchens and the sites where food was distributed to the needy. Many just walked the streets with no purpose, as they had nothing to do at home.

The numbers of beggars grew. Some walked around and begged from passersby, others stood or sat on the sidewalks, near the walls of the houses, asking for a handout. Among the beggars there were many children, alone or in groups, sometimes members of the same family. As the number of beggars increased, the number of contributors decreased. How long could this go on? The number of people selling in the street also grew. Here, too, there were many children. They hung boxes of cigarettes or candies around their necks or set up tables on the sidewalks, where they displayed their wares. If a person gave any indication that he might want to buy something, peddlers would attack the potential customer from all sides and he wouldn't know what to buy in the general confusion.

I walked more and more among the crowds, observing everything that went on in the street. In our courtyard, there were no more musical groups, but every day, singers and accordionists, violinists and other musicians would sing and play, begging, most of them children who sang and then asked for help in high-pitched voices, looking up at the windows of the apartments. These children would have accepted anything; they said, "Don't throw away your trash. Give it to us. Even if it is just a moldy piece of bread or potato skins." Every day the same two children would come to the courtyard, about six years old, perhaps seven or eight, probably a brother and sister, and sing the same song:

Oh, buy, buy papyrus
Completely dry, not wet,
I ask for mercy,
Save us from death.

There was something special about these two children that aroused affection, and they received a bit more food and a few more coins than the others. One day they stopped coming, and we wondered what had happened to them. We assumed that they had died of illness or hunger.

Many things had changed in our courtyard, but one thing did not change — the children continued to play, and their voices could be heard all day; only the games changed and were suited to the times. Instead of playing "cops and robbers," the game changed to "the Gestapo and the Jews." In this game, the children would curse in German and shoot the Jews. I continued to sit on our terrace and watch the courtyard, and from time to time, I would turn to the window on the third floor, watching for the head of the girl of my dreams.

After many nights of quarrels, my mother decided to send Mottel to the town of Turobin, my father's birthplace. My father's sister promised to take care of him. It was difficult to understand my mother's decision — to be separated a second time from Mottel, and this time, on her own initiative. Who knew how long the separation would be? And deep in my heart, I feared that we would never see him again. But it seemed that my mother not only feared that Mottel would be taken by the Germans and sent to a work camp — people were now saying that these camps had been set up in the area of Lublin — the lack of food in our home was becoming more and more serious, with no hope of improvement. Mottel had grown very tall and was very thin. He was nervous and restless and greatly needed both more food and more freedom. There, in an out-of-the-way town, Mother hoped that Mottel might be able to get a bit more of both. And perhaps Mother expected the worst, and did not think that we could hold out and wanted to save whomever she could?

Sending Mottel out of the ghetto and to Lublin, and from there to the town of Turobin, was not simple, and required a great deal of money, but Mother acted decisively. She sold possessions to obtain the money, made contact with smugglers, and then one evening we again said goodbye to him, weeping, one question echoing in our hearts: would we ever see each other again?

This time I wasn't envious of my brother, as I had been when he had left home with my father. This time, I pitied him as he was being forced to leave home and to live with an aunt whom he barely knew. I was glad to be staying at home with my family. I was sorry that Mottel was leaving, I worried about him, and I prayed that he would get to Turobin safely. I would miss him, yet I felt more comfortable and freer without my brother at my side, because when he was at home, I always felt as though I were under his critical eye. He also was a barrier between my mother and me, whose closeness I needed now. Now that he wasn't at home, I did become closer to her: I went with her on errands, I stayed with her at the Wolicka Street market selling household items; I spoke to her more. It was good for me to be in her company, and it seemed to me that she enjoyed my company, as well.

Winter came all at once and with great force. White snow covered everything and the terrible cold ruled the streets and seeped gradually into the house. The streets emptied. People who had to go out crossed the streets quickly. Stubborn peddlers who wouldn't give up stood near the walls of the buildings, jumping from one foot to another to warm their legs, and with them stood the beggars. The Jews of the ghetto welcomed winter with worry and fear: how would they heat their homes when there was neither coal nor wood? We had a small store of coal and wood, but even the most economical use of what we had would not enable us to heat the apartment for more than a short time. And what would happen then? What about the long winter months? It was decided to heat only one room, and grandfather, who had years of experience dealing with the heater, was in charge. "This heater loves to eat a lot, but after it satisfies itself, it heats for a long time," said Grandfather. "We will try to trick it. We'll give it a small amount and let's see what we get." Grandfather put long, thin branches into the heater, put some thicker branches on the top, added a few lumps of coal, considered for a time, added another lump of coal, and then, lit the fire and waited for it to spread to the top of the pyramid. He then closed the first lid, again waited for the fire to become stronger, and then covered the bottom lid and the two protective doors, which prevented contact with the burning hot lids. Grandfather looked happy when he finished his work. Everything seemed to be in order, and now we waited for the heater to warm the room. After a few minutes I walked over to the heater and put my hands on the outside tiles to test whether they had heated up, but Grandfather laughed at me, saying that we had to wait a few hours. In fact, the heater became hot quite quickly. After less than an hour, we could warm our hands on its tiles, but it never really spread the heat. We waited in vain for the room to become warmer, so that we could walk around in our shirts. When the heater had been lit before the war, the room had become so hot that we sometimes had to open the window; now we were dressed in warm coats and we still felt cold.

The experiment with the heater led us to the conclusion that we would have to suffer this winter, and after analyzing the situation, we understood that the big beautiful heater required a great amount of coal, and if it were not filled properly, the minimal heat that it gave off would mostly go out through the chimney, whose sloping bricks would not absorb the heat and spread it throughout the room. So we bought a simple iron heater, put it in the center of the room, and attached its chimney to the chimney of the larger heater. It looked terrible and was uncomfortable — the chimney was not stable and we had to tie it with iron wire at the sides, but the heater itself warmed up quickly and we only had to put some paper into it for the chimney to warm up and for the room to be warmer. The new iron heater also served as a cooking stove and filled the room with smoke and smells, but it did not stay warm; when something was burning in the heater, it was so hot you couldn't go near it, but the moment that it burned out, it didn't retain any heat, and the cold ruled again, with all of its force. In addition, the heat that the iron heater emitted could only be felt when you were standing next to it — the minute you took a step away, you couldn't even tell that the heater was burning, and it was as if the heat had only been an illusion. To heat the room you had to let it burn day and night, and that was something we couldn't do. Most of the day, we froze. We used the heater only at certain hours. We lay in bed, covered up to our noses until late in the morning, and then my mother would light the heater and we would all jump out of bed, straight to the heater, each of us vying to find a better place to get warm.

I was lucky. I slept in the living room and I was first to see my mother lighting the heater, so I could get to it first. But there was another reason that I would get out of bed earlier: at ten o'clock, I had to be standing in Muranowski Square to listen to the announcements on the loudspeaker. At home, everyone made fun of me for leaving the house in the freezing cold to listen to the radio, and my mother begged me not to go outside, but I felt that I had to get information from any possible source: deep within, I was hoping that something positive would happen which would change our lives, and that I would be the one to bring the news home.

I wasn't the only one. Every morning in the square, a few other men would gather to listen to the news the German government provided for us. After listening to the news, I would take a walk through the surrounding streets, sometimes walking down Muranowska Street, sometimes choosing Mila Street in the direction of Zamenhof Street, but usually to Nalewska Street, where I had always enjoyed walking. People hurried down the street, their faces hidden by the collars of their coats, so that it was difficult to identify them. Peddlers and other people stood in the doorways of the buildings, jumping from one foot to another from the cold. Beggars, among them many children, dressed in rags, asked for money in weak voices. Sometimes you would bump against someone lying in the snow. Passersby would stop for a moment, take a look, sigh, and continue on their way, wondering if the person lying there was alive or dead.

Before going home, I used to stand for a time near the gate of the ghetto at the corner of Bonifraterska and Muranowska Streets and watch the other side. The German guard standing there was always dressed like a bear — over his boots, he had heavy boots of straw, and over his coat, he had a fur coat — but the Polish policeman and the Jewish policeman standing next to him were dressed lightly, and they, too, jumped from one foot to another and rubbed their hands. I would arrive home feeling like an icicle and my mother would remonstrate, "Look at the boy, he's completely frozen!" She would leave everything to start taking care of me, rubbing my hands and feet, trying to warm me, pouring me a cup of hot tea, and I would feel happy: it was good to get out of the house and good to return.

The winter always seemed threatening to me. I had heard many frightening stories about people who had frozen to death, or whose hands and feet had frozen and had to be amputated, or who had held their frozen ear and it had come off in their hand without feeling any pain. When my ears hurt from the cold, I was afraid that I would lose one of them or perhaps even my nose, and I would hurry home. Every disaster that occurred seemed to happen to people when they weren't at home, exposed to the cold, and unable to find shelter. Home had always been a fortress, a defense against the cruel winter, and the pleasant heat that prevailed was the only compensation for the cruel winter. Now there was cold at home, almost as cold as the outside, maybe even colder, because if you were going outside you would be dressed warmly from head to foot and you could be constantly moving around, while at home, you could not be dressed as you were outside, nor could you be in constant motion. Of course, you wouldn't freeze to death at home, but the cold never left you for a moment, and it seemed even worse than the hunger — you didn't feel the hunger constantly, it came and went, sometimes with more intensity and sometimes with less.

I imagined that if I hadn't been hungry, I would have suffered less from the cold, but the food I ate satisfied me only for a few minutes. The moment I had finished the meal, my stomach seemingly full, I would be attacked by hunger as before, and I would have eaten anything in the world, no matter what it was. I had never known what hunger was. Food was always the last thing that interested me; now it became the most important thing in my life, something that never left my thoughts.

The coal was completely used up and it could only be bought at a very high price. The wood for heating was disappearing, as well, and we still had the long winter months ahead of us. I began searching for something to burn. Every day, after listening to the news on the loudspeaker in the square, I would search the ruins of the buildings that had been destroyed during the bombing, and the empty lots, looking for something that would burn. The snow, which covered everything, made it more difficult for me. The year before, Warsaw had had a shortage of heating material, and people had already taken everything that could be burned, but even so, I sometimes found pieces of wood that I would bring home quickly. Even though the wood I found didn't belong to anyone, I was always afraid that the street children or the police would take it away from me.

I felt happy about my contribution to heating the house, and even more so about the fact that I was able to do something for the family, but anything I did manage to accomplish was just a drop in the ocean. The house continued to be unbearably cold, which prevented us from keeping as clean as we should have. We changed our underwear infrequently; we couldn't launder our clothes during the winter, nor could we bathe very frequently. And so, eventually, we began to itch.

At first, we found just one louse, but then, there were more and more. Initially, we were upset and ashamed: could it be that we had…lice? Dvora burst out crying and threatened to leave the house if we didn't get rid of them. My mother tried to fight the plague: she undressed us, put us in bed and covered us, and shook out the lice from our clothing, but they reproduced at an alarming rate and my mother's war against them had no effect. One evening, Mother made her greatest effort — she lit the heater and warmed the house, and we all washed ourselves with hot water and put on clean clothes. For a while it seemed that the lice were all gone, but…wonder of wonders, after a few minutes we all began to itch again, and we scratched even more than usual. Mother continued to fight and the lice continued to win. It became clear, however, that the fight against the lice was being waged not only in our home, but throughout the building, and perhaps, throughout the ghetto.

During the summer, we could see the sun on the highest floor opposite us in the morning, and the golden patch grew and covered one window and then another until, by afternoon, half the building opposite and half the courtyard would be drenched in sunlight. In the afternoon, the rays of the sun left the courtyard and the patch of golden light would become smaller and smaller until it disappeared over the fourth floor, to the right of our apartment. Now, in the middle of winter, after the snows, the sun returned and appeared in the courtyard, but didn't touch the ground. It again appeared opposite, but at a sharp angle, coming down from the roof until, in the afternoon, its rays created a sharp angle which reached the second floor — and at the center of the angle, on the third floor, was the window of the girl of my dreams.

On clear days, I would enjoy the patch of light that the sun would cast opposite me and the sight of the girl looking out of her window. It would seem to me that in her apartment, it was warm and pleasant, while I was shivering from the cold at our window. Every day, I would measure the angle of the ray of light. I knew that the sun would get higher and higher in the sky until it would light the asphalt pavement of the courtyard — and then, at last, summer would come at last and end the suffering. But the angle grew so slowly, and the cold went on and on and it seemed that it would be with us forever.

The winter months slowly passed. The short days and the long nights had no end, and neither did the suffering and pain. Why do good things pass so quickly — and bad things last so long? People said that there hadn't been such a difficult winter in years. Had we sinned so greatly that God was punishing us?

At last winter was over. The pleasant, sunny days arrived and people went out into the streets. The houses were still very cold, but the sun warmed the avenues and put a smile on the pale faces. Melting ice dripped from the roofs and windowsills, and drops of water fell from every direction. Only a bit of slush remained of the snow. There were puddles of mud everywhere. The sun warmed our bodies, but our feet were still frozen.

On one such day, I stood for more than an hour in line to exchange our food coupons. It was pleasant to feel the sun warming my face, but my feet, which were standing in a puddle of mud, were freezing. I jumped around to no avail. I wanted to cry from the pain, but these were the last pains of winter. The coffeehouse politicians came back after the cold winter had chased them out of the courtyard, where they now gathered to analyze the situation and to argue about our future. The stream of news, which had diminished during the winter, returned in the spring — it was as if everything and everyone were awakening from a winter sleep — and news flowed from German sources, as well as from underground sources. The residents of the building collected these pieces of information and added their interpretations. Most of the news was bad: the Germans had been victorious and had captured more and more territory; the Italians, led by Mussolini, had joined the war alongside the Germans. But the politicians of our building maintained that the Germans were in a bad state, bolstering this argument by pointing out the difficult economic situation of the Aryan side of Warsaw. The more the Germans confiscated and robbed, the more this was interpreted that they were having difficulties. Even when a group of Germans broke into the ghetto and killed Jews in the street, this was understood to be a sign of their difficulties, which caused them to take revenge on the Jews; we would just have to hold out — salvation was on the way!

The hard winter had forced people to sit at home and paralyzed their ability to try to improve their situation. With the coming of spring, everyone felt that the time had come to find some sort of employment, to earn some money in order to support his or her family. People bustled with activity, searching for a job or a deal. My aunt Sarah and her husband, who had had a clothing store on Nalewska Street, opened a restaurant on Muranowska Street, near our home, investing all of their money in it. I visited it every day, and found that very few people came to eat there. At the beginning, my uncle and aunt had been full of energy and optimism, and the restaurant was sparkling clean, but gradually the place became neglected. My uncle stopped coming to the restaurant, and my aunt was always angry and crying.

My mother forbade me to eat in my aunt's restaurant, as it was a business and everyone who ate there should be a paying customer. I obeyed her, but my aunt started offering me soup, as it was already prepared and she had nothing to do with it; in any case, she said, no one would come to eat. I pitied my aunt and helped her, and she confided in me. We were friends again, just as we had been in the past. But after two months, she and her husband were forced to close the restaurant and they lost everything they had invested.

My grandfather began manufacturing cigarettes. As far back as I could remember, he had always made his own cigarettes. He would buy different types of tobacco, mix them together, and put the mixture onto a strip of newspaper. He would then put some water into his mouth and spray water on the tobacco, filling the room with a pleasant smell. He also sometimes bought strips of paper especially for making homemade cigarettes and filled them with a tobacco mix, using a special tool. Now, after a long period during which he would leave the house in the morning and return after a few hours, bitter and sad, without having done anything, he went back into action: he brought home a large quantity of tobacco and boxes of paper strips, arranged everything on the big table in the living room, and began working energetically. Producing cigarettes required skill, as tobacco that was too wet could not be compressed into the paper shells and would tear them, and dry tobacco would become like dust and spill out of them. You had to fill the shells correctly and carefully with the special compressing tool. Grandfather sat at the table, filling cigarettes, cutting and straightening their edges, and then he packed them in boxes so that they looked like factory-produced cigarettes. I sat by his side, watching him work and trying to help him.

I hadn't seen Grandfather smile since we had come from Lodz. I had often seen tears in his eyes. He had become a bitter, helpless person. He often sat with a Torah open in front of him, but he didn't seem to be able to concentrate, appearing to be deep in thought. Abruptly he would get up and say, "I have to go!" as though he really had something to do, but as there was actually nothing for him to do he would go out and come back, embarrassed that he had lied to everyone and to himself. Now Grandfather had changed completely. I don't know how much he earned producing cigarettes, but he was full of energy. He went out every morning with a package to sell and would return with a package of raw material, arrange it quickly on the table and sit down to work. His mood improved and the bitterness left his face. While he was working, he would sometimes forget himself and start singing. I loved seeing him like this.

There were so many cigarettes left around the house that I was seized with a desire to smoke. I had already tasted a cigarette at school. A group of children had bought one cigarette, lit it and each of us had inhaled a few times. I had experienced a bitter taste that I still remembered, but even so, I was attracted to the cigarettes. One day, I took a cigarette and went out into the stairway, where I lit it with shaking hands. I inhaled several times, put out the cigarette and went back into the house. All of a sudden, I began to feel ill. I felt weak and my legs were buckling. I couldn't move at all and I had trouble lifting my head. Cold sweat covered my face. I felt frightened and I didn't quite know what to do. I remembered that I had had a similar feeling, but much less intense, when my sister had cut her finger and I had seen the blood: I had immediately felt ill and gone pale. Everyone in the family had laughed and said that seeing a drop of blood was enough to make me faint. This feeling, however, was more intense and was lasting longer.

I lay down in bed and felt as if I were lying in thick, hot cereal that was pasted to my whole body. When my mother saw me, she was alarmed. "Berale, what happened to you? What's wrong? Tell me." I said that nothing had happened, and that I felt fine. Mother ran and got a wet towel to wipe my face. "Look at the boy," she said, "His face is so pale. What could have made him faint?" I didn't tell her what had happened, and she seemed to be very worried. The attack of weakness passed quickly, and even though my mother watched over me carefully and worried, in spite of the terrible experience, I wanted another cigarette. Since I was more afraid of everyone's reactions if I should faint than I was afraid of actually fainting, I took a cigarette and found a hiding place behind a bombed-out building, where I sat on a pile of bricks and lit the cigarette. I smoked it slowly, serenely, and waited to see what would happen. After I had finished smoking, I felt ill again and cold sweat again covered my face. I sat quietly until the disconcerting feeling had passed, and then I walked home. I began smoking a cigarette or two every day, and I stopped having any unpleasant reactions.

Again, we had to prepare to celebrate the holiday of Passover, the holiday everyone loved best, the holiday of freedom and of the beauty of nature. How different this holiday was from all those which had preceded it! We were sealed in a ghetto; our freedom and liberty and been taken from us. We searched for signs of spring in the streets of the ghetto — we had no hope of seeing the fields turning green, the wild flowers blooming along the paths, the flowering of the fruit trees. We could not breathe the scent of the fields, the forests, the lilacs in bloom. We were imprisoned and we could not see a ray of hope. We couldn't even compare this holiday to the one we had celebrated the year before, in spite of the fact that we had already been under German rule, and limited by their decrees. Last year, we were not yet living in a ghetto, and Jews tried to celebrate the holiday as it should be celebrated. There was even a sort of holiday atmosphere in the streets. This year, Passover could not be celebrated. It would have been ridiculous to say "We were slaves to Pharaoh in Egypt" when our situation now was worse than slavery. The eight days of holiday, which should have been eight days of happiness, became eight days of spiritual and bodily suffering. The prohibition against eating *chametz* was added to the normal everyday hunger, and kosher-for-Passover foods were not to be found, leaving us hungrier than ever. Due to the emergency situation, the rabbis permitted eating beans and other legumes, but that did not make much of a difference. The Seder was short and sad.

Without our noticing it, our situation went from bad to even worse. That spring of 1941, which brought people out into the streets, also exposed their distress. Each day, the numbers of people whose starvation was visible increased. Their sunken cheeks, pointed heads, and bodies so thin that they appeared to be sticks bore witness to their hunger. The streets were full of people begging, many of them children. Each day, there were more and more funerals, and, in contrast to the past, people did not stop anymore and join the mourners, walking for some distance in respect for the dead; no one paid attention to funerals anymore. Simple wagons pulled by people, two or three crates on them, collected the dead with no ceremony, no decorum. In our courtyard, not a day passed without a dead person being taken out of one of the apartments; sometimes more than one was taken out. The funerals were quiet, without cries or sobbing. The mourners accompanied the dead in silence, almost hiding, as though they were embarrassed that this had happened to them, and all the others made believe that they didn't see and distanced themselves from the mourners as if they were carriers of a plague. Among the people in the streets, you could see many whose faces showed that they would soon be dead, but no one did anything to stop the death. People were quietly dying in droves.

Rubinstein, the "crazy man" of the ghetto, wandered the streets, and wherever he was, people gathered around to listen to him. He stopped beside a death wagon while two young men, along with a policeman, were picking up a dead man from the sidewalk and putting him in one of the crates, and said to the dead man, "Hey, my friend, lie on your side! Leave some room for the others!" The people standing around broke into laughter, and Rubinstein continued: "Everyone in the ghetto will die…only three people will remain alive — the head of the *Judenrat*, Czerniak, the head of the *Chevra Kadisha*, (the Jewish burial society), Pinkas, and I, the crazy man of the ghetto…," and again, everyone began to laugh.

It was unbelievable. Just a short time ago, I was afraid to even think about death. It had seemed so far away. Now, whenever I went walking in the streets, I saw dozens of dead people. At the beginning, I would turn my head away and walk quickly, so that I wouldn't see the body. Now I looked at the bodies lying on the sidewalk, some of which had been covered with pieces of paper by the police — others were completely exposed — and I didn't even react. Had I gotten used to living with the dead? I wasn't the only one. People walking down the street passed the dead with complete indifference and didn't stop their conversation, but only tried not to bump into the body, as though it were some object that had been thrown onto the sidewalk. The gap between life and death had greatly narrowed, but the struggle for survival was very strong — every family fought the war for existence with all its strength. The slogans were: carry on; get through this difficult period; it is impossible that they will let half a million Jews in the ghetto die of hunger; something has to happen, help will come from somewhere. But no one knew from where, or when.

Begging children sang crazy Rubinstein's song:

Oh, food coupon.
I don't want to return the food coupon.
I want to live a bit longer.
Don't return the food coupon.

Not all of the Jews were close to death, however. There were those who worked in the Jewish community institutions, or in the factories that produced materials for the Germans. Some lived by trading on the black market, and there were those who had enough money to last for a long time. Whoever had money did not have to go hungry. It was said that rich Jews spent their nights at wild parties.

I used to spend many hours every day at the gate of the ghetto at Muranowska and Bonifraterska Streets, not far from my home. I would jealously watch the world of freedom on the other side, and I would observe the young boys in their smuggling attempts. Many of them were my age, and some of them were even younger. The smugglers would stand at the entrances of the houses near the gate of the ghetto, watching what was going on at the guard post, ready to jump out at a moment's notice. When the surroundings were peaceful and the German guard and the policemen were busy with something at the guard post, a group of boys would suddenly appear from every side, run to the opening of the gate and go over to the other side, and before the German or the policemen could move, they had disappeared into the alleys.

They didn't always manage to get away. Sometimes they were caught by the policemen, who would search them, take all the money they had, and then beat them. The boys who succeeded in getting to the "Aryan side" of the city had to be careful not to get caught by policemen, or German guards, or by the groups of Polish boys who lay in wait for boys who had run away from the ghetto; whenever they caught one they would take his money, beat him, and threaten to turn him in to the Gestapo. The young smugglers had to make good contacts with Polish merchants to sell the merchandise they had smuggled out of the ghetto and to buy necessities for a fair price with the money they had received. I would see the serious faces of these boys, and I could feel the weight of their responsibility. For a moment, it reminded me of the game the children would play in the courtyard, "cops and robbers" — who would have thought that children would turn this game into something so real? What great courage and resourcefulness they needed.

Not long before, some boys had been shot and killed while trying to get out of the ghetto, but this didn't prevent others from making the attempt. For a long time, I had planned to join these boys and try my hand at smuggling. I felt that the situation at home was deteriorating; we were selling everything we had, but our hunger was still getting worse and worse. Why couldn't I do what those boys were doing? I kept thinking about smuggling. When I would imagine leaving for a smuggling operation, I would become excited. My heart would beat faster and fear would overwhelm me, but I continued to think about the idea. The quick passage to the other side looked relatively easy for me, and not frightening. What I feared was being on the other side, among the non-Jews. How should I act there? How would I make contacts? Where would I buy supplies? I had no idea. And what if I were caught? Would I be taken to Gestapo headquarters and killed there? No one would know why I had suddenly disappeared...

I thought about it a lot, and finally concluded that I was just making excuses for myself. I was simply a coward! After much hesitation, I told my family about my plan to smuggle food into the ghetto, and that I would need money to buy these necessities. My mother was shocked and became pale, and I felt as though I had been caught committing a crime. I tried to explain that boys were smuggling food into the ghetto daily, but my mother interrupted me and said that she didn't want to hear another word about it. Smuggling was very dangerous. Every day, boys who smuggled were getting killed and others were disappearing. I shouldn't worry. We would get by.

My sister Dvora also opposed my smuggling idea. I was disappointed. My mother and sister didn't trust me to do anything. The idea of smuggling did not leave me. I continued to be envious of the boys who crossed the ghetto border back and forth. I experienced every move they made, was happy at their successes and felt the pain of their failures. Once I said to one of them that I wanted to smuggle, too. The boy began to laugh. "You," he said, "are not made for smuggling. You're too delicate. With your Jewish face, they'll catch you quickly. Listen to me; get that idea out of your head." In the end, I did give up the idea.

My mother, who was always looking for ways to earn money, brought home a food grinder. It looked like a home meat grinder, but it was bigger and at the top there was a large bin for grain. The rotation handle was also very large, and the opening for flour to come out was different than in a meat grinder. A large flat dish came with the grinder to hold the ground flour. I considered this primitive grinder a very valuable item — at last, our home would see some activity — and I was proud of Mother's resourcefulness. The operation wasn't easy. One of our friends made contact between my mother and the owner of a bakery who was connected to smugglers who brought grain into the ghetto. The owner of the bakery, who did not want to risk a large amount of wheat at once, divided the work among several people whom he trusted, and my mother was one of them. This was kept secret, so that no one would inform on us. The dangerous part of the grinding was transferring the grain from the bakery to our home and returning the flour to the bakery, which my mother did. At home, the work was divided between the three of us, my mother, my sister and me.

My mother would grind in the early hours of the morning — I never knew when she began — and in the late hours of the evening. I would take her place after breakfast, when she would go on her errands, and I would work until the afternoon, when my mother would return and take my place. Dvora worked in the evening. The work looked easy at the beginning, and it was, for the first few minutes. The handle turned easily at first and the flour would pour into the dish that I turned from time to time so that it would fill up evenly. When I got tired, I changed hands, and I felt that I could work the whole day. But after some time, my arms became tired and the number of times I could turn the handle before changing arms became fewer and fewer. And the farther we got from breakfast, the hungrier I felt and the harder the work became. I would count the revolutions I had done with one hand and try to get to the highest possible number. When my hand felt like it was going to explode from the pain, I had to change hands after only a few revolutions. My mother would usually stop me when I felt I couldn't go on. After lunch, I felt stronger and I could continue working for some time.

That short period of grinding wheat, which lasted for a month, was relatively good for us. We earned enough to live on and we felt secure. Mother brought home fresh bread every day, and the meals were more satisfying. This ended abruptly, however; the bakery owner disappeared and the bakery closed. According to one version, he had run away; according to another, he had "been taken" by "the Thirteen," as he had not paid his "tax" to them. The only source of our support had vanished and my mother was forced to start selling our possessions again.

We had been living in the ghetto for almost a year. The situation was worsening from day to day. All hopes were false and all positive rumors had proved wrong. On June 22, 1941, the German army invaded the U.S.S.R. and advanced quickly, smashing the Soviet army to pieces, and taking hundreds of thousands of soldiers prisoner. One more hope had been shattered. Help would not be coming from the Russians.

The appearance of the streets of the ghetto was terrifying. People were lying on the streets, entire families, half-naked, some of them skeletal, their hands and feet like toothpicks, some of them swollen with hunger like balloons. Sometimes it was difficult to tell who was alive and who was dead. The wagons of the burial society, the *Chevra Kadisha*, were kept busy collecting the dead. And the children — so many children, without parents, in groups and alone — filled the streets, begging for food in cries that sounded faint to the indifferent passersby.

And even then, hope was not lost. People believed that there would be a change for the better, and struggled on stubbornly for survival with slogans such as "We must go on" and "We will not return the food coupon," which meant life.

One day, my mother came home crying and despondent. She had waited for hours in the market, had managed to sell one of our possessions, and had bought bread. On the way home, in the middle of the crowded street, a boy had attacked her, grabbed the bread from her hands — and didn't even run away. He just stood there and ate the bread. My mother struggled with him, hit him, but he just kept on eating the bread, without paying attention to her blows. Mother managed to take a few pieces out of his hands. We tried to comfort her, but in vain — she was so upset and depressed. From then on, I accompanied her when she went shopping.

The "thieves" had already left their mark on the ghetto. Most of them were young boys who wandered around, hungry, in the streets, followed women who had bought food, especially bread, and grabbed it from their hands, eating it on the spot quickly, so that no one could take it back from them. The thieves didn't care about what would happen to them as long as they got something to eat. One day, on Mila Street, I saw one of these boys grab some bread from a woman and begin to eat it. A Jewish policeman and other people beat him on his head and on his hands and tried to take the loaf out of his hands, but he held it stubbornly until it disintegrated into crumbs and scattered on the ground. The boy fell down, injured, and began to gather the crumbs of bread from the ground, eating them one by one.

The courtyard had changed; there was less activity. People who passed through the yard no longer stopped to ask how others were doing, as if an infectious disease was going around and people should keep their distance from one another. I sat on the terrace and remembered better times, when I had enjoyed sitting there and watching the busy courtyard; those days were over. Now it was silent and depressing, and only the sounds of the beggars and the crying children were heard. "I'm hungry! I'm hungry!" — you could hear the cries from morning to late at night. The rubbish bin, which was once such an attraction for the cats that I was afraid to throw out the garbage for fear that a cat would jump out at me, now lured adults and children, who rummaged in it looking for a morsel of food. And what could you find in there? I couldn't look at the people rooting through the rubbish, which smelled terrible, feeling around with their hands, putting "finds" into their mouths, spitting them out and continuing to search. I tried not to look, but my eyes kept returning to the horrible rubbish bin; sometimes my vision became blurry and I wasn't sure whether these were people or cats.

The girl of my dreams had long since disappeared from the window, never to be seen again. My heart told me that something terrible had happened there, in her home. A few times, when I had seen her, she seemed to be ill. I sought her in vain — there was no way of knowing what had happened to her. But one day, when the *Chevra Kadisha* wagon entered the courtyard and took out a body from the right stairway, opposite ours, I knew that the body was hers. Lately, bodies had been taken out of our courtyard every day, but I had never asked who they were. This time, I hurried to the yard and asked someone who had died. He said that it was the girl from the third floor, who had been ill for a long time. I was in shock. Even my beautiful private dream, the dream no one knew about, had been taken from me. For a few days I felt empty and I lost interest in everything; my efforts to continue imagining fantasies with the girl didn't work. For the first time, it occurred to me that it would be better for me to die.

We were getting hungrier and hungrier. Any possession worth selling had already been sold, and now my mother couldn't even buy us bread. We were constantly hungry. Mother was so thin that her clothing hung on her like a sack. Yankele, who had once been chubby with a face as round as a ball, became gaunt, his face lengthening and his eyes becoming bigger and bigger. My sister Dvora, who had always been thin, did not change much. I couldn't see myself, but I must have looked very bad, because one evening my mother asked me if I would like to join my brother in Turobin. I couldn't believe my ears. The thought of leaving my mother and the family was unthinkable. I didn't answer and my mother didn't pressure me. But from that evening, the idea of leaving the house kept going through my head, and I decided that I would never agree. A few days later, Mother said that she had decided to send me to Turobin, to be with Mottel until times got better. It was obvious that she had actually decided some time ago to get me out of the house and to send me to Turobin; she had even found a way to get me there and had prepared the money that was needed. I didn't want to leave the house and live with people I hardly knew. I didn't want to leave my mother, Dvora and Yankele. I didn't understand why I had to leave. I wanted to tell my mother that I didn't want to leave, that I wanted to stay with her, and the rest of the family, but when I looked at her and saw her imploring eyes, I couldn't refuse. There was always something about my mother that didn't let me refuse her, as though she had hypnotized me. I obeyed her as if she had given me an order that I couldn't say no to.

It is difficult to imagine what my mother went through before she came to the decision to send me away. My father was dead, Mottel had left home and I was a weak child, attached to my mother and to my home, and if she sent me away, she wouldn't be able to take care of me any longer. Who knew if we would ever see each other again? The flight from the ghetto and the journey to Turobin would be very dangerous. It may be that, in those difficult days, my mother felt that she herself would not have been able to carry on much longer; and as she saw no possibility of supporting us, and considering that we had received good news from my brother, she decided to try to save me in spite of the dangers involved. I knew that the decision had been made and that I had only a few more days with the family, but I was still hoping that the plan would fail. Terrible and frightening thoughts attacked me. My mother kept me even closer to her than usual, as if she wanted to give me enough love to last for a long while, and I continued to hope for some miracle that would keep me at home.

The miracle I was waiting for didn't come. I stood, dressed and ready to leave. Everyone kissed me and cried. It was all so emotional that I lost my train of thought. I stood like a statue until my mother led me from the house, carrying a package of clothing she had prepared for me. We walked out into the courtyard. Who knew if I would ever return? We went through the streets of the ghetto, walking quickly so that we wouldn't meet anyone who would stop us for conversation. My mother led me, holding my hand, and I didn't even notice where I was going. Finally we entered a courtyard and walked up the stairs to the building. Mother knocked on a door. A woman opened the door and asked what we wanted. Mother said something to her in a whisper and we were led into the house and told to sit and wait. We sat without uttering a word. We were afraid to speak lest we would start crying and we wouldn't be able to separate from each other. A young man came into the room and shook my mother's hand, looked at me from head to toe, thought for a moment, took a chair and sat down next to me and said, "Listen, young man! Listen closely to what I am going to tell you, and if you do as I say, everything will go smoothly. We'll wait a few hours, until the beginning of the curfew for the Poles. (The curfew for the Jews began at seven and the Polish curfew began at nine.) We want as few as possible Poles in the street. We will take you out to the other side of the wall. There, a Polish policeman will be waiting for you and will walk some distance ahead of you. You will walk after him. If everything goes well, he will lead you to the Central Railway Station. Don't be afraid if the policeman comes up to you, grabs you by your coat and leads you like a prisoner. And if the policeman disappears suddenly, you will have to go on walking by yourself, avoiding the German guard posts."

My face must have shown my fright. The man said, "Don't worry. Everything will be all right. Just don't be afraid, and remember, from the moment you leave the ghetto there is no way back in." The smuggler continued: "When you reach the railway station, go straight to ticket booth no. 2. One of our men will be there. Give him your identity card (my mother had given me my identity card with some money in it) with the money inside. He will give you a ticket without asking questions. The train to Lublin should leave at eleven. But the trains don't leave on time these days, so listen to the loudspeaker, which announces the time the train leaves. Sit in a corner and wait until your train arrives. When the train comes in, many people will be trying to get on. You must get on the train at any cost. Remember, if you don't succeed in getting on the train, you are lost! But that won't be a problem for you. You are short and certainly agile."

The man asked me if I knew the way to the station. I had been there when I was a young child, and I only remembered how the building looked, so I answered that I did not. He wasn't happy and he explained to me which streets I had to walk down, just in case I was left alone. Afterward he told my mother that she could go home and that everything would be all right.

Mother didn't want to go and asked permission to stay with me until I left. The man agreed. The tension lessened a bit. My mother spoke to me about trivial things, but didn't mention the painful subject of our separation. Suddenly the man came and said, "Let's go, kid!" I sat frozen, unable to move. I wasn't ready to leave my mother. The man shouted, "Come quickly!" and Mother and I parted in haste, without saying a word. I ran after the man.

We went down to the courtyard, and from there, to another yard, which led us down into a cellar, and we walked through a dark tunnel. We finally stopped. The man told me to wait and not to move until he came back. I don't know how long I stood there, trembling with cold and fear, perhaps a minute, perhaps an hour, until I suddenly saw a beam of light coming from the ceiling. The man took my hand and pulled me over to the opening in the ceiling, grasped my body tightly with both his hands, and whispered, "Good luck." Then he lifted me out through the hole. I was outside the ghetto. The lid was replaced — and there was no way back. The policeman who was standing next to me gave me a short look, and without saying a word, began walking. I walked after him. The streets we passed through were dark and empty. I walked as if I were almost blind, not knowing where I was going. We turned onto a central street, a bit more brightly lit, but empty and quiet, when suddenly a door opened and strong light flooded the street. A group of Germans, with Polish girls, left a house. They were talking loudly and laughing. I didn't manage to avoid them and walked straight toward them. They were all speaking at the same time, and for a moment it seemed that one of them had spoken to me, and everyone laughed, but finally they passed me and I continued on my way, walking down the street. The policeman had disappeared. I was in a panic. I didn't know where I was or how I would reach the railway station. How happy I was when I saw the figure of the fat Polish policeman appear suddenly from a side street! I continued to walk behind him through streets that had no end. Slowly I began to recognize the streets we were passing. In the distance I could see a strong light and I heard loud noise — it was the Central Railway Station of Warsaw. The policeman stood at the corner of the street, looked at me and disappeared into another one of the streets.

This time, I didn't care that he was gone. Walking quickly, I went into the station. I didn't think about anything, not about my mother, not about home. My mind was a blank. I only remembered what the man in the ghetto had told me. The heat, the noise and the crowds stunned me. Poles and German soldiers in a variety of uniforms filled the main hall of the station, and I, a Jewish boy who had run away from the ghetto, was standing among them. I walked straight to ticket booth no. 2; I gave the ticket seller my identity card with the money inside and asked for a ticket to Lublin. The ticket seller looked at me, took out the bill from the identity card and tucked it into his pocket, took more money for the ticket and then gave it to me. When I asked him when the train was leaving, he answered that it would not be on time and that I would have to listen to the announcements over the loudspeaker.

I didn't know what to do. I saw Germans everywhere. I quickly learned to tell the difference between Germans who were traveling, and were not interested in anything, and Germans who were guarding, who walked back and forth with rhythmic steps, slowly, their weapons in their hands, looking around them. I avoided them, but I didn't know where to hide until I saw people sitting and lying on the floor, leaning against the walls. I sat in a dark corner among other people who were waiting for trains. The loudspeakers kept announcing trains that were arriving and departing and delays and changes in schedule. Most of the announcements were made in German and only a few were in Polish. I listened to all of the announcements attentively so that I wouldn't miss the train to Lublin. I lay on the station floor, my head on my parcel. All at once I was very tired and wanted to sleep, but I knew that I didn't dare fall asleep. If I missed the announcement about my train, I would be lost. At the same time, I felt as though I wanted to fall asleep and not wake up, not to be facing any more danger. The German guards marched in front of me, back and forth, sometimes so near me that they almost stepped on me. I pretended to be asleep. What if they identified me? What if they asked for my papers? And what if I didn't succeed in getting on the train, or if I missed it? Or if someone on the train knew who I was?

I knew that my mother had done everything she could for me, but I didn't understand why she had sent me from home to face all of these dangers. It would have been so comforting to be at home right now, near my mother and family. I fought sleep, dozing off for a moment and then waking up. The sound of the loudspeaker woke me up time and time again, and I listened intently. I was afraid that the train to Lublin had already left — and I had been left behind. I didn't want to ask anyone, and I certainly couldn't go to the information desk. But the thought that I had missed the train was so unbearable that I gathered the courage to ask a man who was sitting near me. He calmed me, saying, "Don't be afraid, boy. The train hasn't arrived yet. We are going to Lublin, too." I felt calmer and I was now completely awake.

When the loudspeaker announced the train to Lublin, there was frenzy in the waiting room. At first, I didn't understand what was going on. In an instant, mobs of people stood up, picked up their parcels and crowded into the exit to the platform. Everyone in the room seemed to have been waiting for the train to Lublin, and I hadn't known! I jumped up and quickly pushed into one of the exits. In a minute, I was standing on the cold platform, which had quickly filled with people. The crowds and the darkness enabled me to easily stay out of the sight of the German guards. The train arrived noisily and filled the platform with smoke and fumes. Once again, chaos. People set upon the doors, pushing one another, and entered the train on top of each other. I was pushed among them into the train entrance and ran with them into one of the railroad cars, which quickly filled up. I stood next to the window between two benches. When I entered I could have found a seat on one of the benches, but I let others sit down and remained standing.

I felt relieved. I was inside the train! The train abruptly began to move and those who were standing almost fell on those who were seated; I barely managed to avoid falling on a seated woman. People arranged their parcels, sitting anywhere they could, including on the floor of the carriage. I sat between two pairs of legs, breathing in the foul odor. I pretended to be asleep so that I wouldn't have contact with anyone in the car, but everyone was tired and fell asleep immediately, including me. I fell into a deep sleep. When the ticket collector passed through, I was awakened, and my neighbors laughed when they saw that I had no idea where I was. The woman next to me said, "Give your ticket to the collector. Do you understand?" I took out my ticket, gave it to the ticket collector and promptly fell asleep again. When I woke, it was already morning. The train had slowed down and people were preparing to get off. I, too, got up and looked out of the window. We were in the country, in a place I had never seen before. The train stopped and the travelers left the cars quickly. It was very early in the morning. I didn't see anyone in the street and I had no idea where to go. I started walking quickly in the direction that seemed to lead to the center of the city. The hard part was over. The flight from the ghetto, the railroad station, the journey — they had passed uneventfully. Now if I could only be at home for a while, and tell everyone what I had been through…

Suddenly a Polish policeman appeared, stopped me and asked, "Jew?" He requested my papers and asked where I was from and where I was going. I stammered that I had come to stay with my uncle in a town near Lublin. The policeman, ignoring my answer, said that he knew that I had run away from the Warsaw ghetto, took me by my coat and led me to the police station. I was upset. After all I had gone through to reach Lublin safely, thinking that I was out of danger, now I had been caught by the police? I blamed myself for carelessness. If I had been more attentive, I could have avoided the policeman in time. On our way to the police station, the policeman met an acquaintance and stopped to speak with him. The man asked, "Who is the boy?" and the policeman answered that I was a Jew who had run away from the ghetto and had arrived on the train to Lublin. The two of them laughed. All at once I knew that I had to get away from these two Poles. I slipped away and began running as fast as I could. I could hear the policeman shouting, "Stop, you disgusting Jew! I'll kill you!"

I ran into another street. I kept running until I saw a Jewish man, and I stopped him. The man was as surprised as if I had fallen from the sky. I told him from where I had come and that I was running away from a Polish policeman. I showed him the slip of paper on which my mother had written the address of our relatives in Lublin. The Jew asked me about what was happening in the Warsaw ghetto. After I had given him a short account of the situation there, he sighed and told me how to reach the home of my relatives. As I approached the house, I saw only Jews in the street and began to feel better. Jewish children brought me to the house of my relative. When I opened the door, I smelled the aroma of fresh bread just out of the oven, and I was dizzy for a moment. It was bedlam in the house; this was not the best time to enter a strange house whose residents had just gotten up, washed and dressed. I was embarrassed. I introduced myself to the woman of the house and she hurried to tell her husband that the son of Moshe, son of Reb Leibish from Turobin, had just arrived from Warsaw.

I had not eaten anything since the afternoon of the day before. I hadn't been hungry during the trip except for a few moments at the Central Railroad Station in Warsaw, when a family sitting near me had eaten. When I smelled bread and sausage, I had felt as though my stomach was turning over. Mother had prepared something for me to eat, a few slices of bread, but these were wrapped in my parcel and I was afraid to open it in the railroad station. The hunger had left me during the night, but now, again, I was so hungry I felt that I couldn't move, not even to say a word. I had to eat something. There were children of all ages in the house. The little ones came closer, looked at me and ran away; the bigger ones looked from afar, came closer and greeted me. Their father, our relative, welcomed me, said that he knew what had happened to my father and brother and asked if I wanted to go to services at the synagogue with him. When I didn't answer, he said, "You should stay at home. You're probably tired. We'll talk after breakfast." After he had gone, I took out my *tefillin* and started praying the morning service. In the meantime, the table was being set, and I couldn't take my eyes off the bread, butter, cheese and other food being set out. The sight of food was like the sight of Paradise, and if I hadn't been embarrassed, I would have said, "Give me something to eat quickly. I'm starving!"

When we finally sat down to eat breakfast, I was so involved in eating that I didn't see or hear anything. Suddenly I was aware that there was quiet around me. I lifted my head and saw that everyone was looking at me; I blushed in shame. I stopped eating and refused to continue in spite of the insistent pleading of my relatives. After breakfast, I told them about what was happening in the Warsaw ghetto and how I had been smuggled out, about how I had reached Lublin, and how I had run away from the policeman. They complimented me, spoke of me as a hero, and I felt good. In the city, the news spread that a boy had arrived who had run away from the Warsaw ghetto and people kept coming to visit. I had to repeat the same story over and over. People asked me about their relatives in Warsaw but I couldn't give them any information.

I enjoyed being in the home of these relatives, whose welcome and admiration had made me feel better. The next day, we parted warmly. My relative took me to the wagon depot, negotiated with one of the wagon drivers, and paid for my trip. I protested and said that I had money and tried to return his money, but he refused to accept it. "We are relatives," he said. "I knew your father when we were both children. Keep the money you have. You'll need it."

We said goodbye, and I was alone. We had to wait a long time for enough people to fill up the wagon. The wagon was padded with straw, and three boards across its width served as benches. A heavy woman whose age I couldn't tell sat beside the wagon driver. In the second row sat a young woman and her son, about nine years old, and in the third row, I sat alone. When we started out, the wagon driver said, "You are sitting like noblemen. I could have charged you double. People don't travel much these days." The horse could barely pull the wagon and I remembered that, when I had been a child of six or seven, we had vacationed in a summer village near Warsaw. Every day a wagon would arrive, bringing merchandise for the grocery store, and we children would ask the wagon driver to take us for a ride. The man was good-hearted and liked children, and he would put us in his wagon and take us for a short distance.

One evening, as he was leaving the grocery store, he invited us to get into the wagon and said, "This time you can have a longer ride because I have to come back here." We happily traveled down a dirt road among the village houses until we reached the fields and headed for the forest. It was quite late. The sun was already setting, and the forest had begun to appear magical. The wagon driver stopped, got out of the wagon, and told us to wait for him; he was going to say his evening prayers with a rabbi who lived nearby and would be back soon. We were not happy with that; we had been riding long enough and began to feel afraid. We sat quietly and waited. Night fell. Everything was blurry, and dark. We couldn't see the rabbi's house any longer. We only saw flickering lights from among the trees, lights that seemed very far away. One of the children began to cry, and we all followed suit, one after another. Meanwhile, our mothers had gathered and were worried. We should have been home before dark, but none of us had come back. Our mothers shouted to us, but we were too far away to hear. At last, the wagon driver reappeared and acted surprised when he saw us fearful and crying. To calm us down, he apologized and gave us candies, and we returned home. My mother was waiting for me at the door and I was afraid that she would hit me, even though she had never done such a thing, but she only said, "You have given me such a fright! Go wash up and sit down to eat."

The woman sitting next to the wagon driver spoke without stopping about the prices that were being charged these days. She had apparently been trying to make a living by buying and selling and was used to traveling back and forth. She also asked all the travelers about themselves and where they were going. I didn't want to tell her my story, and I only said that I was going from Lublin to Turobin. This didn't satisfy her and she kept asking me questions, which I answered briefly.

We traveled down a dirt road through fields of stubble, groves of trees, and streams. On the way, we passed wagons loaded with straw, and I filled my lungs with the smell that I loved so well. We passed villages, near and far. I watched farmers, women and barefoot children. The wagon driver said hello to all of them, and here and there, exchanged a few words and smiles. Did he know everyone? We took a side road. In the distance, I could see a town. When I asked if it was Turobin, I was told that it was Zolkiewka, also a Jewish town. We finally reached Turobin in the evening.

# Turobin

## Autumn 1941—Spring 1942

Turobin resembled the scores of Jewish towns that were scattered throughout the Lublin region in eastern Poland. These towns had no government agencies, post offices, police stations, hospitals or clinics. No roads led to these towns, nor did trains pass through them. Those who stayed within the boundaries of their towns did not know of electricity or gas, never saw trains or cars, nor had any idea what radio was. A few received newspapers, but even these were several days late. All of these towns were under the administrative umbrella of the regional city of Krasnystaw. Turobin stood on the plains that stretched between these towns. At the heart of the town was a very large market square, surrounded by single-story wooden houses. Only two houses were two stories high. One of them, constructed of wood, had a large porch, and banquets were held on the first floor, with guest lodgings on the second floor. The other two-story house was made of bricks and belonged to the governor.

From the market square, nameless roads ran in all directions, and unnumbered houses were scattered among them in no real order. The houses had no plumbing, no sewage system or toilets, and the residents would relieve themselves behind their houses. Those who lived near the well would pump the water themselves and carry their pails back to their houses. The rest would purchase water for a small sum from the water-carrier, who would circulate the town in a wagon with a barrel of water. Wastewater would be spilled into the streets. This way of life had been going on for centuries; progress had not reached this remote corner of the world.

Only a few hundred families lived in Turobin, almost all of them Jewish. Aside from the innkeeper, all of the Poles lived on the outskirts of the town. Most of the Jews were Chassidim, some of them Chassidim of the Rabbi of Porsov and some Chassidim of some other rabbi; others were simply God-fearing Jews. Among the Jews of the town were craftsmen who supplied the needs of Turobin and the surrounding towns as well, but most worked in commerce. Some were wealthy merchants, but most of the town's Jews only eked out a living. Any change occurring in the surrounding farms, such as an increase or decrease in the harvest or a disease that spread among the animals, directly influenced the livelihoods of the town residents.

My family, the Freibergs, had many branches, scattered all over Lublin and outside it. Many of our relatives would stay at our home in Warsaw, and later on in Lodz, whenever they came to town. From my early childhood I had the feeling that there was no city or town in Poland that didn't have a member of my family living there. I only knew a few closely. In Turobin, my great-grandfather had lived with his children and grandchildren — a large family — but during the First World War and later, some of his family had left. My grandfather and my uncle Feivel moved to Lodz. My father stayed in Warsaw when he was released from the army. One of my father's cousins emigrated to Eretz Israel, and one to Argentina. Three of my father's female cousins drowned together in the river. The family grew smaller. Only two of my aunts, Rachel and Sarah, and my uncle Michael were left. One summer, in my distant childhood, we stayed for a few months' vacation in Turobin. It was our first visit since my father's marriage. We stayed with my grandparents, when they still lived in the town. I remembered both good and bad things about the town. I loved the open spaces, the beautiful scenery, and my uncle Feivel, who took me on visits to the villages, to meetings of the Betar Zionist youth movement. But the children my age, even my relatives, taunted me. At first I was respected and included in their games, and I taught them new ones. Afterward, they began to make fun of my "city" speech, my dress, and even call me names.

Three events that occurred in Turobin during that early visit had quite an impact on me. The first was the wedding of the governor's daughter. A few weeks before the wedding, the town residents were already busily involved — merchants stored luxury foods and drinks, tailors sewed dresses for the women and *kapotes* (long, black coats worn by Chassidim) for the men, and shoemakers worked day and night to finish all their orders by the night of the wedding. Many of the residents who were able took advantage of the wedding to earn some money. Many out-of-town guests were expected to attend, as the groom was not from Turobin. As the date approached, rumors and gossip spread daily and were avidly received: How many guests would attend? And which important ones would be there? How many chickens and ducks would be slaughtered? What would the bride wear? How big a dowry would the governor provide?

On the day of the wedding, a festive air enveloped the town. People rose early, cleaned the front yards of their homes, polished their boots and wore their finest clothing, ready for the event-laden day. The governor had rented every wagon available for transport of his guests — it was even said that he had brought klezmer musicians from Lublin, who would play music every time a wagon full of guests arrived at his house. The wagons of guests began arriving in the early morning. Some were put up in the governor's big house, and some were distributed among the residents. By dusk, the small community was full of visitors strolling the square and chatting with residents. Laughter and joy was everywhere. In the evening, people streamed, family after family, to the governor's home. My mother didn't want to go, saying it wasn't her place to attend, but my aunts, who had never seen such lavish beauty, pleaded with her and convinced her to accompany them, and she took me with her. Our entire family was there. Gas and oil lamps and candles lit the entire area. Everyone sat at long, food-laden tables and the klezmer musicians played; a sermon was given, lecturing the bride and groom in sad tones, which made several women weep. Then the ceremony under the *chuppah* took place in earnest, and when the groom broke the glass, everyone broke out in shouts of *mazel tov*!

During the wedding feast, a jester climbed up on one of the tables to amuse the guests. He blessed the bride and groom, the parents and the important guests, mixing his blessings with jokes and small asides that insulted no one. He broke down the name of every person he blessed into separate letters and reconstructed them to form blessings and omens for good and long lives, to everyone's enjoyment and to my great wonder. At the end of the meal, the jester presented the gifts and read out the names and good wishes of the benefactors with charm and witty jokes, and the audience waited for each name in suspense, to know who gave what to whom, with exclamations of wonder now and again. Singing and dancing continued until the early hours of the morning. I came home enchanted.

The second event that moved me deeply in Turobin happened quite suddenly. One lovely summer morning, three of my father's female cousins, two of them sisters, all young girls, went down to the river to swim, as was their habit on hot summer days. My mother, who usually joined them, for some reason decided not to that day. While swimming in the river, one of the girls called for help when she was suddenly dragged into a whirlpool and started drowning. Her sister swiftly swam to her and grabbed her arm, but she too was quickly dragged into the whirlpool. The third cousin, who hurriedly swam over to help the other two, drowned with them. A friend who was watching from the shore ran for help. The best swimmers and divers of the town rushed to the river, but they were too late; all they could do was to pull the three lifeless bodies from the river. An atmosphere of mourning fell heavily upon the town, and within minutes all the stores closed and the peddlers disappeared from the market. Neighboring farmers, who had brought their goods to sell, also packed up and left the town. The market square was empty. The townspeople gathered near the home of my cousin Aaron, whose two daughters had drowned. The men recited passages from Psalms and the women wept aloud. The sight of the entire town grieving was terrible. Everyone accompanied the three bodies to the cemetery, and I remained behind in the empty town with the other children my age. The suddenness of this enormous family tragedy shocked me. Girls I had seen laughing that morning were brought for burial a few hours later. And even more shocking was the thought that my mother might have been a victim, as well, and only by chance had she not gone with them to swim in the river.

The third event that had had a great effect on me was the annual fair, which happened to take place during our visit. The fair was such a central event in the life of Turobin that the year could be divided into two periods — before the fair and after the fair. Many weeks before, the townspeople busily began preparing for it. Craftsmen worked day and night to produce a large stock of products; merchants filled warehouses; stores displayed items that hadn't been seen all year. Everyone prayed for a successful fair, which in turn meant good profits.

The square took on a different appearance: stalls sprang up around it, and a section of it was cordoned off for animals. A circus arrived and set up camp. The day before the fair there was great commotion at my grandfather's house, as relatives from neighboring towns who had come for the fair were our houseguests. My grandparents prepared the goods they were to display in their market stall. That evening the house was full of people, and due to lack of space, we children were sent to sleep in the attic. When I awoke the next morning the house was quiet; only my mother greeted me when I came down. But when I left the house, I was amazed by the sight of so many people and wagons — when did they all arrive? It seemed that all night they had flowed into the square and filled it, and still wagons and people continued to stream in from every street and alley.

My mother warned me not to stray far from the house, as I

might get lost in the crowds. The market square looked like a stage, decorated in all colors of the rainbow. The sounds of chickens and their chicks, pigs, cows and horses mingled with the shouts of people and various whistles and strange horns that were being sold for pennies to delight the children. Jews in *kapotes*, farmers, women and children mingled in one great mass of people, all joyous, chattering, bargaining, and I wandered among them as in a dream. I spent the whole day among the stalls and farmers' wagons, enjoying the sight of the chicks and poultry as they cheeped from within boxes and baskets; I looked at the horses and colts, and I watched the farmers' young children, with their round heads and cheeks rosy as apples, hair as fine as silk and eyes blue-green; they seemed alarmed, as this was the first time they had left their village and come to the big city.

And I, a child of Warsaw, the largest city in the country, who was used to seeing interesting sights — trams and wagons in the noisy streets, store windows displaying the latest styles — wandered this small town full of wonder at the simplicity of the sights which were spread out before me. The colorful image of the town fair was etched in my memory for a very long time.

And now, our wagon entered the market square, the same square I remembered from my first visit to Turobin. Nothing had changed. It was the afternoon, and only a few people could be seen in the market square. The wagon driver stopped not far from my aunt Rachel's house, where my brother was staying. I debated what to do. I knew that my two aunts, Rachel and Sarah, had been quarreling for years. Had nothing in their relationship changed since then? My mother told me to go first to Aunt Sarah, where I was to stay, and only afterward could I go to see Mottel, but here I was, so close to my brother and I so wanted to see him! Aunt Sarah's house was farther away, at the other side of the square, and although I knew that that was where I should go, my feet carried me to the house where my brother was staying.

The doors to the store were open. I stood in the doorway, hesitant, and then went inside. I immediately recognized Aunt Rachel, who stood inside the store. It seemed to me that she was wearing the same dress and boots she had worn during my first visit. She didn't recognize me, just looked at me quizzically. "I'm from Warsaw..." I began, and then all at once her expression changed and a cry came from her lips: "Berale! Mottel, come quickly, your brother Berale has come!"

My brother came into the store and we fell into each other's arms. It was hard for me to keep from crying. It was so wonderful to see my brother after so many months. Mottel had put on weight and looked at ease, like one of the family. After being there only a few minutes, I felt good, as well. I would have gladly stayed with my brother, but I was bound by my mother's command and so I rose and said that I had to go to Aunt Sarah, as my mother had instructed.

Silence fell, as though I had said something forbidden. "You can stay here with us," said my aunt. "We have room for you too, praise God. We don't lack a thing." I thanked her and said again that my mother had told me that I had to stay with Aunt Sarah, and that I had to do as she said.

"As you like," said Aunt Rachel, "but if you don't feel comfortable there, know that you will always have a place here."

When Mottel and I stepped out and turned into the square, people stopped us and asked him who I was and where I had come from. They did not speak to me but to my brother, and he answered them briefly. I was glad I didn't have to answer them. He was already one of them. I was a stranger.

It was good to walk with my brother, good to feel again that I had a brother, a friend and protector, and best of all, that I was no longer alone. How much time had I actually been alone? Only two days. But they seemed such a long time! When we neared my aunt Sarah's house, Mottel said that he wouldn't come inside. "Why not?" I asked in astonishment. My brother explained he had somehow been dragged into the longstanding feud between the two families. This saddened me very much: would the two of us also have to cut ourselves off from each other? Mottel read my thoughts and said: "Don't worry, I'll meet you tomorrow morning and we'll go for a walk and talk about everything."

I knocked on the door of my aunt Sarah's home with a pounding heart. My uncle opened the door, looked at me and called to his wife, "Sarah, come here. I think we have a guest," and as my aunt approached me he asked, "Are you Moshe's son?"

"Yes," I replied, and my uncle let out a sarcastic laugh. "You see? I told you he would come, and here he is." "Yes, you always know everything," said my aunt, hugging and kissing me. Afterward she took off my coat, sat down next to me and asked about the family. Sarah soothed some of the tension I had felt upon entering her home, but every time I met my uncle's eyes and heard his voice, I felt very ill at ease.

During supper my uncle interrogated me thoroughly on events in Warsaw and asked me about myself: What did I know? What had I learned? He asked strange questions, as if he wanted to know everything at once. I got the impression that he didn't believe what I said, and this feeling caught me off-guard. My replies became more and more terse, even curt. My aunt tried to protect me from her husband and asked him to let me eat in peace, as my journey had been long and tiring, but he protested, "I'm stopping him from eating? I can see he's eating very well!" and laughed.

Aunt Sarah's two children, ages seven and five, pestered me like their father did. Luckily, everyone went to sleep directly after supper. This was prefaced by an argument between my aunt and uncle in the next room. I didn't hear what they said, but I knew it was about me, and the next day I understood that they had been discussing where I would sleep — my aunt had wanted to put me up on the sofa in the guest room, my uncle had said I could sleep in the attic. Seeing as I had slept on the sofa, my aunt had won that evening, but the next day I had to make up a bed for myself in the attic.

I wasn't used to going to bed so early, "with the chickens," but this time I was relieved to lie down and be alone. I didn't want to fall asleep. For the first time since I had left my home I was free to reflect over the events of the past two days. It was difficult for me to organize my thoughts — the reception I had received at my uncle's house gave me more reason to worry about things to come. I went over every single detail of my flight from Warsaw: leaving our house; sitting in the room with my mother and waiting for the smuggler who would sneak me out of the ghetto; walking at night through the streets of Warsaw outside the ghetto; the long, difficult hours at the Central Train Station; the journey to Lublin by train; being stopped by the policeman and escaping from him... It seemed to me that I wasn't the one who had experienced these things, I was just witness to them. Had all this really happened, or was it all just a dream? I was proud of myself. If I could only tell my mother about it all! Tomorrow I would tell Mottel everything and see what he said.

I awoke the next morning haunted by a mysterious dream. I dreamed that I was in a field, surrounded by forests and other fields; I didn't know what I was doing there, and I was hurrying home. The scene changed to my being in a big city, an unfamiliar one, with unfamiliar and strange faces, and trams traveling back and forth, unceasingly. I jumped onto a moving tram. We sped through various streets, some wide and then some so narrow that the trams almost touched the walls of the houses; I searched for a familiar landmark, but didn't know where to get off. The tram stopped and everyone got off, and having no choice, I did as well. All at once I realized that I was at the last station of the tram garage, near our home in Warsaw. I ran home quickly and opened the door, but no one was home. I went into the kitchen: no one there, either. In the middle of the room, on a chair, however, was a big bowl of fried meatballs. The wonderful aroma filled the room, as if they had just that moment been removed from the skillet, and it whetted my appetite. I was intensely hungry. I ate a meatball; it was spicy, with lots of garlic, just the way I liked them. I ate one after another, ate without stopping...and then other things happened in the dream, but I couldn't recall them when I awoke.

When I got up, my aunt greeted me cheerfully and told me

I'd slept a long time, probably from fatigue. She added that my uncle had gotten up early and traveled to the village on business, as if to make it clear to me that I had nothing to be afraid of; I could relax. And my aunt Sarah's company truly was nice. I enjoyed eating breakfast and chatting with her, accompanied all the while by my memory of the dream of meatballs.

When I went outside, Mottel was already waiting for me. We left the town quickly so we wouldn't run into anyone. We walked along the path between stubble fields, a warm sun shining and a cool breeze blowing. I looked at the wide, scenic plains, strewn with hills like waves upon the sea — a beautiful world, as ever, a world I hadn't seen in two years and whose existence I'd almost forgotten. Here were my brother and I, just the two of us, here in the great plains — then suddenly, images from the Warsaw ghetto flashed in my mind: the masses in the streets, the dead lying on the sidewalks, the children burrowing in the garbage cans in our courtyard, the hunger, the gloomy atmosphere in our house, my mother's pinched, worried face. From here, in the serene, wide-open fields, I saw these images clearly, so sharply they hurt.

I told Mottel of my "meatball dream" from the night before. He burst into laughter and I joined him, the two of us laughing unrestrainedly, laughter that brought tears to our eyes. Afterward I told him in minute detail all that had happened in the ghetto, and about our situation at home, and he listened somberly, his face pale. When I told him of my escape from the ghetto and my adventures on the road, he praised me and I blushed. My brother asked how I had been received at our aunt Sarah's and how I felt there. "Terrific," I said. "Aunt and Uncle gave me a warm welcome!"

I lied because I didn't want to worry him. When he had returned from being imprisoned, we had distanced ourselves from each other and hadn't found a way to get close again. Now, here in Turobin, I felt we were closer than ever.

My uncle returned from his business in the village in a rage, cursing the farmers, the merchants and the Jews all together. Occasionally he would give me a look as if I were the reason for his troubles. I felt totally superfluous in that house. When night fell, Aunt Sarah told me that she had made up a bed for me in the attic. Her voice and expression revealed her feelings of guilt and her inability to change the situation, but I was actually pleased to be alone and see less of my uncle. Now and again, I was startled by the flutter of wings from a bird that had come in to build a nest in the attic, or by the rustle of mice, but I was glad to open my eyes in the morning and see the sun's rays coming through the lattices, to smell the aroma of straw, and mostly, to find myself alone.

I did my best not to be a burden and to help around the house, despite the limitations of my weakened body. I wasn't great at cutting wood. My uncle couldn't stand the way I chopped — he would grab the axe from me, swing it high and land it with great force on the splintered wood, which would crack into pieces, and then mumble, "I see that in Warsaw they raise them weak." Nothing I did pleased him. With every step I took he would provoke and tease me; he would test me with difficult questions from the Torah, which I couldn't answer, and he would say, "I thought they taught better in Warsaw." He told me to teach his children the Torah, to read and write in Polish, and arithmetic. I tried to teach them, but they refused to pay attention; they were headstrong children who needed to be handled strictly, which I couldn't do. Only after a long while did I gain my cousins' trust, and they began to learn something, except by then, my uncle's patience had worn out — he wanted swift results and blamed me for their not making an effort to study.

The atmosphere in their home was not pleasant. My aunt and uncle would often quarrel, and I couldn't get used to it. Only a long time afterward did I learn that my uncle had a reputation in town for being very mean and miserly. And it was true; in his house, which was considered one of the wealthiest in town, I went hungry almost the entire day. During meals my uncle would slice the bread and hand it out, and as he did so would look at me and decide how large a slice I deserved. In these surroundings I missed my home more and more every day. My thoughts wandered constantly to

Warsaw, to my mother, my little brother, my sister, my grandfather, even to the courtyard at no. 1 Pshebyeg Street. I began seeking out advice on how to return home, to the ghetto.

Mottel worked in my uncle's business, but we still managed to meet almost every day, and these were my best times. We would find a place outside the town and would sit there and chat and reminisce about home before the war. My brother described everyone in our family for me, and told me about the meals at different townspeople's homes, to our great whoops of laughter. For a long time I didn't tell him of my suffering at our uncle's home; I would lie and say that everything was fine, as I didn't want to worry him. In addition, it seemed to me that in this situation we were on two sides of the fence — the homes of my two feuding aunts — and I couldn't betray my aunt Sarah by claiming that I wasn't happy. Besides, it might have gotten back to her, and my situation would only get worse.

However, Mottel sensed that something wasn't right and tried to help me. I think he also knew — I don't know how — that I was starving. Aunt Rachel's house, where my brother was staying, was full of delicacies, and when I visited they would serve me fresh-baked goods right out of the oven. The aromas whetted my appetite, but I would swallow my saliva and refuse to eat, and when I was urged to take something with me anyway, I only took a little bit, so they wouldn't think I was hungry. In any case, when we would meet and go for a walk, my brother would bring cakes, fruit and sweets with him, and would eat enough to show me that he was eating as well, but actually he had brought it all for me, in an attempt to raise my spirits. It was useless; I felt awful. I was overcome with homesickness.

The town seemed peaceful, as though cut off from the outside world, so much so that it was possible to think that it and the remote neighboring towns had disappeared from the eyes of the Germans — but this was not so. A German command headquarters in the regional city of Krasnystaw controlled all of the towns, and in each one a *Judenrat* (Jewish council) had been set up. The Germans imposed payments of large quantities of gold and goods on the Jews, and they would imprison distinguished Jews to illustrate their power and threats. The town Jews argued among themselves as to who would pay what, but the German orders were filled. The Germans also imposed various regional labor tasks on the Jews, and the *Judenrat* in each town would assign them to the residents. Every Jewish inhabitant was responsible for contributing to the labor, but the town wealthy would not go out to work — they hired poor Jews to work in their stead.

One day my uncle told me that I must go out to work for one night in the town synagogue, which the Germans had converted into a granary. There they gathered all the grain they confiscated from the village farmers. This assignment was to fill the sacks with wheat and load them onto wagons. The work took place in two shifts, day and night. My aunt, who usually gave in to my uncle's decisions, objected strongly this time, saying she would not permit a weak child to go out to perform manual labor. My uncle lost his temper and screamed at my aunt: "You will not interfere. Times are hard. What do you want; do you want me to work at night myself?" During a break in the argument I told both of them that I wanted to go to work, which calmed them both down immediately. Before I left for work my aunt served me a good supper. This time I ate my fill.

From the look of the synagogue the Germans had confiscated it a long time ago. The building was like a deserted ruin, all of its windowpanes shattered, the windows boarded up with planks. Only the eastern wall with its Holy Ark testified to the nature of the place. The hall was full of grain. Next to the eastern wall the wheat piled up to a height of two meters. I arrived as the shifts were changing. People came and went and I stood on the side. A Polish supervisor and a Jew from the *Judenrat* were in charge of the labor, and people crowded around them. Someone asked me, "Boy, what are you doing here?" "I came to work," I replied. "Who are you?" asked the man. "I came in place of my uncle Mendel." "The one who deals in furs?" he asked. "Yes," I answered. "Ah, you're the one from Warsaw." The man said with certainty, "Your uncle can afford to hire someone to work instead of him. He's not 'sick' enough to send a boy to work rather than come himself. Go sign up with the Pole." There were about twenty people there, mostly adults, some in their early twenties. At the time I was fourteen and a half, but as I was short and skinny, I looked only about eleven or twelve, and as I had garnered the sympathy of the people there, they wouldn't let me work hard. Usually I would hold a sack, someone else would fill it, and others would tie it and drag it to the doorway, ready for loading onto the wagons that would arrive in the morning. The people gave me tea to drink, and I actually didn't feel bad at all.

Toward morning I saw some people secretly tying the ends of their long undershirts together at the bottom and filling them with wheat. From the outside nothing could be seen. I did as they did. I tied my undergarments and filled them with wheat up to my crotch. The weight made it difficult for me to walk, and truthfully, I didn't know why I had done what I did — perhaps only to prove to myself that I could do what the others did? The sun rose as I was walking home. The town was still asleep and its houses looked more beautiful in the grey-purple light of the dawn. From the chimneys of some houses rose thick, black smoke. The crowing of roosters could be heard everywhere. Tired from the sleepless night and the labor, I dragged my feet with difficulty, the grain in my undergarments making each step heavier, and I was terrified it would spill out on the way. At the same time, I was satisfied with myself: I had stood up to the task. I was able to do something and could be independent.

My aunt and uncle were already awake when I let myself into the house. They looked me up and down, and I said I needed a bowl to spill the grain in my undergarments into. They stared at me in amazement. My aunt gave me a sack and I spread it out on the floor, untied the knots and emptied my undergarments of grain. Both of them burst into laughter. "What a hero!" said my uncle, and I heard the first positive word come out of his mouth. "*Nu*, Sarah, you see? We'll make a man out of Berale yet," he said in triumph, as if the decision to send me to work had been the right one.

One day a wagon stopped next to the house, and a woman and three children stepped down from it. The woman entered the house and began to cry. She was Uncle Mendel's sister, a widow who lived in one of the neighboring towns, where she had a small farm. She told us that the farmers there had been threatening to kill her if she didn't leave the town. She had ignored their threats, but the night before they had set her granary on fire and had told her that if she didn't leave her home, they would come back the next day and burn it down with her and her children inside. That morning she took her children and their moveable goods, left everything else she had behind, and here they were.

The woman was domineering and her presence was felt everywhere. She even dominated her brother Mendel, who would grind his teeth, but obey her. The atmosphere in the house, which was now filled with children, became insufferable to me. The worst thing was that the woman and her children were put up in the attic with me. I had lost my private, quiet corner. And autumn was here; the cold already penetrated the attic through the roof lattices — what would happen in winter? We couldn't stay in the attic; we would all have to sleep in the guest room.

During one of my visits to Uncle Michael's house, I told them of the situation at Mendel and Sarah's house. Uncle Michael suggested that I move out and stay with them. His house was small and humble, only one room, not very large, with a wide bed that took up half of it, where Uncle Michael, his wife Esther and their daughter Mirale slept. The furniture in the room was a collection of disparate pieces, purchased separately at different times. No chair resembled another, and none of the chairs matched the table.

There was also a commode in the room, a large trunk and various chests. I had no idea how they would find a place for me to sleep in this house. My aunt was known to be ill and suffering, her face often pinched with pain. Their daughter Mirale, who was my age, was introverted and shy, and since I had come to town had hardly spoken to me at all.

Uncle Michael, a strange, eccentric man, was known as the "good-for-nothing" son of the family, but as I could no longer stay at Aunt Sarah's house, where there was just no room for me, and feeling that I had no other alternative, I unwillingly moved to Uncle Michael's house. My aunt suggested that I sleep on top of the trunk, which was next to the bed — its sleeping area was narrow and although I was short, I had to sleep with my legs bent. Every evening I would come to sleep there and every morning I would return to Aunt Sarah's house.

After I had gotten used to my aunt Sarah's house, to her mean-spirited and miserly husband Mendel, to the difficult children whose sympathy I had already won, I now had to get used to my uncle Michael's family. The eccentric Michael lived in seclusion and imposed seclusion on his wife and daughter, as well. No one came to visit their home and no one in the house ever left it. Uncle Michael was very devoted to his wife and daughter and was willing to sacrifice his soul for them, but he dominated them with a strong, merciless hand. Although he welcomed me warmly and was ready to help me, I was always afraid, for his laughing face, his sparkling eyes, in a flash, with the most minor of incidents, would spark with rage and spit fire. There was constant tension in that house.

In time, a strong friendship developed between Aunt Esther and her daughter Mirale and me. It was the kind of bond that could only develop among people who have suffered. A partnership was woven between us in which my uncle had no part. When he was away from home, a pleasant, free atmosphere reigned, and the moment he returned home, he brought tension and depression with him. More and more I felt the love of the woman and her daughter for me — the two of them would almost compete to take care of me; they would launder and mend my clothes, serve me a glass of milk with cookies before sleep, and more than once at night, I would feel my aunt cover me with a blanket. Her love for me touched my heart to the point of pain, as it made me remember my mother, and my homesickness grew tenfold.

I didn't notice exactly when the bond between my cousin Mirale and me became stronger. One day I just realized that under those ugly clothes and awkward shoes hid a beautiful, delicate girl, her eyes filled with tenderness. I came to realize that she wasn't always quiet and shy; she also knew how to be happy, and even to sing. I loved watching her on Fridays, after she had washed her hair and the light from the gas and the Sabbath candles shone on her combed-back hair and her shining face, smooth as marble. In the evenings, before we went to bed, we would sit outside on the stairs at the front of the small house and chat. Actually, I would do the talking, and she would listen. I told her about my past. I even confessed things I hadn't wanted to tell her, and she listened intently. She was sensitive — more than once I noticed tears in her eyes; but she spoke little.

It felt good to tell her things, and she listened avidly, absorbing every word and storing it deep inside. I knew she would never reveal a word to anyone. Sometimes we would sit very close to each other, even touching — I could feel her through my clothes, and occasionally my hand would brush hers and a shiver would pass through my body. It was even nice to sit with Mirale without uttering a word. She agreed with me and validated everything I said, objecting to one thing only — my intention to return home, to Warsaw.

I had never for a moment accepted being in Turobin; my thoughts were always on returning home. I had no idea how I would do this, but deep inside I believed it would happen. Once I told Mottel of my intention to return to Warsaw. He became alarmed and for a long time tried to convince me that it was impossible and that I must get it out of my head. I never discussed the matter with him again, but my homesickness did not decrease. On the contrary, as time passed it grew stronger and took on a bittersweet dream-form, which stayed with me constantly.

One evening I told Mirale of my desire to go back to Warsaw, and I expected her to understand me and agree with me in this, as well.

"They will kill you on the road," she said decisively and burst into tears, and I was amazed by the intensity of her reaction. I tried to calm her, but she wouldn't listen to me and kept sobbing.

That same night I couldn't sleep. Mirale's words took on real meaning in my mind: the Germans might kill me; they might shoot me in the road like a stray dog. That same night I also understood for the first time how important I was to Mirale — I understood that she loved me.

The town of Turobin, although completely free of any military presence — no walls or German guards — was, despite this, amazingly closed and sealed in. Its residents rarely traveled from place to place. A sort of latent fear would not allow the people to leave their homes. The news that reached the town was sparse. There were no radios or newspapers. The only source of knowledge about what was happening was the rumors that made their way to us from neighboring towns, and these said that the Germans were advancing at an alarming rate into the heart of Russia, and were already at the gates of Moscow and Leningrad. Other rumors came, rumors of the Germans' mass slaughter of the Jews every place they entered. It wasn't difficult to believe the truth of these rumors, although everyone assumed they were exaggerated. Occasionally news would come of the Germans' attack on one of the Jewish towns and the slaughter of the Jews there. This news triggered fear and terror. Because of these rumors, whoever could build an underground shelter did so, to hide his family members in case of attack, until the rage had passed.

The news of what was happening in Warsaw was sparse. Letters that arrived from my mother said that all was well at home and everyone was fine, and that we shouldn't worry about them; but I knew the situation I had left them in, and I would imagine terrible things happening until another letter arrived and calmed us a little.

I soon reached the conclusion that no one would help me return to Warsaw, and if I didn't save up some money, I wouldn't be able to leave. One day I happened to pass a Polish inn. The man was unpacking crates of drinks from a wagon and asked me if I could assist him. I helped him unload the wagon and bring the crates of bottles inside, and he then reached into his pocket and gave me one zloty. It was my first taste of earned wages, a taste of my own money, and it gave me the hope that I might earn more. If only I could find some work and save enough money to get myself back to Warsaw! Sometimes I let my optimistic thoughts wander and I saw myself earning enough money, and returning to Warsaw, sneaking easily into the ghetto, bringing home good things and giving my mother the money I had left.

When I considered the idea, I realized that I had no chance of finding work in Turobin, and even if I did earn money, I would have to turn it over to my uncle. Therefore, my first goal must be to get to Lublin, a big city with many Jews. In Lublin, I could find work, and from there I could get to Warsaw.

I made a new friend, named Leibl. He was my second cousin, the son of my father's cousin Aharon, and his parents had three sons scattered all over the world — Yerihemiel was in Israel, having gone to Eretz Israel as a pioneer; Yakotiel was in Argentina (I remembered that he and his wife had stayed with us in Warsaw on their way overseas); and Avraham was in Russia, where he fled to when the war began. Leibl's two sisters were the ones who had drowned in the river. Only the parents and their youngest son, Leibl, remained in the big house. I loved visiting this house, which was full of warmth, and although Leibl was two years older than me, we spent a lot of time together, and a friendship developed between us. He and his parents suggested more than once that I move into their home, and there was no doubt that the suggestion made a lot of sense. In this house I could sleep in Leibl's room, in my own bed, not on a trunk with my legs bent. However, by this time I had become close to my uncle Michael's family, and my heart told me that it would not be fair to leave them just because I had found better lodgings. It was also good to be close to Mirale, to sit with her in the evenings before sleep, to hear her breathing in the bed next to mine.

One afternoon, while wandering aimlessly in the market square, I suddenly heard gunfire and shouting and saw everyone running. I also began running — to my aunt Sarah's house — and as I ran I continued to hear the gunfire. On the way I saw a German car, left open, with no one in it, parked next to the house opposite my aunt's house. Right next to her house lay a heavy woman, face down, her head surrounded by a pool of blood. The door to our house was broken and ajar. I jumped over the woman and went in; no one was there. I didn't know what to do. I knew that in my uncle's bedroom there was an opening that led to an underground hiding place. I entered the bedroom: complete silence. I heard only the pounding of my heart. I didn't dare shout, "Open up, let me in too!" and so I ran up to the attic, where I lay trembling, my heart beating quickly. Then I heard people speaking German next to the house. I crawled to the edge of the ceiling, where I had a narrow view of the area beside our house and the house opposite. I saw the Germans bringing more and more people, pushing them into the house with shouts and blows. When they had finished gathering all the people, the Germans stood beside the car, discussing something. Then one of them approached the house, opened the door, threw a grenade inside, bolted the door and ran back to the car.

I heard an explosion and then shouts from inside the house. The German went back up to the house, opened the door again and threw another grenade inside. Another explosion and more shouts and crying. The German spoke to his friends and they burst into laughter. He prepared a chain of grenades, threw them all together into the house, and all of the Germans ran some distance away. A huge explosion shook the house. For a moment I thought our house would collapse, as well. The door of the house opposite was torn from its hinges, fell onto its side, and grey smoke, smelling of soot and fire, billowed out of the house. All was silent. The Germans spoke among themselves, laughed, got into their car and drove away.

I continued to lie there in the attic for a long time, close to the slat through which I could see what was happening. All around was a deathly silence. After some time, people began to gather next to the house, and their weeping rose and fell until it turned into a terrible wailing of the entire town, continuing far into the night. People searched for their missing relatives in the pile of crushed body parts and called out the names of their loved ones, in the hopes that some of them might still be alive.

It seemed to me that they were calling my name, "Berale, Berale," or perhaps they were calling "Perele," or "Mirale"? I came down from the attic. All the members of my family were at home. They stared at me and cried in unison, "Berale!" "Were you here the whole time?" asked my uncle. My brother burst into the house — before the shooting began I had been at his house and he was very worried about me — and the two of us fell into each other's arms and stood there embracing for a long time. Afterward, I accompanied Mottel to Uncle Michael's house. The odor of soot still hung in the air. Crying and wailing accompanied us. Neither of us spoke a word on the way; we just held each other's hands, tightly.

When I entered Uncle Michael's house, Mirale fell into my arms and hugged me so tightly I choked and almost had to push her away. She kissed me and I felt her tears on my cheeks. At that moment, something happened inside me; tears poured from my eyes as from a spring and I couldn't stop them, and they mixed with Mirale's tears. The two of us stood and cried and cried. Afterward, I sat and told Mirale, in great detail, all I had seen. The image of the German tossing the grenades into the house, the loud explosions and the smell of soot stayed with me through the entire night. At daybreak I finally fell into a deep sleep, and woke up late. I saw Mirale and my aunt sitting in the corner, crying. My uncle paced the room back and forth, like a caged animal, his face red and his eyes sparking. I attributed this to yesterday's disaster.

And then Uncle Michael stopped, turned to me and said,

"Berale, I want you to leave our house and find another place to sleep."

When my uncle was excited, his words became jumbled, and even now only single syllables were uttered. I was in shock. I couldn't understand what had led to his decision. I looked at Mirale and my aunt, but they wouldn't meet my gaze. Their eyes were rooted to the floor. My uncle continued speaking, and now his words were clearer. He came up with all kinds of excuses — that the house was small, that there was no room to hide in case of danger… I left the house without saying a word, but outside I grew angry with myself for not being able to say anything to anyone. I hadn't even said goodbye.

On the morning of the day after the massacre, as the townspeople prepared to bury their dead, a message was passed around that no one was to go to the cemetery except for immediate family members, in order to avoid a concentration of the town's Jews, which might serve as an easy target for the Germans. No one left his home unless it was urgent. Each person mourned and grieved alone. Wagons full of bodies left the town on their way to the cemetery.

Aside from grief over the victims, the townspeople were left in shock. Until now they had only heard about German brutality. Now they had felt its cruel hand on their flesh, and all this with a feeling of helplessness and lack of knowledge as to what the following days would bring. There was no one to turn to, no one to complain to. One could only pray for mercy from the heavens.

I wandered the market square without knowing where to turn. I felt humiliated, and also guilty, although I didn't know what I had done wrong. I was ashamed to tell my brother that Uncle Michael had thrown me out of his home, but I still found myself walking to his house. Mottel was astonished to hear that on a day like today, after yesterday's massacre, our uncle still felt he could throw me out. He comforted me, saying that with an eccentric like Michael one could expect anything. Then he began to interrogate me about my relationships with the family, especially with Mirale. This questioning embarrassed me, but then I came to realize why my uncle had thrown me out.

My brother and I went together to my father's cousin, Aharon, my friend Leibl's father. I didn't tell them the real reason I wanted to live with them; I only said that I wished to sleep in their home because winter was coming and the conditions at my uncle Michael's house were not suitable for winter living. My request was readily accepted, with no questions, and I moved into Leibl's room, into a bed with a mattress. From now on, I could stretch and straighten my legs as I wished.

Fierce winter winds came, wild as whirling dervishes, blowing everything away and cleansing the entire town. Afterward, the rains fell ceaselessly and the town sank into mud. Then came the frost and snow, which covered the town with a sprinkling of white. The little houses sank even further into the snow and the town was entirely cut off from the world outside. Only on days when the frost eased could one see a few wagons and sleighs, in which farmers brought what meager agricultural goods they had for sale. The farmers hurried to buy the groceries they needed and rushed to return to their villages that same day, as winter days were short. Activity in town ground almost to a halt, even more so than in years past. People weren't occupied with business or crafts, instead dedicating more time to prayer and the study of Torah, either at home or at the *beis medrash* (religious college) — perhaps God might hear their words and save them from evil.

As before, people prepared for winter. Food and other sundries were not lacking; the only thing missing was security. A deep disquiet had wormed its way into everyone's heart since the Germans' grenade massacre in the town. The rumors that reached us of the murder of Jews in eastern Poland, and the occupation of Russian lands, only increased our worry.

The winter severed our outside contacts completely. We had no news of what was happening around us. No news of what was happening in Warsaw. My heart went out to my loved ones there, but my plan to return to Warsaw seemed less and less likely, and more and more like an unfeasible dream. Still, my desire to go back didn't lessen. I believed with all my heart that someday I would return home, to the ghetto.

During my childhood visit to Turobin, the local children had not accepted me as their friend. Now, too, I was unable to make friends with the local youth. I could only feel a meaningless hatred toward me, perhaps due to the jealousy and feelings of inferiority the town youth felt toward every city kid, while ironically I felt myself to be inferior to the local youth, whom the adults considered more worthy, stronger in both body and in common sense. Frankly, I didn't care for their coarseness and crudity. An exception was Leibl, my roommate, with whom understanding and mutual trust was developing. The two of us were soul mates. Also, the atmosphere at Leibl's house was pleasant. I felt free and at home there, and the long winter evenings passed with a pleasure I had never known before. We always found something to talk about, and Leibl knew how to spread a little joy in our lives, and again I was able to laugh.

In the room where our beds were, we told each other every detail of our lives, we considered things together out loud, we asked questions we didn't know how to answer. When I told Leibl of the situation in the Warsaw ghetto, of the people dying of hunger, of the children dying in the streets, he asked how it could be that God saw all of this and did nothing; or maybe there wasn't any God at all?

I was astonished to hear the doubt that Leibl cast on the existence of God; although these thoughts had already sprung up in my own mind, I knew it was forbidden to think them and I repressed them quickly. Hearing these doubts spoken aloud by my friend caused me pain and fear, as if Leibl had touched upon the foundation of things and undermined it in such a way that the entire structure might collapse upon us.

We spoke of this no more, but the question of the existence of God continued to bother me, despite my desire to repress it.

All winter the thought bothered me that I might have done

Mirale and my aunt an injustice and caused them anguish, even though I didn't really know what my sin had been. So I sought a way to speak to Mirale and explain to her that if I had hurt her and her mother it was unintentional, and to ask her to forgive me. But perhaps this was just an excuse, because the truth was that I wanted to see Mirale again, to feel her, to touch her, to be in her company. I wandered around and around in the market square, nonchalantly passing Mirale's house and praying with all my heart that she would appear.

But all my wandering was to no avail. She didn't appear. And then, one morning when I left Leibl's house, I saw her standing nearby. Surprised to see her, I asked, "What are you doing here?"

"I'm waiting for you," she replied, and seemed about to burst into tears. I held her hand and walked her away from the house. I was afraid we would be seen together. Her hands were as cold as ice, her face red from the frost, but the soft warmth in her eyes suffused my whole body. I felt a strong desire to hold her and kiss her, and restrained myself with difficulty. I told her I had been looking for her all this time, to tell her I was sorry for all the anguish I had caused her and her mother, and I asked for her forgiveness.

Mirale burst out laughing. "Fool!" she said. "*You're* asking for forgiveness? If anyone should ask for mercy and forgiveness, we should. We treated you cruelly!"

Then she added, "On the day of the tragedy, after the Germans had finished their massacre, we found out that it had taken place at the home of Rabbi Velvele, opposite Aunt Sarah's house. I was terribly afraid that something might have happened to you. I told my father I was going out to find out how you were. My father insisted that I wasn't going anywhere, and I, a fool, said, 'I am going!' and I tried to leave the house. My father grabbed me and slapped my face. He was upset and lost his temper, shouted that he didn't want to see you anymore, that he would throw you out of his house. My mother tried to intervene on your behalf, but he shouted at her too. It's all my fault," she said, and began to cry.

I hugged her and kissed her forehead and eyes. I told her that nothing was her fault and that I was happy here, at my cousin Aharon and his son Leibl's house, and that Leibl and I were good friends. We parted with good feelings.

The winter came to an end. The snow blackened and slowly disappeared, and the town was again sunk in mud. Then came warm days of sunshine that dried up the mud. The town came back to life. The wounds of the massacre had healed a little — life must go on! My uncle Mendel bought and sold furs, my aunt Sarah bargained when the farm girls brought her butter and eggs for sale. My brother traveled with my uncle to the villages, where they bought what they could and filled the storeroom. Children played outside. Traffic in the town increased. Wagons came and went.

With the renewed contact with the outside world, we began receiving news, mostly bad, on the persecution of Jews, on the banishing of Jews from the towns to the ghettos, on the concentration camp, Maidanek, that had been set up next to Lublin. In a letter we received from Warsaw, my mother wrote that everyone was healthy and that we shouldn't worry about them, but the letter was briefer than usual and its style was worrisome. Mottel and I read it over and over without saying a word to each other.

After two years in the ghetto, I had forgotten what spring was like. Here in Turobin, I experienced its full charm and glory more than I ever had in my life. During the many walks I went on with my brother or with my friend Leibl outside the town limits, I saw how nature shed and took on form, I smelled the fragrance of the wet earth warming in the sun, I noted the buds proliferating, growing, the fields becoming green before my very eyes, I smelled the fragrance of the blossoms. I was enchanted by the wonders of nature, but at the same time filled with sorrow.

One day I noticed a gathering near the *beis medrash*. As I drew closer I heard arguments and shouts. It turned out that an unfamiliar Jew had come there and told them of a place called Belzec, where the Germans had been bringing Jews, killing them and burying them in huge pits. The people of Turobin refused to believe the Jew's story and interrogated him thoroughly. The man could not prove what he knew; he only claimed that what he had said was true and its source reliable. But the people fell upon him and said he was lying, that such a thing could not be, that he was only spreading rumors, and banished him in disgrace. For a long time afterward the Jews stood next to the *beis medrash* and gave valid reasons why the senseless rumors were not to be believed. Even after the Germans had killed Jews in our town, even after knowledge of the horrible things the Germans were doing reached our town day after day, it was still inconceivable that the Germans had set up a special place to purposely kill Jews. It couldn't be true.

The pleasant days of May arrived. Town life went on as usual. One might have gotten the impression that the Germans had left us alone. Only the news that reached us from outside disturbed our peace of mind. Everyone constantly spoke of "something" that might happen to all of us, of some hidden threat hanging over us, without being able to say what this "something" actually was or what hidden threat was involved. And the news that the Jew had brought from Belzec, despite the distrust it aroused, came back and sank into our consciousnesses. In almost every house a hiding place was prepared in which to find refuge, if necessary. Some also arranged places at the homes of farmers they knew in the villages. The alcove in which Leibl and I slept was windowless, and every evening we would have a cabinet moved to hide the door. Leibl also told me that in an emergency he would flee to a village where he had friends and would take me with him. Mottel also told me that if anything bad happened he would flee with our uncle's family to one of the villages.

One day in May, at dawn, my aunt Malka moved the cabinet that hid the door to Leibl's and my alcove, came into our room, her face pale, and told us that the Germans had encircled the town that night. She said that the *Judenrat* members were going from house to house, ordering everyone to gather in the market square, and take with them supplies for a journey and packages one could carry. Cousin Aharon stood stone-faced and silent. We dressed quickly.

I peeked out the window that looked out on the market square. Families with their children, bundles in their arms, marched to the square, urged along by shouting German soldiers.

"I'm not going out to the square," said Leibl. "I'll run away to the village. I have friends there, and you're coming with me." He turned to me. His tone was determined and I went along with his order. Then a neighbor came into our house and told us that the *Judenrat* members were walking around with lists, and that not everyone had to congregate in the square. She was told that those who were evacuated would be taken to Lublin, where a ghetto was being set up for the Jews.

Now the time had arrived for me to decide what I was going to do. Leibl was a good friend in whom I could trust. On the other hand, if we really were being taken to Lublin, that would bring me closer to home, to Warsaw. Lublin was a big city, where I could certainly find some kind of work and save up money to travel. Then suddenly a thought popped into my head: perhaps we wouldn't be taken to Lublin, but to the Warsaw ghetto? The Germans had already brought many Jews from small towns to Warsaw...

"No," I said to Leibl. "You run away to the village, and I'll go to the square." "Why?" shouted Leibl, and continued to try to persuade me to escape with him, but I wasn't listening anymore. At that moment I remembered my brother. I left the family quickly and went outside. The house and shop where Mottel was staying were on the other side of the square, which I couldn't cross, as the Germans had encircled it. Hundreds of people had already gathered in the square, where shouts, the crying of children and gunshots could be heard. I ran behind the houses, sometimes hiding from the German guards, and arrived at my aunt Rachel's house. The door was unlocked. I went inside. There was no one there. I went from room to room, I opened the door that led into the shop — all was empty. A few scraps of food were scattered on the kitchen table; it looked as though they had eaten not long ago and had left in a hurry. I knew there was a hiding place in the house, but I didn't know where it was. I called out the names of my relatives and listened — perhaps a reply would come from somewhere — but nothing did. Tears choked me. I so wanted to see my brother. I was positive he was hiding, and not in the square, and here I was, alone again. Then I remembered that I had nothing with me; the few clothes I owned were at my aunt Sarah's house. Again I ran through the alleys, between the houses, but when I got to the house it was locked. The shutters were latched shut. I called out the names of my family but no answer came. There was a sheet of paper stuck on the door with an official stamp. I didn't bother to read it.

Now I had nothing — no Sabbath clothes, no good shoes, no family pictures that were so dear to me. I suddenly felt a terrible loneliness. I burst into tears and couldn't stop crying. After I finally recovered, I went to the market square.

The flow of people was increasing, among them old people, the disabled being helped along by their relatives, babies wrapped in blankets. And in the square, there was mayhem. People ran to and fro, mothers looked for their children, children for their parents. People had crowded into one corner of the square. The representative of the *Judenrat* read names from the list of people who were permitted to return to their homes. People were pushed, and begging, shouting and cursing the *Judenrat*.

I wandered around, looking for my brother in the crowd, running from one corner to another, although I was sure he wasn't in the square and that he had probably hidden somewhere or gone to one of the neighboring farms. There was no doubt; my uncle's family treated him like a son. But I so wanted to see him, even for just a moment, to exchange a few words, to hear him say something. But he wasn't the only one I couldn't find; I didn't see anyone from our family. And I was concentrating so hard on my search for Mottel that I wasn't even aware of what was happening around me. It was as if I weren't a part of it. I also looked for Mirale; I needed her, as the only soul in our large family in the city whom I felt good around. I could tell her almost everything, she felt my pain, shared my joy. I needed her to look into my eyes with her own dark, understanding eyes, and then I wouldn't be alone again.

I finally gave up. I stood in the square, reconciling myself to the situation, my mind empty of everything, only my eyes following what was happening. Most of the people were poor, ill or crippled. Some were brought in wheelbarrows, others in their beds. It seemed that the wealthy, including my family, had been permitted to stay in the town.

Some SS men walked along and inspected the people carefully, shooting the ill. The people standing nearby were in shock, frozen in place. Close to me sat a Jew in a wheelchair, paralyzed from the waist down. He was about sixty, well dressed, his beard well groomed and a nice cap on his head. He sat alone and looked around him with sorrowful eyes. Our eyes occasionally met. All at once a fat German about thirty years old approached him, looked at him and smiled. He took out a pistol, remove the man's hat with the gun barrel and put the barrel to his head. Then he asked the man if he wanted to live, laughed aloud, and pulled the trigger. Nothing happened. There was only a click from the gun. The German laughed and repeated his game again and again. Tears fell from the Jew's eyes. Finally, a bullet sliced into the Jew's head and a spurt of blood gushed over his body. I stood two meters away from the wheelchair. I didn't react. I was frozen in place, like a statue. My senses went dark. The image was etched into me so deeply that even today, some forty-five years later, I can remember every detail and every line on the Jew's face, every emotion that played over his face, even the shudder that went through him when the trigger was pulled.

I stood paralyzed next to the dead Jew in the wheelchair, perhaps for minutes, perhaps for hours, not seeing or hearing a thing. Thousands of images raced through my mind, crowding one another. How could it be, that I was here, alone amid all these strangers, while Germans walked among them and shot them? Maybe it was a good thing that no one was with me; I didn't want to see anyone. I didn't care what happened. I was overcome by a complete indifference.

Suddenly there was a great tumult. Everyone rose to their

feet and looked down the road. Hundreds of Jews were arriving from the neighboring town of Wysoka, accompanied by Germans on motorcycles. We heard orders, shouts of "Get up!" "March!" "Quickly!" "Quickly!"

Confusion reigned; shouts and crying filled the air. The entire crowd began to move. Next to the *Judenrat* table, people tried last-minute arguments to be permitted to stay, but the Germans pushed them on, and the square quickly emptied out. The Germans had promised to bring wagons for the old and the sick, who stayed in the square, waiting for them. A number of Germans walked around and shot all those who remained behind.

We left the town. Families walked together in groups, so they wouldn't lose each other. Everyone carried his own bundle. Germans on motorcycles rode past us, back and forth, in an ear-splitting roar. The farther we got from the town the quieter the people became; even among themselves, they spoke in whispers. Only the occasional crying of children was heard. It was a typical spring day, a spring day you could only experience out in nature. The skies alternated between clear blue and cloud-covered, and the fields changed color accordingly. The Polish farmers laboring in their fields stopped working to stare at the strange procession. The women and children stood next to their houses, looking at us in astonishment, parents calling back the children who ventured too close to the road. One could see that at the appearance of our column, some people argued among themselves, some laughed, and some crossed themselves. Some of the towns we passed bordered the road, and there we met farmers face-to-face. Most of them taunted and cursed us, but there were also some whose faces showed sorrow and pity. My eyes met those of a young woman, who began to cry. I turned my head away from her, so as not to cry, too.

After several hours of walking, many of the people grew tired and began throwing away their thin bundles, to lessen their load. The old and the weak, who didn't have the strength to continue, sat on the side of the road, and we sometimes heard shots from behind us. People supported their weak relatives with all their strength, marching in silence, not knowing to where, without asking why, as if a stroke of fate had come down from the heavens, not to be pondered. The wonderful, heartwarming May sun became cruel and struck us without mercy. More and more of us weakened and were left at the sides of the road. The shots behind us increased in number.

The Germans ordered us to sit. People opened their bundles, gave their children food and ate quietly. Those who had nothing to eat wandered among the others, begging a piece of bread. I was very hungry. I hadn't eaten a thing since yesterday, but I was too ashamed to beg. Nobody offered me anything, but there were those who asked me, "Boy, where are your parents?"

After some time we were ordered to get up and continue marching. When I arose, I spotted Mirale about a hundred meters away from me. My heart filled with joy. I made my way toward her and when I was near I saw my uncle Michael walking upright, a huge sack on his back. He was a strong man, used to long journeys. My aunt Esther walked bent over, dragged her feet with difficulty and looked ready to collapse at any moment. Mirale walked behind them, wearing a winter coat, black wool stockings and an old knapsack on her back. When she saw me a smile spread over her face and her mouth opened wide for a few seconds, as if she wanted to say many things at once and didn't know where to start. I wanted to tell her I'd been looking for her, thinking of her, that I loved her. She finally began with, "Don't you have anything? Have you eaten today?" and without waiting for an answer she reached into her pocket and took out a handful of cookies, which I quickly devoured. I greeted my aunt and uncle, and my uncle said, "It's good that you found us. We must stay together."

I was pleased that his anger had passed and I asked him if he'd seen anyone else from our family. "They are not here," he said bitterly. "They have money. They managed."

Mirale and I walked close to one another. I told her everything that had happened to me since that morning, and the more I told her, the better I felt. Walking became more pleasant, as if we were strolling together, not noticing what was happening around us.

In the meantime we neared the town of Zolkiewka, where more Jews joined us. The column grew in length. Mirale asked me where they were taking us, as if I knew all the answers.

"I don't know," I said. "I heard they were taking us to Lublin. From there perhaps it will be easier for me to get home to Warsaw."

The reminder of my plan to return to the Warsaw ghetto saddened Mirale and she fell silent. I didn't have anything to say, either. All of a sudden my plans to return to the ghetto in Warsaw seemed foolish, with no way to realize them. However, I believed in my ability to get by in the new place we would be taken, and I was pleased to be free of the aunts and uncles in town.

On the road, as we were passing a large forest path, a young man suddenly fled into the forest, and some other young men followed swiftly after him. The Germans shot at them, but it looked as though they had gotten away. The Germans were too few in number and couldn't control the entire long column and run after them, as well. Whoever wanted to run away could have. But to where?

By the time we reached the regional city of Krasnystaw, evening had fallen. The entire crowd was led into a large yard beside some railway tracks. People didn't know what to do and ran back and forth, looking for water, a place to relieve themselves, a place to sit, to eat something, to rest and to sleep. People lost each other in the dark, and it took a long time until everyone managed to get themselves organized somehow beneath the dark sky. We also found ourselves a place and my uncle gave everyone a piece of bread.

Suddenly people began running. I ran as well, to see what had happened. In the middle of the yard there was a gathering of people, and everyone pushed and shoved to get to the center, where the Jewish community of Krasnystaw had brought bread and coffee and was distributing it. I went back and told them that bread and coffee was being given out. I didn't feel the need for either bread or coffee, but I wanted to do something for the family, to show them I could be useful. I asked for a pot and said I would bring them back some of each. I ran back. In the brief time I was gone, the number of people pushing had grown into a tightly packed mass. Everyone was shouting. I knew I had to bring something back to my family; I pushed with all my might into the mob of people and in a flash I was being pushed and shoved in all directions and I was helpless to do anything about it. Using all my strength, I pushed my way out of the human mass until I found myself outside again, but I didn't dare go back empty-handed; I had to prove to them that I, too, could provide, and not just take. I ran around the crowd, looking for an opening. In the meantime, a group of muscular food attendants tried to enforce some order, striking the pushing mass on the heads with sticks. The people pushing forward now began pushing backward to avoid the blows, and the entire mass swayed back and forth.

Taking advantage of this, I dived in between people's legs and found myself next to the serving table. I received half a loaf of bread and coffee was poured into my pot. The way back was easier, and feeling very strong, I quickly found myself a way outside the jostling mass, but not much was left of the coffee. I felt victorious, but when I got back to the family, they were all asleep. I was angry at them; I had done all this for their sake, and I had wanted their reaction, some words of praise, but all my efforts had been for nothing.

I looked about me. Most people were lying in groups, on the ground, under the sky, sleeping. I heard snores and groans everywhere. Apparently, a long time had passed since I had gone to fetch the coffee. My anger dissipated completely and was replaced by pity for these poor people, who had been abruptly banished from their homes, their beds, and now lay on the ground, following a long day of suffering, in an exhausted sleep. I looked at the people stretched out on the ground. Only yesterday each of them had had a home, a bed, a clothes closet, a gas stove and dishes, things that they had acquired over many years. Suddenly and for no reason, the Germans had come and banished them from their homes, their possessions, transporting them to who knew where, what or why, and were murdering some of them in front of everyone, with no fear of reprisal from God or man.

All day, the image of the man in the wheelchair had haunted me — the tears streaming from his eyes. From childhood I had been taught to be proud to be a Jew. I loved everything to do with Judaism, I loved our way of life, the Sabbaths and the holidays, the family and the home; I had spun dreams of the future, each one more beautiful than the one before; the world had seemed like Paradise on Earth — but what was happening to us, the Jews? And what had happened to me? Blows were falling on me from everywhere. After my father had been killed I had thought that I wouldn't be able to live without him, that nothing could be worse than the situation I was in then. After that there was the period in the Warsaw ghetto, the hunger and the cold, and then the escape from the ghetto, the separation from all my loved ones, from my mother, from my sister Dvora, from my brother Yankele; now I had also lost my brother Mottel and my friend Leibl. I was all alone, among all these strangers. And where were we headed? According to a rumor I'd heard on the way, they were taking us to the Ukraine — even farther from Warsaw, and from there it would be twice as hard to get back home. And I only wanted one thing — to be with my mother, with Dvora and little Yankele. All at once I remembered our home in Lodz, before the war, with all the family gathered around the table…

Mirale slept quietly. It seemed to me that she was smiling in her sleep, as if she were having a good dream. Her cheeks were glowing in the night, and she looked more beautiful than she ever had before. A strong desire rose within me to lean over her and kiss her, but I lay down far from her, closed inside myself.

The whistle of a locomotive engine that was maneuvering along the nearby train tracks woke us with the dawn, while the mists were still dissipating. It was freezing cold. In the light of day I could see the crowd scattered around the area, with one side bordered by high buildings and the other side by railway tracks. Because of the fierce cold, people lay close to one another, to keep as warm as possible. Here and there people rose, to look for a spot to relieve themselves, to wash — there were no amenities for the large crowd. Men put on prayer shawls and *tefillin*, stood and prayed the morning prayers. With no *tefillin* and no prayer book — I had been left with nothing and had brought nothing on the journey — I stood and prayed wordlessly, not knowing what to pray for. Suddenly I felt that God was not listening to me, just as He wasn't listening to anyone else. God had forsaken us. Otherwise, how could He let us suffer like this? I had a daring thought — perhaps God was on the Germans' side, and not on our side?

While I was pondering this, a troop of soldiers in black uniforms approached us, armed with bayonet rifles and led by a German officer. They stopped not far from us, and after performing some drills, spread themselves out along the railway tracks. Apparently, these were Ukrainians serving in the SS. Afterward, a group of SS officers arrived. The locomotive engine, which maneuvered incessantly among the freight cars, finally attached itself to a long line of freight cars along the tracks at the edge of the big yard. The Germans ran back and forth along this train, and we realized it was meant for us. Everyone packed their bundles and readied themselves for travel; the people were anxious to set out, if only to get to wherever we were headed.

Sudden orders were shouted: "Get up! Get on the train! Quickly! Quickly!" The Germans and the Ukrainians pushed and prodded us with shouts and blows. The freight cars were high, without steps, and it was difficult to climb into them. People helped each other, many getting injured, and the Germans pushed more and more people into the boxcars, endlessly. I walked together with my aunt, my uncle and Mirale to the freight car, climbed inside quickly with my uncle and helped my aunt and Mirale climb up. For a few moments we were all together, pleased that we were already inside, but the car filled up quickly, and the Germans pushed more and more people inside, as many as possible. The pressure increased, and with it, the fear and the shouts, until finally the heavy door was slid to shut us in. Gloom was all around us. There was only a tiny knothole at the corner of the car, near the ceiling. It was hot and suffocating in the car and a terrible odor washed over us. I felt nauseated and I was sure that I was going to throw up.

Time seemed to stand still. We all stood crowded together. I was pushed against Mirale, against my will, and I was ashamed to look her in the eye, ashamed that we had both been placed in this situation. There was nothing I could say to her.

Next to me a woman fainted. Someone shouted, "Jews, a woman has fainted, move aside, give her a little air!" People made an effort to make a little room for her, but in vain. There was nowhere to move to. Suddenly we felt a strong push, which toppled us all on top of each other at one end of the car, like a pile of rags, and then we immediately fell back to the other side, where there was a little space. The train lurched forward. We had begun to travel. Fresh air seeped into the boxcar and the travelers thanked God that they could breathe.

One major question was in everyone's hearts: where to? Some people were standing next to the knothole in the corner of the car, and now and then one of them would be lifted up to peek outside and try to identify our location and direction of travel. After many attempts and arguments, a man declared with satisfaction, "Thank God, we're not going to Lublin. We're going in the exact opposite direction — apparently to the Ukraine!"

I had actually wanted to go to Lublin, as I still held hope that I might get from there to Warsaw, but now I understood why it was a good thing we weren't going there: because in Lublin there was a concentration camp called Maidanek, and people had told tales of terrible things happening there.

# Sobibor

## May 1942—October 1943

The journey in the boxcars continued, with all of us horribly packed together, hungry but mostly thirsty, surrounded by suffocation and stench, close to losing consciousness. I don't know how long we traveled; probably hours. It seemed to me that this torturous journey would never end. The shouting had died down, the children had stopped crying, and silence prevailed. Everyone had either grown used to it or grown tired. Somewhere the train slowed down and stopped, as if in the middle of its journey, in a spot that was completely silent. We tried to hear what was happening outside and the sounds that reached us were of cows, chickens, the barking of dogs, and especially the chirping of birds. It wasn't difficult to guess that we were in a rural area. The man who peeped through the knothole said that he saw only fields and forest. The smell of greenery and pine trees wafted into the car.

Our locomotive moved to and fro, each time pushing more boxcars, until finally our car, as well, went through a gate into a closed camp. The door of the boxcar opened noisily and we were greeted by shouting in German: "Out! Out! Quickly! Quickly!" A dog as big as a calf, held by an SS officer, barked and threatened to attack us. We all tried to get away from the boxcar and to move forward. My aunt, my uncle, Mirale and I walked together. Germans in green uniforms and Ukrainians in black uniforms, whips in their hands, urged us forward. We came to a small gate. On the other side stood a German and a Ukrainian, quickly separating those who entered — women and children were sent to one side and continued to walk straight, men to the right. I walked to the right with my uncle, with the men, and all this happened so quickly that we didn't have a chance to react, to say anything to one another. No one realized exactly what was happening; why were they separating us, to what purpose?

I followed Mirale and my aunt with my eyes, but after a few seconds they disappeared. The men were instructed to sit on the ground in a long, roofed barrack. From where I was, I could see the long line of women and children continuing on their way and disappearing as they left the courtyard. It was early evening. The barrack filled with people. We sat crowded next to each other, in shock, not understanding what was happening. Where had the women and children disappeared to? Perhaps they were on the other side of the courtyard? We tried to listen but couldn't hear a thing. The Ukrainians who guarded us with rifle bayonets wouldn't let anyone get up or move from his place. When someone needed to relieve himself, he had to ask permission and wait for a long while to get it.

Night fell. We were tired, hungry and thirsty. My uncle sat and stared into space, like a stone statue. We didn't exchange a word. The Ukrainian guards marched around us, back and forth. Those who approached the Ukrainians wanting to know what was happening and where they had taken the women and children were answered with shouts and blows, and returned quickly to their places. Now and again, Germans came, checked us over and left. One German took some young men with him and after a short time they returned with a few pails of water. There was a commotion — people pounced upon the water — and then quiet again reigned. We sat on the sand, under the roof, waiting for the unknown. No more children crying, no more women sighing. Complete silence, as if no one was there. We heard only the hum of a motor that operated nonstop, accompanied by the croak of frogs, a sound that was somehow both monotonous and terrifying.

The Ukrainians found a man who seemed to be mentally ill

and began amusing themselves with him, torturing him until the poor man began to cry and scream like a slaughtered animal. They laughed aloud and he cried for a long while in an odd voice that cut the silence like a sharp knife. All night long, I slept and awoke alternatively, hearing the unceasing noise of the motor and seeing the image of women and children marching and disappearing at the end of the yard, among them my aunt and Mirale.

In the morning a group of Germans arrived, among them *Oberscharführer* Wagner. They selected the skilled workers from among us — carpenters, metalworkers, electricians, tailors, shoemakers and others. I, too, wanted to leave, but I didn't have a skill. People got up and were placed in a line, and then Wagner passed among them and chose young men and told them to join the skilled workers. Something inside me made me push forward. Compelled by instinct, I jumped up and stood among the chosen. The skilled workers were taken to workshops in the camp and the rest were divided into groups. Four fellows, myself among them, were taken by a German, *Oberscharführer* Frenzel, who ordered us to dig a pit. The shovel I picked up was heavy. I could hardly lift it, and then, when I brought it down, it refused to penetrate the earth. Suddenly I felt a sharp blow to my head. The German had struck me with his whip with all his might and yelled, "I'll teach you how to work!" For a moment, I thought my head had split open and I didn't know what to do, but my body filled with superhuman strength and I began to dig swiftly. Then Frenzel fell upon some others, whipping and shouting at them, particularly the older man among us. The man fell to the ground and Frenzel kicked him, shouted at him to get up and continued hitting him.

In the afternoon, the Germans gathered all the work groups together in a field. We looked at each other — within a few hours we had changed. We were beaten and bruised, most of us without coats, some of us bareheaded, all of us in shock. We were ordered to stand in line and we received a bowl of soup. People told of the brutality of the Germans and the Ukrainians and showed each other the wounds from their blows. But the main question everyone asked was, what was happening in this place? What was the fate of the women and children who had disappeared yesterday? What was the fate of the men who had disappeared today?

There were some among us who told of their work gathering clothes in the courtyard — women's, men's and children's clothing, both inner and outer garments. One, in tears, said that he had recognized the clothing of his wife and children. That seemed to mean that the people had undressed in the yard and from there had walked naked to some other place. We were gripped by fear. Could it be that they were killing everyone? But we had not heard any shots or explosions. No, something like this could not be happening; it just wasn't logical. And there were those who told us that a German had said that the people who disappeared were taken to a bathhouse, where they had received new clothes and were put on a train to the Ukraine, to work. In answer to the question of when we would see our families again the German had laughed and said, "You have nothing to worry about. Very soon you will join them."

The story sounded fanciful and inconceivable. New clothes? A train leaving from the forest? And we had not seen or heard a thing! It was simply incredible. But still people grasped at the story as a ray of hope that their family members might still be alive.

When we returned to work after the lineup that afternoon, my entire body was sore and I felt unable to stand on my feet. Only fear gave me the strength to return to work. This time, our guard was a Ukrainian, who prodded us on incessantly and occasionally struck me and the others with his whip. I was on the verge of collapse more than once. At the end of the work detail, we were made to stand in line again. A group of Germans stood before us and to the side stood a group of Ukrainians. Frenzel taught us parade exercises: at attention, at ease, face left, face right, hat off, hat on… We weren't skilled at our parade exercises, and Frenzel grew angry and shouted, and the other Germans laughed, so he began a series of punishment exercises — he ran us around the field, ordered us to fall and rise, to crawl, to jump with bended knees. Some of the Ukrainians ran beside us and whipped all those who could not follow orders. At last, Frenzel returned us to the parade ground and Wagner told us, "You have been selected for work. Those who work well will be treated well. Those who don't work will be put to death."

Then Frenzel ordered us to sing. No one uttered a sound. Frenzel shouted, "Sing! Sing!" No one knew what to do, what to sing, how to sing, so Frenzel ordered us to run and then punished us with more exercises, returned us to our places and again ordered us to sing. One Jew stepped forward, turned to us and said, "Jews, sing!" and began singing a Polish song about a shepherd. Not many knew the song, but it was an easy one that repeated itself. In the beginning only a few joined him, but Frenzel shouted, "Everyone sing!" and we all joined in, at first half-heartedly, and then loudly, over and over. Frenzel could not be satisfied. "Sing!" he shouted over and over. And again the Jew stepped out and began to sing, this time a Chassidic song everyone knew: "Purify our hearts that we may worship Thee in truth…" And everyone sang until the German calmed down and released us.

We were put into a barn for the night. Broken physically and spiritually, we went inside and were left alone. People prepared places to lie down, formed groups along the walls, and saved places for loved ones. I didn't know a soul. I was lonely and I didn't know what to do. I felt like a stranger. My whole body ached. Some people sat and consumed the coffee and bread they had received; a few took out morsels of food they had found among the bundles others had left behind. I sat on the floor, not eating, not drinking. I wanted to die. I felt that I couldn't live in this place, that I was not made of the same substance as the others, who knew how to get by in the situation we had found ourselves in. I felt like I was choking. Tears fell from my eyes.

And then a Jew sitting nearby said to me, "Boy, you'll never survive that way. Eat the bread you got and drink the coffee." I did as he said. Afterward the man told me to lean on him and go to sleep, and again I obeyed him.

At the morning parade, a large group of Germans and Ukrainians again came, made us perform parade exercises for a few minutes and counted us. One was missing, so they counted us again and again with great tension, until they finally understood that one of us had stayed in the barn and not come out for parade — perhaps he had died in the night or committed suicide. But then, that afternoon, the craftsmen told us that the man had been found alive, and right in front of them he had been dragged out of the barn by the Germans, beaten, and led to the forest, where shots were heard. It seemed that the man had decided to put an end to his life.

We were divided up into groups and led to work. I walked with a large group to *Lager* (Camp) 2. *Scharführer* Groth and some Ukrainians led us. When we started walking, Paul Groth commanded us to sing. Someone started to sing the Polish military song, "How Is It in a Good War," and we all joined in. Then we sang another military song, "It's Great to Be in the Infantry," and the German looked satisfied. He laughed and we got the impression that he was not a bad man.

We arrived at *Lager* 2, which was about a hundred meters from the barn where we had slept. We found ourselves in an area next to a broad courtyard, in which stood a large wooden structure. On the other side stretched a long field, and four hundred meters away there was forestland that continued up to a barbed wire fence. On the other side of the fence the train tracks continued from Poland, along the Bug River to the Ukraine and Russia.

We were brought to newly built barracks, four meters high, with a pit inside that was two meters deep, about six meters wide and some fifty meters long. Outside, next to the barracks, rose a large, rectangular pile of suitcases, packages and various objects. These were the belongings of earlier transports of Jews, who had been brought here a month before us. Our job was to move the belongings into the barracks and arrange them from the ground up to the roof. The sun and rain had already left their mark on a large portion of the belongings. The bundles and suitcases were stuck together, and when we separated them they disintegrated and we had to make new bundles. Based on the contents of the bundles and suitcases and from the documents we found, we knew where their owners had come from — some were from small towns around Lublin, and some were Jews from Czechoslovakia and Austria. The various belongings gave testimony to the extreme poverty of the Jews from Polish towns. Their bundles were tied with rope, leather straps or strips of cloth; in the cheap, old suitcases we found a few old, patched clothes, mended shoes, a few prayer books, holiday prayer books. The Czechoslovakian Jews' suitcases held belongings that attested to a rich religious life. Among the clothes and valuables, we also found prayer books and many valuable religious items. The Austrian Jews' suitcases held expensive clothes, perfumes, pictures and many documents, but few religious items.

We were forced to run while we worked. Paul Groth, whom we at first thought to be a pleasant person, in a flash became crueler than anyone we had yet encountered. He and the Ukrainian, whose name was Taras, beat us incessantly. Paul — as everyone called him — would sometimes order one of us to lie down and then would give him twenty-five lashes on his backside, and when he tired he would hand the whip to Taras. The screams of the victims were horrible. The fear of the whip was so intense that instead of working, everyone looked for a way to get away from Paul and Taras. We all ran back and forth insanely. I tried to get away, but Paul called me, "Come here, you, the little one!" and when our eyes met he said with a laugh, "Yes, yes, you're the one I want!"

My heart stopped beating. Next to me stood a suitcase and Paul ordered me to lie upon it and count. With the first lashes, I felt as if my flesh was being cut to pieces. I screamed and counted, "One, two, three..." every time the whip landed on my body. When my pain passed a certain threshold, I stopped counting and just screamed nonstop. Finally, Paul told me to go. With my last remaining strength, I fled and continued to run and bring bundles from the pile to the barracks. My entire body was in pain, and each movement increased it. I wanted to lie down and die. But the fear of another whipping somehow gave me the energy to continue running and the strength to hang on.

In the barracks I saw a man hiding among the bundles. People warned him that he would get caught and be shot, and tried to convince him to get up and continue running with the bundles, but he was unwilling to listen and begged us to leave him alone. After some time Paul discovered the man, and he and Taras beat him mercilessly until he was battered all over. "Taras, take him to *Lazarett*," said Paul to our astonishment — we thought he meant the German field hospital called *Lazarett*. And then Taras lowered his rifle from his shoulder and pushed the man with it toward the forest, where they both disappeared. Within a few moments we heard shots and Taras returned alone.

I kept looking toward the forest at the right-hand fence of the camp, and the train tracks on the other side. Some time earlier, we had seen a passenger train move from west to east, in the direction in which Taras had taken the man — where *Lazarett* was meant to be. From the other side of the entry to the forest, the left side, there were two rows of barbed wire, two meters apart, leading to a spot close to us, where they joined with the closed yard next to where we were working. I saw two Germans, *Oberscharführer* Bolender and *Oberscharführer* Getzinger, with his big dog Barry, crossing the field and entering the forest at its left corner. After a few moments, horrible screams cut through the air, worse than I had ever heard before. My heart told me that there, in the forest opposite, terrible things were happening.

The hopes that the people who had arrived with us and disappeared were still alive vaporized. We were in Hell on earth, and I wondered again and again if it was real or a dream — was I alive or dead and in Hell?

After work there was another parade, this time directed by Paul. He ordered us to perform parade exercises and accompanied his orders with curses and insults, to the enjoyment of the Germans. Then he turned to us and asked, "Who is sick? Who is tired? Who doesn't want to work anymore? Who wants to sleep? Step out of the line."

He spoke slowly, quietly, came up close and looked into the eyes of each one of us. He stopped next to one of the men and said, "You don't want to work anymore. You are tired. You wish to sleep. Come, step out." He spoke softly, as if he wished the man well, but the man begged him, "No, I'm not tired. I'm healthy. I wish to work!"

It was futile. Paul took the man out of the line, then selected three more, all older men, and the four stood there before us with pale faces. My heart took pity at the sight of them.

"Taras, take them to *Lazarett*!"

Taras and another Ukrainian took the four and walked toward the forest.

Paul, who seemed amused, turned to us almost in a whisper, "Do you know where they are going?" — he stopped speaking for a moment and waited as if we were meant to guess, and then he continued — "They went to *Lazarett*. Do you know what my *Lazarett* is? Anyone who goes to my *Lazarett* does not come back, does not work anymore. He sleeps in peace."

Paul left us standing in formation until we heard the shots from the forest. Only then were we released. After the parade we returned to the yard beside the barn, when I began to feel how my body ached. I couldn't sit, nor could I lie on my back or my side. The only way that my body hurt less was to lie on my stomach. I felt better standing up, but I didn't have the strength to stand. And my ears still echoed with Paul's words, "Who wants to sleep? Who wants to rest? Who doesn't want to work anymore? Step out of line!" Why didn't I step out of line? I so wanted to sleep and not get up anymore!

Bread and coffee were distributed and we sat in groups and ate, each man concentrating on his food, as if it were the most important thing in the world. Two days had passed since we had been brought here, and already ten of us were gone. If things continued in this fashion, none of us would be left in two weeks. All signs pointed to the fact that none of the people who had come with us in the boxcars were still alive, but we refused to believe, we were unable to believe that here, in this place, they killed everyone who was brought here. Neither did we know how they were killed. Some Jews who worked in the forest told us they heard people's voices, claiming that therefore the people were still alive, thus giving us a spark of hope — maybe, maybe they were alive? And I remembered Mirale, and the last time I saw her seemed so long ago. A thought passed through my mind: perhaps I would see her again and would tell her of all my experiences?

Over the last two days I hadn't thought of anyone. I hadn't thought of anything. All was a blur. Now, as if by chance, I remembered Mirale, followed by memories of my mother, my sister, my brother, and again I began to cry uncontrollably, and again the man from the day before approached me. He already knew my name, and he said, "Berale, you're not a child anymore. You must get hold of yourself. To stay alive."

We were all in a strange dream, in which so many strange things happened that were impossible in reality, beyond human understanding. We were exhausted in body and soul, and functioned by instinct. It seemed that we had not yet analyzed what was happening; we had not yet given ourselves an account of our experiences. For some reason, we all fell asleep immediately at every spare moment, and from sleeping mouths I could hear only sighs and groans. I fell asleep and woke up several times; my pains wouldn't let me sleep. In the morning, at the parade, Wagner called the work groups and people with jobs to step forward. For the two days our group had been in the camp, many had been given various jobs, and in the work groups, Wagner named the skilled workers: shoemakers, carpenters, builders, tailors, a gardener, a stockman, a pig sty worker, a worker in the German kitchen, a worker in the Ukrainian kitchen, pharmacist, goldsmith, chief of the burning pit. Afterward Frenzel selected young, healthy boys for the *Bahnhofkommando* (railway station unit).

I belonged to the group for *Lager 2*. This time we were led by *Unterscharführer* Steubel, a tall, thin Austrian. Some of the group continued to transfer bundles from the pile to the barracks, while others, myself included, had to sort the bundles. Steubel arranged us into about ten sorting stations, and in the beginning he explained and demonstrated to us how to sort each article separately — new clothes, used clothes and unusable clothes, which he called *Lumpen* (rags).

Any object of value was sorted separately — shoes, hats, spectacles, wallets, belts and many other items. Steubel explained to us that we must search each bundle and piece of clothing for valuables like gold, silver, coins and valuable notes; all were to be brought immediately to the suitcase that stood open before him. He warned us that if any of us tried any sabotage, we would be killed. He also explained that the old clothing had gold and silver coins sewed into them, and if, following the sorting, these were found in the clothing, it would be considered an act of sabotage, and the sorter would immediately be put to death.

We sorted the clothing of the people who had been brought to the camp and disappeared into the forest, and who had almost certainly died. Everything went past us. I held the clothes of men and women, outerwear and undergarments, clean and dirty, children's clothes and toys. I searched pockets and folded hems of old and dirty clothing, and I found gold coins, paper money, dollars, British pounds and other currencies that had been sewn in by the town Jews. Strangely enough, in the expensive suitcases that were full of high-quality clothing, we almost never found gold coins or banknotes. The Germans were most interested in the sorting work, it seemed, as all day German officers came to the sorting points and inspected the work. Steubel explained to them what he had explained to us, and they seemed satisfied. Among them was also the camp commander, *Hauptsturmführer* Wirth, riding a horse and dressed in a white uniform with a cape over his shoulders.

Our sorting work was apparently important to the camp. All of the Germans walked around with loaded automatic weapons, and toward afternoon each SS *Oberscharführer* passed us on his way to *Lager* 3: Bolender, Gomerski and Getzinger, each of them with automatic weapons. Afterward we heard the whistle of a locomotive and we knew that a "transport" had arrived.

My heart began beating rapidly. After a short time we heard the voices of women and children in the yard next to us. We heard how *Oberscharführer* Hermann Michel shouted, "Quiet! Quiet!" and when there was complete silence, he told the women that they were in a transit camp, and from there would go on to the Ukraine, to work, and that now they must undress and go to the showers, but first arrange their clothing in a way that would make it easy to find them when they returned from the showers. "Silver and gold, rings and watches," he told them, "put in the basket. Now hurry, hurry, we have no time!"

An almost complete silence fell over the yard; only the crying of children was heard. Suddenly we saw naked women and their children walking between the two barbed wire fences in a column that filled the entire path, until they finally disappeared into the forest. And then the gates of the yard opened and Steubel shouted to us, "Quickly! Gather everything!"

I saw two women running, a Ukrainian behind them, whipping their naked flesh.

The yard was strewn with piles and piles of clothing, and we gathered everything quickly, afterward raking the yard, exposing silver rings and gold items that people had hidden in the ground in the hope that they would find them again when they returned from the showers. This entire operation took only a few moments, until the yard was once again empty and clean, as if nothing had taken place there. And then a second group was brought into the yard, and this process repeated itself for hours — after all the women came the men; all took their places quietly and in an organized manner; only here and there were the shouts of the Germans heard, and between the two barbed wire fences we saw naked men marching to *Lager* 3 and disappearing into the forest.

From the forest we could hear shouts and crying. We didn't know who was crying — the people shipped in or the workers there. The entire transport, a few thousand people, were killed that day. Afterward, during the parade that followed our work, Steubel taught us the German military song "The Blue Dragoons," whose last verse went, "The Jews are dragged here/ They come from the Red Sea/ We will beat them/ And there will be silence forever." Steubel changed the last words for us to, "Man lives only once/ And no more."

We learned the song until we could sing it satisfactorily, and we were marched around the parade ground and sang it, and during the breaks in the song, we heard from afar, from the direction of *Lager* 3, the same song sung by others.

In the evening, in the barracks, people who worked in the forest that bordered *Lager* 3 told others that they had heard, and even seen, people engaged in the digging of a huge pit that stretched over the entire area — the height of the earth dug out of it was several meters high. There, apparently, they buried the slain. The things we witnessed in *Lager* 2, along with the information given to us by those who returned from the forest, completed the picture now. There was no doubt about what was occurring in the camp we had been brought to, the death camp Sobibor.

On the Chelm-Wlodawa railway, near the small town of Sobibor, the Germans had confiscated a large, wealthy woodcraft farm, into which an offshoot of the railroad tracks led in order to enable the loading of logs cut in the forest into freight cars. There were buildings for management, a stable, workshops and an agricultural farm. The Germans had encircled the farm with barbed wire fences and hung a large sign at its gate, "Sobibor, Transit Camp, SS *Sonderkommando.*"

And inside the Sobibor farm the Germans had established a well-designed factory for the extermination of human beings.

At first, we didn't know the method of execution, but we were already witness to the disappearance of thousands of people, who were marched, naked as the day they were born, to their deaths in the forest, without a shot being heard, without a sound; and at the entrances to the camp there was no sign of what was happening inside — everything looked rural, serene and calm. Opposite the branch of railroad tracks stood *Lager* 1, a group of wooden country houses serving as lodgings for the Germans, the kitchen and their canteen. This site was well tended. The fronts of the houses had rows of flowers, low wooden fences and paved paths. Jakob the gardener and his assistant worked there, tending the gardens and growing vegetables for the German kitchen. Further on stood the workshops where Jews now worked — sewing suits and making shoes for the Germans and their wives. Between *Lager* 1 and *Lager* 2 the Germans had set up an animal farm, where the Jews raised pigs, fattened geese, tended horses — all for the SS in the camp. Near the railway tracks, not far from the German lodgings and the Jewish barracks, a big barracks was built to house the Ukrainians, and next to it, a smaller building — the Ukrainian kitchen. Opposite the barracks stood a small building that served as a guardhouse, where *Oberscharführer* Graetschus sat, in charge of the Ukrainian guards, and on the other side, toward the German lodgings, stood the weapons warehouse.

In *Lager* 2 stood a lovely, big wooden building with a porch extending along its entire front facade. The building faced the yard where the people undressed, and in it were secretaries and the warehouse for money, gold and valuables. The Jewish goldsmith worked there, sorting the valuables and packing them for transport. In the same building, there was the medical storehouse as well, where the pharmacist, a Jew, sorted medicines, drugs, perfumes and cosmetics and packed them for transport. In charge was *Oberscharführer* Michel, known as "the Preacher," as he was the one who exhorted the people before their march to death. On the other side of the building stood barracks filled with clothing and possessions that had belonged to the people in the transports, and from there was the path to the forest, the path to *Lager* 3.

In the evening of the day that the purpose of the camp had finally become clear to us, people said Kaddish for their relatives and soft weeping was heard from every corner. That day's transport had been indicative of the fate of our own transport, and the fate of the next one. All at once, we realized that we had been left alive for a short time only; it seemed obvious that people had worked in this place before us, and had been executed. The Germans seemed to replace the workers after a brief period. Even today, two were taken from us to *Lazarett* for no reason.

Now I understood what foolishness it had been for me to jump up and join those who had been selected for work. Here I could already have been "past it all." I was convinced that my death was imminent.

We moved into new barracks. Our carpenters had built a barracks to serve as storage for straw, and inside were included three layers of bunks all along its length; the place was encircled by a barbed wire fence and in the fence, a gate had been cut. We were moved to our new barracks after work. A group of boys grabbed the good places. I waited until everyone had finished getting organized and then lay down in a bunk in the second layer, next to the door.

Toward morning, when someone got up to relieve himself in the pails that stood by the door, he bumped into the body of someone suspended from the middle of the ceiling. The man emitted a brief cry and within moments everyone had awoken. We looked at the man hanging there. I knew him; he was one of the solitary men, like me. He was young — in his twenties. Most of the men didn't say a word. There were those who muttered that it was a good thing he had done, that now he wouldn't have to suffer anymore. I also thought it was the best solution for someone in our situation and I began to consider this solution myself.

But I continued to live. I knew that at any moment I might die; I even hoped for it. After every day that passed safely I was amazed that I was still alive. My physical health worsened. I was beaten almost every day. My whole body ached; it seemed to me that I was beaten more than anyone else. Others knew how to get by, somehow. They made sure to follow the German who supervised them; when the German turned his back, they didn't do anything, and when he turned toward them, they worked quickly, with all their energy; that's how they escaped beatings. The beatings were given to me and other workers like me, who didn't know how to work the system.

Transports of Jews continued to arrive from different areas of Poland, from Germany, from Czechoslovakia. The death camp operated smoothly. Here, at Sobibor, it was as if we were at the end of the world — multitudes of people were executed and nobody knew, nobody opened his mouth. The Germans and the Ukrainians tortured their victims in their last moments before death, and afterward tortured us, the ones left alive. Bolender, whose nickname was *Der Beder* (the bathhouse attendant), while on his way to *Lager* 3 or on the way back, would set the dog Barry on one of the workers. You could go out of your mind from the horrible sight of Barry attacking a man, tearing his clothes, biting his flesh, as the victim screamed horribly and was usually taken to *Lazarett* afterward.

One day, Paul came to us with the dog. He sat opposite us and laughed, the dog lying at his side. Now and then he would set the dog upon someone. "Man, catch the dog," he would order Barry. Paul was amused. Sometimes he would set the dog upon someone, then call him back when he was close enough to touch the victim; sometimes he just let the dog sink his teeth in and then he would pull him back. But sometimes he would let the dog attack someone without intervening. The fear of the dog's bite was so great that that fear alone could drive you insane.

Then suddenly, I saw Barry coming straight at me. A weakness ran through my limbs. The dog jumped up on me with such force that I fell to the ground, and he tried to bite me between my legs. I fought with him and pushed his head to the side, and then his teeth sank into my thigh until I felt them hit bone. I turned his head aside with all my strength and then he bit my backside. I don't know which was greater, my pain or my fear. Again, I thought this was the end, but after the attack I continued working, my blood flowing into my pants. Later I changed my pants to a pair that I had taken from the ones I sorted.

After work, during the parade, Paul asked again, "Who wants to sleep? Who is tired? Step out of the line!" To our surprise, one man stepped out. On his face was an apologetic smile, as if he wanted to say, "Forgive me for not being able to stand it any longer…" Paul praised the man and said he would no longer be tired; he would sleep in peace. And then he selected two others from our lines and sent the three to *Lazarett*. In a few moments we heard the shots.

I didn't step out of the line. And Paul didn't take me out of line.

In the evening, as I lay on my bunk and groaned with pain, I heard a conversation between two Jews who lay above me. One said, "This boy, down below, won't last much longer. A few days at most…" "A shame," said the second, who agreed with his companion's opinion. "He seems like a good boy."

When I was a little boy, I overheard a conversation between my mother and her girlfriend. My mother was talking about her children, and of me she said, "Berale isn't handsome, and he's a very delicate child." When we got home I stood in front of the mirror for a long time. I couldn't decide if I were handsome or ugly. I believed my mother. I wasn't angry with her, but I did care. Now, after the two Jews had decided that I wouldn't last, that I would die soon, I resigned myself to their opinion of my fate without protest, as I had resigned myself at the time to my not being "a handsome boy," and I saw myself on the road to death.

My condition did indeed deteriorate. The wounds from the dog bites filled with pus, and the sharp pains made me limp. I was also suffering terribly from loneliness. Without knowing why, I was unable to form bonds with the other young people among us. When I asked them a question, I was rejected rudely and with curses until I didn't dare go near them. I was unable to understand how they could treat me that way, when I received help and words of encouragement from people older than they were.

In the evenings, I would see groups of people lying on their bunks and having feasts, opening canned goods, slicing sausage, even drinking wine or vodka. All these things they found in the transport bundles and smuggled into the barracks; many of them collected gold rings and dollars and hid them in the barracks and outside it. But all that occupied me was death.

One morning, I awoke and felt something dripping on me. I rubbed the liquid between my fingers and saw that it was red and thick. I was sure that the serving of jam that had been given out yesterday had spilled from my neighbor above, and I said to the fellow next to me that jam was dripping on me from above. My neighbor jumped up from his bunk quickly and shouted, "He's dead!"

The man in the upper bunk was lying in a pool of blood. He had cut his wrists. He was a man who had come from Austria or Germany and was one of the solitary ones, those who didn't have any close contacts in the group, and who hadn't made friends with anyone. And again I was jealous of the man for whom everything had ended. The idea of suicide obsessed me. I thought about it constantly and looked for a way to kill myself quickly, without pain. Cutting my wrists seemed brutal, something I couldn't do. During our sorting work, I looked for poison, but I didn't find any; I didn't know exactly what I was looking for. Hanging seemed to me the best way to commit suicide, but I couldn't do that either. I thought about how nothing would be better than not waking up in the morning.

And in the meanwhile, I continued to live and be tormented. Something that I had forgotten, that one of the people brought to my attention after the suicide, was that according to Jewish law, it is forbidden to commit suicide. The man murmured to me, "It is a great sin!" I knew that already; I had even heard that suicides were not buried in the cemetery with others, but in a special place, near the fence. This had made a great impression on me, but now

I paid no attention to this religious law, just as I paid no attention to the fact that I was not eating kosher food; none of us, aside from two or three who ate only bread and nothing else, were keeping kosher. And yet the man's words on the seriousness of the deed I wanted to commit made me think, and also reminded me that, from the moment I had arrived at Sobibor, I had not prayed or thought about God. And yet in my worst moments, whenever I came up against something difficult in my life, I always asked for God's help!

Strange that here, in Sobibor, in this hell, I had forgotten God as if I had lost all contact with Him. When I saw how the Germans treated us, how we ran like panicky sheep, falling, rolling, jumping like frogs at the Germans' orders; when I heard their screams and mine when we were beaten or torn apart by Barry's teeth, it seemed that we had ceased being human; we had lost our human forms. We were in the kingdom of Satan.

No, it wasn't human, what was happening before our very eyes, and we did not see God's role here. From my childhood, I had learned that humans must fight the devil, and not let him control them. Now I prayed to God and asked Him to forgive me for my sins in neglecting Him. And I also asked God to take my soul and allow me not to wake up in the morning.

A sudden thought tortured me: Why? Why didn't God do anything to stop the extermination? Why was God punishing the people of Israel? It couldn't be that our sins were so great that we all had to be killed. I was taught that God loves the people of Israel, that we were chosen from among all the nations. How could God sit in the heavens and watch a small town called Sobibor destroy the entire nation of Israel, all of them, men, women and children, without exception? Perhaps our God was weak, and the German god was stronger, and our God sat up there and cried and could not do a thing?

On the first day the Germans had entered Lodz, our neighbor, the *Volksdeutsche*, said to my mother, "Our beloved God cannot see our suffering anymore and has come to liberate us." My mother told us this with a bitter smile on her face, but we were taught that the God of Israel was the Lord of the world and He could do anything. I remembered a song we sang in the synagogue, "There is none like our God, none like our Master, none like our Savior..."

And perhaps God was cruel, without mercy, and not as it was written in the Holy Books, and, at His orders, the Germans were destroying the Jewish nation? And maybe there was no God in the heavens? Because God couldn't be bad, God couldn't be weak, and God wouldn't destroy His chosen people. But it also couldn't be that the very thing my father, my mother, all my family and the entire nation of Israel had believed in for thousands of years was a mistake — and didn't exist at all!

When I was a child I once asked my father, "Who created God?" My father answered me, "It is forbidden to ask questions like these and forbidden even to think about them," and I tried not to. Even now, I tried to push these thoughts and my skepticism away from me, but they wouldn't let me be, and it was as if the devil had settled within me.

On Sunday we worked half a day. This day was meant to be a day of cleaning and rest. In the afternoon each of us occupied himself with cleaning up and hygiene; we knew the Germans would come for inspection, and everyone did as ordered to the best of his abilities. When a group of Germans, with Wagner at their head, entered our barracks, some were still cleaning, some were lying on their bunks, and some were sitting outside, in front of the barracks. The manner of the Germans' walk and the looks on their faces boded ill. Wagner, who directed the parade, was upset and shouted rudely. He ordered us to collect all of our things and stand at parade again in another two minutes. People ran quickly and brought their things. I didn't have anything other than two blankets, but others had quite a few possessions — I had no idea of how they got them or what they needed them for. People were afraid to bring everything into the yard and left some in the barracks or threw some away on the ground, mostly gold rings and money. The Germans wandered among us, inspecting every item, sometimes catching someone in the act of throwing something away, then beating him and making him stand to one side. When we all stood outside with our bundles, some Germans went inside the barracks and searched it. Another group of Germans passed from person to person and searched each one from head to toe. Those who had forbidden things on their person were made to stand to one side. There were two unpleasant redheaded brothers, who had become close to the Germans and whom everyone feared; the Germans found a treasure trove of food, gold rings and money on them. Both of them were given a terrible beating. They cried and fell at the Germans' feet, begging mercy, but were taken aside and shot to death.

Wagner ordered a bench to be brought and stood in the yard. Everyone who had been found with forbidden items was whipped with twenty-five lashes — he forced every one of them to take down his pants and lie on the bench. Two people held the transgressor on each side, one at his head and another at his feet, so that he couldn't move, and then two Germans whipped him. They lashed their whips on the victims with all their strength, and the victims couldn't move; only their buttocks would jump with each blow. The people screamed until their screams became wails. The Germans grew tired and sweaty, and then called over two Jews who had been used before as their assistants in certain situations. One was named Pozhycheki, a boy of twenty-something from Warsaw, in Sobibor with his father, who was a shoemaker, and with two younger brothers also in the work group. The German gave his whip to Pozhycheki, who whipped the ones being punished with all his might, like the German. The second one called from our midst to whip, named Benno, seemed ashamed. His blows were weak. Frenzel stopped him and said to him, "I'll teach you how to hit!" He ordered him to lie on the bench and Frenzel whipped him with all his strength, asking him with each blow, "Now do you know how to whip?" Benno's whipping improved, but didn't reach the level of Pozhycheki's efforts.

The whipping parade lasted a long time, accompanied by screams and crying. Afterward, Steubel took over, took us out to an open yard and ordered us to sing. We already knew a few songs, but our singing wasn't at its best. There was no harmony, and Steubel became angry and shouted, ran us around and made us do punishment exercises: "Run! Fall! Crawl! Jump like frogs!" and again we were marched and we sang, and were again made to run, and again we sang…

This lasted for a long while. Not far from us marched a Ukrainian unit singing songs in three-part harmony. Not far from them, on the other side of the barbed wire fence, village children led cows from the pasture, and their voices sounded like bells.

I had been in Sobibor for ten days and I was still alive. Each evening I asked myself how I had not died yet, and how long I had left to live. I knew that death could happen at any time. Many of those who had arrived with me were no longer alive. What did it mean, that I, weak and beaten, asking to die, was alive, while others, stronger than I was, fighting for their lives, fell every day like flies? But what difference did it make? We were all condemned to die; one of us would die a day earlier, another would die a day later.

The Jews who were made to work at Sobibor were divided into three groups; one group included the skilled workers, such as tailors and shoemakers, who served the Germans' personal needs. This group's situation was better than anyone else's in the camp, as, like those who observed from the side, they performed their crafts without being involved in the horrors that were occurring around them; they had a chance to live longer, relatively — until the order to execute them came. The second group included those selected to serve in the camp at various duties, such as kitchen workers, *putzerim* (sanitation workers) for the Germans, warehouse workers, cattle-pen workers and duck-pen workers. These went out each day to work but were not involved in the extermination process, and, as long as they did what they were ordered to do, they had a chance of surviving for a relatively long time; to their disadvantage was the fact that they could easily be replaced.

The third group, which I was a part of, was made up of the simple work force, of which there were so many in the death camp; these could be replaced within moments by others selected from a new transport, and indeed ninety percent of the Jewish workers killed in the first ten days were from this group. And members of this group were tortured by the Germans to satisfy their own cruel impulses. According to what we were told, the Germans replaced their staff of Jewish workers every two weeks, exterminating all the veterans. However, since the arrival of our transport they had come to the conclusion that for reasons of efficiency they should let us stay alive longer. This consideration began, of course, with the skilled workers and those with set duties, not with the simple workers like those in my group, and indeed, we found ourselves in a continuous replacement process — we were killed daily, and new workers were brought in daily. We were hanging on a thread between life and death.

Another transport arrived, this time before sunrise. The whistle of the locomotive moving cars into the camp woke us from our slumber. Within a few moments everyone in the barracks had awakened. We all paled. Although we were living in Hell, although we all knew what happened here, we felt the full significance of our misfortune every time a new transport arrived. Each time it seemed to me that I was one of the people in the new transport — that I would have to walk together with them to death.

Frenzel suddenly entered our barracks, called for the *Bahnhofkommando* and led them to work before the morning parade. I heard the voices of the people descending from the boxcars and then the thought popped into my head: Perhaps my mother was in this transport, my sister, my brother, Yankele? Perhaps my brother Mottel was there? How could this possibility not have occurred to me before? Truly, I couldn't have borne it if my family had been in this transport, but the thought that it might be so would not leave me. I washed and dressed, drank my ration of coffee, stood for parade, walked with the group to *Lager* 2, and my only thoughts were, "Perhaps my family is going to die now." More than once, people had found their relatives' clothes in the piles. There was also the opposite case — one of the shoemakers asked Wagner to remove his wife from the transport, and, wonder of wonders, Wagner granted his wish, searched for and found the woman and put her in the work group. I imagined to myself how happy my mother would be to see me alive, I imagined Yankele running to me…but then I remembered that my only chance to see them would be when they marched naked between the two barbed wire fences. How could I get near them? Should I join them on their walk to their deaths in the forest? But the Germans would never permit me to approach them; they would simply take me to *Lazarett*, and as a consequence I would only cause my loved ones more sorrow.

But how could I even think that they would be in this transport? Perhaps I had gone insane? I heard the women in the yard, I heard *Oberscharführer* Michel shouting, and afterward I saw naked women walking between the two barbed wire fences, but I hung my head; I could not look at them. Immediately afterward the gate to the undressing yard was opened and we ran inside — to gather the clothes.

A group of Jews was taken from one of the transport arrivals for work, to replace those who had recently been killed. Among the new workers was a man named Moshe. During his first evening with us he sat and cried. He told us that he was from a religious home and that he ate only kosher food, and asked us to give him something to eat. In our transport was a man named "Tzigayner" (Gypsy); it was said that he was an orphan. (Once, a gypsy circus had visited Lodz, and an orphan boy ran about among them, and when they left the town the gypsies took him with them. He wasn't missed until a few days later, and by then any search for him was futile. The boy lived with the gypsies until he was grown, and he said he lived very well and learned much from them; yet he still returned to our town to live.) Tzigayner was a talented man, who knew how to do everything; he was kindhearted and everyone loved him, even the Germans. Wagner wanted to make Tzigayner a Kapo, but Tzigayner decided there was no way he would be a Kapo. During one of our parades, Wagner called to Tzigayner and ordered him to whip a certain Jew with twenty-five lashes. Tzigayner refused, saying he couldn't do it, but Wagner would not let him be and placed the whip in his hand. Tzigayner whipped lightly, even ridiculously lightly. Wagner went crazy, shouted at him to lie down and whipped him with all his might.

Tzigayner didn't emit a sound. Wagner continued to whip him and Tzigayner continued to remain silent. At a certain point I thought Tzigayner was dead; how could one stay silent when receiving those blows? (Afterward, whenever I was whipped I told myself before each whipping: This time I won't scream; I'll be silent like Tzigayner — but I could never keep it up after more than seven or eight lashes.) But when Wagner ordered Tzigayner to get up, he did so immediately. Wagner ordered him to whip the same Jew, and Tzigayner again hit him lightly. I was sure Wagner would shoot Tzigayner on the spot, but that didn't happen. Wagner told him to return to his place in line and asked, "Who knows how to whip stronger than Tzigayner?"

And then, from among the rows of men, Moshe stepped out — the man who had cried and didn't want to eat anything non-kosher — reached his hand out for the whip, and whipped harder than anyone else had. Wagner made him a Kapo on the spot. A few days later, Moshe was made head Kapo. Frenzel called him "Governor General" and ordered the tailors to sew him a special suit: pants with red stripes on the side, a coat with sparkling buttons and red suspenders, a hard, round hat with a red stripe around it and three stars on his chest.

Moshe "Governor General" quickly became a cruel ruler, and omnipotent in the camp. The Germans supported him and put out a decree: Whoever addressed Moshe had to remove his hat and call him "Herr Governor General!" Everyone he passed had to remove his hat as well. Anyone who didn't follow these instructions could expect twenty-five lashes.

The Germans knew no limits in their torture of us. They did not let us rest for a moment. Several brave ones among us committed suicide; we were all jealous of them. Some went insane. One man, about thirty years old, approached a wall in the afternoon, right in front of us, and banged his head against it. People attempted to restrain him, but with an amazing strength he held everyone off and continued bashing his head against the wall. Covered with blood, he was taken to *Lazarett*.

One man began screaming in the middle of the night and tried to break out of the barracks by force. People had to hold him down physically until he fell asleep. One had an attack of uncontrollable giggles and continued to giggle during parade. *Oberscharführer* Michel approached him, lashed his face with his whip and ordered him with a shout to stop laughing. The man quieted. "You are an idiot!" Michel said to him, and then asked, "What are you?" and the man answered the German, "You are an idiot!" and resumed his laughing. The German hit him again and asked *"Vas bist du?* (What are you?)" and the Jew answered him, *"Idiot bist du!* (You are an idiot!)" The German continued to beat him until his laughter suddenly turned into crying and he fell to the ground, unconscious.

An older man, short and thin, did sorting work with us. I've forgotten his name. He inspected and packed the clothes determined to be rags. One day Paul gave him the name *Lumpen-Koenig* (King of Rags) and from then on never let him alone, arranging "games" with him. When German officers visited the camp, Paul would present the man as *Lumpen-Koenig*, would order him to sing and dance, and the man would do as ordered. Paul would make him eat all kinds of inedible things, like soap and various creams, or a pot of grease, or would order him to drink various liquids, medicines and perfumes, and the *Lumpen-Koenig* would beg him, "Shoot me, I don't want to live!" but he would eat and drink everything Paul would give him. Sometimes *Lumpen-Koenig* would turn as white as a sheet and fall down as if dead, but then Paul would order someone to bring water and splash it on the unconscious man; after some time he would regain consciousness and continue to work. Once Paul ordered *Lumpen-Koenig* to shave only the right side of his face and head — one cheek, half a moustache, one eyebrow and half his head, and let the other half grow. Paul again changed his name and called him *Der Schrechlicher Ivan* (Ivan the Terrible). His appearance became more and more monstrous.

The Germans found themselves another victim, a very tall, very thin Jew, calling him *Der Grabowiecer* as he came from Grabowiec. This man was ordered to shave only the left side of his face and head, and during parades *Der Grabowiecer* and Ivan the Terrible were called to step out of line, and the Germans would inspect them to see how their hairstyles were progressing. Pozhycheki's family, the father and three boys, would also be called to step out of line. Steubel would present them in a ridiculing fashion and the German guests would laugh out loud.

Somehow, I don't know how or why, my loneliness ended. As each day passed I made friends with more and more people. I was surprised and amazed when people began to call me by name and ask how I was. After work, the elder Pozhycheki, the shoemaker, called to me and told me to enter the workshop, where his son, the Kapo, also was. The old man brought me a bowl of soup and a slice of bread. I stood in amazement, but the old man said to me: "Eat, eat, Berale. You need this," and the Kapo son said, "When you're offered something to eat, eat it!"

In the brief time we had been at Sobibor, a division had developed between the veterans and the newcomers. We, who had arrived only two weeks before, were already considered veterans. We all knew each other, and everything we had gone through together had bonded us into a tight-knit group. Even Moshe "Governor General" and the Kapo father and son Pozhycheki treated us better than they did the newcomers, who had arrived only a few days later.

On the bunk beside mine was a new neighbor, a boy named Monyek, who was two years older than me and had arrived in the last transport. We immediately became friends and spent every free moment together. Monyek told me he had come to Sobibor with his family — his parents and four brothers and sisters. When Wagner had selected him for work, he hadn't wanted to separate from his family, but his father had made him go. Monyek cried all night and said over and over, "It can't be that my whole family is already dead." He ate almost nothing, and I did my best to make him feel better. I knew that if he kept on this way he wouldn't make it. We talked a lot. "It isn't worth being here for even a moment," he said. "The solution is to kill ourselves."

I knew he was right. I had already come to this conclusion, myself. And yet I tried to dissuade him from these thoughts. Until then, I hadn't kept for myself any of the things that had passed through my hands during the sorting work; I didn't need anything. Now, when I found something good to eat, I would hide it despite the danger of being put to death, and I smuggled something to the barracks for Monyek every day. But he didn't want to eat, although he sometimes ate to please me.

One day, both of us returned from work in bad condition. Barry had bitten Monyek. While he was sitting in the latrine with a few other workers, Bolender came from *Lager* 3 to *Lager* 1, sending Barry ahead of him to the latrine. Everyone fled, holding their pants in their hands, but Barry caught Monyek and bit his backside and his thighs. That same day, I had brought a pile of papers to the burning pit and exchanged a few words with the *Feuermeister* (fire foreman), Meir. I hadn't seen anyone around, but when I left the pit, Frenzel appeared all of a sudden, fell upon me and whipped my head and face. The whip was torn and the edge of a nail cut my cheek (the whip was made of multiple layers of beaten leather, held together by nails, with wide layers next to the handle and narrow layers at the free ends, and covered with soft, beautiful leather; after much use, the soft coating had been torn and the connecting nails were exposed). When I returned from work I saw people looking at me worriedly. They all wanted to help me and called the medic, who bandaged my wounds and Monyek's. The two of us lay on our bunks and cried together.

I was very worried. My wounds weren't as bad as they seemed at first, when they had bled profusely, and after bandaging, the pain subsided somewhat; but a terrible fear washed over me at the thought that I might lose Monyek. My heart told me the worst. All evening we hardly spoke. I had nothing to say; it seemed to me that anything I might say would be foolish and would only anger Monyek, who was constantly moaning. I was afraid he would do something to himself during the night and I decided to watch over him, but I couldn't stay awake — I fell asleep but woke up several times, each time checking to see if Monyek was lying beside me and if he was breathing.

In the morning, at dawn, Monyek refused to get up. I threatened him that Moshe "Governor General" was already walking around and whipping anyone who had not yet gotten down from his bunk. Monyek got to his feet, but his behavior was strange, as if he didn't care about anything.

I had already learned that people who sank into apathy about themselves usually died quickly. I felt I was losing Monyek. I prayed that he would be sent to work with me; perhaps I could succeed in saving him. But Monyek was sent to work in the forest.

When I returned from work, before anyone said anything to me, I knew that Monyek was gone. I saw it in everyone's eyes. Everyone knew that we had been like two brothers. People who had worked with him came up to me and said that he had been taken to *Lazarett*. Everyone said they thought that he had been the instigator — he had wanted it. From what they told me, he refused to work and by morning had already been given twenty-five lashes by Kapo Benno. Benno, who also approached me, said, "I didn't have a choice. I got orders from Getzinger. I tried not to hit him too hard. I told him that if he didn't work they would kill him, but he didn't care. He killed himself."

"Monyek is better off," someone said to me as if to console me on the loss of my friend. "He won't have to suffer any longer. If only we could end our suffering as well."

Monyek's death did not shock me for the first few moments. I accepted the news as something obvious, and, in any case, death didn't frighten me very much anymore; death was a daily reality. But when I entered the barracks and saw my friend's empty bunk, I realized all at once the extent of my loss, the lack of any point in living, and I decided to kill myself that very night. I was energized. My heart pounded. All of my doubts faded; I didn't feel a bit of fear. On the contrary, I was pleased with myself. Whenever I started to feel any qualms, I dismissed them. My mind quickly emptied of any awareness of my surroundings. I even forgot my friend Monyek. All of my thoughts were focused on committing suicide.

I weighed the possibilities. I had no means, no poison to swallow, no razor with which to cut my wrists, no rope with which to hang myself. I was helpless. I could look for something in the workshop, but I was afraid to be seen. I felt that if someone saw me, they would discover my secret. So I lay on my bunk, doing nothing, until I finally decided to use the belt of my pants.

I waited until everyone was asleep. The family I had once had rose up in my memory: I parted from them one by one. I carefully and quietly removed the belt from my pants. It was a good thing no one was lying beside me. Because I was on a lower bunk, I would have to climb onto the bunk above me, to tie the belt to a beam under the ceiling. I threaded the belt through the buckle, made a loop and hung it above my head. I felt the cold leather against my neck. Half sitting and half lying, I didn't move from my position for a long while, as if I were paralyzed. I was unable to go the top bunk to take the last step.

Suddenly I was seized with the thought that I mustn't commit suicide, that perhaps I should stay alive, after all. I had been close to death many times and each time a miracle had occurred. I had survived. Where did the strength to endure come from? After all, I was a weak and solitary boy who had been put with the workers only by chance, and death had taken its victims from those stronger than me, who, it seemed, had known better than me how to survive. Was it only by chance that I had survived until now? And if so, perhaps it was a sign that I was meant to live? And if so, how could one survive in this place? Thousands had already been executed before my eyes, and the site was even being expanded. The Germans, to all appearances, intended to destroy the entire Jewish nation at Sobibor, and perhaps other peoples, as well. What was the point of living in this place any longer?

The barracks were silent. Only the occasional moan from those sleeping, and the Ukrainian guards' conversation from outside, was heard. These cut into my train of thought. I pulled the belt and felt it tighten around my neck. I felt what it was to be strangled, but I didn't move. I had neither the strength nor the courage to get up and climb into the upper bunk, to tie the belt and end it all. Overcome with fatigue, I fell asleep.

In the morning I awoke to the wakeup call. When I remembered the night before, I grew ashamed of myself.

Why hadn't I been able to do it? Why hadn't I had the courage to carry out my decision? I had only to kill myself and I could put an end to everything. If I hadn't succeeded last night, I would have to tonight. Today I had to get a rope — the belt might be too short. In the sorting room there was no lack of ropes.

Another parade, and all sorting workers joined the *Waldkommando* (the forest workers) this time. SS men Gomerski and Getzinger, along with some Ukrainians, led us. We crossed the open area between *Lager* 2 and the forest. On the left was *Lager* 3. We entered the forest from the right side, near the camp fence and the railway tracks, passing *Lazarett* — a small wooden building with a tiled roof. From the roof rose a cross — this must have been a church at a local cemetery. Close by rose a mound of earth next to a pit. This was the pit where our friends had been killed. A shudder passed through my body. Perhaps they had decided to execute us? But we continued marching into the forest. After about a hundred meters, we saw a barbed wire fence on the left and, behind it, a hill of white sand about twenty meters high. Hills of sand are unusual in a forest, and indeed the hill looked suspicious. We were ordered to load logs that had been cut down by the *Waldkommando* onto our shoulders and bring them to the camp, where they were to be used for electricity poles and for the construction of the camp expansion. This loading work was crushing. The Germans and Ukrainians whipped us mercilessly. It was particularly difficult for me, because as I was short, my shoulders often didn't reach the height of the log. As a result I had to walk on the tips of my toes — both to help the others and so that the Germans wouldn't notice that I wasn't helping in the loading. But sometimes the full weight of the heavy log pressed down on me, and every time this happened I was close to collapse.

On the way back from the forest we were ordered to run. While running, my eyes explored the hill of sand to my left, and all at once I heard voices behind it, and shouting in German, then the barking of a dog and horrible screaming and crying, which echoed around us in the forest. Then the barking and the screams and crying quieted, and then began again. This repeated itself over and over, endlessly. Although I was already used to crying and screams — my own and others' — I couldn't stand the horrible sounds coming from the forest. I felt as though I were going out of my mind and deep inside, I cried together with the poor victims. Now the riddle of the disappearance of the people from the transports who had been led into the forest had been solved: the hills of sand had been made by Jews who had been ordered to dig a great pit, where they buried the remains of the dead from the gas chambers, in layers, one on top of another, and over everything, a layer of lime was sprinkled. The happenings on the other side of the hills of sand distracted me from my work, and *Oberscharführer* Getzinger, who noticed this, wasted no time in venting his rage on me and striking me with his cane on my face and body. I fell to the ground, but he continued to strike and kick me. I thought I would never get up again, but when Getzinger shouted his order, "Get up!" I jumped to my feet. I saw that he was holding a gun in his hand, aimed at me. I swiftly resumed my work.

All that day my thoughts were given over to what was happening behind the hills of sand. In my imagination I saw hundreds of thousands of bodies in the pits, and my ears echoed with the sound of crying. It seemed that I could hear the crying of the dead.

After the evening parade, I lay on my bunk and immediately fell asleep. During the night I dreamed that my mother came to visit me with little Yankele. Mother was as beautiful as she had been during the holidays, before the war. She wore a tight, fancy dress and her hair, tied back, set off her high forehead. Her sad face expressed her love for me. Cute little Yankele, who was wearing a winter coat lined with fur, his cheeks red and his face sad, stood without moving, like a doll. I wondered about their visit. A few meters separated us — something kept us from coming close to one another. I wanted to tell them something, but I couldn't speak. My mother looked at me for a long moment and finally said they had to go. I wanted to go with them, but my mother, as if she knew what I wanted to say, told me I had to stay here. "It's good for you," she said, and I couldn't understand why I could not go with them. I started to follow them, but they got farther and farther away from me until they disappeared.

That day I forgot all the pains and blows I had received the day before. I thought only about the dream. I was glad I had seen my mother and Yankele so clearly and up close. I went over every detail of the dream over and over, trying to interpret it. I finally drew the conclusion that my mother and Yankele were no longer alive. My mother had come to tell me not to go with them — meaning not to commit suicide — I had to stay alive.

The dream caused me to give up my idea of taking my own life.

A train had arrived and the locomotive pulled some of the boxcars into the camp, but this time we saw no commotion on the platform — no armed Germans, no Ukrainians, no call for the *Bahnhofkommando* to report for work. We strained to listen, but we didn't hear a sound from the direction of the platform. It was plain that the train had not brought people.

The next morning we had a perfunctory parade. This time we weren't divided into the usual work groups. Everyone, aside from those with special jobs, was divided into two groups — a small one, taken to the platform, and all the others, I among them, taken to *Lager* 2. All of the boxcars were empty except for one, which was full of barrels of lime. The people in the first group unloaded the barrels of lime, and we loaded the empty boxcars with all of the sorted items that had been collected in the barracks and warehouses. We were made to run while we worked — we had to run from *Lager* 2 to the boxcars, a distance of about three hundred meters. All along the way stood Germans and Ukrainians who urged us on with shouts and blows. Boxcar after boxcar was filled with clothes, shoes and other useable items that Jews had brought with them to Sobibor. Everything was sorted and packed, toilet soap separate from laundry soap, men's socks separate from women's stockings, dolls separate from other toys. Even the rags were packed in large packages. Gold, silver and other valuables were packed in suitcases and special boxes, locked and loaded onto a special boxcar.

Although we ran while we worked, without resting for a moment, the work took all day, until evening. While running with a box of rags that was bigger than me, I met Wagner standing in the road. Our eyes met. He looked at me and said with a smile full of scorn, "Run, run, sons of Israel, you are going to Palestine!" More than once I had received blows from Wagner, but these words, which penetrated my heart like a dagger, hurt me the most.

For a long time we had discussed among ourselves the need for one of us escape from Sobibor, to warn the Jews and to tell the world what was happening here. We knew that the people being brought here had no idea where they were being brought and for what purpose. Now an opportunity presented itself to accomplish this, and one of us was willing to try. This man asked us to load packages on him inside the boxcar, to hide him, and promised that if he made it out safely, he would travel from place to place and explain what was happening in Sobibor. We hid him in one of the boxcars, among the packages. The boxcars were closed and sealed and taken out of the camp, where they stood all night. In the morning, before they were connected to the locomotive, the boxcars were inspected by German troops. The soldiers discovered an open window in one boxcar — and for this everyone in the *Bahnhofkommando* was punished at a public whipping in the parade ground. But the Germans didn't realize that one of us was missing — and we knew that our man had succeeded in escaping.

There was a respite from transports. In the camp, building and expansion activities were taking place. The two barbed wire fences that led from the undressing yard to the gas chambers were concealed with branches pushed through the barbed wire, so that naked people walking between them wouldn't be able to see what was happening around them, and they, themselves, wouldn't be seen by anyone else. The construction of a ramp was begun next to the iron tracks, and narrow tracks were laid for boxcars from the larger tracks via *Lager* 2 to *Lager* 3. Next to our barracks, which had once been a granary, shacks were built for the workers' lodgings. In front of the gas chambers — whose roof alone we could see, as trees hid the building itself — the construction of three barracks began. It became obvious that the Germans were planning to greatly increase the extermination capacity of the camp. The electric grid stretched across the site told us that the Germans planned to operate the extermination machine day and night, twenty-four hours a day.

In the meantime, without transports, it seemed to us that our value had increased. The Germans no longer shot people daily, for no reason. There was a lot of work and they needed us.

One Sunday afternoon, Wagner entered our barracks in a good mood, and patiently and magnanimously wrote down everyone's details — name, age, place of birth — all the while making cracks like, "When were you born? Where were you born? Why were you born?" When I told him my name was Berale, he wouldn't agree and tried to think of another name for me, finally saying, "I'll write down 'Boris,' do you agree?" I agreed, of course.

When Wagner left, we gathered around and argued about why

he had come and listed all of us in detail. There was a feeling that our being listed had granted us a special status, and some saw it as a sign that the extermination would stop. It was true that for two weeks no transports had arrived...and perhaps the Germans were going to send us to work in Germany?

It was a passing illusion. The opposite was true: the expansion activity in the camp attested to an extensive extermination plan, and there was no chance that the Germans would let us live. We knew that, aside from the SS, nobody who entered Sobibor got out alive.

A convoy of wagons laden with bricks arrived at the camp. We were called to bring the wagons into the camp, unload them and put the wagons outside, where the Polish wagon drivers waited. The Germans watched over us to make sure we didn't talk to the Poles. Sometimes, when the Germans were bringing people into the camp in civilian clothes, we knew that if they were blindfolded they had a chance to leave, and if not, they would be brought to *Lazarett* and shot. The Germans wouldn't let anyone who saw what was happening in the camp live.

During the break in transports, the atmosphere in the camp changed a little. These days, our lives weren't totally worthless; the Germans or Ukrainians couldn't kill anybody on a whim — for this they would need a reason, such as an injured or sick person taken out to be killed (there were no sick at Sobibor; when the Germans discovered that someone was ill, they killed him that same day). Moreover, every execution required approval from Wagner or Frenzel or another senior officer. Just the fact that we had stopped seeing thousands of people being led to their deaths every day, however, made us feel that we were alive. During that period our social bonds strengthened. In the evenings, we would sit together and talk, getting to know one another, trying to support each other. Even the Kapos became more humane and willing to help, at the end of their workday. Moshe "Governor General" would sometimes burst into tears, ask us to forgive him for his deeds and promise that from now on he wouldn't touch a soul, even if the Germans ordered him to do so (the next day he would go back to being cruel, and strike without distinction). I felt I belonged with the people among whom I lived, as if we were all one family.

Yet even the expansion of the camp didn't stop the Germans from torturing us, and each time, they reached new heights. When the occasional boxcar arrived with construction equipment, we would be called for special unloading tasks, with most of the camp participating, after our regular work hours. To unload a car of bricks we would form two long lines — from the boxcar to the place where the bricks would be put, and we would pass them from hand to hand. At first the passing went slowly, but despite this there were those who didn't manage to grasp the bricks from their neighbor's hands and the bricks would fall to the ground. In these instances, Frenzel and Wagner would shout and hit us; Frenzel even warned that every brick that fell to the ground would bring a punishment of twenty-five lashes. After some time the people became more skillful and the work went smoothly. Wagner suddenly jumped up onto the boxcar and began to urge the man who handed out the bricks, shouting, "Faster! Faster!"

The bricks flew from hand to hand with greater speed until the line of men worked like a machine — all of the hands caught and threw bricks at a uniform speed, and heads moved back and forth, back and forth, unceasingly. How long could we keep up this level of concentration, when the rough bricks were lacerating our hands and the pain kept getting worse? The Germans stood and watched the Jews working like a machine, but Wagner wasn't satisfied with the increased speed — he started handing out bricks himself, and the speed increased until the mind could no longer control the activity; hands and eyes continued to work for a few more seconds, and then we all lost control, bricks flying without our knowing from where, hands not ready to grab them, and they fell all over our bodies. It was bedlam. Bricks were scattered all the way from the boxcar to the pile in a matter of seconds. The Germans fell upon us in a great rage; there wasn't a soul who wasn't beaten. Some were given twenty-five lashes and some were bitten by Barry.

One day, boxcars loaded with cement and barracks parts arrived at the camp. We unloaded the sacks of cement — each one weighing fifty kilos — and ran about thirty meters with them. With my weak body, I had to really exert myself to run with a sack of cement on my back. Then Gomerski came along and decided that fifty kilos was too light a load for me. He ordered two sacks of cement to be loaded onto my back. The heavy load pressed down on me and my whole body trembled. My muscles were pushed to the breaking point. It seemed that if I took one step all my muscles would explode and I would collapse underneath. But with hidden strength that came from heaven knows where, I stepped forward with the load on my back, Gomerski walking along beside me waiting for me to collapse.

After the cement, we unloaded the parts for the barracks. Frenzel was in charge of this work. The barracks components were very heavy and Frenzel decided that several people would carry each one. Because I was short, I sometimes didn't reach the height of the load, and then I would have to rise onto the tips of my toes to help, which sometimes caused the entire weight of the load to fall on me. The roof, which was the heaviest part, took six of us to carry. Once, when the roof was already on our shoulders, Frenzel ordered the two in the middle to move aside. The heavy load now rested on the four of us. And then Frenzel climbed up onto the roof — and we carried him all the way.

Getzinger and Steubel supervised the construction of the sloping ramp. The work was crushing. Passing pails of sand while running is very difficult. But the Germans didn't stop at this. Steubel turned *Der Grabowiecer* — the man who was ordered to shave only half his face and head each day — into a dog. All day he had to run on four legs, bark constantly and catch the others and bite them. It was a chilling sight: the tall man running on all fours and emitting strange sounds while Steubel yelled at him, "Dog, catch him!"

The cruelty of the Germans knew no limits. One day, during the sorting of the victims' belongings, when we had finished taking out the last packages, there was an umbrella left stuck between the roof beams. Paul, who was supervising us, ordered one of the men to get the umbrella down. The roof was six meters high. The man climbed up a side beam, got to the horizontal roof beam and progressed along its length, hanging by his hands, toward the middle where the umbrella was. He moved slowly halfway, until his strength ran out, or perhaps he wasn't agile enough to grab the beam with his hands — and he fell to the floor. It wasn't enough that he was injured; he was also punished with twenty-five lashes of the whip by Paul and bitten by Barry. Pleased by this turn of events, Paul sent for *Oberscharführer* Michel, and then for more Germans, and told them he had discovered "parachutists" among the Jews. Now he ordered men, one after the other, to climb up the beam, move along the entire length of the beam hanging by their hands — and to come down the other side of the barracks. Quick young boys climbed up and moved along the beam without difficulty. I moved along the beam quickly and easily, and Paul ordered me to repeat the whole thing, but many of us slipped and fell from the great height, were badly bruised and bitten by Barry.

Paul was in an ecstasy of cruelty. The barracks was teaming with mice and he ordered us to catch them — each of us had to bring two — then he took five people and told them to tie their pants closed around the ankles and to stand at attention in a row. When we had all caught mice and held them in our hands, we had to drop them into the tied pants of the five standing at attention. The men were unable to continue standing at attention with scores of mice running around in their pants. They rocked, jumped, cried. Their faces revealed what was being done to their bodies and their souls. But Paul shouted, "Attention! Don't move!" and beat the men without mercy. Barry, the dog, also attacked them.

That day we hardly worked at all. It was impossible to work in this insanity. Afterward Paul called *Lumpen-Koenig* to him — the man he had nicknamed Ivan the Terrible — and ordered the Preacher, *Oberscharführer* Michel, who was also in charge of the medical warehouse, to bring certain bottles. When he returned, the two of them made the victim drink from one of the bottles. He drank and only made a face. Afterward they made him drink the liquid in the other bottle. The man took one sip and began shouting at Paul in Yiddish, "Shoot me! Shoot me! I can't drink it! I can't!"

Paul struck the man with his whip and shouted, "Drink — or I'll beat you to death!" The Jew drank the entire bottle, stood at attention for a few minutes, the color of his face turning to yellow, and then wavered for a moment and collapsed to the ground.

Paul shouted at him and beat him. The man didn't react. The German ordered a pail of water to be brought and poured on the man, but he lay rigid, without moving. We were all sure Ivan the Terrible was dead.

The time came for us to return from work to the barracks. Paul ordered us to lay Ivan the Terrible on a plank, and for four of us to bear him on our shoulders slowly. We were all ordered to sing a dirge. All the way, we sang Chopin's Funeral March.

Ivan the Terrible was in a deep coma. Our efforts to rouse him had no effect. At the evening parade, Moshe "Governor General" reported to the German officer Schutt that one man was missing. The officer angrily demanded to know why the man was not standing at parade, and Moshe answered that the man was drunk. The German lost his temper, "What, a drunken Jew?" Moshe explained to him that the man had been made to drink by *Unterscharführer* Paul.

*Oberscharführer* Schutt was a man who liked order. He wasn't willing to accept the absence of a man at parade because Paul had made him drink, and ordered the drunk to be brought out as he was to the parade ground. He was brought and laid down in front of the German, who inspected him from every angle and tried to rouse him. When he didn't succeed, he ordered us to return him to the barracks.

This time we were all sure that the man was dead, but later in the evening he awoke. We gave him water to drink and by the next day his health had returned. A few days after that terrible day,

*Oberscharführer* Michel sent me with a package to take to Paul in his lodgings. The dog Barry lay in the doorway. I was filled with fear. I didn't know what to do. Paul saw that I was alarmed and said to me, "Don't be afraid, the dog won't do anything. Come on in." I gave him the package and he said to me, "Thank you very much." When I turned to leave he ordered me to wait, approached the table, cut two pieces of bread, spread them with butter, placed a slice of sausage on them, put the slices in my hands and said, "Eat, it's good!" I was totally confused.

The method of the Germans, apparently, was to not let us have a moment of free time, to keep us occupied, and to torture us constantly, so that we would be permanently exhausted and depressed. This was especially so that we would not have the physical or mental strength to think about where we were, what we were doing and what would happen to us. During our "free" time after work, the Germans kept us occupied with marches, learning songs, and punishment exercises. On Sunday afternoons the Germans would come to our camp and make us dance to the sounds of an orchestra made up of our men. They didn't let us alone for a second — every free moment was taken from us.

And yet, we were not so exhausted that we couldn't think at all, and so we began to harbor thoughts of escape. The fact that the man we had hidden in the boxcar had managed to get out of the camp — although we didn't know what had happened to him — proved that it was possible. The yearning to escape spread through the camp like a contagious epidemic — each man had his thoughts on how to escape, each man whispering his secrets to his confidants, but the thought was one thing and the deed was another. In actuality, we didn't know what to do to organize a successful escape.

One of our men, named Chaim, and whom the Germans nicknamed *Der Zimmermann* (the carpenter), was an excellent builder of country houses. He was around forty, a Communist with a background in the Underground, who had spent more than a few years in a Polish prison. This man began trying to persuade our men to organize a mass escape. At the same time, the Germans started laying landmines around the camp — in addition to the barbed wire fences, the water trenches and the guard towers — and everyone knew that when the mines had all been laid, escape would become very difficult. One evening, as I was approaching the latrine, I met *Der Zimmermann* and his younger assistant — the two were always together, both at work and in their free time — and to my surprise he turned to me and said, "Berale, we're escaping from the camp tonight. I'm sorry, I tried to organize a general escape, but I saw that it wouldn't work. No one will talk to me. In a few days, when they finish laying all the landmines, it will be impossible. So I've decided to escape with my partner. We're relying on you not to tell a soul."

I heard his words with a nod of assent. When I came back outside, I was so excited and amazed that at first I couldn't think clearly. Things slowly became apparent to me. I asked myself what the two were doing in the latrine and why the man had told me such a dangerous secret, and suddenly the thought came to me: What a fool I was! The latrine was very close to the fence, and the two were surely planning to escape from there! Why didn't I ask if I could join them? Had the man told me of their escape to give me an opening to join them, or perhaps he feared I had discovered their secret?

My heart began to pound. I returned to the latrine, but there was no one there. I didn't find them in our barracks. I didn't think they could have escaped already, and I waited for them in the doorway. When an hour had passed and I didn't see them, I realized I would never see them again. I lay down to sleep, but my thoughts wouldn't let me rest. I was tense; my ears alert to every noise, to the sound of shots, to shouts, but I heard nothing. Did the two manage to escape? Would they be shot during their escape through the fence, or be caught alive?

Time passed and complete silence surrounded me. It looked like they had made it! And I, the fool who didn't understand what the man had meant by his words, didn't express my desire to join them, and they would certainly have taken me with them! I had missed a rare opportunity to escape from the camp — perhaps the only chance.

Many Germans came to the morning parade, all armed with machine guns. There was tension all around. No one knew what had happened and we were frightened — maybe they were going to kill us? Wagner led the parade. Moshe "Governor General" counted the men a few times and reported to Wagner that two were missing. The Germans counted us again and then consulted among themselves for a few minutes. Wagner finally turned to us and said, "Last night two criminals tried to escape from the camp, but we caught them and they were shot on the spot. As punishment, every fifth man will be put to death. And if it happens again — we will kill all of you!"

Wagner and Frenzel passed between the rows and selected the men. In the silence we heard again and again the words, "You, out!" "You, out!" — and the men stepped out of line without a word, as if they had been selected to perform some task. One of the men wasn't sure they meant him and asked, "Me?" and the German said, "Yes, you!" and the man stepped out and joined the others.

Wagner and Frenzel arrived at my row. In a few seconds I would know my fate. The Germans came nearer, ordered someone to step out…they had almost reached me, they were looking at me, passing me slowly. I had been condemned to live.

Those selected for death stood in a row, facing us. None of them said a word. No one cried. Only their faces were white as sheets, some of them smiling a bitter smile. Men who up to a few moments ago had been together with us, among us, like us, men whose fate had brought them to this hell, were going to die. Although we all knew we would die in the end, we had hoped our fate would be shared — together we would live and together we would die. Now the group of Germans and Ukrainians were leading those they had selected to *Lazarett*. After a few minutes we heard shots. Death had already ceased being a threat to dangle in front of us; death was a daily routine, had even become a subject for jokes, but the execution of a group of friends affected us terribly. Men argued among themselves as to whether the escape had been right or not. Some said the two should never have escaped alone, as they had caused men to be killed. Others said that, in any case, people die or are killed every day, so anyone was justified in doing what he could to save himself. We didn't believe Wagner that the two had been caught, because if this were the case, the Germans would have brought them to the camp and presented them to us. We were convinced that they had managed to get away.

One day I was working next to the camp fence. Suddenly I heard children's voices. I raised my eyes and saw a boy and a girl, about seven or eight, leading cows into the field between the camp and the forest, talking to each other and singing. My heart clenched. The children reminded me of the existence of another world, a world I had totally forgotten. We had been so completely cut off from the outside that yesterday's world seemed like an unrealistic dream! I had forgotten the past so completely that I had even stopped thinking of my family, of my home and my wonderful childhood! Everything had been repressed so deeply inside me, as if it had never existed. Now, suddenly, seeing these two free children outside the camp, who were singing for fun, reminded me of the summer of 1939 at the cottage, and of the farmers' children in the neighboring cottage. Beside them all my memories floated up, all the members of my family appeared before me, bringing back to life everything I had experienced since that summer.

The Germans had no time to wait for the completion of the expansion activities in the camp. The transports began again, and not having seen transports for some time, we were again hit by shock and depression. The transports were mostly from Eastern Poland, some from places where Jews had already been transported to; apparently all the rest were now being brought. The behavior of the people in these new transports was different. We realized that these people knew what they were coming to, or at least, they feared the worst. Some of them looked for a way to save themselves at the last moment — they offered sums of money to the Germans if they would only let them go, or tried to hide in the camp.

Some of the boxcars in the train transport were broken, and many Ukrainian guards accompanied it. It turned out that the passengers had broken the boxcars and jumped out during the journey. The Germans in the camp were put on alert, and they all carried loaded machine guns. Any attempt at resistance was put down on the spot. The screams of the people gathered in the undressing yard reached the heavens — people refused to undress, and the Preacher, *Oberscharführer* Michel, tried to convince them that they were not being taken to their deaths. One time we heard him shout, "Quiet, quiet!" and when he was able to quiet them down he said, "I know you are asking to die, but you won't succeed! You have to work and continue working!" In this furtive manner he tried to convince the women to undress calmly — and the women, moved by despair and the spark of hope, undressed quietly.

One time, when the gates of the undressing yard were opened and we sorters entered to gather the clothing, we saw a young girl hiding in the pile of clothes. Michel, who was there, approached her swiftly, beat her and ran her to the opening of the barbed wire fences. Sometimes we would find children and babies among the clothes.

The people in the new transports no longer asked if the water was hot; they asked how long it would take, if death would hurt. People prayed before death, and some shouted, *"Shema Yisroel, Hashem Elokeinu, Hashem Echad!* (Hear, O Israel, the Lord is our God, the Lord is One!)" Some yelled, "Tell the world what the Germans are doing! Avenge us!"

The value of the service workers, our value, again fell to the bottom rung of the ladder. Again, whoever wanted to kill us was able to. Newcomers replaced those who were killed.

Every day food was brought to *Lager* 3, where the arrivals were murdered. Bolender or Gomerski would take some of our men, who would each carry two pails of food. A few meters away from the entrance, the men would leave the pails and return as ordered at a swift run — they were forbidden to even glance in the direction of *Lager* 3. At the same time, some men would come out of *Lager* 3, take the pails and disappear with them into the forest.

Sometimes, when Bolender felt like it, he would take the pail bearers with him into *Lager* 3. We never saw these men again. Occasionally, when I was ordered to carry pails of food to there, I was even more afraid of entering this *Lager* than I was of death.

One day, Gomerski came to the sorting area and selected some men for *Lager* 3. One of the men, whose brother was also in the group, refused to go, crying and begging to be allowed to stay. Gomerski became enraged. His source of pride was his unique new whip; more than one person said that no one could last more than twenty lashes. Indeed, the whip was big and thick, custom-made to special order for its owner. Gomerski lay the refuser down and whipped him with all his strength until his face was red and sweating. The victim stopped responding and looked dead. He was taken to *Lazarett* and Gomerski looked satisfied — his whip had passed the test.

One of the transports arrived from the region of towns where Turobin was located. The Germans selected people from this transport for work, and one of them, who knew my brother and our family well, told me that Mottel and a few other men had fled into the forests and had joined the partisans. He also told me that my family thought I was dead and had sat *shiva* for me. According to him, all of my aunt Sarah's family had been included in his transport. Other people in my group also discovered family members in the transport from the towns, which included the *Judenrat* and all of the wealthy. I tried to find out what was happening in Warsaw, but none of the people in this new transport knew anything.

One transport arrived from the town of Chrubyeshoov, and its people were executed that same day, except for about one hundred men, who were left to spend the night on the train platform. We couldn't fathom the reason for this — these men were not made to join us like the others who had been selected for work, and their boxcars were left inside the camp. The next day, before we set out

for work, Frenzel told us we had to load the boxcars with packages
from the warehouses, and one hundred people from yesterday's
transport would come to help us. "You will not work hard today,"
he said, "most of the work will be done by the people from the
transport, and in order to differentiate between you and them,
wear caps you can take from the warehouses — and they will go
bareheaded."

When we came to *Lager* 2, each of us selected a cap from the
big pile and put it on his head. Despite our situation, we couldn't
help but laugh at the way we looked. All along the way from the
warehouses to the train platform stood Germans and Ukrainians,
who instructed us to walk on one side and not to mix with the
others, and not to run as we were usually ordered to do, but to walk
slowly, while the Jews from the transport were made to run and
beaten nonstop. All of the Germans and the Ukrainians gathered
on the platform and turned the place into a cruel playground that
continued throughout the day. People were viciously beaten, the
dog Barry bit right and left, the people were forced to eat dirt and
other substances and to drink all kinds of liquids. Two of the people
from the transport were hung from electricity poles. The screams
of the people and the laughter of the Germans all intermingled.

The Germans emphasized their good treatment of us that day,
but for me it was one of the blackest days I had experienced in the
camp. The Jews from the new transport, among them old people
and youths, almost children, in their traditional village clothing,
reminded me of my father and my brother, all of my family and all
of my past. This time, while watching from the side, I saw how they
were tortured, how they were brought to the limits of endurance,
how they struggled desperately to survive, while I knew all along
that they only had a few hours left before they would be killed.
This tormented me. I had stopped crying long ago, but that day
tears choked up my throat again and again — and the day was
very long.

On the way from the warehouses to the platform, I bumped
into *Unterscharführer* Steubel, who tended to like me and called

me Franz for some reason (there were certain Germans who would take a liking to a boy in our midst, and whom they treated better; Germans like that would beat their friend's "boy," and the friend would beat their "boy"). Steubel looked at me and said, "Franz, the cap you chose doesn't suit you. Come with me!" He took me to the warehouses, searched through the thousands of caps in the pile, tried dozens of hats on my head until he found a beautiful new cap, light brown, and fussed with it until it sat on my head just right. "Now you look nice," he said, "That's the cap you will wear!"

This same Steubel put a cup on my head one day when I was sitting at work, sorting objects, and told me not to move and not to be afraid and nothing bad would happen to me. He took a rifle from the hands of one of the Ukrainian guards, moved back a little, aimed the rifle at me and fired. The cup fell from my head. Afterward Steubel suggested to another German that he do the same, but the other one said he'd hit my head for sure.

Toward evening, the boxcars had been filled with the possessions of the Jews who had been killed. We returned to our barracks. From the direction of *Lazarett* we heard long bursts from the machine guns, then single shots, and then a complete silence fell over the camp. The faces of the Jews from that transport were etched deep into my memory.

From the news we gathered from outside, a grim picture was developing. Again and again we heard the term *Judenrein* (free of Jews); the Germans meticulously executed the Jews in region after region, and those regions emptied of Jews were declared *Judenrein*. The people who joined our group from later transports told of Jews who fled from place to place, but to no avail, as they were pursued not only by the Germans but by Poles and Ukrainians, as well. We heard stories of Jews who had fled from the ghettoes, eluded the Germans, jumped from moving boxcars, wandered forests and hid in secret places — only to be killed by Polish murderers, or caught by the Germans after Poles or Ukrainians informed on them, or, having no other alternative, returned to areas where there were still

Jews and from there were taken in transports to Sobibor, knowing for certain that they were going to the gas chambers.

But there were also other stories — of Jews living in the forests, where they joined partisan units and fought the Germans, and these awakened in us a desire to rebel, to try to escape into the forests, not to wait until we were killed. With the passing of time we felt more and more like a cohesive group, each of us could depend on the other, and that we could accomplish something together. This strong desire for action triggered more and more daydreams; in my imagination I already saw us fleeing from the camp into the forest, joining the partisans, and there meeting my brother Mottel, who had been with them for some time. Again and again, I would sink into sweet dreams of this kind, which were, of course, senseless and impossible. There wasn't a single person among us with the ability to organize a rebellion or mass escape; it was very possible that none of us knew how to kill another man, even if he were a German. Most of us were youths, and few of us had any adult skills. Over time, the camp had become a veritable fortress. It was surrounded by three barbed wire fences: between the first and second fence patrolled Ukrainian guards; between the second and third fences were water trenches; marksmen in guard towers stood on the other side of the third fence; and a mine strip encircled the entire site. In this situation, we had no chance of escaping, like the two who had succeeded. In order to escape we had to initiate and plan a rebellion.

The strong desire to escape coupled with thoughts and whispers produced an idea. One of the boys, who worked in the warehouses of *Lager* 2, came up with an escape plan: During the day, the youth would prepare two tins of benzene, and he himself would steal into *Lager* 2 after the evening parade, after dark, which was feasible, as guarding inside the camp wasn't meticulous, and set fire to the warehouses at midnight. During the bedlam that would ensue, when the Germans were busy putting out the fire, we would break through the gate and the fences and try to flee.

The plan didn't cover every eventuality, nor was there a solution for every problem that might arise during its operation. How would the Germans react? What were the chances of us remaining alive? The one thing that was clear to us was that that night everyone's fate would be determined — whoever was lucky would escape, and the rest would be killed immediately, but at least not in the gas chambers, and the camp would go up in flames.

The idea excited us. We agreed to do it without questioning the plan too closely. In addition, the personal example of the boy, who was willing to take the risk despite the slim chances he had of staying alive, gave us courage.

Things happened quickly. The boy prepared the tins of benzene. After the evening parade everyone was alert. I dug up a bag of gold rings that I had buried previously, "just in case." Tension was high. The Kapos, led by Moshe "Governor General," sat together with us in the barracks as equals, and the boy was already preparing to sneak out of the barracks and into *Lager* 2. All at once, two prisoners burst in and threatened that if we didn't cancel the plan, they would turn us in to the Germans. We tried to convince them that in any case, we were as good as dead, that we had no chance of surviving, but the two insisted that our plan was nothing but madness, "and if we have a little more time to live, why do you want to kill us today?" All efforts to persuade them were futile. The operation was canceled. Our only benefit from the scheme of the escape and its planning were the lessons we learned for things to come.

During the hot summer days an epidemic struck the camp. People fell ill one after the other; they burned with high fever, became very weak, and were unable to eat a thing. It was said that this was typhus. The Germans didn't keep sick people around — every worker who became ill was immediately put to death. The sick desperately tried to hide their illness and survived for as long as they could. The healthy tried to help the sick by hiding their situation, usually to no avail, as everyone who fell ill reached the stage where he couldn't work. Every day I saw good friends and acquaintances whose death sentence was written on their pale faces or, alternatively, faces that were as red as fire. There were those who succumbed quickly to their fate, refusing to get up and go out for parade and work. We, the healthy, would coax them to get up, would beg them and even shout at them, as we knew that if they stayed in the barracks, Wagner or Frenzel would come quickly and take them out to *Lazarett*. And then there were those who did not want to give in, who hid their illness as long as they could, who pretended and smiled and with the last of their strength went out for parade and work, if only to stay alive.

One day, out of the blue, I had an attack of general weakness and trembling, pain and a heaviness in my head. The thought that I had been struck with the illness pierced me like a sharp arrow. At home, I was a weak boy and fell sick often, but wonder of wonders, I had not fallen sick even once the entire winter and spring since my escape from the Warsaw ghetto. And here I was, stumbling now.

No, I said to myself — perhaps it's something minor; it will all pass and no one will notice. I didn't say a word to anyone and made an effort to hide the fact that I was sick, but in the evening I felt worse. All that night I burned and shook with fever, and in the morning my body was as limp as a rag — I got up on my feet with difficulty like a drunk. The evening before I had been unable to eat my ration of bread, and this morning I was unable to eat, as well — clearly an abnormal situation. And still, I didn't want to give up. Despite my serious state I believed I would get over it. I reported for parade and imagined that everyone could see my condition in my face. I had the impression that Wagner, who stood before me in parade, had looked at me and within a few seconds I would be removed from the line and taken to *Lazarett*. No, no one noticed me, no one saw.

I went to work. For the previous few days I had been attached to the group that prepared wood for heating for the kitchen and reserves for the winter. I sawed logs with a double-handled saw with another worker; I chopped trees with an ax and sometimes arranged the cut logs in round piles. Now I had to cut trees with an ax, but despite my resolve it was hard for me to stay on my feet, and the ax was heavier than usual and refused to obey me. The Ukrainian who guarded us urged us on now and then, and thus my coworkers discovered I was sick. One of them replaced me, so I could do his easier task — arranging the logs in a pile — but this too became too much for me and, at some point, I couldn't continue any longer. Suddenly I realized the pointlessness of my struggle; suddenly I didn't care what happened to me. I wanted one thing and one thing only — to lie down. I knew that lying down or even sitting and doing nothing meant death — and I didn't care. When I reached the area where the logs were being arranged in bundles, I sat beside the pile. It was so good to sit and lean on it. From within a fog I heard my friends say, "Get up, get up, they'll kill you! Get up, keep working slowly. In a while it will be afternoon…," but I continued to sit as if it wasn't me they meant.

The Ukrainian approached me and yelled, "Get up and work!" Then he stood, looked at me, pushed me with the barrel of his rifle, and said in German, "*Krank!* (Sick!)" pointed to the trigger and continued in Ukrainian, "Soon you'll go to *Lazarett*." Again, I didn't care. Apparently, the Ukrainian was waiting for one of the Germans to come to give permission to take me to *Lazarett*. When the afternoon came and no German arrived, my friends picked me up and supported me all the way back to the barracks.

The rumor that Berale was sick spread quickly. People came to encourage me with their words, gave advice on how to help me, and afterward went to Moshe "Governor General," told him of my situation and asked him for help. Moshe didn't hesitate, saying, "We have to help Berale." He came to me immediately and said, "From now on you are not going out to work — I will go out for you. You will stay and clean the barracks, where you can rest and lie down during the day; two boys will do the work instead of you. Just be careful that the Germans don't catch you." He called the three cleaning boys, instructed one of them to go to work in my place and to the other two he said, "You take care of Berale. Work in his place. And if you see a German coming, warn him."

Moshe "Governor General" was also known in the camp as

Crazy Moshe. No one ever knew what his reaction would be. His moods could change in a flash — sometimes he was cruel and beat people senselessly, after which he would come, beg forgiveness and cry like a little boy; sometimes he cursed God, at others he stood and prayed. One day, when he sat with our group, one of them asked him, "Moshe, tell me, why are you so cruel to us? I mean, you don't think the Germans will let you live. You'll go with all of us to the gas chambers." "What do you think," Moshe answered, "that I'm an idiot? I know my fate will be the same as yours. But with one difference: I'll strike and beat you until the last minute at the entrance to the gas chamber, and then I'll go in. Last."

Moshe did like me, but endangering his own life so I would stay alive was an exceptional act. There was no doubt on that day, that by taking my place at work and having me work in the barracks, Moshe the Kapo had saved me from certain death. Indeed, that was only one of many things that saved me during my illness.

During the difficult days of my infirmity, when I was struggling between life and death, I realized that I mattered to a lot of the people in the camp. Many tried to help me, came to visit me after work, asked how I was, and were happy to see that I was alive. They knew I wasn't able to eat a thing and would bring me any tasty morsel they thought I might swallow. Each evening they made me hot tea, and even secretly made me hot soup; once someone brought me a lemon he had found among the belongings of the people from the transports. But I think what helped me most was the words of encouragement people gave me. They simply would not allow me to give up. I very soon felt like a small child whose whole family was taking care of him. More than once I had the impression that I stood at the heart of a struggle between the people in the camp and the Germans — if I remained alive the camp inmates would score a victory, and if not, the Germans would have the upper hand.

Most of the day, I lay in bed and the two boys did the cleaning chores in the barracks. Every time they saw Germans from afar or heard their voices, they would warn me and I would jump up from my bunk and pretend to work. Occasionally, some of the sick would stay in the barracks and not report for parade. These the Germans would take to *Lazarett* at the end of parade. One day, there were two sick people in the barracks — an older man, an excellent builder, who had been sick for a few days and received permission from Wagner to stay in bed; and a young boy, for whom this was the first time he had not reported for parade. Moshe, the Kapo, had reported that the boy was sick. That day I felt really sick and right after parade, I went to bed. From within a dream I heard the voices of Wagner and Frenzel, but only when I saw their boots stop at my bunk did I understand what was happening. I quietly waited for what was to come.

The two Germans asked the boys where the sick were, and I heard them tell the sick ones to get up and go out. The two walked the length of the entire barracks, and before they went out, Wagner asked the boys, "Are there any more sick?"

"No," answered one boy. "If there are any more sick people here, I'll shoot you," said Wagner before he left. He and Frenzel left the barracks with the two sick men, whom they took to *Lazarett*.

My health grew worse daily. I became very weak. I hallucinated from the fever. People told me that I had muttered strange things, that at night I had tried to leave the barracks, and sometimes my behavior was strange and irregular. Once I didn't go out for parade. After the count, it was discovered that someone was missing. The Kapo who entered the barracks found me, brought me outside and took me to Steubel. Afterward they told me that I had stood before Steubel and laughed, and everyone thought this would be my end. But to everyone's surprise, Steubel laughed too and sent me back to my place in line.

Another time, while I was heating up a cup of water for tea, Wagner came into the barracks and saw the cup of water on the fire, but left — apparently he didn't have time. An hour later he came back and asked, "Who was cooking here during work hours?" I knew there was no point in lying. I stood before Wagner and said,

"I was." His face was flushed with rage. "Pull down your pants!" he yelled, "and lie on the bench!"

I lay on the bench that stood next to the barracks, and I don't know how many lashes I received, but the boys said it was at least fifty. My entire backside was one big open sore. Everything was covered with blood. The boys were sure Wagner had killed me, but when they poured water on me I got up. Although my entire body was in pain, for the first time after long days of illness I felt that I was alive, and I said to them, "I think I feel better…" The boys thought I had gone insane and burst into laughter.

The story about Wagner and me spread through the camp, and after work everyone came to witness the miracle: I had remained alive after Wagner's whipping. Everyone praised me for sticking it out, and for many days afterward, they repeated the joke that "Wagner's whipping made Berale well." And indeed, from that day my condition clearly began to improve — my fever went down, I suddenly had a great appetite. My friends made sure I had food and my recovery was swift. True, it took time for my wounds to heal, until I could sleep on my back. Some time later Moshe took me back out of the barracks and returned me to the work cycle.

The camp was in its last stages of expansion. I worked on the completion of the last portion of the narrow iron tracks for the boxcars that would continue from the barracks through *Lager* 2 to *Lager* 3. The work was supervised by *Oberscharführer* Getzinger, who treated us brutally — he would beat people with a hammer.

One day, a new German appeared. His uniform was black, not green like those of the Germans we had known up to then. He was an officer of the rank of *Untersturmführer*, named Schwartz. We had all become accustomed to the brutality of "our" Germans, and we no longer shook with fear when one of them was in the area. The new German, whom I didn't know, frightened me. My task was to move sections of track from place to place. When I saw the new German, I loaded myself up with as many sections as I could — and ran with them. And then the German stopped me and said, "Boy, are you crazy? Why are you taking so many at one time?" I couldn't believe my ears. I was afraid he was attempting to trick me into failing and I didn't do anything. "Throw some of them down," said the German. I threw one section down, and then the German approached me, and taking some more off my shoulders, said, "You don't have to run — we have enough time."

I walked slowly, a light weight on my shoulders, all the time waiting for the blows to strike me. I couldn't believe that a German could behave like that. But no blows came. On the contrary, during work the German even instructed me to rest and gave me a cigarette.

At the end of work I told my friends about the strange German. *Untersturmführer* Schwartz quickly became a living legend — an abnormal German who didn't beat, who didn't shout, who treated us like human beings. The presence of this man in the camp was a mystery to us. A few weeks later, Schwartz came into our barracks one evening and said he was leaving the camp the next day. He had come to say goodbye; he said that when he arrived at Sobibor he hadn't realized where he had been sent, and added that he wasn't capable of being in a place like this. He shook all our hands and wished us well.

An unusual transport arrived from Maidanek. That day, something had broken down in the gas chambers at Sobibor, and those Jews stayed a full night and day in the camp. Everyone was skeletal, dressed in faded striped garments with numbers printed on them. I had seen skeleton-people close to death in the Warsaw ghetto, but they still had had a bit of humanity left — perhaps their clothing preserved the image of the world of the living in them. The people from Maidanek in their striped clothes looked like walking ghosts. There wasn't a spark of life in them. And they all resembled each other so much it was difficult to tell them apart. The Germans and their Kapos beat them mercilessly, but they didn't scream, only moaned and wailed.

In the evening, when I went with some others to distribute a little food and drink to them, it was almost impossible to do so — these skeleton-people, who lay quietly or moaned, suddenly rose as one man, and with the last of their strength trampled each other to get a little food. After the food was given out, there was again such silence that you couldn't tell that thousands of people were lying there.

The next morning the Germans roused them with shouts and blows, and those who knew they had a bit of strength left dragged the weaker ones to the gas chambers. Some stumbled and fell on the way and then got up and continued walking; others stayed where they lay in the road. After a while, Frenzel came and selected twenty boys, including me, and told us that this transport was filthy and full of lice; we must undress and work naked, and transfer the dead left in the area of the camp to the boxcars, which stood about two hundred meters away, and then clean the area and burn the dead people's clothes and belongings.

Frenzel was in a good mood. He joked and said, "You have nothing to worry about. Nothing will happen to you." We undressed, and Frenzel marched us stark naked to the place where the transport people had spent the night. After one day in the camp, there were hundreds of dead and dying. The day was very hot. We worked at a run. The Germans urged us on with shouts and blows. I cannot describe the feeling of carrying dead bodies on my own naked body. I tried to bear it, but it was impossible to transport them humanely — we dragged them over the ground by their feet.

While I was dragging a body on the run, I stood for a moment to rest in the middle of the road, after I had made sure that there were no Germans near. At that moment, the man I had dragged with the full certainty he was dead, sat up on the ground, looked at me with big, wide-open eyes and asked, "Is it still very far?" It took him great effort to say these words, but they were clear, and when he finished, he sank to the ground.

I was so amazed I didn't know what to do. I had dragged a dead man, and here the dead man had sat up and talked to me — and now he had fallen again as if dead. I couldn't just keep dragging him. After a moment, I recovered, lifted the man, put his arm around my neck, held his waist and carried him, his head leaning on me. I felt every one of his bones. I made slow progress. My legs failed me.

Suddenly I felt lashes on my head and back. I threw the man from me — Frenzel yelled and whipped my naked body. The man tried to get up, and then Frenzel took out his pistol and shot him dead. I grabbed both of the dead man's legs and dragged him to the boxcars.

How much time had passed in Sobibor — two months, three, maybe four? I couldn't measure the time. I had nothing to relate it to. The concept of time also had no importance — not the past, not the future. The only important thing was in the question: When will death come — tomorrow or in another month? It was unbelievable; I had been sure I wouldn't stay alive in this place more than a few days — and here I was, still alive.

During this time a pronounced change was occurring in me. I was no longer Berale the weak and under-confident, the Berale who did not know how to adapt to unusual situations, who received more blows from the Germans than anyone else, the Berale who begged for death as the only solution. I realized that I had held on better than many stronger and wilier than me; I had become stronger than ever, I had developed a remarkable threshold for suffering, and most importantly, I had many friends. All this gave me self-confidence and the desire to live. I knew for a certainty that I could withstand the toughest conditions. Although logic told me that we would all be going to the gas chambers, I developed a strong hope that never left my heart for a moment — that we would succeed in escaping from the camp.

Senior German officers would often come to Sobibor, as well as people in civilian garb. These would arrive in planes that landed in the field between *Lager* 2 and *Lager* 3 and, based on the preparations made for them, one could gauge their importance. The guests always went to *Lager* 3, and sometimes visited the entire camp. During one of these visits, the guests — including senior officers — spent the entire day in the camp, seeing everything. One time there were some brown uniforms, and two civilians accompanied them.

I saw them when they visited *Lager* 2, where I was at work, sorting things. The guests spent a long time there, inspecting everything, and passed from warehouse to warehouse. In the afternoon, they returned and observed the food distribution, even asking some of us if the food was good — the food that day really was good, better than it had ever been, although there was always an improvement in the food on visiting day.

Toward evening, when the visitors had left the camp, I saw the Ukrainians doing punishment exercises for quite a long time. The next day, at morning parade, Wagner took me and another boy named Tsudik out of line and told us that from that day on, the two of us would be cleaners in the Ukrainian barracks. Later I found out that when the guests had toured the Ukrainian barracks they had found it filthy, hence the punishment of the Ukrainians. We had been selected to serve as cleaning staff for them.

At the front of the Ukrainian barracks we were greeted by *Oberscharführer* Graetschus, the head of the Ukrainian guard. He gave us a brief speech, told us that the barracks was dirty and we were to clean it — he would come in the afternoon to inspect our work. He also told us not to make the Ukrainians' beds and not to polish their boots, as this they had to do themselves.

Tsudik and I both stayed there next to the barracks, embarrassed, not knowing where to start. The Ukrainians, however, now exempted from cleaning their barracks, greeted us happily and brought us cleaning tools. We swept the rooms and washed the floors, and then suddenly heard Graetschus, who was standing at the end of the barracks, shout, "Cleaners, come to me!" We ran to him. He took us into one of the rooms and showed us that the floor under the bed had not been washed, and that the windowsills were dusty. He then ordered me to bring his whip from the guardroom. All the way back I tried to figure out how I could avoid a whipping, but when I returned, Tsudik was already lying face down on the table top, and Graetschus immediately began whipping him. While this was happening, I ran to get a pail of water, crawled under the bed and washed the floor. Graetschus whipped and Tsudik screamed and cried — and I continued to lie under the bed. When Graetschus finished whipping, he left the room quickly. Only then did I get out from under the bed, pleased that my fate had been to escape the whip.

After a few days, we learned how to clean the barracks to the Germans' satisfaction — at first, Graetschus and Wagner would come to inspect the results of our work, but in time, they stopped coming almost completely. Aside from cleaning the barracks, we had to make sure there was hot water in the boiler in the wash-rooms all day, and clean the area. Although it was forbidden to serve the Ukrainians personally, we made their beds and shined their boots, as we could not refuse. No doubt, it was one of the best work assignments in the camp — we worked there without the presence of Germans, the work wasn't particularly difficult, and when we had gotten the hang of it, we were even left with free time. The Ukrainians, who were pleased with the service, gave us food and cigarettes. But the most important thing about this job was being away from the execution process. Although the barracks we were working in stood between the platform and *Lager* 2, and from here we could see everything that was happening in the camp, I was not involved in the activities. I was an observer, on the side.

Early one evening, we heard the familiar locomotive whistles announcing the arrival of a transport. The train boxcars stopped next to the platform, as usual, but this time something unusual took place — up to then, no transports had arrived in the evening, and when one arrived at night, the boxcars were left outside the camp and only brought inside in the morning. Furthermore, all of the transports had been carried out with boxcars; this time they were regular passenger cars. It was strange to see lights shining from the cars. The people descended quietly. They were dressed like normal travelers — the men wore nice coats, caps, ties; the women and children were well dressed, too. For a moment, one might have thought that these people had come for a visit.

Frenzel appeared and took the *Bahnhofkommando* with him. The platform area was lit up, as was the road to *Lager* 2. We heard no shouts of "Get out of the cars!" — everything took place quietly and politely. After the people had descended from the cars, the *Bahnhofkommando* gave out bread and jam and hot coffee. The people thanked them graciously. Afterward, the Germans handed out postcards for them to send to their relatives and children — one can assume that these people wrote that they had arrived safely and had been well received. While we stood, wondering where this fancy transport had come from, our hearts wrenching with the bitterness of their fate, Frenzel and Steubel approached and called us to parade quickly, without the count and other preliminaries. Frenzel ordered all of the barbers to step forward, and without waiting to see who would step out of line, he approached one of the boys and said, "You are a barber!" The boy said, "No, I'm not a barber," and then Frenzel shouted, "You are a barber, I said!" and asked, "What are you?" Now the boy replied, "I am a barber!" And so Frenzel continued to select barbers, and it was my fate to be selected as one of them.

Everything happened quickly. Frenzel took us — we were about twenty men, including boys — and led us to the undressing yard in *Lager* 2. The yard was lit up and empty. For a moment I thought Frenzel would order us to undress and we would leave this place naked, like all the others, but he led us through the gate, next to an area with a sign that read "Accounts." We walked between the two fences leading to the gas chambers. A shudder passed through my body as I walked this path toward *Lager* 3.

There was silence all around us. Only the monotonous hum of the generator and the sounds of the crickets could be heard. We didn't know what we were being led to. Finally, we reached three sheds that had recently been built. The first two were lit up and empty. We were put into the third shed, which was connected to the gas chambers by a small corridor. In the shed were two rows of benches, one at each side. Frenzel divided us up and stood us behind the benches. Gomerski entered from the corridor doorway with a box of scissors. Frenzel gave each one of us a pair of scissors and said, "In a little while, women will arrive. They will be naked and you will cut off their hair. We don't have a lot of time. This has to be done very quickly. It should only take seconds. Do you understand?"

We stood behind the benches in shock, the scissors in our hands. We could hear the voices of the women from the shed next to ours. In the first shed they removed their shoes, and in the second one, their clothes. Now they began to enter our shed, unclothed. When they saw us they were embarrassed, covering their bodies with their hands, surprise in their eyes. Frenzel ordered them to sit and said he was sorry, but for hygiene's sake it was necessary to cut their hair.

We began shearing off their hair. Apparently we were too hesitant, gentle and slow, as Gomerski angrily stopped our work and ordered us to watch him — he took a pair of scissors from one of the boys, approached a woman, gathered all her hair in both hands, passed it to one hand, and in a few movements of the scissors, cut off all her hair, telling us, "This is how I want you to work!"

Gomerski and Frenzel urged us on, "Quickly! Quickly!" The scissors sheared off the hair of both young and old, and their appearances changed all at once. Like a conveyor belt, the women entered one after the other from one door and left through the other door, heads bare, into the corridor. The tension in the barracks was so high that I could hear my own breathing. Frenzel tried to break the tension with crude jokes. To one of the young women he said, "Don't be sad. Your hair will grow back quickly, and more beautifully" — and she gave him a simple smile.

The Germans had no patience; perhaps they just wanted to finish and go to sleep. Their rudeness increased. They whipped us and the naked women, the scissors sheared, and the shed filled with piles of hair. From the corridor we could hear the women screaming before they entered the gas chambers.

And then suddenly it was over. Silence. The last of the women left the shed. We gathered the hair in sacks, and our group gathered the clothes and shoes from the first two sheds.

The frightened faces of the women, their eyes full of shame

and surprise, would not leave me. That night, I again begged for death.

The group Frenzel selected that night became the regular group of barbers. My work as a cleaner at the Ukrainian barracks exempted me from this, though, and I was never called to do this work again.

The extermination machine was working at full speed. Transports arrived from Holland, France, Germany, Czechoslovakia and Poland itself. Extermination went smoothly. Each transport was treated in its own special way — there were transports where the people were greeted politely, with bread, jam and coffee, and from the undressing yard we could hear applause after Michel the Preacher's speech before the new arrivals — all so that the work would go swiftly and smoothly. Thousands of people disappeared completely, within a few hours, in wondrous silence. But some-times the Germans and Ukrainians would meet the transport with armed machine guns, the trains would be under heavy guard, the boxcars would be broken, and from the moment of their arrival the Germans would shout, beat and shoot at the crowd.

The Germans tried everything they could to frighten people, to keep them quiet, to prevent rebellion. Mostly they succeeded. People wanted to end their lives as swiftly as possible. By that time, the Jews of Poland knew they were going to die. Still, there were some who resisted, who fell upon the Germans with empty hands, who tried to escape into the camp, but the bullets caught them; some also tried to hide here and there in this hell — and so the Germans would constantly be shooting. More than once it took them some time to succeed in getting all of those condemned to enter the gas chambers.

Ever since I had been delegated to work as a cleaner at the Ukrainian barracks, my emotional state had changed. Before then, I had felt with each transport that I was one of those being brought to die, except that my situation was even worse, as I had been given an extension of suffering before the end. In my new work assign-ment, despite being in the center of Hell — a few meters from the platform — standing in the Ukrainian barracks, I would watch the boxcars entering the camp and the people descending from the cars, I would hear their words, I would see them on their way to *Lager* 2 — but I no longer identified with them, I was no longer someone who was going to die along with them.

Of course, deep inside, I knew all the time that in the end I would die. True, the feeling wasn't linked to the transports — we understood that we, the camp workers, would be put to death by special order. Now I watched one of the transports as an observer. My heart cried for them and not for myself, and as I wasn't under German supervision, I could watch what happened. There were moments when I could no longer stand to look, and then I tried to look and yet not to look at the scenes, not to hear the voices outside. But I always returned to observe the unending tragedy.

One of the transports from Holland brought in the entire staff of a Jewish hospital — doctors, nurses, management and patients. The hospital management organized themselves swiftly. Before the people had even finished descending from the boxcars, the hospital was already functioning. A table was set up in the open area next to the barracks, someone sat at it — apparently the hospital director — and around him stood doctors and nurses in white uniforms, checking lists, giving out medicines, administering shots. The place was converted into a field hospital. Nurses helped patients walk to *Lager* 2 and some were taken on stretchers. The management staff occasionally addressed the Germans — apparently they requested items needed for the sick — and it appeared as though the Germans had succeeded in pulling the wool over their eyes until the last moment. In a short time everything had been moved to *Lager* 2. The area was empty of doctors and patients. Only the unique smell, particular to hospitals, remained for a while in the air.

Once, one of the transports included an institution for the mentally retarded. This was an opportunity for the Germans to amuse themselves and they didn't miss it. From the moment the inmates descended from the cars, the Germans and Ukrainians taunted and beat them. Their reaction was chilling. They ran around crazily and screamed inhumanly — and the Germans laughed aloud.

In one of the transports, I saw a woman of about sixty standing and crying, and the man who stood next to her, probably her husband, said something to Wagner in excitement and rage. Apparently whatever he said was sharp, as Wagner struck the man with his whip and yelled at him, "Cursed Jew!" and then lost his temper, took out his gun and shot the man. The man fell and the woman threw herself upon him.

Wagner, despite his relatively low rank — *Oberscharführer* (Senior Squad Leader) — controlled the entire camp. He would suddenly appear anywhere and we never knew when he would reveal himself or from where. His expression was always severe, and when he smiled it was a bitter one. In the evenings, after we had been locked in our barracks, Wagner would sneak by and eavesdrop on our conversations. He had learned Hebrew in the camp in order to be ready in case Field Marshall Rommel occupied Eretz Israel. His cruelty knew no bounds. When we saw him angry in the morning, we knew that on that day something terrible would happen, and that he wouldn't be calmed before he had killed someone. Our fear of him was so deep that we would occasionally change his nickname. In the beginning we called him "Velvel," and when he would approach us we would let each other know by whispering in Hebrew, "Velvel is walking!" After a short time he came to us and said with a bitter smile, "Velvel is walking!"

Next we changed his nickname to "Vikra." "Vikra's coming, Vikra's coming!" we would whisper to one another when we saw him. And again, after a short time, Wagner came to us and said victoriously, "Vikra's coming!"

Hundreds of people from the transports from Holland, France and Germany were selected for work and lodged in the new barracks. A large group from the women was also selected, all young girls, and put in the side barracks called the women's barracks. During parade the people were divided into work groups called "blocks." Every block group was made up of about eighty people.

The Germans spent many hours training the new workers in parade exercises and German songs. On Sundays, in the afternoon, one could see the groups marching here and there under German, Ukrainian and Kapo supervision, in the area between *Lager* 1 and *Lager* 2. Shouts and orders were given nonstop: *"Links! Links!* (Left! Left!) *Marsch!* (March!) *Links! Links!"* One group sang "The Blue Dragoons," other groups were made to run, and people fell and got up, crawled and jumped, and the orders followed each other closely, *"Hinlegen!* (Lie down!) *Auf, marsch! Marsch! Hinlegen! Auf, marsch! Marsch! Hüpfseil!* (Jump rope!)"

The groups changed places — one group marched and sang and the other did punishment exercises, and afterward everyone marched together, sang, ran and threw themselves on the ground and crawled in unison.

I didn't know how I had looked when I arrived at Sobibor, nor did I pay attention to the appearance of others. I was too occupied with my own concerns. Now I looked at the people in the transports with a more discerning eye. People who arrived a day ago, well-dressed, with fashionable hairstyles, behaving with good manners, changed overnight, unrecognizable in their appearance and behavior, in their struggle to survive.

Here, in Sobibor, every layer of good manners and educated and cultured behavior was peeled off. Even the laws of religion were broken in the camp, although there were some religious people among the arrivals who prayed daily, and even kept kosher. Here, in the camp, everyone was stripped down to the core of his character. Here, new criteria were formed, not by lawmakers, not by the learned and philosophers. We, the little group standing at the edge of the gas chambers, judged each individual by his deeds. Everything was exposed and in the open. Nothing could be hidden. Most people behaved according to our criteria. There were those who showed nobility and self-sacrifice. There were also those who lost all humanity, for whom not a smidgen remained. The workers from Western Europe found it particularly difficult — they had come from regular, comfortable lives, more or less, and had not learned to suffer like the Jews of Poland. It was pitiful to see them struggle to keep going with all the beatings and torture. Many of them were sent to *Lazarett*, and a new wave of suicides broke out among us — all of them newcomers.

Among the arrivals were many artists. A well-known painter arrived from Germany and the Germans exploited his talent — they set up a studio for him and there he would paint their portraits and those of their families. The elderly painter, a severe expression on his face, worked day and night to supply the requirements of his masters.

The Germans selected musicians and established a small orchestra, which would play on Sundays. More than once we were forced to dance to its music. And sometimes, when transports arrived, the orchestra would be called to play, to the wonder of the people in the transport. A cabaret singer — from Holland or France — also arrived at the camp, and she sang in many languages. Sometimes all the Germans would gather, the orchestra would play and the singer would sing. Her voice was pure and deep and she sang plaintive songs, and although I didn't understand their words, they made my tears catch in my throat. This was the first time I had ever heard someone sing in a performance and I was enchanted by her, but it seemed that others were also enchanted, as at the end of each song our applause was joined by the applause of the Germans as well. After a short while, the singer was taken to *Lazarett* and we never heard her voice again. It was said that one of the Germans got too close to her, but the Germans couldn't permit this, so she was killed.

A similar affair involved Paul, the terrible sadist. He took a beautiful young girl as a cleaning woman in his apartment and quickly fell in love with her. We didn't understand what had happened to him — the man changed completely, ceased his beatings, stopped setting Barry upon us, and even gave out cigarettes and talked to us. In our barracks we heard questions like "What's happened to Paul?" and some interpreted this as clear evidence that a change for the good in our general situation had come. After some time, we found out that the reason for the change was that Paul had fallen in love with the Dutch girl — she had influenced him for the better. The response of the Germans was not long in coming. One day, after Paul had driven into town, Wagner came and took the girl to *Lazarett*. Within a few moments, we heard the usual shots. When Paul returned from town he went to his lover's quarters — perhaps he had even brought her a gift — but outside he found a group of SS men and inside was Wagner, who taunted him and asked him, "Paul, where's your beloved?"

From that day on, Paul reverted to being much more of a sadist than he had been before — so much so that he hampered the smooth process of the work — and for entire days he was drunk. The Germans had no choice but to remove him from the camp. Eventually we found out that he had been transferred to Treblinka.

Two new SS men arrived at the camp, *Untersturmführer* Neumann, who was second-in-command of the camp, and *Untersturmführer* Weiss, a tall, thin German, polished from head to toe, whose position was not clear to us — we never saw him deal with transports, nor was he ever in contact with us; he would wander the camp and speak to the Germans, and they treated him with respect.

One Sunday evening we were called to parade. All the Germans were present in the parade ground; it was plain that something was about to happen. After we had performed our regular parade exercises, *Untersturmführer* Weiss got up on the stage and said, "Attention, I want to teach you a song!"

It was strange that a senior SS officer would teach us a song, but he stood and read us the words:

> Oh, return our Moses to us,
> To the people of your faith
> And again the waters will part
> And will stand without moving,
> Steadfast like a craggy bluff.

And through the narrow passage
All the Jews will pass.
Close the passage
And all of the nations will rest.
Jerusalem, hallelujah, amen.

The melody of the words was serious, and sounded like a prayer.
We sang each verse of the song to the accompaniment of different
body movements, like raising our hands, stooping, getting down
on our knees and bowing to the ground. Every verse was practiced
several times, and we worked on it for many hours, until the song
was in complete harmony and the drama was perfect.

After this serious, heavy-melodied song *Untersturmführer*
Weiss taught us a fast, upbeat song:

I am a Jew, you can see by my nose.
It appears crooked on my face
And during times of war it is cautious like a rabbit
And during times of decision it states its condition.
I am from Israel,
I scorn honesty.
One is like two, and I don't eat pork.
I am a Jew and I want to be a Jew.

This song was taught much more quickly. Weiss wasn't pedantic
and didn't insist on every detail — apparently he didn't consider it
as important a work of art as its predecessor. From what was said,
*Untersturmführer* Weiss had composed and written both songs
himself.

My work cleaning the Ukrainian barracks changed my lifestyle,
not only because the more practiced Tsudik and I became at the
work, the more free time we had, but first and foremost because it
freed us from the constant supervision of the Germans. We weren't
actually under anyone's charge now. *Oberscharführer* Graetschus
would come to inspect our cleaning weekly and was satisfied by our

work. Wagner would sometimes come and inspect every corner, but never found a speck of dirt. The Ukrainians treated us well, usually even the cruelest of them, like Taras and Roktsuk (this nickname stuck because he was always shouting at us *Rok-tsuk!* — Quickly!). Roktsuk and Taras carried out most of the killing orders. Roktsuk loved to stab people with a bayonet, and even I felt his stabs now and then. Once I saw him stab to death a baby who was left in the undressing yard.

The Ukrainians' humane treatment of us surprised us. One day, Roktsuk called me to his room and cut a piece of sausage with his bayonet and gave it to me. I didn't understand what he wanted and I thought that in a few seconds he would plunge his bayonet into my stomach. But he only smiled a quick smile, as if to say: You see, I can also be good.

The Ukrainians grew accustomed to us as they did to their dogs. As long as we did what they wanted, they treated us well and sometimes threw us a bone. We also got used to them. The work was fairly comfortable and we couldn't compare it to what was happening a few steps away from us. The two of us, Tsudik and I, were like on a desert island, surrounded by a sea swarming with sharks.

I didn't need a lot of food to satiate my hunger, and so I could give my daily ration of bread and soup to a good friend I had made during my illness, who was like a brother to me. When I was ill, everyone in the camp helped me, but one of them, a quiet, religious boy, older than me by a few years, named Avraham, became particularly devoted to me. Avraham sat next to me and ate with me all the time I was ill. He gave me water to drink, wiped away my perspiration, made me feel I wasn't alone. More than once I asked myself how I could repay him, and now, an opportunity presented itself to me to do something for him. Other than my daily ration I would bring him cigarettes every day. And not just to him, but to all my other friends. I collected the cigarette stubs from the entire area, and sometimes I would find almost whole cigarettes. I begged cigarettes and food from the Ukrainians, and every day, at the end of work, I would come back to the camp laden with goods. If I had been caught, there is no doubt I would have been killed for it, but our lives didn't have much significance anyway, and Tsudik and I smuggled things into the camp every day — dozens would wait for our arrival to enjoy a cigarette or at least the stub of one.

As time passed, my appetite increased. We began to make deals with the Ukrainians — we brought them gold and dollars from the camp and they brought us food and cigarettes from the village, which we would smuggle into the camp. Sometimes I would return from work with my pants full of pieces of meat and cigarettes. On the way, if I met Wagner or Frenzel, I would be positive they saw what I was hiding, and that at a moment my end would come, but every time this happened I passed them safely and, with a sigh of relief, I would tell myself I had to stop this smuggling, but the next day I would do it again.

One Sunday afternoon, I saw pails full of cooked meat standing next to the Ukrainian kitchen. I asked the Ukrainian cook whom they were meant for and he answered that he was sending this food to the pigs. I asked his permission to take two pails and he agreed. After I got them, I considered the risk of walking to the camp with two pails in full view, and I didn't know what to do. This time it wasn't just a piece of sausage, cheese or bread, which I could give out as I pleased — how and to whom could I distribute the contents of the pails? There was hunger in the camp, and every time I brought food, everyone would look at me with hope that they would receive some of the bounty.

I found myself in a complicated situation. I walked with the two pails, barely able to carry them, and after I had passed everyone I went right up to Moshe "Governor General" and gave them to him. I knew that not necessarily the people who deserved to enjoy the food would do so, but I had no choice and I was happy to be free of the pails. I had no idea what was about to happen to me.

During the evening parade, Frenzel suddenly called all the cleaners to step forward. We all stood in a row next to him, and then he asked loudly, "Which one of you brought food from the Ukrainian kitchen?"

"I did," I said, and I felt I was giving myself a death warrant. "Come here!" shouted Frenzel.

I approached him and stood in front of him. Frenzel whipped my head and face a few times and ordered me to turn around and face everyone. Then he turned to everyone and shouted, "I ask you, who is the boss here — me or *der kleiner Hundputz* (the little dog vulva); who gives out food here, me or *der kleiner Hundputz*? And each time he would whip my head, and then burst out laughing and point to me and declare, first with a laugh and then with the utmost seriousness, "Look at him! If this happens one more time I'll shoot you!" He added a few more lashes and sent me back to my place in line.

None of us understood what had happened — how after committing so serious a crime, Frenzel was letting me live. Many said it was a miracle from the heavens, and some claimed I was lucky Frenzel was drunk and didn't act his usual self in these instances.

This was the second time Frenzel had saved me from death. Once, when I was a clothing sorter, Frenzel came and called for ten men. Because I was standing near him, I went and stood in line, but he sent me back to work and took someone else instead. Afterward, we saw the ten men walking toward *Lazarett*. The shots were heard only in the evening, and then we understood why Frenzel had taken these men — when the pit at *Lazarett* was filled with bodies, they would take ten men to cover it and dig a new pit, and the diggers would be the first occupants of the pit, shot to death.

Eventually I found out that the *Bahnhofkommando* had been angry that they had not received any of the food I brought, and their Kapo complained to Frenzel. That evening some of the *Bahnhofkommando* came and apologized to me, saying that they had no part in what had occurred.

None of us believed that we would live this long in the camp, but actually, only a few of the veterans survived — these were the craftsmen and men of position in the camp, like cleaners, assistant cooks, warehousemen, cattle workers and geese workers. Hundreds of other workers were killed daily during the months I spent in the camp and were replaced by others. We all knew our fate was sealed, that we would soon die, that it was just a question of time. The Germans told us that when our work in the camp was finished we would be sent to Germany, to work in factories, but we didn't believe one word.

Tzigayner wrote a song and sang it when we sat together:

How happy are our lives here.
They give us food to eat.
How pleasant it is in the green forest,
The place where they kill all the Jews…

In one of the transports from Holland, a German soldier arrived, wearing civilian clothing, and he was one of the ones selected for work. The man was surprised to find himself in any camp whose nature he knew nothing about. He showed us his personal papers as a soldier in the German army and told us that when he was on leave he had visited his Jewish girlfriend, and when they came to take her family to the East, they had decided to include him. He was angry that the authorities had not permitted him to go with his girlfriend and had thrown him instead into this place, and he demanded a meeting with an officer, to clear up the unfortunate error. In answer to his demand, Wagner came, and the soldier showed him his papers and explained what had happened. Wagner took the soldier with him to *Lazarett* and shot him.

Alongside the knowledge that we were condemned to die and might do so any day, a fierce desire grew in my heart — and, it seems, in the hearts of my companions — to live — a blind faith, with no logic to it, that we would succeed in an attempt to break out of the camp. We were ready to do anything to escape, whatever the risk or chance of success, but we had no idea of how, and none of us had the ability to organize and lead this kind of mission. However, the thought of escape occupied all our conversations. We dreamed of it. We waited and believed that the day would come that something would happen that would render it a real possibility.

One day an unusual activity occurred — the Germans ran around, a troop of Ukrainians rushed to load their weapons and leave the gate of the camp with the Germans — it was obvious that something had happened. Soon, I saw people crawling through the gates of the camp, accompanied by Germans and Ukrainians. At first I didn't know who they were, and, in the meantime, every work group was returned quickly to camp, from every direction. Within a few minutes the cleaners and others who worked for the Germans had also been collected and returned to the camp, and then some of our group told us bits and pieces: men from the *Waldkommando*, working outside the camp, had killed a German or a Ukrainian; some of the *Waldkommando* escaped, and the rest who had been captured were brought back to the camp. Some of the details were unclear and we didn't know what was true in all we heard. In any case, the behavior of the Germans didn't bode well.

Every German we saw was armed with an automatic weapon and grenades tucked in his belt. We agreed among us that if the Germans wanted to kill us, we would resist and attack them — it was better to be killed that way than to go to the gas chambers. Someone said, "If they take us to *Lager* 3, we'll attack the Germans on the way."

A large group of Germans and Ukrainians arrived at our camp and held a parade, which, this time, was tense and meticulous. We were all counted several times, and afterward ordered to walk. We left through our gate and turned toward *Lager* 2, accompanied on both sides by Germans and Ukrainians whose weapons were drawn and aimed at us. We passed *Lager* 2 and found ourselves walking in the direction of *Lager* 3, but not in between the two rows of barbed wire — rather through an open field, next to the narrow railroad tracks. The tension that mounted from minute to minute reached an apex. Ahead of us we saw the roof of the gas chambers. We were going there! No, it was inconceivable that we were all walking in threes, straight to the gas chambers! There was a feeling that, in a second, something terrible would happen, that in a moment horrible screams would erupt from all of our throats and we would attack the Germans and tear them to shreds, that the machine guns would cut us down and the whole area would turn into a river of blood.

Our feet continued to move to the rhythm of *"Links! Links!"* I was dizzy. Abruptly the order was given, *"Halt!"* Frenzel took over and arranged us in groups. We turned toward *Lager* 3. All the Germans, including the camp commander *Hauptsturmführer* Franz Reichleitner and his second-in-command, *Untersturmführer* Neumann, and next to them a platoon of Ukrainians, stood on the side. Everything was set up like a holiday ceremony.

A group of Jews under heavy guard neared us. They all stood in front of us, about thirty meters away. Some of them were from the *Waldkommando*, but most of them were Dutch Jews. Their faces showed fatigue and resignation to their fate. Wagner gave us a brief speech. "Today," he said, "a horrible offense was committed by criminal Jews. They murdered a Ukrainian solder and tried to escape, but didn't succeed. All were killed or captured. Those who stand here will be shot to death as punishment. I warn you — if one of you tries to escape, you will all be punished. You will die!"

A firing squad positioned itself between us and the condemned. Frenzel ordered them to draw their weapons. The shooters aimed their weapons at the men, and when Frenzel ordered, "Fire!" the targets instantly collapsed. Only one tried to get up, as if he wasn't hurt. Frenzel rushed at him and shot a round into him.

The minute or two of silence that followed seemed like an hour. The sounds of the shots still reverberated in our ears. The bodies were strewn in front of us, unmoving, as if they had never had life in them.

Wagner called to Moshe "Governor General" and handed the command over to him. He ordered, *"Stillstand!* (Stand still!) *Rechts um!* (Right face!) *Marsch! Links, Links!"* and led us back to camp.

We found out the details of the event only the next day, from the Ukrainians who had been there. The *Waldkommando*, which was about thirty men, went out that day as usual, to work in the forest about five kilometers from the camp, accompanied by a German and three Ukrainians. In the early afternoon two Jews went out, accompanied by one of the Ukrainians, to bring water from the well that was about one kilometer from the work site. When they reached the well, the two Jews killed the Ukrainian with knives they had prepared earlier, threw the body into the well to make it difficult to find, and fled.

At the work site they waited for the three until it was finally understood that something had happened. The German sent a Ukrainian to investigate, and he hastily returned, saying he had found the Ukrainian dead in the well. The German hurriedly collected the workers and returned them to camp. Some of the Jews realized what had happened, or perhaps even knew about the pair's plan, and on the way back, fled into the forest in every direction. The German and the two Ukrainians couldn't control everyone; some were killed but others succeeded in escaping. A second group of Jews didn't try to escape — these were Dutch Jews, new workers in the camp. They didn't understand the situation, and they didn't have anywhere to run to — they were unfamiliar with their surroundings and the regional language. These were the Jews who were shot in the field, in front of us.

For a few days we all argued around the question of whether the two Jews had been right to escape. Opinions were divided. In the time we had spent together in the camp, a feeling of comradeship and responsibility for each other had united us. It was on this foundation we nurtured our heart's desire: our fate would be one — whatever would happen would happen, but to all of us together. Yet it seemed that deep inside, we justified the pair that had left the group and fled — whoever could, should save himself! One way or another, we were all already dead. The killing of the Ukrainian and the escape of the two *Waldkommando* Jews reignited our passion to rebel and try to escape. Now we knew that just as Jews were killed, Ukrainians and Germans could also be killed; it was possible that we could succeed.

The women's barracks stood at the corner of our compound, near the shoemakers' workshop. The women's block was out of

bounds to the men, and a visit to their block was strictly forbidden. Still, bonds were formed, and men came and went from the
women's block. There were superficial boy-girl bonds, momentary,
the fruit of the longing of youth to taste love before the end. Under
ordinary circumstances, suitors would try to win girls' hearts with
expensive gifts. Under camp conditions the same principle applied,
except that here a valuable gift could only be food, so those men
who could bring food had the possibility of enjoying friendship
with the girls.

One of the girls tried to initiate a relationship with me, and
I didn't understand why this girl was suddenly so friendly with
me. Only later, Tsudik told me that he "had a woman" and that he
brought her food every day that he purchased from the Ukrainians.
He had told his girlfriend's friend that she should form an attachment with me so she would have something to eat. I was unaware
of this obligation in courtship, and it also didn't seem to me the
appropriate time to have a relationship with a girl; I felt that there
was something ugly about it.

However, there were also real attachments in our camp, which
developed into stormy love affairs. Love is something that adapts
itself to every situation. One of us, a young man from France who
was nicknamed *Der Französischer* (the Frenchman), and who,
even under camp conditions, looked elegant, stood out as a good-
natured person and quickly formed a relationship with a singer. The
two were known to be lovers. One day, at evening parade, Wagner
called *Der Französischer* to step out of line, and the two exchanged
angry words. At the end of the parade, Wagner commanded *Der
Französischer* to come with him, and it was obvious to all that he
was being taken away to be killed. Suddenly the singer burst onto
the scene, ran straight to Wagner and said, "If you take him away,
I want to go with him!" Wagner took them both to *Lazarett*. They
died together in love.

Once, a couple was caught while alone together. Frenzel made
fun of them during parade and said, "They did a forbidden thing.
They should have married first," and issued to them punishment

of twenty-five lashes. The two were laid across benches, their lower bodies stripped. Two Kapos whipped them and their screams blended into one.

Tsudik and I continued to smuggle food into the camp. We had an unspoken agreement — each of us would act for himself, without involving the other, so as not to endanger the other if one was caught. Although we worked together and got along very well, we didn't have a deep friendship. We had nothing in common, and when we returned from work we had almost no contact with each other. Tsudik's father was in the camp, and this was another one of the reasons we did not become close.

Tsudik changed a great deal when he began a relationship with a girl — he was filled with happiness, and one could see that she occupied all his thoughts. He increased his business with the Ukrainians and smuggled large quantities of food into the camp.

His father came to me to ask me to persuade Tsudik not to smuggle so much; he was afraid Tsudik would get caught. I did as his father asked and tried to talk Tsudik out of it, but to no avail. One day, at parade, Wagner called for all cleaners to step out of line. Then he passed among us, stopped next to Tsudik and asked, "Are you Tsudik?" When Tsudik said yes, Wagner told all the other cleaners to step back into line. Tsudik's father understood what was about to happen, and he stepped out of line as well, stood in front of Wagner and tried to speak, asking him to forgive his son just once. When his request wasn't granted, he asked to go with his son. And indeed, at the end of parade Wagner took both of them and shot them. We all knew that someone had informed on Tsudik, but we didn't know who. It was said that one of the girls, who was jealous of all the food her girlfriend received, informed on her to Wagner, but it was never proven.

The next morning, when Wagner ordered "Cleaners out of line!" I stepped out alone and waited for someone to be sent to stand with me in Tsudik's place, but Wagner said to me, "You won't have anyone else. You'll have to get by alone. You live too well."

One day a large crane, with two unusual shovels, was brought into the camp. The crane stood beside *Lager* 2 for a few days, where Getzinger worked on it for a long time, and then it was brought to *Lager* 3. After some time the air around us was filled with the terrible smell of rotting, burning flesh, and thick black smoke wafted over to us from *Lager* 3, covering the sky. I was reminded of my father's burial at the cemetery in the small town of Prushkov.

As it turned out, the camp command had received instructions to exhume the remains that had been buried in the great pit, to burn them, grind the bones, and scatter the ashes in the fields as fertilizer — lest any sign of them remain. From that day on, for weeks and months, the fire did not cease and the smoke continued day and night. When the weather was pleasant, the column of smoke would rise straight up into the sky, and I could see in the columns shadows of adults and children rising to the heavens in an unending chain. There were days when the wind brought the smoke and the terrible odor in waves, and the souls passed through you, touched you, sometimes gently, sometimes roughly, and continued to soar upward, onward. And there were days when everything stood still, nothing moved, and the smoke, while rising upward, slanted down in return and settled slowly over the entire camp until there was no relief from it. This stinking smoke penetrated every corner of the barracks, filled eyes, noses, mouths, every crease in the body, and you felt as if you were wrapped in the smoke of people who had been executed, that inside this smoke you were together with the dead, that you were one of them, and in a little while, you would rise together with them into the heavens.[1]

The burning of the bodies gave us something to think about: Why had the Germans suddenly decided to exhume the gassed bodies from the pit and burn them? There was no doubt that it was in order to erase all signs of mass murder, but it was also possible that the Germans intended to stop the extermination and disassemble the camp, and that for this purpose they had begun to destroy

---

1. Sobibor did not have closed ovens. The Germans burned the bodies on a platform built with alternate layers of logs and bodies.

the evidence. If so, this meant our end was very near, and therefore, we must plan an escape as quickly as possible. In the evenings, in the corners of the camp compound, lying on our bunks in the barracks, we discussed escape again and again. Moshe "Governor General" was also deeply involved in these discussions.

One evening, after everyone had returned from work, a group of Germans armed with automatic weapons entered the camp, led by Wagner. An elderly Jew, a resident of Berlin nicknamed *Der Berliner*, went out to greet them. This man, whom the Germans treated like one of their own, walked together with them now. Frenzel and Steubel marched right into the Kapo room and brought out Moshe "Governor General" and another Kapo. Both men's faces were white as sheets. Moshe was without his starred cap and gold-buttoned coat. *Der Berliner* pointed at various men — all friends of Moshe — and all of them, eight in number, were immediately taken to *Lazarett* and shot.

Again, complete despair settled upon us, and not necessarily because Moshe, the crazy Kapo, would not be the last to enter the gas chambers, as he had imagined, and not because of all the others who had died. Death was a daily occurrence among us and we had already gotten used to it, even gotten used to our great jealousy of the dead, whose suffering had ceased forever, while we, what was in store for us? No, the terrible despair tormented us because yet again we had discovered informers among us — each time, the Germans found someone to tell them everything that was happening among us.

Indeed, it was said that *Der Berliner* was strange and not completely sane — he would say that although he had been born a Jew, he was German and didn't identify with Judaism, and he would certainly return to Berlin and have his honor reinstated. Now, in any case, in return for information and subservience to the Germans, this man was crowned "Governor General," was sewn a special suit and cap, and he, loyal to the Germans like a devoted dog, was mercilessly cruel to us. *Der Berliner* sowed fear throughout the camp. He knew no shame. When he noticed a group of people sitting together, even in the evening in the barracks, he would approach and listen, and ask what was being discussed. Even in the middle of the night he would move among the bunks and check to see that everyone was asleep. He made our lives bitter in the few moments when the Germans left us alone.

*Der Berliner* was so sure of his authority that he permitted himself to break one of Frenzel's orders. Frenzel instructed that the *Bahnhofkommando* be given an extra portion of food one day, whereas *Der Berliner*, thinking they didn't deserve it, ordered the cook not to give it to them. The *Bahnhofkommando* complained to Frenzel, who became enraged and told them to do whatever they wanted to *Der Berliner*. The rumor that a lynch-trial would soon be held for *Der Berliner* spread quickly throughout the camp, the barracks filled with people, and the *Bahnhofkommando* settled themselves outside the Kapo's door. When *Der Berliner* came out of his room, people started insulting him. He was stunned. Apparently feeling that he was entering a trap, he suddenly filled with rage, shouted "Bastards!" and raised his whip to strike aggressively. One of the men grabbed the whip out of his hand, and everyone began to throw the man from one to the other until he had been stripped naked; he was laid on the bench, and he was beaten with fist or foot, with whip or broomstick. The victim's screams grew weaker until they disappeared. *Der Berliner* was dead.

Life in the camp was isolated from the outside world not just physically but mentally as well. The past seemed so far away that sometimes it was as if it had never existed, and in any case, I didn't think about it. For a long while I had ceased to miss my home, my childhood, and anything else that belonged to my past. The memory of my beloved family would pop into my head only for milliseconds. Everything was obliterated, as if it had never been. But then there would be horrible days, days when waves of longing and memories awoke in me and didn't leave me for a moment. It was as if I had discovered something I had lost long ago. I found myself thinking of my family constantly, and I asked myself over and over: are any of them still alive? Everyone certainly thought that I was dead.

The image of our home at Rosh Hashanah and Yom Kippur appeared to me clearly, awakening thoughts about religion. My friend Avraham said that the fact we were still alive was a miracle from heaven, but I rejected this view. I had stopped believing that God ruled the universe. And yet I decided to fast on Yom Kippur, so as not to distress to my family, which was religious. On Rosh Hashanah some prayed a bit before going out to work, and after work as well, and even blew the shofar while another group sang in order to mask the sound. On Yom Kippur almost everyone fasted, and prayed whenever they could.

One day several hundred girls from Trevniki camp were brought to our camp. The Germans put them in the three barracks at the entrance to the gas chambers, and our people brought them food and water every day. The girls did nothing, and we wondered why the Germans kept them alive. At that time, there was a special cleanup action — every corner in the camp was cleaned and polished. A German came occasionally to the Ukrainian barracks to make sure that everything was clean and neat, and I worked hard to satisfy the crazy whims of the Germans. One day all of the work groups were returned to the camps and locked inside their barracks. Afterward *Oberscharführer* Graetschus called me and ordered me to sweep outside, in an area that wasn't part of my responsibility. At the same time a locomotive whistle was heard and a train with three boxcars entered the camp. Graetschus banished me to the barracks, and after a few moments I saw a large group of German officers marching toward *Lager* 2. I could see the short Himmler in their midst. The group stopped, and Himmler peed into a field. Everyone stood and waited for him, then he uttered something, everyone laughed, and they continued on their way to *Lager* 3. After quite a while, the entourage returned from *Lager* 3. The guests, who did not visit any other place, boarded the train and left the camp.

After Himmler's visit, we no longer brought food to the girls in the barracks. They were no longer alive. The girls had been kept in the camp for two weeks to be on hand to demonstrate to Himmler and his men the extermination procedure.

Despite our utter isolation from the world outside, pieces of information about what was happening began to reach us bit by bit from various sources, and they were like flashes of light in the dark to us. It was said that the advance of the German army had been stopped at the gates of Moscow and Stalingrad; that the Germans were suffering heavy losses; that trains full of wounded Germans were flowing nonstop from east to west, to Germany; that on the western front, as well, the Germans were being checked at the English Channel and were unable to cross it; that in Africa, General Rommel had been defeated by the English — apparently the days of German success on all fronts were over! And we also found out that the Allied forces were bombing German cities day and night, turning them into heaps of rubble — an SS man from our camp returned to Germany after his entire family had been killed in one of these bombings. Everyone was most interested when he came back and spilled his guts to the Jews — he sat with his work group, handed out cigarettes and told of the disaster that had happened to him, crying like a small child. The man changed overnight following his trip back to Germany — and he was quickly transferred out of the camp.

We also heard news of partisans roaming the forests, bombing trains carrying German passengers, shooting at German cars. And we noticed that the vehicles leaving the camp to bring supplies were traveling with soldier escorts bearing machine guns. When two Ukrainians from the SS left the camp on vacation and didn't return, some said that they had deserted to the partisans, while others said that the partisans had kidnapped them. Either way, this incident took a toll on the self-confidence of both the Germans and the Ukrainians.

One night, at midnight, we were awakened and quickly taken out to the parade ground. They didn't even allow us to get dressed, and we stood and shivered from the cold. A large group of armed

Germans and Ukrainians surrounded us and counted us several times. We had no idea what was happening, but from the east, from the edge of the forest next to *Lazarett*, the shots of rifles and machine guns echoed. The Germans had positioned heavy mobile artillery at the edge of the compound, and it was aimed at us. It was plain that any moment the order to fire might come and we would be decimated within minutes. Under cover of darkness we circulated an order to get ready to attack the Germans; but in the meantime, we stood shivering. This situation lasted for several hours, until the shooting at the edge of the forest stopped and we were allowed to return to our barracks. Afterward, it was said that partisans had attacked the camp. We didn't know if this information was accurate, but there was enough truth to it to raise a new hope in our hearts: partisans would overtake the camp and release us. Other news that came through reinforced our desire to do something, but we also heard from people arriving in transports that there was no more Jewish presence in the forests, that entire areas had been decreed *Judenrein*, that the Jews had nowhere else to run — local residents, Poles and even Ukrainians, were driving them out and turning them in to the Germans.

Now the transports that arrived at Sobibor were accompanied by many guards deployed along the roofs of the boxcars, and the boxcars themselves were broken; in some of them, which were half empty, lay the dead or wounded, or others who asked to be left to die. The obvious conclusion was there was nowhere to run. It was evident that even if we did manage to escape, our hopes of remaining alive were nil.

Despite this, the intensity of our desire to rebel didn't diminish. Indeed, none of us who dreamed of escape thought we could make it out alive — it was beyond all imagination — but we were seized by the passion to put an end to our captivity in the camp. There was no point to this kind of life, whose end was certain, and we didn't want to wait until the Germans decided to exterminate us. Yet perhaps — one occasionally thought — perhaps, even so, one of the escapees would succeed in surviving?

A strange building was erected next to our barracks: at one end, close to us, there was a room that joined onto the long, rectangular, sloping building. This was a bowling alley, meant to provide entertainment for the Germans during the long winter evenings. It was beyond my understanding why this bowling alley was built in our camp, next to our barracks, and not in the German area. It was possible that in this way the Germans could keep a close eye on us during the long winter evenings to prevent the likelihood of rebellion or escape.

One evening, a large group of Germans came to the entrance of the bowling alley. Somehow Graetschus hunted me down, and he ordered me to accompany him to the building. The Germans brought food and plenty of beer with them and had already been drinking before they entered the new structure. Graetschus explained to me that I was to stand at the end of the lane, where there was a platform marked with circles; I was to set up the wooden bowling pins and return the balls that reached me. I spent all that evening with the Germans, who talked and laughed and mostly drank excessive amounts of beer. Now and then, one of the Germans would give me something to eat and a beer. The drink was bitter and after one bottle my head swam. When the Germans left I had to clean the place. I finally went back to the barracks, my pockets full of cigarette and cigar stubs, and within moments our barracks was filled with smoke.

The presence of a group of Germans every night, next to our barracks, all engrossed in the game, led us to entertain certain thoughts in particular. I was not the only one who was sent to work in the evenings in the bowling alley; there were other young men who worked there, and yet others who interrogated me, asking what was happening there — how many Germans were there altogether, where their weapons were while they played, and other questions along that line.

At first glance, an action against the Germans seemed very simple: A group of SS officers are involved in a game, some of them drunk, their weapons laid to the side; a sudden burst into the room would enable us to kill those present before they could grab their weapons. Afterward, with the help of the automatic weapons that would fall into our hands, we could break through the gates of the camp and escape into the darkness. However, things were not that simple. Obstacles popped up everywhere. Apparently, the Germans had also considered this special situation, because they had assigned a Ukrainian guard to stand at the door. It therefore would be necessary to quietly dispose of the Ukrainian before we burst in. It seemed that at least one German had thought of every-thing and left no room for danger — during the game, Wagner could be seen leaving the bowling alley, walking among the bar-racks, watching and listening — and of all people, he was the one who could sniff anything out.

Moreover, and perhaps most importantly, a takeover attempt, a break-in and an escape like this required a leader who could organize people and dish out discipline, and we had no one like that. We were hard-pressed to find people who knew how to use weapons and could kill someone. We, the young, were willing to do all this if only someone would tell us what and how. In the meantime, all kinds of ideas like these only flew around in our heads; the ability to act on them was far from possible.

One day, after morning parade, when we should have gone out to work, we were returned to our barracks and locked in, with heavy guards around us. Some time later we heard a fusillade of shots coming every few minutes from the direction of *Lager* 3. No transport arrived that day, and we believed that they were killing the work force of *Lager* 3. The next day we found out that some men from *Lager* 3 had planned an escape — they had been digging a tunnel for many months and had already reached the passage to the camp fence. The Germans discovered it by chance — and killed everyone.

Our helplessness to do anything drove us to seek out other avenues of escape. In light of the defection of the two Ukrainians, it was possible to assume that there were other Ukrainians consider-ing the idea of fleeing, and these we searched out. Over time, some of the Jews had forged bonds with some of the Ukrainians on a reciprocal basis — the Jews gave the Ukrainians gold and money, which they found in abundance, and received food in return. Solid bonds also formed between the Ukrainian cooks and their Jewish assistants.

At this time, there was among us a Jew, nicknamed *Der Kapitan*, whose friends said had once been the captain of a large vessel. This man, about forty years old, with a strong, muscular body, stood out among us from the first day of his arrival at the camp, and perhaps because of this, during his first few days, he absorbed murderous blows from Wagner and was bruised all over his body. However, *Der Kapitan* had a great ability to absorb beatings — he was a man who did not give in easily. Even from his initial days in the camp, when he was accustoming himself to what was happening and gaining the trust of others, he began looking for a way to escape. As a leader of the Dutch among us, he swiftly formed bonds with the veterans, asked questions, demanded information and learned about the camp and its surroundings. He undoubtedly was a man who knew what he was facing.

When *Der Kapitan* was told of the Ukrainians who had escaped and learned of others who apparently intended to flee, he made contact with them through our people who worked in the Ukrainian kitchen. One day, there were many more Germans than usual in the afternoon parade — a sign of some event — and indeed Wagner ordered *Der Kapitan* to step out of line. He told him he knew that *Der Kapitan* was the ringleader of a plan to escape from the camp and demanded that he give away the names of his accomplices on the spot. *Der Kapitan* answered that he alone wanted to escape from the camp and knew of no one else who wished to do so.

Wagner was seething with rage. *Der Kapitan* was whipped all over his body, and Wagner again asked him who were his accomplices in the planned escape. *Der Kapitan* remained silent, and then they laid him on the bench, stripped him naked and two Germans whipped him alternately. He didn't give in. It was difficult seeing him beaten and tortured, but at the same time, we were proud of his remaining resolute and stubborn. The contest of wills between Wagner and his men and *Der Kapitan* went on for a long time, and all the while, we all stood tense, waiting to see who would finally prevail — it was obvious to every one of us that his fate depended on the results of the confrontation. Many of us were involved in gathering information for the purpose of escaping, and who knew who else would be called to step forward and be shot soon?

When Wagner realized it was no use beating *Der Kapitan*, he made one last attempt to break him and said, "If you don't give up the names of your accomplices, we will cut off the heads of all the people in your block — and yours will be cut off last!" (There were about seventy men in Block 6, all of them Dutch Jews, some of them from the same transport as *Der Kapitan*, and friends of his.) *Der Kapitan* did not waiver. Wagner ordered Block 6 to step forward, and we watched all of the men from Block 6, with *Der Kapitan*, march toward death, accompanied by a group of armed Germans. Afterward, we found out that Wagner had stood by his word: all of those men were beheaded in *Lager* 3.[1]

Although we were used to death and lived in its presence daily, the executions of *Der Kapitan* and his friends left us in great despair. We lost all hope of our ability to escape from the camp, feeling beaten by the Germans' success in so quickly having discovered our intentions and nipping our plan in the bud, as proven by their lethal reaction. In this general despair, the idea came up to perform mass suicide that very evening by taking a large quantity of poisons from the medicinal warehouse and putting them in the ersatz coffee served to us. But if we could pull this off — said one of us — why not try to poison the Germans and Ukrainians? The idea itself was both logical and attractive, but it stayed in the realm of ideas.

Our attempt at mass escape had failed, but the fact remained that all escape attempts by single individuals or small groups had

---

1. After the war, an SS man by the name of Novak was caught, and a search of his home revealed photographs of the beheadings in *Lager* 3.

succeeded. I began to think of a way to escape by myself or with someone else; however, after weighing the matter, I came to the conclusion that there was no point in escaping alone — even if I were able to get out of the camp, I wouldn't last long outside. I was unfamiliar with my surroundings and knew no one outside; and my typically Jewish looks would give me away. I must find a partner, one who knew the surroundings, and then — perhaps thanks to the gold I had collected and hidden — someone would be willing to hide us.

I discussed the matter with my friend Avraham, but he wasn't inclined to attempt an individual escape and had resigned himself to his fate, which was the fate of all the others. But I did not resign myself. I planned. I accumulated a large quantity of gold coins, packed them in bags, and buried them in the ground at various points in the camp, so that when the time came, I could take at least one of them. I learned the order of the Ukrainian shifts, and by watching the formation going out to guard, I learned that before they went out, Graetschus and Roktsuk allocated bullets to the guards, and this ammunition was returned to its place at the end of the shift. I checked the entire yard strip, I memorized what occurred at the gate, and by watching carefully, I came to the conclusion that a certain section of the fence — near the Ukrainian barracks, along the railway tracks — was not mined, as I saw people walking alongside the fence several times. This spot was far from our own barracks, and for some reason the Germans didn't think it necessary to mine it.

I watched the Ukrainians as they loaded and disassembled their rifles, and noted to myself with surprise that the Ukrainian rifles were left in place in the barracks rooms, unattended; more than once I found myself alone in their barracks and was struck by a desire to pick up a rifle. I knew that if anyone saw me, it would be the end, but my desire was very strong. One day I approached the rifles and, in the beginning, only touched the cold barrel of one of them. Then, slowly, my heart palpitating, I picked up the rifle and tried to cock it like the Ukrainians did — I moved the bolt, and then returned it to its place quickly and put the rifle down again. To the Ukrainians, this rifle was probably light; to me it was very heavy, but I was pleased with myself and even imagined that I had already learned all about rifles. In any case, from that day on I began to watch for the opportunity to practice with a rifle, and I continued to watch the Ukrainians when they used their weapons, convinced that I could also fire when necessary.

Time passed. The failures of the past were somewhat forgotten — and again new ideas of rebellion arose, ideas that couldn't help but come into our minds, if only to sustain our desire to keep on living, and they were fortified by the situation on the war front. The rumors that stole their way to us told of German defeats in Russia, and we, who didn't dare to verbally express hope of surviving — it just seemed too unrealistic — dreamed of seeing the Germans defeated and dying.

During my contemplations on escape, I had an idea for a rebellion, which crystallized and took on a more and more detailed shape. My enthusiasm for this plan grew from day to day, but as I had learned caution from past experience, I kept it a secret. According to my plan, the rebellion would take place on a Sunday afternoon, when the camp was at rest; on that day the Germans rested, and some of the Germans and Ukrainians vacationed away from the camp. One of my work duties on Sunday afternoons was to stoke the hot water boiler, and the Kapo would send me two boys to carry pails of hot water to the camp, and when they returned, he would send another two boys.

My plan, when the first two boys came to collect the pails of water, was to dress them in the black uniforms of the Ukrainians and give them rifles and as many bullets as I could get hold of. When the two returned to the camp they wouldn't arouse attention, and this would give them the opportunity to quietly kill the Ukrainian guard at the gate of the camp. And then another two boys would come to collect water, and they would also put on uniforms and take weapons, enter the guardroom, surprise the guard on shift, and kill him. In this way we would not only acquire more ammunition but could also control the ammunition warehouse, which was nearby. When we had a group of armed "Ukrainians" and we controlled the path, we would break out toward the gate and the German barracks. My plan was based in principle on the element of surprise — in the confusion, the Ukrainians wouldn't fire on other "Ukrainians" for a while and, with the element of surprise, we could also kill some of the Germans, and by the time the rest of them became organized, many of us would have succeeded in escaping the camp.

I was convinced that my plan was a good one, but I was still afraid to tell anyone — I was afraid someone would inform on me, as who was I anyway, to propose a plan for rebellion? Therefore, at first I only revealed my plan to my friend Avraham, hoping for some kind of positive reaction — he certainly wouldn't make fun of me. And indeed, he liked the plan — he was even eager to hear all the details — but also warned me that if I weren't careful, my fate would be the same as those who tried the mass escape. After my conversation with Avraham, I approached Leibl Feldhendler, a man everyone liked, and who, as far as I knew, had already been involved in early escape attempts, and I laid my plan before him.

Leibl listened to me seriously, without interruption, and when I had finished, he said, "Very good, Berale, an excellent plan, I wouldn't have believed that you could plan this. Truly, a good plan..." He then became lost in thought and finally said, "Now I have to tell you something very sad. There is no one to carry out this plan, or any other plan. Although we all wish to escape, although no one here would mind dying during a rebellion rather than being sent to the gas chambers or being shot at *Lazarett*, we don't have people among us who have the experience. Furthermore, we don't have a leader who could organize an action like this and command authority over all of us. And yet," he added, "I believe the day will come when we will succeed in taking revenge on the Germans and escaping from here, and then perhaps we could use your plan."

Leibl also warned me to be careful, and not to reveal my plan to anyone. I had no choice but to quit thinking of escape.

One day, when I was bringing empty bottles to the junkyard and setting them up along the wall, a bottle suddenly shattered on the wall above my head and fragments of glass fell on me. Wagner had thrown it at me, but missed. Wagner approached me swiftly, kicked me with all his strength and shouted, "You are not doing anything!" He grabbed a rake and hit my head with the handle until I was streaming blood. The rake handle broke from the strength of his blows, but he continued to kick me. When he left, I ran to the showers in the Ukrainian barracks. It had been a long time since I had received any beatings, since I had begun working with the Ukrainians. Wagner did his usual thorough job, as if to remind me of where I was. His face had shown his loathing of me; I was only a step away from extermination. The affair ended quietly, but again my whole body hurt and I could neither sit nor lie down.

However, something pleasant also happened about that same time. One morning we heard explosions. At first we didn't permit ourselves to speak, as more than once a mine had exploded when a dog or other animal that had gotten into the minefield stepped on it. In each case, the Germans would rush to the scene of the explosion to see what had happened, only this time many more ran. It turned out that *Oberscharführer* Getzinger, the munitions expert who had laid the mines, had trod on a mine and been killed. The joy in our camp was great — one of the murderers had been killed! And, of course, we only worked a half day on the day of his funeral.

Very few transports arrived that winter, but they resumed again in spring. Apparently, all of central Poland had become *Judenrein*; most of the transports arrived from eastern Poland and the Ukraine — from places the Germans had conquered from the Russians. The Jews there already knew where they were being taken, and the transports arrived under heavy guard. Some of the boxcars were broken and contained dead and wounded — the people resisted as soon as they were taken out of the boxcars. Horrible scenes occurred before our eyes. The phrase *"Shema Yisroel, Hashem Elokeinu, Hashem Echad!"* was heard everywhere — as well as calls of "Tell the world!" and "Avenge our blood!" The Jews in the new transports also shouted to us that the fall of the Germans was near.

One morning, instead of being led to work after parade, we were returned to our barracks and forbidden to step outside. From where we were we could hear the locomotive pushing boxcars into the camp, and afterward we heard a barrage of shots that lasted for a few seconds. And then silence. After about half an hour we heard another barrage of shots, and then silence — this continued for about half a day. Here and there we heard shouts and single shots. We listened and tried to figure out what was happening, but without success. Toward the afternoon, Frenzel came and called for the *Bahnhofkommando* to go out to work. After a short while we were also released for work. Outside, I saw the *Bahnhofkommando* cleaning out the boxcars. We never found out who the people were who were shot in groups, but the more the Germans tried to hide every clue of their identity, the more the victims tried to tell us something of themselves, scratching things on the walls of the boxcars. This time the *Bahnhofkommando* found the words "Belzec, death camp" scratched onto the boxcar walls — Belzec was one of the first death camps, perhaps the first in which people were gassed to death. While I was still in Turobin, a Jew had come to town and told of the extermination of Jews in Belzec, but nobody would believe him.

The men found a letter that had been written in one of the boxcars, during the last moments of the writer's life. It said:

> We are the last ones from Belzec. Belzec is a death camp where hundreds of thousands of Jews were exterminated by gassing and burning of the bodies. They have destroyed the entire camp and now nothing is left to show what happened there. The Germans told us that we were going to Germany

to work. We knew they were lying but we still got
into the boxcars. We do not know where we are. We
hear shots outside and I know they are shooting my
friends. Our turn will come soon. There is nothing
to be done. Do not let them fool you. Take revenge
for us.

The *Bahnhofkommando* said that the conditions in the boxcars
were relatively good. Every car had a table and benches. On the
tables was a lot of food — they even found vodka there.

That day we had seen the possible scenario of our extermination by the Germans. We knew without a doubt that the Germans
would kill us, but we couldn't figure out how they could take into
account every possible reaction from the condemned. Each time
there were rumors that the Germans were going to kill us very
soon, the atmosphere instantly changed — people grew very close
to one another, were more willing to help each other, and the desire
to do something together before it was too late increased.

But we would be overtaken by a feeling of powerlessness, which
even seemed to increase when faced with desperate situations
like these. When we saw death approaching it was as if we were
paralyzed, even though when we talked about it among ourselves
everyone would say things like, "We won't go to our deaths quietly
like 'good children'"; "We will attack them and kill them with our
fingernails"; "We'll die but we won't make it easy for them — they'll
die too."

Now, influenced by the fate of the Belzec transport, although
with no clear signs foretelling it, the feeling that our fate was at hand
intensified, that our days were numbered. But they too, the people
of Belzec, apparently had thought as we did — they wouldn't go
to their deaths quietly — and if so, how did the Germans manage
to trick them? Would the Germans also deceive us the same way?
Were they convinced that we didn't know who the people who
were shot in the boxcars were? They wouldn't succeed with us. We
simply had to have a chance to avenge them before our deaths.

There was another wave of construction at Sobibor camp and again, trains full of construction supplies arrived. Unlike the last frenzy of construction, however, which was intended to increase the capacity of the death machine, now weapons and ammunition warehouses were being built, most of them underground. At this stage *Lager* 4 was set up, which the Germans called Nordlager — northern camp — in the northeast corner of the existing camp, in the open area between the railway platform and the forest, and it continued into the forest, close to *Lazarett*. High-ranking officers landed in light planes and ran around the area with maps and plans, while our SS officers were dragged along behind them. The establishment of ammunition warehouses in a death camp didn't seem logical — was it possible that a foreign party would set up in a camp run secretly by the SS? It seemed likely that the Germans were going to destroy the death camp and turn it into a munitions base.

The work was performed at a swift pace. Before the first bunkers were completed, transports of ammunition had already arrived and were temporarily stored outside, next to the bunkers. According to rumors that made their way into our camp, the Germans had suffered heavy defeats near Stalingrad; the German army was in retreat, and this appeared to be the reason for the establishment of the munitions base.

We knew they would destroy us along with the death camp, just as they had destroyed the people of Belzec; but in the meantime, transports of Jews continued to arrive from all over Europe. From each transport young men were selected for work, and the team of workers at Nordlager grew in number.

One transport was different from the others. It came from Minsk, the capital of Belarus, and most of the people in it were Jewish prisoners of war who had fought in the Soviet army. The Germans had sorted out the Jews from the Russian prisoners of war and sent the Jews to be exterminated. About a hundred strong young men were selected from the Minsk transport for work. I had generally found it difficult to form bonds with the Jews from other countries I had met during my stint at Sobibor, both because of the language problems and because of their foreign ways and different lifestyles. It took me a long time before I could find a way into the heart of these strange types of Jews. But it wasn't so with the men from the Minsk transport. Although some of them spoke only Russian, which was a foreign language to us, and the Yiddish that flowed so easily from their tongues was different from ours, we made friends very quickly. From the first evening they arrived, we were already sitting together and talking. It was obvious that they had no idea where they had been taken. When we told them what occurred at Sobibor, they were surprised and refused to believe it. They told us they knew of the actions of the *Einsatzgruppen* units, who had killed thousands of Jews in the areas captured from the Soviet Union, but they didn't know that the Germans had been killing Jews in gas chambers and burning their bodies. When they told us of the failures of the German army, and that the day of the German defeat was near, a feeling of optimism flowed through us.

I loved being with them. Every day I would bring them cigarette stubs and scraps of food, and their gratitude was unending. They quickly accustomed themselves to their situation in Sobibor. Their suffering threshold was unbelievable: they could withstand crushing work, receive beatings — and still sit and sing every evening.

When I had first come to Sobibor, in shock from the transport and being in a death camp, I had been very attracted to the songs of the Ukrainian guards. I loved the melodies and was impressed by their performance — they sang in two- and three-part harmonies while marching, and always with a soloist. I so loved their singing that I would wait for it, and when they sang I would try to be nearby, even though I was often ashamed to be enjoying the songs emanating from the throats of murderers. When I was assigned to work at the Ukrainian barracks, I learned a different type of song, which I heard them sing in the showers, or especially in the winter, when they would sit and clean their rifles. These were sorrowful love songs, delicate and beautiful, and I would wonder how they came out of the mouths of Ukrainians.

At first, I didn't understand a word. In time, I learned their language and discovered that the words were beautiful, as well. And here, on the Russian-Jewish POWs' first evening with us, after they realized where they had been brought to and the barracks was filled with a heavy, leaden atmosphere, one of the them got up, stood in the middle of the our quarters and began to sing a Russian song — a song about a soldier at the front, in the trenches, a soldier whose life was always hanging between life and death and missed his loved one. At the time I didn't understand the words of the song, but the sad, beautiful melody and the way it was sung expressed all of our tragedies. He sang and we were all mesmerized — I suddenly found myself crying, something that I hadn't done in a very long time. I looked around me. Others were also wiping the tears from their eyes.

The Russian men would return from work tired and beaten. They often lost close friends, who were shot by the Germans. And still, in the evenings they would sing, sad, lonely songs, but also songs of hope and bravery. I sat close to them, absorbing every one. From my childhood, I had loved songs and I loved to sing. Now I fell in love with these Russian songs and quickly learned them by heart, even before I understood the words. I liked these Russian boys, who were suffering heroes in my eyes, and they liked me in return, treating me like a little brother and calling me Boris.

A short time after the arrival of the transport of the POWs, the feeling that something was going to happen increased — people whispered to one another, interrogated each other, suspected each other of keeping secrets. The atmosphere grew tense. The Russian boys said we had to escape as soon as possible — we couldn't waste a day — and asked the veterans for help, as they were experts on every detail of the camp, knew their way around, and understood the language as well. Groups of us formed, planning their escapes, but there was the risk that if individuals tried to break out they would endanger the chances of a mass escape, and cause all the rest of us to be killed, as well.

One man, a little older than his companions, stood out among the Russian prisoners, holding sway over everyone — an officer named Sasha (Aleksandr) Pechersky. Sasha had an excellent grasp of our situation. Through the force of leadership he persuaded the individual groups to hold off and took upon himself the organization of a large-scale rebellion, which would enable us all to escape. Sasha searched and found those among us who could influence the veterans and then gleaned from the veterans every detail about the camp. He became familiar with each German officer, knew who among us could or could not be depended upon, and from whom he must beware. From past experience he knew how dangerous it was to attract attention to the operation, and so he began planning the rebellion and mass escape in great secrecy, with Leibl Feldhendler and two or three more of his men. Of course, the more the detailed the plans, the wider the circle of parties to the secret became. There was no choice but to turn to various people to obtain information and assistance, but these were selected carefully and warned to keep everything strictly confidential.

One evening Leibl came to me, took me to one corner of the barracks and introduced me to one of the Russian boys. The Russian was already acquainted with me and said, "We know each other. This is Berale the cleaner." "Tell him your plan," Leibl said to me, and I told him all about the plan I had come up with, substituting the Ukrainian guards. The man asked a few questions, smiled and said, "Very nice!" I felt like a boy who had done well on an exam. And then Leibl said to me, "Remember, we're trusting you. Not one word to anyone!"

From then on I had a secret, and it seemed to me that most of us did, yet no one knew what his neighbor knew. I was suffused with the feeling that I would be at the center of the rebellion, and this excited me very much. I couldn't visualize every single thing that would happen, but thousands of times I imagined how men would come to me with pails of water and I would give them the

Ukrainian rifles and uniforms. I expected to be called upon again for this operation, but a few days later Leibl told me it would be better if we abandoned my plan, "but don't worry, everything will be fine" — hinting that something was brewing, and I caught similar hints from others. In the meantime, the plan for rebellion, which would involve the entire camp, was taking shape. The combination of an army officer with leadership qualities, a group of soldiers accustomed to war and veterans rich in experience, who knew the camp well and whose skills and positions gave them access to every place in the camp, ensured a fairly high chance of success. Things progressed quickly and Sasha convinced those who wanted to escape alone that it would be better to rely on him — the rebellion would break out very soon and would greatly increase everyone's chances of escape.

The leaders of the operation met every evening in the work-shops and the kitchen, and for this purpose we had to let Kapo Pozhycheki in on the secret plan, so he would help rather than hinder the action. Potato-peeling in the evenings was work every-one wanted, as the peelers always got extra food, and Pozhycheki now chose the leaders of the rebellion for this task — the peelers could discuss the plan without arousing suspicion. One day, Sasha Pechersky and another Russian I knew met me and asked me, by the way, could I smuggle rifles from the Ukrainian barracks to our camp on the day of the rebellion? I was stunned and didn't know what to say.

"Look," Sasha said, "you and some of the other boys working at the German and the Ukrainian barracks have free passage from place to place in the camp, and you're the only ones who can get us a few weapons, and we can't rely on everyone..."

"I'll do anything you say, but how do I move rifles?"

"You'll find a way. You've got enough time. We'll talk about this again," Sasha said, and his friend added, "We knew you'd agree. Remember, ammunition is also really important. Thanks, Berale."

I planned the smuggling of the rifles like this: strewn around the junkyard were all kinds of tin smokestacks, and with them

— inside them — I would be able to smuggle rifles. Once again I was filled with a great excitement, and again I waited impatiently for new instructions and for the big day to arrive. When I bumped into Little Drescher — the boy of the camp, younger and shorter than me, beautiful, sharp and glib, whom the Germans treated like a toy, he stopped me, looked at me slyly, smiled and asked, "Will it be okay?" "Yes," I said, "of course," and we each went our own way. With the exchange of these few words we had revealed each other's secret, and I understood that Little Drescher, who was a cleaner at the German barracks, would smuggle weapons from his workplace. My spirits rose.

The rebellion that was about to occur took place in my imagination from time to time, in various forms, and I usually assumed it would be a bloody event, during which we would kill Germans, Germans would kill us, and that would be the end. I never imagined that afterward I would escape from the camp, that I would be a free man. I didn't believe I would survive, as this seemed a very farfetched idea in our situation. But the success of the rebellion itself would satisfy me. That was all I wanted.

One day, after I had finished cleaning the inside of the barracks and moved on to its surrounding area, Wagner suddenly appeared and began to beat and kick me with increasing rage. He told me to lie face down on the ground and ordered a nearby Ukrainian to stand on my head. As I lay in this state, with my head sunk in the earth under the heavy body of the Ukrainian, Wagner beat me with a thick piece of wood. Those moments were horrible. I felt like I was choking, and my body was exploding with pain. Finally, when Wagner ordered me to get up and the Ukrainian released my head, I felt as though I had been reborn and instead of crying, an irrational laughter burst forth from me that spontaneously expressed my objections and resistance. Wagner shouted, "What?! You're laughing? Lie down again! Now!"

I lay down, ready for another beating, but Wagner ordered me to get up. His rage had passed, I guess, and he made do with a shout: "You piece of shit, enough! You haven't done anything! It's

about time you worked a little! From tomorrow you're no longer
a cleaner, understand?" "Yes," I answered, and Wagner left. I was
broken and exhausted. My whole body ached. My feet barely did
my bidding. I thought Wagner had broken some of my bones,
but the Czech medic examined me that evening and said that, in
his opinion, I would be okay. However, I had already gotten used
to living a little better and not receiving the beatings, so I was
exhausted. I also felt that Wagner had it in for me now — the man
wouldn't rest until he destroyed me — and I also was really sorry
to have lost my good work position as a cleaner. This meant going
back to work in *Lager* 2, where I would be involved in the cycle of
transports and might also have to shave off women's hair. And I
was extremely sorry I had been thrown out of my place of work just
when I was supposed to steal rifles. I felt guilty for what had happened and couldn't meet the eyes of the Russians for the shame.

In the camp, they felt sorry for me and comforted me. The next
day, at morning parade, when the cleaners were called to go out, I
stayed where I was. Another boy was selected instead of me, and
I was sent to work at Nordlager along with a Russian and Dutch
group. I was a digger, and it seemed my strength had faltered with
time; Frenzel, who was in charge of our workplace, shouted on my
first day that I wasn't worth anything and ordered me to bend over.
My body still hurt all over from Wagner's beating and I begged to
be spared from more pain. When Frenzel began to whip me I tried
to arouse his sympathy and shouted, "*Herr Scharführer*, I have an
abscess on my buttocks." Frenzel laughed. With every strike of the
whip that landed on me he shouted, "What do you have? What
do you have?" and he continued to beat me until I was completely
bloody. I was in poor condition. The beatings I had received day
after day before had almost finished me. But now, in contrast to
when I first arrived in the camp, I didn't want to die; I tried to hang
on with all my might. I wanted to see the rebellion break out in the
camp and I prayed it would happen quickly.

The autumn days of October 1943 arrived, dark and cloudy,

rainy and stormy, days when the smoke from *Lager* 3 merged with the clouds and made our feelings of depression even heavier.

Tension in the camp increased. Everything was wrapped in mystery. Rumors abounded — tomorrow? The day after tomorrow? When would the rebellion break out? And what exactly would happen? Few could answer this, but many knew or felt that something was about to happen. Everything seemingly went on as usual, and to my amazement, many among us gave no hint that they knew anything. What would happen to them? Would they also flee? In any case, those who had some inkling of what was to occur prepared themselves and secured warm clothing, while I went back and checked to make sure the bags of gold coins I had hidden in various places in the ground were still there.

At the beginning of October, the leaders of the rebellion completed their plan of the operation to the minutest detail and set the day of rebellion for the fourteenth of the month. Some SS officers were to be sent on vacation at this time, including Wagner, apparently due to a lull in transports, and it was vital to the rebels that as few SS officers as possible be in the camp. One day before Zero Hour, the roles of each of the principals were given out. In the warehouses, scores of small axes and knives were prepared and well sharpened — this was the primary weapon at our disposal when the rebellion broke out — and we had to pass these weapons along to the appropriate places. And we still had to enable the fighters selected by the leaders to get to their appointed positions, to be able to operate a communication system of runners who would quickly report on the situation to the leaders.

After I had worked several days sorting Jewish possessions, a man I knew from the group of Russian prisoners came to me and said, "Tomorrow the rebellion will start. You work in *Lager* 2. Our men will be there and they'll tell you what to report, and you'll run and let us know every important thing that happens." Then he came back and cautioned me to keep everything a secret, and left. Until that moment I doubted we would ever arrive at the day of rebellion. Past experience did not increase my hope that we would be able to do anything; and although this time the organization was thorough and gave the impression that one could trust the organizers, there were still many factors and reasons for it to fail. And still, at work, we were less than a day from Zero Hour — and everything was going smoothly.

It was hard to believe that this was reality and not a dream, that the next day a rebellion really would break out, that all would end tomorrow. I didn't know the exact "what" or "how" of the rebellion, and nobody knew, of course, how it would end. I only knew that the dream I had been dreaming for many months was about to come true, a dream that had given me strength to carry on. Many of the people taken to the gas chambers had shouted to us from the passage between the two barbed wire fences to avenge them. Tomorrow we would do it. We would take revenge on the Germans. We would kill as many of them as we could. Tomorrow we would put an end to our suffering at Sobibor. Tomorrow it would all be over.

That night I forgot my anger at God, forgot that I had cut myself off from Him and that I no longer wanted contact with Him. I prayed to God that there would be no obstacles, that the rebellion would take place and succeed.

The morning of October 14th: rising early, as usual. The weather cloudy, cold and gloomy, like before. The dispensing of ersatz coffee went on, as usual, but for some reason everything seemed to take longer and was more emphasized. I already knew: the rebellion would begin at 4:00 p.m., half an hour before everyone returned from work.

Morning parade took place under Frenzel's command. Other Germans and Ukrainians stood with him. I saw everyone in a different light — all were candidates for death. The Kapos in charge of the block counted everyone, gave a report to the new "Governor General" — an older German Jew — and he reported to Frenzel. The parade exercises took place with precision. Group by group, we set out from the parade ground to work, each group singing a song in a different language.

At *Lager* 2, in the possession-sorting barracks, our group was about twenty men. Our commander was *Scharführer* Kurt-Rudolf Beckmann, a short, thin German with a mousy face. He wore a large pistol on his belt and shouted incessantly, *"Schneller! Schneller!* (Faster! Faster!)"* Each time he would give a few lashes with his whip to one or another of us. Time passed slowly. I counted every minute. The secrecy that we were bound to keep until the last moment increased the tension tenfold. I knew, and my neighbor knew, but we couldn't say a word about what was about to happen. I knew that, right up to the last minute, someone could spoil everything.

At noon, when everyone returned to camp for the afternoon meal, you could immediately feel the celebratory atmosphere. People's faces shone with satisfaction — everything was set, prepared, arranged. Everyone stood ready and yet there was a tempering in the tension, perhaps because people began to believe in the success of the operation. The code of secrecy also relaxed: the prisoners exchanged words, asked questions, wished everyone luck.

After everyone returned to work, the tension gradually escalated. It became very hard to concentrate. Two more hours. An hour and a half. One more hour. People behaved unusually — moved back and forth, lazed too much, and *Scharführer* Beckmann began to get angry. He gave out twenty-five lashes to one of us and everyone went back to work. Beckmann calmed down and the victim blurted out, "I'll kill him today."

I saw two men from the Russian group enter the warehouse next to our Jewish possession shed and disappear inside. I knew that they were going to kill Beckmann. The hands on the clock moved. The time had come. Instead of hours until the beginning there were only minutes. And complete silence around us.

Exactly at 4:00 p.m., Chaim, the warehouse worker, approached *Scharführer* Beckmann and asked him to come inside — he had something nice for him. We watched them. The two entered the warehouse and we immediately heard a blow, a scream that was cut off and another blow. Silence returned. In a minute the two Russians came out, one of them flecked all over with blood and a pistol in his hand. "We killed the bastard," said one of them. "We split his head open."

The rebellion had begun.

The two men asked all of us to continue working as if nothing had happened, and one of them told me, "Berale, run and tell Sasha that we killed the German in *Lager* 2 and everything is fine, and return here."

The path from *Lager* 2 to our camp, which was about two hundred meters away, was empty. I ran it quickly and relayed the information. While there I learned that the camp commander, *Untersturmführer* Neumann, *Oberscharführer* Graetschus, who was in charge of the Ukrainians, and some other Germans had been killed — at 4:00 p.m. exactly, people in every workplace killed the German who was in charge of them. The killings took place quietly, with axes and knives, and everyone continued working as if nothing had happened. *Untersturmführer* Neumann had been invited to the tailor's workshop to be fitted for a suit. He had arrived at 4:00 p.m. exactly, riding a white horse, entered the workshop, opened his gun belt and laid it on the table, taken off his coat and sat in a chair. One of the men, who had been hiding behind a curtain, came up behind him and brought an ax down into his head, but Neumann moved at that moment and the ax hit him on the side of the head, slicing off his ear and part of his head. The German managed to utter a few words, "The horse will testify to what you are doing…," but the second blow split his head in two. The body was hidden and a boy was sent to another German to tell him that the camp commander was calling him to the tailor's workshop.

The German arrived quickly and as soon as he entered the doorway they killed him, too. At the shoemaker's they also killed a German. Within ten minutes, most of the SS officers in the camp had been killed, including the camp commander. At the same time the telephone lines were cut and the electricity lines sabotaged by men who worked there, and even now the silence was not broken, and everything continued as if nothing had happened.

I ran back to *Lager* 2. On the way, I met Little Drescher carrying a stovepipe bigger than he was. We exchanged smiles and I continued to run. When I got back I told everyone that Neumann and many other Germans had been killed. Our hearts swelled with joy. It was impossible to continue working. We all waited impatiently for the next thing to happen. Suddenly a German appeared in the doorway, the man who usually took us from work to our camp. We pretended to be working, but he noticed that something was wrong and with quick steps turned to the door of the undressing room and disappeared inside. We knew that the German had gone to the main office, where the Preacher, *Oberscharführer* Michel, used to give his speech before the people undressed. Five men ran after him and found him trying unsuccessfully to make a telephone call. He attempted to draw his pistol, but the men fell upon him and after a brief struggle overcame him and killed him. He was left lying on the floor of the office, in a pool of blood.

It was time to return to our camp. We organized ourselves in rows of three, one man leading the group, and when we began to march he ordered us with a shout, "Sing!" and we all sang a German marching song, like we did every day. On the way, we saw a truck with Germans driving to the main office. We knew they would find the body of the German and all would be revealed. We quickened our steps to the camp until we arrived at a run. All the work groups had returned to the camp and utter chaos reigned. People didn't know what to do and crowded around the rebellion leaders. The leaders were armed with pistols, a few rifles and grenades, and one Schmeisser machine gun — all of these weapons acquired at the last minute. I cannot describe the height of our exhilaration. If machine guns had cut us all down at that moment, we would have died happy.

Everything happened swiftly. I ran behind our barracks, dug quickly and took out a bag of gold coins and ran back. One of the men climbed the tower and blew the bugle that announced the beginning of parade — meaning that everyone was to gather in the yard and join the escape. The "Governor General," who knew nothing of what was happening, heard the bugle, came running out of the barracks and yelled, *"Eintreten!* (Get inside!)" Some men caught him, covered his mouth, took him back into the barracks and beat him severely. All of a sudden, right in front of me, Roktsuk appeared. He was riding a bicycle, stopped in front of us, his face white as a sheet, turned to us and asked, "What's going on here?" We fell upon him immediately, pulled him off his bicycle, and beat him, some with their hands, some with their feet, some with knives — this man was one of the worst sadists in the camp, especially favoring the bayoneting of men, women and children while they were naked, before they entered the gas chambers. He would stab us as well, and I also was at the receiving end of his bayonet a number of times. Roktsuk was left moaning on the ground.

Suddenly a shout was heard, "Hurrah! Onward!" We all yelled "Hurrah!" and began to run through the gate toward the ammunition warehouse and the main gate. At that moment, we heard shots — the first shots since the rebellion had broken out — and none of us, who up to now had been disciplined and followed orders, quite knew how to behave. In the chaos, the unified group broke up and scattered. Some kept running toward the ammunition warehouse, myself among them, some ran toward the main gate, and some just ran anywhere. I saw two Ukrainians run and crawl under their barracks. The shooting increased. Explosions were heard. Here and there, people fell and cried for help. Our men took over the ammunition warehouse. Someone gave me a rifle and a box of bullets, and I loaded a bullet into the chamber, cocked it, held it close to my shoulder and shot the way I had seen the Ukrainians do it. The noise and recoil in my shoulder startled me. I ran with everyone to the gate. Someone yelled "Scatter!" and people began to run back. I stood for a moment and looked around. I saw a lot of people near the gate, many of them falling. Frenzel had gathered his wits, taken position at a machine gun and fired nonstop into the masses that crowded the gate. When I saw a lot of people running for the barbed wire fences, I joined them.

When I neared the fences I saw people climbing the barbed wire like a ladder. Some hung there and didn't move — they had been hit by bullets shot from the guard tower. By the time I got to the fenced area, the inner fence had already collapsed. I jumped toward the other side of the trench and climbed up quickly. The left guard tower, close to the gate, had been neutralized by our men. On the right side, a machine gun still fired, and the wounded were left hanging on the barbed wire. I passed through the third fence quickly, without noticing that my arm was cut by the barbed wire.

There were constant explosions all around us, after which clouds of smoke rose from the ground. It didn't occur to me that I was running through a minefield, and it seemed that the others didn't care, either. The choice was either to flee or be immediately killed, just as long as we didn't fall into the hands of the Germans, and the ones who led the exodus exploded the mines with their bodies and opened a path for the flight of others. In the direction I was fleeing, the distance from the camp to the forest was a bit more than a kilometer. I ran with all my might and passed everyone, and after I'd run far enough, I stopped for a moment and looked back. Before me was an amazing sight, one that I would never have been able to create in the loveliest dream — along the entire width of the field, from the camp gate next to the railroad tracks to the edge of *Lager* 1, hundreds of people were running toward me and the Germans couldn't stop them. More and more machine gun fire was directed to us from the camp, but it was getting darker, and as people distanced themselves from the camp they were less vulnerable. Rockets lit up the area close to the camp and the glowing strips of tracer bullets continued on forever.

Over and over we had heard those being led to the massacre, in their last moments before entering the gas chambers, say the words, "Tell the world what the Germans are doing!" "Take revenge on the Germans!" These words penetrated our hearts and became the last will and testament of the exterminated. Every one of us dreamed of carrying out this bequest, but none of us ever imagined it would actually come to pass. And here, we had won our revenge. The worst murderers were now corpses strewn about, killed by Jews with axes and knives. We had had even less faith that any of us would get out alive, and here, hundreds of people had escaped this hell and were now running into the forest, to freedom. And we would tell the world what had happened at Sobibor.[1]

---

1. Fifteen SS officers — most of the staff that performed the exterminations, their camp commander *Untersturmführer* Neumann, and five Ukrainian murderers — were killed during the rebellion. Out of six hundred Jews who were in the camp at that time, approximately three hundred managed to escape. The rest were killed in the rebellion. After the rebellion the Germans destroyed the camp and covered up all traces of the extermination machine. Aleksandr Pechersky, the leader of the rebellion, survived and lives in Russia. In 1946, a pamphlet written by him in Yiddish was published in Moscow, called "The Sobibor Rebellion" (*Dar Offshtund ein Sobibor*, 50 pages).

# The Forests

## Autumn 1943—Summer 1944

The sounds of shooting from the camp became fainter. There was complete darkness as we were swallowed up into the forest, and I began to feel more secure. I stopped to rest for a moment with a few other escapees. In a short time, more joined us, until we were more than twenty. We looked at each other, not believing our eyes. Out of breath after running so madly, we couldn't speak. People who had prepared themselves for the flight and worn warm clothing had thrown off their coats and cumbersome garments to ease their getaway; now they were only wearing shirts in the chill of the night. I had kept all my clothes. While I had also taken off my coat while running, I had dragged it on the ground behind me. People were looking for members of their families or for their friends and asked whether we knew anything about the others. In our group, there were people from different countries and some of the Russian Jewish POWs. We had three rifles and a pistol between us. My rifle had been taken from me and given to someone who knew how to use it, but I still had a few bullets in my pocket. We knew there was no time to rest. We had to distance ourselves as far as we could from the camp during the night.

A few said that it wasn't a good idea to travel in a large group and moved on, disappearing into the forest, while others joined up with us. We walked in a line, the armed men up front. Walking through the forest at night was difficult and full of obstacles, but we walked quickly. A few times I thought I had lost the group and

I was terrified. I stayed as close as I could to those who were at the front of the line. We stopped a few times during the night. Once we heard shooting from afar; another time we heard a dog barking. Those who thought they knew argued over which direction we should take, left or right. We were in heavy, wild forestland; the undergrowth was very thick, the earth full of muddy puddles. When we finally decided to make camp in the forest during the day, I fell into a deep sleep. I awoke to the sound of a plane flying over the tops of the trees. I tried to sit up but someone shouted, "Stay down and don't move. They're looking for us!"[1]

The plane, which circled above us, finally disappeared, and people got up to stretch their muscles. I continued to lie there. I was confused, still immersed in the dream I had been having a few moments ago. "I want to tell you about a dream I had," I said, and everyone looked at me in surprise. "I dreamed that everyone had run away from the camp and I was the only one left. I asked myself how it had happened that everyone had gotten away and I had stayed behind. I was standing at roll call, surrounded by all of the Germans, with Wagner in front. They interrogated me and asked me where everyone was, and I answered that I didn't know. Wagner threatened to kill me and I decided that I had to run away. I broke through their ring and ran to the fence. The Germans shouted, '*Halt! Halt!*' and they all fired at me. I reached the fence and climbed up, but got caught in the barbed wire. The more I tried to break free, the more entangled I became, and I couldn't move. The Germans were getting closer…but I was in luck — the plane woke me up, or else they would have caught me!" Everyone laughed, and I just lay there, looking at the treetops, listening to the birds, and smelling the greenery.

---

1. As we found out later, all of the German units that were in the area, along with a number of Ukrainian units, had been called out and sent to search for us, using light planes. They had very little success. They caught people who did not hide during the day but kept on going, and people who were informed on by the farmers. At that time, there were groups of partisans in the area, and the Germans were afraid to penetrate too deeply into the forest.

I was free. There was no barbed wire surrounding me. There was no morning roll call. I would never see Wagner again, nor Frenzel, nor Gomerski. I wouldn't see Bolender or his dog, Barry. I wouldn't have to witness the transports, men, women and children, entering the gas chambers. Eighteen months of Sobibor were behind me. I was happy now and I didn't want to think about the future.

For a long time we sat together, each of us telling the story of his own part in the revolt — each of us had experienced events differently, each of us had lived through a slightly different story, and together all of these descriptions gave us a complete picture. Before long, however, we were assaulted by hunger — since the afternoon of the day before, when we had been given the usual thin soup, we had not had anything to eat. Some of the people in the group had prepared supplies. I had a little bag of gold coins in one pocket and a few bullets in the other, but I hadn't had the foresight to take any food. Those who had bread divided it, so that each of us had a slice, which satisfied our hunger a bit, but not our thirst.

A long discussion began about what we should do and where we should go. No one knew where we were. At the camp, we had heard about groups of partisans in the forests and we wanted to join them, but how could we find them? The Russians said that we should get to the Bug River and cross it, moving eastward. That suggestion frightened me, as I didn't know how to swim. Luckily, many others rejected this idea, thinking that it would be better to reach an area where we might know some of the farmers, and where we could get food and perhaps a place to hide. They also took into consideration the fact that the Germans were probably guarding the riverbanks well. It was finally decided to continue going in the direction in which we had started to move, as far away from the camp as possible, and to look for farmers' houses where we might get some food.

Hungry and thirsty when night fell, we continued on our journey until we reached the edge of the forest and we saw an open area and flickering lights from afar and heard dogs barking — we must have been approaching a village. We naturally began to think about going to one of the houses and trying to get some food, about getting to a well and drinking some water, but after some discussion, we came to the conclusion that the village was too far away and it was too dangerous — perhaps the Germans were waiting for us there. We turned back, reentered the forest and continued walking. We were hungry, but more than anything, we were thirsty. Our throats were dry and we could only swallow our own saliva until, finally, we reached a small pool of stagnant water. We each stretched out on the damp ground and drank the filthy water, spitting out the scum and the insects that we kept drawing into our mouths with the water. I thought that my stomach would explode from drinking so much, but I kept on drinking until I was as full as a barrel.

At midnight, we reached a fork in the forest trail, and there, on a small bridge over a dried-up stream was a sign, "Sobibor Forest — Five Kilometers to the Station." We were shocked. We had been sure that we had distanced ourselves thirty or forty kilometers from the camp, and we didn't have many hours of darkness left. We began to go in another direction quickly, not really knowing where. When the sun came up, we camped in a place that didn't seem very secure, and all day we worried about the possibility of getting caught. When night fell, hungry, thirsty and depressed, we continued to walk quickly, now with the aim of getting food; otherwise, we wouldn't have the strength to keep going.

After about an hour, perhaps even less, we reached the same fork in the road with the same bridge and sign. We felt helpless. We couldn't understand how we had run away from this spot in the opposite direction, but returned to the same place again. It was as if we were the victims of some kind of sorcery. After some thought, we understood that the paths in the forest had diverted us again and again from the direction we had planned to go, and they had us going around in circles. From then on, we paid more attention to our direction, and we reached another forest, around whose edge a few houses were scattered. The four fellows bearing arms approached one of the houses. At first the farmer refused to open the door, but after they threatened to blow up his house, he obeyed. He gave them two big loaves of bread, some butter and some onions, and we drank well water that the men had brought back in milk pails. After two days without food, we ate the good country bread with butter and onion, and we drank our fill. The boys had asked the farmer where we were, and we learned that we had distanced ourselves from Sobibor. Our mood improved. We had more energy now.

The next evening, our lads returned to the farmer's house and again got more food by threatening him. When they got back they said that the farmer had warned them not to go in a certain direction, as there was a German camp there. So we walked in the other direction. We walked in a line, through open country, until suddenly we heard shouts of *"Halt! Halt!"* and then soldiers began to fire at us. One of us shouted, "Lie down!" and we all fell to the ground. Our rifles returned a bit of fire, and then someone shouted, "Run away!" From the camp we heard sirens and shouting in German. We all ran. I ran quickly, and in a few minutes I was alone. I was afraid. I lay down on the ground, and then I saw the group running at some distance from me. Heavy fire was coming from the camp and rockets lit up the area. None of us was hurt. The Germans must have thought we were partisans, but, in any case, they didn't pursue us. We would never know whether the farmer had purposefully deceived us, or whether our boys had misunderstood him.

Four days had passed since the flight from Sobibor and we had been walking almost aimlessly, with no hope of achieving our goal — to join the partisans. The farmers we asked said that they knew nothing about partisans, but it was possible that they did know something but just didn't want to tell us. Perhaps there were no partisans in the area. How long would we be able to wander directionless from forest to forest without being discovered? So we finally decided that we would have to swim the Bug River, as, on the other side, or so the Russian soldiers said, there were certainly partisans. They said that there were narrow places where those who knew how to swim could take the others across.

In the afternoon, one of our guards reported that he had seen a man wearing civilian clothing, but armed with a rifle, moving through the forest. After a short consultation, it was decided to approach him and find out who he was. After all, how could we find partisans if we didn't keep asking? Two of our armed lads took covering positions, and two others, also armed, walked over to the man and shouted, "Hands up!" The man gave up casually, introduced himself as a partisan from a Polish unit, and said that he was happy to meet us. He said his men would be glad to let our men join them. We were overjoyed. Everyone shook the man's hand, and he finally said, "You're probably hungry. Stay here and I'll bring you food and call our commander, and then, we'll take you with us."

The man left and we were excited — we had accomplished our goal! We waited impatiently for the partisans to come and take us, but an hour passed, and then another, but no one came. Suspicions began to assail us. Perhaps the man had been lying and wouldn't be back? When we had given up all hope, the guard finally alerted us that the partisans were approaching. A group of about ten men, dressed in a mixture of uniforms and civilian clothes, a variety of weapons in their hands — machine guns, different types of rifles, and daggers — approached us. We welcomed them joyfully. They brought us food and a big bottle of vodka. An older man, wearing a Polish army cap, who looked drunk, presented himself as the commander. He said that he understood that we were hungry, and suggested that first we eat and then we could talk. Someone began to cut bread and then the Polish commander asked, "What kind of weapons do you have?"

Our boys hurried to bring out the three rifles and the pistol, and the commander said, "Give us your weapons and you'll receive others." The Poles took our weapons quickly, without giving us a moment to think. Then the commander gave a sign to his men, they walked a few steps backward, and opened fire on us. I jumped up and ran as fast as I could until I could run no longer and fell to the ground. After a few minutes, I heard the sound of running feet, and two of our group appeared. The three of us burst into tears. We hoped that more of us had escaped the brutal murderers in the forest. We lay there, listening to every noise, but we saw no one; only the three of us had survived. One was a Russian war prisoner in his twenties named Semmen, large, tall and twice as wide as I was. He moved heavily, like a bear, and I thought he personified the typical Russian soldier. He was cynical and acted as though nothing in the world was important to him. During the revolt, he had killed one of the Germans, but it had been difficult for him to run during the flight, and he had taken off his long overcoat and another shorter coat, and was now wearing only a shirt. The second was Avraham, eighteen years old, two years my elder, a boy with the face of a doll — round head, cheeks full and always red. He was short and chubby, but still half a head taller than I was. He had arrived at the camp a few months after me and had worked at various positions. For a long time he had been part of the *Bahnhofkommando*.

Night fell. The three of us sat quietly, without saying a word. What could we say? The calamity, which had come as a surprise, from a place we had never expected, pained and enraged us. After the success of the revolt and the safe flight from the camp, after tasting victory and the happiness of being free in the forest, we had fallen into this stupid trap — our boys had been killed by Polish murderers. Were those the partisans that we so much wanted to join? What good was it for us to be alive, without weapons, without knowing where we were or what we should do next? My wish to die, which had given way to a desire to carry on, returned. There was no use struggling. Our fates had been sealed.

The first of us to overcome the shock and begin thinking logically was Semmen. He said in his rudimentary Yiddish, "We have to think about what to do. We mustn't stay in this forest, because the killers will surely catch us tomorrow morning. We must get away as far as we can." The three of us walked through the forest, staying close to each other. My self-confidence had deserted me. Every moment I found something to be afraid of, whether it was a butterfly, a bird flying over my head, the rustle of a rabbit or another animal running away from us. I saw someone waiting to attack us behind every tree. After an hour of walking we came out of the forest into an open field. Walking over the plowed land was difficult; our legs slipped among the clods of earth. But for some reason, I felt relieved. I was free of the fear I had felt in the forest.

We passed not far from a village. We saw the flickering of lights and we heard dogs barking and people's voices and even the singing of children, which especially moved me. I remembered the days of my childhood, when we had been on vacation in the village, and I would sit on the doorstep, listening to the sounds of the night. Now I was in the mysterious darkness, and I jealously watched a village in a world where I didn't belong.

Walking through the field exhausted us. We sat down to rest, and our eyes gradually became accustomed to the dark. The shadows of the houses could clearly be seen and we could sense the evening life of the village. We were so hungry that we considered going up to one of the houses and asking for food, but we were afraid to see people, for fear that we would encounter our murderers here, in this village. We knew that we should keep as far away as possible and we kept walking. We crossed plowed fields and fallow ones. We couldn't hear the sounds of people or cattle anymore, which were replaced by the sounds of frogs croaking and crickets chirping. We could hear the distant sound of cars on a road. I kept thinking of the barrage of bullets that had cut us down.

After a few hours of walking, we began to worry that we wouldn't find a forest to hide in during the daylight hours, and when dawn broke, we would be caught in open country. We began to hurry and then, to run. All at once everything became darker, and there was a palpable thickness in the air. We knew that it soon would be dawn, and, luckily, while we were running, blinded by the darkness, we found ourselves in a forest that seemed to spring up right in front of us. We were swallowed up by it.

When we awoke, it was daylight. The three of us lay close together, covered by my coat, the only coat that we had. I lay there for a few minutes, looking around at the total peacefulness. Above me were pine trees laden with pinecones, and the strong scent of the surrounding vegetation filled my nostrils. It was impossible not to enjoy the beauty, and this enjoyment filled me with confidence, in spite of what had happened the day before. We were obsessed by hunger. We felt weak. We hadn't eaten anything since the night before last. I turned my pockets inside out who knows how many times, trying to find some crumbs of bread, but in one pocket I had only the bag of gold coins, and in the other, the packet of rifle bullets. Why I was carrying them, I didn't know. But something prevented me from throwing them away. Avraham said that he didn't like this forest — it was so sparse that we could be seen though the trees from afar. Avraham was restless and Semmen and I tried to calm him. The two of us were indifferent. Semmen said that no matter what, when evening came, we would go into the first house that we saw, even if Hitler lived there, unless we had decided to die of hunger. I agreed with him, but Avraham said that if we entered a house, we would be caught.

We got up and walked through the forest in hopes of finding something to eat. We tried chewing on different plants and wild fruit, but all of these were bitter, especially since we had no water to rinse our mouths with. We finally arrived at a place where we found rags and broken dishes scattered here and there. The undergrowth was trampled, and it was obvious that people had been there. We looked around but we didn't see anyone. We searched the area with the discarded utensils, hoping to find something to eat or an object that would tell us something about the people who had been there. We picked up a piece of paper and saw that it was a page of a *siddur*, a prayer book. There was no doubt about the identity of the people now. Jews had been there! Where were they now? What had happened to them? One hundred meters further on, we again found signs that people had been there, and they, too, had surely been Jews.

We were still plagued by the hunger that tormented us. We were so weak that we felt half asleep. We knew that if we didn't find food soon, we wouldn't have the strength to go on, and we would die of starvation. I fell deeply asleep and woke about an hour later. When Semmen said that we had to get up, there was still sunshine coming through the trees. Avraham said, "What? Walk in daylight? That's insane!" But Semmen explained, "We will walk carefully until we get to the edge of the forest. We'll look for a house, and when it gets dark we'll knock on the door and ask for food. In the evening, people are more welcoming. Late at night, no one will open the door for us." The thought that we would eat soon gave us strength. We walked briskly as the sun sank behind the trees. From time to time, we stopped to listen. Suddenly, we heard a man talking to his horse. We walked in the direction of the voice, which became clearer and clearer, and then, in front of us, there was a peaceful valley with farmers' cottages scattered here and there. We lay down and chose the cottage that was nearest to the forest and decided to knock on the door when it got dark.

Time seemed to stand still. Would it ever get dark? We saw farmers returning from the fields. A boy was driving a herd of cows home from the meadow. We didn't have the patience to wait for complete darkness; we got up and walked toward the hut, even though we could still see figures not far away from us. When we got to the house, we found a large-boned, middle-aged woman. When she saw us, she paled. She looked at us in shock, as though we were monsters, and asked us loudly, "What do you want?" "We want food," I answered. "We will pay you." The woman apparently didn't hear everything I said, because she cut me off in the middle and said, "You are the ones who ran away from Sobibor… Good God, the Germans are searching for you everywhere. Get away from here quickly!" She looked at us closely and seemed to relax her guard; she said, "Get out of here or I'll…," but she didn't finish the sentence. "Give us something to eat and we'll go," said Avraham. And Semmen, who didn't know Polish, said, "*Da!*" (Yes, in Russian.) The woman said, "Wait a minute," and went behind the house. After a few minutes, three men appeared, two adults and a younger man, with pitchforks and an ax in their hands, and from a distance they cursed us and threatened to kill us if we didn't leave at once. We started to back off. The three continued to come closer until we had no choice but to run away. The villagers ran after us a bit, then stopped after they made sure that we were going. Semmen cursed those Poles and told us how he had gone with two of his friends a few days ago, with weapons, to ask for food, and how the farmer and his wife had given them bread and butter and even wished them luck. "If I had a gun, I would have killed all of the people who just chased us away," he said.

After we had calmed down, we decided to ask somewhere else, and we walked to a house on the other side of the village. The house was small and there was a barn and a granary alongside it. There was no one outside, but we could see the light of a candle or an oil lamp through the window. We knocked on the door. "Who's there?" said a woman's voice. "One of us." I answered. There was silence, and then we heard the voice of a man asking again, "Who's there?" I didn't know what to say, but, finally, I answered, "We want to buy food!" "We have nothing to sell. Go away," answered the man's voice. "We are hungry. We haven't eaten for two days. We have gold and we will pay you as much as you want." "Go away. We have no food and we don't open the door at night to anyone. Get out of here or I'll call the Germans!" said the farmer angrily.

We wanted to break in through the door or the window, but we didn't have the physical or emotional strength to do it. We went back into the forest. On the way, we searched the ground for something to eat, and even though we knew that at that time of year we probably wouldn't find anything in the fields, we found a few rotten potatoes in a plowed field and ate them.

Until then, we had always tried to avoid remaining in the same place for two days, as we knew that it was too dangerous. This time, we were desperate, and we didn't care about what would happen to us anymore. We returned to the forest where we had spent the day, and we didn't even walk very far in among the trees. We lay down and slept, feeling completely helpless. After some time, Avraham woke up when he heard voices, and he woke us up. We heard the voices of people working in the fields. "They will catch us here," said Avraham firmly. "We shouldn't have stayed here. We have to get away quickly!" But we were too weak to walk. This was the third day that we hadn't eaten anything except for those few rotten raw potatoes. I was tormented by waves of hunger. Now I understood the people who had come to Sobibor and told of how they had run away from the ghetto and tried to live in the forests, but in the end, had returned to the ghetto and wound up in Sobibor, because their experience had made it clear to them that Jews were not welcome anywhere — they were persecuted not only by the Germans but also by the Poles and the Ukrainians. And in fact, during the few days since we had run away from Sobibor, it had become clear to us, too, that we had no place in this world. We felt so hopeless that we came to the conclusion that we would be better off committing suicide — we would hang ourselves on three trees, and that would be the end of it. We had done what we had wanted to — we had taken revenge on the Germans. We had seen their dead bodies, hacked to pieces like the carcasses of animals. We had succeeded in running away from the camp, as well, and had tasted freedom. Now we could die peacefully.

Yet in spite of everything, we still wanted to live. Instead of fleeing deeper into the woods, we continued toward the voices of the workers in the fields. We went down toward the valley and we neared the edge of the forest, where we saw a farmer plowing his field and leading his horse slowly through the furrows. Suddenly I saw a sack lying under a tree. The three of us walked over to it, opened it and found a big loaf of bread, the kind that the farmers bake themselves. It weighted about three kilos. There was also a big chunk of cheese, and next to the sack, there was a jug of milk. For a moment, we just stood there hypnotized. We couldn't believe our eyes. It was a miracle, sent from above. Each of us tore a piece of bread from the loaf — it was fresh and tasted like Paradise. We drank the cold milk, and only then did we remember the danger.

We grabbed the sack and ran off as fast as we could. All of a sudden, we had been blessed with inhuman strength. We ran quickly. A few times we wanted to sit down for a moment and resume eating, but we kept running to get as far away from the scene of the crime as it took to be sure we would never be caught.

We ate the bread and the cheese wordlessly. We could have finished all of it, but decided to leave half for the next day. After we were sated, we found our desire to live was renewed. The sack of food was a sign to us that we could keep going, that we could continue living in the forest. Deep in our hearts, we knew that a miracle like this, finding a sack of food, couldn't happen more than once, but we considered it as proof that we shouldn't lose hope.

That evening, we didn't seek out food at the farmers' houses. The next day, we ate what was left, and the loaf of bread, which had been so big, dwindled until it disappeared, plunging us into sadness. The next few days, we again asked farmers for food and were refused. We continued to wander from place to place. Here and there, we found items in the forest testifying to the fact that Jews had been there. At one point, we met Polish woodcutters who threatened to kill us. I gave them a few gold coins and they left us alone.

One night, we were walking through open country and couldn't find a forest to hide in. It was almost dawn and we were still running through fields when we finally found a grove of trees. When we walked into the grove, we realized that we were very near a village. Early in the morning, the farmers passed us, along with young boys leading cattle to the meadow, and we were terribly afraid that we would be caught. The whole day we lay pressed to the ground, without picking our heads up. We were hungry again, and the day seemed endless. About three hundred meters from where we were hiding stood an isolated hut in the fields, and we decided that when night fell, we would approach the hut to ask for food.

That evening, the farmers returned from the fields and the cattle returned from the meadows. At twilight we got up and walked to the house. As we approached, we heard the farmer working in the granary. We went in and saw an old man preparing feed for cows. When I saw the pile of beets in front of me, I picked one up and began to chew on it. The farmer looked and me and said, "My son, don't eat that. That's food for cattle, not for people." We told the farmer that we just wanted something to eat, and then we would go away immediately. The old man looked at us, and without asking who we were and where we had come from, said, "Don't worry. You won't leave my house hungry." He called to his wife and said, "Mother, prepare a lot of food for supper. We have three guests and they are hungry."

The farmer finished preparing food for his single cow and told us to stay in the granary until he called us. "You understand," he said, "you must be careful these days." From the granary, we saw someone on a horse enter the yard. The farmer went out to meet him and the two spoke to each other for a few minutes. The man on the horse was the farmer's son, returning from his work in the fields. After about an hour, the farmer came out of the house, strode back and forth, looking and listening, and then came over to us and invited us into the hut. It was very old and small, only one room, which was a living room, bedroom and kitchen. The roof was made of straw. We could see signs of poverty by the light of the oil lamp, which was standing on the table and lit the room. But I felt that we had entered a palace. The pleasant warmth of the home enveloped me and I could smell food cooking. We sat down unceremoniously at the table and the woman brought us bowls of hot soup — a milk-based soup with potatoes, pieces of dough and onion. The table was steamy and I suddenly felt very hot. I broke out in cold sweat, my head felt heavy and the room began to swirl. I struggled to overcome these feelings and get control of myself, but the next thing I knew I was outside, in the cold air, my face wet. Avraham, Semmen and the old farmer were standing beside me and I heard the farmer say, "He's all right now." Semmen bent over me and said, "Now's the time you pick to faint, when someone is giving us food? Come on, get up, the food is waiting for us on the table!"

The bowls were big and they were full, but we ate everything quickly and the woman refilled our bowls, saying, "Eat, there's enough soup." It was very pleasant in the hut. We didn't feel like going outside to resume our wanderings. We stayed seated and told our hosts about Sobibor, about the revolt, and about what had happened to us since we left the camp. The farmer listened closely, sat for a few moments absorbed in thought, then finally said, "The war will be over soon. The Germans are being defeated and in retreat. We have to hold out until then. I will hide you. We'll build a bunker inside the granary and you can be there during the day. I'll bring you bread. Whatever we eat, you will eat."

After our experiences of the past few days, it was difficult to believe that there were also people like this, ready to help us and even endanger their own lives. I imagined that a miracle was occurring before my very eyes, and that the old farmer was actually an angel who had been sent from the heavens. Suddenly there was a knock at the door. The three of us hid. One of the neighbors had come to announce that on the following day, the Germans would come to the village to take *das Kontigent* — the tax allocation that the Germans had imposed on the farmers. Afterward the farmer looked embarrassed and apologized, but said that he could not hide us if the Germans were coming.

We got up to leave, but the old man asked us to stay a while longer, because they had no bread in the house at the moment and he wanted to send his wife out to borrow bread. He also sent his son out on an errand. The woman came back with two big loaves of bread, and his son brought bottles of milk. The farmer put the bread and the milk each into sacks and gave them to us. We said goodbye to the woman and her son, from whom we had not heard a word all evening, and we went out into the night. The farmer asked us where we were going and we had no idea, but answered, "To a big forest, so that what happened to us yesterday, when we couldn't find a forest, won't happen again." The man walked with us a long way, even though we told him to return home. Finally we approached the forest. When we were about to part, I took out some gold coins that I wanted to give to the old farmer, but he refused to take them. "I don't even know if I will be alive tomorrow," I said to him, "and you live in poverty. This money can help you." "I don't need anything," he answered, "This is the way I have lived all my life, and this is the way I will continue to live. And this gold may save your lives. May God keep me from taking money from you."

I very much wanted to give something to the old man. I begged him to take at least one coin, but he wouldn't accept anything. He embraced each of us and kissed us. He cried, his face wet with tears, and I cried with him. For a long time afterward I could still feel how his beard felt against my skin when we parted.

The time we spent with the old farmer encouraged us, and the following days were lucky as well. We were able to get food, usually at a high price, however. Once, after a farmwoman had refused to give us anything, I showed her a gold coin and she brought us bread and meat, and offered us a hot meal for another coin. We agreed, of course, and she asked only that we come at midnight and wait until she gave us a sign with a candle, which she would put in the window. She seemed fearful, and we argued about the wisdom of going to the house at midnight. Avraham said that it was a trap, and that was the only reason she invited us; she would probably bring someone to murder us. However, we didn't want to give up on a hot meal so easily, and instead of going back into the forest, we waited near the house. We watched the house and made sure that no one had entered. The woman came out a few times to draw water from the well, and to bring in wood for the oven. Time passed slowly and, luckily, the woman signaled us to come in before midnight. We entered the house, and we were once again moved by the wonderful feeling of being wrapped in the warmth of a home and the smell of food, a feeling of happiness that is difficult to describe. We forgot all about the decisions we had made to be careful before we came. The table was set. The woman was alone, and by candlelight we could see that she was in her thirties and had a pleasant face. Semmen said to me, "I hope you won't faint this time," and the two of us laughed.

The woman asked whether we wanted to drink anything alcoholic with our meal, continuing that by chance she had a bottle of good vodka, but that it would cost us another coin. Semmen quickly answered *"Da! Da!"* and the bottle appeared. The vodka affected all of us; the meal was tasty and the atmosphere was lively. Semmen invited the woman to drink with us, and after drinking, she, too, became merry. Semmen got up, said a few words in Russian and kissed the woman. The vodka gave me the courage to get up, as well. My legs were unsteady, my head was spinning, but I, too, went over to the woman and kissed her on the cheek. The woman returned my kiss and I was very happy. Avraham also kissed the woman. We were enjoying ourselves and the time flew by. Finally, the woman reminded us that it was late and we had to leave the house. We unwillingly walked outside, our legs heavy. As we left, the woman said that we could come to her home at night whenever we wanted and she would give us food. When we left, I had the urge to kiss her again, to again feel her sweet lips, but I didn't have the courage. The cool night quickly removed all of the effects of the vodka and I came back down to earth. But, on the way to the forest, we continued to joke and laugh.

One day, we passed a solitary house, which appeared to be empty. When we approached it, an old couple came toward us and invited us to come in and eat. Our hosts, who seemed to be poor, didn't look like farmers. Their language was fluent and clear, and their clothing was more suitable to city life. It turned out that they were Polish refugees from Poznan. We stayed with them until late at night. The man taught us how to find our way at night. He taught us how to find the North Star and identify the constellations Ursa Major and Ursa Minor, the "Big Bear" and the "Little Bear." He also taught us that when we were in the forest and we couldn't see the sky, or on a cloudy night, we could find north by checking the moss, which always grew on the north side of the tree trunk, as that was the side that was more shaded from the sun.

We gratefully said goodbye to this wonderful couple who had open-heartedly helped us and who had been willing to endanger themselves for us, but, all in all, people like these were only a small minority compared to the many others who were openly hostile and not only did not help us, but chased us away and, more than once, even tried to kill us. The large numbers of hostile people made those few who helped us seem even more unique, and those who helped gave us the will to struggle for survival and not lose our belief in human decency, in human beings created in the image of God.

Every night for three weeks after we had fled from Sobibor, we wandered from place to place, hiding in one forest after another with no particular objective, and we learned to adapt to the special forest environment. I stopped being afraid of the forest, of its voices, its noises and of the animals that dwelled in it. Now, each time we entered a new forest I felt at home, as though the forest belonged to me alone and entrance to others was forbidden. The forest has a unique quality — from the moment you adjust to it, when you are living in it, it gives a feeling of security. You can always disappear in a split second among the trees and hide in its depth, where you are secure from the outside world.

The three of us were the only survivors of a group that had numbered more than twenty men, and perhaps of the hundreds who had succeeded in running away from Sobibor — and perhaps we were the last three Jews in all of Poland? In any case, the Germans could not reconcile themselves to the fact that we, who had revolted at Sobibor, were still alive. Everywhere we went, we heard people warning, "The Germans are looking for you! Get away from here quickly!" Had the whole German army been commanded to hunt us down, even when they were suffering from so many reversals on the front and were in constant retreat? Was killing us so important to the Germans? They certainly didn't want to leave anyone alive who could tell of the extermination that took place at Sobibor; but in fact, it was important for us to survive precisely for that reason.

We were resigned to the fact that we were the only three left. The chances of finding others like us, who had fled from Sobibor and were still alive, seemed impossible. Now we must fight for our survival in the forest, like every other animal belonging there, and never give up the will to live. Our mood changed according to the measure of our hunger: when we could get food, we were optimistic; when we were hungry, we were depressed and in despair.

We were struck by a new blow, this time coming from the skies. Cold autumn rain began to fall and we had no shelter in the forest. For some time, we could sit under the trees and take refuge beneath their branches, but at a certain point, the branches would release all the water that had accumulated among their leaves and we would be soaking wet and shivering with cold. We would huddle together, trying unsuccessfully to share my one coat — when one of us would pull the coat in his direction, the others would be uncovered. The rain also restricted us to one place; walking in the forest was very difficult, as the branches leaning downward in the rain would block the path time and time again. Walking through the fields was even worse, as our rain-sodden clothes burdened us, and our shoes sank into the mud and got stuck, so that our feet would come out of them if we tried to walk. And winter hadn't really arrived yet — what would become of us when the snow began to fall, when the temperature would plunge to below freezing? We preferred not to think about that. But when the rain stopped and the sun emerged from behind the clouds, we would warm ourselves, dry our clothes, and begin to smile again. The forest was unbelievably beautiful after the rain. The strong odors were intoxicating and the singing of the birds gave us joy.

One day we left the forest to search for food, as usual. Navigating the muddy land was very difficult and we walked slowly. We couldn't find any farmers' homes to try our luck at asking for food. After many hours of walking, we went back into the forest. As we lay down to sleep on empty stomachs, we heard the sounds of dogs barking. Avraham jumped up and tried to convince us that we shouldn't stay in this forest; we should go on walking and find another place to hide. Semmen and I were exhausted and we didn't want to move, even though we could hear the dogs. In fact, the dogs gave us hope that we would find a house the following evening and perhaps get something to eat.

In the morning, as always, we investigated this new forest, and while I was walking and looking around quietly — this forest didn't seem any different from the others — Semmen suddenly saw some crockery hanging from one of the trees. We walked over to see what was inside. It was a jug full of peas soaking in water. We stood there, surprised; the jug was clean, and the water and the peas were fresh, meaning that someone was soaking the peas in order to cook them. Were the people who had hung the jug on the tree in the area, or had they gone? We didn't see any sign of life, so we took the jug with us — that night we would feast on cooked peas! We continued on our way with a strange sensation — who in the world had hung a jug of peas on a branch in the middle of the forest? As we walked, we suddenly came upon a line of bottles filled with water, stuck into the ground, and as we were trying to solve the mystery of this new find, we heard the rustling of branches. As if he had sprung up from underground, a man appeared in front of us. He was short, had an ax in his hand, and shouted at us in Polish, "Hands up!" The man's face was pale and serious, the ax in his hand was lifted toward us, but suddenly he said in Yiddish, "Are you Jews?" "Yes," we all answered at the same time. His pale face broke into a smile, and he said, "Don't be afraid. You are among Jews!"

For a moment we stood there in shock. We couldn't believe that the man who had just threatened us with an ax was actually Jewish. At the same time, another man appeared who did not look Jewish at all — his hair was blond and straight, his eyes were blue, and his broad shoulders and clothing marked him as a farmer. He walked toward us and welcomed us in Yiddish, *shalom aleichem*, welcome, Jews. The two men hugged and kissed us and led us a short distance into the trees. We approached a group of seated men, and before we even had a chance to see their faces, we heard shouts of "Berale! Berale! Avraham!" We hugged one another, weeping — they had all been in Sobibor! Shaya the gardener was there, Chaim the jeweler, another two men from Poland, and two from Holland. We must have looked terrible because they all started shouting, "Give them something to eat and to drink!" One of the fellows poured us some tea, and then gave us slices of bread, saying, "I know that you must be very hungry. Soon, we will all eat. In the meantime, have some bread and tea to raise your spirits." The hot tea in the forest, early in the morning, tasted like the finest wine. As I was drinking it, I had the feeling that I had come home, and that all our troubles had ended. The broad-shouldered man took the jug of peas, poured its contents into a bucket, added some other ingredients and put it on the campfire. The odor of cooking peas filled the area and mixed with the scent of pine trees after the rain.

"Where have you been till now?" we were asked. "It's been almost a month since the revolt at Sobibor." The three of us gave them a detailed account of what we had been doing, and as we spoke, I felt as if we were talking with members of our own families. The group that we met had arrived in this forest about two weeks previously. They, too, had had their share of adventures. At the beginning, they were a large group, but then they split up. Most had gone eastward, planning to cross the Bug River, and these men had gone in the direction of Chelm, led by Shaya the gardener, who had known the area, where he hoped they could find a hiding place in one of the villages whose farmers they knew in exchange for the abundance of money they had. On the way, they had been joined by the two Dutch Jews, and by two brothers, Yozhik and Monyek Serchuk, who had been in the forest for more than a year. The brothers had explained to them how difficult, and even dangerous, it was to try to hide with the farmers. Their whole family had hidden in the village with a farmer, but another farmer had informed on them and the Germans had come and taken them away. Only Yozhik and Monyek were left. Their parents had had a shop selling chickens in Chelm.

Monyek, the older son, had been raised and educated in the home of a relative in Warsaw, where he had studied at good schools and had been an excellent student. When the war broke out, he came home to be with his family during the rough times. He had tried to convince his parents to flee eastward, to Russia, but his father had objected to going to "the land of atheists." Monyek ran away to Russia alone, but quickly became disillusioned with the Soviet government and after a year had returned to Chelm. Yozhik, his younger brother, had helped his father in the shop from the time that he was a child and would travel with him to villages to buy chickens. When he got older, he would go to the neighboring villages alone, which was how he learned about the farmers' way of life and became friendly with them. He had sometimes had to return home during the night, and so had learned to defend himself against attackers, both human and animal. When the Germans entered Chelm, and life became harder and harder for the Jews, Yozhik became the only breadwinner of the family, as his non-Jewish appearance allowed him to continue going to surrounding villages to buy chickens.

In the summer of 1942, when the Germans conducted a roundup of the Jews, the first in Chelm, and the Jews were sent to Sobibor, the Serchuk family had managed to avoid being taken. Yozhik decided to hide his family with Polish farmers, as he sensed that something terrible was happening to the people whom the Germans packed into trains. His good relations with the farmers and the promise of payment had enabled him to find a place with a farmer for his entire family to stay, and he and his brother Monyek went out to work in the fields, returning in the evening, bringing food to the family. One night, when they returned with food, they didn't find their family — the Germans had taken them all. They discovered later that one of the farmers had informed on them. Yozhik felt responsible for being unable to save his family; he was so depressed that he didn't care about staying alive himself, and it was only thanks to Monyek that he recovered.

One evening, they had gone to visit the farmer, but on the way they encountered a German patrol. When they heard the order "*Halt! Halt!*" Yozhik shouted to his brother, "You run to the left and I'll run to the right. If the Germans catch one of us, the other will still live!" The Germans opened fire. Yozhik jumped aside, lay flat on the ground, crawled for some time, then got up and ran. Monyek ran in another direction but didn't take cover. The Germans saw him, fired on him, and he was wounded in his thigh and fell. When the Germans saw him lying wounded, they asked him who he was. He answered that he was the son of a farmer from a distant village. When they asked him why he hadn't stopped when they had ordered him to, he had no answer. He was taken to a nearby village and left under guard; the Germans planned to interrogate him on the following day. The guards, aware that their prisoner was wounded, weren't concerned about his running away. Monyek, who knew that the next morning his identity would be uncovered, managed with great effort to jump from the window, and it took him many hours to crawl to the nearby forest.

Yozhik, who didn't know that the Germans had injured his brother, walked to the edge of the forest where he and his brother used to wait for each other. When some time passed and Monyek hadn't arrived, Yozhik began to worry about him and finally realized that the Germans had caught him. Suddenly, from out of the terrible silence, he heard groans. When he walked in the direction of the sounds, he found his brother, lying wounded. Monyek, who was a pessimist by nature, told his brother that he shouldn't try to save him — that he was dying. But Yozhik didn't give up. When he examined Monyek's leg in the dark, he found that the bullet had entered his thigh from the front, leaving a small wound, and had exited from the back, where there was a large wound. He carried his brother to a good hiding place, built a fence of branches around him and walked to the city of Chelm, about fifteen kilometers away. He reached the city early in the morning, and even though the city had been "cleared of Jews," he walked to the city center, without trying to conceal his identity, and went to a pharmacy. When he was inside, he took a knife out from under his coat and held it against the stomach of the pharmacist, saying, "Give me everything necessary to deal with a bullet wound, and enough to heal the wounded man. If you don't give it to me quickly, I'll stab you with this knife!"

The frightened pharmacist packed boric acid, salves, absorbent cotton and other medical supplies, and Yozhik left the city quickly. When he reached the forest, he found his brother struggling with a wild boar that had been attracted to the smell of blood from Monyek's wound. Yozhik chased the boar away and treated his bother's wound as the pharmacist had instructed. Monyek, who had lost quite a bit of blood, was very weak, and Yozhik brought chickens, eggs and milk products from the farmers at night to help his brother regain his strength. In the forest, without help, Yozhik succeeded in healing Monyek, and they promised each other that they would never separate — they would share the same fate, whatever it might be.

The feeling of being among fellow Jews again was wonderful. It was like a dream to hear people speaking Yiddish, to see self-confidence in their faces, to sit with them around the campfire in the forest. We had never dared to hope to meet any Jews in the forest; in fact, we never really knew what to hope for. We had even stopped thinking. We had been living a life of following our instincts, like animals.

We ate the pea soup that Yozhik prepared, delicious and nourishing, and in spite of the fact that it was very hot, we swallowed it so quickly that everyone around us kept watching. Yozhik made sure that we were satisfied. "Eat, children, there is enough!" he repeated again and again, and then he brought out a bottle of vodka and said, "We have to drink l'chaim in honor of our guests!" I took a sip of the vodka and suddenly felt as though I had been hit by a heavy blow. My head was spinning and I had no control over my tongue, and could only mutter a word or two. "The boy is already drunk," I heard someone say. I lay down flat, my eyes turned up to the tops of the trees, but the forest wouldn't stand still — it moved up and down at different speeds, and it seemed to me that I was falling into an abyss, that I was holding on to the earth, that everything, the trees and the people sitting around me, were all moving incessantly. I finally gave in to the strange feeling and began to enjoy it, feeling like a child in a rocking cradle.

Suddenly a vision appeared to me from my distant childhood: I was very young, in summer, at a vacation village near Warsaw called Machlin. We stayed there with a few other families who were our parents' friends, in rented houses. The women and children were there all summer, and the men worked in Warsaw during the week and came up on weekends. The houses were in a forest, and one Shabbat, when we had returned from synagogue, someone suggested bringing the tables outside so that all of the families could sit together under the shady trees. Everyone pitched in — the men carried the tables, we children took the chairs, and the women brought out all the food they each had prepared. We were all buoyed by enthusiasm. Wine flowed like water, everyone laughed and joked and I felt overwhelmed. Now, in this forest hideout, I could clearly see the table and everyone sitting around it. I saw my father, sitting at the head of the table, my mother, pink-cheeked, serving the food…and suddenly the picture changed: I was working in the forest, in Sobibor, near the fence of *Lager* 3. I saw the ridges of the piles of sand at the edges of the pits filled with human bodies. I heard the Germans shouting and the dog, Barry, barking. I heard the terrible screams of the workers and I knew that the dog had sunk his teeth into them — and the tears flowed from my eyes and slid down my cheeks uncontrollably. As I lay there, crying, undisturbed by anyone, I fell asleep.

Yozhik and Monyek had built themselves a bunker in the woods where they could live through the winter. The bunker was bigger than they needed, as they had prepared a place for the uncle, his wife and their son hiding in the home of the farmer in the nearby village, and for other Jews who might pass that way. The bunker had been carefully built — the earth that had been dug up was scattered far from the site of the bunker, and the opening was well hidden, so that someone standing over it couldn't tell what was beneath. When the first group from Sobibor arrived, the two brothers had given them the bunker, and they, themselves, had continued sleeping outside. At night, Yozhik would buy food from farmers for the whole group. The people from Sobibor had money, and Chaim, the jeweler, had taken a large amount of gold. Yozhik would usually go alone, but occasionally Monyek would go with him; very infrequently, they would take someone from the group to help them carry sacks of food from the villages. Yozhik said that people who were not used to the forest would become frightened at every hopping bird and every passing squirrel, and that the Sobibor people didn't know how to behave in the villages, and so it was better for him to go out to get food alone.

It was November. Yozhik said that there would soon be heavy rain and storms, and that snow might even begin falling any day. We would have to quickly build another bunker at a distance from the existing one. Thus, if one of the bunkers were discovered, this would not endanger the other. A chill went through me as he spoke about the possibility.

We went out with Yozhik to look for a place to build a bunker. We had no idea what a "good place" was, but Yozhik knew; it would not be obvious, but it would be high enough so that rainwater wouldn't penetrate, and it wouldn't be easily accessible nor near a path. Yozhik went from place to place and we followed him until he found a site that satisfied him, and when he asked what we thought, we all agreed with him, of course. In the short time that we had been with him, Yozhik had earned our trust and we all accepted him as our leader. We agreed with anything he said. That evening, we started digging, which meant, for the most part, chopping the roots of trees with an ax. The earth we dug out was put into sacks and carried far away from the site. At night, Yozhik and Monyek went to the village and came back before dawn, bringing tarpaper for sealing roofs. The next day, we worked all day under the guidance of Yozhik, who already had experience building the first bunker, and by evening, construction was complete, and the bunker was roofed and well camouflaged. The entrance was through a tree, and it couldn't be seen from two meters away. Inside the bunker, there was room for eight people to sleep, four on one

side and four on the other — heads near the walls, feet meeting in
the center. In time of need, another person could sleep between
the two rows of legs.

We entered the bunker, Semmen, Avraham, Yozhik, Monyek
and I. It was damp and there was a strong smell of the roots of trees,
as we had not finished straightening the walls and the floor was
bumpy. It quickly warmed up and gave me the wonderful feeling
of a house.

Strong winds shook the trees of the forest and a loud unceasing
noise, like a waterfall, echoed around us. Heavy clouds covered the
sky and the sun set in the afternoon hours. The wind brought with it
traces of rain that could hardly be seen, but which wet the trees and
changed their color. The sprinkles quickly turned into large drops
of heavy rain, which became a flood. Thunder echoed through
the forest and lightening turned it into a magical place. Everyone
sought shelter within the bunker and only I stayed outside for a
few moments more. I stood, bewitched, watching the wonders of
nature. Wet and shivering with cold, I went down into the bunker,
and everyone laughed. It was warm and pleasant inside. Protected
from the rain and the cold, we congratulated ourselves on having
completed the bunker the day before. For a moment, I pondered
whether the meeting with Yozhik and Monyek, which led to building the bunker before the rains began, was a kind of miracle, but
the thought of God reminded me of Sobibor, where I had stopped
believing in miracles. In Sobibor, after much thought and many
misgivings, I had come to the conclusion that there was no God. I
had imagined that my inner debate had ended, but here and there,
reasons for believing in God would confront me, and I would have
to deal with the question over and over, as everything beautiful that
I remembered from the past was connected to religion, and those
I had most loved believed in God with such complete faith that it
was difficult for me to deny their belief.

Rain fell for two days without a break. We were low on food
and it was impossible to cook. But inside the bunker, it stayed
warm and pleasant. Each of us lay in his place and talked about

himself and his family. When my brother Mottel had come back from prison and told us about his adventures, I had been envious of him, because he had already experienced life, while nothing had happened in my own life. If someone from my family had been present now — my mother, my brother or my sister — I would have told them everything, leaving out no detail. But where were they all — what had become of them? Here, in the bunker, I had heard from my friends that the Jews of the Warsaw ghetto had been taken to the death camp at Treblinka, and that, in April of this year, there had been a revolt in the ghetto, after which those who remained were killed. What had happened to my mother and my little brother, Yankele — had they been taken to Treblinka, or had they died of starvation in the ghetto? What about my sister; Dvora surely would have been among the rebels, but who knows? And my brother Mottel? Someone had told me in Sobibor that Mottel had fled and joined the partisans. Perhaps he was alive somewhere, in one of the forests?

While I was in Sobibor, I didn't worry about the fate of my family. It wasn't that I didn't think about them — but while I was on the verge of death and watching everything around me being destroyed, we shared the same fate. When a transport arrived at Sobibor from Turobin, and I was told that my family thought I was dead and had sat *shiva* (the mourning period) for me, I felt the pain that my brother, who had considered himself responsible for my welfare, had felt. And perhaps the news of my death had reached Warsaw, and my mother. I imagined her suffering and that of other members of the family, and Mother's feelings of guilt at having smuggled me out of the ghetto. Now, sitting in the bunker, looking at Yozhik and Monyek, who had spent more than a year in the forest, and hearing about the defeats of the Germans, about their continual retreats, I felt a ray of hope that I could stay alive — and I began to worry about my loved ones.

If the war ended and I survived — who else would be left in my family? It wasn't possible that I would be the only one. But the more I thought about it, the more I understood that the chances of anyone surviving were small, and perhaps nonexistent. I couldn't accept this conclusion, and time after time, I imagined that a member of my family had survived — my brother or my sister — and then, I was ashamed of having decided, in my imagination, who had lived and who had died. I was envious of Yozhik and Monyek, who had both survived, two brothers connected to one another like two limbs of one body. And, meanwhile, the war was still going on and who knew how long it would continue, how long we would have to hide like animals taking cover from hunters, with no assurance of survival for any of us.

Yozhik had good connections in all of the villages. He knew every farmer and he knew who was trustworthy. He also had contacts with Jews who were hiding with farmers, including his uncle, aunt, and their child, and another uncle who had been alone since the Germans had killed his family. Yozhik looked after them, visiting them from time to time and making sure that they were all right. He also said that there were three Czech Jews in hiding, who had had professions that were useful to the Germans; the Germans had kept them working in one of the camps until the Gestapo had demanded them. They had found out in time that they were to be taken and had run away, and for the past half year they had been hiding with a farmer. This farmer told Yozhik that he wanted to go on giving them shelter, but that his wife, who feared the Germans, gave him no peace, and they would have to leave. The Czechs told Yozhik that the real reason the farmer wouldn't harbor them any longer was that their money had run out, so Yozhik had asked the farmer to keep them there for a few more days and gave him money to buy food for them. Now that the bunker was ready, he intended to bring them to the forest.

When the three arrived, they were in terrible physical condition. For six months they had been in a cellar, never seeing the light of day — only at night would they walk a bit. Now they were feeble and could hardly stand. The three were older than us — over thirty. The youngest, Krichona, had an athletic build, and his lined face indicated that he had been working since he was very young.

He was a mechanic and there was nothing he couldn't do. He had grown up in a secular Zionist home and knew very little about Jewish customs. The second, Schnabel, was about forty years old, heavyset, with a face that was always sad. He was the son of a Christian father, an estate owner married to a Jewish woman who had converted. Their home was Christian and he knew nothing about Judaism. The Germans had discovered that he had a Jewish mother — and he and his family were sent to Poland with the other Jews. His family went to Sobibor, but as he was a building engineer, he had been taken to a German camp to work. The third man, Solomon, was a carpenter. He was a tall, thin man, with glasses. He was not religious, but he had grown up in a religious family and knew Yiddish, so it was easier communicating with him.

For the first few days after the three men had joined us, the atmosphere in the bunker was tense. The three Czechs felt like strangers and spoke little. But being together constantly quickly broke down the barriers among us, and we found ways to communicate with one another.

Yozhik brought another new resident to the bunker, an older man, over sixty, and it was hard to make room for him. We had already heard about this man, a professor. He arrived dressed in nice, clean clothes, and his appearance called for respect. He had been a noted architect in Czechoslovakia and had drawn up the plans for several well-known buildings. In Poland, the Germans had kept him employed until recently. It was very difficult for him to adjust to living in the bunker, and he had an especially hard time with the sanitary conditions — he couldn't understand how we could live without showering every day. On his first day in the bunker he began his war against the lice, and we couldn't help laughing the first time he felt something crawling under his shirt. He took it off, examined it carefully, and said loudly, "I found four lice." He was surprised, and happy, as well, that he had been able to kill all four. After an hour, he undressed again, and once more went searching for lice, and we watched as he fought his losing battle. That time, he announced that he had killed twelve lice. After a few hours, the professor said brokenly that his war had been lost; he had found so many lice in his latest search that he was unable to count them all.

The one remedy we had against every discomfort — the terrible odor, the sleeping conditions, and even the lice — was "Samogon," the evil-smelling, sharp-tasting, but intoxicating homemade vodka. Yozhik made sure to keep supplying it every evening. Drinking always led to a more congenial atmosphere in the bunker; those who were quiet all day became talkative, told jokes and sang songs. Monyek would recite Polish and Yiddish poetry, and sometimes, poems he had written himself. Those were the ones I liked most, as they expressed what we were experiencing. When he recited these, he would become tense; the veins in his forehead and the sides of his neck would become prominent, his eyes would fill with tears, and each of his words sounded like a treasure. When he finished, he would walk over to me and ask, "Berale, what do you think? Was the poem a good one?" He knew that I loved his verse, but he wanted to hear it from me again and again. He would say, "They don't understand any of this…" Sometimes, it seemed to me that he wrote his poetry for my ears only.

One day, toward evening, we heard a noise outside the bunker. At the opening, we could see a pair of naked legs. Then, the rest of the body of Shaya the gardener appeared, completely naked. He had been living in the other bunker and when we saw his pale face, his shivering, unclothed body and his eyes, which were those of a person who wasn't completely sane, we all knew that something terrible had happened.

Shaya wanted to speak, but he was unable to. Instead, he burst into tears and we could not calm him down. When he was able to talk, he told us that, in the morning, a gang of Polish robbers had fired into the bunker, took out the men, one by one, ordered everyone to get undressed — and had killed them. Shaya told them that he had hidden some gold under one of the trees. The robbers ordered him to undress too, and he began to lead them to the place where the imaginary gold was buried. At one point, he was able to get away from them. They fired at him, but luckily, he wasn't hit. He had spent the whole day wandering around the forest with no clothes on, freezing in the cold, until he had found our bunker.

For a few minutes, we were in total shock. Until then, we had been living under the illusion that here, in the forest, nothing could happen to us. It was true that Yozhik had often said that he was afraid of Polish murderers, but none of us took him seriously, and I even dared to dream of the day we would go free, and how we would live to see the German defeat. Now it was evident that Polish murderers were killing the last of the Jews who still remained in Poland after the Germans had left it *Judenrein*, free of Jews. No! There was no chance that any of us would survive. That was our fate. We were just as doomed in the forest as we had been in Sobibor: we knew that we were fated to die; we just did not know when.

Semmen recovered first and said, "We should go and see if anyone is still alive. Perhaps someone was only wounded." But Shaya muttered, "They are all dead. They are all dead." Yozhik was deep in thought. There was no doubt that the killers were now looking for us — it was only by chance that they had discovered the other bunker first. And their attack had proven successful, as Chaim the jeweler had had a large amount of gold. First of all, we had to get Shaya dressed in something until Yozhik could buy clothes for him. And we had to leave the bunker immediately, as it had become a death trap.

We managed to get some clothes for Shaya, but he had no shoes. He wrapped his feet in sacks and we all left the bunker, planning never to return. It was getting dark. We could barely see. As I looked around, it seemed as though there was a robber hiding behind every tree. But it was quiet outside. We sat down to discuss what we should do, but actually, we were waiting for Yozhik to suggest something. None of us had any idea of how to solve our new problem. It was still just the beginning of winter. We had left the warm bunker and we were already shivering in the cold. Snow would begin to fall any day now, and it was certain that we couldn't live very long when the temperatures fell below freezing.

Yozhik was silent; he couldn't think of anything. There was a pained expression on his face. Finally, he said, "We must bury our dead. The least we can do is to bury them as Jews. But we will go late tonight. We don't know if the murderers are waiting for us, or for Shaya, who ran away naked. As for us, I have no solution. There is no farmer who would agree to hide such a large group for all the money in the world. Monyek and I already have places with farmers, but I can't leave you. We'll stay with you. But we have to find a way to avoid falling into the hands of those murderers. They haven't managed to catch us yet, but they'll keep looking for us."

Semmen remarked, "If they had had a weapon in the bunker, this never would have happened. We must get hold of a weapon, at any price. And then, let them come..." Yozhik answered that they would make every effort to get a rifle, but, in the meantime, we had no choice but to return to the bunker. From now on, we would post a guard outside who would watch and listen for anyone who might be approaching. This would give us time to get away. Soon snow would cover the forest. The branches of the trees would bend under the weight of the snow and block the paths, deterring anyone from entering the forest. The snow might give us away by showing footprints leading to the bunker, but he had an idea about how to solve that problem: we could make stilts from wood and learn how to walk on them, like clowns in the circus. The marks that the stilts would leave in the snow would look like animal tracks — and whoever couldn't learn to walk on stilts wouldn't leave the bunker. The place we had fled from and which had seemed a death trap was again the place where we must live. There was no other alternative, in spite of the danger. The cold had convinced us to return to the bunker.

That night, all of those who had fled Sobibor, except for Shaya, walked over to the other bunker to bury our friends. We all felt terrible. The closer we got, the more often we stopped, peering into the darkness and listening. Were the murderers waiting for us? It seemed to me that I heard voices, sighs, cries and other noises. I was shaking with fear. I tried to hide my anxiety and I was angry with myself — what was happening to me? Every rustle, every bird flying from its nest frightened me, just as they had during my first days in the forest! We reached the bunker and we were shocked beyond belief. White bodies were scattered near the bunker; part of the bunker roof had caved in and there were more bodies inside the bunker, fully dressed. It was hard to identify the bodies at night. Silently we put the deceased side by side in the bunker. Semmen told me to take the shoes off of one of the dead men for Shaya, and I removed a pair of shoes. Yozhik began to say Kaddish, the prayer for the dead. We worked for about an hour, covering the bodies — the bunker had become a mass grave — and we left.

After this tragedy, we lived with the constant knowledge of the danger that threatened us and we searched for ways of defending ourselves. Even though we were now guarding the bunker, we felt trapped when we were inside it, and we tried to spend as much time as possible outside, but again and again, the rain and the cold would force us back inside. "If they attack the bunker," said Krichona, "they won't have an easy time of it. We'll fight them tooth and nail. But when will we have a weapon?" Yozhik reported that we would soon get a rifle. He had already paid part of the price to the son of his farmer friend, who had promised to bring the weapon soon; then, let the murderers come to attack us! "Can we do anything with my rifle bullets?" I asked Semmen. Everyone laughed and Semmen said, only half joking, "We could heat them and then they would explode."

The rains continued to fall. A few times, a wet snow had fallen, which melted as soon as it touched the ground. Because of the stormy weather, we had not yet begun to build stilts, and as time passed, the tension lessened and we became less watchful. Laughter was heard inside the bunker again, and the horrible picture of the murder in the other bunker seemed to fade into just another of the horrible scenes we had witnessed up till then.

One morning as I went out of the bunker, I was surprised to see that the forest had changed — large, white flakes of snow were slowly falling from above, white patches covered the ground of the forest, and the branches of the trees were coated with white, as well. I was struck by a strange feeling — the sight was both beautiful and threatening. The snow continued to fall all day, and the forest became whiter and whiter as the branches began dipping toward the ground. I was happy to leave the bunker for my turn at guard duty. I watched the snow falling, covering everything in white, and memories of my childhood enfolded me. How I had loved the first snowfall — waking up in the morning and seeing the snow falling outside the window, the whole world in white. How I had loved to walk the snowy streets rather than go straight home after school! Even now I was enchanted by the sight of the forest, which had turned white in a few hours. But I was also frightened. Up to now, the forest had given us freedom, the possibility of movement and independence, but the falling snow had taken away our liberty and had sealed us in the bunker as surely as a prison.

One morning, Semmen, who had been on guard, came into the bunker and said that he had seen what he thought was the figure of a man — and that their eyes had met for a moment. The man had disappeared and he had not seen him again, even though he had searched for him for a long while. Semmen was not completely sure that it had been a man; it might have been an animal — or an illusion. But Yozhik said firmly, "They have found us! That man has been looking for us. We must leave the bunker!"

We didn't really want to leave the warm bunker, and we knew that we had nowhere to go, but we did what Yozhik told us to. We lay freezing in the snow all day, but when night fell, we began to walk. Yozhik led us to the granary of the farmer from whom he bought supplies, and hid us among the piles of straw. Then he and Monyek went to the farmer's house. He was hoping to meet the son of the farmer, who was supposed to bring us the rifle for which we had already paid "If we had a rifle," he said, "we could go back to the bunker and we wouldn't have to be afraid of the murderers." If we didn't get the rifle, perhaps the farmer's son, who seemed to be a friend, could find us a place to hide. But the farmer's son wasn't at home; perhaps he was intentionally avoiding a meeting with

Yozhik. Because we really had no alternative, and because Yozhik was still hoping to meet the farmer's son, he decided that we would spend the day in the granary. He bought supplies from the farmer, paying a steep price, and then told the farmer that we wanted to stay in the granary until the following evening. The farmer couldn't refuse him and Yozhik thought that we could spend the day hiding in the straw, but after about an hour, the farmer came to tell Yozhik that his wife was afraid and that we would have to leave. We left after a few minutes and found ourselves in a snowy field; snow was still falling and we had no place to go. The cold penetrated our bones and we finally decided to return to the bunker. In the forest, we tried to hide our footprints with branches and we were glad that the falling snow was an accomplice to our task. It was good to be back in our bunker again — each of us took his place, we drank a bit of vodka and it was soon comfortably warm inside. We felt as though we had returned home.

A few days passed uneventfully, with nothing out of the ordinary happening. We all began to assume that the murderers were ignorant of our whereabouts. The figure Semmen had seen had been a figment of his imagination.

One evening, we were all inside the bunker, waiting for darkness and expecting Yozhik and Monyek to return from the village. We were very tense. We could never feel completely secure when Yozhik and Monyek were not with us, and we always waited impatiently for them to return, like children waiting for their parents. Perhaps this time they would bring the rifle, or perhaps some other good news. In any case, another day of tension and waiting had passed — night fell quickly, and we had learned to appreciate the darkness more and more.

Suddenly, a shout! Solomon, who had been standing guard, yelled, "They're coming!" Krichona took the ax standing in the corner and jumped outside. At the same time, we heard a shot, and after a moment, another shot. "This is the end," said Shaya. Semmen and I were lying on one side of the bunker, and Avraham and Shaya were in the corner. On the other side, only the professor was left with Schnabel, who was opposite the entrance. Suddenly, an object rolled in through the entrance and exploded with ear-splitting noise. The bunker was filled with thick smoke and a sharp odor. We felt as though we were choking. The smoke got into our eyes and our throats. We could not breathe, nor could we see any-thing. I felt that this must be the moment of death — the moment that breath leaves the body. The quiet in the bunker made it seem as though everyone was dead, but, after a moment, I could hear moans. Shaya shouted that he was wounded; Schnabel groaned and muttered, "My feet, my feet..." The professor was wounded, as well. When the smoke cleared a bit, I could see that Schnabel's legs were covered with blood, which was flowing onto the floor of the bunker. Schnabel groaned again, *"Oy, oy..."* I pressed as close as I could to the wall of the bunker, but aside from that, I felt completely helpless. There was nothing I could do except to await death, which would come at any moment. I was surprised that I was still alive. Only a few minutes ago, I had thought that we were all dead.

From time to time, more shots were fired into the bunker. Between one shot and the next, there was silence. The men outside were apparently listening, trying to hear what was going on inside. Most of the shots hit Schnabel, who had been opposite the entrance. We tried to move him to a corner, but he had already been hit a number of times. Avraham was crying and he abruptly took bills out of his pocket and tore them to pieces. He then took his watch off and hit the wall of the bunker with it. "The murderers won't get it," he muttered to himself. We shook hands, kissed each other, and waited for death. Suddenly we heard someone shout from outside, "Everyone out! Everyone out!" We looked at each other; none of us moved. It would be better to die here, inside. Again there was a shot and another shout, "Out! Out!" Again, we didn't move. Let them try to come in and get us. We had recovered from the initial shock of the attack. Semmen, who was in the corner near the entrance, was holding a shovel, ready to use it. Anyone who put his hand or foot in would not be able to take it out again. I found a big knife and I was waiting, as well. Again, silence. Perhaps the most difficult were the moments of waiting. All of a sudden, Avraham began yelling. We all joined him, without knowing why — who would hear us in the middle of the forest? And who did we expect would come to save us, the Germans?

Minutes passed, perhaps hours. We lost our sense of time. When we stopped yelling, and there was silence again, we heard the sound of digging. They were afraid to try to come in. Their shots had not had the desired effect; no one had come out. There was only one way to get to us — and that was to take the roof apart! We were already resigned to our deaths in the bunker — but no one wanted to fall into the hands of the murderers. Then I remembered the bullets in my pocket. I asked Semmen if he thought we could fire a shot with one of them. I immediately took out the bullets. I couldn't think of how to hold it. I tried to improvise pliers by using two forks. I gave the bullet to Semmen and lit a candle. Semmen held the bullet in the direction of the entrance. We could still hear the sounds of digging above us as we heated the edge of the bullet. After a few seconds — or perhaps many minutes — an explosion sounded that rocked the bunker. Excited by success, I shouted in Russian, "Semmen, fire! Come here — bring the rifle! Give me the pistol! Fire! Fire!" I shouted as loudly as I could, hoping that the murderers would think that there were armed partisans in the bunker, and, meanwhile, Semmen was heating another bullet, and another shot was heard. This time, I thought that I had been hit and shouted, "I've been wounded." I felt a burning sensation on my skin, but it was only the burning cap of the bullet that had touched me. Semmen continued to "fire" — each shot taking a long time — and the two of us continued shouting orders in Russian. We noticed suddenly that the digging sounds above us had stopped. We listened tensely to what was going on above. Complete silence! We waited breathlessly for a long time, but we didn't hear a sound. "Fire one more bullet," I said to Semmen, and we heard the explosion of the bullet, and again, silence. It had been some time since Solomon had shouted, "They're coming!" There was no light coming into the bunker. Perhaps they had gone. We couldn't take any chances! Perhaps they were waiting for us quietly outside. Perhaps they had gone to bring more ammunition. If so, we should get out and run away.

Semmen tried to put his head outside, but felt something blocking the opening. "They've blocked the entrance," he announced. When he brought a candle over to investigate, he added, "They've blocked the entrance with Kirchona's body!" Semmen tried to move it aside, but was unsuccessful. I couldn't believe that he could not move it away from the opening, so I tried, but I was unsuccessful, as well. Our need to get away from the bunker began driving us mad. All of us tried to move the body, but no one succeeded. There was only one way to get out — and it meant cutting up Krichona's body, but no one dared to do that. Avraham started to take the roof apart from the inside. He tried to free the beam that held the roof up. He began digging under it and the beam sagged a bit. Some earth fell on us from above, and we immediately realized the danger: the roof could collapse and bury us alive. We shouted to Avraham to stop. With a great effort we managed to move the body a bit and pull one of its legs inside, and working even harder, we finally freed the entrance. Bloodstained and perspiring heavily, we went out into the freezing cold. Outside, everything was white and silent. There was no sign of what had transpired a short time ago. It was difficult to believe that we were alive.

We tried to take stock of our situation. The old professor was lightly wounded in his head and hand, and he had probably been cut by shards of the explosive device the attackers had thrown inside. Shaya's wounds were even lighter — they were only scratches that had bled a bit, but the bleeding had stopped. Only Schnabel was seriously wounded: his whole body had been riddled with bullets and his legs were smashed. He was fully conscious and asked that we kill him, as he could not stand any more suffering. We didn't know what to do with him. We were afraid that the murderers would return, and we wanted to get away from there as fast as possible. We told Schnabel that we would come back in a little while and take care of him, and we left Krichona's body above, intending to bury it when we returned.

We stood looking at each other, not believing that we were alive. Avraham broke into tears. Suddenly we heard a rustle, and, as though he had popped up from under the ground, Solomon came toward us, extremely agitated. He told us that the murderers must have known that the bunker was being guarded. They had snuck up quietly, so that they wouldn't be seen or heard, and by the time he discovered them, they were already very close. He was alerted to them by chance — one of them had stumbled over a tree, and Solomon had heard the sound of a branch being broken. There were three of them, each one armed with a rifle. When he saw them, they didn't even try to hide. It was as if they knew that the guard was unarmed. In any case, they continued their approach and it was then that he had shouted to us that they were coming. He himself had run away and had heard explosions and shots from a distance. He was convinced that no one in the bunker was still alive. When there was complete silence, he began to wander in the forest without knowing what to do. He considered going back to the farmer who had hidden him before he had joined us, but he had been drawn back to the bunker to see what had happened. For a time he checked the surrounding area, not daring to go toward the bunker — until he had heard our voices.

We felt that we had to get away quickly, but we couldn't walk very fast — we had to support the old professor and Shaya, both of whom had difficulty walking and had to rest from time to time. Not far from the house of the farmer who sold us supplies, near the big tree that stood at the side of the path leading to the house, we stopped. We had to decide what to do: Go into the granary and hide? Go to the farmer and ask him about Yozhik? Ask for permission to remain in his yard until Yozhik returned? There was no chance that he would agree.

Suddenly we heard steps. Two figures were approaching against the background of snow. We froze. I made our signaling sound and we heard the return sound echo back. The two figures were Yozhik and Monyek, and we told them what had happened. From the time we left the bunker we hadn't spoken about what had taken place. Now, all of us felt the need to tell Yozhik every detail. Everyone was speaking at once, and we kept interrupting each other until finally, there was silence. Yozhik said, "I knew something terrible would happen today. I had a bad dream last night, and all day I said to myself that something terrible was happening in the forest. It's a miracle that you're alive." He had no answer to the question of what we could do now; he decided to hide us for the time being in the farmer's granary without his knowledge. He and Monyek would return to the bunker to see if they could save Schnabel. We wanted to go with them, but Yozhik forbade us, saying, "You have suffered enough today. We don't need you."

We crept quietly into the granary and lay in a pile of straw. Yozhik told us to try to come up with a plan to save ourselves; he admitted that he had no solution. He went to the farmer's house, but he didn't tell him that we were in the granary; he only told the farmer's son about us, and asked him to bring us a hot drink and something to treat our wounds. Yozhik and Monyek went into the forest. We had been freezing outside, but in the straw, we began to warm up. I began feeling drowsy, and I was just dropping off to sleep when the farmer and his wife appeared with pitchforks in their hands, shouting, "Out, Jews! Quickly! Out!" They pushed their pitchforks into the straw and continued to shout, "We know you are here!" We got up out of the straw and told them that we were going, but the woman kept shouting and cursing us, saying that she would kill us if we didn't leave immediately. We left the warm granary and returned to the tree alongside the path, shivering with cold and waiting for Yozhik and Monyek to return from the bunker — and for a miracle.

Yozhik and Monyek returned, and seeing us, realized what had happened. Yozhik told us that they had found Schnabel dead, completely naked, his clothes scattered near his body. It appeared that the robbers had returned to the bunker, undressed him and searched his clothes. We continued to stand by the tree together, shivering in the cold of the winter night, quiet and in despair. We felt that this was a fateful moment — we had been together through so much hardship but to no avail, and it was folly to have imagined that we could survive together. Now our partnership was coming to an end — the time had come to part from one another...

Shaya broke the silence. He said that he and Avraham had decided to go to the villages around Chelm, where he knew many farmers, and the two of them could find a place to hide. Solomon said that he and the professor could go back to the place where he had been hiding before coming to the forest, but that he had no money to pay the farmer. Yozhik asked if anyone could give Solomon some money. I had very few coins left. I gave two gold coins to Solomon and he kissed me.

I looked at Semmen and Semmen looked at me — where could the two of us go? Not to Vinitzia, his home city, nor to Warsaw, mine. Then Semmen said, "Berale, we will go back to the bunker. Whatever happens, happens." "You can't go back to the bunker," said Yozhik. "You will come with us. Whatever our fate is will be your fate, too." We parted from Avraham and Shaya, from Solomon and the professor. We felt that we would never see each other again. We stood and watched the figures going farther away, until they disappeared. We felt as though our hearts were breaking. Why?

It was past midnight. We had to hurry to find a place to hide before the farmers got up to milk their cows. Yozhik led us quickly down dirt paths covered with snow. The cold burned our ears, our noses and our cheeks, but walking quickly warmed our bodies. We walked silently. The images of what had happened in the bunker wouldn't leave me: the explosions, the shots, the shouts, the crying, the acceptance of death, the parting before death, the death of Krichona, Schnabel and his shattered legs, asking us to kill him, Avraham, Shaya, Solomon, and the professor — and taking leave from them at the tree — people I loved and who had loved me. I would never see them again.

I couldn't understand how I had survived until now. Wasn't it a sign that I was being watched over from above? This thought went through my mind again and again, and then I asked myself, why had I been watched over, and not Krichona or Schnabel — was I any better than they were? And suddenly I laughed — it had been the bullets that I had taken from Sobibor that had saved me. Those killers — what cowards — when they heard the sound of shots, they had run away in fright!

I got the impression that Yozhik, who was leading us, didn't know where he was going. From time to time he would stop, stand and consider; sometimes he would change direction and continue walking even more quickly so that we were almost running after him. Finally, we stopped not far from a large, isolated farm, a short distance from the town. Yozhik said, "I knew this farmer well before the war. He's a good man. His name is Karpiuk. You wait here and I'll check out the area and quiet the dog. I'll hide you in the granary, and in the morning I'll speak to the farmer — maybe we can find a place to hide with him." We made our way carefully into the granary. Half of it was filled with bales of straw, and we made an opening in the bales so that we could communicate with Yozhik and Monyek and so that they could pass food to us, but the moment I lay down, I fell asleep.

I woke up in the middle of the night drenched in perspiration, my heart pounding quickly — I had dreamed that I was in Sobibor and I couldn't understand why I was there again, after I had run away. In my dream, I decided to run away again that night. My friends and I were in a bunker under the Kapo's room. Everyone was there in the bunker — Avraham, Shaya, Krichona, Schnabel and others. We left quietly and walked toward the gate. The camp was brightly lit and we could see every detail clearly. I said to myself, "There was supposed to be complete darkness — why is the camp so well lighted?" Suddenly I saw the Germans coming quickly to the gate — Frenzel, Steubel, Gomerski and Graetschus, all carrying automatic rifles. I realized that they had been waiting for us. Someone had informed on us! We changed direction, running along the fence, toward *Lager* 3. As we ran, we found a large gap in the fence and Avraham, Shaya, Krichona and Schnabel ran through. I was waiting for another group that was on the way, and in the meantime I heard singing, coming closer and closer. The singing came from a group of Jewish girls from Holland, singing in Dutch — and I was surprised. What were they doing out here in the middle of the night? Then I saw that Wagner was leading them. Our gazes met and I understood that Wagner knew that I was trying to get away. I stood up and started to run toward the gap in the fence, but Wagner took out his gun and shot me...

That was the moment I awoke, and it took me a few minutes to determine that I was still alive, lying in the bale of straw with Semmen. When I told my dream to Yozhik he declared, "Avraham and Shaya are dead!" and burst into tears. A few days later, Yozhik was told that on the night we had taken leave of Shaya and Avraham, two Jews had been shot by a German patrol.

When I awoke in the morning, I made a hole in the straw to look around the granary. My dream haunted me and I still had difficulty distinguishing whether it was really a dream, or perhaps it was the dream that was real and the reality I had awakened to was actually the dream. Through the opening, I saw Yozhik and Monyek pacing back and forth, near the door, shaking their hands to warm them up from the frost of the night. Yozhik ordered us to stay quiet and not to move — that the farmer would probably be coming in soon to take out feed for his cattle. Indeed, the farmer soon entered. He was surprised to see Yozhik and Monyek, but immediately embraced and kissed them, speaking to them warmly. He then filled his wheelbarrow and left.

After a short time, a young girl came into the granary. Yozhik kissed her and his hand wandered down her back. The girl slapped him lightly and said, "Pig!" and I was certain that Yozhik had done something terrible and that the girl would never forgive him. I couldn't fathom why Yozhik had behaved so rudely, but I was surprised to see that the girl was not at all angry. The opposite was true. She stroked him and kissed him before she went out, and then returned and invited Yozhik and Monyek to breakfast. Semmen and I remained in our hiding place under the straw.

Feeling hungry, we chewed on grains of wheat that we found here and there in the straw.

In the meantime, Yozhik was looking for a way to get food to us. He told the farmer that he didn't want to disturb the household and that he and his brother would eat in the granary, but the farmer insisted that his guests eat at his table, and Yozhik had no alternative but to fill his plate, removing bits of food while the others weren't watching. After filling their pockets, Yozhik and Monyek left the house on some pretext and brought us what they had managed to smuggle out.

The straw was swarming with little grey mice, which ran around incessantly and gave us no peace. I got used to them, but I shuddered when one of them ran into the leg of my pants and climbed upward. I grabbed him through my pants and held tightly while he twitched, trying to get away. If I let him go he would continue upward, but on the other hand, I didn't feel that I could crush him with my hand. In the end, I stretched my pants with my second hand and I was able to free him. I then tied the bottoms of my pant legs, but the mice didn't give up and found a way to get to my body. They just climbed into my sleeves, under my coat and inside my shirt until, finally, I just gave up and let them wander through my clothing.

On the second day in the granary, toward evening, Yozhik ordered us to remain silent, as the farmer would be coming in to take straw for the cattle. Some minutes later, the farmer's daughter came into the granary, placed a ladder against the bales of straw, climbed up, and began to throw some of the upper bales to the floor. We heard her working close by and we held our breath… Suddenly she fell and all of her weight was on us. We looked at each other in surprise for a moment without uttering a sound. I felt the weight of her body upon me, her heavy breathing, and I was afraid to move. She suddenly gasped, "Oh, Jesus!" Semmen replied in Russian, "Don't be afraid. There's a young man staying with you, Yozhik?" "Yes, yes," she replied, and stood up, freeing me of her weight. "So tell him that we have come to visit him and we would like to see him." The girl quickly stood up, jumped off the bale and ran home as fast as she could.

A moment later, Yozhik and Monyek entered and told us to come out of the straw. We had been discovered. The farmer came in and Yozhik introduced us — he said that Semmen was a Russian pilot whose plane had been shot down by the Germans; Semmen and I belonged to a group of partisans and we had come to meet with him. In honor of the occasion he would like to request a good meal for everyone and he would be paying for everything. The idea of having a good meal and drinking a bit appealed to the farmer. Late in the evening, when the whole town was asleep, Semmen and I entered the warm house and sat at the table for a holiday meal. Glasses were filled with vodka from the start of the meal and very quickly, I got drunk. The food was delicious and we had large quantities of it. The atmosphere was merry.

The farmer said that he hadn't known what had happened to Yozhik. "I have known Yozhik for years and he is a decent young man. I knew all of his family; they were all decent people. Yozhik and his brother have been guests at my table and treated as though they were my own children — I gave them as much food as they wanted, and what do I see? They've been stealing food from my table! The moment I turned my head, something went missing from the table. I asked myself, why are they stealing from me? They have all the food they need! I got angry and I thought about making them leave, and letting them go to Hell! But I love Yozhik more than a son and I couldn't make myself drive them away. Now I understand why they were stealing food — these two were in my granary the whole time — and you, Yozhik and Monyek, were stealing for them, and don't tell me now that they have just arrived this evening to meet with you..."

As Karpiuk spoke, we understood that he wasn't so concerned that we had hidden in his granary; the solution to the mystery was much more important to him. Yozhik broke into laughter, walked over to the farmer and shook his hand. "You're an intelligent man, Mr. Karpiuk!" he proclaimed, and the farmer began to laugh, as well, and we all joined him. Yozhik poured another round of vodka and the atmosphere became even warmer.

Yozhik had not for a moment forgotten what our situation was. He declared that Semmen really had been an outstanding pilot, that he had bombarded Berlin several times, had parried an attack of six German war planes all alone and had destroyed three of them before being shot down. The farmer, who was already saturated with vodka, asked Semmen if the stories were true, and Semmen kept repeating *"Da, da!"* He was embarrassed to hear the imaginary stories that Yozhik was inventing about him, but Yozhik exclaimed, "Don't be modest!" and continued his tale: "The war is almost over, and Mr. Karpiuk and his family will be invited to Moscow, where they will receive a medal from Stalin himself for having helped the illustrious pilot, Semmen."

Now it was my turn. "You see this young boy?" exclaimed Yozhik to the farmer, "He is the son of the owner of the largest factory in Lodz. There are important streets which belong entirely to them, and when the war is over, you will no doubt receive a house or two as a gift." I sat blushing and going pale in turn. It was a good thing that the light in the cottage was dim, because it was really difficult for me to listen to Yozhik's exaggerations. "Tell me, why would I want a house in Lodz?" asked the farmer. "You could always sell it and buy whatever you need," replied Yozhik with equanimity.

We stayed in the farmer's house until the late hours of the night, without anyone mentioning our problem. We finally got up and went to sleep in the granary. In the morning, when I awoke, I noticed that I couldn't feel the lower part of my right leg. At first, I shook my leg, which I assumed had "fallen asleep," but with no results. It became apparent that during the night, while I was asleep, I had pushed my leg out from under the straw and that part of my leg had gotten frostbite. Yozhik and Semmen massaged my leg for a long while with snow, until it became pink and the blood started flowing back into it. It was very painful, and I wasn't sure whether this was from being frozen or from the vigorous massage

The door opened and Yozhik was swallowed up inside. He was in there for a long time. At last, when we had lost patience, he appeared, with a smile on his face. "We have found an excellent place to stay," he announced. "Two women and a small child are living in the house. They are very poor and they have nothing to eat. I promised them that, if I stayed with them, they would eat like queens, and that from now on, they would lack for nothing. They are willing to do anything. I have already slept with one of them, and she was fine…" Everyone laughed, but I couldn't understand — we were all hanging by a thread, between life and death, looking for a secure refuge, if only for a few days — and he was playing love games? But maybe that would help us more than any promise?

"I didn't tell them that we were four, to keep them from panicking," Yozhik said. "At the beginning, I only told them about me. Afterward, I told them that I had a brother, and I have come out to get Monyek. Monyek and I will sleep in the house. I'll sleep with Yanka, the one I have already slept with. And you, Monyek, if everything goes well for you, can sleep with the other woman in the second bed. And if not, you can sleep on the floor. You, Berale and Semmen, can spend the night in the shed. Tomorrow morning, we'll all start to dig a bunker for you inside this shed, and, in time, when we win the hearts of these two women, we'll let them know that we really are four."

There were a few bales of straw in the shed. We prepared a place to lie down in one of the corners, but because of the bitter cold, we weren't able to fall asleep and we remained awake all night. The wind and the cold penetrated the shed from every side. My leg was aching badly. In the morning, Yozhik and Monyek came out and we all began to dig. The ground under the shed wasn't frozen, and we managed to dig deeply in a short time. We knew that even if we weren't able to cover the bunker on that day, we would be warmer inside the pit.

Later on, Yanka came out to the shed and brought Yozhik and Monyek something hot to drink. I managed to hide, but she saw Semmen, and Yozhik quickly introduced him as a Soviet pilot whose plane had been shot down. Yanka murmured, "I don't understand. When you arrived, you said you were alone. Then you told us that you had a brother. And now, there is someone else? How many are you, actually?" "That's it, we are three!" replied Yozhik. But shortly thereafter, the other woman, Yula, came into the shed. She probably had come to see the third guest, Semmen, but she found me, as well, in the bunker pit. "Bastards!" she shouted. "How many are you?" Yula called out to Yanka, who came running. "There's another one!" Yula announced. Yozhik swore to the two on everything that was dear to him that there were no more people in his group. We were four, and no more. No one else was with us! He introduced Semmen and me to Yula and Yanka, but they had already lost their faith in us and went looking for others in every corner. Finally, when they had found no one else, they burst into contagious laughter, and we all laughed together.

As in Karpiuk's yard, after we had dug one meter, water began to appear in the pit and we couldn't continue working. When evening fell, Yozhik, Monyek and Semmen left to get provisions from Karpiuk. Because my foot ached so badly, I stayed in the shed. I placed a layer of straw at the bottom of the damp pit and I tried to lie down on it and sleep, but no matter how much straw I added, it was soon sodden with water. After a while, Yanka came to visit me and when she saw the state I was in, she took pity on me, and saying that there was no point in my remaining in the shed, invited me into the house.

It was an odd feeling to find myself alone in the company of these strange women, the one so different from the other. Yanka was in her twenties, tall and well formed, and her size made her look older than she really was. To me, she symbolized the strength of women. She had wide shoulders, and her arms and legs were heavy. Her head was round and her nose wide and upturned, and her grey eyes were always watery, as though she were about to cry. Her voice was deep and quiet. She was shy and spoke little. Yula was short and very thin, flat-chested, her face wrinkled, her nose small and sharp, her eyes blinking and always a bit closed, her hair

versation flowed until, at a certain moment, the guest asked us if we would be ready to join him in a small burglary that he and his friend Vladek were planning to carry out. Yozhik answered without hesitation that we would be ready to participate in any burglary — and glasses were raised to celebrate the new partnership. Although we were all sitting together, Yozhik and Stashek carried on most of the conversation. Stashek said that we would soon meet his friends, Pan Folka and Bronek, who were "great guys." "It's been a long time since I've seen them," said Yanka. "Who knows if they're still alive?" The guest then told us that he had his eye on a small farm belonging to two old people and their daughter. "There isn't too much there to take, but they have a pig that's not bad, and geese, and that's what we need right now. Their hut is some distance from the village, and the work will be easy, but we need a few men to carry it out — two or three can catch the pig, kill it and cut it up into pieces, and two will keep a lookout for unwanted visitors. And then, they will help us carry the pig, as it's quite a long way."

"We will be three," said Yozhik, and when Stashek looked at the four of us in surprise, Yozhik added, with a wave of his hand in my direction, "We won't take him with us. He's still a child." Stashek agreed. "All right, he can stay and watch over the women," he joked. Everyone laughed and I didn't know how to react, I was so embarrassed. It was agreed that on one of the following evenings, Stashek would come, accompanied by his friend Vladek, and the whole group would go together to carry out the small robbery. After Yula's brother left, we continued to sit and drink with the two women. The vodka had had its effect on everyone. Yanka and Yula were surprised that we had never heard of Pan Folka. "He's famous. He's the greatest burglar in the whole area. Even before the war, the authorities offered a large prize for anyone who could lead to his capture. He's always the commander," said Yanka enthusiastically. And Yula, who had been sitting quietly, added, "He's got a woman in every village — and Yanka was once one of them." Yanka didn't disagree, but only added that it had been a long time since Folka had visited them.

"And what about Bronek?" asked Monyek. "I'll tell you about Bronek," said Yula. "That bastard was once a respected man, but he has hot blood, and when the blood rises to his head, he gets involved in brawls. Once, during the wedding of one of our friends in the village, a quarrel broke out. Bronek was involved, as usual. One of the young men insulted Bronek, and Bronek doesn't like being insulted. He grabbed the young man and cut off his finger with a knife, in front of everyone. The young man who was cut belonged to a rich and powerful family, and Bronek had to leave the area for a long time. After more than half a year, when it seemed as though the incident of the finger had been forgotten, there was another wedding in the village. Bronek arrived, happy to meet his friends, and he drank quite a bit. The young man whose finger had been cut and his family were at the wedding, too.

"The wedding ceremony was uneventful, and everyone had the impression that it would continue peacefully. But during the dancing the family of the young man whose finger had been cut off got up and attacked Bronek, who was pretty drunk by then. They beat him and tied him up, and brought a plank and an ax and put them in the middle of the floor. They then brought Bronek, trussed up like a sheep — he asked for help, but no one had the courage to help him. Two young men put his right hand on the plank and, when the father gave the command, they cut off three fingers of his hand. That night Bronek swore to have his revenge on the family. He waited a long time, until his wounds had healed, and then bought a gun and practiced shooting with his pinkie on the trigger. When he was ready, he set a trap in the forest, near the path leading from the village to Chelm. In the evening, by the light of a full moon, when he saw the family returning from the fair in Chelm, he killed them all — the father, the mother, two sons and the wife of one of them, and two horses, as well. From that day, Bronek has been wanted by the police throughout the area, living in hiding and never sleeping for two nights in the same place. He became friendly with Folka and now, he is a thief, as well."

We weren't told very much about Vladek, the third in the group

boots, the top of a sewing machine. Stashek suggested that we divide up what they had taken, but Yozhik replied that we could do without the clothes; we would be satisfied with the geese.

The late-night feast that was served was wonderful. The organ meats of the geese were delicious. During the meal, Stashek remarked, "It doesn't matter that tonight wasn't a total success. What is important is that we saw that we are a good team and that together we can do great things. We'll plan the next job, to steal a good pig, soon, and this time he won't get away from me." Before a week had passed, Stashek and Vladek appeared again, ready for action. "Boys, we're going out on a job," said Stashek. "And this time, I picked a good farm. There are a few pigs. One minus is that the farm is inside the village, but this village is close to the forest, and we have an easy walk." He seemed excited and added, "This time, we'll need the boy."

His words struck me like a blow. My heart began to pound and I was sure everyone could hear it. I tried to hide my strong response. I had wanted to go along with everyone else to commit the first robbery, so why was I feeling so upset? But Yozhik quickly answered, saying that my leg was wounded and I would have to stay behind.

"Can you walk?" asked Stashek, and I, out of fear that if I didn't go with them this time, they would never let me go with them, replied that I could walk. "We are too few," explained Stashek. "I want this to be a quiet job. We won't enter the house. Three will guard: one by the door, one by the window beside the door, and one by the window at the back of the house. Three will go into the pigpen. We'll pick out the largest pig and I'll slaughter it, then we'll pack it up and get out. Everyone understand?"

"Yes," replied everyone in unison. No one asked any questions. We got dressed and were on our way. It wasn't terribly cold. The moon was full and we could see for a great distance over the snowy expanse. From time to time, heavy clouds hid the moon and we had to feel our way in the dark, but when the clouds passed, we could see clearly again.

It was quiet. I only heard the sound of our steps in the snow, the dogs barking here and there, and the low humming sounds of automobiles coming from the far-off road. The sound of cars took me back to our home in Lodz, on the day that the Germans entered the city. It was the day after my father and Mottel had fled the city. As we sat in the house — Mother, my sister, Dvora, and my little brother Yankele — we heard the sound of automobiles and tanks passing unceasingly in the street below, a sound like molten lava, flowing down the slopes of a volcano and covering the land. Memories and scenes, as though from a film which had been speeded up, continued to flicker through my mind, scenes from the years since then: the flight to Warsaw, burying my father at Prushkov, life in the Warsaw ghetto, the flight from the ghetto, Turobin, the eighteen months of hell in Sobibor, the revolt and the flight from the camp, life in the forest, the bunker, the attack, Avraham, Shaya, Krichona, Schnabel…

Had all this really happened? And if so, how could I still be alive? And what about now? Was I really walking with a band of robbers to steal a pig? No, no, this couldn't really be happening. It was more reasonable to assume that this was a dream, a crazy hallucination.

We reached the forest and walked along the outskirts. Stashek stopped, explained that we were close to the village and this would be our meeting place after the job, whether we had succeeded or failed. He divided up the tasks among us: he, Vladek and Yozhik would go into the pigpen and slaughter the pig; Monyek, Semmen and I would keep guard on the house. We moved on and passed a few farms that stood at some distance from each other. Although it was still early in the evening, the village was completely silent and we didn't see the gleam of a light in any of the houses. We stopped by the house that had been targeted, and Stashek went on ahead to calm the dog — he had a way with them — and after a few minutes he returned and sent Monyek to guard at the back of the house, placed Semmen at the door, and I was to stand at the window. Stashek, Yozhik and Vladek, armed with two rifles,

one of the sacks, and I brought it to the pen, but after everything had been cut up and packed, Stashek and Yozhik decided to kill another pig. I took everything that was packed and ready to a spot some distance from the house, and I was then left to stand guard while the four others returned to slaughter another pig. Unlike the first robbery, during which I had been trembling with fear, for some reason I was now calm and relaxed; even though I was guarding alone, I was not afraid. There was complete silence around me. I had the impression that everyone on the farm was fast asleep. When I heard the sudden squeal of a pig and then, a return to silence, I knew that the second pig had been killed. A short time later, I saw the others coming toward me.

It was late and we still had fifteen kilometers to walk — with the heavy burden of two slaughtered pigs and a sack full of geese, we couldn't hope to get home by morning. Yozhik found a solution to the problem. He led us for some time until we stopped at a farm that I immediately recognized — it was the farm that we had used as a meeting place while we were living in the forest; it was here that we had parted from Avraham and Shaya, and now, we were standing there, a pack of thieves. Yozhik hid some of our haul in the barn; the rest we carried all the long way home, which we reached toward morning, the home of Yanka and Yula.

We spent the next day eating until we were completely satiated. We were all happy and in good spirits. The night, which had begun as a complete failure, had ended in complete success. Stashek could not stop praising Yozhik, saying again and again that we were his best friends, and he spoke of our operations to come. Amid the high spirits, and everyone drunk, some more and some less, someone noticed that I was the only one of the group with a Jewish name. Both of the women called me "Barak," which sounded more Polish, but it was still a Jewish name. Now they decided to find me a purely Polish name, and the names of the saints were suggested, one after another. In the camp, Wagner had called me "Boris," Steubel had called me "Franz," and Frenzel had always used some vile epithet. Now they were looking for a Polish name for me, but none of them seemed to suit my Jewish face. When Monyek suggested the name "Bolek," which was a short form of "Boleslav," it sounded a bit like "Beral" or "Barak" to me. I intervened in this conversation for the first time, immediately agreeing to be called "Bolek," but Yula said that she didn't know of any saint called "Bolek" or "Boleslav." Monyek explained to her that in Polish history, there had been two Polish kings, King Boleslav Chrobry, and King Boleslav Krzywousty, and it was unanimous that I be renamed "Bolek." Again the glasses of vodka were raised to mark the occasion.

In the evening, Stashek and Vladek left for home, Yozhik, Monyek and Semmen went out to bring home the pig that we had hidden in "our" farmer's granary unbeknownst to him, and I stayed home. The state of my leg had gotten so much worse that I couldn't even stand on it or take a step.

After the group had taken the pig quietly out of the granary, Yozhik went to visit the farmer. The man innocently told Yozhik that a band of thieves had been wandering around the area and that no one could feel secure of his life or his possessions. "Yesterday," he related, "there were two robberies in the area. In one of them, the robbers had already gotten into the pigpen. By chance, the farmer's son had just been returning home, and he struggled with one of the robbers and overpowered him. He called for help, and the villagers were able to chase the robbers away. In the second robbery, the gang came late at night, when everyone was asleep. They surrounded the house, went into the pigpen and slaughtered two pigs. The squealing pigs woke up the farmer, who went to the window and saw the armed robbers first wandering around the farm, and then leaving with the dead pigs, but the farmer didn't do anything — he was afraid that the robbers would try to break into his home, and was happy when they left with the two pigs."

We had experienced a great deal since our flight from Sobibor. We had learned to quickly adjust to every situation, but who could have imagined that we would join a band of thieves? Robbery had always seemed to me such an act of cruelty and thieves were

that we had a chance of surviving the war and seeing the Germans defeated.

But in spite of this hope, and in spite of the comfortable conditions in which we were living, the danger to our lives was increasing from day to day. Every so often a stranger would come by, and in the surrounding villages, there were rumors that Jews were hiding out in the isolated little house of the two women. One day, when I went out to bring water from the well — I was dressed in women's clothes, with a kerchief on my head, as I usually was when I left the house during the day — a man suddenly appeared behind the house, went to the door, and entered. I froze in my tracks. I had no doubt that the man had seen me, but had ignored me. I was certain that he had discovered all of my friends, but when I came back into the house with a bucket of water, I was surprised to find that everyone had managed to hide, and I stood at the door, not really knowing what to do.

The man said, "Good morning, miss," with sarcasm in his voice. "Good morning," I replied, attempting a feminine voice, but the man burst into laughter and said, "You can take off your rags. When I saw you outside, I knew that you were no woman." At that moment, Yozhik came out of hiding, and Semmen and Monyek followed, and after a long conversation, punctuated by glasses of vodka, the man received a pair of boots. We parted in friendship, and he swore to us, by all that was holy to him, that he would never tell anyone about us.

In response to the rumors going around the surrounding villages about Jews in the house, we started rumors that a partisan headquarters was located in the house, and anyone who uttered a word about what was going on would be endangering his life. But the various rumors about us spread quickly and grew. Strange stories were told about the house; there were those who had seen units of partisans going in and out at night, and the house was guarded by partisan guards armed with machine guns. There were those who had seen people pass the house and disappear. People were afraid to come near it, and anyone who had to pass by our vicinity would keep his distance to avoid the danger.

The rumors had their effect. Yanka and Yula began to be afraid, and the possibility that the war would soon be over caused Yanka her own disquiet, as well. She was very much in love with Yozhik, and one day she said, "Now you say that you love me, and you treat me like a queen. But when the war is over, you will leave me. You will find a Jewish woman and get married to her..." Yozhik pretended to be angry and left the room in a huff, and Yanka, looking worried, sent me to see what he was doing. Yozhik wet his cheeks with saliva, and I returned to Yanka and told her that Yozhik was crying. Yanka held her head in her hands. "Oh, God, what have I done?" she cried. "I shouldn't have said that to him. Go, bring him back." I went and came back. "He doesn't want to come," I said. Weeping, Yanka ran to Yozhik, kissed him and begged him to forgive her.

Another time, she told Yozhik that she knew he didn't really love her, but only wanted to stay in her house until the end of the war. Yozhik was so insulted that he took a knife and began to sharpen it, shouting, "I have nothing to live for!" We jumped on him and held him down by force, and he struggled with us, trying to commit suicide by stabbing himself, shouting again and again, "I don't want to live!" Yanka, shaken by Yozhik's reaction, announced in a voice trembling with feeling, "If anything happens to Yozhik, I'll kill myself, too. I am to blame for everything." Again, she begged Yozhik to forgive her, and in a few moments the two were sitting and embracing on their bed.

But the clashes didn't stop. Semmen and I began to feel unwelcome in the house. This was especially reflected in the food we received. Each of the women made sure that her "man" received the best food, while Semmen and I got leftovers and sometimes we even went hungry. One day Yanka said, "I am ready to put myself in danger for my Yozhik, and if the Germans catch us, let them kill us together in bed." Yula responded, "I am ready to endanger myself for Monyek, too. But why should we be in danger for Semmen and

came, we would call for a midwife, although the chances of finding a midwife for Yanka when she needed one were slim.

One evening, quite late, Yanka began having labor pains and asked us to call a midwife. This wasn't possible — who could go to the village to call a midwife in the middle of the night, and even if one of us did go, it would take a long time, and by the time a midwife came, it would already be too late. Yanka was frightened and miserable and we pitied her, but we didn't know how we could help her. We thought that Yula would act as a midwife, but she refused and said that she didn't know what to do. Yozhik decided to be the midwife. He ordered us to leave the room and to pray that everything would be all right, and he told Yula to prepare hot water and a clean sheet and to be ready to help him. He took off his clothes, scrubbed his hands, put on one of Yanka's nightgowns and went to work. We stood tensely outside the door, listening to every noise from inside. We heard Yanka's cries until suddenly, there was quiet, and afterward, we heard Yozhik shout, "Very good! Yanka, you have a son!" Yozhik continued to care for the new mother for some time — he cut the umbilical cord and tied it, washed the baby, and finally came out to us with his face shining and proclaimed, "*Mazel tov*, we have a bastard!"

Pan Folka and Bronek had been gone for a long time, and we hoped that we would never have the opportunity of seeing them. We hadn't seen Stashek for a long time, either. And then, late one evening, after we had all gone to bed, we heard people outside, calling for Yanka and Yula to open the door. Folka, Bronek, with his cut fingers, and Stashek had arrived by surprise, but the former two didn't have to be introduced. I knew who Bronek was immediately when I saw his right hand, which was missing fingers. He was in his twenties, short, with a constant smile. Pan Folka appeared to be over forty, of medium height, chubby with a small potbelly. He was dressed in a short leather coat and fine quality boots, and, in addition to a rifle, he carried a pistol under his coat. He looked serious and boastful and he gave the impression of complete authority — Bronek and Stashek looked like messenger boys next to him.

The suddenness of their arrival and their friendly behavior made us forget the danger for a moment — the armed robbers could have killed us in a moment — but a few quick glances were sufficient and each of us made sure to be on different sides of the room. The women set the table and we all drank in honor of Yanka's child, in honor of our friendship, and in honor of the commander, Folka. Yozhik quickly became friendly with Folka, and the two sat together in a corner of the room and decided to go out on several robbery jobs in the coming days. Then Folka said, pointing to me, "We won't take the kid with us." Again I was a child. When would I ever be old enough not to be thought of as a child? Stashek said, "This kid was with us on our last job and he was fine." I was happy to hear the compliment, but Folka cut into Stashek's words and said, "Don't stick your nose into what doesn't concern you." And to me he added, "Don't be afraid. I'll make a man of you."

After we had finished eating and drinking, Folka stood up, went over to Yanka and told her to come with him. Yanka was flustered and told him quietly that she had given birth just a week ago. Folka didn't say a word, but just looked at her — and she stood up and went to the hallway with him. After Folka and his friends left, Yanka burst into tears and said, "If I hadn't gone with him he would have killed me."

A few days after the meeting with Folka and Bronek, the enlarged gang, under the direction of Folka, began to go out on jobs at least once, and sometimes twice a week. The robberies were committed in a wide area after getting information on what the possibilities were. At first I was embarrassed just sitting at home and waiting for my friends to return late at night, relating their experiences and what they had taken in the robbery. Although I wasn't too enthusiastic about stealing, and my health was still bad — my leg hadn't healed, I found it hard to walk, and the scabies were all over my body — I wanted to be an equal partner with my friends in everything they did, good or bad, and not be a child who had everything done for him. So I begged Yozhik to convince Folka to let me join the band, and, in the end, he agreed.

humor. Bronek grabbed the bride, pulled her against him and tried to kiss her. The girl resisted and was slapped. The groom tried to defend her, but was also struck and then thrown into the cellar. Pan Folka stood like a proud father watching the antics of his children. Bronek dragged the bride over to a bed that stood in the corner of the room. The girl struggled and shouted, "Take everything, just leave me alone!" But Bronek hit her again, and raped her. Then Stashek raped her, as well.

Sometimes I found justification for the robberies we carried out — why should only the Jews suffer? Let these non-Jews get a taste of our suffering. I saw our deeds as a kind of retribution for the "Polacks" who had helped to destroy the Jews, but I couldn't stomach the cruelty of Bronek and his friend, Stashek, and the suffering of the girl. In the camp, whenever terrible deeds occurred in my presence, I found refuge in working at an insane speed; this was the only way I could overcome the awful things that were happening inside me. Now, too, I began taking things out of the house, running to and fro insanely.

We emptied the house of everything that had been prepared for the wedding. We loaded crates of excellent vodka onto the wagon, along with sides of smoked meat, baked goods and sweets of all kinds, and we left in a wagon that was filled to capacity. For a long while, I kept hearing the screams and sobs of the bride and reliving the scene of Bronek with his pants pulled down.

We came home laden with treats, but our hearts were burdened with terrible feelings. We didn't exchange a word on the way home. We had shamed ourselves. We had seen our partners in the robbery at their cruelest, and we had cooperated in their horrible deeds. With what speed we had passed from one side to the other, from the robbed to the robbers! But we could think of no way to end this partnership before summer, when we could go back to living in the forests. And, on the other hand, we were living comfortably in our present situation; we had gotten through the hard winter peacefully, in a warm house, eating our fill. And Folka, Bronek and Stashek had treated us as equals — we never heard them use the word "Jew."

The next evening Folka, Bronek and Stashek came to visit, and a party began which went on all night. The vodka was of excellent quality, unlike the "Samogon" vodka that the farmers made, and which we had become accustomed to. This time we drank a stronger vodka that didn't smell bad. We drank great quantities; all of us got drunk, and Folka burst into song:

In a hiding place time flies; we should enjoy the riches of the world —
A wedding today, tomorrow death, when an ax is suspended over your head.
Oh, my princess, of great splendor, one hair will not fall from your head,
And you wait for death at any moment — your end will be bitter...
They came to the ball at the palace, warriors and graceful women, as fresh as the dew.
Suddenly shots were heard; our swords were pulled out and held high.
The men threw their weapons to their feet, and their money, as well.
The women removed their jewels and took off their gold...
And when we had finished our work in the palace, my band and I were already in the forest.
A young girl appeared before me, a jug of raspberries in her hand, dearer to me than all else.
"Bring me your jug, my one and only young maiden, my sweet —
And I will give you gold, and an abundance of love..."

Folka sang the song with pride but seemed troubled. Perhaps the words had reminded him of something. Even a man like Folka, a

to see us was deep and sincere. They begged us to stay with them, and we said we would.

Two days passed — and then Stashek burst into the house and told us with tears in his eyes that Pan Folka had been killed. After we had poured him a glass of vodka and he had calmed down a bit, he said that he had gone to meet Folka at the home of one of his mistresses, but when he had reached her village, he had been told that at dawn, policemen from the neighboring towns had arrived and had surrounded the house, calling on him to come out and give himself up. Folka opened fire on the police. There was a long battle, and at some point Folka jumped from the back window of the house and tried to get away, but the house was completely surrounded. As he ran, he was shot, wounded and fell to the ground. He continued to fight, wounded, until he had used up his bullets — but he reserved the last bullet for himself. He shot himself in the head, and died. Four policemen had been killed. It was later said that one of his mistresses had informed on him in retribution for his having left her.

We were in shock. Folka had been killed! It had only been a week since Bronek had been killed! Stashek was miserable. Folka and Bronek had been his only friends on earth. He was on bad terms with everyone in his village — everyone hated him — and now he didn't have anywhere to go. He went from village to village, took part in every brawl and got himself into every dangerous situation he could. As the war was reaching its end, violent clashes between the Poles and the Ukrainians in the neighboring villages became worse and worse. Night after night the sky would redden here and there, as one village was burned by the Poles and another by the Ukrainians, and we would stand watching and trying to figure out which village was going up in flames. And there was almost no village burning that took place without the involvement of Stashek — either helping to set the village on fire or helping to put the fire out — until, in the end, the Ukrainians caught him and threw him alive into a burning house. He was burned to death and no one cared. After Folka and Bronek had died, Stashek had become superfluous and we, who had wanted to be rid of them all and to sever our relationship with the thieves, were freed from them all within a month. Our feelings toward them were mixed. On the one hand, they had always been fair with us, much more than many more respectable people, and we had even felt friendly toward them; but on the other hand, their merciless cruelty had greatly troubled us — they treated human life as if it were worthless. We were glad that our forced partnership with a band of thieves had ended.

After the deaths of our partners in crime, we had relative quiet, but it was clear that it couldn't last. The summer had brought people out of their homes to work in the fields and we could see people making their way to their fields not far from our house, working in the surrounding fields, and more than once it seemed that they had turned their glances toward us. We often saw people walking in the direction of our house, and we tried to identify who they were while they were still far away — were they men or women, armed or not — but just as we were preparing to hide, they would change their direction and disappear into the distance. Yozhik contributed to the atmosphere of tension with his nightmares, which he would relate to us from time to time, and then he would warn us of a coming danger. One summer morning, he awoke and said that he had had a terrible nightmare and announced that this was the day that something would happen. For the rest of the day, we kept watch, keeping track of what was happening outside. But nothing happened and we taunted Yozhik and made fun of him and his dreams. Toward evening, as we were sitting down to eat, we suddenly heard a loud explosion and it seemed as though the house was about to collapse around us. Fragments of the walls and ceiling fell to the floor. The door, which had been closed and bolted, flew open. I was sure that the Germans had thrown a grenade or a bomb into the house. Each of us scrambled to hide, and I unthinkingly crawled into the baking oven. After a few minutes of quiet, I heard Yanka calling us to come out. "Nothing has happened," she assured us.

I tried to crawl out of the oven, but I wasn't able to — I was stuck inside. I heard someone asking, "Where is Bolek?" I shouted, "I'm here, in the oven, and I can't get out!" They all grabbed my legs and slowly pulled me out. As I was freed, everyone burst into a laughter that continued through the evening. I was as black as coal and no one could understand how I managed to get into the oven.

We could have left the house and lived in the forest, and we told each other that the time had come to leave and that it was too dangerous for us to stay where we were, but we put off leaving from one day to the next. We had gotten accustomed to the good conditions and we were happy together. Each of us had prepared a hiding place in the small house — behind the stove or in the attic. I found a loose plank in the floor, near Yula's bed. I lifted it up and dug enough earth out from under it until I had sufficient room to lie down. German soldiers from the units camped in the area wandered through the villages trying to get eggs, butter, chickens and other supplies, and they didn't miss our house. Whenever we saw them coming, we would hide and they would come in, ask for food, see that they could get nothing, and leave.

One day, two German soldiers came into the house and started to fool around with Yanka and Yula. One of the Germans sat on the bed with Yula, and sand and dirt fell over my face continually through the cracks in the floor. I couldn't move, but I needed to sneeze and to scratch myself. It was hard for me to hold on until they left. Another time, two German soldiers surprised us — we saw them too late, as they were looking through the window from outside, and there was no use in trying to hide. Yozhik ordered us to scatter to the corners of the room, and he picked up an ax and sat near the door. We had no idea whether they were just strolling around the area or if they had come to take us, but if the latter proved to be true, we would attack and kill them. The two Germans knocked at the door. Yanka opened it and they stood in the door-way, their weapons slung on their backs. They looked at us, and we at them. Just as we were preparing to spring at them, they paled as though our faces had betrayed our intentions and one of them asked if we had any eggs or butter to sell. Yozhik answered that we had nothing to sell and they left quickly. That was the first time I had ever seen fear in the face of a German soldier.

Obviously, the visit of the two Germans would not go by without a response. The two couldn't help but notice that we were neither farmers nor sons of farmers; apparently, our unusual appearance frightened them and we had no doubt that they wouldn't hesitate to report their discovery. We didn't know how much time we had, but we knew that we had to leave quickly. We told Yanka and Yula that they had to leave the house, as well, for a time, and we said goodbye with the hope of meeting them soon. They were to take their children and go stay with Yanka's mother, who lived about ten kilometers away. Without waiting for dark, we left the house and walked through the fields, keeping away from the villages and from the farmers working in the fields, until we reached the nearest forest, this time with the feeling that we would never again go back to our refuge.

At last, the Soviets began their attack along the front. They crossed the Bug River, and the Germans, unable to stop their advance, were forced to organized new lines of defense again and again. During the nights, we could hear a low rumble, unceasing, that sounded like stones rolling down a mountainside or like thunder announcing an approaching storm. We listened closely to the sounds, which for us, were like messages from heaven saying, "We are coming to bring you freedom."

I don't know whether or not we would have been able to return to living in the forest as we had lived before, had we not known that the day of our release was approaching. It didn't even occur to us to build a bunker. Each morning we would only think about how we would spend that day and night. In the evenings, we visited farmers we knew, who were receiving us more and more warmly now that the fear of Germans was gradually disappearing. We also became less careful, sometimes daring to go about in broad daylight, as people do when they are free, when in actuality with the Germans in retreat it was even more dangerous. There were many Germans encamped in our area, and with the increase of partisan activity, the Germans were harsh in their search for suspects. Day after day, we heard shots and explosions, and we were told that the Germans had attacked a large unit of partisans that had been operating from one of the forests.

One evening, we went back to visit Yanka and Yula. We had assumed that we would find the house deserted, but, to our surprise and delight we found the two women at home and our meeting was boisterous. They told us that the day after we had left the house, the Germans had come, broken in and turned the entire house upside down in their search. The women had come back after a week, and they begged us now to stay with them. We refused but promised to come and visit them from time to time.

One day, we were awakened by the hum of automobiles and the sound of German, spoken by people who sounded close by. Peering out from among the bushes and trees, we could see German soldiers walking through the forest and preparing to set up camp. We quickly retreated to the deepest section of the forest, but there, too, we felt ill at ease. The Germans might reach us here, as well. We felt that our liberation was almost at hand, and that in a few days there wouldn't be any Germans in the area, but it was just at this stage that we couldn't find a place to hide. The Germans were everywhere, and many of them were staying in the forests to avoid being seen by Soviet pilots, and to seek shelter from the heat of the sun. Many of them visited the houses of farmers, as well.

Luckily, the wheat in the fields had grown to a height of half a meter or more, and at night we would choose a large field of wheat, walk to the center, straighten the stalks that we had trampled, and lie down to sleep. The forest was a Garden of Eden compared to these fields in which we were finally forced to spend both day and night, lying down without being able to raise our heads. The sun beat down on us mercilessly and the multitude of insects refused to allow us to lie there peacefully. At first, we panicked every time a rabbit or some other small animal ran by us, but our greatest fear was of people, who sometimes passed not far from us — we could hear them walking through the fields, talking; sometimes it would be children walking through the field for the fun of it, and we knew that if we were discovered, we would be lost. In the fields, unlike the forest, there was nowhere to flee. In moments of danger, we had no alternative but to cling to the ground, hold our breaths, and wait until the human voices had gone on.

In the evenings, swarms of mosquitoes would attack us, with their unceasing buzz, and there was no chance of getting rid of them. There were also days when we were left without water. The sun dehydrated us and we could think only of our thirst. One day, when I was particularly thirsty, I prayed for rain, and lo and behold, a cloud passed over us in the middle of the hot sunny day, covering the blue sky from horizon to horizon, bringing a cool wind. It was as if a miracle had occurred — God had heard my prayers, and large drops splashed onto my face. I took a folding cup out of a box in my knapsack and placed the cup, its cover and the box on the ground to catch the rainwater. I stretched out on my back and opened my mouth to receive the gift from the skies. The rain became heavier, falling in large drops on my face until I could lick them. Soon there was heavy rain with thunder and lightening and I drank my fill. But the miracle of rain that I had prayed for became a curse, as if vengeance had been taken for my trivial request. We all got soaking wet, the ground became muddy and we sank into it, and the wind and rain pushed the corn down and we could easily be seen.

The day went on endlessly, the rain didn't stop falling, and Yozhik said that all signs pointed to a steady downfall for three days. And so it was. When night came we got up with difficulty. Our clothes were sodden and stained with mud and they added to our suffering. We tried to find a farmer who would let us come in and dry our clothes, but we found no one who would agree. The next day we went back to lie in the muddy field — and the rain continued to fall. Again I prayed, but this time for the sun to come out from behind the clouds to dry me out and warm me up. All at once the rain stopped, the clouds began to disappear, the sun came out from time to time, and my body trembled at the change — the sky became blue again and the sun shone warmly. Once more I lay on my back, this time enjoying the caressing sun. Our clothes began to smell and we took them off, piece by piece, until we were completely naked, protected by the stalks of wheat that now stood upright around us like a wall.

A month ago it had seemed as though the war would be over in a few days, but it went on endlessly and the fighting was now very close. Again and again I was assailed by feelings of despair. My heart told me that we would never be able to survive until the Russians captured the area. The grain in the fields had ripened, the harvest had begun — where would we hide after the harvest? In the open fields of stubble? In the evenings, Yozhik would find out which fields were being harvested the next day, but even so, we couldn't always be sure that the field we were hiding in wouldn't actually be harvested. In any case, as each day passed, the number of remaining fields became fewer and fewer and we turned into field mice, fleeing at the last moment from the blade of the sickle.

One night, we felt that the front had almost reached us. We heard the artillery fire clearly, and we could see the flashes of the explosions. The distant sky suddenly became red with the flames and heavy smoke. The farmers said that the Germans were exploding stores of gasoline before their retreat so that they wouldn't fall into the hands of the Soviets. We watched the flames as though hypnotized, and in my imagination, I seemed to be able to see the entire German army exploding into fragments. That night, we knocked on Karpiuk's door and he cheerfully brought us inside. He told us that the Germans who had been camping in the area had left, heading westward, and we in our great happiness got drunk. Karpiuk suggested that we sleep in his home, but we preferred to sleep in the fields nearby. We felt that at any moment, we would be free. And I, Berale, was close to achieving the realization of an insane dream — I was going to stay alive, to survive, to be a free man; I was going to be witness to the German defeat.

But mingled with my feeling of happiness was the fear of wondering what would happen after the liberation. Since I had been smuggled out of the Warsaw ghetto, I had had one dream — to go home and to tell my mother, my sister and my brother everything that had happened to me. Over the course of the weeks, the months, the years, my dream had become less and less realistic and had become a cloudy hallucination, but, in spite of everything, from time to time, it provided me with some seconds of pleasure just before I fell asleep. All this time, I had known that in the end, I would die, sooner or later; now that it began to seem that I would live, would there be anyone left to tell my experiences to? I could see the sadness on the faces of Yozhik, Monyek and Semmen. They, too, like me, were frightened that they might be the only ones left of their families.

All the next day the sounds of fire and explosion gradually got closer, and the retreat of the Germans began to turn into a rout. Convoys of German army vehicles were retreating on every road and path, and even being in an open field became dangerous, so we made our way carefully to Karpiuk's house. In the evening, the stream of retreating Germans became larger. We watched from the window as they retreated in wagons and on foot. They walked quietly, looking more like a caravan of gypsies than like the lauded German army, and we sat in Karpiuk's house, endlessly sipping vodka, as we really didn't know how to react to what was going on. We wanted to be happy, but there was something inside that would not allow us to feel joy. Only the vodka helped us escape our confused feelings, blurring our senses and keeping us in a fog.

We drank and laughed. Fear had left us completely — in spite of the fact that the retreating Germans passed by the house and could have come in and killed us easily at the last moment before liberation. Suddenly Monyek got up and went outside. We thought that he had gone to relieve himself, but when he didn't return, Yozhik and I went outside to see what had become of him. We were shocked to see him standing next to a wagon in which a German soldier was sitting. Monyek was holding the reins of the horses and speaking to the German. *"Deutschland kaput* — Germany is finished — give me your horses!"* commanded Monyek, and the soldier, with a rifle slung over his back and grenades stuck in his belt, shouted in German, "Hans, they want to steal the horses!" We jumped on Monyek and pulled him away and into the house as fast as we could. But he, completely drunk, was angry and shouted that he could have taken the horses from the German and we had ruined everything.

The next morning we were awakened by explosions that shook the house. We looked outside. We couldn't see any Germans. We went outside and we couldn't see anyone although the day was summery, clear and warm, and the sky was blue. The Karpiuk family was hiding in a dugout meant for potatoes, some distance from the house, and we stood in the field, alone, like lords of the manor, trying to understand what exactly was happening. We were in the area between the two forces. Shells passed over our heads in both directions, but the real battle was taking place on a side hill where we saw shells exploding one after the other against the background of the sound of machine gun fire. Some shells fell in our vicinity and then one exploded next to us. A shock wave hit us, then stones and clods of earth showered us. It was only then that we realized the extent of the danger. What was the use of dying a meaningless death from a chance shell falling on us moments before liberation?

We quickly jumped into a crater left by an exploding shell and watched as dozens, perhaps hundreds, of burning shells flew over us and landed on the hill, which was covered with billows of smoke. These were katyusha rockets. Then there was quiet. At the beginning, we saw nothing, but suddenly we heard the sound of galloping horses. Three Russian horsemen were moving quickly toward us and reined in with difficulty when they saw us. The Russian soldiers had the faces of children, but they looked serious. Their uniforms were minimal, but they were carrying rifles. We wanted to assail them with hugs and kisses, but they only asked if there were Germans in the area and continued to gallop onward. So we attacked each other with hugs and burst into tears. We had been liberated!

The Soviet army passed us quickly, rushing after the retreating German army. The Soviet soldiers looked nothing like the Germans who marched into Lodz wearing smart uniforms and carrying fine-looking weapons. They were poorly dressed and their weapons looked wretched. We even saw soldiers whose rifles were hanging by ropes, rather than leather straps. But this was the army that had overcome the Germans. We wished them well as they passed, but they paid no attention to us and only a few responded to our greeting.

We were liberated, but we didn't know what to do. We wandered the paths in broad daylight, aimlessly, if only to get a taste of being in public, where anyone could see us, without fear. A family of farmers walked toward us and when they reached us we exchanged greetings as though it were the most natural thing in the world, but this was a new experience for us and it even seemed to us that they had stared at us with fear in their eyes. Evening was falling and we returned to Karpiuk's house. Semmen said that he had to hurry and rejoin the Soviet army so that he could still manage to fight the Germans. When we tried to argue that he shouldn't leave so quickly, that we should stay together a bit so that we could enjoy our liberty, he replied that he was a Soviet soldier and his place was with the army. Yozhik and Monyek had the two uncles who had been hiding with farmers and they wanted to visit them the next morning. Exhausted after a night of wakefulness and from a day filled with events, we ate supper, drank vodka and went to bed in the granary.

I woke up late the next morning. No one had disturbed my sleep. Yozhik and Monyek had gone to find their uncles. Semmen was not there either — he must have gone to find out what he had to do to regain his place with the Soviet army. When I left the granary, I saw a Soviet sentry with an automatic rifle standing at the entrance to the house. I walked in and discovered that the house had been turned into a clinic. The odor of disinfectant and medication filled the air, and a woman in a soldier's uniform with a white coat worn over it — apparently a doctor — was treating an officer sitting on a chair. The upper part of his body was bandaged and the doctor was bandaging his arm, as well. The patient seemed to be a senior officer, as time after time, officers came in, saluted, stood at attention and reported to him.

Karpiuk came into the room and said to the officer, "You see this young man? He is a Jew who ran away from the Sobibor death camp and has been hiding here." The officer looked at me and continued to sit with a frozen expression on his face. The doctor gave me a long, sympathetic look and I was embarrassed. However, I was happy just to be in the room. I was happy to be near Russian soldiers, and I couldn't stop looking at the doctor, a woman of more than thirty, heavy, but not fat, her face the face of an angel or of a Greek statue — a sculpted face, her rosy complexion smooth as silk, her brown hair pulled back, her eyes large and black, her clothes ironed and shining clean, the white coat highlighting her beauty. At a certain point, when the injured officer and I were left alone in the room, he suddenly spoke to me, and said in Yiddish, "Come here, *yingele* (my boy)." I began to tremble. I walked over to him and he took my two hands in his, looked at me tenderly and asked, "Are there many Jews left?" "We are four, and I know of another three that are still alive," I answered. He looked at me and nodded his head. I wanted to go on talking, but he looked away and the frozen expression returned to his face. Our conversation had ended.

The officer left the house. The doctor treated a few more lightly injured soldiers and when the room had emptied and a soldier had collected the equipment and had left, the doctor, who remained sitting on the table, called me over and asked me to tell her about what had happened to me. I didn't know how to begin, nor did I know what she wanted to hear. When she saw that it was difficult for me to begin, she gently asked that I tell her about myself and my family.

I started hesitantly to talk about my family before the war, and slowly I became more articulate. All of a sudden I wanted to tell this woman everything that had happened to me during the five years of the war. She sat opposite me, her eyes not leaving my face, absorbing every word without stopping me, as the expression on her face turned from a beaming smile to a shocked, greyish pallor. Her eyes filled with tears, and in spite of her attempts to retain control of herself, she started to cry.

I stopped talking and looked at her. I didn't understand why, she, a Russian officer, was crying. The woman wiped her tears and said, "I am also Jewish!" She hugged me tightly and kissed me, then got up and held my hands, asking that I come with her. On the way, she told me that she lived in the city of Astrakhan, on the Black Sea coast. Her husband, an important engineer, had been forced to remain in his factory, so he wasn't serving in the Soviet army. We reached headquarters. The doctor introduced me to her colleagues and everyone looked at me as though I were some kind of strange exhibit until I began to feel uncomfortable. She brought me to a field kitchen, and again introduced me and asked that I be given a large meal. We sat down to eat, but she couldn't eat anything and only whispered, "Eat, my son, eat."

I wasn't hungry, but I couldn't refuse her and I ate until she was satisfied. She then said, "Now I need to arrange a special military order so that they send you straight to my home in Astrakhan. You shouldn't stay here, on this accursed land, for even one day more." I tried to explain to her that I didn't want to go anywhere, that I was here with another three friends, with whom I had been through hell and I didn't want to leave them; and that first of all, I had to look for members of my family who might have survived, but she answered that we would talk about everything when we met at ten that night, after she had made all of the arrangements.

When I returned to Karpiuk's house, I found Semmen there and I was happy to see him. It was as if I were returning from a dream to reality. He explained that he had been told to come to army headquarters in Chelm, where he would be mobilized again, but before he left, he wanted to see Yozhik and Monyek. The two brothers hadn't yet returned, and in the meantime, I told him of my meeting with the Jewish officer and the Jewish doctor, and about her plan to send me to Astrakhan. Semmen laughed his cynical laugh, which I had heard so many times before. "You've found new parents very quickly," he said, and then became serious and added, "Go. It will be good for you."

At ten, I met with the doctor. She was troubled. In the light of the moon, I could see that she was unhappy and on the verge of tears. "You know," she said, "We have anti-Semites, too. Our commander, who is a good man, is not here. He has already advanced and is at the front. He would have arranged your trip with no problem. I asked his assistant, but he said that it wasn't an emergency military matter and that there was no need to give you a special permit. I begged him, but to no avail. We are moving out tomorrow at dawn, and I don't know what to do." She was so upset that I pitied her although I had no intention of going to Astrakhan. When I told her that, in any case, I wouldn't have gone, she asked why. I told her that I had to find out if anyone in my family had managed to stay alive, and besides, even though I didn't know exactly why, I couldn't just leave everything; I needed time, I needed to try to clarify what I wanted to do, and I couldn't leave my friends.

The officer tried to convince me to accept her offer and said, "Look, Bolek, I am a doctor and my husband is an important engineer. The war will be over soon, and I'll go home. We have a lovely house in Astrakhan and everything we need. But we have no children. You, Bolek, have stayed alive by some miracle and you've gone through hell. You're still so young. You could have everything you want with us. You'll be able to study. We'll help you make up the years you have lost. You'll grow up to be an important person. And from our home, we can search for your family together." I was silent. After a few minutes, the doctor asked me to continue telling her about my life. I acceded, and spoke without stopping for a few hours. I didn't leave out any period of time, as if I must tell her everything, and she sat opposite me, looking at me constantly, and from time to time, wiping away a tear.

A heavy grey light filled the sky, a sign that dawn was near. I finished my story. We sat in silence. She took out a piece of paper and wrote her address and the telephone number of her house and her sister's in Astrakhan, pushed it into my hand and said, "I must move to the front, but the war will be over soon and then I'll be home. Go to Astrakhan, Bolek. Our home is yours. You will be like a son to us." The two of us knew that I would not go to Astrakhan and that, when we parted, we would never see each other again. She gave me a bundle with a white shirt, a towel and some soap, and apologized that she had nothing more to give me. The village roosters crowed, and on the horizon, a strip of grey light was spreading across the sky and getting lighter. The two of us stood there, facing each other, not wanting to part, and suddenly she pulled me toward her and hugged me tightly. She covered my face and my head with kisses, and I returned them. On my first day of liberty, I had been washed with abounding love.

I returned to Karpiuk's granary, my head whirling. I lay down beside Semmen in the fresh straw and I tried to reflect on the events of the day that had just ended, but I fell asleep immediately. Semmen woke me up, annoyed with Yozhik and Monyek, who had not yet returned. "I am afraid," he said, "that the war will be over before I have a chance to be a part of it. I want to reach Berlin. I don't have the patience to keep waiting for them; I'm going to Chelm. Wait for them here, and I'll wait for all of you in Chelm." Semmen left and I went back to sleep. I woke up in the afternoon. Yozhik and Monyek had still not returned. Only an old woman was left at home; Karpiuk and all of his family were working in the fields. I felt lonely. The events of the day before seemed very distant.

I, too, lacked the patience to sit, doing nothing, waiting for Yozhik and Monyek to return. I was also a bit worried about them even though I knew that there was no reason to be, as the Germans had gone. I went out for a walk, perhaps wanting to go to meet my friends as I had gone out to meet my father when he came home from a journey. I walked freely, admiring the beautiful scenery, but inside, I felt emptiness and unease. Until now I had had something to look forward to. I had had a clear purpose. Now that I had reached my goal, I didn't know what awaited me or what I should hope for. The image of the injured Jewish officer and the few words that he had said in Yiddish, "Are there many Jews left?" returned and haunted me, and the tears of the doctor inhabited my thoughts constantly. I remembered the feel of her smooth, cool cheek and the odor of soap emanating from it…

Suddenly I heard the sound of squeaky wagon wheels and the whinnying of horses. An army convoy was approaching; the square caps identified them as a Polish unit. At the head was a Polish officer and after him rode a horseman carrying the red and white Polish flag. I stood at the side of the road. The officer greeted me in Polish and asked how I was, and I waved my hand — I was the only one to meet the Polish army returning to its homeland. At that point someone jumped off his horse, approached me and asked if I were Jewish, saying that he had seen immediately that I was. When I confirmed it, he shouted, "A Jew!" and instantly the convoy stopped in its tracks and soldiers jumped from the wagons and horses, running toward me. They completely surrounded me, all of them speaking at once in Yiddish or Polish, asking me what had become of the Jews of their towns; perhaps I had met their families… How had I survived? Were there others like me?

The chaos around me compelled the officer to get off his horse to find out what was going on. He ordered his men to return immediately to the convoy and continue on their way, but a Jewish officer said that the unit would be camping near the town and asked me to come to visit them in the evening. The Jewish soldiers asked me to come, as well. I was excited to be meeting so many Jews, and wondered briefly if the entire Polish army was made up of Jews. Impatient for the evening and the meeting with the Jewish soldiers, I didn't feel alone anymore.

Toward evening, I washed up and put on the white shirt that the doctor had given me, and I was basking in the odor of soap and the feeling of cleanliness. Some soldiers were waiting for me outside of the camp and brought me inside to meet with the soldiers, where once again I was deluged with questions about their loved ones and their cities and towns. They wanted to know where I was from and how I had managed to stay alive. It was suppertime. A Jewish officer bought me a plate of food and sat down to eat with me. Someone asked the soldiers to let me eat in peace, but they came one after another, each bringing me more and more food. By the time night fell, a few hundred Jewish soldiers were gathered around me. We sat in a semicircle and the Jewish officer who had organized the meeting said, "The boy, Bolek, who has by some miracle remained alive, will tell us what he has seen."

Silence fell upon the group. I didn't know what to say, where to begin. Just yesterday, I had spent the whole night telling the Russian doctor about what I had gone through — and now, I was at a loss for words. Finally I began to talk about the Warsaw ghetto, but I felt that I wasn't able to describe what had actually happened, and so I moved on to Sobibor. I related how hundreds of thousands of Jews had been killed in the sophisticated death factory that the Germans had constructed. I told of the transports that reached Sobibor from all over. Each time I paused, I could feel the tense silence, and I saw the pain on the faces of my listeners, their cheeks wet with tears. I kept talking, jumping from one subject to another haphazardly. I felt that I had to get everything in. When I described the revolt and the escape, I felt a rustle and I saw the gleaming eyes of the people around me. I concluded by recounting what had happened after the revolt and when I was done, there was complete silence for a few minutes. No one asked a question. When we got up, however, soldiers approached me and continued to ask if, by chance, I knew anything about their relatives. Everyone shook my hand and hugged me and two officers walked back with me to Karpiuk's house. Before we parted, they gave me a pair of pants and a new shirt, but asked me not to wear them until after they had gone.

Yozhik and Monyek returned full of energy and plans for the future. They had been to Chelm and had found fifteen Jews who had survived in the city jail, and, after the liberation, had received a large house that had been the German headquarters. Yozhik brought his uncles there. Monyek had decided to join the Polish army and to help build a new Socialist government in Poland. Yozhik tried hard to persuade him not to enlist, arguing that since we had survived we shouldn't willingly throw ourselves into new dangers, but Monyek had made up his mind. Yozhik had already managed to make a few business deals: he had bought clothes from Russian soldiers, paid for them in vodka, and then sold the clothes to Poles. He had also bought kindling stones cheaply, and because they were hard to find in the area, sold them for ten times what he paid for them. His pockets were jingling with money and he bought gifts for the Karpiuk family and for Yanka and Yula.

The next day, early in the morning, we said goodbye to the Karpiuk family and we went to take our leave of Yanka and Yula. We were all very emotional, as though we hadn't seen one another for many years. The two women laughed and cried simultaneously and Yula said that she had been convinced that she and Yanka would never see us again. Yozhik told them that we were going to Chelm, and that when we were organized, we would bring the two of them there, but brought no comfort to Yanka, who lamented, "I always knew that when the war ended Yozhik would leave me. He will find himself a Jewish woman and marry her. I have just one request: Let me be a servant in your home. I won't disturb you. I will just serve you and your wife..."

Yozhik again promised Yanka and Yula that immediately after we had gotten settled in Chelm we would bring them and "have a wonderful time." But our hearts told us that we were leaving them for good, and it was hard for us. The two of them cried.

Although I knew Yozhik and Monyek, Shaya the gardener and

a few others who had come from Chelm — all of them regular people and some even extremely intelligent and even sophisticated — from childhood I had always thought of Chelm as a small, provincial town, whose inhabitants were simple and odd. Now I wanted to see the city with my own eyes and find out whether the stories of "The Wise Men of Chelm" that I had heard in my childhood had any basis in reality.

# Chelm

## Autumn 1944—Winter 1945

We walked the few kilometers to the road that led to Chelm — the road from which we could hear the noise of German vehicles when we walked at night from forest to forest. Now we could stand calmly at the side of the road and watch as the Russians' cars passed by us. Yozhik took out a bottle of vodka, waved it, and within seconds a loaded truck stopped for us. Yozhik let Monyek sit in the driver's cabin, while the two of us climbed up and got settled in the back with the freight. The outskirts of Chelm were very similar to the outskirts of Lodz — small farms crowded next to one another, a few workshops and factories — and for a moment it felt as though I were coming home after a long journey. We reached the city quickly. The truck stopped and we got off in a quiet street with only a few people about. I felt a frightening foreignness; not only was the city completely different from what I had imagined, it also bore no resemblance to any Jewish town I had known.

The three of us walked down the street, and everyone we passed looked at us as if we were strange creatures, perhaps because of the way we were dressed, perhaps because we were Jewish — Jews had not been seen walking the streets of Chelm freely for a long time. It is true that neither Yozhik nor Monyek looked like Jews, but where I was concerned there was no doubt, and everyone probably wondered where a Jew had come from. In any case, I strongly sensed that people were looking at me from every window and doorway, staring at me, until I wanted to run back into the forest, to the fields, to Yanka and Yula.

When we arrived at the building where the twenty-five Jews were living, those who had been living in the jail and Yozhik's relatives all came out into the yard to greet us. They knew Yozhik and Monyek, and when they saw me, they asked, "Is this the boy from Sobibor?" and bombarded me with questions: Maybe I knew their relatives? Maybe someone was still alive? My answers caused a sadness to settle over everyone, but it was still good to be among Jews and to hear Yiddish spoken around me. The building and courtyard reminded me of our building in the Warsaw ghetto, although there was no physical resemblance between them.

Yozhik's aunt, who had hidden in a cellar at a farmer's house for two years, hadn't seen the light of day all that time. She now found it difficult to be in the light and her eyes were always half-closed. She and her husband seemed desiccated, their eyes sunk deep in their sockets, their bodies bent, their steps strange. But his aunt was always smiling; she greeted me warmly and decided that I was one of the family and would sleep in their apartment.

Yozhik gave me money and sent me to buy cigarettes. The gate to the courtyard was open. There was no German guard there. I was a free man. I had nothing to be afraid of, but I was reluctant to go out into the street and have people look at me again and whisper among themselves. When I went into the grocery store, the women there looked at me in wide-eyed amazement. The grocer looked at me and said, in Polish, "Is the gentleman a Jew?" But it wasn't a question. It was as if he had said, "I know you are a Jew, but how is it that you are alive?" Everyone looked at me and waited for my reply. "I am a Jew," I answered, and one of the women said triumphantly, "I knew right away that he was a Jew!" The grocer called his wife from the back and said, "We have a guest — a live Jew!" and he asked me, "How did you manage to stay alive?"

One of the women said that she had heard that in Chelm there were fifteen Jews left alive. I looked everyone in the shop in the eyes and got the feeling that I embarrassed them. When I left, I had the impression that simply by being able to stand face-to-face with a group of Poles, I had had the upper hand of the situation. I came back from the shop with a spring in my step. I felt the urge to yell, "I won the war! I'm still alive and I'm not afraid of anyone!"

Semmen came and told us that the next day he was leaving to join his unit. He could have done so earlier, but had deeply needed to see us first. Yozhik and I had each tried to convince him not to enlist, but in vain. He remained resolute. Semmen was like a brother to me; for ten months we had been as close to each other as identical twins. In our most difficult moments we had understood each other completely. Now I didn't want to lose him, because everyone who had ever left me up until now had never returned. I had a terrible feeling that I would never see him again.

That same day a boy and girl arrived at the house together. The two of them looked like typical Aryans; I would never have suspected either of them of being Jewish. The boy, my age, named Yanek, was very thin, with a sharp, upturned nose, green eyes deep-set in his face, well dressed, and constantly smiling. The girl, Wanda, two years younger then me, was plump, her head round as a ball, with blue eyes, a small nose that hardly protruded from her face, and silken hair falling evenly around her head. Wanda was dressed in rags and looked very neglected. Everyone in the building went out into the yard to look at the new guests, and only when they began to tell their story in simple Yiddish did we believe that they were indeed Jews.

Thanks to their Aryan appearance, both Yanek and Wanda had been able to escape death. They learned to behave like Poles in every way — they each knew all the Christian prayers by heart — and they wandered from place to place until they each managed to find shelter with farmers, by coincidence, in the same village. The two would meet in the field when they took the cows out to pasture. Neither of them knew the other was Jewish, and each pretended to be Christian, until one day, Wanda ran after a cow that had separated from the herd, tripped and hurt her foot. When she screamed with pain, Yanek rushed over to her, and at the sight of the blood flowing from her foot, he blurted out *Oy Gottenyu!* (Oh, God!) in Yiddish. The girl was surprised to hear Yiddish coming from the mouth of a Polish boy and asked him how he knew Yiddish. Yanek asked her, how did she know the words were Yiddish? Wanda answered that she knew some Yiddish words as she had had Jewish neighbors, but from that same moment each one suspected that the other was Jewish. The two found discrepancies in each other's stories and interrogated one another while they continued pretending to be non-Jews, until finally, after a long time, they revealed to each other that they were in fact Jewish. From then on it was easier for them to deal with their surroundings, as they could help each other.

Wanda had had a very hard life at the farmer's home where she was taken in. The farmer worked her from early morning to night without a break, and now she looked very worn. Yozhik's aunt immediately took her under her wing and made up a place for her to sleep in the room where I was sleeping.

Yanek had joined the *Armia Krajowa*, the Polish Home Army, a right-wing Polish partisan organization that was also very anti-Semitic. This organization didn't accept Jews into its service, and more than once had killed Jewish units when it encountered them in the forests. Yanek joined the organization because the farmer whose house he stayed in was a member. Being a quick, intelligent boy with exceptional courage, he excelled as a fighter and was particularly good at stealing weapons and ammunition from the Germans. The partisans loved him and his host also treated him with respect.

One day the Germans caught Yanek trying to steal ammunition from a tank and ordered a heavy guard around him. When the partisan command found out that Yanek had been caught and that the next day he was to be brought before the Gestapo for interrogation, they feared his captors would succeed in forcing him to confess the names of the people in the underground. That night they attacked the German guard, in an attempt to either free Yanek or kill him, to ensure that he didn't divulge any sensitive information. During this attack on the guard, some Germans and some partisans were killed. Yanek himself managed to escape and he was considered a hero. None of the partisans knew that they had saved a Jewish boy.

That evening, we all gathered together. We were twenty-five in total. While there was a general feeling that we were the only ones who had survived out of the tens of thousands of Jews who had been residents of Chelm and the surrounding areas, we still hoped that soon we would be joined by other survivors like Yanek and Wanda. The fact that we were a large group strengthened our spirits. Yozhik's aunt served us all soup that reminded us of the taste of years ago, of home. We ate, and drank vodka. The four of us — Yozhik, Monyek, Semmen and I — sat close to each other. We knew that the next morning we would part from Semmen, but in the meanwhile, it was good to be sitting together. Little by little, our hearts warmed and our mouths loosened, and by morning light we had told unbelievable tales of our history during the German occupation.

The Soviet army continued to hit the Germans and to push them westward to Warsaw. The Russians occupied eastern Warsaw — the part of the city called Praga — and stopped at the banks of the Wisla River. In Chelm we didn't feel the war except for the few times German planes suddenly appeared, usually at night, to bomb sensitive areas. People went down into bomb shelters, but I loved to watch and follow the big spotlights that sought out the German planes, and the anti-aircraft artillery that shot at them.

The first time I saw a group of German refugees being led down the street, I lost my senses, burst into the columns and hit the Germans as hard as I could. I kicked one of them and he began to cry. Two Soviet soldiers rushed over and pushed me away with shouts, but people standing at the side of the road applauded me. Overcome with shame and embarrassment, I quickly fled.

Over the next few days individual Jews who came from partisan units and a variety of hiding places joined us. Among them were some who appeared Polish and who, with the help of false papers, had lived like Poles. Most of these were women, but there were a few men who did so as well, some even undergoing complicated surgeries to wipe out all traces of their Jewishness.

Every Jew who came to us in Chelm was greeted as a hero who had helped to defeat the Germans by staying alive. The additional people enlarged our group of survivors considerably, but ultimately we were only a few individuals left of an entire people. As the days passed, Jews coming from east of the Bug River also arrived. These were mostly people from partisan units. Some stayed with us in Chelm, and some continued on their way to Lublin. The building was by now completely filled, with people sleeping on every spare section of floor. Others found themselves places in neighboring buildings, but we all met at "our" house, which we called the *Komitet* (Committee). Jews who came by chance to Chelm, mostly Jewish soldiers in the Polish and Soviet armies, came to the *Komitet* every day to look for relatives, to search out other Jews, and to hear the latest from its residents. The yard was full of people all day, and in the evenings, we all gathered together to tell and listen to stories. Someone would always bring vodka or something to eat, and the stories flowed one after another, each one seemingly fabricated from a world of fantasy — and none of the storytellers or listeners tired of hearing them.

Yozhik didn't waste any time building his new life. He completely dedicated himself to "commerce" — he bought and sold everything he saw. He bought from soldiers and sold to civilians, bought from farmers and sold to soldiers. He brought home ducks and chickens, and filled the house with all kinds of delicacies. His pockets bulged with money and we ate and drank to bursting. Monyek, who didn't want to live at his younger brother's expense but didn't know how to deal in business, rushed to join the *Armia Krajowa* despite Yozhik's pleas not to. I tried to help Yozhik with his business, without much success. I hated commerce, as it was all based on bartering, but I had to make a living. I got to know the soldiers who needed money and were willing to sell everything they had just to buy vodka. I would wait for them at the corner, before they reached the market, and would buy their clothes from them. Sometimes they offered me the new shoes they were wearing, and when I bought them I offered them old shoes so they wouldn't have to return to their camp barefoot.

I had to be careful of the Soviet military police; they chased me once, but I managed to avoid getting caught. One day some of their officers came looking for me in the *Komitet* courtyard, bringing with them a soldier from whom I had bought a new pair of shoes. Some residents warned me away in time, and I didn't sleep at home for several nights.

I would give all the goods to Yozhik — he was better than I at bartering and selling. But what I did was nothing in comparison to what Yozhik accomplished — he was in contact with all kinds of suppliers and city merchants, and while others didn't have a penny, the two of us had lots of money, and we ate and drank to excess, inviting anyone we saw to join us. For breakfast the two of us would eat an omelet of twenty eggs and a half-kilo of sausage, and to that, we added a few glasses of vodka. At lunch we would devour a big roast duck, and in the evening we would continue the eating and drinking. It's a wonder we didn't get sick or explode.

After Semmen and Monyek each joined their respective armies, the bond between Yozhik and me immediately strengthened. We both felt that this link was all we had left in the world; we were compelled to hang on to each other and thought that we would stay together forever. And yet, inside I felt a hidden force beginning to create a distance between us. Without my realizing it, I had became a popular character among those who came to the *Komitet*, most likely due to my past, which I spoke about during our long evening gatherings. I made many friends — there wasn't a soul at the *Komitet* who didn't know me and exchange a few words with me; there wasn't an event I wasn't part of, no bottle of vodka was opened without me being invited to join in. I made particularly good friends with Yanek, who quickly became my best friend. Behind his hard, almost crude façade, Yanek turned out to be a sensitive, vulnerable boy. The two of us loved to take off and wander around the city, go to the movies together and afterward sit someplace alone and talk. Our mutual stories of our loved ones were an unofficial secret between us. We knew neither of us had a chance of finding any of our family alive, but we still hoped for a miracle. Yanek would tell me about his family, of his father and mother especially, in great detail — every bit of trivia was of infinite importance — then he would see images from the corners of his eyes, go quiet, and finally say, "Shit, what am I telling you all this for? Let's go look for something to drink."

One day the famous Russian-Jewish writer Ilya Ehrenberg visited Chelm. He was accompanied by journalists from the Soviet government's daily newspaper *Izvestiya*, and had gone out to gather testimony against German war criminals. I wasn't at the *Komitet* when the delegation arrived from Moscow, and people were sent to go get me. I wasn't familiar with the name Ilya Ehrenberg; I was only told that important people wanted to interview me. I went into the room and found the writer, some journalists, a photographer, and the residents of the *Komitet*. "This is the boy from Sobibor," was how I was introduced to the guests, and Ilya Ehrenberg, speaking in Yiddish, asked me to tell him about Sobibor.

I wanted to tell him everything — I felt this was my chance to tell the world of the terrors there — but for some reason we didn't click, perhaps because I was already used to people listening to me attentively and not dissecting what I said, and perhaps because he kept interrupting with irrelevant questions, as if to say, "That's not important, I already know that." I got the impression that the writer felt that my story was less important than his questions, and it disturbed my concentration and made me feel that I wasn't expressing myself well. When I finished, Ehrenberg thanked me and said the things I had told them were very important, as the world should know what the Nazis had done, but I came away from the meeting with the feeling that I had failed, that in fact I had not been able to make the world understand what I had experienced in the German extermination camp.[1]

Some time later, an entertainment troop from the second front at Belarus came to Chelm, more than a hundred people. All the members of the company were of high rank, and they wore crisp, ironed uniforms. Many of them, including the orchestra leader, were Jews, and many came to visit the *Komitet*. I made friends with them quickly.

One day, some of the people in the company came to us excitedly and showed me an issue of *Izvestiya*, where, right on the front page, was my testimony to Ilya Ehrenberg, my photograph in the middle of the article. They said it was a great honor for me to appear in *Izvestiya*, especially on the front page. The news spread quickly and people gathered in the yard, everyone crowding together demanding to see "the picture of Bolek in the paper." One of the members in the military band read Ehrenberg's article out loud, and the more I heard what he had written, the greater was my impression that these were not necessarily the things I had told him...

The band members wouldn't let me be, and I was coerced into joining them and going to their lodgings, where I was received warmly. Everyone came up to me, shook my hand, kissed me, turned me into a hero. The old orchestra leader came over, shook my hand heartily and gave me two tickets to the company's premiere performance. Everyone at the *Komitet* was jealous of my getting tickets, especially for the premiere, and in the third row, yet!

Yozhik, who was supposed to attend the concert with me, couldn't go, as he hadn't come back yet from an out of town busi-

---

1. Ten years later a friend of mine from Sobibor, Meir Zeiss, came across a pamphlet in Yiddish in a used bookstore in Tel Aviv, entitled *Murder Fan Falkar* (Murderers of Nations), which had been published in Moscow in 1945, with testimony gathered by Ehrenberg that same journey. My own testimony on Sobibor, bearing my name, was at the beginning of the pamphlet.

ness trip. I considered whom to take with me in his stead. A beautiful girl had been living in the *Komitet* for a time, one of the "gang"; she dressed in Russian military clothes and had many admirers. She was older than me — about eighteen or nineteen — and I had never dared to approach her. Her name was Raya, but everyone called her *Partisanit*, as she had come to Chelm with a partisan unit that operated on the eastern side of the Bug. Her smooth face, large eyes, hair that fell about her head, and ample bosom worked their magic on me, as well. I loved to feast on her with my eyes. Now, with the two tickets in my hand, I invited her to accompany me to the concert and she happily consented. We both arrived at the municipal theater early — the audience had just begun to assemble at the front of the building — and telling *Partisanit* that I would be right back, I went to relieve myself in one of the nearby yards. Suddenly, a dog that was tied to a chain charged at me and tried to bite me. I jumped back, but the dog managed to wound me — not only that, but half of my trousers remained in his mouth.

I was stunned. The girl was waiting for me, the show was about to begin, and I couldn't appear in public like this! I ran as fast as I could back to the *Komitet* — luckily nobody saw me in the dark — found someone's trousers in one of the rooms, put them on and flew back. I got to the theater just as people were entering the hall, but Raya the *Partisanit* greeted me with an angry face and asked, "Where were you?" I made up a story about a good friend I had suddenly met and had to take to the *Komitet*. Luckily, there was no time to discuss it further — the two of us entered the hall and a severe-faced female soldier took the tickets from me. She looked at the tickets, then at us closely, and then back at the tickets and at us suspiciously from head to toe, but finally led us to our seats. The hall was filled to capacity, mostly with Russian and Polish officers, but there were also civilians with their wives, wearing evening clothes, and the fragrance of perfume hung in the air. In the first few rows sat distinguished guests, high-ranking officers, important city personages, and Raya the *Partisanit* and me.

When we sat down, I felt pain in my leg and blood running down into my boot, but this wasn't what worried me; I only wondered at my bad luck. When I finally had a rare chance like this to go out with Raya to a concert, to be alone with her for a full evening, and maybe, after the concert, take a stroll and make small talk — the whole thing had gone wrong. She was angry at me, and certainly wouldn't forgive me for abandoning her. I was quiet and she also kept silent. I knew that anything I said would only make her more upset.

On the stage, in front of the curtain, a Soviet officer came out and a spotlight illuminated his face. The hall went quiet. The officer greeted the audience and introduced the company and its leader, to the sound of applause. The curtain went up. On the stage were the choir and the orchestra, rows and rows straight as a ruler, all in identical Soviet military uniforms — the dress, the caps, the boots and belts looking exactly alike. I knew many of them personally, but it was hard for me to identify them up on the stage. The old orchestra leader took his position and again there was applause, but he immediately raised his baton and the orchestra began to play a sad melody. The choir, which up to now had stood without moving, like statues, began to sing a quiet song, almost a whisper coming from a distance, then grew louder, into a roaring wind, strengthening until it became powerful singing, making the heart tremble. The orchestra leader gave gentle directions, drawing a beautiful sound from the choir as if by magic. For an entire hour the choir sang and the orchestra played heroic war songs and Russian folk songs full of longing and love, and I absorbed this wonderful poetry, more beautiful than anything I had ever heard. When I looked over at Raya, I saw that she was no longer angry. Our eyes met and she smiled at me.

At the end of the first half of the show, an intermission was announced. People got up and left the hall, but I didn't want to leave. It felt good to sit in my seat, the sounds of the choir and orchestra echoing in my head, good to sit next to Raya, to feel her body close to mine. I was happy. I didn't want to change a thing.

Suddenly my leg hurt. The affair with the dog seemed like something that had happened a long time ago and I told Raya the story, and she burst into laughter that made me laugh as well. The second part of the evening consisted mostly of beautiful folk dances, performed with great accuracy, and skits mocking the Germans; but it was the choir that had won me over; the magical singing granted me something I had never experienced and opened up a new musical world to me.

For a long time, Yozhik and I had been wanting to bring Yanka and Yula to the city, to Chelm, to have fun together; we even planned to rent an apartment for them in the city and help them get settled. We finally managed to bring them for a visit. The two of them, big Yanka and sharp-tongued Yula, were as shy as little children when they arrived in the city. We brought them to the *Komitet*, and as soon as we entered the yard people came out to see who had arrived. Immediately someone blurted out, "Where did they find those monkeys?" We explained to the people who gathered around us that these two had hidden us in their cottage and saved our lives. People shook their hands, but I heard some people, on the side, making fun of us. The two women felt uncomfortable in this atmosphere, so Yozhik and I took them into the city, bought them presents, and treated them to a meal in a restaurant and a movie. In the evening we met with some soldiers in our apartment, and they brought vodka. The two women got drunk, and Yula started singing baudy songs while the soldiers joined in the merriment. Yula snuggled up to me, hugged and kissed me and declared aloud, "Bolek, tonight I will sleep with you!" Everyone laughed and I was so embarrassed I didn't know where to look. The evening continued and I felt a growing worry — how could I get out of sleeping with Yula?

Yozhik and Yanka disappeared somewhere. The soldiers continued to drink and to get Yula drunker, and I wondered what the night would bring. At that point Raya came up to me and said, "I can see that you don't feel like sleeping with that old woman. So come sleep with me in the attic. I'm afraid to sleep there alone."

Raya's suggestion shocked me. Up till now Raya had been sleeping with a soldier who served in the city, and I had thought they were a couple. Recently I had noticed that they'd been mad at each other, and now she was asking me to sleep with her. But I didn't know how to sleep with a girl. I didn't know how to act, how to begin, how to continue. The thought that we would be sleeping together made me so excited that I could hear my heart pound. I became very concerned that she would laugh at me, but at the same time I couldn't refuse this beautiful creature. I liked her so much.

"Don't be afraid, Bolek," Raya said, as if reading my thoughts. "I won't do anything with you, and it's only for tonight, as tomorrow morning I'm leaving here."

Yozhik's aunt and uncle went into the next room to sleep. The party continued in the front room and I was pleased to see that Yula felt good, surrounded by soldiers. I was afraid that if I took blankets, Yula would discover that I was going to sleep somewhere else, and perhaps everyone would find out that I was going to sleep with Raya, but no one noticed us. The two of us lay on the blanket, close but not touching. Raya told me that the soldier she had been sleeping with was a scoundrel; she didn't want to see him anymore and that's why she was leaving — she meant to go to Lublin the next morning. "And now we'll sleep," she said, and turned onto her side, with her back to me.

I don't know how long I lay there without moving, my thoughts tormenting my body, Raya lying quietly next to me, deep in sleep. The summer was nearing its end; the nights were already cold, and the chill penetrated into the attic. With a quick movement Raya snuggled her back into me, and a sweet current passed through my body. Without my changing position, my hand rested itself on her hip and without obeying me continued to move until it lay across her breasts. I hugged her to me gently, kissed her back through her shirt, and fell asleep happily.

I awoke late the next morning. Raya was no longer beside me. I went over the night before and a feeling of shame washed over me. I was angry at myself. Raya was probably already gone, and what had happened remained a secret between us, but I felt a strong urge to see her before she disappeared. In the morning Yozhik and I accompanied Yula and Yanka on their way back to their home. When we said goodbye, we promised we would visit them there and have fun like the old times. Later, I went with Raya to the train station. I carried her small cardboard suitcase, which was light and probably half empty. Raya wore her Soviet military uniform, and a military coat hung on her arm. We walked without speaking. Raya, who in my eyes was a model partisan — self-confident, fearless — suddenly seemed like a small child whose parents had abandoned her and didn't know her way home. The military train entered the station. Raya hugged me, kissed me soundly — and jumped onto an open car loaded with artillery. Soviet soldiers held out their hands to her and pulled her up.

The war was not yet over. The Nazi monster had absorbed blows from all sides. In the west the Allied forces fought on Italian and French territory, pushing the "invincible" German army back into Germany. Germany was bombed constantly, day and night, and German cities were turned into hills of rubble. On the eastern front, the Soviet army was stationed all along the Wisla, planning a large attack, whose goal was Berlin. But Hitler, like a wounded animal, would not give up. He concentrated his remaining forces to continue the fight. The Third Reich, which was supposed to have lasted a thousand years, was about to crumble, but still the Germans continued their cruel, oppressive deeds and their destruction of the Jewish people. Every day, trains full of Jews traveled to Auschwitz and other extermination camps.

While the Soviet army stood on the other side of the Wisla, which intersects Warsaw, the Polish underground in the city began an uprising on the instructions of the Polish Nationalist leadership in London, to ensure Polish political rights at the end of the war. The Poles hoped the Soviets would come to their assistance, but the Soviets, who had no interest in an independent Polish party sharing in the victory over the Germans, did not lift a finger. Just as in the ghetto's Jewish rebellion, when the Polish underground had not helped either with forces or weapons, watching as the last remnants of the Jews were destroyed in the ghetto — now the Russians stood and watched indifferently as the Germans repressed the Polish uprising.

While the Polish uprising was at its peak, a group of us went to Warsaw — a Jewish officer in the Polish army, a Soviet officer serving in the Polish army (many Soviet officers served in the Polish army in Polish uniforms), Yozhik, a boy named Grisha and I. It was a business trip — the two officers took us to sell us goods they had warehoused in the Praga quarter in eastern Warsaw.

The nearer we got to Warsaw, the more military units we saw in the area. Again and again we were stopped to have our papers checked. We arrived in Praga in the late afternoon. From the west side of the city we could hear explosions — German planes were bombing rebel positions. We could hear bursts of gunfire from various points. The officers led us to an old four-story building — it looked like our old apartment building. We went up the curved staircase and made our way down the long, dark hallway. The officer knocked on the door. For a moment, I imagined how my grandmother would open the door. Three young women greeted us. The two officers kissed them. Everything in the apartment reminded me of my home — the doors, the windows, the furniture... Only the Polish women seemed out of place, as if I had suddenly been thrown years back in time. I went to a window and looked out over the western side of the city, "my" side, and then the Jewish officer asked me, "You're from Warsaw? Come, I'll take you to a place you can see the city from."

The officer went downstairs with me and led me through a few streets to a deserted building, where we climbed to the top floor, entered an apartment whose door was open, and went out onto the balcony. In front of me flowed the Wisla, and on the other side stretched the city. I needed some time to orient myself and identify some sites — the fortress, and on the other side of it a large area of ruins, probably the ghetto — and there, among the ruins, stood my home. A rush of memories passed over me with clearly detailed images: I saw myself strolling with my father in the big park next to the fortress, where a policeman approached my father and ordered him to get out quickly if he didn't want to get into trouble. On the way we saw policemen, running, chasing boys, beating a young boy; we got away from there quickly and my father explained to me that the police were chasing Communists who had gathered in the park. And here I was in Bonifraterska Street, teeming with people, small crowded stores pushed up against one another, with many vendors in the street, the fragrances of bagels and hot sausages rising into my nostrils… I got closer to our street, felt the whip of the wind in my face — when I walked with my grandfather in the evening, from the synagogue, I would be afraid the wind would lift me up and I would hang on to his hand tightly…

And here I was in the tiny, quiet street, where almost nobody was seen; I heard the sound of the workshop machinery making copper parts, I smelled the cookie factory in the basement, I entered our yard — it was a hot summer day, windows were open, I could hear a woman singing and the hum of sewing machines… The milkmaid passed with her canister of milk and her white cat crawled after her, the vendors, beggars, musicians, craftsmen — all of them, all of them known to me. I sank deeper and deeper into the past, inundated with images I had repressed and which now appeared before me, drawing me like a magnet deeper and deeper into those days that had once been, and were no more. I saw my grandmother dressed festively, wearing her funny cap and walking to the synagogue, my grandfather winding the clock on the wall, my mother and father, my sister Dvora, my brothers Mottel and little Yankele sitting at the table on Friday evening, and again I saw the ghetto, the crowded streets, the human skeletons lying on the sidewalks; I heard children say tearfully, "We're hungry, give us something to eat!" I saw people digging in the garbage crate in the courtyard and felt the hunger and the cold that prevailed in our house — I saw everyone before me.

The ruins stabbed my eyes like nails — was there nothing left? Out of that entire multitude, not one person had survived? From my entire family, only I was left? How could this happen, that everyone had died and only I was left alive? Me, the weakest of them all? Perhaps I had gotten it backward — perhaps everyone else was alive and I was dead? How had they died? From hunger in the ghetto? Or at Treblinka, where most of the Jews from the Warsaw ghetto had been taken and exterminated? Did my mother and Yankele walk together to the gas chambers, or had they been separated, each one forced to walk alone into death? My sister Dvora certainly wouldn't have let them take her to Treblinka… Perhaps she had participated in the rebellion? She always was rebellious, a member of *Hashomer Hatzair* — and perhaps she had survived? What right had I to be alive when all were dead? I was overcome by a feeling of shame that I was still alive, that my fate hadn't been to be with them — what was the point in living all alone, without any of your loved ones? What did I have left to look forward to in this strange world? I was convinced that in the end I, too, would die: I had to be killed somehow; it just wasn't logical that I of all people would remain alive.

We returned to the women. Yozhik was inspecting and sorting a pile of dresses, coats and other clothing, and I went over to help him pack the goods in bundles. Yozhik told me that he had bought a large quantity and that if we succeeded in getting it all to Chelm, we could make a lot of money. In the evening, the city was under curfew. There was no electricity. We ate our evening meal around a table lit by candles, and thanks to the officers, we had plenty of vodka and good food. We raised our glasses to the Polish army, to the Soviet army, to victory, to Stalin, and the bottles emptied one after the other. The room also had a wind-up Victrola phonograph with a large outer horn, two records of romantic Polish songs from before the war, and a Russian record that had apparently been brought by the Russian officer. We continued toasting — to the women, to each one of us, to the record player playing — every-one laughed and joked. I drank too much and my mind wandered among the ghetto ruins. All of a sudden one of the women turned to me and said, "You know? You look just like a Jew…" There was a silence. I immediately told her, "Yes, I really am a Jew." The woman said apologetically, "It doesn't matter...," and then Yozhik said, "You know, I'm a Jew too!" "No," said the woman, "that's not true. You don't even look Jewish." Grisha, who looked like a typical Pole, responded with the declaration that he too was a Jew, and the Jewish officer also confessed his Jewishness.

The women were embarrassed. They didn't believe that we were all Jewish and one of them said coquettishly, "You're making fun of us! You're not Jews! Even Bolek isn't Jewish; he just looks like a Jew..."

The atmosphere was ruined. We continued to drink, but I couldn't be sated and drank too much. The Soviet officer put the Russian record on the player. We heard a sad song about soldiers and a nightingale at the front, which captivated me, and the officer played it several times. The women left to go to sleep in the other room, and the song put the others to sleep, on the floor of the room. Only the Russian officer and I stayed at the table and continued to drink and to listen to the soldier's song:

> Nightingale, nightingale, do not bother the soldiers,
> Let the soldiers sleep a little,
> Because spring has arrived at the front
> And their eyes have known no sleep.
> And not because of the roar of the artillery
> And not because...

The officer sat with his eyes closed, a glass of vodka in his hand. I thought he was asleep, but every time the song ended he put his hand out to the Victrola's arm and set the needle at the edge of the record. I sat opposite him, listening to the song, my head spinning. Everything spun around me, the table, the record player, the officer, every object in the room rose up and down at varying speeds, as did the thoughts in my head, from subject to subject in no order; all became mixed in my head and it was as if I no longer existed...

I awoke with my heart pounding, covered in a cold sweat. I had dreamed I was in Glowno, the town we stayed in when we fled from Lodz, my mother, my sister, Yankele and I sitting at a large table. The wagon driver came in and told us to go out to the wagon. We all took up our bundles and went out. As I got up to go out, I suddenly saw *Oberscharführer* Wagner in the doorway and wondered: How can this be — I am again in their hands? I have to get away from him! I jumped through a window and ran in an open field. I looked in vain for shelter to hide from him. Suddenly I saw an outhouse, ran inside and peeked through the cracks. I was in Sobibor. I knew my end had come. I heard Wagner's footsteps. He came closer to the toilet. He stood in the doorway, all in a rage, pulled his gun from his holster, aimed it at me and shot me… I sat up and looked around. I hadn't remembered lying down on the floor. Next to me lay Yozhik and Grisha. "What happened?" asked Grisha. "Nothing," I said. "It was just a dream."

I was afraid to go back to sleep, in case my dream returned, but I fell asleep again quickly. The dream haunted me all the way from Warsaw back to Chelm. Wagner would not let me be. He had always wanted to kill me, and now continued to haunt me in my dreams.

I was glad to get back to Chelm. It felt like I had been gone for a long time. It was good to see the friends I had made in this place once more, all of the lonely ones, each one with his unbelievable story, each one a survivor pulled out of the fire, a survivor of a large family, one of a city, one out of an entire region, all of them now living with no clear goal, not knowing what the future would bring. I loved them all and felt that they all loved me.

Yozhik took me with him to the market to sell the goods we had purchased in Warsaw. He took a huge pile of clothes and gave me a smaller quantity, telling me more or less the price I should ask and how low I could go. We stood a few feet apart. Yozhik called out the goods he had in a loud voice and within a few moments was surrounded by men and women, and quickly sold item after item. All that time, I stood like an idiot next to my pile. Once in a while a woman would come and search through my pile, ask me the price, leave and go to Yozhik. In two hours, Yozhik had sold almost everything he had, while I had only sold one dress, and at a low price. I felt ashamed and helpless. Why was I such a failure? I told myself that I would never again enter the market as a merchant. Yozhik, understanding my predicament, took all my goods from me. I stood aside and enjoyed watching him perform miracles of salesmanship. When he demanded a high price for a dress from a woman who approached him, and she offered him a lower price, he stood his ground and suggested that she leave. "Why don't you sell to her," I asked him, "the price she offered was good!" But he answered, "Don't worry, she'll be back and she'll buy the dress" — and it was so.

Afterward he showed me a flowered dress that was torn and not worth a penny, and said to me, "You want to see something neat? Watch how I sell this!" He held the dress folded in his hand and yelled, "A wonderful dress for a cheap price, almost for nothing!" Women ran to see the dress and to inspect it, but Yozhik wouldn't let it leave his hand and the women were left with their arms out, reaching for it. A competition quickly began between them, each of them wanting the dress until its inspection became almost incidental. Women crowded around him, offering him money, until to everyone's envy it was finally awarded to a lucky woman. After a second, the customer realized she had a torn dress in her hands, and flushing in anger she came back to complain to Yozhik. He just chuckled and said, "Blind people shouldn't play cards!" Everyone laughed, but Yozhik didn't want to hurt the woman's feelings. He returned her money and was rewarded by all with compliments on his honesty.

The goods we had brought from Warsaw earned us a lot of money, but I knew I had contributed nothing to our business success. Yozhik actually had known that he couldn't expect any help from me in selling, as I had no talent for it, but he didn't mind. He enjoyed his ability to provide me with my needs. I did try to help him wherever I could, but I couldn't bear living off his charity. I had

# German court convicts then frees Nazi guard Demjanjuk

4:21pm EDT

By Christian Kraemer

MUNICH (Reuters) - A German court convicted John Demjanjuk on Thursday for his role in the killing of 28,000 Jews in the Sobibor Nazi death camp, then set the 91-year-old free because of his age.

Holocaust survivors at first welcomed the Munich court's verdict that Demjanjuk, who was exonerated in another war crimes case in Israel two decades ago, was an accessory to mass murder as a guard at Sobibor camp in Poland during World War Two.

But they then expressed dismay at Judge Ralph Alt's decision to free Demjanjuk despite handing down a five-year sentence.

"At the end he threw everyone in the courtroom a curveball and destroyed the hopes of the survivors of Sobibor," Martin Mendelsohn, counsel for the Nazi-hunting Simon Wiesenthal Center and the lawyer of two co-plaintiffs in the case, told Reuters.

Demjanjuk showed no reaction while the judge read out his verdict. It said guards played a key role at extermination camps like Sobibor, where at least 250,000 Jews are thought to have been killed despite only 20 German SS officers being there.

Prosecutors had faced several hurdles in proving Demjanjuk's guilt, with no surviving witnesses to his crimes and heavy reliance on wartime documents, namely a Nazi ID card indicating he worked at Sobibor which experts said appeared genuine.

Defense attorneys said was a fake made by the Soviets.

Defense attorney Ulrich Busch told the court that even if Demjanjuk did become a prison guard, he did so only because as a prisoner of war he would have either been shot by the Nazis or died of starvation.

Demjanjuk emigrated to the United States in the early 1950s and became a naturalized citizen in 1958, working as an engine mechanic in Ohio.

(Additional reporting by Reuters TV; writing by Eric Kelsey in Berlin; editing by                and                .)

Demjanjuk was initially sentenced to death two decades ago in Israel for being the notorious "Ivan the Terrible" camp guard at Treblinka in Poland. The guilty verdict was overturned on appeal by Israel's supreme court in 1993 after new evidence emerged pointing to a case of mistaken identity.

The Ukraine-born Demjanjuk has been in a German jail since he was extradited from the United States two years ago and his lawyers had sought his release on age and health grounds.

He attended the 18-month court proceedings in Munich — the birthplace of Adolf Hitler's Nazi movement — in a wheelchair, and sometimes lying down. He denied the charges but otherwise did not speak at his trial.

JUSTICE, NOT REVENGE

Stephan J. Kramer, secretary general of the Central Council of Jews in Germany, told Reuters that the verdict was "not revenge but the execution of justice, even 65 years later."

Victims' groups said the main point for them was the guilty verdict and they refrained from criticizing the decision to set Demjanjuk free.

"It's inappropriate that he be freed, but I'm not going to question the German judicial system," said Elan Steinberg of the American Gathering of Holocaust Survivors and their descendents.

Vera Dejong, whose family were Sobibor victims, said she was "very much relieved I don't have to have all the stress every time I have to come and sit here and hear all the horrible things that happened during the war and to my family."

A U.S. Justice Dept official praised "many years of extraordinary work" by German and U.S. authorities in the case.

"It serves notice on all human rights violators that the passage of time will neither erase the world's memory of their terrible crimes nor end its commitment to holding them to account," Eli Rosenbaum said in a statement.

Demjanjuk, who was once atop the Wiesenthal Center's list of most wanted Nazi war criminals, said he was drafted into the Soviet army in 1941 then taken prisoner of war by the Germans.

His son, John Demjanjuk Jr., said in an e-mail before the verdict that his father was a victim of the Nazis and of post-war Germany. "While those who refuse to accept that reality may take satisfaction from this event, nothing the Munich court can do will atone for the suffering Germany has perpetrated upon him to this day," he said.

LEGAL HURDLES

to make my own ends meet. But what could I do? I had no skills, no education on which I could base any kind of employment. I was jealous of Yanek, who was earning his living by writing. Some went to work for the police and the UBP (Public Security — the Soviet-sponsored secret police). I was also offered an enlistment in this service, but it didn't attract me, so I had nothing left to do but to deal in commerce.

Around this time, I made friends in Chelm with a group of Jewish partisans who had served in the famous unit that had fought east of the Bug. These fighters were to leave for Moscow soon to receive decorations for their heroic efforts, but meanwhile, they were looking for ways to save a little money. They asked me to get some Russian currency for them, and in return were willing to pay a little higher than the official rate. To that end, I visited a few shops in the city and bought Russian currency for more than the bank's rate. At first, I needed to find the courage just to enter a shop and ask the owners if they wanted to sell Russian currency. Since I had left the forest as a free man, I had avoided coming into contact with the Polish population, and actually with anyone who had no idea of what we had gone through; I only felt comfortable among Jews, who had suffered as I had.

Trade in foreign currency was forbidden and entailed a risk, arousing the suspicion of the shop owners, but I quickly gained their trust. I ended up being a welcome guest — when I entered a shop I would be greeted with "Welcome, Mr. Bolek," and a wide smile, and there were merchants who offered me a glass of liquor and good conversation. My aversion to meeting people soon subsided. On the contrary, I began to enjoy my contact with strangers, with whom I had no conflicts, perhaps because I didn't have to explain anything to them, but also because they treated me like an adult. Even the question that used to irritate me so — "How did you stay alive?" — no longer bothered me.

There were a few stores in Chelm where I felt intense anti-Semitism as soon as I entered, and these I did not visit again. However, I saw a blessing in this "business." On the days that I made my rounds in the city, the shop owners would prepare their Russian money and I would buy all they had and sell it to the partisan group, making a good profit. There were some who asked me if I could obtain dollars and gold coins, as they no longer trusted the new Polish currency. I knew two Jews who dealt in foreign currency, and so I entered into this business as well. Indeed, dealing in foreign currency attracted me from the beginning, even with the tension and risk that kept one alert, and demanded constant vigilance. The prices fluctuated like mercury, and whoever was ahead of the fluctuations knew what to buy and what to sell and was rewarded. I liked the game of it, as well as earning money independently, with no one's help, not even Yozhik's. The dealers in foreign currency were all older and made fun of and teased me at first, but swiftly began to treat me as an equal. Because I was able to gain people's trust, many preferred to deal with me.

Monyek, Yozhik's brother, completed his officer's course and came to visit. He was an honor student and was proud of himself. At first glance, everything seemed to be going well, Monyek was happy in the army and intended to continue in a military career, but after a few sips of vodka and conversation into the night, it was revealed that the new Polish army was anti-Semitic. Monyek had to cope again and again with this hatred of Jews, but wasn't always successful, and expressed doubt as to whether he would last; only his stubbornness and the faith that he would eventually attain a high rank, where he could change things, kept him going. Monyek also told us that the main role of the Polish army was to fight right-wing nationalist underground forces, which proliferated in the region, and he had already been in many battles of this kind. I had been aware of underground activities before this, but I hadn't known that their scope was so large.

Yozhik was proud of his brother, the officer, but was also very worried and said he felt something bad was going to happen. Yozhik and I both begged Monyek to leave the army, but our pleas fell on deaf ears.

It was a wonderful feeling to be together again. The three of us were a unit, strong and complete. I was only sorry that Semmen wasn't with us. Since he had reenlisted in the Russian army, we had lost all contact with him, and wondered what had happened to him and why he didn't write — perhaps he had been killed? I felt that the four of us had to live, and to live together.

Monyek made fun of my dealing in foreign currency. "I would never have believed it of you," he told me. "Yozhik has been a salesman since childhood and will always be one, but you mustn't do this kind of work. You're young, you're only seventeen. You must study and become a productive person."

I enjoyed the fact that Monyek worried about me. No doubt, we were brothers, heart and soul. During those days of Monyek's leave, we found out that some SS men who had been captured when the Soviet army entered the concentration camp Maidanek, near Lublin, were going to be hanged. We decided to go to see the event. At dawn the next morning, we walked to the train station and jumped into one of the army freight cars, where we met a woman of about thirty with a young boy. Spirits were high — we were traveling to see revenge being taken on our murderers! We ate from a basket we had brought with us and gave some to the woman and boy as well.

Time passed quickly. Suddenly, just before a station at a small town on the outskirts of Lublin, the train slowed. We heard a wrenching sound, as if many things were being broken, and when I looked in the direction of the noise I saw the cars in front of us toppling over, one after the other, and falling onto their sides like dominoes. At the same instant Yozhik shouted, "Jump!" Yozhik, Monyek and I jumped from the car, and a second later it toppled as well. I sprained my ankle when I landed, but other than that, we were fine. The woman who had been with us, however, did not jump out, and was crushed and killed on the spot. I didn't see the boy. Yozhik and I wanted to run from car to car to see if anyone needed help, but Monyek told us to get away fast if we didn't want to get mixed up with the security forces.

We arrived in Lublin a few hours later and missed the hanging. We went to Lublin's Jewish *Komitet*, a large building filled with people, and there I met people who had been in Chelm. They told me that some survivors of Sobibor were in Lublin, among them Leibl Feldhendler, one of the leaders of the revolt. We met with them in the evening. Although we each had already known that the other was still alive, the meeting was emotional. We decided to organize a gathering of all Sobibor survivors.

The assembly of Sobibor survivors took place in Lublin about two weeks later. There were close to twenty participants. Leibl Feldhendler was there; Yitzchak the shoemaker and his wife, Ada; Zuckerman the chef and his son, Josef; Samuel, who tended the horses; Esther, Zalma and Ola, three Dutch women; my friend Meir Zeiss; and Shkelrik, Avraham Margolis, and others. From those present, I found out that another ten people or so from the camp were still alive, among them the leader of the revolt, Sasha Pechersky. What had happened to the hundreds of people who had managed to escape from the camp during the revolt? Some had been caught by the Germans in the great hunt that took place immediately after the revolt; others were caught by the Germans over the course of that year, most because locals informed on them; some had been killed by Russian and Ukrainian murderers and during battles in partisan units they had joined, and some had just disappeared, as if the earth had swallowed them up alive. That evening was all too brief a time to hear everyone's survival story. People told of how their friends were killed and I told of our group of escapees, of which only three survived, of the massacre in the second bunker, of Shaya the gardener and Avraham, who were killed one day after they had left us.

Only the year before, we had all been together in Sobibor. None of us had dreamed we would get out of there alive, and here we were, sitting in Lublin, free people! Unbelievable. Again I heard people calling me Berale, my nickname from childhood, which I had not heard since the robbers' party when my new name, Bolek, had been chosen; I was again surrounded by the affection I had been shown by the people in Sobibor. I remembered the help these people had given me in difficult moments, without which I would have been dead long ago. And suddenly it seemed that we were in Sobibor again, that we had never left... I heard the whistle of the locomotive bringing boxcars into the camp, people getting off the cars quietly and orderly, marching family by family, Wagner in a corner of the shed separating the men from the women and children; I saw them undressing and arranging their bundles according to *Oberscharführer* Michel's instructions, and then they were walking between the two barbed wire fences to the gas chambers...

"Berale, what's wrong with you?" someone asked. "You look as if you're about to burst into tears. You should be happy. We managed to stay alive!"

A week later I was shocked to hear that Leibl Feldhendler had been killed. Before Leibl and his family had been taken to Sobibor, they were able to move some of their possessions to a village, to one of their farmer acquaintances. Leibl was negotiating with the farmer regarding the return of his possessions and had traveled to the village, meaning to return to Lublin that same day. When he didn't arrive, his friends went out to look for him and found him dead at the side of the road, not far from the village.

From the moment I was free, I couldn't really believe I was alive. I was always haunted by the thought that I must die, as everyone else had, and that my place was with them; this wasn't normal, my being alive. Recently, I had dreamed that I was in Sobibor and yet knew, even while I was dreaming, that I had been in this camp once but had escaped, and I couldn't understand how I could be back there again. All of these dreams ended in my death. Leibl's death reinforced these thoughts.

Rumors that reached us of the murder of Jews in Poland after the release from Nazi occupation convinced me that I should get hold of a weapon. Among those who frequented the *Komitet* was a young Russian Jewish pilot, a tall thin man with a youthful, smiling face, who didn't speak Yiddish and knew nothing of Judaism, yet came to spend time with us at every free moment he had. He would bring food and other things he could obtain, and would eat with us and sometimes sleep with us in the *Komitet*. I made friends with him quickly. Various soldiers I had known whom I had asked to get me a gun had refused steadfastly, and even made fun of my request — but not my pilot friend. When I explained to him that even now we were living in insecurity, and that I needed a gun for self-defense, telling him about Leibl's recent murder, he didn't ridicule me or get angry. His expression grew serious and he was lost in thought, finally saying, "I'll get you a gun."

And indeed, after a few days he returned, and leading me to a secluded place, took out of his pocket a beautiful little pistol that looked like a toy and two magazines of bullets, and gave them to me.

I was as excited as if I had received a holy artifact, and I asked my friend how much I should pay him. He laughed and said, "I'm happy to give you this pistol as a gift, but be aware that this is a real gun, that it can kill. Don't tell anyone I gave it to you, otherwise I'll go to jail." The pistol became part of me. It never left me day or night.

Rosh Hashanah and Yom Kippur were approaching. The *Komitet* was turned into a synagogue. A Holy Ark was set up in the large hall, and benches were set up in the hall and in the yard. From somewhere, someone brought a Torah, prayer books and a shofar. We had everything we needed. We expected a large crowd of Jewish soldiers from the Polish and Soviet armies. The holiday made me feel sad and unsettled; I didn't know what to do. I had stopped believing in God in Sobibor, so what was the point in participating in the prayers? I didn't feel that my place was among the faithful and therefore, I should distance myself from prayer and synagogue. But at the same time, I was attracted to the synagogue; I missed the prayers, the special atmosphere of Rosh Hashanah and Yom Kippur, the thoughts of which brought me back to days gone by, to my home and family. I couldn't disappoint my parents and all my family, who had died believing. I couldn't cut myself off from Judaism. I was lost in indecision and didn't know what to do.

Rosh Hashanah eve arrived. Everyone prepared for the holiday, cleaned up and dressed as festively as possible. Yozhik's aunt lit candles and cried and blessed us all with a Happy New Year. In the synagogue hall, many memorial candles were lit. Yozhik's uncle gave me a prayer book. Everything was just as it had been at home on Rosh Hashanah. I looked at Yozhik's uncle and aunt, at Yozhik and at Monyek who had come on leave, at the girl Wanda — and I saw my father, my sister and brother in our house in Lodz on the eve of Rosh Hashanah, saw my mother lighting the candles and all of us walking to the synagogue...

In the yard I met Yanek, all polished, standing alone in a corner. "Are you going to pray?" I asked him. "Of course," he answered. "Aren't you?" "I don't know," I replied.

The two of us stood in the yard, watching people come and go. We knew everyone except for the officers and soldiers, who were coming here for the first time. The cantor opened with a prayer and the congregation prayed with him. I didn't open my mouth; I only watched the praying. Was something wrong with me? Everyone around me was praying together as they had from the beginning of time, praising and glorifying the good and merciful God who took care of us — as if nothing had happened over the past four years. Didn't we have any argument with Him? Weren't we angry with this omnipotent God, who sat on high and watched the Jewish people being destroyed, his chosen people, men, women and children, sinners and righteous, all, all of them together with no exception — and didn't raise a finger? Shouldn't one of us have risen and shouted to God in the name of all the survivors, "We don't want you as our God anymore!"

I asked myself these questions silently, but around me people continued to pray as in olden times, to the same God, until I couldn't help but wonder if something was wrong with my soul.

On Yom Kippur eve, throngs of soldiers and officers of all ranks came to the *Komitet* and filled the hall and yard to bursting. Many had to stand outside the yard, in the street. A group of high-rank-ing Soviet officers stood out among the rest. I looked at these hun-dreds of soldiers and officers: most of them weren't praying, they only stood there, proud, decorations of bravery waving on their chests. All of a sudden I understood that most of this congregation had not come to pray to God. These people had come to say, "We are Jews! We are with you! We are one nation!" At that moment I loved them all.

After a long struggle, thanks to contacts with important people in the city and with the help of the police commander, a Jewish partisan, Yozhik was able to get his parents' house back. Yozhik and I went to live on the second floor of this house, which held a bedroom and a kitchen. The shop on the ground floor remained in the hands of a Pole who had come there to stay during the war. The first thing we did was to get a crate of vodka and lots of food, and the place quickly became a hostel for people who had nowhere to live. Each evening friends gathered, among them military people, police and security forces. Each one brought other friends. The feasting and drinking continued on into the early hours of the morning. Some were so inebriated they were unable to go home and they went to sleep on the floor. From being a private lodging, the place had turned into a kind of branch of the *Komitet*. More than once we agreed, Yozhik and I, that we couldn't let this situa-tion continue, but to no avail.

Occasionally Jews from east of the Bug came to the *Komitet*, some of them continuing on their way to Lublin after a brief stay, others staying in Chelm, crowding into the *Komitet* rooms, the big lobby that during the day hummed like a beehive and at night became one big bedroom. People were waiting for the Soviet army to leave on an offensive to conquer the rest of Poland, and then they could go to the large cities, to Warsaw and Lodz.

One day Yozhik told me that he had decided to allow a couple he had met in the *Komitet* and had liked to lodge in our home. "They will live in the kitchen and we in the bedroom," he said.

"The woman will run the house and cook for us, and the house will begin to be a real home."

The two had arrived in Chelm the week before and had been staying in one of the corners of the lobby at the *Komitet*. The man was about forty, tall and thin, handsome, with a shining face, the woman a little younger, short and plump, average-looking, and it was difficult to tell what kind of person she was. From the details I had gotten from the couple I learned that they were from Lodz and that she had converted. Their names were Harry and Ola. When Yozhik asked me what I thought of them, I had reservations; I had been biased about mixed marriages from childhood. Therefore, I just told him there was no need to rush. First we should see what kind of people they were. But Yozhik had already made his decision. "My heart tells me they are good people," he said firmly.

When the two of us approached the couple and Yozhik invited them to come to live with us, they both stood amazed, not knowing what to say. Yozhik invited them to come see the house. The man came with us and when we were inside the house he asked what the monthly rent would be, adding that he didn't know how long they would be living in Chelm — the moment Lodz was won back from the Germans, they meant to return there.

"You needn't pay a thing," Yozhik told him. "All I want is for the house to be run as it should be, and if your wife would care to cook for us, I'll bring all the ingredients she'll need and I'll buy kitchen utensils." "It's a deal," said the man. "I assure you, it will be a wonderful home. When would you like us to move in?" "Now," said Yozhik.

The four of us moved their things. Harry and Ola each took off their *kopikoat*, the winter jacket stuffed with cotton batting, and began to vigorously wash and scrub the apartment, and we were drawn into the work with them. Quickly the house took shape and looked as clean as on Passover eve. It was hard to believe such a dramatic change could take place within a few hours. Harry disappeared and came back with loads of groceries. Yozhik wanted to pay him for them, but Harry said with an affronted expression,

"What, do you think I'm penniless? I have enough money to keep the four of us going for a whole year!" and to prove it he took a few gold coins out of his wallet.

That evening we didn't want any guests. When someone knocked on the door, Ola went to open it, and when the visitors were surprised to see an unfamiliar woman and asked for us, she would answer that we weren't at home. Ola cooked and set a table fit for a king. Cleaning the house together had brought us a little closer, and Harry, who we discovered had a sense of humor, kept us entertained. Thus, the ice was quickly broken between us, and our first meal together passed in an open and happy atmosphere. When the frank confessions began, however, the laughter stopped.

Harry told us that he was a textile engineer; his family in Lodz had had a large textile factory. When the war broke out, he and his wife fled to Russian-occupied territory, and when the Germans conquered eastern Poland, they again fled and hid in various places. Yozhik told of his family and his life in the forest, of how he had met me, Semmen and Avraham, and what had happened to us later. I also told about myself. Harry and Ola sat spellbound on the other side of the table, and the entire time I spoke they didn't utter a word or move, their eyes locked on me — and I talked and talked until the early hours of the morning.

That night marked a change in my life, but I didn't realize it until later. These two people, Harry and Ola, spread their wings over us, especially me. To them, I was still a child who needed caring for and saving from straying from a straight and narrow path. The two kept a close eye on me, but I was completely in the dark about it. Ola took on the role of housewife, put everything in order and worked nonstop — cooking, cleaning, washing, ironing and mending our clothes. She also made demands — she ordered us to be at meals on time, not to drink too much, to keep our bodies clean, as well as our clothing and shoes, and she checked us each morning before we left the house. And before we returned to the table to eat, we had to wash our hands, on her orders.

At first we took all her demands lightly, but Ola wouldn't let us get away with a thing and we finally had to do as she asked. Over time, her demands increased until they affected every aspect of our lives. Every man or woman who came to visit us passed her scrutiny first: Ola would interrogate them, and those she deemed decent and nice she would encourage, and whoever she didn't, she would reject and demand that we stop being friends with them. Often we couldn't meet her strict standards, and more than once I got angry at her for her overbearing bossiness, which was eating away at my personal freedom. In the end, however, I would forgive her for everything because of her devotion to us, and because both Yozhik and I realized her demands were for our own good. Harry didn't interfere in these struggles. Often, when we weren't inclined to obey her, she would say to Harry, "Maybe you could speak to the children?" and he would reply, "I can see that you're getting along fine without my help. I'll only ruin things." Harry never demanded anything from us or rebuked us for anything, always seeming to stay on the sidelines. Still, he had a great influence on us. His elegant manner, his vast knowledge and ability to analyze impressed us again and again. Every conversation with him was an experience. I felt that I was milking him for knowledge to fill my empty head.

Harry spoke to me about the possibilities that would open up at the end of the war — something I hadn't yet considered. He drew his forecast of the future Poland and said the government would try to rehabilitate the country's economy, which had been destroyed in the war and during the German occupation; there would be a great shortage of professionals, of technicians and engineers. The government would have to permit throngs of young people to study the necessary skills, and whoever studied could be sure that all doors would open before him. Harry was referring to the general situation, but his words suggested that a conclusion be drawn about my own path. He also spoke of the possibility of leaving Poland and going to Eretz Israel, where he had relatives, or perhaps to America.

The long winter evenings brought me closer to Ola and Harry.

I grew accustomed to them and we lived together in complete harmony, and I allowed Ola to try again to "make a mensch" out of me. After some time, when Monyek again came to visit and saw the change in our lives, he said, "You aren't free people anymore — this woman has control over you."

The struggle between the Polish security forces, with Soviet officers at their head, and the right-wing underground and gangs of robbers got worse. Confrontations between them, attacks, murders and arrests became a daily routine. Anti-Semitism also reared its head. Despite the small number of Jews that had survived, attacks on them increased until they became a common occurrence. Again and again, I heard of Jews being murdered seemingly everywhere. The Polish security forces moved constantly to flush out the underground groups, and Monyek, whose army unit dealt with this problem, would come home to us, exhausted and tense, never sleeping without first loading his gun. Every sound would make him jump up and reach for his weapon. Yozhik and I, witnesses to his constant nervousness, became very worried and again pleaded with him to leave the army. Monyek refused, citing the necessity to "purify the land from the ruling enemy" and insisting on his commitment to do this, saying it wouldn't take long.

Only a brief time passed before an officer came to our house with the terrible news — Monyek had been killed "while fighting for his homeland." His funeral took place with an impressive military ceremony. His unit commander delivered a eulogy and said that "the army has lost a good officer, who fought heroically for the new Poland," and added that Monyek had been posthumously promoted to the rank of captain. Yozhik said Kaddish for his brother, the only member of his family he had left.

Monyek's death hit us hard. I had learned to be on intimate terms with death, and to meet it often. I had become so used to death taking my close friends, one after another, and although I continued to live and to struggle for my own life, I was unable to resign myself to Monyek's death. After all we had been through together, how could he have been killed now, after the war? What had we remained alive for? I had thought that the four of us — Yozhik, Monyek, Semmen and I — would always live together, and if we died, we would die together. And now Monyek had been killed and we knew nothing of Semmen's fate. Life had lost its flavor; in the end, I had been correct in my thinking that we wouldn't stay alive for long, either. We were all of us condemned to die. Our place was among them.

My heart wrenched every time I looked at Yozhik. I knew how much he had loved and admired his brother, how proud he was of him. How would he live without him now? Yozhik, the strongest one of us, the master of resourcefulness, the man who had taught us not to be afraid, not to lose hope in any situation, to rise above everything, now sat for hours and hours lost in thought, completely silent, as if he had ceased to exist. I couldn't do a thing for him. I felt helpless. I didn't have one word to comfort him and I was constantly worried that he would punish himself by committing suicide. Indeed, Yozhik blamed himself for his brother's death — that he hadn't managed to convince him to quit the army. "I should have forced him to leave," he repeated over and over.

After a long mourning period at home, cut off from life, Yozhik got up one day and went out into the street. He resumed his mercantile activities with his usual zeal, but a long time passed before I saw him laugh again.

One day, when I was at the *Komitet,* I met an unfamiliar family — a father, mother and daughter — who apparently had only just arrived in Chelm. When I saw the daughter, I couldn't keep my eyes off her. Her beauty, the likes of which I had never seen, stunned me. The girl wore ankle boots of fine leather, tight against her legs, with a beautiful tailored coat, and between the coat, which reached below her knees, and her boots, were two lovely legs. On her head she wore a fur hat that covered her forehead and ears a little, and from under it flowed blonde hair, in waves. Her face was delicate, pink from the cold, and her cheeks had dimples. She was different from any of the other girls I had known, who had dressed shabbily and looked coarse. In my eyes, she represented the height of delicacy, and reminded me of girls I had seen on the streets of Lodz before the war. I observed her with pleasure, like seeing a beautiful painting or sculpture, until she suddenly turned her gaze to me, a sharp, clear look. Her eyes shone and her cheeks reddened, and I had to turn my eyes away from her.

From that day on this beautiful girl disturbed my peace and added new color to my life. I longed to make contact with her, but at the same time I was afraid to meet her face-to-face, as I had no idea how to act and what I should say to her. I was afraid of failure.

Yozhik was the first to notice the change in me. "What's happened to you? Perhaps you're in love?" he asked one day, and laughed. My behavior had indeed changed. I began to take notice of my appearance, and Ola was pleased that I shined my boots every morning and dressed well. She took the credit for this small victory: in a brief time she had succeeded in teaching me to be neat. At that same time a few fine hairs had began to appear here and there on my face — my beard had begun to grow. I looked in the mirror and saw myself as more ugly than ever. I asked my friend Yanek to shave me, but he just laughed and said, "You have nothing to shave. Come back in another six months. Maybe then you'll have to shave. If you start to shave now," he warned me, "your beard will grow and you'll have to shave every day."

I visited the *Komitet* often in hopes of seeing the girl, but when I saw her I didn't dare seek her company. Sometimes I saw her in the company of other boys, who conversed and laughed with her freely, and I was jealous of them. I wondered if I would ever be with her, as I was a hopeless failure. And then, wonder of wonders, one day I came to the *Komitet* and met her face-to-face, and with no self-control I opened my mouth and blurted out, "Good morning!" The girl answered me with a smile, asked if I lived at the *Komitet*, and we began to talk.

"My name is Bolek," I said.

"And mine is Zoshia," she replied. "I've heard a lot about you.

I know you've been through a lot in your life. I know you were in Sobibor and in the forests."

Her eyes shone like the first time I had seen her and her face was as red as fire. When I asked her how she knew so much about me, she replied, "I wanted to know and I asked about you. Everyone here knows you and your friend Yozhik. They say you are a good person."

Now it was my turn to blush like a beet, and then Zoshia suggested we go for a walk and I consented, of course, after berating myself for not having suggested it first. We went out into the street, which was white from the snow. Luckily, it wasn't snowing then and there was no wind. We walked slowly, close to each other. A wonderful warmth washed over me. Zoshia began to tell me about herself without my asking. She was from Warsaw. She and her parents had fled east to the Russian-occupied areas, and when the Germans had conquered eastern Poland, the three of them had hidden in the home of a Polish family. Now they were waiting in Chelm for the Soviets to take Warsaw.

At this stage of our walk, we had neared a café that Yozhik told me was owned by a Jewish woman who was able to hide her Jewishness and run the café during the occupation. Even now she continued to pretend she was Polish and didn't want to be exposed as a Jew. I invited Zoshia to come in and have a hot drink with me. When we sat at the table, I was reminded of my mother's story of the first time my father had taken her to a café, on Marynarska Street in Warsaw.

That day I was happier than I'd ever been in my life.

The Soviet army's expected attack finally arrived and shook the ground of Poland. The German defensive collapsed before the Soviet thrust like a pack of cards. The sections of Poland that had been conquered as quick as lightning by the Germans were now taken from them at the same speed. The Poles got their land back, and red and white flags waved again across the land. The Soviets "appropriated" the western Ukraine from the Poles, an area that had been Poland's corn basket, and in exchange "gave" them the

German Silesia. Convoys of German prisoners were sent east, into the depths of Russia, and the battered German army retreated back into Germany to try to draw a new line of defense in their own land. Poland went back to being an independent country, and although it was under the harsh command of the Soviets, it again had its own government, army and police forces. The administration was again Polish. Poles who had been banished or who had fled from the Germans returned to their homes, their jobs and businesses. The German masters were swiftly removed and replaced by Polish masters. Life quickly got back on course.

The few Jews left in Chelm, Lublin and the surrounding areas didn't feel a real connection to the place. The Polish population ostracized them, and they felt foreign and superfluous. Now they no longer had non-portable assets, the sale of which before had presented a problem. They didn't even have anything to pack — every survivor could pack all his possessions in one suitcase. Therefore, most Jews went west, following the Soviet army — to search for a future in the big cities.

I found myself at a crossroads. It was time to make a fateful decision regarding my future. I loved Yozhik heart and soul. He was very dear to me, but in my heart I had known for quite a while that our paths would have to separate. His lifestyle didn't suit me, and I had enough sense to know that the longer I stayed with him the more dependent on him I would become. I had no choice but to sever my ties with him.

Harry and Ola asked me to come with them to Lodz, to live with them in their home, and to decide on my path in life there. They also asked Yozhik to come with them; he didn't refuse their offer, he just said he would join them at a later stage, and urged me to go with them immediately. It was hard for me to leave him on his own. We were like two brothers who only had each other left in the world; deep down, I was still struggling with the fear that if we parted, we would never be together again.

Harry went to Lodz alone, to assess the situation firsthand and to prepare our accommodations. Yozhik traveled somewhere on business, and I was left at home with Ola. In the evening, next to the warm oven, she told me her life story.

Ola's father had been a guard at Harry's father's factory, and her mother had also been employed there as a factory worker. They lived at the factory, in a house next to the gate. Harry, the youngest son, and a student, often visited the factory, and he and Ola fell in love. The affair was complicated. Ola's parents were totally against any kind of relationship between their daughter and the factory owner's son — they were afraid they would be fired because of it. Harry's parents and family were also against their son's relationship with the non-Jewish guard's daughter, and tried to end it any way they could. The situation became even more difficult when Ola became pregnant. As she didn't want to add to their romantic problems, she had an illegal abortion and almost died from infection. She recovered, but would never be able to have children. After Harry decided to marry her, his whole family, who were devoutly Jewish, ostracized him for a long time. Ola, who wanted so much to be accepted into a loving family, and for Harry to be accepted back into the family as a beloved son, decided to convert, even though Harry didn't ask it of her. She went to Krakow and studied Jewish law from a rabbi for months until he agreed to convert her, and then they married, with a *chuppah* and *Kiddushin* prayers. Still, neither Harry's nor Ola's parents attended the wedding.

Ola told me painfully, but also proudly, how she and Harry had endured all their difficulties. Love had overcome. "It's all thanks to Harry," she emphasized, "he is the one who gave me the strength to go on" — and she began to cry bitter tears over her inability to have children.

One morning, there was a knock at the door. I opened it and was surprised to see Zoshia. She was somewhat embarrassed, perhaps due to the surprised look on my face, and said in an apologetic voice, "We're leaving Chelm soon and going to Lodz. I came to say goodbye."

The two of us stood in the doorway, looking at each other, and then Ola invited her in — in my embarrassment it hadn't occurred to me to do so — but Zoshia refused, saying she didn't have time. They were leaving very soon. I walked back with her, and wanted to tell her now, in the few minutes I had left alone with her, many things — everything that was in my heart that I had longed to tell her for weeks and hadn't — but somehow the words stuck in my throat, and despite everything I wanted to say, I couldn't even form one sentence.

We reached the gate of the *Komitet*. Zoshia offered me her hand. It was warm, and I was trying to hang on to it for just another moment, and finally I said, "Zoshia, I'll come to Lodz soon and we can keep seeing each other."

She moved her face closer to mine as if to kiss me or to receive a kiss, but I wasn't prepared for this and by the time I realized what was going on, it was already too late — she withdrew from me and disappeared into the building.

All day, I was angry at myself; I couldn't forgive myself for my foolish behavior, for not being able to say a word to her, for not kissing her goodbye and for making her think, no doubt, that I was an idiot. And indeed — I was an idiot.

Harry came back from Lodz with good news. He had gotten his parents' house back, a large, three-story building at no. 8 Poludniowa Street. He would also be the manager of his parents' factory. Harry tried until late into the night to persuade Yozhik and me to abandon everything and accompany him and Ola the next morning to Lodz. Yozhik assured him that he and I would come to Lodz very soon and might even stay there. Harry and Ola tried to take me with them at least, and part of me really wanted to go, but I didn't want to leave Yozhik all alone, and I was afraid he wouldn't follow us to Lodz if I left him.

Only after Ola and Harry had gone could we really appreciate all they had done for us. It had been so nice to come home knowing that someone was taking care of us, that every corner of the house was clean and neat, that meals were regular and the atmosphere was one of family. Now we went back to the way we had been before, and the house quickly deteriorated back to being a hostel for random visitors. The two of us missed Harry and Ola, who wrote and told us they were waiting for us to come every day, that all was ready for us — "your beds are all made up and waiting." And indeed, within a short time, we packed our things and left for Lodz.

We were joined on the way by two other men. For a bottle of vodka we were able to hitch a ride on a Soviet military train to Lublin, and from there, we went to the train station and continued on to Lodz. The station was full to capacity, and we were told that people had been waiting for days to board a train. In order to obtain a ticket, you first needed to get a permit from the *Kommandatura* — the Soviet military government. We had neither permit nor tickets, but the ever-resourceful Yozhik did not despair. "Follow me closely," he ordered, "and everything will be fine."

Yozhik began to make his way through the throngs in the station with sure steps — and we followed him. Occasionally he would shout, "Excuse me! Excuse me! Make way! Excuse me! Excuse me!" continually cutting through the sea of people. People moved aside quickly and made way for us — and Yozhik pushed through confidently, with us closely following him. He continued moving forward, shouting, "Excuse me! Excuse me!"

The ticket collector, who was standing next to the gate, looked at us in amazement as we passed through the gate without stopping, and by the time he asked for our tickets we were on the platform, next to the train. The cars, some of them for passengers and some for freight, were already packed, and throngs of people on the platform were trying to find a way in. In a flash, Yozhik decided to be a crippled war veteran. He began to limp on one leg and to drag the other behind him, and everyone moved over for him, and we all crammed into one of the freight cars after him, where we found that the crowd was only at the door and in the car itself, people were sitting comfortably on the floor. Yozhik let out a sudden scream of pain and everyone's eyes turned to him. We explained to people that this man was a crippled war veteran, and that apparently his bad leg had just received a blow. Someone next to us thought it was he who had hurt Yozhik and begged forgiveness; he then declared firmly, "We must make room for the cripple!" People moved over until there was space in the middle of the car. We sat Yozhik down and sat down next to him.

In those days there was no travel schedule. No one knew when the train would depart or when it would reach its destination. Every military train was given priority. Our train was taken to a side track, where we waited for hours until the tracks were clear. Yozhik made friends quickly with the other passengers. He pulled a bottle of vodka out of his pack and offered it to all his neighbors, and the others did the same — they pulled bottles and sausages out of their packs and everyone ate and drank and conversed and told jokes and stories until the difficult and boring journey became a joyous party. Next to us sat a woman of about thirty-something, who joined in the merriment and quickly made friends with Yozhik. When I awoke toward morning I saw them lying in each other's arms.

In the morning the conductor came to check our tickets. When he approached us, Yozhik let out a cry — this time he cursed and abused the conductor for hurting his injured leg. The people in the car fell upon the poor conductor and he apologized and left quickly. When we got to Lodz, we took our leave from our friendly companions, left the train station, and when we saw a streetcar, began running toward it. Yozhik forgot that he was crippled and ran as well, and then I saw one of our erstwhile friends on the road make the sign of the cross and say, "Oh my God, it's a miracle! Our cripple is running like a healthy man!"

Again I was filled with amazement at Yozhik's resourcefulness, and wondered where he had the talent to overcome every obstacle, to cope successfully with every situation, to make friends with everyone with ease and to be loved by all. The man had turned a long, difficult journey in a freight car into a pleasant experience that made everyone forget the time, allowing it to pass quickly. I wasn't made of the same stuff as he was; I would have traveled the entire way without uttering a word. Nevertheless, although I truly admired Yozhik, I didn't want to be in his shadow. I wanted to live my own life, as I wished; deep down, I had already decided to part from him.

# Lodz

## Spring 1945—Winter 1946

The tram that stopped for us was filled to capacity. I could neither move nor see a thing; I only knew where we were by the ticket-seller calling out the names of the streets we passed. After some time, a seat near a window became free and I sat down and looked outside, beginning to identify streets. When we entered Piotrkowska Street, everything became familiar. The tram traveled toward Plac Wolności (Liberty Square) — which had been called Hitler Square when the Germans occupied the city. As we neared the square, everything became more and more familiar, until I could identify every house. When the tram stopped at the square, we got off.

I stood in front of my grandfather's house and looked around. Everything was the same: the iron gate, the lamp post in front of the house, the stores, the church at the corner of the street, the tram bell and the sound of its screeching wheels on the iron tracks around the square. The only thing missing was the statue of Kosciuszko, which the Germans had blown up right after they occupied the city. I looked up at the windows of their apartment, and the images of my grandparents and their son, Uncle Feivel, appeared to me. When was it? It all seemed so long ago — what had happened to my grandmother and grandfather? How had they died? Of hunger? Had they been shot? Gassed? Apparently, I would never know, just as I would never know the fate of my mother, my sister and brothers, and all the rest of my family.

The place had not physically changed, but its character had changed completely. Everything was quieter, and although the stores were open, the atmosphere was like Sunday morning (when, in a Catholic country, everything is closed). I searched for Jewish faces among the passersby and those standing in the doorways of the shops. Everyone looked Aryan. I remembered this street before the war, when it was full of life — elegant women and men in modern dress, Jews in *kapotes* with round, tiny-brimmed caps, Polish children going to church, and Jewish children. The street had been full of people every hour of the day, people rushing on their way to wherever. Now it seemed that even the smell of the street was different. Suddenly everything was foreign to me, as if I had never been here before — and again my mind was pierced by the thought that I belonged with those who would never return. Why, oh why, had I been fated to return here and not to die with everyone else?

When Ola saw us from the doorway of their house, she cried out in joy, embraced and kissed me as one kisses a small child, and said, "My children have returned to me!" She led us into the room meant for us and we could see that she had readied it for us with great thought and love — two beds all made up, a wardrobe, dresser, table and chairs with tablecloth and flowers… When had she and Harry had time to prepare it all? Our room was nicer than theirs.

Ola quickly took charge. Declaring that we were "dirty," she heated water and sent us to bathe, took our shirts and undergarments and gave us others in their place. Where had she gotten everything — had she prepared all of this for us? After the time we had spent alone, and at the end of our long journey, it was wonderful to experience the feeling of being home and of a woman taking care of us. Harry arrived in the afternoon, and we celebrated all over again. The first words he said when he saw us were, "I told you they would come!"

That afternoon, tired from our journey, clean and fed, we lay in our spotless beds and slept until evening, when we took Harry to the cinema. We saw a Soviet war film about the cruelty of the Germans and a group of partisans who triumphed over their enemy in the end. I really enjoyed the film and was surprised to hear the Poles in the audience laughing at the Soviets. It angered me, as after all, it was they who had freed Poland from the Germans. The Polish hatred of the Russians was strong and deeply rooted in the history of the two peoples.

At home, Harry lectured us on our options. In his opinion, I could choose to study any skill I wanted from a variety of courses, but it would be better if I first made up the general studies I had missed during the war years. He was willing to help me in my studies and to sit with me every evening. To Yozhik, he suggested opening a shop in their house, adding that the two of us could continue, of course, to live under their roof.

The next day, Yozhik and I went out for a stroll. It was a spring day. The sun appeared intermittently and sometimes there was a cleansing rain that sent people running for cover into shop and house doorways. I wanted to go to my own house, but I was worried about how I would react face-to-face with the past, so I decided I should go there alone, and put it off for another time. We strolled the streets aimlessly when suddenly I heard a shout, "Bolek!" — and it was Semmen's voice. Was this a dream?

Opposite us stood a Russian soldier leaning on crutches, his military coat open, and under it, hospital pajamas. "Semmen!" Yozhik and I cried at the same time, and we fell on each other, the three of us standing on the sidewalk embracing, to the amazement of passersby who stopped to watch this strange scene.

We entered one of the cafés and ordered vodka and something solid to eat. Our Semmen had changed a great deal. He was thinner. His shaved head made him look ugly, and his smile was so sad that one could see that he had recently been through difficult experiences. When he asked how Monyek was, Yozhik burst into tears and I did too, and then so did Semmen — the three of us sat and drank and wept. If Monyek had been with us, the meeting

with Semmen would have been joyful; without Monyek, the unex-
pected meeting with the fourth member of our group was deeply
sad.

Semmen told us his story: On the day he had rejoined the
Soviet army, he was interrogated for many hours; he told the Soviet
officers how his entire unit had fallen prisoner to the Germans,
how he had spent time in various prison camps, how he had been
sent to the extermination camp Sobibor because he was Jewish, and
how the Germans had selected a group of around a hundred men,
including him, for a work detail at Sobibor. He also told his interro-
gators about the camp, the rebellion and life in the forest until the
liberation. At the end of his preliminary interrogation, Semmen
was sent to jail along with the Ukrainians who had served with
the Germans, and he, who was no stranger to suffering, said that
those had been the worst days of his life — he had been charged
with collaborating with the Germans and jailed with Ukrainian
murderers.

Semmen's interrogation lasted several days, and finally, he
underwent a quick military trial and was sentenced to twenty years
imprisonment, but his verdict was converted to a month's service
in a penal unit.[1]

Semmen also told us that in one of the attacks his unit had
made on a fortified German position, only he and one other soldier
remained alive. Semmen was a veteran and a battle-experienced
soldier, and was lucky enough to be wounded in the last battle and
taken to the hospital as the Germans retreated. He showed us the
medals he had received and said that everything was all right, the
wound wasn't serious; soon they would remove his cast and he
wouldn't be sent back to the penal unit.

For the first time, I was angry at the Soviets, whom I had

---

1. During the war, the Russians established penal regiments, comprised of
prisoners with long or life sentences. These regiments were given the most
difficult and dangerous of missions. The fighters' chances of survival were
very slim. Some of these prisoners excelled in heroic acts, but most were cut
down by German fire when they went into battle.

admired up to now. How had they dared treat Semmen as they had when he was guilty of nothing? I had encountered anti-Semitic Russians before, but thought they were few in number. Semmen's case suggested that Soviet anti-Semitism was systematic and that his was not the only case. We continued to sit together in the café, oblivious to everything. The time for Semmen's return to the hospital came and went. He told us that after the cast was removed from his leg and he was declared healthy, he would be sent to Russia for continued treatment and vacation, and we knew that we would once again have to leave one another, and who knew if and when we would meet again. We accompanied Semmen back to the hospital, but left him at some distance from it so as not to "complicate things," as he said. The next day we met again, and the three of us strolled down Piotrkowska Street looking for a place to sit and have a drink. Yozhik liked the Grand Hotel, and when I explained to him that it was not for the likes of us, but rather for important persons, he said, "What, we are not important people?" and pulled us in through the heavy revolving door.

The large, elegant hotel entrance looked empty at first, and only when our eyes had become accustomed to the dark could we see people sitting here and there in heavy leather armchairs. Total silence reigned and our entry in heavy boots attracted everyone's attention. Everyone looked at us, including the waiters and other employees in their ironed uniforms, who, when they saw us, began whispering among themselves. We found an empty table and sat in the armchairs surrounding it. An elderly waiter approached us, greeted us with a severe expression and asked how he could serve us. Yozhik ordered a large bottle of vodka, an omelet with twenty eggs and sausage, and also asked if we could have "some kind of good smoked meat." The waiter listened attentively to the order, was quiet for a moment and said, "You will please excuse us, but we do not serve food here. If you wish, you may have dinner in our dining room, which will open in about an hour, but I suggest you go to a restaurant not far from here, and there you can find what you wish."

"And what can we get here?" Yozhik asked the waiter.

"Here you can have soft drinks and hard liquor, but you should know that our prices are very steep."

"Thank you very much," said Yozhik, "We won't be needing anything," and the waiter left, pleased that he had gotten rid of the strange characters.

"Wait for me here," said Yozhik then and got up. "I'll be right back." He left the hotel and I saw the waiter describe to his friends what had happened at our table, and how they laughed.

I knew Yozhik was up to something; otherwise he wouldn't have asked us to wait for him here, and indeed, a few minutes later he returned with a smug look on his face, and set down a bottle of vodka, some sausage and a loaf of bread. It wasn't hard to guess that this wouldn't go down well; it was unreasonable that a group of strange characters like us could turn the elegant lobby of the Grand Hotel, one of the finest hotels in Lodz, into a common snack bar. Before the war, the waiters would have called the police in cases like this and we would have immediately been arrested; now, only a few weeks after the city had been taken back from the Germans and before the policies of the new government had been determined, the hotel staff didn't know how to handle us.

No doubt, Yozhik was looking for a fight, or perhaps he wanted to protest against the world, which was continuing to live peacefully without Jews, and to show that we still existed. The entire hotel staff gathered at the reception desk and consulted with each other on how to handle us. And then Yozhik summoned a waiter, and when one of them approached, ordered him to bring glasses. The waiter brought glasses on a tray and placed each one on the table without uttering a word. When I said "thank you" to him he was very surprised, as if his enemy had offered him a hand in peace.

We sat in the comfortable chairs and drank. While in the company of Yozhik and Semmen, I felt confident. I was impressed that the hotel staff had resigned themselves to our presence and had decided to leave us alone, but after a few glasses of vodka, when our voices began to rise, a waiter approached us and reminded us that we were in a respectable establishment and asked us not to make noise. Yozhik asked, "What, are we in a church?" and the waiter answered, "No, we are not in a church, but we are not in a synagogue, either." The waiter had hit our most sensitive spot. The three of us rose as one, ready to attack him.

"You lousy bastard," Yozhik cursed him, along with a few more juicy epithets, and the waiter, who wasn't expecting such a reaction, went pale and wavered, not knowing what to do. He finally moved away, but not before turning toward us and muttering, "Dirty Jews!"

At that moment, Yozhik punched him hard in the face and the waiter flew backward and fell to the ground. He tried to get up, but now all three of us fell upon him with our fists and feet. Other waiters came to his assistance, a real fight broke out and from all corners of the beautiful lobby people gathered around us to watch the exchange of blows. The injured waiter got up, pulled a knife out of his pocket and approached Yozhik. Other waiters tried to stop him, and in the meantime, Yozhik grabbed the neck of a vodka bottle, hit the bottle on the table edge and broke it in two, waving the jagged bottle neck in the direction of the waiter. Who knows how things might have ended if a tall Russian officer hadn't suddenly appeared and shouted, "Stop!" Everyone froze in their places, and then the officer came over and stood between us and the waiters. Without waiting for any explanations, he turned to us and said in Russian, "Get out of here immediately!"

Semmen stood to attention, saluted the officer and began to tell him about the behavior of the "fascist waiter," but the officer cut him off and said, "I don't care what happened. Get out of here immediately!" We left the hotel through the revolving door and out in the street we began laughing hysterically. We marched happily, arm in arm, as if there were no one happier than us on the face of the earth.

Those were the most wonderful days of our friendship. Each

morning we met Semmen and spent the entire day together, wandering the streets, visiting restaurants and cinemas. For me, our being together was the most important thing in the world. I felt so close to my two friends that it seemed that the only time I was able to feel truly good was when I was around them. Actually, we all knew deep inside that these days of happiness would soon end; the trio would be separated, and it was possible that we would never be together again. When Semmen's cast was removed, we took our leave from him with a mutual promise to stay in touch. Then, some time later, Yozhik told me that he had to go to Chelm to "take care of things"; he also confided that he was undecided about what to do with his life and where to make his home.

The good days I had spent in the company of Semmen and Yozhik were over. I was overcome with loneliness. With my friends gone, somehow I saw no point in life and I had nothing to hope for. The feeling that I didn't belong in the world around me returned and took control. The great prize I had won by staying alive seemed like a punishment. Harry and Ola did all they could to make things easy for me by pampering me like a child, and I thanked them with all my heart and truly appreciated their efforts, but somehow their love made me suffer. More than once, I felt the urge to run away from the home of my hosts and never to return, but I couldn't hurt them like that.

May 8, 1945: The war was over. The radio announced that the Soviet army had entered Berlin, and that a Russian flag waved from the Reichstag. The Germans had signed an unconditional surrender on all fronts. In the streets a joyous holiday atmosphere reigned. The city was decorated with flags. Loudspeakers were set up around Liberty Square, and toward evening, crowds of civilians and soldiers filled the square and the surrounding streets. Music blared loudly from the speakers; soldiers fired pistols and rifles into the air. The city of Lodz rejoiced — and I passed among the revelers like a mourner, like an uninvited guest to a joyful event that he had no part of. I told myself I should celebrate, that a once-inconceivable dream had materialized — I was able to witness the German defeat — but I remained heavyhearted, saddened to tears.

If Yozhik and Semmen had been with me I would have been happy, without a doubt. If Monyek had been with me, or Avraham, Shaya, Krichona, Schnabel…if my brother Mottel, my brother Yankele, my sister Dvora, my mother…if even one of these people had been with me! But no — I was alone. It was just me. I quickly realized that my place was not among the revelers. I was the only one in the square who moved in the opposite direction — from the inside outward. The crowds grew thinner and the joyous cries faded. I kept walking. I remembered the first day of the war, September 1, 1939, and it was amazingly clear, as though it had happened just the day before. I wanted to freeze the surge of memory within me, but it passed and was replaced by one memory after another, images from the war years, too many to count — was it possible that all this had happened to me? When Mottel had returned from German captivity, I was jealous of his having such special experiences to relate to us — how we all sat and hung on his every word! Now, I remembered my many experiences, but I had no one to tell them to.

I found myself walking down a darkly shaded, quiet street. I didn't see a soul. A strange, free-floating fear of something I couldn't determine took control of me. I hurried back home.

I had been in Lodz for a month and I still hadn't visited my home. I had wanted to visit from the moment I arrived, but had postponed it from day to day, and even avoided entering our street, Listopada. The day finally came when I could no longer come up with an excuse not do it. I stood at the tram stop, but a moment later I left and kept walking quickly, not looking to either side. When I heard the bell of the tram approaching from the other side of the square, I ran to the next stop, but it left before I got there. I continued walking hurriedly and stopped only when I was very near the building.

Where was I going? Would they let me in? What would I say

to the people who lived there now? Why had I come? What was I really looking for? Did I really expect to find my family there?

To buy time I crossed over to the other side of the street. A little wooden house stood in front of ours, looking nicer than I remembered. It seemed to have been repainted in light brown and the sunshine gave it charm. When we had lived there, I hadn't noticed it; to me it had just been a passage on the way to the building, which stood in the yard. I stood rooted to the spot for a few moments, my eyes gazing at the building. I was afraid someone would recognize me, would come over and start asking me questions, but nobody noticed me, and I saw no one I knew. I suddenly needed to find someone who knew me from before the war and to show them that I was alive. I scanned the faces of passersby in vain — no one looked familiar.

I decided to find out if the gatekeeper from my childhood was still there. I knew she lived in the attic of the tiny house, but I had never visited. I entered the corridor and went up the dark stairs. Since childhood I had hated dark stairwells, and even now I felt uncomfortable. I knocked on the door. No answer. I went back outside and approached the front of our building. I looked for someone who could possibly answer my questions. The hat shop and the delicatessen in the front were closed.

At the corner of the building I saw a small restaurant that hadn't been there before the war, and behind the counter I saw a woman who looked somewhat familiar. I approached her and asked if she knew where I might find the gatekeeper. The woman burst out laughing. "Why do you need the gatekeeper?" she asked, continuing to laugh. Her voice also seemed familiar. Was this the gatekeeper? Before me stood a woman in a flowered dress, her lips and cheeks rouged, her hair lighter in color — no, this wasn't the same woman...

And then the woman stopped laughing and said, "I'm the gatekeeper of the building. And who are you, sir?"

"I am one of the Freiberg family boys, who lived in this building."

The woman's face grew serious. "Yes, yes, I remember them," she said. "Your mother was a very nice woman. Are you the elder son?"

"No, I'm the middle one."

"Yes, certainly I remember you. A thin boy. You used to play with my son. Now you have grown. My son has also grown. Is anyone else from your family alive?"

"I don't know. I wanted to ask if anyone had visited you?"

"No, no, no one has visited me and no one has asked about you."

I wrote down my address on a piece of paper and gave it to her. I asked her to give the address to anyone who asked about me.

"You didn't recognize me," said the woman, "I now own this restaurant and I live in the big building, in an apartment like yours."

She looked at me, expecting a reply, but I didn't have any interest in her. I told her that I wanted to see our apartment.

"What," she replied, "you want to get your old apartment back?"

"No, I just want to see it…"

The gatekeeper was willing to accompany me, but I asked to go alone. My nervousness was completely gone. I crossed the yard and climbed the stairs calmly. Then when I knocked on our door and waited, my nervousness returned. I heard footsteps. From the other side of the door I heard a woman's voice calling, "Who's there?" I stammered and managed to get out a request for her to open the door. She opened the door a crack and peeped at me.

"What do you want?"

"Nothing… I used to live here, and I'd like to see the apartment, if I may."

The woman hesitated, not knowing what she should do; she looked at me as if trying to read my mind and finally opened the door and invited me in. When I went in, she told me that she and her family had moved to the apartment several months ago, after a family of Germans who had been living there had gone back to Germany.

"The apartment was completely empty," she said. "I guess the Germans took everything. All the furniture you see here we brought with us…" I cut off her stream of words by saying I had no interest in the furniture and wanted nothing; I came only to see the place where I had once lived. We quickly passed through the rooms and the kitchen. I felt no connection to the place; it was all strange to me. Only the large oven took me back six years.

I stood embarrassed, smiling a silly smile at the woman. She returned the smile in kind. All of a sudden the pointlessness of visiting was clear to me, and I felt a strong urge to run. And then a foolish thought popped into my mind: before we left the apartment I had placed a bundle of things high above the oven. Perhaps they were still there? I told the woman about the things I had left. She understood what I meant, but asked in wonder, "How can we reach that high? I don't have a ladder."

I gently suggested that she let me bring the table standing in the center of the room close to the oven and place a chair on it — that way I might reach the top. The woman immediately agreed and even helped me move the table. I climbed up, but found nothing. When the woman, whose curiosity had been aroused, asked if there was anything there, I answered sheepishly that it was silly to think I might still find something after six years. She commiserated with me and asked if there had been anything of value. I explained that they had been toys and souvenirs of no monetary value. I thanked her for her hospitality, and left. What a fool I am! I thought when I was back outside. I was glad that no one had been there to make fun of me.

The end of the war brought waves of Jews returning to Lodz from east and west. From the west came individual Jews and small groups, the survivors of concentration camps and extermination camps scattered across Germany and Austria, from weapons factories, from coal mines, from agricultural farms. The Germans had worked all these people like slaves in the war state until the very last moment, and then intended to exterminate them, until finally, the end came and they weren't able to. These survivors were mostly residents of Lodz and its surrounding area, and had come back to search for whatever members of their families might still be alive. From the east came Jews who had fled to Russia at the beginning of the war, and had stayed alive thanks to the Soviets, who had banished them to central Asia and Siberia, but were now permitting them to leave the Soviet Union and return to their homelands as expatriates. They came to Lodz in large groups, making their way across the Soviet Union in freight trains for weeks. All of the arrivals searched for relatives, acquaintances, or, at least, fellow members of their cities and towns, wandering the streets of the city from morning to night, particularly Zawadzka Street, where many Jews used to live. They stopped every Jew they passed and asked him where he was from, where he had been during the war years and if he had, by chance, come across a member of their family. Those who had photographs pulled them out of their pockets, showed them and waited for a response.

The obsession with searching for surviving relatives led to a magic phrase that spread quickly and made it easier for Jews to identify themselves to each other for their mutual interrogations: "Your people?" When you met someone who looked Jewish, you uttered this expression as a question, and if they were Jewish, they would immediately reply, "Your people!" and instantly there would be a sense of mutual brotherhood, enabling an intimate conversation. More than once I heard this Jewish identification exchanged between people whom I would never have guessed were Jewish. From experience, I learned that non-Jews almost never acknowledged the words "Your people?" when spoken near them, or at most, reacted with a stolen glance or turning of the head, while Jews always reacted quickly and warmly.

The identification of Jews using the phrase "Your people?" was often a game of suspense for me, the code for success or disappointment. One day, on the tram, I stood beside a man who I was convinced was Jewish and uttered the password in a confident tone. The man looked at me as though I were from Mars and said,

"Excuse me?" I was so embarrassed I wanted to disappear. Another time, when I was waiting at a tram stop, a Polish-looking woman stood near me. Something in me made me utter, "Your people?" to her, and she turned to me and answered "Your people!" and began talking to me in Yiddish. Then my joy knew no bounds — this time I had gambled and won.

The most important site to look for relatives was the Jewish *Komitet* on Śródmieście Street, where dozens of clerks recorded every survivor who stood before them. The walls of the *Komitet* were completely covered with notes written by people searching for their families, some with photographs. Jews returned to this place, studied the lists of names, scanned the new notes, and asked each other, "Who knows…?" For a while, I, like many others, visited the *Komitet* every day and witnessed emotional events occurring round-the-clock, when friends and family members met for the first time after years of separation, when someone found out that one of his relatives was alive and well, or the opposite — dead, exterminated. Cries of joy and sorrow, laughter and sobbing, mixed with each other at all hours of the day in a great commotion — but the silence of the solitary people, who formed the majority of those searching for relatives or acquaintances in low voices, carrying their pain inside and hoping for a miracle, drowned out the noise around them.

Again and again I saw people reuniting with their relatives and I was happy for them, but I was also filled with a stormy jealousy and I asked myself, why wasn't I meeting any relatives or friends? I, who up to now had been convinced that I was the only one of my family who had survived, and only seldom experienced a passing hope that I would ever see one of my family again, was suddenly obsessed with the belief that someone in my family was alive and that I must find them. Slowly I wove my illusion: My sister Dvora is alive! Of all people, she had the best chances of survival — she was a young girl, full of energy and stamina in difficult times, a member of a pioneer movement. In my mind, I saw her fighting in the Warsaw ghetto, and afterward with the partisans... No, my sister Dvora would not be one to give in easily!

My conviction that Dvora was alive grew, giving me no rest during the day and invading my dreams at night. Every day I went to the *Komitet*, checked the lists again and again, studied the notes that I already knew by heart — everywhere I went, walking down the street, traveling on trams, in cinemas, in restaurants, I looked for my sister. I dreamed of meeting her by chance. Every girl with a similar figure made my heart pound and I would rush to look at her from up close, only to be proven wrong. I so wanted to keep the image of her face in my mind that it seemed her face was being wiped from my memory, and my confidence that I would recognize her when I saw her in the street disappeared.

One day I saw a girl who I thought looked like my sister. I approached her, said to her, "Your people?" and was answered by "Your people!" When I asked her where she was from, she said, "Warsaw." I felt that I was going to faint, but when I asked what her name was, it was plain that we weren't related. Only when I thought about it afterward did I realize that this girl didn't look like my sister at all. And still, despite all the failures and lack of logic, my belief that Dvora was alive didn't fade — one day I would see her before me. This belief, it seemed, would continue to obsess me all the days of my life. Then one day, quite abruptly, without understanding what or why, I grew tired of going to the *Komitet* and I never went back there again.

Harry's family had been lucky. His older brother Josef returned from a concentration camp in Germany and moved into the building. His second brother Ignatz sent greetings from Russia, with the news that he would return home soon. Harry's niece, Ireka, eighteen years old, who survived thanks to Polish friends of her family who had hid her in their home, came to live in the building, as did Harry's cousin, the family who hid Ireka, Ola's sister, and a few other acquaintances. The three-story building with dozens of rooms was filled with family and friends, and Harry helped everyone to get by, finding jobs for most of them. I became friendly with my neighbors, who grew close to me and tried to give me a feeling of belonging to the family. As Harry's government salary was not sufficient to support all of the families he was sponsoring, he made contacts with factory managers and businessmen, made deals on the side and sold goods without the authorities' knowledge in order to increase his income.

I was his assistant. I initiated contact between Harry and factories and merchants; I would transport goods to various places, and quickly learned the "ways of business." I was pleased that I was no longer accepting charity, and also enjoyed my contact with people, but Harry was not pleased with my situation. The first time he sent me to deliver a package somewhere, he only intended it as a one-time operation, but things changed and these missions tripled in frequency until they became routine. Harry didn't want me to engage in illegal business, he wanted me to study; he also feared I would be caught. But he had no choice — he needed my help. Harry told me more than once that I had to make preparations for the next school year, and even bought a few textbooks for me, wanting to set regular hours for study under his tutelage, but I felt a strong inner resistance to studying. I was ignorant and uneducated, embarrassed to be in this position, and I tried to hide the fact of my ignorance as much as possible, first and foremost from myself. I didn't believe I would succeed at my studies and feared failure. Another reason that kept me from studying was that it would return me to the status of a child taken care of by Ola and Harry, living at their expense, and in actuality, would make me their son. I couldn't live with that.

After their many attempts to convince me to study had borne no fruit, Harry and Ola resigned themselves to my not getting an education, at least not in the near future. But Harry could attest to one significant victory in his attempts to impart a bit of knowledge. Although he didn't have much free time to read books, he would always read while resting and before he went to sleep, and sometimes he recommended a book he thought I should read. Under his influence, I picked up my first book, and when he saw that I had begun to read in the evenings and at night, he filled the house with the finest literature, and I devoured book after book, everything I saw. I immediately felt my general knowledge expanding and deepening — and realized how completely uneducated I really was.

Despite his failed efforts to send me to school for regular studies, Harry did not give up trying to provide me with vocational skills. He kept telling me that a man had to have a profession, as there was nothing like a skill to give one faith in life. He told me that although he was a textile engineer, he had survived the war thanks to his being an electrician, as well; while he was living under the Soviets, he worked in the fields. Harry asked me what profession attracted me and what skill I wanted to study, but I had no answer. I didn't know what I wanted. One evening, while sitting together with our neighbor, the watchmaker, Harry asked me, "Perhaps you'd like to learn to be a watchmaker?" and when I didn't refuse, he asked the watchmaker to teach me. The watchmaker agreed, and I didn't protest, as I knew and liked the man. For two days I sat for long hours next to him, watching him use his tiny tools and miniscule watch parts, with a magnifying glass in one eye socket, and I was amazed by the speed and practiced movements of his fingers, but I couldn't see myself sitting morning after morning for long days, doing this kind of work. My second day with the watchmaker was also my last.

Harry came up with a new idea for me — I would learn a profession in the knitting field. He sent me to one of his friends, the manager of a major factory for knitted garments. The man received me warmly, took me on a tour of the various departments and then to the department where large, round machines stood, producing cotton clothing. The manager introduced me to an old man, the *meister* — only later did I find out he was the most skilled person in the factory and that the machines in his charge were the most expensive ones — and he said to him, "I am leaving this boy in your care; he's the son of a good friend, and I want you to make a good craftsman out of him." The old expert assured the manager that he would do the best he could.

From the moment I entered the factory and during my tour of its departments, I had a feeling of contentment and curiosity. The sound of the machines, the smell of wool and cotton from one and machine oil from another were familiar to me and awakened in me longings for my parents' little factory in the days before the war. The *meister* asked me if I had ever worked machines like these, and I told him that I had grown up living beside sweater-knitting machines and had seen how they worked, but that machines like these I had never seen in my life. The old man told me to first watch the actions of the machines; afterward, he would begin to explain and to teach me. It was agreed that I would work every day from 8:00 a.m. to 2:00 p.m., unlike all the other workers who toiled from 7:00 a.m. to 4:00 p.m. My salary would be like that of an unskilled worker and would be calculated according to my work hours. The manager promised me that if I progressed in my skills, my salary would increase.

I was seized by a strong desire to learn the profession. I saw this as a challenge and test for myself — this was how I could prove that I was able to learn anything at all. And somewhere, deep inside me, was the wish to begin to put down roots and become strong — I remembered that, before the war, my father had expressed a wish to purchase machines like these and to produce machine-woven clothing; perhaps I would fulfill his wish and carry out his destiny? Thus, for the first time, I felt the desire for something concrete, and this desire took the form of an inclination to study knitting skills and to open my own factory — as my father had done at the beginning of his career in Warsaw. At dawn every morning I traveled to the factory by tram, arriving early, wandering around outside, smoking a cigarette, and, a few minutes before eight, I would enter the factory area and hurry through several departments where scores of men and women were already toiling, most looking at me as at a stranger who didn't belong, and making me feel uncomfortable. But when I entered my own department I would feel my heart lightening and I would be immediately engrossed by the commotion of the machines, by the spools of cotton thread and bolts of material being knitted.

The old *meister* explained every action of every machine part slowly and carefully, and instructed me on how to deal with each problem and prevent it from occurring. I absorbed every word he uttered and my workdays passed swiftly. Harry and Ola were delighted that I was learning a skill and happy for me, and their manager friend reported to them that I was a good student and that the *meister* was very pleased with me; I was one of the best students he had had in the past few years. Ola pampered me even more. Each morning I found clean, ironed clothes, and waiting for me on the table was breakfast, as well as sandwiches for work. When we sat long into the evenings, Ola would scold Harry and say, "The boy has to work in the morning and should go to sleep," and when she saw light in my room at night she would come in, take the book out of my hand and turn out the light, saying, "Sleep, my child, enough reading." In the evenings she awaited my arrival, and would serve me dinner, bringing a bowl of warm water to my room for me to wash my feet. Once she even asked if she could wash them for me. I refused sharply to make sure she didn't try again.

There was a girl working in one of the departments who wasn't particularly pretty, but she was charming, and something about her captivated me until I couldn't help but pay attention to her. Every day, when I passed her, she would smile at me and I would return her smile. When I went out to the yard for a cigarette, she would come out too, and walk past me, and again we would smile at each other. One day we exchanged a few simple words and introduced ourselves. Maria — that was her name — was seventeen. From that day on, she would bring me a cup of tea to my workplace every day and sometimes a homemade cookie, as well, and I would offer her chocolate and ice cream during our brief breaks. The attachment between us quickly grew. I couldn't figure out what Maria saw in me, when she was surrounded by tall, young, good-looking Polish admirers, which I couldn't help noticing because they all grew angry whenever she spent her spare time with me. I enjoyed every minute Maria was near me.

I liked girls but I was afraid of them, as I didn't know how to court a girl. To me, a woman's body was something shrouded in mystery and every date with a girl was accompanied by an unexplainable fear. My first physical contacts with Maria weren't stressful, as they were all furtive — we always had only a very few minutes and every meeting was only a surreptitious opportunity to express mutual affection, like a quick sip from an alcoholic beverage, which leaves you with a warm feeling all through your body, and your head remains dizzy for quite some time. In these brief touches, there was no time for the awakening of fear of the need to "continue" what I obviously didn't know how to do. But my heart fell for Maria. I longed to be with her more than just a few stolen moments, but I was afraid she would discover I was a good-for-nothing who didn't know how to court a girl, and she would rebuff me. Finally, I invited Maria to a film. She told me she could only go to the first showing, as she had to be home by ten, "otherwise my father will kill me."

Early that evening I went out to buy a pair of tickets and for a long time, longer than forever, I waited for her to meet me before the show. She finally arrived, a little earlier than we had agreed upon. When I saw her I was shocked — I had never seen her look so beautiful! It was hard to believe this was the same Maria I knew from the factory. "Why are you looking at me that way," she asked, "is there something wrong with me?"

"Just the opposite," I said, and told her, "You look like an angel!" She laughed.

I took her to a café. We sat opposite each other at a small table and drank coffee. Full of joy, my eyes took in her face, more beautiful than ever, and she seemed happy as well. In those moments of happiness, I didn't have a care in the world. It was enough that the two of us were together.

At the entrance to the cinema, people stared at us. At first, I didn't understand why, but then it hit me that they were surprised and angry to see a Jewish boy out with a Polish girl. I felt uncomfortable. My moments of happiness were interspersed with feelings of tension. To our relief, we were finally able to enter the cinema, which was dark. We sat next to each other. I was very tense, and my words froze in my mouth. At the factory we spoke and laughed freely, and now, when we met outside the workplace, I didn't have anything to say. And all because of the fear I felt from being with a girl, a fear I was unable to shake.

The film began. I looked at the screen but nothing registered. My thoughts were all on Maria, sitting beside me. Somehow our hands touched and caressed each other. Our fingers interlaced and we held hands tightly. I looked at her face in the darkness and she smiled at me. On the screen, people were shooting and attacking enemy positions, but it was Maria's hand that moved me and made my heart flutter. Suddenly Maria took my hand, placed it under her blouse and moved it over her body. I was burning with a pleasure I had never known before.

On the way to the tram we kissed. Her lips were like sweet wine and I could not be sated. I told her I loved her and she said she loved me, too. Leaving each other was very difficult. Afterward I continued wandering the streets to prolong the feeling of having been with her only a moment ago. I didn't want to let go of her. All at once completely different thoughts popped into my mind, erasing the beautiful dream I had woven with Maria at its center. What was wrong with me? How quickly had my relationship with Maria developed? Less than a month had gone by since I had first seen her smile at me next to her machine at the factory, and this evening we had already grown close and declared our love for each other! But I was a Jew and she was a Christian! How could I have ignored that? If my father and mother had been alive, they would have cut off all contact with me for going out with a Christian girl, and, in any case, it would still be better for me not to complicate matters with a serious relationship. I was only eighteen. I still didn't know what was in store for me. Maria was a good girl and I loved her. I mustn't disappoint her. Maybe I should cut off contact with her now, before it would be too difficult for either of us to do so? But I loved her! She gave my life substance. Already I was sorry that the next day was Sunday and we wouldn't be able to see each other for a whole day.

That night I dreamed I was in Sobibor, and in my dream I asked myself how I could again be in the camp, as I had already run away once. No, I would not stay in Sobibor for one moment longer. I would escape immediately. I was working in the Ukrainian barracks. I went outside with a pail full of empty bottles, but instead of walking to the camp, I turned in the direction of the camp's barbed wire fence. I heard the singing of the approaching Ukrainians and I walked faster, faster, until finally I was running as fast as I could. But when I reached the fence I saw *Oberscharfürher* Wagner slowly approaching me and I understood that I was doomed. This was my end. My legs failed me. My body was paralyzed. Wagner stood before me and smiled slyly. Then he slowly took his gun from his holster, aimed it at me and fired…

I awoke covered in perspiration, shaking all over. I was afraid to go back to sleep, in case the dream might resume. I tried to keep my eyes open, but fell asleep again quickly. The next day I tried to review my evening with Maria, but I couldn't shake my nightmare of the night before. Images of the magical evening with Maria were pushed away by images of the camp. Wagner's face appeared before me time and time again, and the image of his shooting me repeated itself over and over. Wagner continued to torment me in my dreams since my escape from Sobibor, as if he had not forgiven me for staying alive. And although these were only dreams, there was enough in them to unbalance me. Strange, but the more time passed, the more I dreamed of the camp, and in every dream, Wagner was trying to kill me!

I had been invited to dinner on Sunday evening at the apartment of Mrs. Shumanski, the woman who had saved Ireka. Almost all of the building's tenants were there, all of them Harry's relatives, all happy and joking. I wanted to take part in the merriment, but I was overcome with sadness. Both my nightmare and my future contact with Maria worried me so, that I couldn't break free of them. Everyone was busy with his own concerns and nobody noticed me — only Mrs. Shumanski noticed that I was troubled, and made an effort to keep my glass filled. I drank more and more, getting very dizzy. All of the people, the furniture, the room, danced around me at varying speeds, and I spun around with them. I tried to control myself, but was swept into the whirlpool, and among the blurry faces dancing around me, Maria and Wagner appeared, as well…

I felt like I was suffocating. I got to my feet with difficulty, excused myself by saying I was tired, and began moving to the door. Ola got up and said she would come with me. I asked her to leave me be and said I would manage on my own. Harry also told her to stay. Mrs. Shumanski accompanied me to the door and kissed me goodnight. I went out, and when I got to my room I sat in an armchair and burst into tears. I cried for a long time, and I fell asleep still sitting there.

The next morning I awoke from a deep sleep refreshed and in a good mood. I told Ola that I didn't remember getting into bed and she told me that she had found me asleep, half of me in the armchair and half of me on the floor. She and Harry had undressed me and put me into bed. I was embarrassed and angry at myself, but Ola said, "Don't be silly. You're only a boy!" I told her that, in my childhood, I had loved to fall asleep in my clothes and feel how my mother undressed me and put me to bed.

Free now of any doubts or negative thoughts, I hurried to the factory to see my Maria. I entered her department, passed between the two rows of machines near the machine she worked at, and when I reached her I said, "Good morning," and waited for her smile. But Maria continued to work, her face turned toward her machine. She couldn't have not heard my greeting — up to now she had sensed me as soon as I entered her department — and I repeated my "Good morning" and waited. Maria turned to me for a moment and then I saw tears in her eyes. "Go away," she said.

I didn't understand what had happened. I looked around. Most people avoided looking at me and others gave me looks of hatred. I continued standing next to Maria, trying to understand — had I hurt her somehow the evening before yesterday? Everything had been wonderful when we parted from one another! I felt compelled to speak to her, to hear what had changed in a day, but she only repeated in a soft voice, not angry, "Go already, go."

The old *meister* greeted me with a smile as always and asked how I was, but when he noticed that I was troubled he left me alone. I was restless and unable to work. I had to find out right then what had happened. When I went out to the yard to smoke a cigarette, I heard Maria's footsteps behind me and I thought she would come up to me and we could talk. But she only passed by me, giving me a folded note, which told me to meet her on a side street outside the factory during our break.

When I got there, she was already waiting for me. She stood next to the entrance of one of the houses, her arms folded as if trying to warm herself, her face troubled, and before I could say a word she blurted out quickly, "Some boys who work in my department have been bothering me for a long time because I'm seeing a Jew, but I ignored them. Yesterday they found out we had been to the cinema together and they came to my house. I used to go out with one of them; I had liked him before I met you. They attacked me, called me a whore and said I was sleeping with a Jew — and all within hearing of my parents and neighbors. They threatened that if I went out with you one more time they would kill me, and kill you, too. They also said that they would make sure you were out of the factory. I'm scared. They'll kill us. We have to stop. We can't see each other again."

Maria looked as if her whole world had fallen in on her and I didn't know what to say. "Maria," I said, "but I love you!" She burst into tears, said, "I love you too, my darling," and ran back to work.

Later on that day, the factory manager called me and told me that he had received an anonymous letter on behalf of a group of employees, complaining that a young man was being trained on the newest machines while they, who had worked there for years, were still working on the old ones. They felt one of the veterans should learn to work on the new machines and they were demanding that the situation be rectified.

The manager tried to hide his nervousness, but I could see that he was troubled by the letter he had received. He said that he hadn't yet decided what to do. "I'm not afraid of hooligans," he said. "This is not the Poland of before the war. This is Socialist Poland and there is no room here for anti-Semitic elements." While he spoke he raised his voice as if making a speech before an audience, then suddenly went silent and sat thoughtfully. Afterward he turned to me and added, "Listen, Bolek, regarding you, I cannot disregard the slightest threat and I have no choice but to suggest that you stop working here." He also asked if, by the way, I knew the reason for the threatening letter and if anyone in the factory had provoked me up till then. I didn't want to tell him about my romance with Maria and the chain of events. I told him that nothing special had happened, but they had never been friendly toward me.

"Who is 'they'?" asked the manager.

"The ones who work next to my department," I said.

But apparently the manager had his sources, who reported to him on what was happening inside the factory walls. "You," he said, "are going out with a girl from the sock department, Maria. This Maria had a boyfriend and you stole her away from him."

I had no desire to discuss the matter and I said, "That's irrelevant."

"No," said the manager, "it's very relevant. It may be the principal reason you're not wanted here."

I didn't answer. I wanted to run away as quickly as possible, just not to be interrogated by the manager and to have to tell him about Maria. I got up and left the room. I went to the old *meister* and told him I was quitting work as of right then. He didn't question me. I thanked him for the effort he had invested in me and praised him. He complimented me in return for being a good student, said he had enjoyed working with me and even predicted a good future for me if I continued to learn the profession. This man — the only one in the factory who parted from me in friendship — was, to everyone's scorn, a German who had happened to be in Lodz during the First World War and had stayed.

I left the factory without looking at anyone. I got on the tram, which at that time of day was almost empty, and sat in the back with a feeling that it had come especially for me, to take me away from that horrible place and to bring me somewhere safe. I was unable to think about anything, I only felt relief. People got on and off and I saw them as through a translucent veil, hearing their voices as if they came from somewhere else. When the tram stopped near my building, I stayed glued to my seat. I got off at Nowomiejska Street, on the other side of Liberty Square. This street, where the Jews had had their businesses, had once been one of the busiest streets in Lodz. Every building and yard had had shops and workshops from the first floor to the very top floors, and one could buy things at half the price demanded on Piotrkowska Street. All the farmers in the area and most of the Jews in the city used to come to Nowomiejska Street to buy their goods. The smell of leather, rubber and cotton goods had been intermingled with the fragrance of perfume and the aroma of sausages and spices. Now the street was silent, most of the shops were closed, and the smell of mold and rot was everywhere.

In my childhood, my father would sometimes send me to Nowomiejska Street to buy things he needed urgently, and in those days, there were shops I hated going to, where I was treated like a small child, where I was questioned and laughed at, as well as shops I loved going to, where I was treated like a regular customer and was even given a special pencil or a sharpener, just because. Didn't even one of these shopkeepers survive?

I continued walking toward Baluty, where the poorer Jews had lived in difficult conditions before the war, and where the Germans had set up the ghetto, cramming all the Jews of Lodz and the surrounding areas into it. My father had once taken me on a visit to the home of one of his friends, a resident of this quarter, whose wife was seriously ill. He lived in one room with his wife and five children, and this room served as a leather workshop, as well. On one side of the room stood a large work table, piled high and surrounded by packages of furs of every type and tools, and on the other side were two large beds, in one of which lay the sick woman. My father asked how she was, and the man answered, his eyes lifted upward, "Everything is in the hands of Heaven." Other people joined us and we all prayed *Mincha* (the afternoon prayer) and *Ma'ariv* (the evening prayer) and read chapters of Psalms for the sick woman's health. We wished her a speedy recovery, although we all knew her days were numbered. I thanked God then that my mother and father were healthy and not poor.

I now found myself walking down streets where the homes were completely destroyed. Very soon, I no longer knew exactly where I was. I didn't see a soul, not even a dog or cat. I felt as though I were in a cemetery and my instincts told me that under the ruins were shriveled bodies like those I had seen in the Warsaw ghetto. I grew afraid and hurried to return to living people. During my walk, however, I had gone over the events of the last few hours in my head and as everything became plain to me, I was suffused with a strong feeling of guilt. I was the guilty party in all that had happened. Acting without thinking had made Maria suffer, she who had been so good to me; I had caused the manager distress; and now I had been dealt a blow that put me back in my rightful place. Why hadn't I understood that as a Jew it was forbidden for me to have a romance with a Polish girl?

And yet, maybe all this had been for the best, as my eyes had now been opened. In a short time, I had distanced myself from my Jewishness. From morning to evening I had been spending my time with Christians, and in the evenings I was with a few Jews who, like me, were in the process of immersing themselves in Polish society. I had dissociated myself from the Jews I met in the street, not to mention falling in love with a Christian Polish girl. If what had happened that morning hadn't happened, who

knows where things might have led. When Fate had chosen me
and decided that I would be the only survivor of my entire family,
should I be distancing myself from all they valued?! Besides, how
could I even dare to flee from my people? I was ashamed that the
Poles had had to remind me of all this today. And what should I
do now? How should I change my ways? If I wanted to live among
Jews, I must separate myself from Harry and Ola. This would hurt
them very much. The two of them treated me so well, with such
great devotion. Under their roof there was nothing I lacked. How
could I explain to them that I loved them and I was happy with
them, but that I still had to leave?

Hunger began to plague me, so I went home. Harry and Ola
already knew what had happened at the factory — the manager
had called Harry and told him — and they were worried that I
hadn't yet returned home. When I came in Harry, Ola, Josef and
Mrs. Shumanski all looked at me in surprise and concern, which
made me feel like a child who had done something wrong. Ola
hurried toward me, hugged and kissed me and murmured while
her tears moistened my face, "Thank God you've come home, my
child."

The tense atmosphere dispelled and quickly developed into a
discussion about anti-Semitism and the way to fight it. Josef said
that the Poles had always been anti-Semites and always would be.
Nothing had changed and nothing would help; he thought all the
surviving Jews in Poland should leave the country. The others disagreed. Harry said that I shouldn't worry, that he intended to buy
me a knitting machine that I could operate myself. "The *meister*
said you had learned the profession very well," he said. But my
thoughts had already flown on to other destinies.

The next day I went to the *Komitet* and again scanned the lists,
wandered through the crowds and heard stories of people who had
assembled from Russia, from Germany and from Austria. Aside
from those who had come from Russia, most had come to seek
their relatives, with the intention of returning west in a few days,
to Germany. They said that in Berlin and other German cities,

refugee camps had been set up by the United Nations Relief and Rehabilitation Administration (UNRRA), and the large Jewish-American aid organization, the Joint Distribution Committee. The Jews in these camps were waiting for the chance to go to Eretz Israel, or even to immigrate to the United States and join relatives there.

From the *Komitet* I walked to Zawadzka Street, where Jews stood and argued about the situation in Eretz Israel, about the struggle of the Haganah and the Irgun, about the British White Paper policy, which had locked the gates of Israel to Jewish refugees, and about the emissaries from Israel, who had come to Poland to organize Jews to leave for Israel. On the street I ran into a couple from Sobibor, Edda and Yitzchak Lichtman, whom I had first met in Lublin, where they had told me that both of them had fought in a partisan unit. Now Yitzchak had opened a shoemaker's workshop in Lodz. I also met a man I had known in Chelm, who invited me to his home, where he introduced me to his daughter and his aunt. My friend's apartment was large, expensively furnished and full of valuables. He told me that he made trips back and forth to Berlin, smuggling gold and dollars into the city and clothing and cigarettes out. He offered me a job smuggling with him and invited me to live in his apartment.

That day, I realized how cut off from the Jewish world I had been, and all at once, I felt myself belonging again. I swore that I would never isolate myself from that world again. However, although I had decided to leave, I put off the actual leaving daily. Harry and Ola were close to me in heart and soul, and I couldn't suddenly say, "Goodbye, I'm leaving you!" In the meantime, out of guilt that I was intending to go, I tried to do all I could for them. I brought home flowers and exotic fruits, and I volunteered to make all their deliveries. Ola would beam with happiness and say, "The boy has gone mad!" She pampered me as she would an only son, and it was hard for me to bear, until I finally worked up the courage to tell Harry that I wanted to leave Poland and go to Israel.

When Harry heard this, the smile disappeared from his face.

He sat opposite me, looking at me sternly, and was silent. For several days I had been practicing a speech for just this moment, and now I could only think of a few words to say. To my surprise, after a few moments the smile returned to Harry's face and he said that he too wanted to go to Israel. "We can all go together," he said, adding, "but there's no need to rush. First we should wait until the situation clears up and conditions improve. And in the meantime, I have an offer for you: There is an empty shop in our building. You can open a shop for knitted goods. I have solid contacts with a lot of manufacturers and they'll flood you with merchandise. This way you can make a little money until the time comes to travel. And so it won't be too difficult for you, I have a candidate for a partner for you, Mrs. Kasja, Ola's sister. She's a good woman and you two will get along well together. By the way, don't say anything to Ola for now about your wanting to leave, and think about what I've told you." "Of course, of course, I won't say a thing to her. And I'll think about what you told me," I answered quickly.

Harry's offer to open a shop in the building banished sleep that night. To leave home and to go on my way without a cent in my pocket didn't seem the most intelligent move, and the chance that I could earn some money, as well as the challenge of running a shop, appealed to me, overpowering my desire to leave Poland as quickly as possible.

The next morning I informed Harry that I accepted his offer, and from that moment I put all my energy into preparing the shop, which was completely empty and seemed fairly spacious. All that day, I went in and out of shops to see how they were built and organized. Harry brought in a carpenter and a painter, bought me goods that we temporarily stored at home, and introduced me to a few merchants of ladies' and men's undergarments and socks. I asked Mrs. Kasja to make an inventory of every item in the shop in notebooks I had purchased for this purpose.

In ten days, the shop was ready to open. The night before the opening, I had another sleepless night for the excitement. And I was also anxious, as along with the goods, I would be on display, as well. What if I didn't make a good impression on customers and they made fun of me? And perhaps I wouldn't know how to sell, as I had already proven in the market in Chelm? I got up early, chose my clothes carefully, and stood before the mirror to inspect every inch of my appearance. I wasn't satisfied. I left the house quietly, went down to the shop and entered through the back door, checking to make sure everything was ready. I enjoyed seeing the shop all clean with the goods set up on the shelves, on the counter a notebook, pencil and ashtray. Everything was in place. When I returned home, Ola scrutinized my appearance, she *was* satisfied, and immediately ordered me to sit and eat, as later I wouldn't have time to do so. Mrs. Kasja, my partner, came in festively dressed, her face heavily made up, all smiles and pleased with herself. She leaned toward me to kiss me and a sharp odor of cologne nearly suffocated me. "Aren't we a great pair?" she asked. Although she was Christian, Mrs. Kasja looked like a Jew — her eyes were black, her hair brown and her nose long. During the German occupation, she had been arrested several times on suspicion of being Jewish.

At 8:oo a.m. exactly, I raised the heavy metal shutters and opened the store. All of the building tenants came and brought flowers and bottles of drink. Ola brought a cake and a bottle of vodka. The shop, which had seemed large when it was empty, looked small filled with merchandise. Passersby stopped and peeked in to see who the new shop owner was. The barber from across the street also came in and asked who the new owner was, shook my hand and wished me luck. He was our first customer: he purchased a pair of socks. He was also the first to say he'd never seen such a young shop owner.

"Excuse me for asking," he said, "but how old are you?"

"I'm already over eighteen," I replied.

"And I thought sixteen at most." Everyone laughed, he shook my hand again and went back to the barbershop. In a short time Mrs. Kasja and I were alone behind the counter, waiting for customers.

Many people stopped at our display window, peeked in and continued walking. An hour passed and no one came in. Why? Because of the way I looked? Desperate, I smoked cigarette after cigarette while patient Mrs. Kasja tried to calm me down. Then three women entered, one after the other. The counter was strewn with goods, two of them bought something, and paid the price I asked. When they left, I hugged Mrs. Kasja and kissed her cheek. As the day passed, more customers came in, time went by quickly and the turnover wasn't bad.

The period after the war was good for commercial activity. People were hungry for every product and, as they didn't trust the new banknotes the government had printed, they bought every-thing they saw. The flow of customers through our shop increased daily and the goods disappeared from the shelves. The problem wasn't to sell, but to obtain stock frequently enough and in large enough quantities. With the help of Harry's contacts, and sources I found myself, I was able to get the merchandise, some officially, with packing lists and invoices, and some without documents and without the knowledge of the authorities. Profits were much higher than expected, and in a short time I had accumulated assets. I never thought it would be so easy to make money, and I realized I was capable of running a business. But the business took all my free time, from dawn to dusk. Mrs. Kasja was nice and willing to do anything, but she wasn't very talented at winning the hearts of the customers and would tell me of customers who came in when I wasn't there, asked disappointedly where "the young man" was and left, saying they would come back another time.

I was so immersed in the business that I didn't have time for anything else, not even to enjoy my money, and I wondered what all this money was for; but the shop wasn't just about accumulating money. I had thought that I would never take a risk, but here I was successfully managing a shop, enjoying my contact with scores of people every day, enjoying the trust people had in me when they asked for my advice and acted on it; and the praise I received, particularly from women, more than once made me blush.

One day the shop door opened and in came Zoshia. She approached hesitantly and stood before me, smiling her familiar smile, bordering on tears, her cheeks on fire. How could it have happened that I had forgotten all about her ever since she left Chelm? I hadn't thought of her even once since then, and when I came to Lodz I hadn't looked for her, either. Was it because, in recent years, I had become used to not seeing anyone again after I was parted from them?

Zoshia stood before me in a summer dress, her arms and legs bare. I had known her in the winter and remembered her wearing a heavy coat and boots. Now she seemed exposed and more beautiful than ever. "Zoshia!" I cried, just one word, and she also replied with one word, "Bolek!" and we both knew that we would renew our friendship.

As we began telling each other what we had been through since we were parted a few months ago, I put Mrs. Kasja in charge of the shop and went outside into the street with Zoshia. We strolled together for many hours. I was suffused with a new happiness in her company. She told me that she was a member of the Zionist organization *Ichud* (Union). In the evenings they had activities — lectures, Hebrew lessons, poetry and dancing. That evening, she said, her group would meet at the local chapter of the movement and she begged me to go with her. I agreed, and we decided that I would pick her up from home. But from the moment we left each other I felt uneasy. I was afraid to meet a group of young people I didn't know. Would I be able to fit in? Wouldn't I disappoint Zoshia by being there?

I forgot all about the shop. I suddenly felt I had nothing to wear, and decided to buy some clothes. I looked in the mirror and saw a beard just starting to grow in on my cheeks. I had wanted to shave for some time, but everyone told me I didn't need to yet. At home I had shaving gear that I hadn't used yet, but I was afraid I wouldn't know how to use it correctly, so I went to the barbershop across the street. I was embarrassed to ask for a shave only, in case they made fun of me, so I asked for a haircut, too. The barbershop staff greeted me with respect. The owner himself came to cut my hair and started a conversation with me, telling me about himself and occasionally asking gently, was I Harry and Ola's son? And how did I meet them? During my haircut a girl came up to me with a small table with various instruments on it, and sat down next to me on a stool. When she asked for my hands and inspected them I finally understood that she wanted to do my nails. "Thanks very much," I said to her, "but there's no need, I only came for a haircut and a shave," but she smiled and said: "Don't be afraid, sir, I won't put red polish on your nails, but your nails are neglected. I'll take care of them and push back the dead skin that has grown around them."

I regretted coming into the barbershop, but I couldn't take back what had been done. I gave in and let the barbershop staff do whatever they wanted with me. The barber spent a whole hour cutting my hair. When he put a hot, wet towel on my face I felt like I was being suffocated but didn't say a word, again giving in to my fate.

"This is the first time the gentleman is shaving," I heard the voice of the barber. "I'm sure the gentleman has an important date with a girl…" I didn't answer and he continued, "That's when everyone starts shaving." Afterward he sprayed cologne on me and combed my hair for a long while. When I rose from the chair, all the staff looked at me carefully and expressed satisfaction. When I glanced in the mirror, I saw myself well-groomed and looking completely different. I gave large tips to everyone and rushed out.

In the evening, I walked with Zoshia to the *Ichud* chapter, where she introduced me to her friends, all of them around seventeen or eighteen years old. They were dressed nicely and looked like they came from good homes — none of them looked like the boys and girls I had known in Chelm right after the war. In Chelm, everyone was a sole survivor, with whom I instantly felt a common bond and easily made friends. Here, in Lodz, the young people at *Ichud* seemed from another world, which wasn't my world. If not for Zoshia I would have fled immediately. A man slightly older than the others opened with a review of the situation in Israel, and spoke about how the British had closed the gates to Jews, and the underground organizations like the Haganah, Etzel and Lechi, which had begun to act against the British, of protest movements that had begun around the world, demanding that the British government allow immigration of Holocaust survivors, and the Anglo-American Commission of Inquiry, which had been set up to look into the problem and to find out where the remaining refugees wanted to go.

From time to time, I had read newspaper articles about what was happening there, as well as articles against British government policy, but the review I heard at the *Ichud* branch drew a clearer picture for me and increased my desire to reach Israel as soon as possible. At the end of the lecture, the members sang Hebrew songs that I had never heard before, and then formed a circle and danced — boy took girl, girl took boy — each holding the waist of the other and everyone dancing together in the circle, changing partners again and again. This dancing game seemed simple and childish to me, and I hoped no one would pick me, but when it was Zoshia's turn to dance she chose me and I bounced around the circle with her and then took another girl to dance. Afterward, everyone danced the hora and dragged me into the circle, too, although I found it hard to keep in step, as they knew the dance well and I was unfamiliar with it. We danced until we were drenched in perspiration. When we left the chapter we walked in a group and I treated everyone to ice cream.

I kept going to the *Ichud* chapter with Zoshia, becoming active and accepted by everyone. After a while, I began to join in on the activities of the older group as well, most of whose members were students at Lodz's university and technical college. They, too, accepted me as their friend, perhaps because of the money I had in my pockets, which I was always willing to shell out whenever they were penniless.

My circle of acquaintances grew. I was invited to parties; we had fun at plays, films, cafés and restaurants — I didn't have one free evening. Many were the times I returned home late, in various stages of drunkenness, and Ola would always be waiting for me with cake and a glass of milk and warm water in a bowl and a towel to wash my feet before I got into bed. I asked her a thousand times not to wait up for me, but to no avail. All I could do was to pity her and kiss her goodnight.

When I was finally alone in my room, however, I would sink into the armchair to rest, my throat would choke up and my eyes would stream tears like an overflowing spring, and there I would sit, crying quietly without knowing why. The shop, which so brief a time ago had been my whole world, and into which I had invested all my time and energy, interested me less and less. I was tired of meeting with merchants and businessmen. I preferred to go out and have fun, and not to worry in the least about the selection of stock in the shop. Mrs. Kasja saw how I was neglecting the shop and looked at me sorrowfully, but she couldn't do a thing.

One day, I was traveling by tram with Harry's "undocumented" goods, which I was to deliver to one of the shops, as I had done dozens of times. When the tram stopped next to the store, two young men suddenly stepped out of the entrance to the building and introduced themselves as policemen. They asked me where I had brought the goods from, who had sent me and where I lived. I knew we had more merchandise at the house, and if it was found, it might lead to Harry's arrest, so I told them I worked with Mrs. Kasja — whose name was on the shop's lease — and that she had sent me with the goods to this store. When asked where I lived, I answered that I lived in the same building as Mrs. Kasja's shop. I assumed that when I saw Mrs. Kasja I would tell her what I had told the policemen and she would confirm what I said, and the police wouldn't come to our house and find the merchandise. The policemen brought me home, but refused to let me go up to Mrs. Kasja's apartment with them. One of the policemen guarded me and the other went upstairs to ask Mrs. Kasja if she had sent a boy with goods to another store. Unaware of what was going on, she said that she hadn't sent anyone anywhere. The policeman came back in a rage that I had deceived him. They took me to the police station, where I was interrogated again about where I had brought the goods from, and again I said that I had brought them from the same building.

We went back and forth on this point until the two gave up on me for the meantime, one saying, "Tomorrow we'll get the truth out of you." I was ordered to empty my pockets, remove my shoelaces and my belt and hand them over. During their search, they found American dollars. "A young man like you with dollars!" they said and took everything from me. They led me into the basement, put me in a small room with bars on the door and locked me in.

I was alone in the cell, relieved that I would no longer have to deal with their questions and the humiliation of it all. The coolness of the cell dried my perspiration. The cell was completely unfurnished. At one side, a spread blanket took up the entire length and half the width. In a corner, by the door, stood an empty pail. Dim light came in from the hallway. I paced back and forth in the tiny room and tried to consider my situation. Much had been written in the papers recently about the war on the black market, and in some court cases, there had been convictions and lengthy sentences. Was this, then, to be my fate? Would I rot in a Polish jail? I felt horrible for Ola and Harry. I knew how they would suffer knowing their Bolek was in prison.

This time, I saw no reason to blame myself for what had happened; it had never occurred to me that I might be arrested. I remembered the group I had met at the *Ichud* chapter — the ones who had danced those childish dances. How would those children react to my arrest? And Zoshia, what would she think? Would she come to visit me in jail? I already imagined the entire group making their journey to Israel — and me staying behind, locked up. But when I thought more about it, I was sure that I would quickly be freed. Harry wouldn't allow me to stay in this situation; he was bound to find a way to get me out, if he managed not to get arrested himself.

I don't know how long I was in the jail, as they took my watch from me. The cold slowly penetrated my bones. The blanket on the floor stank of urine and disinfectant. I stood there and shivered with cold until I grew tired and sat on one corner of the blanket and covered myself with the rest of it, but I continued to shiver. I was unable to think about anything, but I was also unable to sleep. Suddenly I heard screaming, and two policemen came dragging an older woman behind them, with wild hair and a torn dress. She looked drunk; she resisted them with all her might and showered them with a steady flow of curses until I could hardly keep myself from laughing. The woman was put in the cell next to mine, and even after the policemen were gone she continued to curse, insult and utter obscenities I had never heard before. Now I forgot about everything — I was wholly absorbed in the woman in the next cell. I was amused by her collection of expletives and rich vocabulary of obscenities, and I listened attentively to every word. After a while, she stopped cursing and began to cry pitifully, and then her sobbing slowly changed to a heavy, irritating snoring. I finally fell asleep, as well.

When I awoke, there was a policeman standing next to me, ordering me to come with him. He led me upstairs, to the room where I had been interrogated the day before. It was daylight, and sunshine was coming from outside the window into the room. Behind the table sat a police officer I had never seen, who wrote something down in a notebook before him, raised his eyes for a moment and instructed me to sit down. I was sure that this police officer had come to interrogate me and I tried to think of what to answer to the questions he would ask. Then another policeman came into the room and set the bundle of my things on the table. The thought crossed my mind that they were going to move me somewhere else. The officer finished writing, turned to me and said curtly, "The man is released!" He made me sign the notebook, where he had written that I had no complaints about my treatment during my incarceration, and I got back everything that had been taken from me.

I couldn't believe my ears and continued to sit until the officer said to me, "You're free to go." I took my bundle and left the station. Harry and Ola were waiting for me on the other side of the street. Within a day their faces had changed beyond recognition, as if they had suddenly grown old. My sympathy went out to them.

Harry never would tell me how much he had paid to secure my release, but, no doubt, it had been a large sum.

Around that time, Ignatz, Harry's brother, returned from Russia, bringing with him a heavy bag he carried on his back and a heavy wooden suitcase. He was dressed humbly. The people in our building joked about it, saying that Ignatz had come with a lot of possessions, but his brother Josef said that his bag and suitcase only held rocks. When we asked him, Ignatz said, "Ah, I have some very valuable things. Rare books that were very difficult for me to find." Everyone burst out laughing, and Harry said it really was like his brother to bring books instead of other belongings. Harry and Ola held a homecoming party for Ignatz, and all the survivors in their family, as well as friends from the building, attended. The party was very successful — food and drink were in abundance, and I drank glass after glass, enjoying the company. There were the three brothers, Harry, Josef, and Ignatz, who had each survived in different ways; Ireka and her savior, Mrs. Shumanski; and other more distant relatives, all sitting together at the table and reminiscing about their home before the war. I remembered my own family, none of whom were alive except for me. The image of Sobibor appeared before me. I saw my mother and my little brother Yankele walking between the two barbed wire fences to the gas chambers. I saw them burning and smelled the smoke rising into the sky. I saw my brother Mottel being killed in the field. I saw my father's body in the graveyard in Prushkov, and the odor of the rotting bodies returned to my nostrils. Suddenly, I saw nothing around me and I burst into tears, silencing all the revelers.

Within seconds, I came back to reality. I saw the guests sitting as silent as stone, everyone's eyes upon me, and realized what an inappropriate thing I had done. At once, I rose and ran outside, where I sat in the dark and empty yard. A moment later, Mrs.

Shumanski stood before me and asked if she could sit next to me. In the company of this woman, with whom I had exchanged only a few words and hardly knew, and who did not know me, to whom I owed nothing and who owed me nothing in return, I felt free of all shame and fear. She sat next to me, lay her arm lightly around my shoulder, and I began to sob again. She didn't say a word, didn't try to comfort me, didn't ask me to stop crying, and I cried in her arms until I could cry no more.

The next day I was ashamed to face anyone who had been at the party. For a long time afterward I couldn't forgive myself for my behavior that evening. I was particularly ashamed to face Ignatz, the guest of honor, whose party I had ruined. This man, who didn't know me, what could he think of me? Probably that I was some "spoiled child!"

But when Ignatz came to share my room, I saw immediately that not only was he not angry with me, but that he had a real affection for me. We became fast friends. I also came to realize that Ignatz was a special person, broadminded, from whom one could learn much. During our first evening together, he asked me to tell him my story. I talked until late into the night and sensed how attentively he was listening to me. He wanted to know everything and wouldn't let me skip over any details. Here and there, I felt he was cross-examining me to make sure I was telling the truth — he simply refused to believe that all I told him could be true. Again and again, he repeated, "Who would believe it, that the German people, with their high cultural values and beautiful manners, would deteriorate and turn into a nation of murderers! And our own culture isn't worth anything if it couldn't prevent the Holocaust..."

Finally, after I had finished my story and gone silent, he said, "Bolek, you are a very valuable person. You have been a witness to it all. You must write down everything for posterity. No detail must be omitted, or no one will know how millions of people simply disappeared!"

And he added, "Bolek, you are not only extraordinarily lucky that you survived; you are a man of integrity, who has remained true to himself after everything that has happened to him."

Ignatz decided to cram me with knowledge from every sphere. He elaborated upon everything we touched upon in our conversations and our daily lives — actual and abstract, technical and spiritual. An expert in every subject, be it history, geography, art, music or theater, mechanics or electricity, he explained everything thoroughly and wouldn't let me be until he was sure I had understood everything he taught. My empty head absorbed his teachings like a dry sponge hitting water. This man, who spoke seven languages fluently, had traveled the world, and had spent two years in Israel. Aware of my intent to go there, he decided to teach me Hebrew and English because he felt these were two languages I ought to know. He bought a blackboard and hung it on the door, opposite our beds, and when I came home I would find words and passages written on it, one day in Hebrew, the next day in English. Each day he would speak to me in the language that was on the blackboard, and I had to read, write and speak back in the same language. At first it was like an amusing game, but also interesting; after a while I realized I had acquired a fairly good vocabulary in the two new languages, and could already handle a simple conversation in both. This awareness made me regard my new studies with more respect.

Ignatz told me of his life in Israel, of the kibbutz and the moshav, of Tel Aviv and Haifa, of the Galilee and the Jezreel Valley, of Jerusalem, holy to three religions, of the Sephardic and the Yemenite Jews. He said, "Life in Israel is hard, but you'll love it. Besides, we Jews have no other place to live but in Israel. Don't wait for Harry and Ola. Harry wants to go, but if you wait for him and Ola you'll never get there."

Autumn came. The streets were covered with the yellow-brown of fallen leaves that the brisk winds blew down from the chestnut trees. Furious rains fell without pause. In the meantime, the Soviets established their hold on lands that had been freed from the Germans, setting up Communist governments where they pleased.

Not even a year had passed since the end of the war, and on the western borders of the Soviet bloc countries the Iron Curtain fell, sealing them off quickly. And the British, who had won the arduous war with the Germans, very soon began to see their empire crumbling and the loss of their colonies in Africa and Asia, which demanded independence. The British, however, wanted to maintain a presence in valuable, strategic lands, among them Israel, where they carried out an anti-Jewish policy that stirred up rebellion among the Jewish settlements, particularly when they closed Israel off to Jewish immigration.

At the end of the war, the Jewish Agency sent Haganah representatives to Europe, teachers and spiritual leaders, with the objective of organizing the refugees, Holocaust survivors who sat in DP (displaced persons) camps in Germany and Austria, and helping them to immigrate to Israel, legally or not. These survivors — who had returned to Eastern Europe from concentration camps, from the forests where they had hidden like hunted animals or had fought in partisan units, from the cellars of noble people who had taken risks to give them shelter, and as refugees who had spent the war years in the Soviet Union (which had opened its borders to those fleeing from the German occupation and thus saved tens of thousands of Jews) — had no living relatives; their possessions had been destroyed or stolen, their homes appropriated; the local population did not welcome or understand them; their places of birth had become large Jewish cemeteries. The great majority of survivors and returnees no longer wanted to live there, and those who did wish to put down roots in these places were met with hostility from both the local population and the government. Anti-Semitism turned its ugly face toward this wretched remnant: Attacks on Jews in Poland, mostly murders, were a daily occurrence in the villages and towns, and reached a peak in the pogrom that took place in the Polish city of Kielce on July 4, 1946, where forty-two Jews were killed.

How foolish the Jews were during the German occupation, having thought that, after the war, the survivors would be carried home on people's shoulders. No, the stench of the war still remained in the air; the few survivors had not had time to count their dead before they were being persecuted again. Most of the Jews in Poland, therefore, sat on their suitcases, seeking a way to get out of the country with no knowledge of what their fate would be afterward. Thus began, as if of its own accord, a mass wandering from town to town, from country to country, from Eastern Europe to Central Europe, from the center, the south, to the ports of the Mediterranean — before it was too late, before borders were solidified and closed forever.

It was during this time that the *Bricha* (escape), illegal immigration, was organized among the refugees, expanding across Europe under the command of the Haganah, aided by the Jewish Brigade, emissaries from Israel, and hundreds of devoted, local activists, with the support of American Jews. This great organizational machine, which secretly set in motion tens of thousands of people over thousands of kilometers, on foot or by car, through forest and over snowy mountains, included border smugglers, document counterfeiters, border guards, police and army staff, train station managers and local government officials of all ranks. Thus, the remaining refugees in Eastern Europe wandered through the Valley of Death, more than once disguised as German and Austrian refugees returning home, to DP camps established in Germany and Austria, where they waited for months or even years until their turn came to set out on the golden path — to the Land of Israel.

I should have been happy with my life; everyone said how lucky I was. Young people were jealous that I had everything I needed. I had been adopted by a wonderful family, which did all it could to help me get an education and get on with my life; I was the owner of a successful business; I was well dressed as only a few of my friends could allow themselves to be. (As winter approached I ordered a pair of boots from one of the best shoemakers in town, and when I wore them, there wasn't one person who wasn't impressed. I even bought an expensive leather coat.) My circle of friends expanded;

popular and in demand, I was invited to meals and parties, I was out every evening until late, I had a steady girlfriend, beautiful and charming, desired by many. What more could I want?

Yet in spite of it all, I was a miserable, tormented person, with no self-confidence. I could not relinquish my history. I was under constant siege by the past — the images from "there" accompanied me everywhere, whether I was awake or asleep. I had the terrible recurring nightmare in which I was back at Sobibor, and at the end of the dream, I was always killed, waking up in a sweat, my whole body shaking. But even when I was awake, I couldn't quite believe that I had survived, that I had been given the gift of life — that my death was not imminent. I felt empty and depressed. I was convinced that I would never be able to function with other people. Life had no meaning, as I had no idea what to hope for; more than once I was sorry I was still alive, and many times considered suicide.

The longer I was with Harry and Ola, the stronger our bond grew. Ola treated me like her only son in every way. I couldn't handle the guilt this brought me — it made me feel like a traitor to my own dead parents, as if I had chosen other parents in their place. I also felt guilt over the fact that I was setting my benefactors up for a great sorrow by letting them love me as a son who would always be near to them, when, in fact, I already had the earnest desire to leave them and Poland, and to set out to Israel.

As I thought about my deepening relationship with Harry and Ola, which I had allowed to develop, I hated myself. My shop, whose tremendous profits helped Harry and Ola to make ends meet and was a source of my own pride, quickly went downhill, due totally to my neglect. I was tired of the shop without knowing why — was it because it stood as an obstacle to my plans to leave Poland? I finally decided to hand it over to Mrs. Kasja, who wanted to turn it into a bar.

A strange thing was also happening in my relationship with Zoshia — when I was with her for a long time I would feel the need to get away, but after a few days of separation, I would again feel how much I missed her. Our relationship became a nerve-wracking game: sometimes she couldn't stand it and she would come to me; sometimes the opposite — I would rush to her hoping she wouldn't send me away. During that period, Mrs. Shumanski's niece arrived from a small town to stay with her aunt so she could study in the city. Helena, as she was called, was my age and had typical Slavic looks — very light blonde, silky hair, tied back in a braid, a high forehead, a pug nose, blue-green eyes, fair skin and plump. She was blessed with a particular beauty that one sees only in country people. After the scandal with Maria, I steered clear of Polish girls, but I couldn't stay composed around the girl who lived nearby and whom I saw often. Whenever I ran into her, an electric shock would run through my limbs and I would immediately be embarrassed, and the more impressed I was with her, the more excited she grew to see me.

Very soon, I was faced with a struggle between my common sense and fairness to my Jewish girlfriend, Zoshia, and my strong attraction to this beautiful village girl, whose eyes beckoned me. The country girl won, and I found myself visiting Mrs. Shumanski's apartment more and more often. I would make excuses to Zoshia about being busy on the evenings I spent with Helena, and Helena returned affection for every bit of attention she received. Very quickly, everyone in the building knew that Helena was in love with me and I became alarmed — would I get mixed up again with a Christian girl, a relative of Mrs. Shumanski, and who admired me so? Logic lost out to emotion — I couldn't cut myself off from Helena, and found a way to divide my time between my two radically different loves, who, of course, knew nothing of the other's existence.

I learned about life from both of them. Zoshia, always surrounded by admirers willing to take my place, enjoyed and encouraged the battle over her among the boys and I had to fight for her again and again; when I came out the winner she was pleased, but when I was the loser — and more than once I lost these battles, as I wasn't practiced in all the rules of the game — she would be furious. Actually, I never understood why Zoshia didn't leave me and choose a better looking and more refined boy than me. Helena, in contrast, never looked at another boy once she met me, and waited for me day and night, greeting me with a smile on every visit. She was willing to give me everything without asking for a thing in return, and did everything she could to make herself attractive. Although she was always neat and well-groomed, she would run off for a few moments when I arrived and return with her hair perfectly combed. Helena ate up every word I uttered, agreed with everything I said and never opposed me. However, she did notice one of my flaws right away — I didn't know how to court a girl.

I would "begin" but not know how to "continue"; my hands and tongue would become paralyzed and refused to do my bidding, even though my entire being longed to be with her. Sometimes I would catch myself acting aggressively, awkward and excessive, and once I even treated her unkindly. She was hurt, but she quickly forgave me and only teased me by saying, "That's not the way you behave with a girl. You have no idea what love is." At that moment I felt just like I had when I came to my grandfather's house, when he would ask me questions about that day's Bible portion and I wouldn't know the answer, and he would tease me. Helena then added, "Don't worry, Bolek. I'll teach you how to behave with a girl if you want to win her over," and I was ashamed and angry with myself for my uncouth behavior and for not knowing how to control my urges. Although Helena had forgiven me, I felt I wasn't worthy of her forgiveness. I thought that I would never be able to meet her gaze again, but I was even more attracted to her than ever and quickly went back to her. Until this day, I am grateful to Helena for what she taught me about love.

The Anglo-American Commission of Inquiry was about to visit Lodz to assess the mood among the refugees left in the city, and in the *Ichud* chapter we prepared for their visit. When the Commission arrived in the city, they stayed at the Grand Hotel, which raised the American and British flags from its towers in their honor. The Zionist organizations initiated a demonstration against "imperialist Britain," having first obtained a permit from the authorities. In the morning, organized groups from all of the Zionist movements and organizations gathered in Zawadzka Street with their various flags, among them unaffiliated Jews who had answered the call to come and protest. The crowd was large and the demonstration impressive. We marched along Piotrkowska Street carrying signs that called for the opening of the borders of Israel to the remaining refugees, condemned Britain and declared that the Jews had only one homeland — the Land of Israel. It was the first demonstration in Poland since the beginning of the war. Passersby stood amazed, asked the reason for the parade, and refused to believe that the authorities had permitted the demonstration to take place.

Among the observers was Helena, who, when she saw me among the demonstrators, approached me and asked me how I was connected to the marchers. Zoshia, who was marching not far from me, noticed Helena speaking to me familiarly and overheard my explanation of the reason for the demonstration. I had hoped that Helena would leave then, but instead she announced that she identified with the demonstrators' cause and would stay with me throughout the protest. She marched at my right side while Zoshia followed us with her gaze, making me far from comfortable. At the Grand Hotel we stopped and boisterously shouted out our slogans: "We want to go to Israel! We want to go to Israel!" Helena shouted along with me and it was all I could do to keep from kissing her. Members of the Anglo-American Commission came out onto the hotel veranda and waved at us. Our shouts rose in volume until the Commission members agreed to receive a delegation from the demonstration. After it was over, I explained to Zoshia that Helena was my neighbor, had asked me to explain the demonstration and had joined us in solidarity with our cause. Zoshia listened to my explanation, but she obviously sensed that there was more to it than that.

I had scarcely finished handing the shop over to Mrs. Kasja, determined to leave Poland soon and get to Israel as swiftly as possible, when a young man named Marin, a relative of Harry's who had just moved into our building, offered me the opportunity to open a sweater-making factory with him. He was able to convince me that it was important to have a profession when I got to Israel, not to mention the amount of money we could make, as sweaters were scarce. I was attracted to the sweater production business, having grown up with it, and I postponed my plans to leave. I had an excellent relationship with Marin and his wife Eva, and this time, unlike the knitted goods shop, where I had carried most of the responsibility, Marin took on most of the bother. He purchased the raw materials, made the sweaters, and sold them — while I only invested money and worked a little. Marin's forecast was borne out; the goods were quickly snatched off the shelves and sold at a good price. We were able to sell as much as we could produce, but we didn't want to expand the business, only take advantage of the season and then close up shop.

I passed the winter months in the sweater business, spending time in various social and Zionist movement activities, and dividing my evenings between Zoshia and Helena. And I still felt the spiritual disquiet; I still could not rid myself of the feelings of insecurity, self-doubt and guilt that I was "having fun" while my entire family had been killed. My heart told me that it wasn't logical for me to have survived; one day, and soon, my time would come and I would die, too. My nightmares, which were a mixture of past and present, and ended in my violent death, would not allow me to leave my past behind. I very often could not distinguish between my real life and my dreams.

With the spring, a new wave of emigration from Poland began among the Jews, and this time included all walks of life. The *Bricha* increased its activities. Organized groups of youths and adults left Lodz in secret, went out to neighboring cities and after crossing the border were smuggled west, most to the American-occupied areas in Germany. Families and individuals contacted smugglers and paid them huge sums of money to get them out of Poland.

Every day I heard about acquaintances I had seen only yesterday or the day before who had disappeared from the city during the night. Everyone asked each other, "So when are you leaving?" or, "What, you haven't left yet?" A mania to leave Poland was in the air.

And me? For a long time I had struggled with my conflicting urges: on the one hand, the intense desire to fulfill my destiny in the Land of Israel, but on the other, the fear of leaving the warm cocoon I lived in, surrounded by affection and love, to give myself up to loneliness, to an unknowable fate. But I knew that I had to put an end to the close ties with my beloved benefactors, who were suffocating me. I had to get free, to seek and find my own strengths and path in life.

We closed down the sweater factory, but Marin, who had repeatedly reminded me that he wanted to leave Poland, decided to remain for the time being and offered me partnership in a new business — to purchase and operate a machine for winding thread.

I steadfastly refused. My life in Poland was finished. When I told Helena that I had decided to go to Israel, the land of the Jews, I assumed she would be angry with me and try to get me to stay with her in Poland. To my surprise, she said without hesitation, "Bolosh, I'm ready to come with you to Israel!"

I explained to her that Israel was a hard and dangerous land, that the Jews there were fighting against the British, but she remained resolute: "If it's a good place for you, then it's a good place for me." I wasn't prepared for this response. Helena knew that my place wasn't in Poland, but in Israel, and like Ruth, the Moabite, she was willing to follow me. But to where? I didn't know myself where I would end up on my journey — how could I take responsibility for a Polish girl? I kissed her, told her she was the best girl in the world and that I was crazy about her. She did not ask if I would take her.

And Zoshia? Zoshia told me her parents had decided to immigrate to Argentina, where they had family, and she was going with them. Zoshia's decision not to go to Israel severed our romantic relationship completely. We still spent time together, but a wall had come up between us. And once she told me that she knew I loved the *shiksa* who had marched at my side in the demonstration — and I remained silent.

It took a few crazy days and sleepless nights before I got up the courage to tell Harry that I was leaving him and Ola, and I did it without meeting his eyes, and with a shaky voice. He was not surprised. He already knew I wanted to go — it wasn't the first time we had discussed the matter, but still, the final determined announcement, spoken in private, shocked him. His face went pale. His smile was regretful. He said, "I knew this day would come. I can't say whether this is a good decision or a bad one. Times aren't normal and it's hard to say what a Jew should do. I know I'm also thinking of going there, but our time hasn't yet come. You must do what your heart tells you to do." I didn't say a word in reply. I knew that any word that came to my lips would be foolish.

Harry told me he would break the news to Ola, and he promised to help me as much as possible to prepare. He also offered to keep my leaving a secret until the last moment, as we never knew what obstacles might come up.

The next few days were difficult. Ola cried incessantly and I couldn't comfort her; I could only tell her that I would write and that we would be together again soon. I didn't know what to do about Helena. Should I tell her — and add that I didn't want to take her with me, that I didn't want to stay with her? Was there an excuse for the pain I would cause a girl who loved me? I thought that I loved her, and if so, how could I leave someone I loved? I intuited that I was afraid to tell her because I thought she might convince me to go back on my decision.

Harry and Ola bought me clothes for the trip, but I explained to them that I didn't want to take a lot with me. I converted my cash into gold coins, and my friend Yitzchak from Sobibor, who was a shoemaker, fixed them into the heels of my boots. I also bought a few pieces of valuable jewelry, and Harry and Ola gave me a diamond ring as a gift, which was also easy to hide. I packed a bag with the necessary clothing and decided on my course of travel — I would go to Stettin, and from there proceed to Berlin.

The preparations for the trip were carried out in a race with time. Every extra day I was forced to spend in Lodz seemed to last an eternity. I tried to advance my departure date as much as possible, so that nothing could come up to disrupt my plans. All of my prior feelings of doubt and guilt disappeared. Only one thing occupied my thoughts — leaving Poland; and only one thing disturbed my peace — Helena. I lacked the emotional strength to stand before her, face-to-face, and tell her, "My beloved, I'm leaving you!" I was also afraid that I just wouldn't be able to do it, that at the last minute I would abandon my travel plans.

At dawn the next morning I shouldered my pack, which, in addition to clothes, also held a large loaf of bread, a long sausage and a small bottle of vodka, and like a thief slinking off, without taking leave from my loved ones, or from my beloved Helena, I left the house quickly, not looking back. I crossed the street as one pursued, boarded the tram and rode to the train station. The train to Stettin wasn't leaving for more than an hour. I wandered impatiently here and there in the station, already feeling alone in the world. But there was no way back. And as in the flight from the Warsaw ghetto, I felt a strength rising inside me in anticipation of what was ahead.

Policemen patrolled back and forth in the train station, glanced at me occasionally, then approached and asked me to present my documents, asking me where I was traveling to and the reason for my trip. I did as they asked, while images flashed through my mind of the night I had spent in the Warsaw train station, which had been full of the Germans I was hiding from. Then, I had left my home and loved ones against my will; my mother was the one who had made me flee the ghetto, to save me from death by starvation. Now, of my own free will, I was leaving a home that was all comfort and pampering by those who loved me, and going out to face a multitude of hardships in an unknown world. And unlike when I left the ghetto, this time I had no wish to return; this time I did not regret leaving for a moment. On the contrary, I was glad that I had stuck to my decision and I wasn't worried about the future. With unbelievable speed, everything linked to Lodz — my friends, my home, Harry and Ola, Zoshia, even Helena — seemed far removed in time and distance, although I occasionally searched among the train passengers for Helena's face...

Stettin, annexed from Germany by Poland with Soviet encouragement, seemed like a ghost town. Most of the German residents had either fled or had been exiled. Destruction and desolation was everywhere. The streets were almost completely empty. The few Germans left in the town were almost unnoticeable and the Poles had only just begun to settle in the district. In Lodz I had been told of a building that stood not far from the Stettin train station, where some Jewish families lived. There I was directed to a man, to whom I paid a large sum of money, and who assured me that, the very next day, I would leave with a group for Berlin. In the meanwhile, he instructed me to go to a certain house and rent a room for the night.

A woman of about fifty opened the door and greeted me in German. At my request, she readily rented me a room. It was late in the afternoon, and the building was gloomy. The woman asked me to wait in the guest room and returned a few moments later with a lighted lamp. She apologized that there had been no electricity since the battles that had been waged in the city, and that she was saving kerosene, as it was expensive. By the light of the kerosene lamp I saw a room full of heavy furniture, ceramic statues and family photographs, drawings and pictures hung on the walls. I felt dwarfed by all the furnishings. The woman, with the lamp in her hand, led me to my room, which had a large, very wide bed, covered with a feather comforter. On one side of the bed stood a dresser with family photographs on it. On the other side was a window with heavy drapes. There was no doubt that this was the master bedroom.

The woman invited me to have tea with her in the guest room.

I was hungry and thirsty. I had bread and sausage in my pack, but I wanted to postpone my meal until much later, when I could be alone in my room. I entered the guest room and sat in one of the deep armchairs. The woman brought tea and a young woman of about twenty entered the room with her and was introduced as her daughter. The three of us sat at the table to drink. Here I was — in a German house, drinking tea with German women! As we drank, the woman told me her tragic story in detail. Her son, twenty-five years old, had been killed at the front. Her husband had disappeared at the Russian front and not a word had been heard from him. When the Russians entered the city, they pillaged her home and she had nothing left to live on. "And now," she said in tears, "we are hungry for bread…" Instead of feeling a sweet revenge, I saw before me a starving woman and daughter, and forgetting for a moment that they were German, went into my room, brought back the bread and sausage, and gave the woman half of each. The woman, dumbstruck, got up, kneeled before me and kissed my hands.

The moment of pity left me quickly. I was angry at myself that instead of taking revenge and killing Germans, here I was feeding them. I felt such deep shame at myself and frustration at what I had done that I got up and went to my room.

Only a few minutes went by before someone knocked at my door. The door opened and the daughter came in, wearing a nightgown, her hair loose. She said that her mother had sent her to dress down my bed, and she removed the feather comforter from the bed and arranged the pillows. I tried not to take notice of her; I was still full of anger at myself for giving food to them. But the girl didn't leave the room. She wandered around as if waiting for something and finally stood before me and said, "Would you like me to stay with you tonight?"

I looked at her, not believing my ears, and she rested a hand on my shoulder and said, "Don't worry about my mother. It's all right."

For a second a struggle went on in my mind. I felt a rising

passion to sleep with this pretty young woman who was asking to come into my bed, but to make love with a German girl? This meant forgetting all the Germans had done to us! "No, get out of my room!" I shouted. Trembling, the girl quickly left.

I was very tired. I hadn't slept a wink the night before. I lay in the big bed, the two large pillows at my head, one next to the other, as if expecting someone to come and sleep beside me. The bed was clean and white as snow, with the fragrance of soap rising from it, but I felt that I was lying in filth. I couldn't close my eyes. That morning, I had still been in Lodz, living a normal life, surrounded by love and friendship — and by evening I was stuck in a strange, foreign city, filled with ghosts, sleeping in a German house, eating supper with a German family, speaking German, and a German girl had asked to sleep with me. Could all this really be happening? All of a sudden I realized — the mother had sent the daughter to me! Could this really be so, that a mother would send her daughter to sleep with a strange man?

In the morning, I took my pack and paid for my lodging. The woman invited me to stay for breakfast, and at least to have some tea, but I could not look the two German women in the eye. Out of shame for them I left the house.

Some people had already assembled at the smuggler's house, and one group had even set out already. A Soviet military truck stood next to the house. A Soviet officer went in, shook hands with the landlord, and afterward inspected us as if he were going to buy us. We got on the truck, which was half-filled with crates and sacks. They put us deep inside and then arranged the crates and sacks in front of us, concealing us, covered the back opening with a piece of tarpaulin — and we set out. We couldn't see a thing and had no idea of where we were. Sometimes we stopped and I heard voices asking for papers, and sometimes we stopped and the officer and driver got out of the truck and returned some time later. From the noises, we knew we were crossing villages and towns until suddenly we heard the tumult of a large city, the roar of many cars and the bells of trams.

The truck slowed to a crawl, turned around and stopped. The tarpaulin was removed from the opening and a blinding light shone in. We were taken off the truck next to a big, beautiful old building, surrounded by a wall. When we asked what city this was, we were told, "Berlin!"

# Berlin

## Spring 1946

As we stood outside the building, two young men with serious expressions came to welcome us and led us into a large hall with many white doors, and benches along the walls. A woman brought us coffee and sandwiches. A man wrote down our personal details and asked additional questions. He informed us that we were to wait there until someone came to get us, and ordered us not to leave the building and not to wander around the streets. "You're in the Russian-occupied area, and it is advisable not to get into trouble."

We quickly found out that we were in a building that had served as the Jewish hospital in Berlin, established by Rothschild and bearing his name until Hitler's rise to power. The Nazis had confiscated this institution, as it had all other Jewish property. After the city had been occupied by the Russians, they returned the building to the Jewish community, which had begun to reorganize, and now it served as a hostel for Jews returning to Berlin and a transfer station for Jews coming from Eastern Europe and traveling onward, to the American sector of Berlin. In addition to our group, there were other people in the hall, most of them older German speakers, but also older people speaking Yiddish, who immediately asked us whether we had any gold or dollars to sell.

After a short wait, we were called to get on another truck, this time an American army truck — like smuggled loot, we went from a vehicle belonging to one army to a vehicle belonging to another.

One of the two men who had welcomed us was traveling with us. The driver, who wore an American army uniform, was also Jewish and spoke to us in Yiddish. The American truck was covered with a sheet of canvas, but the rear opening was left uncovered and I got a hasty glance at the streets of Berlin. The people looked poor, even destitute. Berlin, which I had imagined as a city of strength and power, wealth and opulence, its streets filled with SS soldiers, other army personnel and elegant women, seemed grey and defeated. The wretched people I saw in the streets had been, just yesterday, rulers of the world, rulers of unbounded cruelty. Now, I was proud that I had been able to see this sight.

The truck left the heart of Berlin and entered an area covered with greenery and trees, checkered with luxurious villas surrounded by gardens, and with a river flowing down the center. We had reached the suburb of Wannsee, where the decision to completely eradicate the Jewish nation had been made. This area was under American control and American flags fluttered above a large number of buildings. We continued traveling and reached Schlachtensee, a suburb similar to Wannsee, which was also very green, and was the site of many army camps. The truck entered a camp with a sign at the entrance road, reading "Displaced Persons Camp Schlachtensee." In the not too distant past, this had been an SS camp. We could see two-story buildings standing close to one another and, at some distance, an office building, a kitchen and a dining hall, a movie theater and lecture halls. The truck stopped near the office building. We could see people strolling about, or sitting at the doorways of the buildings, and there were children playing outside. The residents of the camp surrounded us and asked us where we had come from, what the situation was like in Poland, and perhaps we knew someone named… Others asked if we had something to sell, or if we wanted to buy anything. Everyone in the camp was Jewish and it reminded me of the ghetto. Even the police were Jewish, just as they had been in the ghetto.

Even though I didn't know anyone there, I didn't feel uncomfortable. It seemed to me that I had returned to a place where I belonged. Again, our personal details were listed, we received blankets, toothbrushes, toothpaste and other necessities, and we were housed in one of the buildings, four to a room. I put my belongings on one of the beds and went out to walk around the camp and get acquainted with it. Near the gate, there was a group of young men and I heard them laughing. I walked past them without getting too close. One of the group, short and thin, dressed nicely, came up to me and asked, "Are you new here? Did you arrive today?" When I answered that I had, he extended his hand. "My name is Schneider," he said. "Mine is Bolek," I answered. We strolled together and Schneider told me that he was the only one of his family to survive; they had all been killed in Auschwitz. He had been in Auschwitz for some time himself and was then sent to a variety of work camps whose names I had never heard of as he listed them, one after another. At the end of the war he reached Berlin and had spent some time in the Russian-occupied area. In Berlin, he said, you could make a lot of money, as the city was divided into four sectors, each one controlled by a different Allied country, and there were excellent possibilities for smuggling; he, Schneider, bought and sold anything, from cigarettes and coffee to cars and motorcycles. When he had enough money, he planned to open a large shop in the heart of Berlin. Schneider added that life in the camp was good because we were protected by the Americans, and he suggested that I start working in "business" as quickly as possible.

I explained to my new acquaintance that I had come to Berlin as the easiest way to leave Poland, and that I had no intention of remaining here; I wanted to move on as soon as possible to Italy, from where I could get illegal passage into Israel. Schneider interrupted me and asked me where I had been assigned a room. I pointed to one of the houses and Schneider said decisively, "You'll come live with me. Come on, let's get your things." I didn't object. It was natural that two young men like us, each of us being the only one of our families to survive, would want to live together, even though I had met him only a few minutes before; it was as if we had met in the forest during the war. On the way Schneider told me, "I understand why all of a sudden everyone has turned Zionist and wants to go to Israel. But I didn't stay alive just to get killed in Israel by the Arabs or the British, or to die there of malaria." I wanted to ask Schneider how he was able to live among the Germans, not to mention opening a shop in this country, but I didn't want to get into an argument so soon after I had met him, and I didn't say anything. After a minute, though, Schneider continued, although I hadn't prodded him. "I don't want to stay here and live among Germans forever, but right now I don't have a choice. What can I do in this wide world with no education and no profession — clean latrines, maybe? That's what the Germans taught me to do well. Here I have the chance to make money, and after that, we'll see."

Schneider lived alone in a large room, half of it taken up by suitcases and boxes full of all kinds of merchandise, but the room was orderly and clean. He led me to an adjoining room and gave me the key to the door as though he were the owner of the house. Afterward, he invited me to eat with him. He had a large stock of different types of food. We sat down to eat and Schneider didn't stop talking. He told me about what was going on in the camp, about the Germans and the Americans and the Russians. He said that in Berlin every German woman, from the youngest to the very old, was ready to sleep with anyone, without exception. I said that he must be exaggerating; it wasn't possible that every woman would be ready to sleep with anybody. In the end, we wagered a bottle of vodka and Schneider took me into the city. We went to the light railway station. At the station and around it, there were dozens, perhaps even hundreds of women, one prettier than the next, all nicely dressed. I thought that they were waiting for the train but Schneider said, "All of these women here are waiting to catch an American soldier who will take them for a night, or even for a few minutes. We'll wait and you'll see what happens when the train pulls in."

He was right. When the train arrived, many American soldiers got off. The girls pushed their way through and tried to attract the soldiers, but only one or two were lucky enough to find a customer. Many of the soldiers already had beautiful girls with whom they were walking arm in arm, and what especially impressed me were the number of black soldiers with their arms around blond girls.

We left the station and walked down a lovely, quiet street, which appeared to be decent and respectable. Schneider suggested, "Take a good look and choose the most beautiful woman, one who looks completely respectable, and point her out to me."

There weren't many people in the street, and hardly any men at all. I looked carefully at every woman who passed by. They seemed to be normal women, as might be found anywhere, but most of them were dressed very nicely, in clothes which were rarely seen in Poland. From time to time, I wanted to point a woman out to Schneider but I kept on walking, and sometimes I didn't dare to believe that a woman I had seen would accept an offer to go with us. After some time, a woman appeared coming toward us who was beautiful, dressed nicely but modestly. I looked at her delicate face and I couldn't help but be impressed at the perfection of her beauty — she looked like a picture in a magazine advertisement. "That one!" I exclaimed to my new friend. He smiled, turned back and the two of us walked after her. I was ready to hear an angry reaction and leave in shame, but when we went up to her she turned her head and looked at us. Again, I was struck by her delicate, wondrously beautiful face. Schneider greeted her in German and suggested that she come for a walk with us. She stopped and asked, "Why should I go with you?" and there was a hint of anger in her voice. "We have American cigarettes and real coffee," replied Schneider. The girl stood hesitating for a moment and said, "But there are two of you and one of me. Come with me and I'll call my friend." I had lost the bet.

When we returned to the camp I heard the sound of music. Schneider led me to a dance hall, where dozens of couples, young and old, were dancing to the sound of an orchestra, and others were sitting on benches or standing along the walls. This was the first time I had ever heard American music and it grated on my ears. Schneider knew many of the people and introduced me to some of them. He encouraged me to dance, but I refused. I was a poor dancer and, until shortly before, hadn't known how to use my legs at all; every attempt at dancing ending in terrible failure. Only recently had I learned to do the tango and the waltz, and now, I didn't really want to dance with anyone. I just enjoyed standing there, not knowing anyone, watching people dancing; soon I even began to get used to the style of the music. All of a sudden, the images before my eyes changed; I saw these people dancing in the undressing yard of Sobibor, and *Oberscharführer* Michel was shouting at them to remove their clothes quickly. The music turned into a loud scream of people entering the gas chamber. I was angry at myself for having had thoughts like these and I made an effort to repress them, but they wouldn't go away. I finally told Schneider that I was tired and went back to the room.

I had no intention of staying in Berlin a day more than was necessary. I wanted to continue on my way south, to Italy, so the next day I went to the office building to find the soldier from the Jewish Brigade that Schneider said was the one who dealt with issues concerning Israel; he took groups from Berlin to West Germany and organized question-and-answer sessions in the camp.

The office building was still empty, but clerks and soldiers were beginning to arrive and to fill the rooms, and people from the camp began to arrive with their questions and problems. I stood at the entrance and watched them impatiently. Finally the soldier from the Brigade arrived in a jeep along with other military personnel. I wanted to speak to him right away, but I didn't dare stop him — I just stared at his English army uniform, his beret, and especially his sleeve, on which was sewn a yellow Magen David against a blue and white background — the same symbol that we were forced to wear in the ghetto and which shamed us before the Germans. The yellow star now filled my heart with pride, and the young soldier wearing it, short and thin, just a few years older than I was, seemed to me an adult with authority. What great strength can be endowed in a small symbol! A few months before, two Brigade soldiers had come to Lodz. The news of their arrival spread through the city and people hurried to where they were staying and waited for hours to feast their eyes on Jewish soldiers from Israel. I had also gone there a few times, waiting with the others to see them, but I never did. Now, here I was, standing face-to-face with a Jewish Brigade soldier. I waited for a few moments at the entrance before I went inside to his office, and before I had even managed to utter a word, he welcomed me and put out his hand. "My name is Ze'ev," he introduced himself. "Ze'ev Geller." "And mine is Bolek," I replied. The soldier told me to sit down. "Are you new here?" he asked. "I haven't seen you before. When did you arrive, yesterday? Have you come from Poland?" I only nodded my head in reply, and, in response to his questions, I told him about the situation in Poland and how I had gotten to Berlin. The soldier asserted that all of the Jews from Eastern Europe should be brought to the West as quickly as possible, as the routes might soon be blocked.

We began to converse excitedly, exchanging information and opinions, to the point that I had forgotten what I was doing there. Finally, he asked me why I had come, and I answered that I wanted to emigrate to Israel, and that I was hoping that he could help me get to Italy, from where I could get passage on a boat. The soldier replied, "You think you can get to Italy, and by the next morning, be on a boat to Israel? Impossible. Not even in a week or a month. There are thousands of Jews in DP camps in Italy, and more and more are coming every day from Germany, Austria and Yugoslavia, and they're all waiting for the chance to get to Israel. *Aliyah Bet* — that's what we call the illegal immigration — can only handle a small number at the moment. The chances of immigrating from Italy or from Berlin are the same. The most important thing we can do now is to prepare people, and especially young people, for immigration, to help their adjustment to Israel when they get there."

The soldier spoke seriously and enthusiastically in broken Yiddish with a sprinkle of Hebrew words, and he gave me the feeling of partnership in a mission: "We can do… We have to prepare young people…," he had said, and I thought to myself, Who are the "we"? He and I? "I have a suggestion for you," added the soldier. "Help me set up a youth group and prepare them to establish a kibbutz in Israel." I agreed to this proposal on the spot, without considering exactly what I was doing, without asking a single question. The Brigade soldier was a representative of authority for me, and a symbol of Israel, and Israel was the only solution to the problem of the Jewish people, and certainly the only solution for me. I was ready to do anything the soldier demanded of me. He seemed pleased, and then, offhandedly, as if he had just remembered something, asked, "What kind of name is 'Bolek'? Is that what they called you at home?" I briefly explained how I had gotten the name and he asked, "What did they call you at home?"

"Berale."

"In Hebrew, that's Dov," he remarked. "I'll call you Dov (bear) and you call me Ze'ev (wolf)." I didn't react; I thought it was a joke. Ze'ev told me that he already had a few candidates for the kibbutz, and that he was about to get a house where all of the kibbutz members could live together. I left, excited and confused, as though I had drunk too much. I had no idea what was to happen. I felt only that, from now, my life would change. I wasn't sorry that my plan to get to Italy had been canceled; I was waiting impatiently for the next move. I told Schneider about my meeting with Ze'ev from the Brigade and about the kibbutz that we were going to set up and I suggested that he join us. "It's not for me. Don't waste your breath," he said. He invited me to go into the city with him and we took the light railway. There were many civilians and soldiers getting on and off at the stops, speaking a variety of languages. At one of the stops, a few young people got on, speaking Ukrainian. When I heard the language, my heart began to pound. I looked at their faces. Perhaps I knew them? Ukrainians, Poles and others who had been Nazi collaborators had found refuge in Berlin and were being sought by the authorities. They were posing as anti-Communist refugees who had fled the Communist regime in their countries. They were able to hide their past and were being helped by the authorities of

Western countries, and were even being given immigration permits to the United States and England. I didn't recognize any of them, but their coarse language and loud laughter reminded me of the Ukrainians who had served in Sobibor.

As we moved from the suburbs into the city, we saw more and more buildings in ruins, or perhaps it only seemed like more because there was no greenery to hide them. My eyes were focused out the window. I observed what remained of the legend of the opulent and powerful Berlin. Even the buildings that had been left standing looked like corpses. Few people walked the streets and only military vehicles were on the roads. We walked down to Alexanderplatz. Here we felt the pulse of modernity; the shops were open and we saw more people in the streets. Many of them weren't German and they spoke a variety of different languages. Business was being conducted in the shops, in the entranceways to buildings and in other corners of the street. Schneider knew many people in this area, stopped to talk, and, now and again, he entered some of the shops. I tagged along after him, disinterested; all of my thoughts were centered on the kibbutz we were going to set up.

Schneider took me to a restaurant where old people were sitting and drinking soup in a large room smelling of sauerkraut. The owner of the restaurant welcomed Schneider warmly and led us through a dark passageway to a small room with a few nicely set tables. At one of them, people were sitting and drinking wine. The owner of the restaurant announced happily that he could offer us veal steaks, which by chance he was able to get, and he brought us wine. I ordered vodka. Eating in the back room of the restaurant endowed the meal with an intimate and mysterious atmosphere. The food was good and the vodka had its effect on the two of us. "You know, Bolek," said Schneider drunkenly, "too bad you're leaving me. We could have been good friends." "I think you're right," I answered, drunk as well, and I was sorry that we had to part ways.

The meeting of kibbutz candidates drew more people than we expected. Some of the candidates brought friends, most of them lone young people, but there were also some older people and even two married couples. Some of those who came had been members of youth groups in the past, such as *Hashomer Hatzair*, and they had some idea of what pioneer Zionism and the kibbutz were, but for most of them this was the first time they had heard of life in a collective. Ze'ev, who looked happy and excited, gave a short explanation of the objective of the meeting in broken Yiddish, and explained the importance of setting up a seed group for the future kibbutz here in Berlin. He told us that in West Germany, training camps with working farms had been set up, and young members were working the land, raising cattle and managing their farms on their own. The goal was to assemble a group in Berlin who would be willing to live together and be transferred in the near future to West Germany, where they would receive a farm in one of the villages and live collectively, preparing themselves for the establishment of a kibbutz in Israel. He added that he would manage the group and help them get organized for the first few days only; afterward, they would choose a secretariat, which would be responsible for management.

When Ze'ev finished speaking, everyone got up and gathered around him, offering their opinions and asking questions. He stayed with us for a long while, during which people became acquainted with each other and asked one another about where they had come from and what their story was. People who had been complete strangers to each other only a few minutes before now felt close, aware of the one objective uniting them all.

That evening I wrote a letter to Ola and Harry. I asked them not to worry about me as I had everything I needed and I was happy, and I told them that I would be living on a kibbutz. I wasn't sure that they would understand what a kibbutz was; I was worried that they might think it was some kind of orphanage — even I had begun to think that it really was an orphanage, as we were all orphans, although we were not children. The next day I left Schneider and moved to the kibbutz house. Ze'ev spent the whole day with us, helping us to get organized, and bringing us craftsmen to renovate the building. He had managed to get furniture and worked with us arranging the house and cleaning it inside and out, emphasizing that we had to serve as an example to the entire camp.

In a short time, the number of people in the seed group had increased to fifty, mostly young people about twenty years old, some older, twenty-five to thirty, and among those, a few married couples. There were people who had come from Russia and had served in the Soviet army, those who had served in the Polish army, partisans, concentration camp and death camp survivors; some made friends quickly and formed small groups, some remained solitary and it wasn't easy to get to know them; some kept their past tragedies buried and didn't utter a word about themselves. There were unusual and odd types among us, with different backgrounds, each with his own tragedy, each, for the most part, the only one who had survived out of entire families, each uniquely affected by his war experiences. Naturally, there were those who were ready to take on responsibility for managing the kibbutz, and Ze'ev made certain that everything was done democratically. He organized the kibbutz meetings in which the Secretariat was chosen unanimously. There were also those among us who knew how to draw, how to sing well, how to recite, and on Friday nights, we had *Oneg Shabbat* (Shabbat Delight) parties, which were open to all of the young people in the camp, even those who didn't belong to the kibbutz.

Ze'ev devoted most of his time to the kibbutz, taught us Hebrew and Israeli songs, lectured to us about life in Israel, about kibbutz and the smaller *kvutsa*, individual and communal moshavim, about the Haganah and the Palmach, the Etzel and the Lechi, and he filled us in about the various Socialist doctrines of working-class Israel as much as he could. He got us a ping-pong table, a volleyball net, a chess set, checkers and dominoes, and I discovered a great appetite for sports and games, for music and for literature, and for all of the social activities that I had never tasted. There was no kibbutz activity in which I didn't participate — the days and nights were too short for me to do everything I wanted to. I quickly made friends with everyone; I loved contact with people, younger or older, and I enjoyed visiting the married couples and feeling a family atmosphere. I made several close friends, all survivors of concentration camps, all alone, all the only survivors from their families.

One of my friends was Yossel, who was born in Lodz. He was a bit older than me, and shy; sometimes he appeared depressed, sometimes he would joke and participate in pranks. He didn't talk about the time he had spent in Auschwitz, as testified to by the number tattooed on his arm, and, in general, he didn't talk about his past. Another was Nachum, a youth I met on his first day. I had noticed his insecurity as he walked around trying to familiarize himself with every corner of the camp. I walked up to him and started a conversation. He was my age, perhaps a bit younger, but taller and broader than I was. Nachum related that he had been born in Warsaw, had been in Maidanek, and in other camps, and only he and his uncle, whom he had found by chance, had survived from his family. Until recently, he had been living in a city in eastern Germany and had served as a translator at the Soviet headquarters there, but now he had come to Berlin with his uncle. When I told him about my kibbutz and suggested that he join us, he agreed immediately, just as I had agreed to go with Schneider. Nachum left his uncle, took his suitcase and came to live in my room. We quickly became good friends.

Another friend, Yisrael, had also been in Auschwitz and in other camps, and he too was the only one left of his family. While I pondered my future and had not yet decided on my personal philosophy, Yisrael, who was a dreamer, strongly believed in Communism; he was a strong supporter of the Soviet regime and a great admirer of Stalin. He was convinced that Communism would swiftly take over the world and justified every act of the Soviets, and he blindly believed that "the ends justify the means." I couldn't understand what attracted this youth to kibbutz and why he was planning to immigrate to Israel, and not to Russia. When I asked him, he replied that, in any case, Communism would reach Israel; but my opinion was that in spite of his great love for Moscow,

Zionism pulled at his heart, and he wanted to live among Jews. Yisrael and I grew close and he became my closest friend. Even though he had lived in the ghetto and in Auschwitz, he asked me to tell him about my past and listened closely, hungry to know every detail, as though he had come from a different planet and was hearing about these horrors for the first time. The two of us discussed many subjects, and we argued a lot, but we had a relationship based on trust and understanding and we enjoyed one another's company.

Yisrael had a friend named Berale, who had been with him in Auschwitz. Although Berale was on good terms with everyone, he never became close friends with anyone. He trusted no one and continued to live his life as if he were still in a concentration camp or in the ghetto. He lived in the kibbutz house, but he also had a room in the Russian quarter of Berlin. He kept a suitcase full of food under his bed, and every day he took bread and other foods to the dining room, where he exchanged the stale food for fresh, trying to prevent other people from seeing him. When we came to dinner, Berale didn't sit with us, but sat at an empty table so that he wouldn't be disturbed while he was eating. He would have two or three bowls of soup — the soup was given out freely at meals — and then after the main course, he would rest a bit, take off his coat, and go get another bowl of soup; perspiring, he would wait again, then hesitantly take off his sweater and his shirt and go up to get another bowl of soup, eating slowly, pausing, sitting and waiting; then he would suddenly get up and walk back and forth across the dining room, his expression serious, as though he had a difficult problem to solve; and finally, take his bowl from the table — and go up to get another bowl of soup. We sat watching Berale's struggles with his portions of soup — he was so engrossed in eating that he saw nothing except his bowl.

Berale told me that he had a radio that he wanted to donate to the kibbutz and other belongings that he wanted to bring from his room in the Russian sector, and asked me to see if Ze'ev Geller could arrange a car for us. A few days later, the three of us left in a car belonging to the camp administration, and Ze'ev suggested that we use this opportunity to take a trip around the city. Berale, who had been in Berlin for a year, was our guide and led us, explaining as best as he could. For half a day we rode around occupied Berlin, divided and controlled by four countries, and we saw a city in ruins, the remains of magnificent buildings.

During the tour, I felt moments of indescribable satisfaction alternating with deep sadness. Since I had left Poland and stepped onto German territory, I had been unable to bear the Germans' behavior. The subservience, the attempts to hide the past and to appear incorruptible which seemed to characterize every German, without exception, increased the disgust I felt. Every German I conversed with — without my having asked — immediately apologized, saying that he, personally, knew nothing; only Hitler and his gang were responsible for everything, and they alone had brought disaster on everyone. Everyone, every German, lied shamelessly. The destruction of millions of people, which had gone on for years, was not something that could have been hidden.

It was also impossible for me to understand the self-abasement of the Germans, who were willing to bow before you and to kiss the soles of your feet just to get a cigarette; they were ready to sell body and soul for any minor necessity. When I traveled by train in a car filled with Germans and took out a cigarette, everyone sitting near me would offer me a light; sometimes I would give each of them a cigarette and they would thank me profusely — old people would get up and offer me their seats. Most didn't even smoke the cigarette I gave them but would carefully put it into their pockets, excusing themselves and saying that they would smoke after they had eaten. Once I lit a cigarette and after several puffs, I threw it onto the floor of the car. A few Germans bent down to pick up the half-smoked cigarette and when I hurriedly crushed it with my heel, their faces were surprised and saddened. When one of them asked me, blushing, why had I done it, I answered, "The Germans taught me to do it." "Where?" asked the man.

"In the death camp where I spent time, the Germans used to

do it," I replied. And again, the usual reaction — everyone said simultaneously, "We here did not know anything... Hitler, he is the one who did all of those terrible things..." Just as, in the days of their "greatness," the Germans knew no limits to their arrogance and humiliation of others, now, they had slipped to the lowest level of degradation.

In the DP camp people spent their time aimlessly, waiting for what was to come. There were some who smuggled and dealt on the black market that had developed in carved-up Berlin. From time to time, the American Military Police (MPs) would enter the camp, carry out searches looking for smuggled merchandise, and arrest suspects. From time to time, there were disputes between different groups of camp inhabitants, which evolved from verbal arguments to blows and sometimes, to unsheathed knives. The quarrels mostly broke out for no particular reason, over trivialities. On one of the dance evenings, a group of young people, known as "the group from Bialystok," entered the hall. They stood in one corner and a different group was standing in another. One of the Bialystok group asked a girl who was dancing with one of the other group to dance. He walked over to the couple, breaking in as was usual, and the girl started dancing with him. The first youth was angry and broke in on them, so that the girl was dancing with him again. The anger on both sides escalated and turned into a quarrel that quickly came to blows. Friends on both sides joined the melee, and within moments the dance hall had become a battlefield. There was no alternative but to call the MPs, who came quickly in a convoy of jeeps. The sound of the sirens rising and falling was enough to scatter the fighters.

The kibbutz began to take shape. A group of people, different from one another and foreign to each other, learned to live together and to form a cohesive unit, in no small part thanks to Ze'ev Geller, who devoted all his energies to us and gained the trust of every member. Ze'ev drafted a charter, and after much discussion, we decided to call our kibbutz "Talba," a Hebrew acronym made up of the words "It is good to die for one's country" (*Tov Lamut B'ad*

*Artzeinu*). The secretariat organized a celebratory evening to formally establish the kibbutz. The hall was decorated. At the official table sat Ze'ev and the secretariat. All of us members were called up, one by one, to sign the kibbutz charter, and Ze'ev pinned a badge representing our movement on each of us. Our movement was called the United Pioneer Youth Movement (*Noar Halutzi Meuchad*). When I was called up and Ze'ev attached the pin and shook my hand, I knew that I was joining an undertaking of the utmost importance and that I was obligating myself to give up my private life for the good of the collective.

All of the kibbutz members were invited to participate in a Passover Seder led by the chief rabbi of the American army. The Seder took place in a large hall in one of the palaces of the Wannsee suburb. The hall was decorated and flooded with light. The tables were set and candlesticks with lighted candles stood on each table. A number of army officers welcomed us and sat us at the main table. It was an unbelievable experience — hundreds of Jewish soldiers sitting down to the Passover Seder, and I was among them!

The rabbi, who sat at our table, read the *Haggadah*. I heard him reading, "This is the bread of affliction which our forefathers ate in Egypt..." I closed my eyes and I saw myself sitting at the Seder table of our home in Lodz. I heard my father's voice reading the *Haggadah*. I saw my little brother Yankele asking the Four Questions with an anxious look on his face, my mother serving the meal; I again experienced the holiday atmosphere, the exhilaration of everyone sitting at our Seder table; I could see the beautiful multi-colored dishes, the special foods...and then I saw the Seder that we organized in the ghetto, without Father. My grandfather led the Seder, and we were all very sad as we sat around the table. How could we sit at the table when my father was not with us? But he had died and was gone! The room was dark and depressing, but I was still sitting with my family... Now I was sitting at the Passover Seder with hundreds of people I didn't know. No one was left of my family. They were all dead. They had disappeared as though they had never existed. Only I was alive. Why had I survived? How could I continue to live without them? How could I not be ashamed to joke, to sing and to laugh, when they were all buried under the ground or their ashes had been spread by the wind?

Yet — why was I to blame for staying alive? How many times had I been just a step away from death — and death had passed over me. Had I done anything wrong by surviving? Why was I torturing myself? Why were others happy about being alive? But perhaps they were thinking these same thoughts and just not mentioning them to anyone, as I was not mentioning them.

# Schesslitz

## Summer 1946—Summer 1947

The day we had been waiting for had arrived. Heavy American army trucks came noisily into the DP camp and stood parked in a row. Ze'ev had announced to us several days before that we were to prepare to leave, and we were packed and ready to go. We stood in festive formation as we lowered the flag, and, carrying our suitcases, we each boarded a truck. We started out on our journey with singing, but we didn't really know where we were going. Ze'ev had told us about the *hachshara* (training) farms of the United Pioneer Youth that had been set up throughout Germany, but it still wasn't clear to us what the meaning of *hachshara* was. One thing was certain, however — we had taken one more step on our way to Israel.

On the day that I found out that we were going to leave Berlin, I met with Schneider and tried to convince him to leave his business deals and join us. He refused to listen, saying that he would leave Germany only when he had enough money to live on for the rest of his life. Now, just as we were leaving, he came to say goodbye and didn't leave until the convoy began to move. I saw him standing by the truck, the eternal smile on his face, but he looked very sad to me. For a moment it seemed that if I had said at that moment, "Come with us, just as you are now!" he would have left everything and jumped into the truck. I pitied him and I blamed myself for leaving him behind in this accursed place.

The convoy left the streets of the city and moved out into open country. I did not look back even once. I hated the city from which all our troubles had come, even though sometimes I felt that my greatest vengeance was my very presence in Berlin as a free man, while the Germans were defeated and their country occupied. We passed green fields, streams, lakes and forests, quiet villages with church towers above them, and it seemed that the war had passed these places by; the fields and lakes appeared indestructible. Once, when we entered a thick forest in the afternoon of a clear day and the world suddenly darkened as though it were evening, we saw huge piles of ammunition that seemed to go on forever on both sides of the road. No one was guarding the ammunition. No one had any need of it.

Traveling through such scenes of natural beauty made me feel as if I had drunk a great quantity of wine, and I was once more accosted by visions and strange thoughts, one pushing the next from my mind, some happy and some depressing. Then all at once the fields and streams disappeared, the village scenes ended, and I was awakened from my daydreams. We entered a densely built up area, made up entirely of burned-out structures — skeletons of tall buildings, solitary standing walls, chimneys scattered through the area. We crossed through this industrial zone just outside of Frankfurt and entered the city proper, which was also in ruins. The sight of the rubble was threatening; it was like entering a city of Hell. At first it seemed that most of the houses were left standing, but then I saw that their interiors had been bombed out. The walls of the houses seemed to be skeletons punctured by gaping windows, row after row of facades of buildings four or five stories high and on the verge of collapse, and behind them emptiness. Berlin had been destroyed, as well, but there, sections of streets had been left untouched by the bombing and there were still scenes of normal life. Here, in Frankfurt, I did not see one building left intact. Although I was pleased to see Germany destroyed, riding through the ruins was a depressing experience.

We passed through the city and were once again riding through lovely village scenes, but the memory of the bombed-out city stayed with me for a long while. After many hours of travel with almost no break, we reached the Jewish DP camp in Bamberg, Bavaria. It was evening and darkness was falling. Exhausted, we got out of the trucks and were immediately surrounded by people shooting questions at us: "Where are you from?" "Where are you going?" "Maybe you have seen…?" "Perhaps you heard about…?" Groggy from travel, I answered mechanically, "No, I haven't seen…" "No, I didn't hear…" DP camp personnel took those in the convoy who were not part of the kibbutz. We remained standing near the trucks. Night had fallen. It seemed to me that we waited for hours, but actually, after about half an hour, another truck rolled up, and two men came out of the driver's cabin and ordered us to climb in. The truck was small, and we had difficulty making room for everyone. The man who had met us calmed us down, saying that we didn't have very far to go, and we would just have to put up with it a bit.

The truck began to move and Yisrael, who was standing next to me, whispered that he felt like we were being taken to Auschwitz — the crowded truck reminded him of how they had taken him and his family in the roundup of Jews in Lodz. I shouted at him to stop comparing everything that happened to the Holocaust. Even in Berlin, I couldn't stand his habit of comparing everything to the days of the ghetto and the camps: when he wanted to say that someone worked in the administration of the DP camp, he would say that they worked in the *Judenrat*; when there was someone he didn't like, he called him an SS man. I despised these remarks and I argued with him about them, and he would retort that the war hadn't done anything to me, and, in spite of everything I had been through, I remained "a momma's boy." But in the crowded truck, not a moment had passed before I, too, began having visions of the railroad car taking us to Sobibor, hearing the shouts of "Air!" "Water!" and "Help!" The smell of sweat and urine in my nostrils brought a return to the anxiety of a journey to the unknown. I felt horribly suffocated the entire way, and when the truck finally stopped, I was anticipating shouts of *"Raus! Raus! Schneller! Schneller!"*

The house where we had stopped was brightly lit, and, for the first few moments, it seemed to me that it was the only house in an area of darkness and wilderness. But after our eyes got used to the black, we could see that we were on a road dotted with rows of small houses, some of which had small lights on inside. We walked into the yard and I could smell the odor of barns and hay. We walked up to the second floor and we entered a large lighted room with long tables. A pleasant warmth surrounded me. We were welcomed by a group of Hungarian, Czech, German and Yiddish speakers who had reached the site two or three weeks before us, and who had prepared the houses for us. Hungry, we attacked the warm, tasty and abundant food they served us, and then each group was led in turn to houses in the village.

Sunshine and the sound of work in the neighboring yard awakened me. At first, I didn't know where I was. From the window of my room I saw a church tower with a clock and the neighboring yard, with chickens wandering freely about. The sound of hammering could be heard from a storeroom. A woman went out the door, crossed the yard and returned after a minute. I hadn't imagined that this was the way the training farm would look. I expected an isolated farm, surrounded by fields, and here we were in the middle of a village, among German farmers.

Someone came to take us to the main building, where we had eaten the night before, and we again crossed almost the entire village. Unlike in a Polish village, where wooden cottages stood at a distance from one another along a dirt path lined with wooden fences, the German village was intersected by a road of square stones, and on both sides of it were sidewalks and white, two-story houses. On the way, I saw two *Biergartens*, a beauty parlor and a few places of business. The war had not left its mark on this village. All of the houses were standing; the town had not been touched. As we walked, we met some Germans dressed in short leather pants held up by suspenders — like the ones I had worn in childhood — who greeted us as we passed.

We learned that we were in a village in southern Germany called Schesslitz, not far from Bamberg, between the city of Bayreuth, where Richard Wagner, the composer adored by the Nazis, had lived, and Nuremberg, where the Nazis had passed the anti-Jewish laws known as the "Nuremberg Laws" in 1935. Schesslitz had had a few Jewish families before the war, and all of them had been killed, their houses and possessions confiscated by the Germans. At the end of the war, the Nazis disappeared, vacating the Jewish homes. The inhabitants of the village had taken the animals and some of the possessions. Jewish Agency emissaries and United Pioneer Youth leaders had been searching for places to train young survivors for kibbutz life and agricultural work in Israel, and when they found out about the Jewish properties in Schesslitz from Jews living in Bamberg, they requested them from the American occupation authorities.

The Jewish property consisted of four houses in the village and a large farm with a big two-story house, a barn, a stable, granaries and fields near the village, and the Americans transferred this property to UNRRA and to the Joint Distribution Committee ("the Joint") to serve as an agricultural school to train Jewish refugees. The Germans returned the agricultural equipment, cows and horses; and only a German woman and her two daughters were allowed to remain temporarily in the central building, in two rooms that were allocated to them by the American army.

In the Bamberg DP camp, a group of people had been chosen to act as a seed group for the Jewish agricultural school, as our group had been, and so the two groups met in Schesslitz and formed one consolidated group whose objective was to immigrate to Israel and to set up a kibbutz. There were also a number of refugees who had become bored with doing nothing in the DP camp and found a place where they could live a better, more productive life and perhaps earn some money from crops they raised. This second group — like most of our seed group, before they had come to

Berlin — had no Zionist background and most of them had no intention of living on a kibbutz after they immigrated to Israel. Some members of this group had grown up in the Carpathian Mountains, a rural area between Hungary and Czechoslovakia, and many had been farmers there, so they were very knowledgeable about agriculture.

All of the authorities had a vested interest in the success of our kibbutz — and of, as they called it, the "agricultural school." UNRRA, which managed the DP camps, was interested in proving that under their administration, the refugees were not only being supported, but were being prepared to reenter normal life; the Joint wanted to help turn the Jewish refugees into productive individuals wherever they lived, and the Zionist leadership saw us as an especially positive seed group among the refugees and wanted to help us progress. UNRRA and the Joint provided us with material assistance, and the Zionist leadership sent us emissaries from Israel to teach us about Zionism and kibbutz life. All these were factors in our success, of course, but the main reason was the composition of the group. We were a mosaic of many different people, each of whom contributed to the collective. The older individuals among us had been active in Zionist youth movements before the war, and some of them even knew Hebrew. There were also older members who had sound business skills, and some who had been raised in rural areas and who quickly dominated all sectors of the agricultural work. We also had a sports coach, and those who had no professional training but who were ready to do any kind of work and learn anything.

The kibbutz also hired an agricultural instructor, a young agronomist, the son of a Jewish father and a German mother, who trained us in fieldwork and taught us a bit of theory. We worked energetically to rehabilitate the farm and turn it into a prosperous agricultural settlement. We all shared the ambition to be an excellent kibbutz and to prove to the German residents of the town that we could manage a farm better than they could. We quickly earned a good reputation, earning us visits by many respected guests.

An administrator of UNRRA, an older English officer, visited us often. As no one in the kibbutz could speak English, I was nominated to be translator, thanks to the few words I had learned from Ignatz; somehow, we understood each other. The officer told me that when he was tired of all of the problems in the DP camp under his jurisdiction, and he was about to break from the nervous strain, he would visit us; walking around our farm calmed him and he drew renewed strength from those visits.

In addition to working in the agricultural divisions of our farm, we had wide-ranging cultural and sports activities, we learned Hebrew language, folk songs and dances, we heard lectures and we had artistic evenings. Whoever had had the idea of setting up training kibbutzim throughout Germany after the war could not have possibly known how well they had targeted the needs of young people like me. There was no place where I felt as good as I did on kibbutz, after the war. I took part in every type of activity, at work, in our social activities, in cultural events and in sports; I was protected from dealing with the daily life of a world about which I knew nothing; I didn't owe anything to anyone; but, first and foremost, on the kibbutz I was not out of the ordinary, nor was I an object of pity.

Life in the village, work in the fields, being close to nature, cooperative living, the common goal, the sports that were a large part of the day's activities, and which had been lacking in the years of our youth — all these helped to release us from the burden of years of war, its terrors, and from the adulthood that was forced upon us too early. In the German village of Schesslitz, I experienced days of happiness, and to a certain extent, I was disconnected from my terrible past. There, too, I continued to have the nightmare about Sobibor, waking up just at the moment that I was to be put to death, my heart beating out of my chest, but the dreams didn't haunt me for a long time. And although at the kibbutz, too, images from reality and images of horrors from the past followed each other in my imagination, there the images of the past didn't over-whelm me — they were only flashes, which passed quickly. It was unbelievable: I, a prisoner at Sobibor, was now living in a German town, next door to a German home, meeting Germans every day in the street and exchanging greetings with them.

A German doctor treated me, and when necessary, I was hos-pitalized in a German hospital. I bought supplies from Germans, had my hair cut by a German barber. I drank beer in a German *Biergarten* where the other customers were German. But I made sure to keep my distance from Germans as much as possible; I wanted no genuine contact with them. At kibbutz meetings, we often spoke about what our conduct toward the Germans should be, and our guidelines were simple: as we were forced to live for a certain amount of time in a German town, we must behave with decency toward our neighbors and we were not to act on feelings of vengeance; but under no circumstances would we develop close relationships with them, nor would we make friends with them — we must not forget for a moment what the German nation had done to us.

Most of our members followed these principles. We lived in the German village, but we remained a closed group. We ignored our neighbors and we had contacts with them only when necessary. But there were those who behaved otherwise, whether by relating to them expressions of vindictiveness and open scorn, or by becoming too friendly with a German who might say, as they all did, that he "liked Jews" and "had no idea about what Hitler had been doing to the Jews." But slowly, some of us developed a new habit — at first, just a few of us, but later, more and more of us — young men began to disappear in the evenings, after dinner, even skipping kibbutz meetings, as they were going out to spend time in the fields or in farmers' homes with village girls. It might have appeared as though our boys had won the hearts of the local girls, but it seemed to me that it was the girls who had won the hearts of our boys. The girls would seek out the boys anywhere and at any time, and when night fell, there were many who disappeared. On Friday evenings, when we had *Kabbalat Shabbat* (Welcoming Shabbat) parties which went on into the night with singing, performances and a festive meal, the girls of the village would wait outside until "their" boys could come out. Not only did this contradict our expressed principle of not having relationships with Germans, it also affected their connection to the kibbutz, as these boys participated less and less in kibbutz social life and in important discussions about kibbutz problems, and they sometimes even "lifted" kibbutz supplies for their girlfriends. The secretariat decided to fight these attachments in any way they could. Special meetings were called to discuss the problem, and there was great personal criticism directed against the boys who had German girlfriends; they were threatened with disciplinary action, including being expelled from the kibbutz.

One of the reasons our young men sought out German girls was that the female members of the kibbutz were a distinct minority. It was pretty obvious that if we wanted to set up a kibbutz in Israel, we would need an even ratio of young men to young women. Therefore, it was decided to wage a campaign to bring more females into the kibbutz: any boy who knew a Jewish girl, from anywhere, was sent out to attempt to recruit her; boys were sent to other kibbutzim and to DP camps to try to convince girls to join us; and the central administration of our movement, located in Munich, tried to direct girls to us. However, the only result of our efforts was the addition of a few new young women. Unlike most of us, the girls arrived with their families, as almost all of them had reached Germany from Russia, where they had fled to during the war. So the success of the DP campaign could be considered only modest.

My friend Yisrael and I brought in one girl we found in a Jewish children's home we visited. Since we had failed to find enough girls to even things out, Ya'akov, who was a member of the secretariat, and I went out on a special mission to meet a convoy of participants in the *Bricha* from Poland, which was to arrive at a DP camp before they were sent to other locations. We were directed to the administrator of the DP camp, who had been apprised of our coming. Ya'akov informed him that "the two of us have come to take fifty girls for our kibbutz; we do not want children, older women, and certainly not men." The administrator, who was facing us, jumped up as if a snake had bitten him and shouted, "What is this, a cattle market? You choose who you want to buy and who you don't want? Perhaps you want to check each one to make sure that she's good enough for you?"

The atmosphere was tense. The negotiations were not going well. In the end, the administrator said that we could take fifty percent girls and the rest, "other people." In Berlin, our group had been formed from people who had seemed suited to kibbutz life — and now we were going to accept people sight unseen? I whispered to Ya'akov that I was going to "check out the goods" and that he shouldn't come to any agreement before I returned. I left the room and entered a long wooden house where the new arrivals were waiting. I looked the boys and the girls over, I heard them speaking and observed their behavior. I wasn't impressed; they didn't seem suitable for kibbutz life. I didn't see a single pretty girl, or even one who looked pleasant, among them. Afraid of the disappointed reactions of our friends if we brought these people to the kibbutz, I hurriedly called to Ya'akov and told him what I had seen and expressed my strongly negative opinion about bringing any of them. Ya'akov was not convinced. "What did you expect to find, movie actresses? I've already agreed that at first, we'll accept thirty girls and boys who will arrive in the next few days, and if everything goes well, we'll take a second group."

On our way home, I was in a terrible mood. I felt that I had failed and I was angry at myself for not having prevented the arrival of the new group. How foolish of me it had been to dream about bringing girls, each of whom would be lovelier than the next! But as the journey continued, I reached the opposite conclusion — what made me think that I had the authority to determine that these boys and girls were "not good enough" and "unsuit-able" for kibbutz life? Perhaps the administrator of the DP camp was right when he compared Ya'akov and me to cattle dealers? What did I actually know about the quality of these people? Who knew what they had gone through in their attempts to reach the West, and wasn't it possible that after they had washed, rested, gotten dressed and combed their hair, they would look completely different?

The first group of "reserves" reached us after a few days. My fears, unfortunately, were borne out. The new people behaved strangely and had no desire to fit into our group. Quarrels and disagreement broke out between "us" and "them." There were robberies, and food supplies and clothes disappeared. The situation became untenable — and after two weeks they were all sent back.

While they were with us, an incident occurred that upset me very much. Among the original members of the kibbutz in Berlin was a married couple, Marisha and Izo. She was from Warsaw; during the war she had been in the ghetto and later survived by masquerading as a Polish girl. He had been an officer in the Polish army. In Berlin, I had been so friendly with the couple that I was almost a member of the family. In many ways, all of the members of the kibbutz were like one big family, who celebrated every marriage and every birth. When Marisha and Izo had a baby boy on the kibbutz, we were all very excited, and I felt as though a boy had been added to my own family. Everyone prepared for the *brit milah* (circumcision) ceremony, and the married women got together and prepared a festive meal for the party that we would have.

But all of our plans were canceled, as the baby was born with a heart defect and died when he was ten days old. The entire kibbutz was plunged into intense mourning. The baby's casket was placed in the dining hall on a special stage, wrapped in black, with lighted candles placed on either side. All of the kibbutz members attended the funeral, which took place in the small Jewish cemetery of the village. I was terribly upset at the death of the baby. I, who had seen literally thousands of dead people, and had experienced the loss of my entire family, whose friends had died one by one before my very eyes, had thought that nothing could horrify me again, but I broke down at the death of a baby a few days old who was not related to me and whom I had only seen once or twice when I had visited Marisha, his mother, in the hospital. Had everything I had been through not changed me a bit? I was ashamed at my reaction and I tried to conceal my feelings from everyone.

One day, a woman in her thirties arrived at the kibbutz with a sixteen-year-old daughter and a son who was thirteen. When I returned from work, I was told that a beautiful girl had come to the kibbutz, and like all of the other bachelors in our group, I was impatient to see her, but she had been ill when they arrived and she was in her room. In the evening, it was suggested that I bring a kerosene lamp to the new family, so I was one of the first to see the girl, who really was impressively beautiful. All of the boys, myself included, tried to start a relationship with her; not only was she beautiful, she also knew how to sing and dance well, and was lively and effervescent. I wasn't aggressive nor did I make obvious efforts to be in her company, but secretly I tried to be near her. The victor in the struggle to win her turned out to be Nachum, my friend from Berlin; he was tall and nice-looking, and the fact that he owned a motorcycle and a camera added to his "points" and helped him to victory.

The summer passed quickly and our farm flourished. We reaped the wheat that we had planted, filling our granary with grain and hay, and we harvested potatoes, beets and other vegetables from our fields. Our storerooms and cellars filled up. All throughout the summer we also participated in many sports activities and had organized our own entertainment, sometimes forgetting ourselves and acting like children. We enjoyed living in Schesslitz. We were quite cut off from the outside world, and we sometimes forgot what we were doing there and what our ultimate objective was. However, when fall came with its unceasing rains, work in the fields came to a halt, and our priorities were now studying, cultural activities and discussions about the future of our kibbutz, discussions which became more serious when the administration of our movement informed us that it would soon be our turn to immigrate to Israel with the organized illegal immigration project, *Aliyah Bet*.

Emissaries from Israel visited us to educate us, and one of them, a music teacher, set up a kibbutz choir. As someone who joined every social activity, and who had loved to sing from childhood, I as a matter of course joined the choir, whose members spent many hours learning songs in harmony. We were immediately invited to sing before our friends at *Kabbalat Shabbat* parties and on other occasions. But our teacher would not let us appear until we had mastery of a full repertoire. Our first appearance was at the Hanukkah party and we had many invited guests, among them members of the Zionist leadership, officials of UNRRA and the Joint, and Jewish officers of the American occupation forces. At the meal, as at every celebration and holiday in our kibbutz, there was an abundance of food and a variety of dishes. There was an unwritten law in our lives — which clearly stemmed from the need to recompense ourselves for the years of hunger we had all experienced — that food would always be in abundance and of good quality, and so, on every holiday, our kitchen was the scene of culinary competition among the married women.

The Hanukkah party opened with communal singing and with speeches by the honored guests and the kibbutz general secretary, all of us sitting around food-laden tables. After we had filled our stomachs with the delicious meal and had drunk our fill of wine to ensure a merry atmosphere, we began our artistic program. Our member Yehudit movingly recited literary excerpts, and Anshel read some amusing anecdotes, but the repertoires of the two were already well known to us. Then the choir took the stage. Concentrating intensely on our conductor, we opened our program with the melancholy song, "How Long Will Our Nation Live without a Homeland." In the course of our singing, we overcame our nervousness and sang well. We completed the program to deafening applause. After this success, the choir was invited to sing at other kibbutzim and at the Bamberg DP camp.

At one of the kibbutz meetings, a proposal was made to institute complete communal life, to forbid private property and to obligate all of our members to contribute their money and valuables to the communal fund. We had a stormy discussion. Members who had no possessions supported the proposal warmly while those endowed with material wealth rejected it aggressively. Three evenings of discussion were devoted to the proposal, and we finally came to a compromise: for the next month, members would be able to use their money to buy personal items — and afterward, none of us would be permitted to retain personal money. Those who had larger sums of money were asked to contribute it to the kibbutz in order to purchase necessary equipment, and I unhesitatingly took the gold coins out of the heels of my boots and gave them to the secretariat. Evidently, I was the only one to do so; others bought themselves clothes and jewelry or hid their money.

The financial situation of the kibbutz was good. The secretariat requested that the relatively large sum that we had in our communal fund be used to buy equipment, but there were those who proposed spending it on clothing for members or on other items. At the kibbutz meeting it was decided to first purchase machines and equipment for a carpentry shop and a metal shop, and to send these ahead to Israel, to Kibbutz Mishmarot, which we were in contact with via the leadership of our movement.

At the center of interest during the idle winter months were the competitions for chess and ping-pong championships, but these weren't substantial enough for the long winter, and so a profound issue was raised to fill our evenings — a mock trial was convened to judge the behavior of the Jews during the Holocaust. The trial was organized and conducted by members of the secretariat: Zalman and his friend Yitzchak, who had fought in a partisan unit, Yitzchak Fishman, who had been an officer in the Polish army, and Ya'akov, our leader — all older than us by a few years and all with a background in Zionist movements. The idea for the trial came from Zalman, born in Latvia, who was both educated and had excellent speaking ability. The prosecutor Zalman chose was Yitzchak, our Hebrew teacher, who was also a talented speaker. After explaining to me the importance that he saw in carrying out the trial and the emotional difficulties involved in it for those who participated, Zalman asked if I would be willing to take an active role. An inner compulsion and a feeling of moral-social obligation led me to volunteer to represent the defense. In Zalman's opinion, I was well suited for the role, but he hoped that the unavoidable airing of the terrible past would not be too much of a burden for me.

The decision to carry out a public trial spread among the members like wildfire, and led to disagreements and even serious quarrels, mutual accusations that led, more than once, to blows. My life in the village had so far helped me repress all of my traumatic memories, but now, again, I relived my past with all of its intensity. Thoughts of the war years gave me no peace from the moment I opened my eyes until, completely immersed in these thoughts, I tried to fall asleep at night. I felt strongly that the honor of those who were gone depended on my success or lack thereof. Listening closely to the debates among my friends, I discerned the arguments I would have to refute. A strong claim was that already by 1925 in his book *Mein Kampf*, Hitler had argued the need to destroy the Jewish nation; and in the early 1930s, the first years of his rule, he proved that he was determined to turn his principles into reality — Polish Jews knew of the pogroms he had carried out against German Jews, the revocation of their civil rights in the Nuremberg Laws, and their humiliation, events which were repeated in Austria and Czechoslovakia. But the Jews of Poland had not learned their lesson, they had not drawn conclusions, they had not foreseen the Holocaust.

The prosecution also accused all streams of Jewish leadership of disappearing from the first day that the Germans invaded Poland. Not only hadn't they warned the nation of the horror that was to come, but when it did come, they were useless; they did not lead the hopeless nation nor did they provide direction — whether to flee or to fight. There were accusations of collaboration with the Germans on the part of many Jews, of assisting them in their Final Solution. But the main accusation was that the Jews had gone to their deaths like lambs to the slaughter, without putting up an active resistance.

My thoughts went back to the past and focused on the war years, but now, I attempted to examine events from the standpoint of the Jewish leadership. I clearly remembered how the war had begun, with the lightning conquest of Poland by the Germans, which hadn't allowed the Jews enough time to flee enemy forces. I remembered that night in Lodz that no one had dreamed would come so quickly — only a few short days after the invasion had begun, the Germans were already at the gates of our city, on the heels of the fleeing remnants of the defeated Polish army. The streets of the city had been filled with Jewish men fleeing eastward out of the city, trying to avoid capture by the Germans. Indeed, only two days before, as we were leaving the shelter after the air strike, Father had said that if the Germans were successful, he wouldn't stay and be under their control; he would flee with my older brother, Mottel, reasoning, "There will be no danger to Mother or the children..." On that horror-filled night he had taken Mottel and joined those escaping without a second thought. But they didn't get far; the Germans had captured the expanses of Poland so quickly that they were able to overtake those who were fleeing and had, on that very day, shot my father to death along with another two Jews and three Poles.

Thousands of innocent people such as my father and his comrades were killed in the first few days of the invasion, but everyone had assumed that these deaths had occurred in the heat of battle, as soldiers under fire are "permitted" to do as they please. The new German rule would be established quickly, and as Germans were known, after all, to be a cultured nation, the danger would pass and life would return to normal.

The first days of occupation were characterized by daily humiliations and persecution. Each decree the Germans issued was worse than the one before. Had the general paralysis of the Jews been inevitable — brought on by the heavy punishments imposed on disobedience, by the disappearance of Jews and Jewish leaders with no knowledge of their fate, and especially by uncertainty of what the next day would bring? What should the Jews have done — declare war on Germany? During this period, thousands of Jews had run away, most of them young people whose families were unable to care for them, going eastward, intending to cross the border into the Soviet Union. Some of them succeeded, others wandered along the border for weeks until they returned home. Everyone had hoped that the superpowers — Britain and France — would defeat Germany quickly and peace would return to Poland.

These thoughts led me to Warsaw. When our family arrived, the capital had seemed like Paradise in contrast to Lodz. There was no ghetto, nor was one being discussed. The Jewish shops were open; the streets were filled with Jews and Poles. But the situation changed in Warsaw, as well. The ghetto was established; the daily struggle became more and more difficult. The money we had thought would last us through the dark days, until the Allied forces had won the war, was exhausted and we had to sell every possession that was worth selling. And we were far from alone. People were starving; they turned into walking skeletons or swelled up like balloons — and died. At the beginning, a "Committee for Mutual Aid" had been set up in every building, and whoever was able contributed to the needy; then the contributors became needy themselves, and there was no one to help. Parents who sacrificed themselves for their children died of hunger, and their children walked the streets until they, too, died of hunger and of the cold; at night I could hear the sound of children crying, "I'm hungry... I'm hungry..." And even then, people lived with the slogan "We must carry on!" "The Germans want us to die? We will not give in!" The situation was terrible, but it never occurred to anyone that the Germans would destroy all of us. What could we have done that we didn't do? What did we do that we shouldn't have done? What could we be accused of?

In Turobin, one of the hundreds of Jewish towns scattered around Poland, where I had fled to from the Warsaw ghetto, the strong arm of the Germans was not felt. Getting to the town was difficult, as it was far from the railroad and the road, and in winter, it was completely cut off from the outside world. At the same time that so many people were dying daily in the ghetto, life went on as usual in Turobin — shoemakers made boots for farmers, tailors made them coats; my Uncle Michael traveled around the village, walking stick in hand to chase away the farmers' dogs, selling notions. The Jews of the town continued to pray each morning in their synagogue. There was poverty, but no one was starving. The Germans forced the villages to supply them with a quantity of gold or merchandise such as leather or pelts, and threatened them if they refused — and the rich complained, but they paid. From time to time, the Germans imposed compulsory work details and later, the SS passed through the village and killed dozens of Jews for no reason, but life had somehow returned to normal. No one in Turobin, or in the many similar villages, could imagine that their days were numbered, that the Germans were going to kill all of the Jews without exception — could a normal human being imagine such a thing?

And when we were stuffed into boxcars, suffering in subhuman conditions on the way to the extermination camp Sobibor, someone had said, "Thank God, we are going eastward! They are apparently taking us to the Ukraine, and not to Lublin, to Maidanek, which is rumored to be a terrible place." And on the way, when people collapsed of suffocation, and we were confused and frightened of what was to come, still, no one had supposed that in a few hours, all the women and children would be lying dead in gas chambers.

And in Sobibor, when the doors of the boxcar had finally opened and we could breathe fresh air again, the Germans had stunned us with shouts and blows...then they had taken the women and children and disappeared with them into the forest... For some days we had hoped that they were still alive; we were still unable to fathom that we were actually in an extermination camp. Prisoners working in the forest said that they had heard the voices of people and children crying from within the forest, which we interpreted as evidence that they were still alive; only after some time did we understand that these were voices of people burying corpses...

The more I thought about those days, trying to reconstruct our situation as it had been then, without the benefit of the knowledge we had now, the more I tried to recreate and relive the past, the more I saw the trial as an act of foolishness. Jews were murdered during the Holocaust through no fault of their own — and we were going to grope through the past, investigate whether their behavior had been "correct"? Who had the right to determine what their behavior should have been? Who could judge how a human being, hungry day and night for months, for years, should act? Who could say what a man or woman standing at the entrance to the gas chamber or before a firing squad should do? What were the criteria for evaluating courage? Should men have fled to the forests, to the partisans at the price of leaving their wives and children to their fates? Did that take greater courage than standing by their sides as they trudged to the gas chambers?

Judging by the disagreements that broke out between my friends and me, I came to the conclusion that there was a great divide between us. No explanation could bridge the gap — no one who hadn't undergone these experiences would ever understand. All of my efforts at explanation were rejected — was it my inability to express my thoughts? How could I explain that the standards and rules existing in normal times were not applicable to "there"? In the ghetto and in the camps, rules of behavior evolved which were suited to the situation, and people behaved according to these. It was completely clear who was living according to the rules and who was not, and each man was judged by society in conformity with his behavior.

The day of the trial was nearing, but as it approached, our kibbutz members recoiled more and more from bringing the subject up for discussion. They were tired of the stormy arguments and, deep inside, they wanted to keep postponing the trial until it would be forgotten and ultimately canceled. But to cancel the trial completely after we had made the decision to hold it was impossible. Thus, on the scheduled evening, all of the members of the kibbutz gathered in the dining hall along with some guests from outside the kibbutz.

The argument of the prosecution was restrained. Yitzchak emphasized the possibilities for Jews of the Volin ghetto to leave and to join partisan units that were operating in the area, possibilities that very few took advantage of, and in contrast, he spoke of the important activities of Jews who had joined the partisans, making the implicit contrast of those who were willing to fight and those who weren't.

When I stood up to address the audience, I again felt the divide yawning between us. I felt to my very core that what I had been through was something utterly foreign to them, something beyond their ken; it was useless to try to describe it. Despite all my thought, I couldn't find the right words, I had difficulty deciding which event among all I had experienced to relate. Everything I could think of suddenly seemed inconsequential; my friends would never be convinced by my account. I briefly summarized the situation of the Jews in Poland at the beginning of the war, but then I suddenly jumped to another subject, and then skipped from one subject to another without fully explaining anything. I felt that no one could really understand what I was saying, and that the attention they were paying me only attested to their patience. I swiftly described, in a few words, the war years, as though something was impelling me to finish quickly, and it was only when I turned to the rebellion at Sobibor and the flight into the forests that I became more detailed and I spoke at length. Suddenly I was aware that I had established contact with my listeners, as if I had only now begun to speak in a language that everyone understood. I spoke of the uprising in great detail, and as I completed my speech, there was applause.

In spite of the fact that my friends offered me compliments, I knew that I had failed to accomplish the task I had set out for myself. I was furious at myself for not being able to explain the mass suffering and the noble behavior in difficult times. I promised myself that never again would I take upon myself tasks that I was unable to carry out.

The trial was over. The heavy atmosphere of uneasiness that had permeated the kibbutz as a result of our grappling with our open wounds was soon replaced by merriment — the Purim holiday was approaching, and we began to make our preparations. Everyone was discussing the upcoming party and deciding on costumes to wear. The cultural committee decided that we would put on a comedy written by Shalom Aleichem as the centerpiece for the party. I was given the main part, the *shadchan* (marriage broker). I accepted the part although I had no idea how to act and had never before appeared in a play. We put great effort into the play, holding dozens of rehearsals. Purim arrived, and the Purim party, and as always we had invited many people from outside the kibbutz and the hall was full.

After a good meal and unlimited drinking, Yankel, our director, introduced the play and the curtain went up. I appeared on the stage as the marriage broker of the town, dressed in a *kapote* and a wrinkled top hat atop my head, an umbrella in my hand and a pointed beard on my chin, and my appearance amused the audience. I took my watch out of an inner pocket and stared at it as if I was waiting impatiently, and I felt the expectation of the watching crowd. There was a knock at the door. Paula, who played the servant, entered the room. She only had five words to say — "Reb *Shadchan*, the groom has arrived!" — but someone in the audience caused her to burst into uncontrollable laughter, which infected the audience. The groom, Yoash, came on stage and saw Paula laughing, and began to laugh, as well. Sarah, who was supposed to come on stage next, left in anger, and that was the end of our first performance. But we didn't give up. A short time later, we performed for the other kibbutzim in the area with great success.

Life in the isolated town, in a community of people whose situation was similar to mine, influenced me for the better by filling my life with positive activity. However, I sometimes felt caged in, that I was living a life I had chosen out of fear of being exposed to and dealing with reality. From time to time, kibbutz members traveled to visit relatives and friends in a variety of places in Germany. I had nowhere to go. So when our kibbutz general secretary asked me to travel to Munich for some errand at the central chapter of our movement, I immediately agreed.

One afternoon, I left Schesslitz by local train to Bamberg. It was stormy and in the train, consisting of four tiny cars, there were no more than ten people. Snow mixed with rain was falling and strong winds bent the tops of the trees. From the window of the tiny train we seemed to be traveling through a whirlpool into an abyss. From Bamberg, I continued on to Nuremberg on a regular train. The strangers I was traveling with and the changing scenes didn't disturb me. The opposite was true — they gave me the isolation to be with my own thoughts, to ponder and to dream.

So, in a railroad car filled with Germans, on the way to Nuremberg, I took stock of my situation. I thought of all the beloved friends I had left behind in Poland. How they had disappeared from my thoughts... Yozhik, from whom I thought I could not conceive of being separated — what was he doing now? And what about Semmen? Would the three of us ever meet again? I remembered Harry and Ola, Mrs. Shumanski, Maria from the factory, Zoshia and her shining eyes, and Helena, the lovely village girl. I had loved them all, and they had loved me, but I had left them behind and had almost forgotten them. When I was reminiscing about the girls that I had loved in Poland, I realized that from the liberation until I had left for Germany I had always been in love with someone; and now, for the past year, I hadn't fallen in love with any of the girls I had met.

I was on good terms with all of the girls in our kibbutz. I had even spent time with a few here and there and had felt that they were attracted to me, but none of them had managed to capture my heart. Undeniably, there had been one who had caused me excitement and insomnia: Sarah, the beautiful girl who had arrived with her mother and her brother, but my friend Nachum had won her and I had given up, ending my attempts to be near her. But when I saw her from time to time, my heart would still pound. Recently, the relationship between Sarah and Nachum had seemed to have hit a snag. Nachum had found out that his father was still alive, in Poland. He was planning to immigrate to the United States, and Nachum was considering going with him. As a friend of them both, I was aware of the problems this move would cause them. As I was trying to help them get over these problems, somehow Sarah and I had become closer. Now, in the train, I began to think that maybe Sarah and I were moving toward something more than just friendship.

The train arrived at the Nuremberg station, where I had to change to the train to Munich, and I entered a crowded car. I sat between a heavy woman, in her thirties, and an older man. In the aisle between the benches, people were standing crushed together, so that I couldn't move my feet. During the first few moments I enjoyed the warmth that enveloped me, as though I had gotten into bed and was lying between blankets. After a short time, however, I felt pressed in on all sides. I could only move my head. Strange, horrible odors filled my nostrils. I was afraid to move my limbs. I felt like a brick in a pyramid — if I moved, I would undermine the whole structure. I became tired and fell asleep, awakening from time to time. Every so often I tried to change my position, as did my neighbors. The head of the older man fell onto my shoulder at times, and the weight of his body pushed me into my neighbor on the other side. I couldn't push him back; he just pushed me away. I finally fell into a deep sleep, and I must have slept for a long time, for when I woke up when the train stopped at one of the stations, I found myself leaning on my neighbor, my head on her shoulder. I immediately sat up straight and looked at her. At first, I thought she was asleep, but her eyes were wide open and she smiled at me warmly. Before we got off the train she asked me if I was an *Auslander* — a foreigner. "Yes," I answered, "and I am Jewish." She looked at me and invited me to have a cup of coffee at her home. I politely refused.

When I left the train station in Munich, it was not yet light. I had two addresses: one, of the movement's main office, to which I had been sent, and the second, of Berale, from Berlin. He hadn't wanted to join the kibbutz, but often visited us and had invited me to be his guest. As it was too early for visitors, I remained in the vicinity of the station, observing the awakening city, and finally entered a café. A waitress approached me. I asked for coffee and cake. "With or without butter?" she asked me, and explained that if I wanted cake made with butter, I had to give her a butter coupon from my food card. I said that I had no food card, but I was ready to pay. She thought for a moment and agreed. The coffee was tasteless, the cake inedible. The events of my trip, from its beginning in the storm and up to the smile of the woman on whose shoulder I had awakened seemed a nightmare to me. What a stupid thing I had done in accepting this errand!

The movement's main office hummed like a beehive with so many busy people, hurrying from room to room. Some of the employees who had visited our kibbutz recognized me, welcomed me happily and invited me for breakfast. I heard that progress was being made, and things were not stagnating, as it had seemed to us on the kibbutz. Groups of movement members were leaving Germany on their way to the ports of southern Italy and France, where they were getting on illegal immigration ships sailing eastward, trying to avoid the sea blockade that Britain had imposed on Israeli seaports; when they caught a ship with illegal immigrants, they sent them to DP camps in Cyprus.

I was supposed to take material to bring back to the secretariat of our kibbutz, and I had to wait until late afternoon to get it. As I didn't want to make the return journey traveling all night, I decided to sleep at Berale's home. When I reached the house where he lived, which was located in an older neighborhood of four-story buildings, an old woman with a serious face opened the door of the apartment and told me that Berale had not come home yet. I went downstairs, considering whether I should wait for him or go back to the railroad station. Night had fallen, and while I was pacing back and forth, trying to decide, I heard Berale's hoarse voice from afar. He was approaching his house, accompanied by a girl of about fourteen or fifteen, and when he saw me, he ran up to me and hugged me, and then introduced me to the girl. The three of us went up to his rented room in the old woman's apartment. The room wasn't large, but it was completely filled with furniture, pictures, other items and a wide, nickel-plated iron bed.

The girl, whispering something to Berale so that I couldn't hear, looked angry, but then the two of them laughed. In the electric light the girl seemed a bit older, perhaps seventeen. She was pretty, but neglected; her dress was too short and narrow, old and cheap, her shoes were old and the heels were bent. I understood that I had done the wrong thing by arriving unexpectedly, so I told Berale that I had just come to see him and that I planned to leave this evening.

Berale started laughing. "You're not going anywhere," he replied. "You're staying here tonight. The bed is wide enough for the three of us. A minute ago I had problems with her, and now you're giving me problems?" Berale's sleeping plans were not acceptable to me — we would both be sleeping in his bed with the girl between us? After a short argument, Berale agreed to let me sleep on the floor. He made us dinner and put a bottle of vodka on the table. The girl ate quickly and managed to swallow a remarkable quantity of food; I got the impression that she had been hungry for a long time. I was more affected by the drink than usual, perhaps because of my exhaustion. When we had finished the bottle, the three of us were drunk and we were overwhelmed by waves of laughter. Berale suggested going to bed; the girl went to the bathroom, and I got undressed and climbed into bed. When the girl returned, Berale told me to go to the bathroom and to wait until he called me, and when I returned he got up and left the room. The girl came up to me, her body burning. For a few minutes, I forgot about the world around me. Afterward, I was attacked by a wave of exhaustion, but the girl lay close to me and didn't let me sleep, wanting more and more.

When I awoke, Berale and the girl were sitting at the table and eating breakfast. The girl said in German, "Good morning, my love." The German words were like a sword stabbing my heart. I felt like a traitor.

The entire way home from Berale's house, thoughts of the previous night disturbed me. How could I forget everything and have relations with such ardor with a German girl? I, who had condemned those boys who went out with German girls, who had sworn to myself that I would never have any contact with German women, had forgotten everything. I had held a German girl in my arms and had had the greatest of pleasure with her! I tried to console myself with the excuse that I had been drunk, but I had to admit that even though my head had not been completely clear, I hadn't forgotten any detail of the previous night. On the other hand, I asked myself, why did I want to be different from the rest? Boys whose past was similar to mine, whose entire families were killed by Germans, were having fun with German girls, and their consciences were not bothering them...or were they? In any case, I was ashamed of what I had done, and I promised myself not to get too near German girls.

After the trip to Munich, I went on additional errands here and there, to Munich again and to other cities. Although it was always difficult, and each journey made me promise myself that it was the last, I always agreed to any suggestion to get out, as the aspect of adventure continued to attract me.

Spring arrived. Nature thawed from its freeze, and we absorbed the beauty that heralds life and continuity. Hearts were filled with gaiety. Two years had passed since the end of the war, and nations that had known suffering and destruction were rebuilding; ruins were being cleared away and new houses were being built, more beautiful ones, with the security that no one would destroy them in the near future. The defeated Germans, whose country had been divided among the four conquering allies, were rehabilitating their lives, with the help of those who had defeated them and who now had nothing to fear. Millions of German refugees and displaced persons, who had found themselves scattered throughout Europe, had returned, for the most part, to their homes. It was the Jews who had managed to survive — a small number in comparison to the millions of Jews who had been obliterated from the earth — who were still suffering. They were living in DP camps, mostly in Germany and Austria, among their murderers, not far from the concentration camps where they had spent the war years, and were living in subhuman conditions, with no privacy, with no possibility of beginning new lives, waiting for the day when they would leave for Israel.

But the British had locked the gates. Their large war fleet had one more assignment — to prevent illegal immigrant ships from reaching Israel. The British Intelligence system had one more mission — to discover when and where a ship carrying these refugees would approach the shore.

The heavy hand of the British and the exile to Cyprus of the immigrants they caught did not deter us. We had nothing to lose. We were determined to struggle until the end. Instead of remaining in DP camps in Germany, the illegal immigrants had been moved eastward — to DP camps in Cyprus, where the living conditions were far worse than those of German DP camps, where they became prisoners of the large British army who guarded them.

In the kibbutz, we continued to raise animals and to till the soil. Emissaries from Israel continued to teach us patriotic songs and tell us about the land we were hoping to reach, but, all this time, we had been preparing for immigration at an increased pace. We had already purchased the machinery and equipment for the carpentry and metal shops to be set up when the kibbutz members reached

Israel. With the money that our hard work earned us, we ordered clothing and high quality boots for our members. We sensed that our time to immigrate was drawing near.

My relationship with Sarah became closer, and soon we were lovers. In our nights together, we could not be satiated, and we dreamed of setting up a family in Israel. For the first time in my life, I felt that a loving partner was giving me undivided attention. It was wonderful to return to my room and to find the signs of her love — a few flowers in a cup, a package of ironed laundry on my bed, no shirt missing a button, every sock darned. But Sarah, from the moment that she was completely mine, demanded that I would be completely hers, and in those wonderful days of love, I suddenly felt that I was losing my liberty — I was distanced from friends, I stopped participating in the activities I loved so much, and each night after dinner, the two of us would leave the dining hall to be alone together. But I wanted both love and freedom. I enjoyed my relations with my friends; I still wanted to be involved in everything. From time to time, I tried to break the wall that I had erected, but this was always at the price of a quarrel.

One evening in the dining hall, while I was sitting and playing chess, Sarah came up to me and suggested that we go outside. I replied, "Wait a few minutes. I'm almost finished," but I was so involved in the game that I forgot everything else. Sarah returned and reminded me that she was waiting for me and I again sent her off, with "Soon," and again became involved in the game. She lost patience and she left the dining hall angrily. When I had finished the game, I hurried to her and found her sad and disappointed. It took me a long time to placate her, before we again knew moments of happiness in each other's arms.

On one of our enchanted nights, on a bench that stood under a tree, Sarah related to me her family history. Their city, Brisk, was only in German hands for a short time; it was quickly granted to the Soviet Union when Poland was split up between the Germans and the Soviets. Sarah's father, a Zionist leader, was arrested by the KGB with other Jewish leaders, Zionist and non-Zionist, and all of them were sent off to who-knows-where. Shortly after that, the Soviets rounded up the families of the prisoners and transferred them to Siberia, where they settled them in an isolated town, and still, nothing was known of the men who had been arrested. Two years later, all of the men except for one, who had disappeared with no trace and was probably dead, were released to join their families in Siberia. After some time, they were arrested again, this time along with some of their wives. When the war ended, they were permitted to leave Russia and were repatriated to Poland.

My friend Eliezer and I were chosen to participate in a movement leadership seminar that was to take place in Munchberg, not far from Nuremberg. I was glad to have been chosen. I couldn't give up participating in the seminar, but my separation from Sarah was difficult. The two of us were tense and sad as though we had been sentenced never to see each other again.

The seminar was led by soldiers of the "Brigade," Zvi Gershoni of Kibbutz Nir-Am, and the poet Michael Deshe, both of whom established an atmosphere of comradeship. Others also helped run the seminar, and we studied about Israel and Zionism from every aspect. In addition, we went on hikes and learned to find our way in the fields and we improved our physical fitness. When I returned from the seminar to the kibbutz, I found Sarah full of pain and happiness, and again, we experienced wonderful days, new heights of love. But not for long: I was soon chosen to accompany another kibbutz member, Anshel, to the city of Buchholz, in the British sector of Germany — near the border with the Netherlands — where there was a transit camp for people with permits to enter Israel. The camp was also used as a transit point for equipment and other articles being sent to Israel. We were told that our job was to assist with the sending of the kibbutz equipment and to make sure that it passed through British inspection procedures. I didn't quite understand how we could help, but I didn't ask questions. We were told that our tasks would be explained, and our contact person would determine when we could return to the kibbutz.

Near Buchholz, there was a British army camp with a sign over the entrance: "Palestine Transit Camp." There were storehouses and many offices in the camp. Next to it, there was a small camp of wooden shacks where Jews were waiting their turn to travel to Israel. We found the representative we had been told about, and we were housed in this camp. He grilled us about who we were and he announced that, from now on, we would be porters and we would work on his orders. I protested that we had come to send our equipment to Israel, and he replied that he knew very well why we had come, but that our equipment would have to wait and, in the meanwhile, we would work as porters or the British would hire Germans. This was undesirable as the work was very important and required secrecy.

The atmosphere in the camp was official and tense. Many British soldiers were about, and we got the feeling that they were watching us closely. Even though I was not there alone, I felt lonely and foreign. Conditions were awful; the food was awful, as well, and the portions small; the yellow cornbread they gave us was disgusting. I missed Sarah, the merriment of kibbutz life, activities, friends and good meals. In the evenings, I yearned for Sarah so much I was unable to read a book or fall asleep.

Twice a week, British officers came to the camp, and, at their command, we had to open crates for a check of the contents. After checking the equipment was passed to the other side of the shed, where a partition separated the checked from the unchecked crates, and the checked crates were then loaded onto trucks. We soon realized that we were participating in a smuggling operation of the Haganah, which was being coordinated by the man in charge of us, but we still didn't know exactly what our role was. Our commander knew the British inspection procedures so well that although the officers assumed that they were the ones choosing which crates to be checked, in actuality, we were the ones choosing the crates which were opened. We had learned to read every hint given by our commander and we knew which crates to move nearer to the British, and which to move away. Our commander made it clear to us that this operation would serve Jewish settlement in Israel. At the end of a successful day of smuggling, he would bring us good cigarettes, and sometimes we would have a drink in honor of the Jewish settlement of Israel, to the success of the Haganah and its Palmach units, and to the success of our work.

One evening, our commander came and took us to his room, where he told us that he had to speak to us about a matter of utmost secrecy. "Until now," he said, "you've helped a great deal by smuggling arms to defend Jewish settlement, and I am very pleased with your work. Most importantly, you do what you have to do without asking questions. Until now you have been smuggling on a small scale, because we couldn't endanger this important route. But the struggle between the Jews, the British and the Arabs is growing more intense from day to day and there is a great shortage of decent weapons. Every piece that we succeed in sending increases our strength. So, it has been decided to send a relatively large shipment. I've already planned how to do it, but I need your help. However, I must warn you that there is some danger in this plan for all of us. If the British catch us, we may find ourselves in prison. So you must decide whether you agree to participate in this mission or not."

There was silence in the room. I lit a cigarette to gain time. What had I had gotten myself mixed up in? I had read somewhere that the English sent their prisoners to prisons on isolated islands in the ocean. Instead of getting to Israel, I might find myself in some jungle on a godforsaken island off the coast of Africa. A chill went through me. Why did it have to be me? On the other hand, how could I refuse? The two of us were chosen for this mission because they completely trusted us to do whatever we were called upon to do. Could I return to the kibbutz and say, "I came back because I was afraid to do what they asked of me"?

I looked into Anshel's eyes. He looked tormented, as though he were suffering from an unbearable stomachache. His eyes seemed to be asking for help. I knew him well; I knew that he would do as I did. In the end, after a long silence, I answered, "I agree." Anshel looked at me and said, "I do, too." "Very good," said our commander. "I knew you would agree." The tension broke at once. Self-confidence took the place of fear. We smiled at each other. The commander explained his plan in detail: we would have to pass several crates of agricultural machinery through the checkpoint, but inside the crates, there would also be very important items for the Haganah. "On Sunday," he said, "the storeroom is closed. The English have a day off and only one English soldier guards the storeroom and a few other sheds. On Saturday night, we will steal into the storeroom. That won't be difficult, I've already done it several times. You will enter through the window, which won't be locked. We will do nothing that night, because it is very quiet and any noise we make can be heard from outside. We'll wait until morning, and then we'll take apart a section of the partition dividing the two parts of the shed — the part with crates that haven't been checked and those which have been checked. We'll transfer our crates to the checked area, we'll reassemble the partition, and in the evening, in darkness, we'll leave the shed. Do you have any questions?"

Anshel asked what would happen if the British caught us. The man smiled and responded, "It will be bad. You don't know very much, and since you haven't asked questions you won't be able to tell very much to the British. Tell them that you don't know anything. You worked for me and you did what I asked you to do… I hope that everything will go well. Today is Friday. We will begin tomorrow evening."

We went back to our rooms. Through the wall, I could hear our neighbor saying Kiddush in a tune I recognized, which reminded me of my father. I remembered Sabbath eve in our home in Lodz, all of us seated around the long table. Only now could I feel the atmosphere of holiness that had surrounded us in those moments, the divine spirit hovering over our home. I saw my father and mother, glowing with happiness. I wanted the image to remain, not to disappear, to experience more and more of that happiness, but my thoughts led me down the path of torment of the war years, and I wasn't able to re-create the image of Friday nights in our home.

My memories plunged me into the depths of the Holocaust. Such a short time had passed since these horrors had taken place, yet it was difficult for me to believe that it had all actually happened, and even harder to believe that I had remained alive. I didn't understand how I was supposed to go on living completely alone, with no member of my family; it would appear that I simply did not understand anything about the essence of life. My thoughts quickly passed on to what we were going to do the following evening and my heart began to pound. I feared that we would fail and I already saw myself taken by the British and sent to one of their territories, to rot in jail.

The next evening we went out to the storeroom. We stopped at the fence, close to our objective, and our commander told us to lie down. There was an opening in the fence that he had obviously prepared in advance. We heard the steps of the guard. When we saw him walking away, our commander told us to crawl through the opening and to climb into the storeroom through the window. Within a minute, I was inside. Anshel came after me, and then the commander. We made room for ourselves among the crates, and I was glad that, in the darkness, no one could see my pale face. Outside, I could hear the guard walking back and forth. Eventually, the sounds that were coming from outside silenced, and I finally fell asleep.

The world had awakened. In spite of the fact that it was Sunday, we heard noises — the sound of motors and work tools, the crying of babies, the songs of children, and all these merged into one unceasing, monotonous sound.

We went to work; two of us worked, and one guarded. We removed a wooden board that was nailed to the wooden frame of the partition and then we took off some parts of the frame, as well, which were attached with screws and nails. A few screws came out easily; others were more difficult to remove as they were more deeply embedded in the wood. We couldn't use a hammer, of course, so we made small holes around the heads of the screws with knives so that we could pull them out with pliers. We gathered every sliver so there would be no sign of our work.

Time flew by. After a few hours of work, we had succeeded in taking apart a section of the partition and we could pass anything from one side to another as we pleased. After arduous, uninterrupted work, making every attempt to be as quiet as possible, we had transferred all of "our" crates and placed them among the crates that had already been opened. We then reconstructed the partition. Only when we were finished did we realize that we had worked all day without a break — we hadn't been aware of the time passing. Tired and hungry, we slipped out of the storeroom in darkness, left our commander and returned to our room. I fell asleep with the wonderful feeling of having done something for our country.

That night, I dreamed that Anshel and I were working in the storeroom. There were many British soldiers around us. An officer called me over and ordered me to open one of the crates. I was afraid that the arms would be discovered and I was looking for a way to escape. While the British were talking among themselves, I jumped out of the window, but I couldn't find the opening in the fence. I ran to the back of the shed and suddenly realized that I was in Sobibor, near the Ukrainian barracks. I hid so that the Ukrainians wouldn't see me, as they knew me and would certainly ask where I had been. I didn't understand what I was doing in Sobibor. I had to escape and I ran frantically about the camp. The air was smoky; I smelled the odor of the burning bodies. I saw members of the kibbutz digging a pit and wondered if the Germans had been able to put them in Sobibor, as well. I ran, and then suddenly I found myself near the gas chambers. I turned right and ran straight into the fence, where Wagner appeared in front of me as though he had popped up from under the ground. When I saw him, I knew that all was lost. My strength failed me. I stood frozen to the ground and my legs were paralyzed. I couldn't move. Wagner stood opposite me, his eyes gleaming with anger. Slowly he took out his pistol from its holster and cocked it. I wanted to run away, but my legs wouldn't move. I wanted to tell Wagner that the Germans had lost the war and that his end would be bitter, but I couldn't utter a sound. I saw Wagner aim the gun at me and fire…

At that moment, I awoke, my heart beating like a hammer inside my chest. I was shaking. I sat on my bed and looked around to reassure myself that I was not in Sobibor, that I was still alive. As usual, I was afraid to go back to sleep, afraid that I would dream of Sobibor again. The nightmare destroyed my good humor. Even though it wasn't real, it still had the same effect on me: the images of the dream did not go away; and once again I interpreted this dream as a reminder that I belonged "there," that my place was among the dead; my staying alive was a fluke. I was overwhelmed with shame for being alive when all of the others were dead, feeling that I had betrayed them. Again I was accosted by doubts about being alive. I imagined that death was waiting for me somewhere in the corner.

One morning a pounding on the door awakened us. In the doorway stood Shmilka, the kibbutz's German driver. He told us that that evening the whole kibbutz was leaving Schesslitz, and he had been sent especially to Buchholz to bring us back immediately. He had spent the whole night driving and now he wanted to sleep, but only for an hour — we had to leave for our long journey soon, otherwise we wouldn't get there in time and our friends would leave without us.

We were extremely happy. The day had come when we would leave Germany to immigrate to Israel. We ran to tell our commander from the Haganah about our leaving and to say goodbye. He thanked us for our good work and hoped to meet us again in Israel. Shmilka put his foot hard on the accelerator, and the little old kibbutz car raced ahead as its driver requested, doing its best to cooperate so we would reach Schesslitz in time, but it was a hot day, and we were forced to stop several times to let the motor or the wheels cool down. We reached the kibbutz in the late evening, and as we were getting out of the car, we heard someone shout, "They've arrived!" followed by a shout of general happiness from everyone, as they accosted us with hugs and kisses. It was wonderful to come home, to people who cared for you.

We entered the dining hall, accompanied by our friends, and I looked for Sarah, but didn't see her at first. She suddenly appeared at the door to the kitchen. She looked at me and quickly disappeared. I left my friends and hurried to the kitchen and I saw Sarah standing by the window, tears falling from her eyes. I hugged her tightly, and for a few minutes we stood without moving, pain and happiness filling our souls and our bodies and uniting us as a single being. The color came back into her cheeks, her face relaxed and a smile appeared in her eyes. Hypnotized by her face, I forgot the world around us. But Sarah brought me back to reality, reminding me that we were about to leave the village in a short time; she had packed my bag — all of my clothes had been laundered and ironed. She sat Anshel and me down at the table and placed a delicious meal in front of us, the remains of the feast that the kibbutz members had prepared after they had slaughtered all of the chickens in the henhouse and emptied the kibbutz storeroom of food. In Buchholz, we hadn't had one decent meal.

We were soon called to get into trucks, which were waiting for us, everyone dressed in dark green clothing and all of us wearing the same boots, while each of us carried his own knapsack. The convoy started moving as the motors snorted and disturbed the quiet of the village. Just as we had arrived in the village of Schesslitz at night, when the village was sleeping, so we left it. It was night and the main street was completely empty. Only Rexie, our dog, ran after the trucks for a long while.

The period of relaxation, the period of peacefulness and lack of worry, of release from the nightmares of the past and fear of the future, of the unashamed return to the adventures of childhood, was over. The kibbutz in Schesslitz was a rest home after a serious illness, a transit point before dealing with the life awaiting us. We knew that we were not leaving for a vacation trip, as the journey would be long and difficult, and marked by dangers. We knew, as well, that life in Israel would be difficult. But the strong desire to live in our own land, our belief that we were doing the right thing, our certainty that there was no other path open to us, strengthened us in our confidence that no obstacle would stop us from reaching the Land of Israel.

# Salon, Near Marseilles

## June 1947

After a few hours of traveling, we stopped at a DP camp near the city of Ulm, where we were placed in a large hall. More and more trucks arrived from all parts of Germany and discharged groups of immigrants — kibbutz members, residents of orphanages, organized groups from a variety of refugee camps. No one knew exactly what would be done with us or where we were headed. The only thing that was clear was that we would not spend much time in this hall, as no arrangements had been made for us. So many immigrants arrived over the course of the day that it appeared that every Jew in Germany had been organized and sent here. The men of the *Bricha* coordinated the operation with impressive order. Group after group was assembled at the side of the road, food was distributed quickly, and each of us received a new identity card with a fictitious name. We were told to memorize the names and other details on the card. To my great surprise, my new identity was that of a woman, Rachel Garka, and although I tried to exchange my card for one with a masculine name, I was unsuccessful.

All day long trucks had been entering the camp and now dozens were parked in a long line. When night fell, we boarded the trucks and began to travel, accompanied by motorcyclists who whizzed back and forth along the line of trucks and lent an air of mystery to the operation. I sat with Sarah near the opening of the truck and we held on to each other tightly as we looked out into the night. A full moon was out, sometimes disappearing and then coming out again, and by its light, we could distinguish mountains and a valley and sometimes a river in which it was reflected. The scenery seemed enchanted. When we entered a mountainous area, we could see the curving snake of light from the convoy, crawling here and there against the background of the black mountains. When the convoy of trucks finally stopped, the motorcycle riders told us that we had reached the French border — it was forbidden to get off the truck or to speak.

We were very excited. We were going to enter one of the Allied countries, a land of beauty and romance. Our truck neared the border crossing point and halted. A French border policeman peered inside the truck with flashlights, wrote something down, and gave us a sign to continue. We had left Germany and, at that moment, I promised myself never to set foot on German soil again.

I looked for indications that we were in another country, but the moon had disappeared and in the dark, we couldn't see anything. Even so, it seemed to me that there was a different scent wafting in from the fields. In the light from the headlights we could see that the French road was as narrow and full of potholes as the German road had been. Suddenly the convoy stopped, and a motorcyclist braked next to us and asked if there was a doctor among us. Although the journey was being carried out carefully and methodically, a fatal accident had occurred: a boy in one of the trucks had leaned out of the back and the truck following behind had crushed his head, killing him. After a short time back on the road, we were stopped again; this time, a large truck was blocking the road. The French truck drivers were on strike at the time, and although our convoy had received special permission from their union to pass, the driver of the French truck was drunk and wouldn't listen to anything that was said. In the end, there was no choice but to take the keys of his truck by force and to move it off the road. The French driver resisted and finally our people were forced to beat him.

At midnight, we stopped at the railway station of Strasbourg, where we got out of the trucks, shivering in the cold night air that penetrated our bones. The light of the station blinded us. A long table had been set up inside the station, and men and women, nicely dressed, gave us hot cocoa and fresh sandwiches. The cocoa, and even more so the knowledge that someone was caring for us — one of the women urged us on, saying, "*Es, es, kinderlach* (Eat, eat, children)" — warmed our hearts. Near one of the platforms, a special train was awaiting us and we filled its cars completely. Anyone who couldn't find a seat sat down on the floor of the car, in the entrances and in the passageways. The train left the station and we all fell into a deep sleep.

A new day awakened us: a day on French soil. These were seemingly the same fields, the same patches of forest, the same hills and rivers as in Germany or Poland, but in each of the countries, there was different scenery, and the more I observed the more I could distinguish the differences and the uniqueness. As in my childhood, I still enjoyed watching the changing scenery, the farms and the villages, the people and the farm animals we passed. Sarah's hand rested on mine, and together we looked outside, filled with happiness and optimism, as if our next stop would be the railroad station in Jerusalem.

Everyone in the railroad car was in good humor, and we began to sing loudly. At the Marseilles station, trucks were waiting for us and we left quickly this time, in only two trucks, traveling until we reached the town of Salon. We stopped near a wall. An iron gate creaked open for us and we entered a large yard with a spacious two-story house in the middle, something between a palace and a ruin, and around it, tall trees and greenery growing wildly. Near the house, I could see a fountain with marble stairs leading to it and benches scattered on both sides of the door. Only after some time did we discover that we were staying in a palace that Napoleon had built for one of his mistresses, and he also had stayed here from time to time.

A serious boy of around twenty, named Uzi, gathered us together and told us in broken Yiddish that he was from the Haganah and had been sent from Israel. From now on, we were under his authority, and all of the regulations of the Haganah applied to us, as well. "Soon you will be sailing to Israel," he announced, "but it is not yet possible to determine how long we will have to stay here, and so we will use this time for organization and for training." He emphasized the need for complete secrecy — no one was to leave the yard; it was forbidden to phone outside; it was forbidden to send letters. He read the schedule to us, which included a wake-up hour, physical exercise, meal times, training and lights out. At the end he stated that any member who did not follow orders would be punished according to the regulations of the Haganah.

The young Haganah representative with the Hebrew name, whom we didn't know, and who represented Israel, imposed his authority on us with a few simple words in ungrammatical Yiddish, but his words gained special significance when we looked at his serious and determined face. I understood that my period of freedom had ended. Indeed, we had found ourselves in an army camp, and we were to be turned into disciplined soldiers in the struggle for our future in Israel, with all of the responsibility that entailed. The feeling of responsibility was accompanied by a feeling of pride in belonging to the Haganah.

In an operation unprecedented in its scope, the Haganah had assembled thousands of immigrants in Marseilles and its surroundings, in complete secrecy. They rented any place in which it was possible to hide a group of people and were organized so that they could assemble us quickly and get us onto a boat when the time came, but in the meantime, they prepared us for the difficult journey ahead. The abandoned and unnoticed palace and its large yard surrounded by a wall was an excellent place for training exercises. At first, we worked for a few days cleaning the area and preparing the house to be lived in, and the beauty of the place was unveiled. The schedule was fixed: we were awakened at a very early hour in the morning, we took a morning run around the yard and did physical exercises, learned to stand in formation, had training in self-defense, lectures, meal times and rest hours, and then, lights out — and all under the strict authority of Uzi, who tried to make us conscious of the need for order and discipline.

Uzi told us that we should be ready to move at a moment's notice, and exercised us in formation with loaded knapsacks. One day, one of the young men slipped away and got on a train to Paris to visit his uncle. When he returned two days later, I was envious of him for having seen Paris. Not Uzi. He called us for a special formation and with a face more serious than we had ever seen, he ordered the boy to leave the ranks and to stand aside. He told us that by leaving the camp without permission, he had committed a serious breach of orders, and accused him of treason. Uzi read the relevant clauses from the Haganah by-laws determining that heavy punishments might be imposed in times of emergency, including the death penalty, and he announced that by virtue of his authority as commanding officer of the camp, he imposed expulsion from the camp forever on the person who had committed the offense.

This verdict sounded to me like a death sentence. The boy was ordered to get his things and to leave the place immediately. He passed in front of us carrying his knapsack on his back, his head lowered, and we followed him as though his head were about to be removed by the guillotine. Uzi, who had been sent to Europe, like his comrades, to organize the illegal immigration operation, was not acquainted with people who had been in concentration camps, who had suffered through the Holocaust, and initially he behaved toward us with great severity, as he would have behaved toward military recruits. In time, however, he got to know us, and understood our strong desire to reach Israel and our readiness to do anything demanded of us, and he became closer to us and more lenient.

Inside the palace and in the yard, it was impossible to be alone, and when Sarah and I wanted to be by ourselves, we would slip out of the house after lights out and find a hiding place in the yard, among the bushes. Uzi, who checked the yards every night, passed close by us, shined the flashlight on us, and then continued on. We thought that he hadn't seen us, but the next day he met me and said in a friendly way that he didn't want to see Sarah and me outside the building after hours. I greatly respected Uzi for behaving with tact and not reacting severely to our offense when he found us; but when more serious orders were violated, he reacted with great severity.

One afternoon, Uzi assembled us and announced that within a few hours, that very night, we would embark and sail to Israel. He added with pride that our ship was the largest and fastest of any used in the immigration operation and the number of passengers would be the largest in the history of the operation. If we got into a struggle with the British, we would be able to carry on for a long period of time, and we should consider ourselves lucky that we were sailing on this particular ship. Uzi divided us into several groups and appointed me in charge of one of them. The group leaders were to make sure that everything was in order on the journey to the port, the embarkation and during the voyage.

We all roared with happiness, but in a moment, there was quiet and tension filled the air: What was going to happen? What did he mean by "a large boat with the ability to withstand a struggle"? How would we battle the British on the sea? What would we be fighting with? Would we succeed in reaching Israel or would we be sent to Cyprus?

Everything was vague. We had no idea of what was to happen. But I was not apprehensive; I had blind faith in the Haganah and in Uzi, our commander. I was convinced of the wisdom of the path I had chosen and I didn't allow myself to feel the shadow of a doubt in our ultimate success, just as, in my childhood, I told myself that I could not doubt the existence of God.

Late that night, two trucks entered the yard, one covered and the other open. Sarah and I climbed into the open truck. The road was empty and the trucks traveled with great speed. The cold was unbearable and the wind slashed at our heads. Sarah and I tried unsuccessfully to snuggle together and protect each other from the wind. With morning, we traveled in mist, and the dew in the air drenched us. We came to life when the sun rose, and we finally stopped at the small port of Site, near Marseilles. The trucks approached the pier and we could see a large boat, its lower part iron, its upper part wood; on one deck were small windows in a row, and above, a large black smokestack. When we approached the boat, I tried to tell the young man standing at the gangway that we were a group and we wanted to remain together on the boat. Before I could utter a word, the young man shouted, "*Arein! Arein! Schneller! Schneller!* (Get in! Get in! Faster! Faster!)" put out his hand, and pulled me inside the boat. It was dark inside, and in the narrow passageway stood more young men who urged us to move faster and pushed us toward bunks with shouts of, "Lie down and don't move."

I felt a terrible sense of helplessness and loss of identity. For a moment, I remembered the transports to Sobibor and the shouting of the Germans, but this passed with a feeling of great shame for even having made the association. I picked my head up from my bunk and saw how the boat was filling up. All of my friends had found places near me. With exemplary teamwork, the men of the Palyam, the naval division of the Palmach, filled the ship with 4,500 people, placing them in three-tiered bunks that had been constructed in rows from floor to ceiling with narrow passages in between them. The boat, which had once served as a ferry on the Mississippi River and was meant to hold only a few hundred people, had been purchased by the Jewish Agency and had been prepared especially to serve in the immigration operation. British Intelligence had observed the process of refurbishing the boat with interest. The boat sailed under a Panamanian flag and the Palyam had moved it from port to port to cover its tracks until it had been brought to Site. But the size of the ship meant that it couldn't be hidden, and British Intelligence, which had men stationed at every port in the Mediterranean, had pinpointed it. At this stage, the British government had heavily pressured the French government, threatening to cut off diplomatic relations if it allowed Jewish refugees to sail. The officer in charge of the area had therefore received an order from Paris to prevent the boat from sailing, in spite of the confirmation it had previously issued. But this order had been received when 4,500 people were already on their way to Site, and some of them had already arrived and were on the boat. It was impossible to stop the operation and change plans, and it was decided to continue quickly loading people on board and to find a way to get it out of Site. The Palyam sought and found a navigator who agreed to take the ship out of Site secretly, at midnight, for a large sum of money, half of which he received in advance and the other half to be paid after his work had been completed.

Everyone had embarked that day, the ship was completely filled, and everything was made ready for sailing. In the evening, the captain, "Ike" (Yitzchak Aronowitz), and his men inspected the ship and made sure that everything was in order. Ike, a young Palyam officer, wore shorts, a jacket and a captain's hat, all of which were too big on him. He looked more like a little boy wearing a costume than a real captain, but his serious face and his decisive manner of speaking attested to his status. The passengers, who had received instructions to neither move nor to get out of their bunks until sailing, were disciplined, lay quietly, their heads out, trying to see what was going on.

The Palyam waited in vain for the French navigator, and finally went to find him, with no luck. He had disappeared with the money he received. The commanders of the operation had a difficult choice to make; it was very logical to assume that if the ship didn't sail that night, it would never be permitted to sail. Removing the passengers from the ship and sending them back to the camps would cause them emotional distress and would harm the entire immigration operation irreparably. On the other hand, leaving the port without the aid of a navigator was considered dangerous and almost impossible, as the boat might run into an obstacle and be damaged. Finally, it was decided: Ike, the captain, would himself navigate out of the port, taking a heavy responsibility on his young shoulders.

Those of us below deck knew nothing of the drama that was taking place above us. We only knew that we weren't sailing, and

we could see the worry and tension on the faces of the leadership
and the crew. Finally, when the nature of the situation was revealed
to us, we feared a return to Salon, or even to Germany. But now the
heavy motors were humming, motors that had been made especially for the ship to increase its speed and maneuverability. The
anchor was raised and in a few nerve-wrenching minutes, we heard
the ship clanking, its sides ramming the walls of the underwater
pier, each collision rocking the ship. We moved forward, backward,
and then forward again. Looking through one of the narrow windows I saw how the ship seemed to be struggling like an animal
attempting to escape from a cage. We were struggling against time,
as well. We could only leave the port at night, while the coast guard,
the police and the port crew were asleep, thinking that the ship
would never put out to open sea without a navigator. Suddenly the
ship picked up speed and went forward quietly, before the sun rose
— we had safely left the port, which was disappearing behind us.
We were in open sea. I heard the laughter from the crew on deck.
They were drinking "*l'chaim.*"

# *Exodus* 1947

## July 1947—December 1947

Hebrew songs broadcast over the loudspeakers awakened me. Dawn was breaking on the horizon. The ship, rocking from side to side, made me feel as if I were drunk. The rays of the sun penetrated the small windows. I looked out and saw only sea and sky. The songs stopped, and an announcer requested that we listen to the instructions of the Haganah. A voice welcomed the new immigrants and told us animatedly of the obstacles that we had faced on our way to Israel, about the British efforts to prevent our sailing, and the success of Captain Ike in navigating the ship out of the port. We burst into applause and the excited voice explained that our ship, the *Exodus (Yetziat Europa* in Hebrew), sailing under the command of the Haganah, was the largest vessel, with the most immigrants aboard, since the *Aliyah Bet* operation had begun. The announcement ended with the playing of *Hatikvah* and we all joined in, singing loudly.

I felt uplifted. Every word that the announcer said seemed to have come from the depths of my heart. We were still avidly discussing the events of the night before when we heard the drone of a plane flying overhead, circling around, and then going over us again, this time flying very low. The plane repeated this several times and then flew off. It had borne the emblem of the RAF, and there was no doubt that it had been photographing us. The British were aware of our location and weren't about to leave us alone, but nevertheless the atmosphere on board was wonderful. Their efforts to stop us had failed: we had successfully left the port.

The loudspeakers announced orders for the use of bathing facilities and toilets. People began to accustom themselves to the especially difficult conditions; they went to wash up and arrange their bunks for an extended stay. A group of young people was called on to do various jobs, and here and there faces became pale as they succumbed to seasickness. After a few hours had passed, we saw a ship approaching us at great speed. So many people rushed to see the approaching ship that our vessel listed to the side, the water line almost reaching the small windows. Over the loudspeaker the order quickly came to return to our places, and the ship stabilized. In the meantime, the other ship had drawn closer and we saw that it was a British destroyer, silver, with cannons and machine guns prominently on deck. The destroyer slowed its pace and sailed parallel to our ship, at a distance of a few hundred meters, as though it were tied to us with a rope. "That destroyer won't leave us," said one of the crew. "She'll accompany us to Israel."

From the first day we set sail we were guarded by the British against the possibility of escape, but this didn't overly concern us. We were filled with a blind optimism that stemmed from our belief in the justice of our objectives, justice that was bound to triumph.

The waves that came in the wake of the big destroyer disturbed us; our ship, which was top-heavy, began to rock back and forth like a cradle. Many of us felt ill and ran to the railing to throw up, and those who couldn't make it to the sides vomited on the way, or in their places. People lay helplessly on their bunks, sighing and groaning. I prayed that I wouldn't get seasick, but that afternoon I, too, felt nauseated, had a stomachache, and was dizzy. The ship continued to list from side to side — one moment we could see only water, the next only sky. When I was called to the upper deck for a group leader briefing, I told myself that I had to overcome my nausea. I went up to the deck, my head spinning and my legs trembling, trying to avoid people, who might see me and say, "You, too, Dov?" On the upper deck, at first the nausea intensified and I was so dizzy I couldn't stand up, but after a time I began to feel better, and my nausea passed.

Our first day at sea was over. Most people lay on their bunks, feeling ill. The sun had set; night had fallen and darkened the sea. Everything was so black that the line between sea and sky disappeared. Only the British destroyer, lit up from fore to aft, could be seen at our side, like a house alight hovering in the air. In the silence, we could hear the bow of our ship cutting through the water and the waves hitting its sides. In our corner, some of the crew had gathered, including "Captain Short Pants," as we called Ike, and our young people gathered around as well. Someone brought a guitar and began playing softly and we joined the quiet singing. One of the crew, a bearded, well-built American, took out a bottle of whiskey and everyone had a drink. Initial contacts between the sabras of the Palyam, the American volunteers and us, the Holocaust survivors, consisting of embarrassing questions innocently asked but going unanswered, and the laughter that covered the pain and embarrassment only emphasized the gulf between us. But over the course of the evening, as we sat there together, exchanging words, calling each other by name, the feeling of mutual affection and the desire to get to know one another lowered barriers and brought us together.

The next morning a second British destroyer appeared, similar to the first one, and sailed on the other side of us. We were surrounded, but it didn't greatly excite us, and we even reacted to what was going on with ridicule: "What? One destroyer isn't enough for them to guard us?" Indeed, the second destroyer gave us something else to watch on the monotonous sea.

The ship commanders, who tried to improve services and maintain cleanliness, were assisted by the kibbutz members, who were easy to mobilize for any mission. We did the best we could, but the resources on the ship were not sufficient for such a large number of people. The number falling ill increased daily. The ship's small hospital worked day and night, treating the sick and dispensing medication, but it, too, could not stand up to the pressure. The toilets and the water taps stopped running. Sanitary conditions worsened by the hour. We were able to tolerate these difficulties only because we knew we need hold out only a few days longer, and our spirits remained as high as they had been at the start. In the evenings we sat with the crew, sang to the accompaniment of a guitar and a harmonica, told jokes and drank coffee long into the night.

Sarah and I couldn't find a secluded spot to be alone together on the ship. We took advantage of the late hours of the evening when we would stand by a window, leaning our heads outside and whispering together until the cold of the night would chase us back to our bunks.

The inevitable moment of confrontation with the British was approaching. No one deluded himself into thinking that we would be able to escape from ships of the British fleet and secretly approach the shore and debark. On the third day, two more British battleships joined our bizarre convoy. It was clear that the moment we entered British territorial waters we would be attacked. The strategic plan was to prevent the British from boarding the ship by battling them in any way we could. Meanwhile, our ship would sail with all possible speed to the Tel Aviv coast, where we would run into a sandbank. Jewish settlers would be called out to the beach in great numbers to prevent the British from gaining control of the ship, and the Haganah would be mobilized to take the passengers off the beached ship and get them to the shore, where they would blend into the crowds. A separate strategy was to arouse worldwide public opinion to support the struggle of the DP camp dwellers, Holocaust survivors, for the right to enter Israel, and increase the pressure on the British to open the gates of the country to immigration.

Now we devised tactics for the decisive moment of our operation. We worked mostly at night to hide what we were doing from the British, who were constantly watching us. We blocked all of the passageways with wire, boards, anything that was available.

On the lower deck, which was impossible to completely block off, we poured thick oil on the floor and boarded the doors shut. We wanted to force our attackers to come aboard from the upper deck only, where we would be waiting, hundreds of young men and women, to fight them in any way we could. The work at night, in the darkness, was difficult and slow. My hands were cut by wire and pounded by hammer blows, but I felt great. We felt as though our work was something holy and blessed.

The last day before Zero Hour arrived. Tension was high from the early morning hours. Two more British destroyers, larger than the four already accompanying us, joined the convoy. A plane observed us from above and dived down from time to time toward the ship, perhaps to frighten us and to make it clear that there was no point in resisting. On the ship, a general mobilization was called. Most of the work was to bring up the "weapons" and the "ammunition" — sticks, our principal weapon, supplemented with cans of preserves, potatoes, onions and pieces of iron. We emptied the storerooms of anything that could be thrown, as we wouldn't need them for food any longer. We piled the "ammunition" along the upper deck.

Many of us packed our knapsacks and dressed as though we were going to leave the ship, even though we had received no order to do so and there were still many hours before our confrontation. Here and there, quarrels broke out about trivialities; our nerves were on edge.

At three in the afternoon we were called to the upper deck for a final briefing. All of the Haganah people, the ship's crew, the leadership of the kibbutzim, the youth group leaders, and the heads of other groups were present. The Haganah commander described the expected struggle to come. The assumption was that the British would not use lethal weapons against us, and so we were instructed not to use weapons, or at least, not knives or anything that could cause a British fatality. We were, however, ordered to fight with all of our strength to prevent the British from gaining control of the ship.

I listened to every word attentively, trying to imagine what was going to happen. The upper deck was divided into sectors; each kibbutz or youth group was given a sector to defend. Our kibbutz was assigned to defend the rear of the ship, including the blue and white flag flying on its pole, and we were filled with pride. I had never, neither in Sobibor nor afterward in the forest, dared to dream such an unbelievable dream. I had been convinced that if the Germans were defeated and I remained alive, the free world would receive me and others like me with open arms, and we would live in a paradise. And now, two years after the liberation, my friends and I found ourselves sailing as exiles, in shocking conditions, and our desire to settle in our homeland, a difficult and dangerous land, had no hope of success. We were surrounded by real war ships, capable of shelling us once or twice and sinking our ship without leaving a trace.

But another thought passed through my mind during those moments — what magical strength was hidden in the words "the Land of Israel" and in the blue and white flag, that we were ready to fight with no hesitation, refusing to consider logically the results of a battle between such unequal adversaries? We, who had spent the war years in a superhuman struggle just to stay alive, were now ready to sacrifice ourselves for a homeland whose sovereignty was still not in our hands and before we had even taken one step on its soil.

The tension rose as the loudspeakers blared out orders frequently: "Tonight we will reach the shores of Israel — everyone should be dressed and ready to leave the ship!" "Everyone must remain in their bunks!" "Do not walk around the passageways! Do not go up on deck!" and on and on. Evening fell. There was an abnormal silence on the ship. I took my leave of Sarah, who was responsible for keeping order inside.

Some of us were called to close a gap in the lower deck and we worked quickly. We didn't want to be isolated, cut off from the action. I wanted to be on the upper deck with everyone else. Work progressed slowly and it seemed to me that we would never finish

— I was afraid of missing something. Finally we were ordered to stop our work and join the others.

The upper deck, quiet and dark, at first glance appeared almost empty of people, but as I walked, I saw that it was full and people were sitting or lying near the piles of "ammunition." The members of our kibbutz were gathered at the flag and I joined them. The breeze dried the perspiration that covered my body from my work below. The lights of the destroyers, which had illuminated the previous nights, disappeared. There were no lights on our ship, either; it was pitch black outside. The darkness and the silence created a mysterious atmosphere, which stimulated my overactive imagination. According to the plan, we were due to reach territorial waters in the early morning hours, and then the battle would begin between the British, who ruled the country, and us...

Suddenly the darkness was rent by the beam of a spotlight directed on us from somewhere and approaching us quickly — it was the British destroyer, which was sailing parallel to our ship. Through loudspeakers it was announced that we were nearing the territorial waters of Palestine, and we were commanded to obey the orders of the British Royal Navy — otherwise we would be stopped by force.

The announcement was repeated several times. At once, the deck came to life; everyone stood up and one of the crewmembers came out of the command cabin, a loudspeaker in his hand, and replied to the British. We all broke out in whistles and shouts, the spotlight went out and the destroyer sailed off and disappeared. Again, we were swathed in darkness, but we knew — it had started! We stood and waited for what would come next. In a few minutes, the destroyer approached, lit the spotlight and repeated its announcement. We continued to shout and to whistle until it disappeared, this time for a lengthier period. Quiet returned. We heard only the lapping of the waves at the sides of the ship. In one of the corners, I saw Uzi connecting a fireman's hose that was supposed to spray oil at our attackers. Uzi's face was dirty and his red hair blackened.

I sat with my friend Yisrael and we smoked. "If we only had a bottle of vodka now," I said, and he in turn cursed the British imperialists. Then suddenly we heard a ship approaching and we were hit by a strong light opposite us: the British destroyer was almost upon us, all lit up. On its deck stood sailors, standing in a row. We all jumped to our feet — and at that moment we were hit by tear gas bombs and flares. The upper deck was covered in smoke. Here and there, fires broke out. The gas burned my eyes and my throat until I felt that I was choking. Was it possible, the thought popped into my head, that we were going to be gassed to death? A young woman standing near me shouted, "My eyes! Help me! Help me!" and, next to her, a young man had been injured by a direct hit of a tear gas bomb and blood was streaming from his forehead.

Our ship sounded a continuous siren, which sounded like the howl of a wounded animal. (I later found out that the siren had broken and couldn't be silenced). We quickly recovered from the attack, however, and we began a counterattack — the deck of the destroyer was lower than ours and we threw anything we could get our hands on, while our shouts mixed with the sound of the sirens. We hit some of the sailors standing on deck and we could see them running for cover. The British again fired tear gas at us and again we choked, but we had learned how to defend ourselves; some of us even succeeded in flinging the tear gas bombs back to the British. We all continued to bombard the sailors with cans of preserves. Suddenly, the lights of the destroyer went out and it disappeared. Everything was quiet, as if everything that had happened just a minute ago had been an illusion.

We soon realized that the British had not waited until we entered the territorial waters, but had attacked us in the open sea. Indeed, in any case, our struggle was doomed to failure, but it never occurred to us for a moment to give in. We continued sailing at top speed. We felt good after the first skirmish. We had responded, and they had fled! After the first difficult moments, we had proven that we could cope with tear gas. We each described our own "method" for dealing with watering, stinging eyes, and each of us had a personal version of the battle and our victory. In the meantime, the wounded were bandaged; a few were taken to the infirmary, but most of them stayed on deck. Our store of "ammunition" had decreased, but we felt that we could stand up to our attackers. Uzi, who was the ship radio operator, broadcast an emotional speech to the Jewish settlement in Israel, relating how the British had attacked us far from the territorial waters of Israel. He called on other nations and governments to demand that the British cease their attack against us in international waters and requested that ships sailing in our area come to our aid.

After a short while, a violent shock rocked our ship and it tilted to one side. Some of the "ammunition" scattered around the deck and loud screams were heard from within the ship. A British destroyer had rammed the *Exodus* at its center. Its sharp bow had smashed the upper part of the ship, made of wood, and had destroyed the wall of the deck, entered the bunk area and destroyed some of the bunks, as well. People were injured, some crushed between the bunks, and many had fallen from the force of the blow. Water began to seep in and for a few minutes, panic reigned. Screams and crying filled the air. People were afraid that the ship would sink. Some ran up to the top deck and shouted at us to surrender.

The destroyer sailed away, but another was approaching from the other side. Again, we were lit up as by the afternoon sun and another relentless tear gas attack began. The upper deck was enveloped in smoke and gas. There was nowhere to run. There was no way to defend ourselves. Someone urinated on a scarf and held it over his eyes, saying that it helped. We all did as he had done. A girl pleaded for anyone to urinate on her scarf. I covered my face with the palms of my hands. I felt the tear gas bombs hitting my back and I pushed them away with my foot. I peeked out at the destroyer — its deck was empty. The bombs were being fired from sheltered positions.

As we were struggling with the tear gas, we heard someone shout, "The English! The English!" At once, the choking gas was forgotten — but perhaps the British had stopped firing or the wind had blown away the clouds of gas — and we all ran to the railing of the deck. The destroyer was very close to us, and its sailors were putting ladders over the side, which could reach our ship, and British sailors were trying to board. In a rage, we attacked the ladders and we threw anything we could on the heads of those who were trying to reach us. Some of the ladders were thrown into the sea with the climbers still on them. Other sailors retreated quickly. Very few sailors succeeded in climbing aboard our ship.

Those who did seemed frightened and surprised and their appearance was ridiculous — they were all wearing white steel helmets, most of their faces were protected by strips of hard leather, and their hands were covered with protectors made from tire parts. In one hand, the British sailors carried a shield, and in the other, a club. They didn't seem to be threatening us with attack, but the anger that had built up needed an outlet and some of our fellows lit into them. One of the Haganah soldiers rescued them, ordering us to detain them and put them into a locked room. In the meantime, the British pulled their men out of the water and retreated.

Although we had succeeded in holding back the British in the second encounter, even taking British prisoners, our mood was no longer positive. Our attackers had exhausted us and we were weakening. The number of wounded had increased, and there were those who had not managed to hold out during the battle and had left the deck. I had completely forgotten that there were thousands of people in the boat on the lower deck, including my Sarah. I was under the impression that our ship had been rammed in the area where our bunks were located, but no one knew what damage had been done or if there were wounded within. I went to the command room, where the crew and the Haganah officers were located, to get an update on the situation. On my way, I saw someone whom I had earlier seen filming the battle, and now, dressed as a priest, he was trying to persuade young boys to leave the deck, but without success.

At the moment I entered the command room, a destroyer approached us and attacked again. It seemed as if the destroyers were taking turns. Again, a large number of tear gas bombs fell on the deck simultaneously, this time accompanied by a burst of machine gun fire. Above the command room, a fire had broken out. The survival instincts I had honed so sharply during the war years made me jump for cover, but at the same time, I felt ashamed — what was I doing? Hiding? I got up and ran forward. The British were trying to move sailors from the destroyer to our ship, and we were fighting them with sticks or even barehanded. A face-to-face battle was going on all over the deck. The command room had been taken over by the British. One of our kibbutz members was running about insanely, with a board in his hand, hitting British sailors left and right and shouting.

Two British sailors ran away and jumped into a lifeboat, which was hanging at the edge of the ship. The boat overturned, and the sailors fell into the sea. From time to time I heard shooting, but I didn't pay any attention to it. Finally this battle, which was lengthier and more sweeping than the others, was over. The British ship sailed off, and again, there was darkness. The results of the skirmish were very serious. One boy of about fifteen years old, and one crewmember, the bearded American who had spent time with us in the evenings, were shot and killed. We had wounds of every type — bullet wounds, tear gas bomb injuries, heads dripping with blood, and broken arms and legs. It was said that the boy who was killed had taken out a knife and stabbed a British sailor, and, at that moment, a sniper had fired at him from the destroyer.

The situation was desperate. We had been fighting for several hours and we were still far from the shores of Israel. Even though none of us wanted to surrender, we began to doubt our ability to stand up to another attack. There was just one hope — perhaps the English were exhausted, as well, and would not attack us from close by; but it was logical to assume that the British knew that they had to get control of us quickly, or otherwise, we would be able to reach the shore. Indeed, a destroyer approached us and attacked again.

We were exhausted and had nothing left to throw at them — we couldn't even shout at them. We got the order to stop fighting, and not to oppose the British any longer. The *Exodus 1947* surrendered to the king's fleet.

There was quiet all at once. British sailors began boarding our ship, undisturbed. I looked at the sailors. My hatred for them was boundless. We saw Uzi, who seemed on the verge of collapse, and we asked him if the battle had ended and we wouldn't do anything more. He replied, "No, we can't do anything more. We have too many wounded, the ship is taking in water and listing to the side. We can't continue to endanger the passengers. They've won, the bastards!"

On the horizon dawn was breaking. The British ships again turned on their lights and we could see more clearly. A look at the faces of our boys gave a good indication of what had taken place that night. All of a sudden, I was cold. I sat, curled up, shivering, alternately dozing and waking until the sun was fully up. The deck was filled with people. Young British sailors could be seen with heads and arms bandaged. I looked into their young faces and could no longer hate them. One sailor stood surrounded by children, giving them sweets. British medics were tending to our wounded. I remembered the Germans in the Warsaw ghetto and in Sobibor, and it seemed that the English were different. Their behavior during the battle and afterward had been fair. When I thought about the experiences of the night before, I laughed to myself — the battle we had fought reminded me of one I had seen in a pirate movie. Nevertheless, I considered myself lucky to have taken part in the struggle. I didn't know what would become of us, but I assumed that we would be taken to Cyprus. That wasn't anything to worry about; it was the knowledge that we had been defeated that bothered me. As it was, the forces were unequal and there was no chance that we could have overpowered the British, but even so, it was a terrible feeling to have been defeated, to be prisoners in the hands of the enemy.

The British ships that had accompanied us on our voyage were now very close to us and we could see what was happening on their decks. Motorboats arrived from the coast, and officers climbed on deck. On the horizon, we could see mountains rising from the sea. Suddenly we could see that the British were nervously running around the *Exodus* command cabin, which they had taken over. A British sailor was holding the wheel and navigating the boat toward Haifa, but the *Exodus* continued sailing toward Tel Aviv. It turned out that the steering wheel in the command cabin had been disabled and one of our men had been steering the ship with another steering wheel. A search was carried out, and the second wheel was found. The last attempt of the Haganah to bring the ship to the shore had failed.

The British officers who boarded the ship walked around, looked at each man carefully, sometimes asking for identification cards, as they sought out members of the Haganah; but they had disappeared as though the sea had swallowed them up. The mountains opposite us came closer and closer. They seemed larger now, and could be seen more clearly until we could even distinguish houses and smoke rising from chimneys and a car making its way up the mountainside. We gazed upon the shore with yearning eyes and with aching hearts; it seemed like Paradise on earth. This was the land we had dreamed of reaching, this was the land that for a thousand years we had been praying, every morning and evening, to return to; and now we were so close, but its gates were closed. A flock of gulls coming from the shore flew over us. The destroyers had gone, and in their place were small coast guard vessels. The ship entered Haifa port. We were so close to land that it appeared to me as though we were entering the streets of the city and that I would be able to touch the houses. People standing with me were wiping away their tears. I felt myself choking up with tears, as well.

The ship was tied to the pier. On the dock sailors wearing red caps were standing in row after row, as though at a holiday presentation. Armored cars with machine guns and a military ambulance were assembled on the dock, and a large number of officers were standing and watching us. The transfer of 4,500 passengers from the

*Exodus* to three British expulsion vessels, *Ocean Vigour*, *Runnymede Park* and the *Empire Rival*, was done quickly and methodically. First, the ill and the seriously wounded were removed, whose large numbers shocked me, followed by the others. We walked between two rows of sailors. Again I considered how foolish I was to have thought that the world would welcome everyone who had survived the Holocaust. I took a last look at our "wounded" ship and I could see the broken bunks through the gap made by the destroyer when it rammed us. A sign was hung on the ship with the words "Exodus 1947" written in Hebrew and in English. A wave of strong affection for the ship washed over me.

We were led to a shed where people in yellow overalls were standing, masks over their faces. They asked us to open our shirts and pants. Using hand pumps, as though spraying to control mosquitoes, they sprayed us with DDT. The strong odor caused us to sneeze, and our hair was colored grey, causing us to smile at each other, but I felt humiliated. From the shed, we were boarded onto a large freighter, led into an area surrounded by barbed wire, and then brought down to a large storage room located in the belly of the ship. Although it was filled to capacity, the British kept bringing more and more people. It was hot and stuffy. Sarah's mother fainted and the British allowed her, along with Sarah and her brother, Yitzchak, to remain on deck. Everyone somehow found a place to sit. We were convinced that we would have a short voyage, as, in a few hours, we would be taken off at one of the ports of Cyprus.

When we surrendered to the British, feeling ourselves defeated, we had no idea that in fact we had achieved one of the most important goals of the Zionist movement. The events on board the *Exodus* (since the best seller written by Leon Uris was published, the Hebrew name of the ship, *Yetziat Europa*, has been forgotten) shocked the world. That very day, the Jewish settlement in Israel proclaimed a general strike, and Jews demonstrated in many places throughout the world. Foreign newspaper reporters hurried to Haifa, and although they were not allowed to approach us, they filmed the rammed ship, the passengers being taken off, the wounded, and the transfer of passengers to deportation ships; they filmed the faces of the young men and women who had been defeated by the British army in a cruel struggle that had gone on for an entire night. The events had been radioed in to the shore by the soldiers of the Haganah, the leaders who had mysteriously disappeared before arrival in Haifa to avoid arrest by the British. Radio stations and newspapers all over the world recounted the story and published pictures of the fate of the *Exodus*, the story of how thousands of men, women, and children, Holocaust survivors, had fought a desperate battle against the British fleet in an attempt to reach the Land of Israel. The naval "victory" of the British became a political failure.

When we were transferred to the expulsion freighters, we expected that in a few hours our voyage would end in Cyprus, where we would be kept in an internment camp, as other illegal immigrants had been. None of us even imagined that we were at the beginning of a journey that would continue long into the future.

The heat and the crowded conditions made us edgy. People quarreled over a place to sit, until everyone had a small space of floor, like sheep in a pen. Yisrael and I found ourselves a place in one of the corners, near the side wall of the ship, but we couldn't lean on it since the wall was burning with the heat of the sun. People began to undress, taking off one article of clothing after another; soon a strong stench filled the air. We were so involved with getting ourselves situated that we didn't notice that the ship had left port. I wanted to see Sarah, who was up on deck. People were waiting in line on the stairs to use the toilets, which were located on the deck. At the top of the stairs there was a closed door with a sailor next to it who was letting people in and out, two at a time. The line was long and moved slowly. There was only one banister along the steep staircase, and if you didn't hold tightly, you were liable to slip and fall. One girl had already fallen down the stairs.

There was a cool breeze on deck. The part of the boat we were enclosed in was separated from the rest by screens and barbed wire. We were a floating prison. Through the screen I saw another two freighters sailing alongside us, and on the other side — again, British destroyers. I exchanged a few words with Sarah and returned to the lower deck of the boat. We had been sailing for many hours, and, according to my calculations, we should have reached Cyprus already. Were we being taken somewhere else? Fear began to steal into our hearts: If not Cyprus, then where? We argued, some maintaining that according to the direction of the sun, we weren't sailing to Cyprus at all, and in the meanwhile, the sun had begun to set and we couldn't see land in the distance.

The British brought us pails of tasteless soup and stale-smelling toast that was hard as a rock. When we asked where we were being taken, we were answered with a shrug of the shoulders; they didn't know. What a great change had occurred in the space of a day! Yesterday at this time, we had been ready to battle the British, believing that we could reach the shores of Israel. Now we were caged in a British ship, without even space to lie down for all of us, without privacy, men and women lying pressed up against each other, being taken to some unknown place.

Exhaustion finally overwhelmed me and I fell asleep. During the night I was wakened by a strange cry, which had come from my own mouth. My heart was beating rapidly. Cold sweat covered my face. People sleeping near me awoke, looked at me, and went back to sleep. For a moment, I didn't know where I was. I wanted to sit up but something was on my stomach — a girl sleeping opposite me had thrown her leg across my body. I removed it carefully, without disturbing the girl's sleep. Two British sailors came running, opened the door, inspected the storage space with their flashlights, and finally left. I hadn't dreamed about Germans for a long time, and now, I was back in Sobibor. Again, as in the previous nightmares, I wondered how I had gotten back there after I had already fled. I was near *Lager* 3, very close to the gas chambers, and I saw Bolender and Getzinger standing at the entrance. The two of them looked at me and I knew that I was lost — they wouldn't let me go back to *Lager* 2. I was angry with myself. I didn't understand how they had managed to catch me. I knew that I had to get away immediately but my legs were paralyzed. Getzinger got up on the large crane that took the bodies out of the pits to bring them for burning. I tried everything I could to get away as the crane was being lowered straight to me, but Bolender, laughing, instructed Getzinger to lower the crane, and then motioned with his hand to stop. Now the arm of the crane came closer and closer to me, and as the arms of the crane began to crush my body, I wanted to scream, but I wasn't able to. With a tremendous effort, I let out one scream…and awoke.

As always, I was afraid to fall asleep again lest I return to Sobibor. I sat, staring at the sleepers by the light coming though the deck windows, which lit parts of the storeroom. The sight of hundreds of people sleeping crowded together in strange positions left me with a terrible feeling, which was connected to the horror of the dream. It was as if I were sitting amid hundreds of dead bodies. I made an effort to banish those thoughts from my mind, remembering instead a slave ship I had once seen depicted in a film. We all seemed to be in a movie. I looked around me; people were sleeping pressed into each other and doubled over, looking so ridiculous that I suppressed a laugh.

I awoke once more, and we were on the open sea, but I could not see water and sky, only iron walls. The line to the toilets snaking up the stairs remained lengthy. Anger swelled and ebbed. All signs pointed to the fact that the ship would be making a long journey — the British jailors had given out dishes and blankets, a group of officers visited us and instructed us to take unnecessary knapsacks and parcels and store them on the deck to make more room for the people.

Someone I had met on the *Exodus* entered the room. It was Mordechai Rozman, one of the *Hashomer Hatzair* leaders in Germany, who had been placed in an adjacent storeroom. He stood on the stairs and gave an emotional speech: "We have not been defeated; although we surrendered, although we are here, in British hands, being led like slaves, our struggle has not ended and we will go on to victory!"

We had all needed some words of encouragement, and Mordechai Rozman expressed them well. Above, on the deck, the British gathered to listen to the speech. Rozman attacked the British for imprisoning us in closed cellars, in floating prisons, under humiliating conditions, without even allowing us to breathe fresh air on deck, which in any case was surrounded by a fence of barbed wire — and that this had been done on the high seas, where we had nowhere to run to. "We will not tolerate this!" he announced determinedly. His words were met with stormy applause, and at the end, we all stood up and sang *Hatikvah*, standing at attention.

We took the hint. Again, we were ready for struggle. A few minutes after the speech, a large group of young people was standing ready on the steps, and the moment a British sailor opened the door, we broke out and did not let it close again. The deck was filled with young people who led the hapless sailor to the opening of the closed off area. At the same time, those imprisoned in the second storeroom also broke out. A warning siren was sounded. Sailors wearing helmets, holding shields and clubs, gathered opposite the closed area and we had the impression that a battle was about to break out between us. Although our hands were empty and we were prisoners on a British ship, we were extremely aware that we had no choice, that we had to struggle against our jailors, no matter what the result would be.

An officer approached and asked to speak to our representatives. After a short consultation, Mordechai Rozman and a man from the organization of soldiers and partisans went forward to speak to the officer, who took them to the ship's commander. On the other side of the barbed wire gate stood the serious-faced sailors, waiting for the order to move forward, and we stood opposite them, a wall of resistance. A few of our people taunted the British, but they remained calm. After a few minutes, the tension lowered on both sides, a few people even conversing with the sailors.

The commander of the ship announced to our representatives

that what we had done was considered mutiny on the high seas and he had the authority to punish us; we had to obey the rules of the ship, or he would have to use force to maintain law and order.

Mordechai answered that we had no wish to confront the armed forces on the ship, but that we could not tolerate being treated as slaves. It was unacceptable that people could not relieve themselves as civilized people, that those who did not feel well in the intense heat of the interior of the ship could not go up on deck to get a breath of fresh air. If the commander wanted us to cooperate during the journey, he would have to leave the storeroom doors open. The ship's commander consulted with the commander of the fleet and informed our representatives that the doors would remain open. During the conversation, Mordechai tried to ascertain where we were being taken. The commander maintained that he could not answer that question, and Mordechai reacted by saying that if we didn't receive an answer by the end of the day, we would begin a hunger strike.

The fact that the British acquiesced to our demands to keep the doors open encouraged us. We could go out into the fresh air and be in contact with the people in the other storeroom. But I still couldn't escape my images of the night — the entrances to the gas chambers, Bolender and Getzinger, the crane coming down over my head. They returned as though I were in Sobibor and on the boat at the same time.

We became accustomed to the special living conditions on the ship with remarkable speed. Each of the hundreds of people who were in the large storerooms made a place for himself that afforded a modicum of comfort. The heat forced people to remove articles of clothing one after another until the men remained only in their pants and sometimes, only in their underwear, and the women also wore bras and shorts or improvised bathing suits. Shame immediately disappeared, and if anyone had stripped the others would have followed suit.

After a few stormy days, we relaxed and accepted our fate. One evening, we met and Mordechai informed us that he had still not received an answer to his question. He proposed that we begin a hunger strike and maintain it until we knew where we were going, and the proposal was accepted unanimously. Again we stood up and sang *Hatikvah*.

Later that evening, Yisrael borrowed a chess set from someone. Everyone had gone to sleep and the deck was empty. Yisrael and I sat alone and played until the early morning hours. The British sailors on duty gave us cigarettes and we exchanged a friendly word or two. From time to time, when I looked around me into the darkness, I saw the lights of the other two ships, which were also accompanied by destroyers. We were sailing west, but where were we headed?

The next day, when the British called our people to take the meals for everyone, no one got up. After a time, they, themselves, brought coffee, toast and jam into the storeroom, but we pushed the food to the opening in the barbed wire fence. The same scene occurred at lunchtime. But even in the morning there had been voices denouncing the hunger strike, and these increased as the day went on. There were those who spoke up against keeping food from children, pregnant women and the weak. There were those who said, in any case, we wouldn't be able to maintain a hunger strike for very long. But that evening, Mordechai was invited to the commander's cabin and informed that we were being returned to France, our original point of departure.

This news was received with mixed feelings. There was frustration at not being able to realize our goal of reaching Israel, and also at not being sent to Cyprus, which was close to Israel, and from where the chance of immigrating soon was a possibility. This frustration deepened with our return to where we had left from, which symbolized the complete failure of our operation. However, knowing that we were not being taken to some godforsaken corner of Africa or Asia broke the tension and ended the guessing game about the location of our exile.

A secretariat was spontaneously formed, with Mordechai at the head, joined by the secretaries of the kibbutzim and the heads of the various movements. Among us there was also a soldier of the Haganah, named Micha, who had concealed his identity and had tried not to be conspicuous, but who was operating behind the scenes.

The exact number of days that had passed since we had boarded the *Exodus* escaped me. I didn't know the date, nor did I remember what day of the week it was. But it was the fourth day of our exile on the *Runnymede Park*, so I knew that we would reach France in a few days.[1]

It was Friday. From the early morning hours, the ship hummed with activity. The members of the secretariat gathered for a consultation in the other storeroom. In one corner, a youth choir was having rehearsals for the *Oneg Shabbat* party the secretariat had set for this evening, and when evening came, everyone gathered in our storeroom.

It was hot and stuffy and people sat squashed together, half undressed. Mordechai Rozman invited the ship's captain to our party, and he arrived with several other officers, all dressed in white dress uniforms. A man playing the accordion stood at the top of the stairs and began to play Shabbat songs. Everyone joined in with loud singing, which warmed the hearts and rocked the ship. Suddenly the accordionist lost his balance, slipped, and fell down the stairs. Slips had occurred from time to time and had always aroused laughter, even though they sometimes resulted in someone being hurt. This time, no one laughed. There was complete silence. Everyone stared at the accordionist, who quickly stood up, went back up the stairs and continued playing to the sounds of applause.

After group singing, Mordechai gave another stirring speech. He opened with a summary of the fate of the Jews through the ages, went on to talk about the period before World War II, pointing out that only a small part of the Jewish nation had joined the Zionist

---

1. The *Exodus* left the port at Site on July 11 and was boarded by the British on July 18.

movement, which strove to entirely eradicate the Diaspora as a solution to the problem of the Jewish nation. He then went on to the Holocaust, during which all the nations watched as the Jewish people was exterminated. And now, two years after the end of the war, we, the survivors, were jailed in a British prison on the high seas for the crime of wanting to live in the land of our forefathers and to rebuild our lives in Israel, which had been awaiting us as a wilderness for hundreds of years. The speech attacked the British, who, because of oil interests, were going back on their promise to allow the Jews to build a national homeland in Israel. Finally, he spoke of our being returned to France, and warned the British government that if they assumed that we would leave the ship of our own free will, they were mistaken. We would struggle. The British would have to carry us out of the ship one by one, using force.

We sat, hypnotized. We absorbed every word and here and there people wiped away their tears. The British sailors, who had gathered on the deck above us, listened attentively, although they didn't understand a word of Yiddish. The audience applauded enthusiastically.

The cultural portion of the evening began. The children's choir from the orphanages sang some songs in Hebrew. A girl told an amusing story written by Y. L. Peretz, and finally a woman named Lola Fulman, about thirty, walked up the stairs. She was chubby, and wore shorts improvised from a flowered skirt, and an open, sleeveless blouse, in the fashionable style of the women on the ship. It was difficult to understand from her appearance why she was on the stairs, but when she began to sing the folksongs of the destroyed world of our youth, in a voice that was strong and clear, a quiver went through the audience. The wonderful evening on the freighter *Runnymede Park*, somewhere on the seas of the Mediterranean, ended with *Hatikvah*.

Living conditions on the boat were difficult; some even said that these were the most difficult days they had ever experienced. I, who had lived through the German hell, found these days pleasantly adventurous, with a few difficult moments, and I was happy to be a part of what was happening. When people equated the British with the Germans, I could find no room for comparison, despite the hatred I felt for them for having closed the gates to our immigration. From the moment I had met the Germans, every German had symbolized death to me; and although I couldn't admit it to people during the *Exodus* affair, I was not afraid of being killed by the British; thus, I couldn't bear the comparisons which some of us made between the British sailors and the Nazis. During the voyage, we even made friends with British sailors and played games with them to pass the time.

The days crawled by slowly. I spent many hours playing card games I learned on the ship, and in the evenings, Sarah and I would sit on the deck and talk, filling each other in on what was going on, and weaving plans for the rosy future that awaited us. Every morning, I would go up on deck and observe the other boats sailing with us, accompanied by destroyers, and try to find some sign of land in the distance. There was only sea and more sea surrounding us. Another week went by and it was Friday night again, and another *Oneg Shabbat* party. There was another wonderful speech by Mordechai and an artistic program. But we were becoming sad. What would be our fate? According to our calculations, we should have reached France already, but the voyage was continuing, day after day until it seemed that we were condemned to sail the seas forever.

One morning the boat stopped moving. We hurried to the deck. It was just dawn, but through the mists we could see lights flickering. Land! The sun soon rose and when it had scattered the mists we found ourselves a few hundred meters from a small port called Port-de-Bouc, near Marseilles. Small motorboats sailed slowly in front of us. Did they know who we were? Did anyone know that we had reached this place? Whenever a boat approached us and got within hearing distance, we would shout in chorus, "We are from the *Exodus*! Let everyone know that we are here!" Suddenly one of the boats quickly came toward us carrying an older man wearing a long coat and a hat, and shouting at us through a hand-held loudspeaker, "Don't get off! Don't go back to Europe! We are with you. The whole world is with you. Be strong and of good courage!" We found out later that this man was Moshe Sneh,[1] leader of the Haganah (Military) Command.

The people in the boat waved at us in encouragement while their craft sailed quickly past the British freighters, until finally a motorboat full of British sailors approached and chased it away. There was no need to instruct us not to leave the ship; we had already decided that we would not. However, the immediate contact with people on the outside, the knowledge that we had not been left alone, made us feel better about our decision. We were emotionally ready for anything. Indeed, one of the most terrible things about the war years was that not only had the survivors not received any help from anyone, but also that no one had come to encourage us, to raise our spirits by saying, "We are with you!" The loneliness, the feeling that we had been abandoned, the knowledge that no one was supporting us, destroyed us spiritually.

During the initial days of the war, I had heard people say, "The world will not let Hitler do whatever he wants." Even later, we kept waiting for the reaction of "the world" to Hitler's acts, and in the Warsaw ghetto, when thousands of people were dying every day of starvation and disease, when the situation was getting worse from day to day, people still expected to hear some words from "the world" — "Where is the world?" they asked; "Where are the Jews of the world?" I am sure that if one small piece of paper had been smuggled in from "the world" expressing empathy and encouragement, it would have given many of us the strength to struggle to stay alive; it would have prevented many from going to their deaths with resignation, accepting the fact that there was no way to struggle against the fate that had been imposed on us. Not one word arrived then, from anywhere. Even today, it is difficult for me to understand. Now, one small boat with a few people waving

---

1. Moshe Sneh, who was born in Poland, was a left-wing activist who would later found the Mapam Party in Israel.

at us in affinity, saying only, "We are with you!" infused us with new spirit.

Mordechai Rozman called us together for a short briefing. "As we have seen," he said, "our organizations are with us. We must be patient and act only according to instructions."

At noon, a boat full of supplies approached us — crates of long loaves of fresh white bread, vegetables, fruit, cheeses, chocolate, cigarettes and other needs were brought on deck, and their aromas wafted throughout the ship. The English inspected every crate, every sack, every basket, looking for prohibited items and expropriating any newspaper or slip of paper. Quickly, the ship turned into a "fast food restaurant." We had not seen fresh bread or any decent food for a long time, and we devoured large amounts of food. I had the impression, to my malicious satisfaction, that the British were envious of us, and when I offered one sailor a piece of chocolate, he considered what to do, and finally, embarrassed, took it and thanked me.

In the evening, we sang loudly, in hopes that we could be heard throughout the port. Despite the precautions taken by the British to isolate us, news from the outside was flowing in and contact was made between the organizers of the illegal immigration project and our secretariat. We discovered that since we had been expelled from Haifa, the "*Exodus* Affair" had not left the headlines in the world press; world public opinion was siding with us and was sharply critical of Great Britain; Britain demanded that the French government readmit the *Exodus* passengers but they were refusing, and, due to discussions between the two governments, we had been sailing hither and yon for some days. British pressure on the French was continuing, and in the meanwhile, little Port-de-Bouc, which had been the focus of publicity throughout the world, had attracted a swarm of reporters. Jews from all of the countries of Europe came to see us and to express their solidarity. Heavy pressure was being put on the British to allow newspaper reporters to visit the ships and to report on living conditions.

The news from the outside warmed our hearts and strengthened our belief in the justice of our cause. It was a wonderful feeling to know that world public opinion was in support of us. However, the descriptions in the newspapers depicting us as heroes were exaggerated, in my opinion, as was the description of our terrible suffering. Citing these depictions, we laughingly nicknamed each other "hero." But perhaps my reservations were uncalled for, as, after what I had been through, my criteria for what constituted "suffering" were probably far different than those of others; what the immigrants on the *Exodus* suffered was bad enough, and perhaps even worse than what was described in the newspapers. In any case, every small piece of newsprint in which we were mentioned became a valuable commodity on the ship. Meanwhile, as the British were asking that we be removed to the French coast, our people on the shore were trying to help us organize ourselves for a long stay on the ships, and in addition to food that was both good-tasting and fresh, we received textbooks for children, writing material, books to read and games.

Some time after we had anchored at Port-de-Bouc, we were told that we would be visited by an official delegation of the French government, and many newspaper reporters were trying to gain permission to accompany them. Someone came up with the idea of preparing a surprise for the guests. Early the next morning, we cleared out an area of one of the storerooms we were living in, spread out four blankets, sewed them together, and with red and white toothpaste which we had found and which was contributed by the immigrants, we drew a large swastika entwined with the British flag. The "drawing" was very impressive both in form and in significance, and when the work was finished, we rolled up the blankets carefully.

In the afternoon hours, we saw a convoy of small boats approaching us. Tension rose. "They're coming! They're coming!" came the shouts from every direction. We quickly brought out the blankets and attached them strongly to the netting surrounding our enclosure so that they wouldn't fly in the wind. On the deck, our young people stood, ready to fight the British if they tried to take the blankets down, but they were too occupied with the guests who were coming up on board. We clearly saw how the eyes of the guests were focused on our large caricature of the Nazi-British alliance. Dozens of photographers snapped pictures of it. The operation was a success!

Next to the gangway, the captain and an honor guard were standing to receive the guests, a long line of people dressed in civilian clothing and a few in military wear. Walking behind them was the small group of reporters who had been allowed on the ship; the rest were in boats sailing nearby. After a short stay in the captain's cabin, the group approached our enclosure and stopped at the door of our storeroom. The visitors, perspiring in their suits, looked at us embarrassedly. The captain announced to us that representatives of the government of France were on deck, and that they had brought a proclamation from their government. One of the members of the delegation read the proclamation, which was translated word for word into Yiddish. The proclamation was long and contained many clauses. Its important points were that the government of France was aware of our suffering and had decided to take the humanitarian step of offering anyone who willingly left the ship full French citizenship. A British officer, who spoke after the French, expressed the hope that we would take advantage of the generous offer of the French government and that we would leave the ship; the crew would provide any assistance necessary for those leaving.

Until this moment, everything seemed to be going according to plan for them. It is possible that some of the English and the French expected that we would line ourselves up, leave the boat, and that would be that. However, at that moment, Mordechai Rozman took the floor and thanked the French government for its generous offer to receive us as citizens; but, he explained, "We must refuse. There is only one place in the world where we want to live, and that is our homeland, the Land of Israel. Only there will we willingly leave the ship. There and nowhere else." There was applause and shouts of agreement everywhere that rocked the ship. All of the tension we had been holding back burst forth at once. There was no doubt that the guests were shocked at the force of our reaction. Mordechai continued, "Each of us is free to do what he desires and if anyone wants to leave the boat, he could do it even now. No one is preventing it." He stopped speaking as if waiting for someone to leave our ranks, but no one moved. He then continued, determinedly, "I tell you that no one will leave this boat in France!" Again there was applause, and Mordechai ended with an impassioned call to the British to take us back to Haifa and let us debark there.

At the end of Mordechai's speech the guests prepared to leave, but we began singing *Hatikvah* and they remained standing. The French faces expressed admiration and exhilaration. The British were burning with anger, but stood at attention like the rest until we had finished singing our anthem. It was clear that we had won this round of the battle. Indeed, the next morning, the newspapers reported that, in spite of the difficult conditions that the *Exodus* passengers were forced to bear and their great suffering, they were steadfast in their refusal of the tempting offer to debark as French citizens.

We had won, but what would come next? How much longer would we have to remain on this damned boat? The British were certain that we would ultimately break down. They were waiting at the gangway and at the opening of the enclosure for those of us who would ask to leave, in order to defend them against anyone who wanted to get in their way and prevent them from leaving. No one spoke to them. On the contrary, we ridiculed and laughed at them. Finally they lost their patience and threatened that if we did not get off the ship of our own free will, they would forcibly remove us in Germany. We had difficulty taking this threat seriously, and stood our ground. Only a few pregnant women who were close to giving birth and two men left the ship.

The next morning, the three exile ships lifted anchor and sailed with sirens of farewell from Port-de-Bouc to the open sea. This time, we left for a long voyage under difficult conditions, and we knew where we were headed, the knowledge of which sent chills down our spines — we were sailing to Germany. In a short time the boat freighter sailed into Marseilles, to take on supplies. All of the ships and boats in the port received us with sirens. Sailors stood on the decks, people left workshops, storage facilities, and ran to see us. Everywhere, people waved hands and handkerchiefs to us and blew us kisses.

Again, we were at sea. The shore quickly disappeared, the gulls that had accompanied us returned to shore, and destroyers, which appeared out of nowhere, took their place. Our spirits sank, as did the temperature when the sun went down. It was Friday, and we intended to have the traditional *Oneg Shabbat* party; it had lost its vitality and we were tired of it, but we had nothing better. The one thing we were not tired of was the weekly speech of Mordechai Rozman, as his words came from his heart and entered our hearts when we needed them, like the air we breathed — we always knew that his words would raise our spirits. This time, he had no good news, but his speech was a well-thought-out self-examination and a clarification of the great contribution that our operation and our efforts were making to the establishment of a Jewish state. Mordechai placed us, the people of the *Exodus*, in the same category as the Haganah and the Palmach; each was a fighter stationed at the front.

We drank in his words, but our spirits remained low. We could not see a way out of the dead end ahead of us. Finally, during the artistic portion of the evening, we had a moving surprise. Lola Fulman sang a new song, "Exodus," which excited all of us. Her husband, Yitzchak Perlov, wrote the lyrics. Perhaps she composed the melody herself, but at any rate, we didn't let her come down from the stairs and she sang the song over and over, until we had learned it and sang it together. Our spirits were lifted and the sadness was gone.

Now that we were at sea, the days of fresh rolls, fruits and vegetables, and unlimited cigarettes were over, and we returned to the tasteless British fare. Boredom filled our days. I was sick of card games and I was not always able to play chess. The well of stories Sarah and I told each other had gone dry; we would look at each other and remain quiet. The hundreds of pairs of eyes focused on us did little to encourage us to speak. The only thing that could lighten the boredom and take me to another world were the books we had received in Port-de-Bouc.

The weather changed for the worse. A strong wind rocked our ship and the waves became higher and beat against the sides of the ship. We rolled up and down, up and down. Many got seasick and threw up; most of us lay without moving, not eating or drinking anything. That evening it rained, and people who were lying on the deck, including Sarah and her family, came down to the storage area. Yisrael and I gave them our places. The next day we entered the Straits of Gibraltar, and toward evening we approached a high mountain, which was wondrously beautiful and hid the sun; then, we docked at the large British naval base, which was full of different types of war vessels.

A company of British troops came aboard to relieve the sailors who had been guarding us since we had left Haifa. These sailors had serious faces and avoided all contact with us, did not react to our requests, and stood guard like inanimate objects. When evening fell a giant spotlight was focused on us, coast guard boats patrolled us, and from time to time depth mines were set off near us, shaking the sides of our ship. No one was able to sleep that night. Outside we could hear the noise of a generator, which reminded me of my first night in Sobibor and the generator in *Lager* 3 that we could hear.

In the morning, when the base came to life, a ship approached and stopped near us. Senior officers came aboard our ship bringing a large number of cardboard boxes, which were placed at the entrance to our quarters. As we were wondering at the meaning of this act, Mordechai was asked to see the captain, who informed him that the commander of the base had asked to give these to us and that they were gifts from the few Jewish families living in Gibraltar — each of us received a box containing a raincoat and a package of cigarettes. Since we had left Port-de-Bouc, our spirits had been low. Returning us to Germany was the cruelest thing that the British could have done — just the thought of stepping off onto German soil, humiliated, as the Germans looked on, was too hard to bear. The stormy weather that had met us as we reached Gibraltar added to our discomfort. Yet now, in the heart of a giant British base, instead of feeling completely cut off from the world, we had discovered a few warmhearted Jews, people of whose existence we were not even aware, who demonstrated their compassion. The sudden feeling that even in a place like that we were not isolated lifted our spirits immediately, and Mordechai made an emotional speech to this effect that evening, which caused many to shed a tear.

The next day I watched the beautiful Rock of Gibraltar which rose above us and I imagined that I could see in through the windows of the houses which dotted the slopes and watch the Jews waving to us in welcome. I wanted to wave back but I was afraid that the other passengers would say that I had lost my mind and that I was trying to communicate with a mountain.

Our sailors returned from their leave and their replacements left the ship as they had come. The ships pulled anchor and headed for the Atlantic Ocean and the English Channel to the North Sea, on the way to our final destination, the port of Hamburg. The Atlantic Ocean was stormy, and giant waves, the likes of which we hadn't seen before in the Mediterranean, washed over the deck. Most of the passengers were ill, and I, who considered myself immune to seasickness, had to throw up as well from time to time and lie down unmoving for hours.

The days followed each other in a routine that never changed. All around us, from horizon to horizon, we saw only the ocean. The number of days we had spent on the sea was calculated according to the number of Friday evening *Oneg Shabbat* parties we had. Passengers lay without moving, sick and weak. The reek of vomit permeated our enclosure. And in spite of it all, our group of young people tried to maintain a pleasant atmosphere and prove to the British that they couldn't break us. As a palliative for boredom and depression, we continued to play childish games on the upper deck with excessive enthusiasm, sometimes with the participation of our guards, while below, people groaned with seasickness. My yearning for dry land increased until, over the horizon, I imagined I saw cities and villages, forests and cattle grazing in meadows, none of which existed. When we reached the North Sea, which was also stormy, we would sail into schools of large fish that jumped up over the waves and gave some life to the monotonous sea.

Every day we were getting closer and closer to Germany, to the port of Hamburg, which was in British control; and there, as governors, they could do as they wished with us. Mordechai Rozman instructed us on how to behave in Hamburg — not to leave the boat willingly, but to make it as difficult as possible for the British and to carry on a passive struggle against being removed from the ship. We would make them take us out one by one. But we were instructed not to use force against British sailors, or we might pay a heavy price. "We don't want any more victims," he said.

One morning I woke up and when I walked up to the deck, I was surprised to see an incredible scene. Our convoy was sailing down a river, in quiet waters, smooth as glass, and on both sides, there were green expanses, villages and towns, and on the river itself there were freighters and passenger ships. At the beginning, I thought I was dreaming, but I soon realized that during the night we had turned from the stormy sea into the Elbe River, and we were sailing toward Hamburg. The beauty of the river scenery dumbfounded me and filled me with wonder, and even cheerfulness, but these feelings were swiftly replaced by sadness and pain — the defeated Germans were serenely living on their land, undisturbed, while we, a remnant of European Jewry, had been wandering the world for two months of suffering, and now we had been returned to the land of our murderers after the failure of our attempts to reach our own land.

We stood ready for the struggle even though we had no idea of what form it would take. We took our baggage, and expressions of worry and anger were visible on each of our faces. We all left the deck and went downstairs to our enclosure. To make it more difficult to take us out to the port, we dismantled the steps leading from the storerooms to the deck except for one flight, which was left for the sick, the elderly and others who might want to use it. British officers came running and tried to prevent us from taking the stairs apart, but they were unsuccessful and they left angrily. A group of young people assembled at the only staircase that remained to obstruct the British as they came to evacuate us.

The ship stopped, but we had no idea where. The British removed the canvas that had covered part of our enclosure and now could see almost everything that was going on in the interior of the ship. Idle waiting and the anticipation of what was to come set our nerves on edge. People lost patience and any trivial thing could destroy their calm. To break the tension, we played cards, made noise and laughed, but it would be difficult to say that this raised anyone's spirits; many only became angrier and shouted, "Aren't you ashamed to be playing cards and laughing at a time like this?" After a long while, we heard steps on the deck and orders spoken in English. A unit of military police spread out above us. The policemen took their positions, set up machine guns and loaded them with cartridges. Although we couldn't believe that the British would actually open fire on us, it gave us a very uncomfortable feeling. The loudspeaker blared that we were to leave the ship immediately, within ten minutes — or we would be expelled by force. Our answer was loud singing of *Hatikvah,* the only weapon at our disposal. Dozens of times we had used this weapon during the journey and every time that I sang it, I was moved anew with the same intensity.

A small group of the elderly, the ill and pregnant women went down to the shore, and again, there was quiet. The rest of us distanced ourselves from the stairs into the inner part of the storeroom. The British waited for others to leave of their own free will, but in vain. No one went up to the deck. And again, the loudspeaker ordered us to leave of our own accord, this time within five minutes. We answered the British with boos and shouts. Within a few minutes, a group of sailors came down into our storeroom and began dragging people up to the deck. A commotion began. Everyone was shouting. There were those who let the British drag them; there were those who struggled and were beaten. Women lay on the floor and were taken out on stretchers. Once in a while a soldier would slip and fall down the stairs together with the person he was dragging. Those remaining retreated to the rear of the storeroom, huddled together, sitting arm in arm, creating a mass of compressed humanity. Resistance grew. Each young man and woman struggled with the soldier trying to drag him or her up to the deck. In reaction, the British used greater force, but had difficulty in tearing apart the human chain we had formed. They took a short break and moved away from us. Then, from above, cold water was sprayed at us under heavy pressure from fire hoses. Again, we used the only weapon we had at our disposal — drenched to the bone, shivering with the cold, we sang *Hatikvah* as loud as we could.

The British waited, but when we had finished singing, they attacked us with clubs and hit our heads and hands. And then it was my turn. Two British sailors took hold of me, another two held my friend Yisrael, and we were quickly dragged up the stairs, where they left us. For a minute, we were free, between two rows of officers and soldiers. I called to Yisrael, "Let's go back down to the storeroom!" and instead of walking between the rows of soldiers to the pier, we turned on our heels and began a mad rush back. Sailors ran after us and tried to catch us. Those who were still in the storeroom urged us on with encouraging shouts. We struggled with the sailors insanely and we were hit. Four soldiers caught me by the hand and foot and carried me up, hitting me continually with their clubs. From behind me, I heard Yisrael cursing in Polish, "Bastards, don't hit him!" and, in spite of my condition, I couldn't help laughing. How could those British sailors understand Polish?

This time, they didn't let us leave the ship by ourselves but carried us down to the pier, where we were placed in a military ambulance standing near the boat. The ambulance was full; there were a few of the leaders and among them, Mordechai Rozman, along with boys like Yisrael, Ya'akov and me, kibbutz members who resisted a bit too much. We were held there for a long time, waiting for others who were placed inside from time to time. All of the other people on the boat were put into railroad cars, guarded by soldiers, while the ambulance brought us to one of the buildings of the port where we were placed in a room with glass walls, and a big table and benches. We were about twenty people. Armed soldiers guarded us from outside. We sat around the table, looking at each other. Everyone's face showed bitter disappointment. The lengthy struggle — it had taken two months — had ended in failure. All of our efforts and our suffering had been futile. We had been returned to the country from which we had left on our immigration journey; and now we had even been separated from our friends, not knowing what awaited us.

A group of officers entered the room and asked which one of us was Mordechai Rozman. No one uttered a word. The British went from person to person, checked us over from head to foot, and left the room. Mordechai had changed his appearance beforehand; he had exchanged articles of clothing with other people, changed his hairstyle, and shaved off his moustache. In a few minutes, the officers returned, stood us in a row, and one of them said that they knew Mordechai Rozman was in the room. Again, we were checked over one by one, again we were asked our names but we remained silent, and again, our captors left the room, disappointed. When they returned a third time, they ordered us to take off our pants, and then they immediately approached Mordechai and told him to come with them. Mordechai had had a lesion over his knee and had been treated by the ship's doctor, and that was how he was identified. We tried to resist, to prevent them from taking him or to go together with him, but the soldiers separated us. Our spirits flagged; we were helpless. After we had gotten accustomed to Mordechai's self-confident leadership, coming to him with every difficulty, minor or major, we now felt orphaned. However, we quickly came to the unanimous decision to wage a hunger strike until Mordechai was returned to us, and when they brought us food, we refused to accept it.

The atmosphere was tense. We sat at the table without speaking to one another, as if we had decided on a "mute" strike, as well. The British were also tense; every movement we made caused them to jump and point their weapons at us. From time to time, officers entered and looked at us through the caged walls of glass. Time crawled slowly by.

I was in low spirits. More than once, in moments of deep depression, such as this, depression that I never expected to experience after the war, I wondered to myself if the four of us, Yozhik, Monyek, Semmen and I, should have stayed in the forest; Monyek wouldn't have been killed, Semmen wouldn't have been sent to serve in a punishment unit, and I wouldn't have turned into a British prisoner... Or perhaps I should have committed suicide after the war with a smile on my lips? After all, although I had overcome the Germans, my reason for living had been lost with the deaths of all my dear ones. And how could I explain the fact that during my stay in the home of Ola and Harry, when I lacked nothing and I was enveloped by love and pampering, I felt miserable — something I had not been throughout the *Exodus* affair?

Our good spirits returned in the evening, when Mordechai Rozman was returned. We ended our hunger strike. Together we had the soup from lunch, and the bread and jam from supper, and we waited for what would happen next. Our glass cage was so brightly lit we were unable to sleep. The British, so it appeared, didn't know what to do with us, and we didn't know what to do with ourselves, either. Bored, Yisrael, two other boys and I began to play a card game which we had learned on the *Runnymede Park* called Dardel — and we became immersed in it completely, excited, laughing and shouting, to the amazement of the British. In the morning, we were put in a closed car and we left as part of a motorcade, a jeep and an armored vehicle ahead of us, and an armored vehicle and a motorcycle behind us. We rode through the streets of Hamburg with sirens sounding to clear the road in our honor.

Indeed, it had been a long time since the Germans had seen Jews being led somewhere, accompanied by an honor guard!

The guard accompanying us led me to believe that we were certainly being taken to a prison, and, in the meanwhile, the journey continued, leaving the city and entering an army camp where we found ourselves together with all of the other *Exodus* passengers. We were received with roars of happiness, hugs and kisses, as though we were heroes.

As though I were drunk, I was pulled along by the large group surrounding us until we reached a shed that had been assigned to members of our kibbutz where I was told that, from the moment of their arrival at the camp, they had begun a hunger strike with the demand to free us and bring us to their camp. We had not been alone.

Our detention camp, surrounded by barbed wire and guard towers, was located near the town of Poppendorf, and on the surface it looked like a German concentration camp. Armed soldiers guarded us day and night. People came in and went out only with special permission. And inside the sheds, there were two rows of bunks with a narrow passage down the center.

I could not understand why we were being held in a closed camp. What were the British afraid of, that we would get back on a ship — "*Exodus II*" — and we would begin the whole affair again? Nonetheless, there was a positive aspect to our being held in a closed camp: we were spared the shame of meeting the Germans face-to-face. I didn't like the comparisons that were being made in the world press between the Poppendorf camp and a German concentration camp; it seemed that the reporters had no idea what a real German concentration camp was like. The external characteristics were similar, of course. And we were prisoners. But death did not hover in the air over the British camp, nor was there the fear of death. When a British soldier passed by, no one trembled. No one was ever cruel to us there.

After a two-month enforced break, Sarah and I could again take walks alone in the evening hours, far from the crowded sheds where we were housed in the camp, freed from the dozens of curious eyes, inspecting and following us. And it was good to be walking on firm ground, to hear the rustle of the birch trees, to pick a leaf, to crush it between your fingers and to taste its bitterness; it was good to embrace Sarah, to hold her close to my heart, to feel her warm lips, the two of us alone together under the sky, to forget everything, past, present and future, as if nothing else existed in the world during those moments of happiness outside the ticking of the clock... The beam of light falling upon us suddenly and the shout of a soldier from a guard tower, "Stay away from the fence!" brought us back to the British-German reality.

The story documented in history books as the "*Exodus* Affair" didn't end with the return of the would-be immigrants to Germany. Ahead of us were more weeks and months of difficult life in a camp and struggles with the British while the affair continued to make waves throughout the world and to undermine the foolish policy of our jailers, struck by temporary blindness out of anger at their inability to cope with moral ramifications of the human enterprise of the *Bricha* and the immigration movement. Reporters thronged to us from all over the world, the Joint sent us clothes, sports equipment, books and learning material. Among the barbed wire fences and guard towers, we were invigorated by a great desire to live, as evidenced by the many cultural and sports activities. We were promised by the representatives of Mossad l'Aliyah Bet, the organizers of illegal Jewish immigration, that they would do everything possible to help as immigrate as soon as possible, which raised our spirits.

The British government had no satisfaction in their dealings with us. They tried to issue us personal documents and to impose order, but we received instructions not to cooperate. The British were aided by a Jewish translator named Bolek who was ferried around the camp with a loudspeaker to make their announcements in Yiddish. But Bolek was a Haganah representative, and he added Haganah instructions to the British announcements. When he was asked to announce that we were to present ourselves to be listed at the camp office in order to receive personal identification cards, he added the Yiddish expression "NO with an *aleph*" and we understood that we were not to use our real names. So, when we came to the office and we were asked our names, each of us chose the name of a movie star or a historical figure, and to the question of where we were born, we answered "in Jerusalem," "in Tel Aviv" or "in Haifa." The British were forced to give up their lists and finally issued each of us a numbered card with a photograph but no personal details, except for the fact that we had been on the *Exodus*. (After we were released from detention, people responded to these unique cards with awe, and they opened many doors for us and eased our way. When we showed these cards to conductors on trains, we were not asked to present our tickets. More than once, people in the streets pointed to us, saying, "Those are Jews from the *Exodus*!")

After some time, we were transported from the Poppendorf camp to a camp on the outskirts of the city of Emden, which was open and unguarded, like most of the DP camps in Germany. Living conditions in the new camp were far superior. We lived in houses of brick rather than in sheds with tin roofs, and we were free to come and go as we wished.

Representatives of the Mossad kept their word. In a relatively short time, they arranged for us precedence in receiving "certificates" — official permission to immigrate issued by the Mandatory Government — and allowed us to use licenses which had been issued to others and arranged forged passports in the names of those who had the licenses. Our kibbutz received twenty certificates. Sarah was chosen to receive one. My friend, Yisrael, received one, as well, but passed it on to me.

The evening before we left for Israel, our kibbutz had a wedding for five couples. We celebrated through the night. The next morning, we left again for Israel, this time legally, although our personal documents were forged. Our first stop was Bergen-Belsen, which, at the end of the war, had served as a DP camp for thousands of Jewish survivors of concentration camps and from Eastern Europe.

Here we received our new passports and we learned our new identities (my name on the certificate was Sigmund Shatzker), underwent physical examinations by the British Immigration Authority, and we waited our turn to immigrate.

The armed struggle of the secret organizations in Israel was at its peak during those days, and another fateful struggle was going on at the General Assembly of the United Nations, which met in Lake Success, New York, to debate the political fate of Israel. On November 29, 1947, a majority of UN members at that time, including the two superpowers, the United States and the Soviet Union, recognized the right of the Jews to have an independent state of their own in a partition of the Land of Israel. A variety of factors led these states to make that decision, but it was clear that the consciences of states that never lifted a finger to end the Nazi destruction of the Jewish nation, or at least to obstruct and to minimize it, states that had closed their gates to those seeking to flee the hell of Nazism, had awoken and expressed themselves at that historic moment. When we heard the results of the vote, even before we understood its full significance, a group of our young people went out for a midnight parade; we awakened all of the residents of the camp, bottles were opened and we all drank to the health of the Jewish state. We sang and danced until morning.

Bearing the forged passports issued by the British, we traveled to the transit camp of Buchholz, where we had stayed before our *Exodus* sailing, and now, publicly and freely, we continued on our way to Marseilles. This time, we stayed in a hotel and we could wander around the streets openly, without secrecy. From Marseilles, we continued on to Genoa, so we passed through the French and Italian Rivieras by train, and in a few days we were on the deck of the Italian ship *Argentina*. The women divided into pairs and receive third class accommodations, and the men slept together in a large room in the interior of the boat, but not in bunks, as on the *Exodus*, or on the floor, as on the British deportation ship, but in real beds with real sheets.

The *Argentina* sailed first to Alexandria, where we were

requested not to walk on the deck, because of the tension between Arabs and Jews in Israel, but my curiosity quickly got the better of me and I went up on deck to get my first glimpse of the Middle East: barefoot porters working sluggishly, singing in a monotone which repeated itself over and over again endlessly. Everything looked so drowsy and slow — a sharp contrast to the European experience.

# Haifa — Mishmarot

## January 10, 1948

The next morning the familiar Carmel coast appeared. A coast guard boat approached and British officers came up on deck. My heart beat wildly. Would we again be arrested and sent back to Germany? The ship entered the port and anchored alongside a pier, as it had then, but now the scene was different. Along with the British guard were Arab and Jewish longshoremen. Two officers stood at the entry to the ship and checked passports. One of them compared the picture in my passport to my face, returned my passport to me and told me to go on. I hadn't gone more than two steps before a man approached me, told me in Yiddish to come with him, and quickly led me to an old bus standing not far away. The man had a serious expression, no smile, and said nothing. When the last person had been brought to the bus, we set out from the port in a tense atmosphere.

We were in the Land of Israel. It wasn't a dream. It was reality. I was reminded of *Oberscharführer* Wagner. One day in Sobibor, when a transport of Jews had arrived for extermination, we were loading all the possessions from previous shipments into the boxcars. We worked at a constant run, and along the way Germans and Ukrainians urged us on with blows. When I passed Wagner at a run, holding a bundle bigger than I was, he looked at me and said in German, "*Läuft, läuft, israelisch Bruder, ihr kommt noch Palestina!* (Run, run, Israeli brother, you are going to Palestine!)" and his words had cut like a knife in my chest. Now I had a fierce

601

urge to shout, "Wagner, I have come to Palestine!" But I sat in silence. Everyone was silent — we neither sang nor were joyous. We were focused on the new scenes of the land we had yearned for.

We quickly left the city and turned south. On our left were the heights of the Carmel, on our right, fields and banana orchards. Suddenly we stopped. Two young men, dressed in khaki trousers and jackets of a thick, coarse material, got on and sat on each side of the front of the bus, next to the windows. Each of them had a British Sten submachine gun with a loaded magazine peeping out from under his jacket. The tension in the bus increased. Armed men next to the windows? Would the Arabs attack us? I had read accounts of these attacks in German newspapers. But no one said anything; their expressions just grew more serious.

We neared an Arab village. Village girls clothed in colors of the rainbow worked in the fields. Village women walked at the side of the road with big bundles of dry twigs on their heads. Village boys rode on donkeys. The sharp smell of smoke penetrated the bus. On the slope of the mountain, above the houses, a shepherd herded black sheep.

No one shot at us. A short distance after we had left the village, we stopped again. The two men bid us goodbye with an apologetic smile and got off the bus, hiding their machine guns under their jackets.

We rode through orchards and rows of pines that shaded us from the sun. The orchard trees were laden with citrus fruit. I was intoxicated with all that I saw around me. I imagined that this was Heaven on earth, the Paradise I had dreamed of in my childhood. I wanted to kiss the ground, to kiss every bush and tree, every person I saw.

The bus entered Kibbutz Mishmarot and stopped next to a circular tower. People gathered and looked at us — and we at them — like the meeting of two planets. A kibbutz member wearing a brimmed hat greeted us in Yiddish dotted with Hebrew expressions that we didn't understand and led us to the dining hall, where the older members came, faces etched in wrinkles, and asked us where we had come from and if we knew members of their families and perhaps knew what had happened to them. Disappointed by our replies, they left us.

At the end of the meal, the man, our guide from the kibbutz, took us to a camp of tents set up among the trees. In each tent, there were four iron beds with straw mattresses. In the clothing storeroom we received blankets, work clothes and high-topped work shoes. We joked about the "apartments" we had received, and we invited each other to our "palaces," but none of us criticized being quartered in tents; we had been expecting something like this. Afterward, Sarah and I strolled the paths of the kibbutz and enjoyed the sight of little houses, with their flower gardens, grass and decorative trees, the chicken houses and cowsheds, the surrounding orchards and fields. The dream of setting up our own kibbutz seemed achievable.

In the evening we gathered for a meeting. Our guide entered, accompanied by the kibbutz secretary and a third man, younger, in his thirties, with an athletic build, a head like a bronze statue and a face that communicated determination and strength. The kibbutz secretary welcomed us and explained the rules of the kibbutz. He said that we would soon be given jobs in the various kibbutz branches, in order to learn how to manage a kibbutz of our own, and in the meantime, we would all work picking oranges. The man with the strong face — the security chief — explained the security situation to us, saying that the Arab countries were poised to attack the Jewish settlements as soon as the British left the country, and in the short time we had until then, we had to prepare for the attack. A few kilometers from us, he added, there was a large concentration of Arabs in the villages of Nahal Iron, and that it was quite possible that the Jewish settlements in the area would have to defend themselves. The settlements were organizing for defense within the framework of the Haganah. Every settlement, depending on its size, trained a squad or division. Kibbutz Mishmarot had a squad, whose members officially served as guards in the Jewish settlement police, under the command of the British. This squad had to be strengthened, and one of us would join it to this purpose.

We looked at each other in embarrassment. Things were happening too fast, it seemed. Aware of our embarrassment, the security chief said, "You don't have to decide now. Let me know who it will be tomorrow." As he said that, I felt with my entire being that I had to volunteer, and that I must do so without delay. I stood up and said, "I want to join the squad." The man approached me, asked my name, shook my hand and said, "My name is Michael. We'll meet tomorrow morning at eight, by the dining hall." For the first time that evening, I saw Michael smile.

That night I dreamed that we were in the Warsaw ghetto. A division of German soldiers was marching down Muranowska Street. The street was empty of people. The houses were deserted; doors and windows were wide open, as in a ghost town. In my dream, I thought: How did I get back to this place, when I had left the ghetto, and escaped from Sobibor? How can I be back in the ghetto? No! I will not fall into their hands. I have experience. I have to find a way to escape from them. But the Germans marching in their hobnailed boots drew nearer, and I knew they were coming to get me. I ran into a courtyard and up the stairs of a building. All the doors were open, all the apartments were empty. I ran from room to room until I reached a large room whose front wall, facing the street, was missing. I heard the Germans marching up the stairs and nearing the room. I felt it was hopeless. I approached the edge of the missing front wall, preparing to jump down, but there, in the street below, I saw a German standing and looking up at me. Suddenly this German rose and flew up from the street and stood facing me in the room, his Schmeisser machine gun aimed at me, an odd smile on his face. At that same moment, without thinking, I kicked him in the groin with all my might. The German let out a scream and fell back, down into the street...

I awoke and sat up in bed. I heard the sound of a strange wailing, a sobbing, getting louder. I looked around. A beam of light shone in through the tent opening. My tent companions were also awake. For a moment I didn't know if I were still dreaming or if the wailing I had heard was real. Our neighbors in the next tent also awoke and we all asked each other what the crying meant. Finally, the kibbutz leader came in and explained with a grin that no one was crying — the wailing sounds we had heard were the coyotes wandering through the orchards.

I lay back and analyzed the dream I had just had. Up till now, all of my dreams had ended in my being killed by a German. This time I had killed the German. I was pleased. But the deserted streets of the Warsaw ghetto continued to haunt me for a long time afterward.

The next day I learned how to use a rifle and throw grenades. I devoted myself to the art of warfare and was very proud to be in the kibbutz defense squad.

That same January day in 1948, so many years ago, a new chapter opened in my life, a chapter filled with wars: fighting from fortified heights, at battle fronts, in innumerable mine fields as a sapper in the Golani brigade — and also the battle to integrate myself into everyday life. I needed to prove to myself that after growing up among the gas chambers, after being so dreadfully humiliated, sorting the possessions of my brothers and sisters who were led to slaughter by the Nazis, after fighting like a wild animal in the forests of Poland for another day of life, after fighting the British, who dared to return us from the shores of our homeland to Germany, the land of monstrous murderers — that I, Dov, son of Moshe and Rivka Freiberg, the last of the Freibergs, had survived and prevailed, and could work, could be productive, and could establish a family in Israel — that I was no different from any other human being.

# Index